Y0-BCC-925

THE MANIPULATORS:

Personality and Politics in Multiple Perspectives

THE MANIPULATORS:
Personality and Politics in Multiple Perspectives

Allan W. Lerner
University of Illinois at Chicago

LEA LAWRENCE ERLBAUM ASSOCIATES, PUBLISHERS
1990   Hillsdale, New Jersey   Hove and London

Lawrence Erlbaum Associates, Inc., Publishers
365 Broadway
Hillsdale, New Jersey 07642

Library of Congress Cataloging-in-Publication Data

Lerner, Allan W.
   The manipulators.

   1. Political psychology.   I. Title.
JA74.5.L47 1990   320'.01'9   89-26045
ISBN 0-8058-0335-1

Printed in the United States of America
10 9 8 7 6 5 4 3 2 1

To *Rachel* and *Ben*

Contents

Preface

This volume has two purposes. One is to shed some light on the impact that manipulativeness has on modern institutional processes. The other is to illustrate the importance of attempting militantly interdisciplinary work on themes that run through a variety of social sciences and related disciplines, as a way of breaking down excessively stifling disciplinary barriers.

Manipulativeness is a connotation-laden notion with shifting meanings across the variety of action contexts, levels of analysis, and disciplinary orientations. It absorbs the idea of strategic-mindedness, rule exploitation, situational advantage seeking, tampering with structure and context, and control of the action climate. In a way, it is a very contemporary interpretation of the theme of power, melding images of control with the experience of pervasive social ambiguity. The concern with the exploitive potential and how it may be managed strikes me as the truly distinct feature in the idea of a political science discipline. The result should be a discipline that looks at social behavior, social institutions and social contexts with an eye for such possibilities and how they come to be checked or focused.

I believe that the meld of political science and psychology is therefore quite a natural one. But at the same time, the practice of these disciplines in contemporary academia presents many obstacles to the realization of their joint potential, despite the valuable and creative efforts of many who work at some of their clearer points of contact: on leadership, ideology, group decision making, mass movements and political violence, to name but a few.

Lingering obstacles in the productive cross fertilization of psychology and political science seem to fall into two categories: levels of analysis complexities, and intradisciplinary cantonization. It has been my concern that matters have been oversimplified in the former case and taken too far in the latter. Some of the limitations of political psychology as it is frequently presented seem to involve difficulties in moving from individual and face-to-face scale settings to large scale, formal organizational, genuinely institutional level images of processes. As a result, considerable attention has been paid to such levels of analysis issues in the pages that follow. Regarding disciplinary cantonization, the intention here has been to deal with it in several ways. The major commitment has been to resist working with only one psychological subdiscipline's perspective. Instead, in what follows, several styles of psychology are brought to bear, and of equal importance to this enterprise, some attempt is made to probe their points of partial overlap and analogy while avoiding the naive assumption of any simple equivalencies. Similarly, care has been taken to mark the current and potential suitability of several styles of political science to the type of psycho-political inquiry undertaken here.

In covering as much interdisciplinary ground as I have attempted to do, it is likely, if not necessarily inevitable, that particular disciplinary perspectives or works may appear at times to have been treated, shall we say, suboptimally. I hope at such times that the larger purpose of what follows is not overshadowed.

ACKNOWLEDGMENTS

This book had many shapes and there are many people to thank in connection with each one. However, I am especially indebted to Ike Balbus, George Balch, Mike Cline, Jamie Eimermann, I.E. Farber, Doris Graber, Rathe Karrer, Laura Lerner, Mark Lichbach, and John Wanat for their particularly helpful assistance at various stages. I am also grateful (for not being indebted) to the Office of Social Science Research at the University of Illinois at Chicago for assistance with some of the early costs of research associated with this project. Of course any shortcomings in this volume are entirely everyone else's fault.

Allan W. Lerner

1

The Problem and Its Many Approaches: Horizontal Divisions Among Disciplinary Approaches

This is a book about the urge to be manipulative in our dealings with other people. Modern Western societies—and many other societies past and present—show great ambivalence toward the manipulative posture in dealing with others. We respect people who are "shrewd," who "weren't born yesterday." No one wants to be "naive," "vulnerable," or "a willing victim." At the same time we value honesty and openness, people whose word is their bond, and with whom we can safely be frank and "upfront." When given a choice in abstract terms, we seem to esteem the tactful more than the tactical, but we also esteem winning and surviving, and we know that situations imposing this crasser test are very common in life.

Tact and tactic can peacefully coexist in the idealized persona of the well-adjusted modern person so long as the idealization is not scrutinized. All that is required is a modest rationale, one that serves best when it is implicitly elevated to a vague maxim for living (an act of casual conceptual inflation that unfortunately occurs all the time).

The modest rationale is that people should be treated in the manner they present. Openness for openness, warmth for warmth; unguardedness for naivete. So it follows also: cleverness should be met with cleverness, scheming with still better schemes, and force with force, to be sure.

This maxim to mirror a counterpart's behavior, to live by "tit for tat," to reciprocate cooperation and hostility each in kind, has taken various homiletic forms and it has the limitations of all homilies. It will not survive close

1

inspection. There are too many necessary ifs and buts for which it gives no guidance. It is a frequent experience that others simply break the rules and take advantage by not reciprocating cooperation. Often others present nothing cooperative to reciprocate. Reciprocating hostility can begin a mutually destructive cycle. Initiating cooperation in the hope of reciprocation can get one killed or worse. Actions and messages can mix several relationship levels simultaneously and it is hard to signal a response on one level without intruding on another. Actions and messages are often unclear and inconsistent. Interpretations by actor and counterpart can differ. People often misunderstand their own interest. When the effects of actions run contrary to the intentions behind them to which does one respond?

The simultaneous attraction to and discomfort with the manipulative orientation toward others cannot be balanced with a simple rule. It is a point of departure for this book to see these dual values as an ambivalence that is inherent in the modern condition. It is a dilemma both felt and reflected in personality and society, and its presence on each dimension perpetuates its display in the other.

Scholarship has struggled to grasp various facets of this phenomenon. Some probe it by first casting it as a drive for domination, aggression, or power, depending on the favored nuance. Some focus on the Realpolitik demands of a harsh world and argue survival as the first value for which the art and science of manipulation is an obvious necessity, and which may in any event be channeled to serve humanistic purposes. Others focus on the reconstruction of social form, or with an institutional emphasis, societal structure, to obviate the necessity for manipulation as a way of life. Others focus on understanding the social dimension of species evolution and see it as a process that will include the extinction of the manipulative orientation that is rooted in primitiveness. Many such theoretical strands of the subject have been raised within disciplines and with various interdisciplinary orientations. The subject of manipulativeness is as broad as it is vital.

The thrust of the approach to be taken in this book is informed by an interpretation of what has been done so far within a cluster of disciplines. We now turn to an assessment of some of those efforts that will be most relevant as orientations out of which has been formed the approach taken here.

GAME THEORY, RATIONAL CHOICE, AND THE REQUIREMENTS FOR A PARADIGM OF MANIPULATIVENESS

Consider "game theorists" and their close social science cousins from the school of "interactive rational choice" (populated by economists and political scientists). As with all academic "movements" considerable variety can be found within their collective efforts. In the main, however, they chart the "game strategies" people employ against one another in playing for predetermined game rewards. This generally involves establishing the successfulness of various sequences of moves in response to counterpart moves and in light of game properties, or game rules. A major interest over the years has been to understand how people may find their way to cooperative play for joint benefit, when playing games set up so that each player would be vulnerable to aggressive, exploitive play by the other as a tempting alternative to cooperative play. Axelrod's (1984) work represents a high point of the genre, consolidating and elaborating its consistent findings. In briefest overview, the work succeeds in providing a demonstration and within its paradigm framework a verification, of the basic homiletic guide for reconciling manipulative and cooperative postures just noted, namely that others should be treated as they present. In the case of the game-theory genre, the limitations of homily do not glare to those immersed in the gaming paradigm because the technique is based on assumptions that exclude the subtler and more troubling concerns for which the homiletic position is inadequate. Axelrod described the superiority of the game strategy "tit for tat," wherein an opponent's aggressive act is met with a retaliatory act, and his cooperative act gains a cooperative response. This is deemed the best road to cooperation over the long term. It is in a sense, the way to harmony and the suppression of tendencies to mutual harm or one party's exploitation.

The problem is that although the game theorist describes such a tit-for-tat precept as a "strategy," in complex social action it is really only a circumscribed tactic. To Axelrod and the school his work epitomizes, relationships are conducted or in subdiscipline vernacular, games are played, according to mutually understood rules that are given, which is to say set beforehand by a vague "others." The rules are communicated by an experimenter serving as a passive agent describing the game form, an experimenter who says in effect "the rules are . . ." rather than "I have decided the rules will be. . . ." With the clear and simple rules of popular rational choice games like the Prisoner's Dilemma or the game of the Acme trucks—two games having each been the format for more than 100 empirical studies (Rubin & Brown, 1975)—what is left to players to "strategize" about is simply the choice of tactics within fixed and narrow game rules that cannot be tampered with. The freedom to strategize or at least simply communicate about what their relationship will be, how they will present, resolve, clarify, or leave ambiguous their preferences for its form, its significance, its inclusiveness, its purpose—its relation to almost an infinity of creative and destructive social possibilities—is taken away from the actors. The meanings the encounter will have for each are pretended to have been decided by an implicit paradigm rule to ignore such issues.

This approach is consistent with a tradition of laboratory research on bargaining and negotiation that has frequently preferred for the sake of manageability, to exclude verbal communication in its laboratory replicas of "negotiation." All that people are left to "strategize" about, is really only an essentially predetermined and limited range of tactics. Axelrod's work is an excellent statement of a now classic approach. However, its inherent paradigm limitations must be taken into account in assessing its relevance for understanding the dynamics of manipulative behavior. The paradigm tends to divert attention from, and it may indeed formally foreclose, an understanding of sophisticated manipulativeness as exploitation of relationship structure—of game*r* properties, in the course of preoccupation with *game* properties. What I have alluded to as strategy, in contrast to mere tactics, may be suppressed by positing a fixed elementary game structure encapsulating an uncreative, strategically barren problem, compared to what life away from the game board can produce. The game can often be quite elegant as the classic "Prisoner's Dilemma" is in a way, but it is an elegance based on the distillation down to a fundamental choice that is the game's essence.

In some respects, this is still a process of severe constraint. These games are often elegant in the sense that the distillation of a problem to "do or die" is elegant, but it is the elegance of a minimalist aesthetic, parsimony at too heavy a price. What is excluded in the rational choice a la Prisoner's Dilemma, are the richer contextual elements that are often employed to create manipulative possibilities: structural vagueness, ambiguous mutual understandings, moves toward a counterpart that may appear concessionary as well as serving a partisan interest, a driving emotionality, and symbolism.

Hacking (1984), in a review of Axelrod's recent book makes two wry observations that speak to these concerns. Dealing with male–female difference in style when playing a variation of the Prisoner's Dilemma, Hacking drew on a vignette from a recent work by Gilligan (1983):

> In part the girls collaborate by trying to change the rules of the game to suit the human beings caught up in it. One of Gilligan's examples is this: the girl said "Let's play next-door neighbors." "I want to play pirates," the boy replied. "O.K.," said the girl, "Then you can be the pirate who lives next door." We certainly need to change games more often than we need optimum strategies. . . . perhaps some ten-year-old girl can help us out of the game. I have done my small bit. At least I have changed the name of the game. It has hitherto been known as the Prisoner's Dilemma. I have been calling it the Prisoners' Dilemma. The two prisoners are in it together. (pp. 26–28)

In Hacking's and Gilligan's context, the point is well taken that genuine cooperation may require substantial creativity in reshaping "the game" itself, and the development of a broader common vision that can reconcile now expanded interests. But from our perspective, the passage just cited underscores other important points as well. Sophisticatedly manipulative strategies aimed at counterparts frequently work through distortion of the rules. The "human beings caught up" may remain one's adversaries if not one's enemies. Games expanded for cooperation may also be expanded for advantage. Clarity of rules is often one of the first casualties, and here nuance figures heavily in achieving manipulative strategies masked as invitations to joint meta-awareness. Consider the pirates versus next-door neighbors dilemma and its resolution. From our perspective, an interesting question is whether the would-be pirate will find himself indeed hoisting the Jolly Roger with his mate at his side, or singing a lullaby to an imaginary pirate baby while waiting for the Maytag man, albeit with a plastic cutlass under his apron. Such is the dimension of issue that the *Prisoner's* Dilemma leaves behind and even the *Prisoners'* Dilemma may underestimate.

Interactive rational choice á la Prisoner's Dilemma exploration offers suggestive insight into the effect of basic situation features on tactical possibilities, and allows for a cooperative assessment of tactical postures under given sets of basic rules. The awareness of possibilities for game linkage and game expansion á la Hacking, aids appreciation of how game properties may be changed regarding the values likely to be associated with them. These may be values held individually or in common by the participants. However, a fuller understanding of manipulativeness, including insight into its relationships with situational properties and possibilities must go further. It must embrace rather than resist, a psychologizing of some aspects of its subject matter. It must include inquiry into the interplay between situational elements and personality proclivities, talents and motives for deviousness, emotionality, and emotional maturity.

On this dimension it is useful to keep in mind, that meta-awareness may facilitate scheming in service of ignoble values every bit as much as noble values. Progress in the understanding of manipulativeness thus requires a still richer framework.

Of course there are many ways to psychologize. Consider the efforts that have recently come to be called *psychohistory*.

THE PROMISE AND LIMITS OF PSYCHOHISTORY

Like many newer academic enterprises, the difficulty in establishing a consensus on what psychohistory is seems matched only by the intensity of an apparently felt necessity to do so, on the part of many of its practitioners. In a 1978 symposium in the *Journal of Psychohistory* aptly titled "The Joys and Terrors of Psychohistory," Lawton (1978) surveyed "roughly 110 individuals worldwide, on how they define psychohistory . . ." (p. 325). Understandably, there seemed to be almost 110 answers to this question.

As one reads the literature of this genre it seems that in the main, psychohistory at its current best is psychohistory at its narrowest: psychobiography. The biography explores the inner life of a historically/ politically prominent individual or an individual taken as representative (i.e., phenotypic, or a historically significant group of persons). The object of inquiry is to link the external actions of such actors to the dynamics of their inner lives. Thus, one probes a president's psyche to better understand the origins of his administration's foreign and domestic policies (Kearns, 1976).

It seems fair to say that so far as this sense of psychohistory is concerned (that is, as biography of prominent psyches) the problem is not with its internal methodology or assumptions (although debates and debatable assumptions are not in short supply). Clearly, people matter in the shaping of historical events and so do psyches, the constellation of individual motives, conscious and unconscious. Prominent people and also key small, relatively homogeneous classes of people representable in a phenotypic exemplar, can be crucial to events. Psychobiographies of such persons can offer valuable insights into such events, even if they do not constitute exhaustive explanations of the events. In this obvious sense psychobiography makes a useful contribution to sociopolitical analysis. This is a rather obvious point; it would be condescending to even state it as if it needed defense—were it not that two cautions follow closely.

The first is that there is a major difference between a useful contribution and a substitution. Psychohistory, as psychobiography based on clinical concepts relaxed for subclinical purposes, cannot explain, obviously cannot supply a comprehensive conceptualization of, the action dimension of institutional-level relationships pondered by the social sciences. Few psychohistorians (but still not all) would disagree with this point as stated. However, ranks break completely and dissent is widespread once one attempts to mark off the domain of the social sciences still further. Thus, much of the psychohistory community seriously disputes the inappropriateness of the psychohistory approach to the study of collectivities—and to put it sharply, very large collectivities—say, the interwar Germans. For such broad categories, there are those who trace action to motive and motive to psyche, reading history thus as a psychohistory of a society (Kohut, 1985). When psychohistorical techniques have their origins in historically clinical tools, the limitations of psychohistory are terribly clear. The traditional psychobiography is limited in the sense that its usefulness is demarcated at the boundary of individual experience. When psychohistory is extended to collective level action in inter-institutional context, there is always a risk of epistemological chaos. When the method does go awry, all is firstly and ultimately psyche-driven.

When this happens, the clinical emphasis on empathy runs a danger of being reduced to a process of willing one's self into the past and experiencing it for truth mining purposes in the present. Explanation then comes from unverifiable "insight," and is confirmed by post-insight exhaustion. Intensity can replace argument. Consider a passage from Binion's symposium contribution on the definition of psychohistory:

> Twice now I have cited Hitler's unconscious rapport with his public . . . I thought and felt myself back into his audiences in the Munich area before the Putsch and across Germany in the late 1920s. After long months of straining my mind's ear I could all at once hear, and shrilly where his call for eastward expansion resonated with a traumatic national experience. This was the 1918 defeat, for which Germans were the less prepared since Ludendorff's subjugation of Soviet Russia had seemed to render them invulnerable. That trauma did not, then, just pop up behind Hitler's expansionist project and introduce itself. It erupted convulsively, a pent-up panic so overpowering when released that I blocked it out again and again before I could admit it to consciousness sufficiently even to identify it. With it, disparate elements of Weimar Germany's troubled and confusing politics rushed to mind, connected up, fell into place. These included a missing link in my evidence that I then had to hunt down: the transition from Hitler's two early repertory pieces to his project for a new eastern conquest. This project was now intelligible as an invitation to a traumatic reliving—one designed ostensibly to undo the 1918 defeat, actually to outdo it. A year or more passed before I realized that I was taking that transition for granted. Then I scouted for documentation. I found it for May 31, 1921, when Hitler delivered those two repertory speeches combined, both for the last time. In vindicating Brest-Litovsk on that occasion he blurted out that the big German loss from the defeat in the west had been the land conquered from the Soviets. And he grounded the point in the very arguments that he later advanced to urge a reconquest.
>
> That documentary find confirmed for me my intuition of the German trauma. True, my final proof of it lay with Hitler registering it and reacting. But the insight had been won through self-projection into his national public. This opened mass phenomena to direct psychohistorical inquiry. (Binion, 1978, pp. 320–321)

The contribution of psychohistory as psychobiography is clear when it stops at the edge of collective/institutional level issues. Indeed, Stalinism is not derivable from probing baby Djugashvili, as Binion noted in an earlier passage. But psychohistory as psychobiography can indeed offer a piece of the puzzle. One may wonder whether it is not in the long run a more useful if modest piece than what can be derived by a "self-projection" into a national public, which claims to open mass phenomenon to "direct" psychohistorical inquiry. Thus, Monaco's (1978) comments on Binion included the observation "Binion emphasizes an approach to causal explanation that is reductionist, with a vengeance. It is a necessary corrective to the last half-century's rampant pluralism dominating the social sciences, and in turn historiography, in search of a multiplicity of casual [sic] explanations. Binion's emphasis on 'empathy,' however, is exaggerated and troublesome" (p. 408).

The issue here, however, is not reductionism but appropriate reductionism, the possible error of reducing collective institutional-level phenomena that have no equivalent individual level manifestations. Monaco (1978) noted this, in a way, as he also observed:

> The greatest problem with Binion's overzealousness for empathy as the psychohistorian's research tool, *par excellent,* is that even in believing that "mind is enough of a kind," we are speaking of the individual mind. Thus, the rub is that while one might become "Lenin artificially," it is far more dubious for one to try to become "Russian society artificially." The individual mind cannot grasp the group mind emotionally; it can do so only intellectually. The mind cannot empathize with that which is other than itself in kind. The group mind does not correspond *to* mind, but implies an entirely different nature derived *from* mind. For the individual to empathize with the group mind would be like empathizing with a flight of stairs; unrewarding for psychohistorians, except for those who might fancy themselves to be neo-symbolist poets. (p. 409)

In discussing the results of his survey of psychohistorians, Lawton (1978) aptly observed: "But if my researches and respondents [only two . . . showed any concern with this question] are any indication, the problem of a theoretical system for psychohistory has been too much for anyone to meaningfully deal with. At this moment in time there is no detailed coherent philosophy of psychohistory" (p. 332).

A candidate for a collective level psychohistory appears in the concept of "group fantasy." An excerpt from Durvin's (1984) article "Group Fantasy Models and the Impostor" reflects this genre:

> Although a modest expansion of established psychohistorical theories of group-fantasies operating through the American political system is the serious purpose of this essay, it may also propose an answer to the more popular question of how a grownup electorate came to choose an aging actor for its president in the waning years of the twentieth century . . .

I should like to see a structuring of group-fantasies to include a fuller range of early psychosexual stages, and it falls to the present essay both to widen the range of group fantasies . . . and to offer a rationale for the basic group-fantasy approach, regardless of what interpretive level one plugs into. (pp. 240–241)

In any case, the concept of *representative* then becomes highly charged with subjective contents or, as we say, overdetermined . . . after a honeymoon phase, disillusionment sets in – necessarily, since the illusory goals of our childhood can neither be later satisfied in their pristine form nor can our delegates accomplish for us what we could not – hence crisis, cracking, collapse; search for scapegoats, magical renewal, offerings of sacrifice; ultimately regicide, war, or martyrdom.

In these various stages people behave in a peculiarly ambivalent way. Leo Rangell in his "psychochronicle," *The Mind of Watergate*, refers to a "dual type of psychic recording" in which events are experienced more or less as they occur, as well as the way one wants to see them. "Opposites never contradict" writes deMause about the group trance. The effects of lapses and distortions suggest that we know more than we let ourselves know but also that we do not know all we may think we know. Group-fantasy analysis resolves some of the confusions, at least for those willing to face the dilemma. What might be added to these endeavors, by way of explanation, is that people apparently given vent to very destructive fantasies – upon which they rarely act, however – toward their representative because he is experienced as a subjective object: as, to put it more emphatically, their own creation. The power to create carries along with it – in effect legitimizes – the power to destroy. (p. 244)

Much of the disillusionment Americans have experienced over the past decade with the Presidency can be telescoped into a sunny Family Romance disintegrating into a turbulent Primal Scene. The healthy as well as the purient curiosity about what went on in the Nixon White House and the disclosures of conniving coverups, dirty-tricks, secrets, and betrayals cannot help but revive memory traces of painful childhood events in which the parents are subjectively experienced as secretly and selfishly loving each other, or more disturbingly, as conspiring against their children. Thus the Nixon tapes reawakened some of our worse misgivings and primitive fears about the perverse nature of adult sexuality, where in place of marital mutuality is revealed and recorded male conspiracy, envy, revenge, and hostility . . .

Thus the collective mythology of that office – created by the public as well as by the occupants – has been modified over the years, and the changes, especially a lessening of aura, idealization, and expectation, can be expected in turn to modify the currents of group-fantasy that continue to operate with a life of its own, though never entirely so. (p. 247)

These passages speak more eloquently than I could to the epistemological work that remains, if "group fantasy" is to serve as a basis for taking psychohistory beyond psychobiography.

Strands of psychology and strands of politics have been woven in yet another design that is again both limited and suggestive for the purposes of this book. Psychohistorians have often underspecified social-level processes when attempting to pull individual, intrapsychic concepts too far up the ladder of levels of analysis. However, traditional organization theorists tend to err in the opposite direction—although it must be added far less egregiously. But, it is not my purpose to conduct a derby of worst examples. Therefore, let us consider what have been the strengths of the traditional organizational literature in blending individual, psychologically oriented concerns with sociostructural, macro concerns.

THE VARIOUSLY PSYCHOLOGIZED STYLES OF ORGANIZATION THEORY

When mainstream organization theory has been concerned with the individual, the focus has been on the individual as an organizational role occupant. The image of generic-role occupant has several usually implicit assumptions attached to it: The individual is basically well-socialized and pre-socialized to organizational life. Organizational life is sensible and not a struggle. Mostly, whatever is at all remarkable can be summarized under the general heading of a certain low level, persistent, or at least periodically recurring, stress. The latter is traceable to the continually communicated pressures to conform to organizational life within the framework of the basic role of the organizational repertory: managerial drone/bureaucrat.

There is a faintly *Kafkaesque* twist running through such a perspective in two senses. The individual's felt stress when it is not traceable to conflicting demands placed on him by organizational life, is traceable to vague, *ambiguous* demands. Kahn, Wolfe, Quinn, Snoek, and Rosenthal's (1964) classic study concludes that the two main stressors of organizational life are role conflict (presumably, "Stand up! Sit down!") and role ambiguity (in effect, "mumble, mumble!"). Academically defined by Kahn et al., *role conflict* is an objective condition and/or subjective experience of pressures on a role occupant stemming from incompatible role expectations. In contrast, *role ambiguity* is defined as objectively prevailing (and/or subjectively experienced) inadequacy of information necessary to role performance.

The theme of such organizational research, in some places clearly bolstered by rigorous and widely gathered survey results and/or depth interviews, is that the stress that poor role communication fosters takes a heavy toll on role occupants. Kahn et al. have shown how it diminishes their performance, distracts them from past performance in favor of shall we say constant role-mending, often makes them sullen and defensive, and keeps the organization from what it might more wholesomely be, both as a place to spend adulthood and as a collective enterprise for pursuing socially constructive goals.

Stress fosters tension, dissatisfaction, inner conflict, task confusion, and status anxiety. It lowers one's sense of personal efficacy. It fosters empathic failure across role boundaries. It splits off innovative from status quo-preserving functions. It does this by leading organizations to throw off discrete roles for each such function. Pervasive organizational stress reflects a widely felt inconsistency between humanistic values that tend to be held more in the work group, and more formal pressures for a less flexible, rule-oriented climate within the organization. Clear lines of authority do not obviate role stress because role occupants see two bases of power in the community of role senders: superiors' formal authority, reward and coercion of course, but also peers' "expert power," "referent power," and indirect influence (Heclo, 1977; Lerner, 1976b).

Conventional organization theory, when it has focused on the interplay of individual-level experience and larger structural pressures has not been insensitive to individual personality variations and even disturbance, in analyzing the psyche-society connection via the individual-organization relationship. Thus, Kahn et al. noted 20 years ago, that to the extent that organizational role relationships pivot on functional dependence and power "psychological withdrawal reflected in a weakening of affective interpersonal bonds" may be expected (p. 221). They find support for the expectation that role occupants under stress would exhibit "avoidance coping strategies — withdrawal, rejection, and evasion" and note that such tactics that reduce communication are likely to perpetuate the very conditions to which they are a response.

It is quite interesting from our perspective to note how such a landmark study conceptualized the impact of variations in individual personality on organizational process in light of the apparent ever-presence of stress in such processes. Kahn et al. conceptualized the personality issue in terms of five dimensions, noting how variations in individual positioning on each of the continua representing a dimension would augur for broadly predictable variations in adjustment to ever present organizational stress.

Thus, on the dimension of "neurotic anxiety versus emotional stability," " 'neurotic' and 'non-neurotic' reactions to role conflict are substantially similar, and . . . sufficient environmental stress may produce neurotic symptoms even in those who show little predisposition to neurotic anxiety" (Kahn et al., 1964, p. 262). Also, "although the neurotic's hypersensitivity exposes him to greater strain than that of his non-neurotic counterpart, his level of tension is not necessarily disabling and it may lead to coping efforts which are reasonably effective for the person and acceptable to the organization" (Kahn et al., 1964, pp. 261–262).

Further in terms of how this exemplary work in the traditional organizational/personality genre treats the interplay of personality and organization as sociotechnical structure (conceptualized in turn as an open system of role relationship networks), consider the implications generated by exploring the flexibility–rigidity dimension of personality in relation to organizational life:

> Not only is the flexible individual more frequently exposed to role conflict, but he is also more likely than a rigid one to respond to conflict by experiencing a high level of anxiety, worrying about what is in store for him and what he can do to make things right. By contrast one who is rigid is more likely to react to conflict by an abrupt rejection of the role senders creating the conflict. The flexible individual, incapable of effecting such a rejection comfortably, continues to comply in word to those role expectations which he can no longer fulfill in deed.

This tone is continued as well, with the positing of a relationship between individual positioning on an "achievement–security" continuum or dimension, and two other dimensions: extraversion–introversion, and flexibility–rigidity. In general they observe that:

> But coping by withdrawal tends to be an ineffective response, because role senders in an effort to control the introvert's behavior only intensify their attempts to influence him.

> Modern industrial organizations face the persistent dilemma of securing conformity to existing organizational procedures while simultaneously making allowances for adaptation to changing environmental conditions. In an earlier chapter we witnessed one attempted resolution of this dilemma through the institution of specific organizational roles, in which innovative behavior constituted a principal role requirement. Organizations may further insure this incorporation of both rigid and flexible behavior patterns through the enlistment of individuals whose personalities predispose them toward one or the other of these behavioral extremes.

It will be most economical in discussing the style of analysis this work represents, to summarize the authors' approach to the organizational end of the individual–organizational relationship that they develop in light of their findings about personality and the stress-inducing realities of organizational life. As Kahn et al. noted:

> The research on which this book is based is in part descriptive, attempting to set out something of the prevalence and distribution of two common conditions of organizational life: role conflict and role ambiguity. Our major emphasis, however, has been on explanation – on showing the organization origins, the immediate causes, and some of the consequences of these two conditions. The practitioner who reads these pages will do so with still a third consideration dominant in his mind: What can be done to reduce the incidence of role conflict and ambiguity, and to make the effects of these conditions (when they cannot be avoided) minimally damaging to the person and to the organization?
>
> The issue, then, is not the elimination of conflict and ambiguity from organizational life; it is the containment of these conditions at levels and in forms which are at least humane, tolerable, and low in cost, and which at best might be positive in contribution to individual and organization. The present research implies four ways in which this goal might be approached: by introducing new criteria of selection and placement, by increasing the tolerance and coping abilities of individuals, and by strengthening the interpersonal bonds among organizational members. The research suggests also that all four of these approaches will be facilitated by a substantial revision of conventional views of organizational structure and by the direct utilization of the role set in bringing about organizational change. (pp. 386–387)

Finally, the practical prescriptions for a more humane, less stressful (i.e., less conflicted and ambiguous) organization are offered. It is worth noting the specifics of these recommendations in the original. In cumulative effect they purvey a perspective on the relationship between individual and organization that serves as an excellent illustration of the strengths and weaknesses of the empirical organizational psychology literature of the 1960s and 1970s. In those vineyards there still labor many a skilled researcher.

In effect, Kahn et al. suggested that a much needed new view of organization must begin with a new answer to the basic definitional questions. They answer their question by stating that organizations must be defined essentially as role networks, with each role envisioned as the hub of a cluster of interactions for which it may be viewed as the focal role. They see role stress, their explicit focus, as partially ameliorable although their work is far broader than that by virtue of the sweeping conceptualization of stress and its context that they offer. However, they note the way to do this may be in a sense to *underorganize* the organization, by which I mean leave more deliberately ambiguous, and by which they seem to mean allow more to remain contingent upon the work *groups* rather than tightly centralized via long, formal, organizational chart connections. They emphasize the need to create what is today popularly called "win/win" situations where the rewards for individuals come from joint undertakings toward common goals, avoiding zero-sum situations for organizational members. Having acknowledged all this, however, one cannot help being reminded of pirates as next-door neighbors, and the ambiguities that remained even in such relatively enlightened arrangements. Kahn et al. emphasized the importance of organizations being open to change and see this promotable essentially through an enlightened, conflict- and tension-reducing, positive, almost therapeutic emphasis on group dynamics. They concluded their work as follows:

> We have interpreted our research data on organizational stress as urging on practitioners of organization the importance of the key concept which has informed the research: the idea of the focal person and role set. We have argued that from this idea stems a new view of the organization, a fuller appreciation of organizational structure, and a more powerful approach to creating individual and organizational change. In urging our views on practitioners with such seeming confidence, we are nonetheless painfully aware that knowledge of human organizations is still fragmentary. That knowledge can best be advanced by research which attempts to deal simultaneously with data at different levels of abstraction – individual, group, and organization. This is a difficult task, and the outcome is not uniformly satisfactory. It is, nevertheless, a core requirement for understanding human organizations. Organizations are reducible to individual human acts; yet they are lawful and in part understandable only at the level of collective behavior. This duality of level, which is the essence of human organization as it is of social psychology, we have attempted to recognize in our theoretical model and in our research design. Our hope is that the effort and its product may contribute to the understanding of organized human behavior. We know of no more urgent problem. (pp. 397–398)

The social psychological orientation to the analysis of individual–institutional relationships a la Kahn et al. and the genre they represent, reflected an emphasis on the generic processes of groups in the organizational context. It demonstrates the importance of the individual–group relationship in the understanding of the group–organizational relationship. Its emphasis on a therapeutic orientation to group dynamics within organizations as the key process in organizational change really betrays a broader view that the key processes of organizations – organizations in action – are actually group processes.

This is both the strength and weakness of the social psychological approach to the workings of organizations as societal institutions. Although we have been letting the strengths speak for themselves, some consideration of the limitations of this genre are appropriate, with the considerable benefit of hindsight. In this genre the frictions and difficulties in organizational life are in large part traced to faulty patterns of interaction at the group level. If we were to use a more psychoanalytical vocabulary, it might be said that in such patterns participants show a lack of empathic support for one another, and this condition is both aggravated by and in turn partially caused by, the formal organizational arrangements that bring them into contact for prescribed reasons in prescribed ways. Further, the concern with structure is basically limited to pointing out this general effect. The remedies have a therapeutic style to them, intellectually. Group dynamics and processes must be made more feeling and open, communications must be more natural and follow the path of parties' healthy needs conditioned by a common desire to work hard and with commitment to common enterprise. Invariably, personal growth and expression through productive work are the universal needs that underwrite the promise of an improved organization and organizational experience. However, this is contingent upon a trusting and indeed faintly clinical reliance, on the power of a properly developed group style reiterated throughout the organization. The implicit model rests at bedrock, on an assumption of generic human motivation and large modern organization, which I can only describe as "homo wholesomus."

In a sense, organizations represent a massive failure to communicate interpersonally. When there occurs what others might label as *deviousness* it is seen as procedurally bred organizational maladaptiveness. It is ultimately rooted in insensitivity, never malevolence. Conflicts become inconsistencies. The remedy is communication wholesomely intended and persistently attempted, indeed organizationally institutionalized.

Among other reasons, this perspective is noteworthy because it implies that manipulativeness is a last (or at least very late) resort when people deal with one another. It is situationally imposed on people. Their problems are created as a macro-organizational consequence of bad communication patterns that come back to torment them in their daily dealings. The answers and clarifications people need are not there in a meaningful way when they need them. At the same time, supercilious amens that they don't need, and externally imposed, inconsistent demands are placed on them as well. Born of stress, the responses people make perpetuate the unhealthy collective cycle, and passively evasive individuals cannot find full relief.

The preceding discussion out of the organizational literature offers a view of individual patterns of adjustment to organizational society. It finds the fundamental rub to reside in a generic, if idiosyncratically modifiable, form of reaction.

In extensions of this genre, the looseness of the concept of organization, with its vague and flexible constellation of implicit referents, invites easy culture-level generalizations and reductionist interpretations as well. It applies to factories, offices, and "the organizational society." Indeed the structure of argument just described has many close cousins intended to explain various levels of organization: Merton's (1968) "bureaucratic personality" of the modern workaday bureaucracy; White's (1957) "organization man" of post-war materialism; Presthus' (1965) further evolved ambivalents, upward-mobiles, and indifferents; Howton's (1969) functionaries in a technological/organizational society, and so on.

PERSONALITY AND SOCIETY WRIT LARGEST: PSYCHOLOGICAL ANTHROPOLOGY

Extending the disciplinary horizons, it is not a very far leap to the most explicit form of grand inquiry into the personality–organizational/societal relationship and the various "chicken or egg" schema by which they shape one another. This is the quest for models of the interplay between individual personality and the cultural context of institutions and collective values: the collections of fields and academic orientations known as psychological anthropology. As Bock's (1980) masterful overview of this field reveals, the scholarly persistence in the quest is matched only by the diversity of models, schools, and shifting disciplinary juxta-positions displayed in its pursuit. This is work on a breathtakingly vast plane of scholarly inquiry, grand theory that is of a very grand sweep indeed. As Bock noted, in building on an earlier overview offered by LeVine (1973; see also, Galdston, 1971) the varieties of models receiving sustained interest spans from the search for basic personalities characteristic of given cultures, through slightly more qualified concepts of modal personality, to isomorphism of personality and culture systems, and national character constructs. These and other variations are in turn associable with various disciplinary orientations from linguistics to orthodox Freudianism, neo-Marxism, and so on, introducing not a few disciplinary frictions along the way. This jarring diversity of fundamental orientations within a common enterprise is not lost on Bock, who concluded:

> Viewed over the first century of its existence, psychological anthropology exhibits two complementary tendencies: It examines in ever finer detail the cultural and interactional constraints on individuals' behavior while simulta-

neously considering the widest possible context for any action (Price-Williams 1975:18). Our survey of issues and approaches in psychological anthropology brings us to this question: *Why does a particular society, or school of thought, or individual choose at some point in history to attribute behavior to a particular set of causes?* To answer this question we would need a psychohistory of the behavioral sciences (see Devereux, 1978:373–375; Coles, 1970). Difficult as this sounds, it may be a necessary prolegomenon to any future synthesis. (p. 250)

I fear that neither psychiatry nor the behavioral sciences, nor certainly the present enterprise can afford to wait for this. However, what psychological anthropology does offer our enterprise is a reminder of the importance of multiple levels of analysis in the personality–society connection. We may see society promulgating, or conditioning, the interpersonal orientation rooted in a generic personality profile that it fosters as a kind of personality template. We may see society as the institutional network whose general form and culturally distinctive features represent a systemic extrapolation from the dynamics of individual encounter which mark out what is most remarkable about life in that culture. Usually we will see both extremes as part of a circular process. What we must supplement this perspective with, or more honestly compensate it with, in adapting this perspective to the examination of manipulativeness, is a concern with middle-level themes. When undertaken for complex modern societies, this approach allows for the extensive use of various tools from a variety of disciplines, but in application to social phenomena of a manageable scope. It is on the middle level precepts that the working tools and concepts of a variety of disciplines have their greatest potential for commonality. Epistemologically, we are free to range up and down the full length of the levels of analysis ladder that psychological anthropology manages so well, from individual personality to macro, social system. But in the pursuit of middle-level themes we travel up and down the ladder carrying less baggage. We study not the whole personality per se but themes within it (i.e., significant trait constellations). We study not the macro edifice of culture and institutions for all their distinctive features in a given society, but those that especially resonate as isomorphic with or fundamentally linked with trait constellations, with personality facets of interest.

Comparative psychological anthropology with a quantitative thrust is often middle-range oriented, but the comparative orientation leads to an epistemological emphasis on horizontal translatability across contexts, rather than on vertical consistency amidst transformation up and down the ladder of emergent properties. To study a middle-level notion like manipulativeness, we need be less concerned with the gamut of personality traits in full complex configuration for individuals. We can dispense with comparative analysis across cultures initially. So lightening the burden however, we do well to retain the levels-of-analysis concern across individual and societal manifestations.

PSYCHOLOGY IN MAINSTREAM POLITICAL SCIENCE

In striking contrast to psychological anthropology's sweeping overview of the interplay between personality and sociocultural institutional processes, stands the orientation to psychology in politics that characterizes political science in its "normal science" mode (Kuhn, 1963). For contemporary, mainstream political science it is reasonable to say there are few major psychological issues perceived and pursued as such. There are rather, somewhat psychologically oriented variables introduced in the study of behavior associated with political institutions and their processes. The paradigmatic political science orientation is typified in this respect by the orientation of its literature on party identification, often more broadly described as the subfield of either "political socialization" or "political behavior." Thus, it is typical to operationalize the concept of "socializing influences" on individuals' party choices, as the record of parents' party membership (Franklin & Jackson, 1983).

Similarly, in a sophisticated and important study of differences in the attachment to the established political parties that were displayed by two successive generations surveyed over 17 years, Jennings and Markus (1984) raised the issue of "psychological ties to political parties" but understand it in conventional political science terms. Focusing on high school students in 1965 and also their parents, and tracing these two groups over 17 years, the authors found that for each generation, party identification increases in stability, or "crystalizes" with the passage of time. At the same time, the filial generation's partisan attachment stabilizes at a decidedly lower level of party commitment. They noted in interpreting an aspect of this pattern: "Between the mid-20s and the mid-30s, moderate degrees of consolidation and constraint begin to replace the attitudinal fragmentation and disorder of the young adult years. In this respect party identification, although special for its relatively greater continuity, is but part of a more general learning process" (Jennings & Markus, 1984, p. 1008). In a footnote immediately following this passage the authors noted that "here as elsewhere throughout this report, the overall findings beg for fine grained analysis of the impact of individual life histories and macrolevel events. We intend to pursue these topics in subsequent reports" (p. 1008). Part of the evidence for the pattern that Jennings and Marcus asserted is the finding that this pattern holds not only for overly political measures, but also for a cluster of measures as well: "self-confidence; personal trust; opinion strength; interpretation of Bible; and church attendance" (p. 1007). Indeed they note that the first and third "are more properly considered personality traits" (p. 1008).

It is playful to note that their professional jargon—with its references to degrees of consolidation and greater continuity replacing a condition of fragmentation and disorder as part of a continuing development, and all the notice of the indirect relevance of self-confidence, opinion strength, trust, measures of religion-related factors and later a discussion in terms of "partisan *objects*"—are faintly reminiscent of the language of psychoanalytic self-psychology, with its emphasis on the narcissistic dimension of personality in all its aspects. Self-psychology is well represented in psychohistory and figures prominently in later sections of this work. Of course, understandably, in the context of the political science of the *American Political Science Review* nothing could be further from the current research frame of reference. The important point from our perspective is that the mainstream political science orientation has a genuine, but clearly a secondary, and relatively passing interest in psychological factors. Moreover in this respect, the field takes in the main, a decidedly "behavioral" stimulus–response interpretation of the dynamics of the political processes under its attention. Thus, among their conclusions, Jennings and Marcus (1984) observed that "As a group, members of the younger cohort have stabilized at a level of partisan loyalty notably below that of their parents. This has led to more volatile voting among younger electors which, in turn has failed to provide the kind of consistent electoral reinforcement required to enhance preexisting attachments to political parties" (p. 1016).

This framework with the emphasis on the dynamics of a reinforcement process in a behavioralistic context makes the potential psychology and politics of mainstream political science much more the psychology of B.F. Skinner than a psychology of complex inner mental states. In social science today as in political science in particular, "the behavior" is the unit of analysis. The dynamics of inner life become either "a black box," or worse yet, are "assumed to have effects randomized in the aggregate," the modern social science equivalent of being vaporized. I do not presume to call this a failing, only one consequence of an epistemological choice to take a different road.

2

Levels of Analysis
and Strategies for Understanding:
Vertical Divisions
in Problem Approach

PSYCHOLOGIZED ANALYSIS, LEVELS OF ANALYSIS,
AND DIMENSIONS OF UNDERSTANDING

If mainstream political science has made the choice to take a road that is largely unpsychologized, the choice, although eminently within the discipline's "rights," is not without its irony. As a past president of the American Political Science Association, Harold Lasswell (1960) wrote in 1930 and stuck by in 1960: "Political science without biography is a form of taxidermy" (p. 1). As one committed both to psychoanalysis and the study of political institutions, Lasswell was not arguing the superiority of some simple reductionism. To explore the implications of his perspective, it is worth excerpting at length from an essay in praise of Lasswell by another former American Political Science Association president, Heinz Eulau (1969). Eulau observed:

> Though Lasswell never explicitly and directly discussed emergence as a philosophical assumption, his frequent use of the terms "event manifold" and "emergent" indicates his acceptance, it [sic] not the doctrine of emergent evolution, at least of the philosophical notion of emergence. For instance: "If the significant political changes of the past were signalized by revolutionary innovations, the future may well follow the same course of development. Hence our "present" would be transition between the latest and the impending world revolutionary emergent . . .

"Emergent evolution" was a philosophical doctrine that was bred by crossing Darwin and Hegel. It implied, therefore, two conceptions—one of *existential* emergence and one of *functional* emergence. These concepts are by no means opposed to each other. Existential emergence means that in the course of development certain qualities, objects, or events come into existence which did not previously exist, and that knowledge about such novel types of existents— that is, emergents—cannot be derived from knowledge of what existed previously. Functional emergence means that the functioning of different types of existents is irreducible, so that no single theory can explain the characteristic functions of all types. These functional discontinuities are due to the existence of "levels of organization," regardless of whether these levels are novel or were always present. If novelty is stressed, the notion of functional emergence, like that of existential emergence, hold that the emergents cannot be explained by propositions that could explain previously existing phenomena; if levels of organization are emphasized, the doctrine holds that explanations of lower-level phenomena cannot be applied to the functioning of higher-level phenomena. But regardless of where the accent is put, the notion of emergence assumes an ultimate pluralism in propositions that are needed to describe and explain the functioning of different types of phenomena. Both existential and functional emergence assert the nondeducibility of the phenomena with which they are concerned. In the case of existential emergence, this nondeducibility can be called "unpredictability." But in the case of functional emergence, it can be called "irreducibility . . .

The notion of emergence has aided in overcoming may old dualisms. Just as such "nothing but" ways of thinking—pluralism versus monism, determinism versus free will, or materialism versus idealism—could be abandoned by philosophy, so Lasswell could dispose of the logic versus free-fantasy dualism and suggest a compromise. In this new mode of though it was unnecessary to make a choice between extreme views. What appears to be antithetical is reconciled on a new plane. It represents a position which Lasswell has repeated time and again in his various writings when he enjoins us to occupy as many observational standpoints as possible in the analysis of individual, social, and cultural phenomena.

But what of the "thorny problem" of research on individual and society that bothered Lasswell? We can see now that it was linked in his mind to the problem of utilizing appropriate ways of thinking about the phenomena involved. In the *Psychopathology* he had probed deeply into the microbehavior of individuals, but there remained the problem of how such knowledge cold be made relevant to an explanation of social entities. Lasswell did not assume as is sometimes assumed by less sophisticated students of individual behavior, that societal phenomena can be explained solely by means of a theory concerning their microstructures. Insight into societal behavior at the level of the individual may be a necessary condition for explanation of social phenomena, but it is not a sufficient condition. Lasswell came to identify classes of events in society and culture which could not be explained by theoretical propositions about the behavior of individuals in terms of personality. His concern, clearly, was a theory of classes of events that were unexplained. Similar concerns were at the root of the doctrine of emergence.

Emergence, we have seen, refers to the process by which *new* effects (or process or events) arise from the operation of antecedent causes (or processes or events). As a result of emergence new *wholes* (or configurations) appear which include or show *novel* properties that are qualitatively different from the sum of the properties of their constituent parts. This is not to say that aggregation of individual properties is not a legitimate operation to describe new wholes. For instance, if we speak of the median age of a group, the property "age" is stated in the form of a summation. But when we speak of a group's cohesion or integration, we do not refer to some arithmetic value, but to something new — an emergent property that cannot be reduced to some characteristic of its individual members. The new phenomenon is a "whole" that cannot be dissected or taken apart and then reassembled like an automobile. We can see better now, I think, what Lasswell meant when he characterized the state as a manifold of events. What he meant was that state behavior cannot be analyzed by disassembling it into parts. In this connection, we must not make too much of Lasswell's use of the term "state," which, at the time, was still the prevailing theoretical concept in political science for what we would call today "political system." A political system can be any political whole whose boundaries are identifiable — the historical "state" as much as a "legislature" or a "party" or a "party system." The important point to keep in mind is that in leading to a conception of the whole, the idea of emergence called attention to the manifold of events that constitutes the whole . . .

. . . If it is correct, then, that in the course of interaction of individual parts new properties appear or emerge that characterize the whole, the behavior of the parts and whole must be analyzed on different levels — a macroscopic and microscopic level. And as behavior on the macrolevel is new and emergent, it requires new descriptive concepts and possibly new empirical propositions that are independent of the concepts and propositions relevant to the microlevel. Confusion of levels has disastrous consequences for scientific explanation and interpretation. (pp. 21–28)*

For our purposes here, the most interesting point in the preceding excerpts is Eulau's suggestion that Lasswell's sensitivity to levels-of-analysis issues and emergence phenomena (with interactive features, no less) led him to a

---

*Reprinted from *The Journal of Politics*, 30(1), February 1968. Copyright © 1968 by The Southern Political Science Association and the University of Florida. By permission of the author and the University of Texas Press.

particular epistemological position: Simple reductionism is impossible and yet a formal levels-spanning, unified theory is also beyond us. The wiser and still enormously ambitious goal is a metaperspective that spans levels not with a "master level" of analysis but with a multilevel awareness—a kind of simultaneous understanding with partial translatability, in comtemplating social phenomena. This is a fluency to be gained, however, by working through multiple analyses of an action system, undertaken at distinct levels and only then assessed in overview. Thus, arises the tendency in such writing to shift from unidimensional analysis to a call for a reorganized disciplinary perspective and agenda. Again, as Eulau (1969) noted:

> If I understand it correctly, the "General Framework" was Lasswell's attempt to come to grips with the problem of interlevel relations. What motivated him to deal with the problem was, I suspect, his desire to avoid the reductionist trap into which his preoccupation with individual psychological mechanisms might have led him, as is indeed the case with many psychologists interested in social phenomena. He was too much of a social and political scientist not to sense that behavior at the level of group or culture followed laws that were quite independent of propositions about microscopic behavior items. Yet, though he resisted reduction, or perhaps because he resisted it, Lasswell recognized problems of interlevel or translevel relations that must necessarily arise if reduction is not feasible. The amazing thing is, I think, that his essay is as suggestive today as it was almost thirty years ago, for we have made little progress in the solution of the problem. Although the essay was reprinted in a volume devoted to political behavior, its original appearance in *Psychiatry* as well as its unfamiliar vocabulary seems to have deterred political scientists from following up on his suggestions; and this despite the fact that political science occupies an eminently interstitial position between the three basic behavioral sciences. I am confident that in the future, as political scientists must come to terms with the interstitial position of their discipline and hence with the problem of emergent properties in the macrostructures and processes that interest them, they will have to turn to the "General Framework" for guidance and enlightenment. (pp. 31–32)

It is to political science's misfortune that the discipline seems not yet to have confirmed Eulau's confidence in this regard. However, the discipline seems not to dispute the merit of his grand view, having elected him its president.[1] The broad implications of level of analysis issues—in political

---

[1] Of course it is also interesting to speculate on the proportion of political scientists acknowledging a debt to Eulau who construe his contribution to rest on some narrow "behavioral" or "empirical" dimension without being aware of the Lasswellian dimension of his perspective in the subject matter of political science.

science in general, and in what might be accredited the "political science perspective" on organization theory in particular—have not been centrally addressed, much less worked through by a disciplinary community.[2] However, the challenge has probably become more difficult if no less important, since Lasswell's writing. As the extended excerpt on Lasswell indicates, his position on how level-of-analysis considerations should be handled is sanguine not only in calling for a systematic disciplinary agenda, but also in several other respects.

MULTILEVEL ANALYSIS AND DEVELOPMENTS WITHIN LEVELS

The "manifold of events" must now include a macrolevel of analysis conceived in terms of highly distinctive emergents far more resistant to integration with individualistic concepts than was available at the height of Lasswell's activity. The multipositioned observer faces an altogether new order of challenge with the advances of general systems theory. It has had a considerable impact on the various branches of political science, albeit an impact currently observable in the field's implicit working assumptions rather than in the jargon of its most current titles as was once the case, from the mid-1960s through the mid-1970s. As the upper reaches of macrotheory in their most elaborate and explicit form, general systems theory is quite alive and well in the multidisciplinary field of organization theory, where the organization as system is already a given for serious theorizing. Lasswell does not offer enough description of his epistemology of multipositioned observation to meaningfully incorporate such a newer level of macroanalysis. Partly as a result of these factors, Lasswell's constructs are not sufficient to build upon. The disciplinary sands beneath them have shifted infortuitously.

To be sure, the principle that political man displaces private matters onto public objects with accompanying rationalizations was an important revelation. And although it now seems obvious only because that is the fate of great revelations that are accepted, the practical matter is that it offers little by way of handholds for current theory building. The latter must span more contemporary interpretations of macrosystemic, organizational, and even intrapsychic processes.

---

[2]Alas, this is certainly still true despite my own writing on the subject, in which I have taken two tacks: first, to turn the emergence process back on the analyst as a phenomenon of reasoning not events, indicating the extent to which micro and macro constructs may be explored as isomorphic abstractions (Lerner, 1982). Second, I have sought to untangle micro- and macroconnotations in the vocabulary of political science, showing the implicit assumptions that considerably distort analysis til one does so (Lerner, 1986).

Lasswelliana in its particulars offers an understandably "old-style" psychoanalytic perspective. Its political science parallel in emphasis is the focus on coercion. The less overtly power-preoccupied constellation of concepts associable with *manipulation* as we see here, is more congenial to a psychodynamic concern not with power struggles analogous to classic drive conflicts, but with self-environment (i.e., "self-selfobject") relations analogous to the currently widespread emphasis on character disorders, narcissism, and the dynamics of the sense of harmony and continuity in the experience of the self in its relationship to the social surround. These are points that are elaborated later. Their simple mention at this juncture is useful in highlighting the last and in some ways most circumstantial development that renders the Lasswell tradition in political psychology both generally suggestive, and unwieldy in its specifics, as a foundation for probing the nature of manipulativeness in modern politics and organization.

Lasswell observed in his 1960 "Afterthoughts" to *Psychopathology and Politics:*

> It must be apparent by this time why the study of politicians (and of politics in general) by methods largely inspired by psychoanalysis has made but modest progress to date. There are thousands of political roles. It is a vast social audit to discern these roles in the conventional or the functional sense. And it is a vast task to ascertain the degree in which these roles are played by power-oriented personalities. It is a huge undertaking to demonstrate the developmental sequence that results in the formation of a power-centered personality at maturity—that is, one who prefers to impose rather than persuade even when persuasion would accomplish every desired outcome (except the opportunity to coerce) . . .

> But the *Psychopathology* obviously did not restrict the definition of political personality to conscious perspective. It examined the results of various observational standpoints in order to bring out unconscious as well as conscious structure. Data concerning unconscious orientation are important in arriving at a final classification of political roles as nuclear or peripheral to a given personality system. The significant question appears to be whether denials of opportunity to play a political role—even a humble one—will destroy the integration of the person. Sometimes the environment performs an "experiment" for us and imposes such deprivations upon the individual—by forcing him out of office, for instance. As a result the person may attempt an extreme internalization (suicide) or display somatic conversion symptoms of a severely incapacitating nature, or become mentally disordered. Some of the cases reported in the *Psychopathology* came to the attention of the therapists precisely because of political reverses. They were power-oriented persons in the fullest sense of our definition, since their capacity to continue as integrated members of society depend upon a social situation in which they pursued and exercised

power with some success. These personality systems were so rigidly oriented
toward the playing of a particular set of roles that they were unable to maintain
their integrity when the opportunities were shut off. (pp. 290–291, 297)

These themes of rigidity and compulsiveness, of repression and blocked
drives, support a psychology of power expression and energy release through
coercion and domination.[3] The recent turn in psychoanalytic theory has
emphasized character disturbance rather than traditional neurosis, and
disturbances in narcissistic development rather than drive conflicts. The
Lasswellian "displacement onto public objects" with accompanying rationalizations seems nowadays to have as a more appropriate social science parallel,
a concern with the dynamics of gamesman behavior (Maccoby, 1976),
manipulativeness, themes of narcissistic disturbance mirrored in shifting
cultural patterns and social/institutional motifs. If Lasswell saw pathology in
the preference of coercion over persuasion, we may suspect pathology in the
preference for manipulation over discourse.

All in all, what Lasswell primarily offers this modest enterprise is an
understanding of the political science–individual psychology relationship as a
levels of analysis challenge and opportunity. Thorough analysis requires
exploring our subject from several vantage points along the levels of analysis
continuum. At the same time, this comes with the caveat that the exemplar
of the macro extreme now as "system," raises very new issues. Also, the
dynamics of inner life that are relevant must be explored in the context of a
considerably evolved theory framework at the individual psychodynamic
level. Its ripples and reflections on the institutional level may correspondingly
require new conceptual themes. These considerations are not primarily
traceable to the mere passage of time; Lasswell was ahead of his time. Rather,
I believe they stem from the fact that Lasswell has been honored more in
myth than in practice in current political science, whose epistemological
casualness, frequent subfield fragmentation, and generally lessened interest
in the connection between inner life and political life, make the discipline less
Lasswellian in practice.

FURTHER VARIATIONS IN APPLIED PSYCHOANALYSIS

If we could in fact find a current representative of social psychology as an
attempt at comprehensive "grand theory" on the societal level, I believe
Lasch's (1978) work on "the narcissistic society" would have to be pointed to
as an example. Work of this type, perhaps because of a concern to keep the

---

[3]For a newer and provocative psychological perspective on "domination" see Balbus, 1982.

popular reader (and also the humanist more than the social scientist), makes the personality–society connection with relatively casual metaphor, with loose imagery, and with highly articulate polemics. Popularization and polemicism are of course honorable traditions in social criticism. Unfortunately for our purposes, the priorities of popularization, polemicism, and humanistic imagery are not always the priorities of social science theory building.

Lasch provided a pointed overview of the increasing prevalence of narcissism-related disorders in clinical diagnosis. He dramatically presented a sweeping picture of the social problems that a "narcissistic" outlook may breed. These observations are entwined—but I believe not inextricably so—with judgments on the price and future of capitalism. Lasch's exploration of "a culture of narcissism" is suggestive for a multifaceted study of manipulativeness in contemporary society, because it explores many interesting connections. His suggestion that shifts in societal patterns of psychopathology reflect shifts in social values and adjustment to them is a well-rooted working assumption in psychosocial theorizing. When used with care it independently supports the case for expecting a link between psychological and institutional/social developments.

The point here is that for theory building, these richly suggestive associations must be explored with epistemological care, anchored in a more manageable focus on a comparatively middle range (if still far-reaching) concept like manipulativeness, and detached from potentially distorted, added meaning in service of a theory of the state—again an honorable, but I believe at this stage, potentially quite complicating enterprise.

The challenge to social science is to mine work on this plane for its insights, albeit its highly stylized insights; to provide a conceptual infrastructure for extending and displaying them, adding to them, cleaning them of polemic, sharpening their epistemologies; and linking them to a broader enterprise. This is in part the difficult process of probing, qualifying, and elaborating notions Lasch leaves in the tone of "the degradation of sport"; "the spread of stupefaction"; "the collapse of achievement"; "the apotheosis of individualism" (Lasch, 1978). These and other nuggets must be sifted, sorted, scrubbed, and strung together, when scientific theory building about the interaction of personality dynamics and social institutional dynamics becomes the aim.

PSYCHOANALYSIS AND ORGANIZATIONS

The last in the catalog of approaches from which this book draws but that subsequently go in directions not satisfactory for our purpose, is a not too large but extremely interesting body of work. It is concerned with what might be described as the intended direct application of psychodynamic theory to organizational analysis.[4]

The title of a fairly recent book by Robert de Board states the focus of this genre of organizational analysis quite straightforwardly. Its subtitle offers a clue to some of the difficulties that ensue and with which we will have to come to some sort of arrangement. The book is de Board's (1978) *The Psychoanalysis of Organizations: A Psychoanalytic Approach to Behavior in Groups and Organizations.*

The application of psychoanalytic concepts directly to organizations is potentially quite important for theory development. As the more conventional organization theory has long recognized, organization is very much the mystery of a structural context shaping and yet consisting of individual behavior pressed into abstract forms (rules, roles, units, subsystems). These are alleged to be more than individual-level determined. Indeed they are presented as resisting definition in simply individual-level terms. Of course this was part of the issue in effecting a Lasswellian, multilevel orientation for a discipline.

If the application of psychoanalytic, and therefore basically individual-level concepts to the study of organizations is to surmount this problem, then there are at least two possibilities for how the world is held together in this regard. One possibility is that an organization as a human collectivity must be directly psychoanalyzeable in some way, based upon psychoanalytic meaning of a group "personality"or "psychologically collective structure" when the organization is the actor to whom the psychoanalytic theories are applied. A second possibility is to see the collectivity, the organization, as somehow having internal processes symbolically analogous to the dynamics of the individual psyche. Then the organizational events could be understood by seeing them as the outcome of organizational processes that relate organizational elements and forces in a fashion parallel to the relationship among individual mental elements and forces that produce analogous states. Then, the organization itself can be in such a sense, "neurotic," "fixated," "hysterical," and so on. In a sense we might thus describe the former literal

---

[4]This is now probably not the first juncture at which it may be observed that as Lasswell's use of the term *state* may be more currently rendered as *the political system* according to Eulau, so the *prevailing theoretical concept in political science* could from my perspective be eventually and to some advantage, be replaced as well, by the term *organization*. In both its micro and abstract macro rendering, it can congenially carry the weight of both "government" and "generic" political institutions. This would fit well with the ever increasing political science interest in politics with a small "p" as well as politics with a capital "G" so to speak, as pertains to the study of government per se. We make use of this sense of the central political domain in several later sections.

application as organizational psychoanalysis while seeing the later isomorphism-based metaphoric application as organizational "psychoanalysis." Literal organizational psychoanalysis is a concept whose plausibility strikes me as curvilinear. I believe those who are extremely naive and those who are extremely wise scholars would tend to see it as impossible. In between these extremes there is work based on the faith that an organization can be psychoanalyzed just as a group could be psychoanalyzed. This orientation draws precedent from Freud's somewhat peripheral but still notable speculations on group processes.

The appeal of this genre would seem to be the prospect of understanding an organization's behavior at the level of the deep interacting motivations of its participants. Its behavior becomes a function of shared inner life. This shared emotional field would have to be understood as a dynamic system representing the interplay among personalities. In this sense there is a psychodynamic system of the whole as well as of each individual. The interplay between individual contributing personalities' states and processes, the shared field, and the external realm as domain for acting out, becomes the ideal scope of subject matter explored with psychodynamic tools.

Now so far, this strikes me as quite plausible and also worthwhile, if ambitious in equal measure. What the success of any such program hinges upon is the ability to account for macrolevel (i.e., institutional level, emergent properties). Then the shared interpersonal field could be seen in its interaction with the multifaceted institutional rule system. The latter is a human product of complex systemic intricacy that has been conceptualized with what many would see as excruciating, comprehensive abstraction, by Etzioni (1971), Parsons (1951), and Katz and Kahn (1978), to name three major variations on the grand theme of organization as system understandable by *system-level processes* (if not "laws").

The major failure of the directly psychoanalytic approach to organization has been precisely the failure to deal with organization as regular system on this macrolevel while absorbing it within the psychodynamic framework. Regarding any attempt at what might be called a *unified theory* that would span individual psyche and macro-system, institutional dynamics, something in fact has had to give, so far, it seems. What gives tends to be a genuine macro-systemic interpretation of organizations as systems.

Thus, returning to the example noted earlier, de Board's very interesting little volume with its fascinating title *The Psychoanalysis of Organizations*, hints at the seemingly standard limitation in this regard in its subtitle, *A Psychoanalytic Approach to Behavior in Groups and Organizations*. It seems basically to turn out that the psychoanalytic interpretation of behavior in organizations is simply the psychoanalytic interpretation of groups restated. Organizations seem to be taken as the context of groups at times, as basically just a big group, perhaps as an implicitly infinite repetition of group behaviors, and at most and *quite* implicitly if at all, as a network of (or group of) groups. This epistemology is implicit in de Board's interesting piece. It is explicit in Eulau's (1964) work. Such an epistemological position is characteristic of the school de Board typifies, whereby the analyst observes the task performance of a group assigned its work within an organization, and that group experience becomes an organizational episode. The effect is that although offered the psychoanalysis of organization, we receive the psychoanalysis of a group, not withstanding that it is empirically plucked from what common speech would concede is indeed an organization. In de Board's case specifically, a work crew taken from a coal company. The problem is it is still the work group and not the collectivity, "the company," as a genuine macro entity whose behavior is analyzed. This is the moat the Laswellian agenda has difficulty crossing.

It may be interesting to note here that an erstwhile candidate for a genuinely psychoanalytically oriented, macroanalysis—the psychoanalysis of mass movements—overshoots the mark, in contrast. It implicitly depends on an institutionless, structurally undifferentiated, underspecified collectivity of *the mass.* It reflects in its way too, the difficulty of reformulating the psychoanalytic perspective to make it apply to generically institutional level, system processes whose workings are conceptualized to operate as processes free of intentionality, motive, and self-consciousness, but according to specifiable relational determinants (Lerner, 1986).

This "conceptual bait and switch" (I describe the error that way to be vivid; of course, I don't mean literally that any intentional deception is involved) also appears as an error in classic macrolevel, systems analysis as well. This happens when the latter fails to sustain its deeper assumptions in the presentation of case studies. What are alleged to illustrate macro, system-level processes in organizations are actually studies of small-group dynamics. In a near perfect example of this problem, Katz and Kahn (1978) in *The Social Psychology of Organizations* offer the same example of coal miner work-group arrangements offered by de Board, as one of the culminating case illustrations in their study of the organization as system. De Board offered the study in his *Psychoanalysis of Organizations.* Thus, Katz and Kahn from their macro-systems perspective on organization, fail to keep their footing and slip down the levels of analysis ladder. This occurs when illustrating the fruits of their systems perspective. They produce a study of small-group dynamics instead. De Board, attempting to offer the psychoanalysis of organizations, failed to attain a genuinely organizational level application, and produced a study of simple, small-group dynamics instead—indeed, the same study. If Katz and

Kahn slipped on the ladder when working from its top, de Board failed to see that the top was at yet a higher rung. One result of this unintended meeting at the middle has been a disproportionately major minor element in the annals of organizational analysis. This is not a picky issue, however.

ORGANIZATIONS AND PSYCHOANALYTIC THEORY: THE EPISTEMOLOGICAL CRUX

The question of whether emergent, systems-level properties of organization can be conceptually linked to psychodynamic processes is a vital question. Without the link there is no psychodynamic theory or psychoanalysis of organizations. There may still be the "psychoanalysis" of organization, that is the establishment of extensive metaphoric parallels in the conceptualization of key processes. This is frequently possible as a device for relating separate and distinct action domains, often when one – and especially if both – are viewed as "systems" in some sense. I believe the reason for this has to do with the tendency to see action realms treatable in the same language as ultimately derivable from one another in principle. Things translatable in the same (analytical) language seem relatable to one another. Ultimately, this may advance our conceptual language more than our power over the empirical domains being translated with it. However, that is a dividend too, and besides, the better the language the better the attack on the empirical realm will be.

I do not know if we will eventually ever psychoanalytically comprehend (i.e., analytically deconstruct and reconstruct) organization qua organization. However, more immediately, we can improve the intellectual grasp of selective areas of linkage. I refer to areas of linkage between individual motives to influence organizational events and organizational–systemic responsiveness to such influence. That is, we may not for a while lay out comprehensive isomorphism maps depicting the parallel between intrapsychic and organizational–systemic processes. Also, we may not for a while lay out a grand unified theory spanning intrapsychic and organizational, systemic processes. However, we can in our eclectic, middle-range themes, discern compatibility or incompatibility between macroprocesses (structural features of institutional systems) and microforces (profiles of individual inclinations: personality profiles, and group developments).

When this perspective is taken in the study of middle-level themes like manipulative behavior in organizational life, analysis proceeds via questions such as these: What features of organizational structure would tend to enhance the manifestation of members' manipulativeness? What structural features—and elements of the value system, and climates of attitude—would amplify the effects of manipulative behavior? Conversely, which such features block, muffle, segregate, and serve to help extinguish such behavior orientations? What general organizational conditions, in terms of relationship patterns, degrees of formalization, structural elaborateness and differentiation, centralization of decision making, conventional or unconventional form—and so on as we see later—produce a hospitable or hostile host/organizational environment for the growth and spread of the manipulative orientation to behavior in organizations? To what personality proclivities for manipulativeness do given structural arrangements provide individual nourishment and circumstances conducive to spread (secondarily through imitation, as well as primarily through the attraction of self-selectively available, appropriate personality types)? In tight turn, what structural features of organization are manipulative persons likely to nurture, or less intendedly facilitate, in the growth and development of the organizational structures they inhabit?

Analysis oriented in these directions throws up two foci for inquiry. For one, we must know the manipulator: his or her personality dynamics, how he or she behaves, and how he or she experiences and reacts to his or her environment. Second, we must understand organizational forms not simply as objects of analysis in themselves, not as "independent explainers" of some organizational product, but as context. The organization's features constitute a configuration of available launching plateaus for manipulation. At the same time that they represent a path of potential handholds for individuals making their way up the organizational mountain, they also offer clefts of refuge from such actors. Their structural configuration necessarily marks the paths that are open, shows that others do not exist, and determines in circular interplay with the creative and skilled actor, what is likely to be attempted and what not. Organizational structure is a set of tools, a set of constraints, and an object of the effort as well.

In order to "know" the manipulator in this sense, and for the analytical purposes indicated, it is necessary to make some research choices with attendant prices for the benefits they promise. The choices I have made in this work were guided by the desire to retain the strong features of each of the styles of psychopolitical inquiry discussed in this and the preceding chapter, while avoiding their weakness and mistakes. The hope has been to advance the technique of psychopolitical inquiry by combining the strengths of various schools to produce a hardy hybrid, to avoid the inevitable weak points of any approach taken alone. Additionally, in the following chapters,

I have sought to match an intense treatment of the micro-issue of manipulative personality, with a genuinely macro-organizational level analysis. This analysis is oriented to the issues raised by exploration of the personality dynamics of the manipulative orientation, but proceeds from concepts formulated for the purely macro-systems level.

SUMMARIZING TO THIS JUNCTURE:
CHAPTERS 1 AND 2 IN PERSPECTIVE

In terms of drawing analytical power from what has come before, there are specific lessons to be drawn from the preceding pages. Game theory and the "rational choice" literature have the strength of clarifying the structure of tactical problems that underlie broadly grouped dilemmas and conflicts. These styles of work are good at isolating the structure of problems in terms of the tactics to which they are responsive or unresponsive. This is true in terms of interaction with a passive edifice of conditions or an interactive counterpart.

This instinct for the tactical structure of a situation, shaped by a competing other or disinterested social circumstances, is a useful conceptual orientation to the interplay between individual and organization or among individuals within organization. It is potentially a useful supplementary understanding of the notion of "organizational structure"—now structure also in terms of the configuration of tactical levers and deadends presented to strategizing participants. What must be added to this is a more sophisticated understanding at two extremes: the organizational context and the psychological dimension.

As contended earlier, it seems that the assumed randomization of psychological factors in game theory and rational choice has made them unnecessarily barren as regards large domains of social science concerns. Rational choice and game theory assumptions might prove far more powerful and interesting with the introduction of greater organizational and psychological considerations. The latter can often be expressed easily in the language of this research tradition that has chosen to exclude them (Etzioni, 1983; Lerner & Rundquist, 1984).

Thus, in dealing with manipulativeness in organizational life I have sought to supplement the tactical crispness of the game-theory approach with a greater sensitivity in two respects. The first concerns a willingness to see wide variations in individual tendency and ability to take subtle and sophisticated, complex, systems-comprehensive overviews of their relations with others. This is the issue of strategy beyond mere tactics discussed in chapter 1.

I have also sought to supplement the merits of a tactically aware view of

manipulativeness by adding as well, concern with the dimension of actors'
inner lives. These are relevant as they bear on the perception of organizational episodes and actors' self-expression through behavior in organization.
The sensitivity to inner life that this study of manipulativeness in organizations tries to incorporate, is not the biographical emphasis of
psychobiography. The latter at its best is a powerful extension of psychoanalysis that makes its contribution to social science suggestively and indirectly
via the humanities. This is not an approach easily compatible with a social
science focus on organizational dynamics that should incorporate an institutional-level set of questions. The appeal here is also not the overly
personalized adaptation of psychoanalytically informed imagination, or what
might be called a kind of "wild analysis" for social science (Kohut, 1984)–a
genre also discussed in chapter 1.

Instead, I have sought to explore issues of inner life related to manipulative
behavior in a way more readily compatible with the contemporary social
science comfort with aggregate data, statistical concepts of correlation and
significance, and generalization from scales yielding phenotypic profiles. The
latter would be based on interpretive guidelines that are both "rational" as the
jargon goes (derived theoretically), as well as "clinical" (based on a long
experience of a professional community dealing with subjects and patients).
At the same time I have sought out techniques of use to the more as well as
the less psychodynamically inclined within the psychotherapy communities.
In short, I have sought to explore the inner life issues associable with
manipulativeness in the organizational context, through the selective administration of projective and objective psychological tests. These are specifically,
the MMPI and TAT, administered to individuals also assessed for manipulativeness, as are detailed in a later section.

There are choices to be made in taking the general, connotatively rich and
scientifically imprecise notion of manipulativeness to a researchable level of
specificity. In casting for an operationalization compatible with the desire to
echo the strengths of several approaches discussed earlier a few criteria loom
large.

Like the psychology of mainstream organizational social psychology that
Kahn et al. (1964) exemplify, it seems that a psychology of manipulativeness
that is most likely to be compatible with organizational analysis, now at a
genuinely macrolevel, would be one able to avoid undue dependence on
concepts of illness, via exclusive derivation from the clinical categories of
serious pathology, that is via grounding in extremes. The roots of a smooth
inter-level linkage between organizational concepts representative of organizations in the main, and individual-level concepts applicable to individuals in
the main, is not wisely rooted in concepts of excessive individual-level

aberrance. The social psychology of Everyman best suits the institutional context of EveryOrganization. Thus, what we have to avoid are three pitfalls. First, "homo wholesomeness" (see chapter 1) is too narrow a spectrum of Everyman personality. Stress and ambiguity may be the culprits in self-report, but even that caution aside, these terms seem to cover a tremendous variety of inner experiences.[5] These various inner experiences are likely to call up a considerable variety of reactions, with many of them stemming from personality orientations we have no reason to believe are conspicuously pro-social. In other words, the Everyman Club does not admit only nice guys. We need a psychology for organizations that is more open to this possibility. At the same time we must remember that "not nice" and clinically patholog-ical are very different.

Second, the Social Psychology, qua discipline, orientation to personality, which so dominates organizational psychology[6] is too narrowly focused on personality as interpersonal posture in social and often task or work groups. This is a very valuable sense of personality for some organization theory purposes[7] but less so for our particular purpose here. Therefore, we need a psychology well suited to explaining the individual perspective including its darker side and not overly confined to the group-compatibility preoccupa-tion of social psychology. This is to say we need a psychology of social interaction that has more clinical depth for normals—a subclinical melding of clinical insights and social psychology episodes. This also rules out the still less-suited psychology of normal political science's "political behavior" dis-cussed earlier. It offers this enterprise still less than the conventional social psychology of organizations, in the matter of a psychological framework for building analysis. However, its concern to construct some phenotypic pat-tern for aggregate empirical data is something of a common denominator.

Thus, we are casting for a phenotypic profile with a broad and dynamic texture not unlike the aspiration of psychological anthropology. However, we want to retain the capacity to speak to a relatively middle range concept—manipulativeness. We want to tie the search for a phenotypic manipulator to empirical methods more compatible with social science as it exists today. Also, we want to retain the ability to understand the tactical prowess and the strategic world view associated with it, and see how they affect organizational life. The latter aim involves a focus on the interaction between a personality

---

[5]Whom for example are we to believe when the going gets tough? A former president? (. . . the tough get going), or a wise tee shirt (. . . the tough go shopping)?

[6]There are a few recent exceptions far more in the spirit of this book: See Etheredge, 1985, and my review of it in *Political Psychology*. See also LaBier, 1983.

[7]I have used it myself: Lerner, 1976a. Also in a slight variation, see Levinson and Rosenthal, 1984; Levinson, 1972.

predilection and the vagaries of specific aspects of organizational structure. We will be able to point to them better once we know the personality factors that give the manipulative profile its particular psychological shape.

These interrelated, multilevel goals require something of a Lasswellian approach. If we begin with the individual personality, I assume that the phenomenon of a manipulative profile can be variously sketched from several disciplinary perspectives within psychology. Each one adds depth at the same time that it shifts emphasis. The picture of the manipulative personality element will become more subtle as various styles of psychological investigation are applied to it. It seems profitable to take a multifaceted approach to analyzing manipulativeness even at the individual personality level.

At the same time, multiple perspectives will not clarify matters unless the perspectives can be related. They will not reduce to one another; there is too much richness, independence, and variety in the world of the disciplines. However, if there is an empirical "it" to study, we may expect that good works from a variety of perspectives on personality can yield their common theme. It can give us a fuller, multifaceted, multilayered picture of the manipulative personality than we get from any one discipline alone. With the multifaceted picture, with each disciplinary view rounding out the others, we have a concept with many features of use in linking to other dimensions of theorizing. This can be of special value for linking the individual level understanding of manipulativeness with the organizational level, where we are concerned with the dynamics that seem to amplify or mediate the expression of manipulativeness, and shape its impact on the societal level.

CHAPTERS 3 AND 4 IN PREVIEW

The next two chapters explore the manipulative personality by linking three levels of personality research: the social psychology; diagnostic and testing psychology; and the depth psychological, psychoanalytic psychology. As every weekend artist knows, attaining a perspective in depth requires reference to some fixed point. Thus, while chapter 3 links a psychoanalytic perspective on the possible personality roots of manipulativeness with a social psychological perspective on the manipulative personality, this is done by anchoring the discussion primarily in the social psychology work. We use the features of the social psychology material as a framework for introducing related psychoanalytic issues and concepts. Chapter 3 necessarily alludes to some clinical psychology test findings that I developed for this manuscript. However, because of the layered intricacy of these issues, I reserve chapter 4, separately, for a full-blown discussion of the clinical psychological material on manipulativeness. Additional clinical psychological test results reported in chapter 4 also tend to support the idea of a link between the social psychological and psychoanalytic perspectives on manipulativeness that chapter 3 links more intuitively and discursively. We turn now to a discussion of manipulativeness as *Machiavellianism* in social psychology, and its relationship to the *narcissistic personality* of psychoanalysis, specifically from the perspective of so-called "self-psychology." The goals are to develop a multifaceted construct that can be used to link with further emergent levels of analysis in the full explanation of manipulativeness in all its meanings. For indeed, they shift, as we see later, as they are refracted through the action contexts' differing densities, which recall Lasswell's manifold of events.

3

The Manipulator:
Perspectives From Social
Psychology and Psychoanalysis

MANIPULATIVENESS AS MACHIAVELLIANISM

Within the discipline of social psychology, the best candidate for operationalizing manipulativeness that I have found is the construct, *Machiavellianism*. It is well suited to serve the multifaceted epistemological purposes indicated in the preceding chapter.

Machiavellianism is a construct born of the social psychology laboratory and social psychology's psychometrics. It is amenable to considerable subclinical elaboration as I indicate here; it is manifest in significant degree in the normal population; and it is suggestively linkable to parallel psychoanalytic conceptualization. Indeed, it seems fair to say that its parallel psychoanalytic manifestations are central to the latest concerns in psychoanalytic theory and general commentaries on Western psychosocial development.

Chapters 1 and 2 offered some discussion of a variety of approaches to the analysis of strategic behavior and to psychopolitical analysis. They suggested that a topic such as manipulativeness could benefit from a sturdy hybrid approach. This begins with an exploration of the social psychology construct, *Machiavellianism*, (now understood in a somewhat trademarked sense) and its relationship to the psychoanalytic concept of the narcissistic personality. Later we elaborate this two-factor hybrid with a consideration of the testing psychology picture of a composite "type." In later chapters the analysis of a resulting phenotypic profile on the individual personality level is supplemented with a companion analysis of the features of groups, organizations, and society that would seem most relevant in the expression of manipulativeness. This includes the development of a picture of the manipulative organization and the manipulable organization, as settings that interact with the manipulative individual. This culminates in consideration of some of the implications of "a manipulative society."

The main statement of Machiavellianism as social psychology is Christie and Geis' (1970) *Studies in Machiavellianism*.[1] Conceived as a study of manipulative behavior, the work presents a fascinating collection of largely laboratory experiments (but also some discussion of survey research and of course, methodological issues in scale construction and refinement) as well as carefully considered discussion of issues beyond the laboratory suggested by the reported findings. The authors developed a 20-item questionnaire, the Mach Test, which was used in most of the Christie and Geis — and all of the later Machiavellianism research — in either the "Mach IV" or "Mach V" versions. The latter was designed to control for the effect of respondents' varying concern to express socially desirable sentiments. The general research strategy in the Mach work has been essentially to administer the Mach test to subjects and then pit high scorers (presumably more manipulative persons) against low scorers. This is done with various refinements in populating the cells of research designs as the reader may imagine. Mach scores of subjects are also correlated with other data on their behavior, to establish the constellation of traits associable with manipulativeness as Machiavellianism.

Nicholo Machiavelli's writings per se are not of interest in this genre of research. It is not concerned with "Machiavellianism" as humanities text or normative political philosophy. However, the authors reported that rereading *The Prince* inspired some items in the Mach Test. Also, the authors' sense of the values implicit in Machiavelli's view of man broadly influenced the general overview of human nature that the authors loosely attributed to their hypothetical profile of successful manipulators in the course of framing their thinking. Thus, although the relationship between the laboratory "high Mach" and Machiavelli's well-tutored prince may be a somewhat interesting topic of speculation, it constitutes no critical test of the social psychological construct in question and is here more a red herring than a research issue.

To present the core background assumptions and major findings in as orderly a fashion as possible, it seems that the clearest way to organize this

---

[1]The book is essentially edited by Christie and Geis with many chapters authored by them in collaboration with a sizeable group of others, with combinations of authors varying over the chapters. For convenience, I refer only to Christie and Geis when discussing this volume.

chapter is to present the major ideas and issues of the Christie–Geis work, punctuating the discussion with observations on later pertinent research by others as appropriate to the phase of Christie–Geis narrative under discussion. One theme in what follows then, is a retracing of the high points of the Christie–Geis thesis, with some updating and commentary relevant to their social psychology perspective.

MANIPULATIVENESS AND NARCISSISTIC DISTURBANCE

There is however, a second, major theme: to point out the parallel between Machiavellianism and contemporary psychoanalytic thinking about narcissistic personalities. Doing so furthers the understanding of manipulativeness not just by providing another way of looking at it, but by allowing the social psychological and psychoanalytic perspectives to enrich one another. It is a sad fact that in the reality of academic life, these two disciplinary perspectives on human personality operate basically oblivious to one another. The cultism even within an individual discipline can make it rare to see the intradisciplinary scope of thinking on a subject seriously acknowledged, let alone worked with evenhandedly to attack a problem. The independent development of the various "psychologies" poses a still greater obstacle to *inter*disciplinary investigation of a generic notion such as manipulativeness.

I raise this because such circumstances require a certain kind of epistemological awareness, a well-considered expectation about what will be produced by combining such perspectives. As noted earlier, these perspectives are too disparate and independent to simply reduce to one another. But the common roots of their empirical focus mean that the best work from the independent perspectives can yield genuine linkages. To get at them we must carefully loosen – without tearing – some knots of disciplinary meanings and preoccupations. After all, these linking concepts are also tied into their parent fields. Thus, while creating a common context for the moment we must remain aware that elements combined in it come from prior contexts of their own which give them their meanings.

We deal with the social psychological (primarily the laboratory analog study); the psychoanalytic (primarily in terms of the newer self-psychology); and what I am calling *testing psychology* (the world of diagnostic testing and its psychometrics).[2]

---

[2]What is involved here are MMPI and TAT data. In contrast to social psychology analog studies and psychoanalytic theory, such data are a sort of knowledge with their own epistemological bases that represent a genre in their own right.

What does it mean to achieve "linkage" across these fields, regarding a subject like "manipulative personality"? This seems basically the question that Lasswell attempted to answer with his imagery of perspective on the "manifold of events" (see chapter 2). It is useful to unpack this kind of phrasing and attempt a more declarative statement of what is involved in this case.

INTEGRATING THREE PSYCHOLOGIES

At the risk of encountering the resistance of a discipline to "being explained," we are dealing with three disciplines, each of which defines the issues in human personality differently. Social psychology is associated with the dynamics of "the situation." The personality is a network of circumstantially explainable responses by subtypes of persons to types of social interactions — to interpersonal or group encounters that are real or imagined between two or more actors. The focus is on the social context of human personality. The concern is with interaction dynamics. In social psychology there is no sound of one hand clapping; one-hand studies (on the inner thought processes of individuals) do not get into their journals.

Psychoanalytic self-psychology, as are all forms of psychoanalysis, is concerned with "inner life," the complex internal mental states of human beings and the dynamics determining their harmony and disharmony, leading possibly to internal senses of well-being or disturbance. It is enmeshed in concepts of personal health and illness. It springs from a Freudian epistemology that was generally committed to the absorption of group, communal, and cultural issues within its purview. However, in the main, psychoanalysis is fundamentally the analysis of the dynamics of maintaining steady inner states and the forces accounting for, and unleashed in, their disruption.

As a result, what psychoanalytic levels of explanation can contribute to social psychology is, depending on how one looks at it, either the following *annoyance* or *suggestion:* Laboratory discoveries of patterns in social behavior may be predictably related to patterns in inner states. The latter can be explained on a psychoanalytic dimension. Social psychology is probably the closest of our "three psychologies" to the conventional observer's posture in viewing the manifest actions of others. Psychoanalytic explanations are the most likely to posit a wide variety of condensations and distortions of conscious patterns now at the psychological "surface." The psychoanalytic approach is more apt to explain manifest behavior by probing with the concepts of unconscious thinking and preconscious awareness. It will find tensions, dialectics, and surpluses of meaning in behaviors that seem forthright at the social psychological level of observation. This is the primary value of linking these styles of analysis: to make the unidimensional multidimensional for the purpose of gaining perspective.

Of course as a practical matter the practitioners of social psychology and psychoanalysis do not frequently interact. Sometimes the disciplinary gap between these two psychologies can be shortened by a bridge. Testing psychology can often serve this purpose. It is relatively bilingual, and can combine with either of the preceding approaches. The field's perspective and methods are often turned to psychodynamic or social psychological questions and purposes. We explore social psychological and psychoanalytic connections in this chapter, and the relationship of testing psychology findings to their hybridized product in chapter 4.

As a general rule, linking these three psychologies means taking every fruitful opportunity to find a connection between an idea about manipulativeness in one of them and to establish its explanatory relevance to an idea in another of the fields. When is it fruitful to do so? When an explanatory theme in one of them entails an anomalous element that insights from another psychology can render an instance of the familiar. Also, linkage enhances explanation when one of the perspectives can be used to specify contingencies and intermediate stages or dynamic processes in place of what the other can only assert as given.

When and where in an analysis, and with what degree of digression, with how much metaphor versus how much data are we to undertake such cross-disciplinary analyses? These are ultimately esthetic questions, judged by the sense of artistic value of the final product. At this level of issue no more rules can be laid down—except perhaps for one more "rule of thumb" that is especially relevant here: The best emendations and supplements of one disciplinary concept by association with concepts of other disciplines are those that can reverberate through several levels of analysis. These emendations and supplements extend the vertical range of analysis up the levels of "emerging" social action, as well as enhance the scope of applicability at a given level of action. These are the considerations that determine when and where to attempt cross-disciplinary theory building. One major tactical principle that is used here, for the sake of orderliness of presentation, is to follow the development of social psychology thinking on Machiavellianism as the centerpiece concept, and to broaden it with psychoanalytic notions and testing psychology findings. This is because manipulativeness and the idea of a manipulative personality per se, as a self-contained isolatable notion, seems to have been most explicitly marked out as an "it" to pursue by the social psychologists studying Machiavellianism. Thus, we use the others to expand, elaborate, and in some ways transform our "beginning" view of manipulativeness, Machiavellianism.

MACHIAVELLIAN THEMES
AND SELF-PSYCHOLOGY CONNECTIONS

In their creative and balanced interplay between empirical study and speculation, Christie and Geis began work from the premise that certain general
characteristics could safely be attributed to the successful social manipulator.
For one, the successful manipulator is likely to view others as objects to be
used rather than as individuals with whom one empathizes. This is to say that
whether the manipulator is amoral or immoral, his or her view of others is
highly utilitarian rather than being governed by a prior moral code. It follows
closely that the effective Machiavellian would be likely to remain free of
ideological bonds. Such schema limit tactical flexibility. Furthermore, many
a modern ideology turns attention to a vague horizon at the expense of
situations to be won or lost that are now at hand.

From this view, Christie and Geis were led to assumptions about the
mental health of the Machiavellian. To be effective as a manipulator it would
serve well to have escaped in general terms, neurosis and psychosis. The view
was based on the assumption that the social perceptions of the successful
manipulator would have a minimal distortion of social reality. One must read
the map accurately to capture the high ground, as it were.

The results of years of research since, have in a way remained true to these
shrewd general insights. However, with the benefit of all the work Christie
and Geis undertook and stimulated others to undertake since 1955 when
construction of the Mach questionnaire began, it is now possible to render
more subtle versions of these assumptions and to thereby understand the
manipulator as Machiavellian in a somewhat different light. In this chapter
we add a depth psychological perspective. In the next we add a clinical
psychology perspective. Consider a first subtlety regarding the idea that an
empathic deficiency and a tendency to view others instrumentally, reflects a
general social orientation that is at the same time distinguishable from "gross"
psychopathology and neurosis per se. This Machiavellian feature is also a
feature in the clinical picture of narcissistic character difficulties, in which
manipulativeness and exploitation figure prominently (Millon, 1981).[3] One

---

[3]Here again, I cite a more "clinical psychological" source. I do so in this case because it offers
a succinct discussion of the manipulative theme in narcissism. It also makes interesting reference
to the more psychoanalytic tracts on narcissistic disturbances. Such reference is predictably
somewhat impatient with psychoanalytic theorists' jargon. As alluded to earlier in this chapter
it is probably impossible to find a significant statement or interpretation in one of these
disciplines that would not require rephrasing and reduction of emphasis to sit right with the
practitioner of another, who is nonetheless "in total basic agreement, except to add that . . ."

portion of the research I report in the next chapter links these two profiles by correlating a scale of narcissistic traits with Mach scores.

From the perspective of psychoanalytic self-psychology, empathic deficiency figures prominently in the causes and in the acting out of narcissistic disturbance (Ornstein, 1978). When empathic deficiency is viewed from this depth psychological level, it becomes a warning. The profile that includes it involves a certain maturational failure. Inherent in this failure to fully and healthfully mature are elements of rage, anxiety, and destructiveness, which linger in a primitive form in the personality. Compared to those with more healthful narcissistic development who experienced and who can express a modulated empathic posture, persons with comparatively disrupted narcissistic development have what may be called a narrow empathic response to others.

This is an important subtlety because it suggests two important caveats to the social psychological perspective. First, a diminished, narrow empathic orientation is always purchased at an inner price, from the depth psychology perspective. To comprehend the total patterns of the empathically narrow manipulator, we should expect that the tensions and maladaptiveness associated with it may crop out under perceived situational conditions it would greatly pay for us to anticipate.

Second, manipulativeness does not occur where there is no empathy. It occurs where there is narrow and immature empathy that is also clever. Thus, the manipulator may see people as pawns, but it is likely that he or she imputes a psychology to pawns. The manipulator's perspective being narrow but also very prescient, has a great deal of emotional energy swirling around it. From this view, the breezy detachment of Machiavellians may involve stronger winds beneath the surface. Thus, the manipulativeness that appears emotionally unencumbered from the social psychological perspective may appear so more as a result of the individual's being emotionally unfinished from the depth psychological perspective. To be unfinished in this sense does imply an encumberance—that of limited adaptiveness further beneath the surface, which some circumstances can bring to the surface, and which even normal circumstances can reveal in diffuse, nonspecific ways that nonetheless have an impact on the social environment.

The latter sense of pervasive deficiency in development short of a classic circumscribed symptomotology felt at a conscious level, is characteristic of the "character disorders" as opposed to the classic "neuroses." In this sense there is consistency with the original Christie–Geis intuitive judgment that the Machiavellian would be free from "neurosis and gross psychopathology." The concept of character disorder admits of manifestations that can be quite compatible with the image of individuals adept at getting their own way to a degree that can be highly serviceable at a superficial level, often causing felt difficulties for those around them more than for themselves, at least at the level of observation that cursory, unassisted self examination is likely to reveal.[4]

PAUSE FOR PARTIAL SUMMARY

To summarize, adding a depth-psychological dimension to the picture of Machiavellianism suggests revised assumptions about the relationship between empathic ability and the concept of maximal facility in manipulativeness: *Narrow* empathic ability would be a considerable asset. It might even be considered a necessity for superior manipulative ability. It is quite compatible with utilitarian interests. The two need not be viewed as extremes of a scale. Diminished, narrow empathic ability as a general interpersonal posture is a prominent theme in a broad category of personality problems central to current debates over some refocus in psychoanalytic theory. This involves some de-emphasis of the theoretical prominence of traditional neuroses. It involves the merits of attaching greater importance to the narcissistic dimension of personality in its healthy and unhealthy patterns of development. Problems on this dimension of personality are associated with character disorders rather than neuroses. Detached manipulativeness often figures prominently in the interpersonal styles of persons of this type.

This interpersonal orientation and broadly speaking, the patterns of social adjustment and personality development behind it, have been taken as an exaggerated, dramatic illustration of a pervasive problem in the social orientation of the general population. This has been done on the principle

---

[4]Regarding the concept of a narrow and neutral empathy which figures in exploitation, consider Kohut's observations, in Goldberg (1980):

> The confusion [of empathy] with compassion . . . rests on the erroneous assumption that because empathy is a prerequisite for compassion, the obverse must also be true. Empathy is, however, not only employed for friendly and constructive purposes but also for hostile or destructive ones. When the Nazis attached howling sirens to their dive bombers and were thus able to create disintegrating panic in those they were about to attack, they used empathy for a hostile purpose. It was empathy (vicarious introspection) that allowed them to predict how those exposed to the mysterious noise from the skies would react. If a salesman uses in quick succession both a firmly commanding and softly cajoling approach, his empathy is not in the service of compassion – it is meant to overcome the sales resistance of the customer. In other words, he – or the supervisor who instructed and trained him, or the industrial psychologist who devised the method – is in empathic contact with the child in the customer who was once made to obey by similar means, i.e., through near simultaneous command and seduction. (p. 459)

that shifts in the leading psychological disturbances of the day reflect shifts in the patterns of development and adjustment pressures which a society requires of the populace. This is the theme that Lasch seized upon to develop his profile of the "narcissistic society" (see chapter 2; Lasch, 1984). In chapter 7 we pursue the issues he raised as part of a societal-level discussion of manipulativeness.

We see then, that several truths are possible at once. Their combination becomes an interesting thesis. The combination represents a deepening and broadening of the manipulative profile. It facilitates an understanding of manipulation at levels beyond the individual. Consider what emerges so far: The intuitive underpinnings of Mach as the social psychology of manipulativeness are proved durable. Yet, in them ambiguities and subtleties remain. These subtleties hinge on issue that are current in depth psychology: the shift of emphasis toward the narcissistic dimension of personality development, so-called "self-psychology." Developments in the latter are in turn source material for a widely discussed psychosocial critique of Western society, Lasch's work. The latter extrapolates from personality research on narcissistic character difficulties to map culture patterns and institutional styles. Within the individual level, Machiavellianism and issues of narcissistic personality development share a number of interesting associations. Their connection already has some empirical support as chapter 4 indicates. This is in addition to the theoretical support of such a connection. The depth psychological supplementation of the Machiavellian picture suggests greater emotional complicatedness may exist beneath the surface, with possible consequences: behavior that the social psychological picture alone would not imply. Testing psychology research expands the personality profile involved and also ties narcissism to Machiavellianism empirically.

An important implication of these connections to be suggested here is the support they lend to Lasswell's approach (as interpreted in chapter 2): The manifold of events, interpretable with a manifold of perspectives, can yield a sense of continuity and multifaceted understanding, especially on the strength of a selective linkage of concepts that share common properties in their deep structure and that are focused on enduring middle-level processes. The dividend in this case is an enriched understanding of manipulativeness through an enriched perspective on Machiavellianism that links it to testing and depth psychology concepts that are recognized to have societal level significance.

RETURNING TO MACH SELF-PSYCHOLOGY CONNECTIONS

But at this juncture, more needs to be said about the basic findings and conclusions in Machiavellian research. The early intuitive context of the development of the Mach scale itself had another belief associated with it: a tendency to avoid ideological zealotry. The utilitarian, pragmatic, emotionally distant stance conducive to accurate situational reading and calculated behavior would be hampered by it. Thus, movements may have their activists, but Machiavellian activists should tend not to be also ideologues at heart.

Now, a further issue worth pursuing in this regard, via the suggestiveness of certain test-devised diagnostic concepts associable with the Machiavellian profile, is an interesting variation on that theme discussed in the next chapter: Manipulators of the Mach ilk may not be zealots, but they may be somewhat susceptible to volatility under the surface in this regard, in the sense of the cynic who would be a true believer were it not for having become somehow alienated, possibly at levels of awareness considerably beneath the surface.

They may have a zeal, however, for movements and leaders who communicate an understanding of how alienated they are. In contrast to the idealogues of movements (and those who affiliate on ideological grounds), the more viscerally attracted rank-and-filers, and the less intellectual activists, may gravitate to movements for reasons of consistent symbolic and emotional meaning. These motives may be predictable like the *principled* zealot's affinity is predictable, but not articulatable and evaluable on the level of ratio-ideological discourse. In these cases verbalization may appear in overlay, but not as more than rationalization.[5]

It does appear that Machiavellianism works its ways providing there is opportunity to improvise (Christie & Geis, 1970). This seems to entail lack of structure in situations. On the organizational level, we might expect variations in the manifestation of loose structuring. There would be a manipulation-conducive effect in each case but with different dynamics. Thus, lack of structure may be manifest as simple insufficiency of structure, or as a flexible but well-developed structure, or as ambiguous structural requirements that may arise from rococo intricacy of structural features. Each variation could

---

[5]This distinction is captured in the reputed origins of the acronym for the Italian fascist secret police. Mussolini is said to have chosen it for the right sound to symbolize the new order of things. The point is also illustrated by the capacity of Stalinists and Nazis to sign a nonagression pact and retain their followings for a now tortured party line. I am calling this kind of a movement bond *visceral* rather than ideological. The visceral bond to a movement would allow for ideological *acceptance* without tactical or belief restrictions. Only the latter make behavior predictable from ratio-ideological tenets. The point is that manipulativeness could accomodate affinity for movements, without signaling tactical predictablity. This is a picture of persons who are ideologically mobilizable, but more in the sense of being susceptible to a familiar signal under some emotional conditions, rather than being *convincable*. Only in the latter mode are followers predictable by knowing their rational belief systems. These are the systems built on rigidly guarded principles maintained, through verbal "exercise regimens" in approved discourses.

nurture manipulativeness but respond best to different tactics. This has implication at institutional and sociopolitical levels of discussion. Although less determinant structure gives the manipulator room to maneuver at the institutional level, widely differing secondary effects may be set off by each of these types of ambiguous structural conditions. We consider them in a later chapter.

We know also about Machiavellians, that in general they tend to orient their social perceptions using themselves as the key reference point. Christie and Geis (1970) suggested that "high Machs size up others *in relation to themselves*" while low Machs ". . . can locate others' relative position in the population, *but not in relation to themselves*" (p. 232, italics added).

Related to this, Geis and Levy (1970) in the Christie and Geis volume, note immediately following their passage just cited:

> A second unanticipated finding was that high and low Machs differed as target persons. These differences in how they were seen by others, combined with their differences as judges of others, shed some light on the high Machs' success as manipulators. First, highs were estimated as less Machiavellian than they actually were. Second, they were apparently perceived as more transparent, understandable, or predictable. In fact, they were less predictable, especially for low Machs. These same deceptively untransparent high Machs were, in turn, not deceived about others. Although they did not discriminate how one target differed from another, they were accurate on the average, and they were also accurate in estimating others as less Machiavellian than themselves. (p. 235)

This description of a deceptive transparency, seems to be of a kind of arid congeniality or affability. It presumably offers an openness that is in fact unresponsive. It would appear to belie a relentless social scanning the better to inform manipulation. Probably it would draw a smile from Lasch, as well as a sad nod from Kohut.

On a related theme, Christie and Geis (1970) note that Machiavellians seem not likely to "invest affect" in others (p. 228). This is one expression of what is called the Machiavellian *cool Mach* syndrome. As Christie and Geis put it:

> In laboratory studies the hallmark of the high Mach has become what we term the cool syndrome. This has gone beyond the original concept. Not only do high Machs remain relatively unmoved by emotional involvement with others; they also appear equally unaffected by their own beliefs and even their own behavior. (p. 294)

At another level of explanation, it has been observed that high Machs show markedly diminished "cognitive dissonance," which is to say of course, lessened concern to behave in a way consistent with more abstract beliefs or interpretations of past behavior, when compared to the current dictates of situational expediency (Bogart, 1971). Thus, it would seem they are less guilt-oriented; less concerned with past conduct or a code derived from it, to which they would then need to conform.

Interestingly, self psychology in its own way observes a decline in the centrality of guilt in modern Western man (Kohut, 1971). However, none of this is to suggest that Machiavellian coolness runs *deeply* under the surface. The autonomic responses under the stress of lying by high Machs appear no different than lows (Oksenberg, 1964, cited in Christie & Geis, 1970). Yet, highs lie more convincingly than lows in the laboratory so far as observers can judge.

Machiavellians display a social independence, especially under social pressure. This seems consistent with an air of grand detachment while participating substantively in a task at hand. On this general theme, the Machiavellian position is marked out in contrast to the low Mach orientation, dubbed *the soft-touch* profile. It appears that non-Machiavellians are more concerned with maintaining an interpersonal bond with action partners, and are consistently "moved by sheer social pressure" compared to high Machiavellians. Christie and Geis (1970) noted two specific cases of this Machiavellian position demonstrated in the research to date: First, "high Machs resist 'unjustified' inducements to lie or cheat" (p. 298). Based on a number of studies of laboratory cheating and confession situations, sometimes involving the experimenter, high Machs seems to resist overtures to lie or cheat that are detached from an individual private judgment by the Machiavellian of a self-interest in doing so. That is to say, lying under social pressure is unfavored as is social pressure of any content, in general.

It seems plausible to speculate in this regard that the appearance of autonomy and the demonstration of resistance to control, rather than aversion to immoral behavior, may well be at the heart of the Machiavellian independence from social pressure. It also seems fair to infer from the social psychological picture, that it is most important to the Machiavellian to establish in the impression he gives to others, that he is his own man, not so much a "good" or "bad" one, but his own. Galli and Nigro (1983) found a significant positive correlation between the Mach V scale in the Italian version, and Rotter's I–E scale. This suggests an association between Machiavellianism and the feeling that others act controllingly toward oneself, impinging upon one's freedom of action. I am suggesting that Machiavellian independence and resistance can be understood as a reaction to that expectancy.[6] Solar and Bruehl also suggested that Machiavellianism is associated with feeling powerless. The depth psychological picture of narcissistic difficulties, which I am suggesting as a parallel and link to the Machiavellian profile, would emphasize that the behavior and attitudes behind Machiavellian behavior of this type may be seen as the product of this fear of powerlessness *as well as the struggle against it*, as a dynamic process of phobic and counter-phobic impulses.

Further consistent with this line of reasoning, Hollon (1983) found Machiavellianism significantly, negatively correlated with *perceived* participation in decision making and job involvement, and positively correlated with job-related tension. In the context of such subjects' self-report measures, it is interesting to note the reactions of students in the laboratory experiments who interacted with high Machs. They consistently expressed a belief that the high Mach subjects must have been confederates because of "the way he just took over . . . he was too confident . . . he couldn't have been one of us" (Christie & Geis, 1970, p. 309).

The depth-psychological picture can provide a supplementing and unifying perspective from the study of narcissistic disturbances, which can account for the contrast between the inner and outer self-images associated with this Machiavellian profile. The outer appearance of take-charge coolness and aggressiveness and lack of vindictiveness on the one hand, and on the other the inner image of tension, being controlled by others and having hostile impulses, form twin profiles in a dynamic process. Their shared theme is more clearly understood as we probe deeper.

Christie and Geis (1970) read the experimental literature to date to indicate that Machiavellian suspiciousness tends to suspiciousness "primarily of people . . . not of events, objects, or ideas" (p. 300). It is equally important to note however, that Machiavellian resistance to authoritative pressure perceived as pure "social pressure" can apparently be loosened by switching the appeal to one based on some sort of rational justification. Thus, it seems to say that the resistance to subordinating one's self to the wishes of another, a kind of resistance of an overtly compliant and dependent posture, can be penetrated by allowing compliance with "the facts" or "the situation" rather than "the *other*." Further, the inanimate basis of authority tends to be less a focus of suspicion for the Machiavellian. It is the live body in its arbitrary insistence that draws the Machiavellian resistance and becomes the instigator of apparent Machiavellian "independence."

---

[6]When the meaning of belief about "chance" and one's actions are included, the picture becomes more complicated but still consistent. See Miller and Minton (1969) and Solar and Bruehl (1971).

In this regard it is interesting to note that the Machiavellian ability in the laboratory to shape interaction towards the Mach's agenda also depends on contacts occurring face to face. This "live" medium is where the Mach features described so far seem to have their most potent effect.

We consider at greater length in a later chapter, but may simply note at this time, that Machiavellian reluctance to be easily persuaded could have subtle but serious effects on deliberative groups, under certain circumstances. This is particularly so because they may show affinity for group interests along the lines suggested earlier (pp. 46–47) while seeming independent at the level of verbal exchange and formal deliberating. As an example of the subtlety this introduces into the analysis of group behavior, consider the implications for Janis' (1982) view of the dynamics of "groupthink." The personality profile we are sketching is likely to resist being counted as a mere yes man or legalist on the verbal/procedural level, preferring a posture of independence. At the same time, he or she may be highly susceptible to unarticulated, subrational bonds of group involvement perpetuating the group cause. In cases such as this, the procedural remedies for groupthink that intrude on rational-level behavior may be incessantly subverted by such persons at the same time that they strike postures of independence. As we see here, this can account for the frequent observation regarding procedural failures despite heavily "checked and balanced" procedures, that "the system worked but the people didn't follow it." The result in such cases with such people can be policies that are clever but not wise. Some researchers have suggested that group level strategic and tactical performance *as a whole* increases as *group-level* Machiavellianism increases (Jones & White, 1983). However, the concept of "group Machiavellianism" raises a whole new level of issue, and we deal with that in another chapter.

The Machiavellianism literature also finds that a lack of concern for conventional morality is associated with Machiavellianism on two grounds. The first is definitional; Mach questionnaire items involve such content. Second, the "affective detachment" attributed to Machiavellians in interpreting their laboratory behavior was read to also suggest a likely unconcern for conventional morality. The assumption is that "they remain unconvinced by the larger social consensus of conventional moral standards" (Christie & Geis, 1970, p. 298). "Unconvinced by the larger social consensus of conventional moral standards" is an intriguing phrase, not only in the context of trying to understand a personality profile, but also for trying to understand institutional dynamics. *What* about the larger social consensus is unconvincing? Is it the implied empirical assertion that there is *a* conventional morality that has a consensus and not a dissensus behind it? It is the content of the standards that is not convincing? Is it the feeling that one is entitled to an exception or tends to receive treatment as if one were an exception, to a consensus that holds and/or ought to hold for others? If we allow for the notion of levels of awareness, levels of experience, and levels of belief and reasoning operating in a person at once, it may be that such questions are not mutually exclusive when asked of Machiavellians.

Of course, to be unconventional is not necessarily wholesome, but at a societal level, to be unconventional is to help society hedge its bets. Machiavellianism as a retention of options for belief and action likely to go against the conventional flow, could serve several functions so long as it were the minority view. In group deliberations it obviously gives new meaning to the role of "devil's advocate." It also provides a brake on the durability of rationalizations by throwing the test of "who benefits?" against them. Machiavellianism also tends to be associated with a relative willingness to question others' definition of "the situation."

Laboratory research also has suggested that Machiavellians are not particularly vindictive. This would not sit well with the argument for an overlap between Machiavellianism and narcissistic manipulativeness. It seems inconsistent with the more common manifestations of narcissistic difficulties (see Kohut, 1978, on narcissistic rage).

However, after detailing several laboratory situations in which high Mach scorers seemed not vicious or vindictive though exploitive, it is very interesting that Christie and Geis (1970) reported the following:

> Wrightsman and Cook (1965) found that high Machs scored higher on Siegal's (1956) scale of manifest hostility . . . It is conceivable that high Machs are indeed more hostile, but that the range of situations in which we have observed them simply did not elicit evidence of it. Our hunch is that they would be more likely to use hostility instrumentally, to achieve some desired goal. In general, they are adept at getting what they want from others without overt hostility. They take what they get cooly and do not reciprocate the generosity, but usually they have not promised reciprocity. (p. 307)

At the risk of a self-serving position, I am inclined to agree that the absence of "vindictiveness" (in some sense of sadistic hostility in retaliation beyond strategic interest) is simply not observed in the range of emotion induced in the small group experimental format. Some TAT and MMPI findings to be presented in the next chapters are indeed consistent with the Wrightsman and Cook findings. However, there may be an important subtlety involved.

I believe clarification of the issue rests in suggesting a distinction between revenging and avenging. The emotional processes involved may include some issues in degree and so what Machiavellian manipulativeness in the laboratory and what manipulativeness stemming from narcissistic difficulties entail may involve *tendencies* more than cut and dried *distinctions*. Let us call retaliation proportionally and in kind *avenging* and retaliation to excess *revenging*. I think it reasonable to suggest that although they may have different emotional tones and social value overtones, the difference between the two can be best understood to rest on a question of degree rather than kind.

Given this lexicon, it would seem that avenging evidences the control of an angry impulse by demonstrating the ability to release it in a measured fashion, "in proportion." Its expression is shaped and delimited. Indeed, high Machs in the laboratory do not break agreements they make explicitly (although they do not operate with *implicit* assumptions of reciprocity) (Christie & Geis, 1970). The adherence to explicit and thus somewhat legalistic "contracting" to control aggressive ploys, changes the tone of their outward emotional expression. It is changed from primitive venting to rationally guided expression (but it is also explicitly imposed "from without" as it were, through formality). In any event, one is still reason-bounded. In contrast, revenge is more a regressive, raw expression of an impulse. Its sense of limit is only intrapsychically, emotionally measured, as a sense of release and calm is reasserted.[7] Thus, avenging involves hostility that can be checked and focused and bonded to the social situation with appropriate rationalizations in context. Of course, there are always eccentric elements in the assessment of that context. Revenge is a less successful — or a less outwardly convincing appearance of — binding hostile impulses. In the laboratory, the hostility of Machs may be high but well bound to situation parameters of games experimenters require. MMPI work reported in chapter 4 suggests that increased hostility is associated with Machiavellianism. However, the phenotypic Machiavellian can successfully rationalize specific situational and individual foci for such feelings. Also, the more one is facile and creative with rules and structure, the more creative one may be in finding precepts and tactical postures which rationalize a change in the emotional tone for an ongoing impulse. Thus the individual may appear cool, exploitive (situationally), "hard-nosed," and so on, but not vindictive. This still allows for considerable hostility. However, the hostility is bonded to a principle larger than the expression of a pure, unrationalized, inner rage.[8] "Revenge-

---

[7]In this context, Christie and Geis' "exploitiveness" simply means the uninhibited ability to see and act upon the sense of where the outermost limits on achievable game advantage are located in a given laboratory situation.

[8]Consider Kohut's (1985) discussion of Mr. P as an example in social conversation of the expression of somewhat sadistically tinged rage. It becomes important to note the outward plausibility of the rationale for Mr. P's provocative conversation at the expense of the victim and

fulness" seems more like the "vindictiveness" Christie and Geis did not discern.[9]

Somewhat related to their subtheme of lack of observed hostility, Christie and Geis suggested that high Machs do not experience emotional arousal in the presence of others when there is information processing to be done. Thus high Machs are portrayed as focusing on task-relevant issues, whereas low Machs, experiencing arousal, fall back into what might be called "ruts" of old behavior, along the lines of the universal effects predictable from the "social facilitation" literature (Zajonc, 1965).

Again however, Christie and Geis also noted an alternate possible interpretation of the Machiavellian experience in this regard. The latter is again more consistent with the interpretive line suggested here, and with the MMPI data detailed in chapter 4. Briefly, it is that personality correlates of Machiavellianism involve the tendency or ability to convey an outward appearance of "holding one's act together" or "presenting well." This squares with the second line of interpretation Christie and Geis offered, to the effect that high Machs' advantage may involve a lack of arousal as noted earlier "*or the ability to control it in social situations* in which information processing pays off" (Christie & Geis, 1970, p. 301, italics added). Information processing may mean having something to bind or devote one's emotions to. It may present an opportunity in a sense, to sublimate one's "arousal" as task preoccupation and information processing. The point here is that the distinction between a lack of arousal and the ability to control it in a social situation where some task theme exists, is indeed a major distinction. The latter alternative fits well

---

discomforted third parties. One should also note Mr. P's initial unawareness of that rage. What Kohut emphasized as true motive is revealed only after a great deal of digging beneath a sophisticated rationalized surface. The laboratory situation in the case of Machiavellians who seem not to show vindictiveness may in this context not instigate a probing sufficiently deep to release hostility as vindictiveness, allowing it instead to be simple tactical retaliation and assertive, exploitive game play.

[9]Thus, Christie and Geis (1970), in noting that low Machs show a greater interest in justice and reciprocity in the laboratory, observe that high Machs are normally more "exploitive" than punitive (p. 309). From a depth-psychology perspective, *avenging* as I have used the term, may be grouped with tensions in maintaining the "nuclear self." It would represent anger on behalf of entitlements. If it served the purpose of restoring a sense of shape and boundaries, its self-limiting aspect might be explainable this way. Avenging would thus be a controlled hostile expression. Revenging would be a hostile expression less successfully controlled. It seems possible to understand Machiavellianism's lack of laboratory-observable vindictiveness *or* implicit reciprocity as a sign of the struggle to formulaically keep any hostility within limits. The avenging posture becomes a naturally limiting and dynamically appropriate form for such a need, should it arise. For a psychoanalytic self-psychology perspective on such issues generally, see Morrison (1984).

with the possible depth-psychological picture that seems to complement the social psychological laboratory picture of Machiavellianism.

Further along these lines, recent empirical work (Jones & White, 1985) indicates a significant positive correlation between Machiavellianism and individual preferences for "forcing" as a conflict-resolution style, when compared to the alternative styles of "smoothing [over]" conflict, and [frankly and honestly] "confronting" conflict in the sense of so-called win-win philosophies (Burk, 1970). Jones and White (1985) observed that the "forcing" mode of resolution preferred by Machiavellians would tend to be effective in formal organizations under severe time constraints. As we see in later sections, Machiavellianism and narcissistic disturbance patterns have associated with them limits testing and the urge to impulsive risk taking. In this context, one must consider the possibility that Machs in positions of organizational authority may tend to exaggerate the tensions, crises, and power elements attached to a problem at hand organizationally. They may then turn to their now seemingly appropriate "take charge" approach, and resolve the somewhat contrived and dramatically enhanced problem/crisis. This process would contain all the elements of the urge to yield to aroused impulse, the control of that arousal through continued constraints of structure, and deadline, the call to action and audience. We discuss such matters further in a later chapter, but note now, that this line of speculation also supports, and can be unified with, the independently developed observations on the "dramaturgy" of overwork often cultivated in modern organizations (Thompson, 1977. Also there is a close relationship to the tendency to generalize expertise as a strategy for gaining power in organizational decision making. See Lerner, 1976).

From the depth-psychological perspective the behavior pattern being described here is not necessarily all "strategic" in the sense of being consciously calculated, of being pure ploy. There may be a clear element of compulsiveness and lack of full awareness of the motives behind such behavior. Chonko (1983) found a significant positive correlation between Machiavellianism and "job involvement, viewed as obsession-compulsion." It is also interesting to note that here again the relationship between Machiavellianism and depth-psychology issues of narcissism surfaces in an interesting way: Chonko (1983) noted, "Job involvement was viewed as obsession-compulsion and was defined as the degree to which a person's work performance affects his *self esteem*. The scales developed by Lodahl and Kejner (1965) were used to operationalize job involvement (p. 1194)." The understanding of job involvement as an issue of self-esteem and its significant relationship to Machiavellianism, once again links Machiavellian behavior and motivations to issues of self.

One of the most fascinating bits of creative speculation offered in the early Mach research is the suggestion that "high Machs are attuned to some psychological equivalent of the .05 probability level, that they know how to push the limits of the possible without breaking them" (Christie & Geis, 1970, p. 303). A previous issue involved a possible tendency to bind hostility by retrieving individual and situationally specific, rationalized foci for it. Now the issue is the possibility of acquired ability to, and predilection to, test critical limits. The latter seems interpretable as an interest in going to the edge, looking over but not going over, so to speak. The clinical psychology profile of the MMPI and the depth psychology profile each support and add to this theme in their own ways. Thus as we see later, part of the MMPI profile suggests that the personality correlates of Machiavellianism include the impulse to thrill-seeking. This could be interpreted as the sign of an urge to release energy pent up and kept under the surface, by individuals who have the ability to keep their hostilities apparently rationalized and focused in the main, thus presenting well, holding their act together. In more contemporary and less drive-release terms characteristic of more recent self-psychology, this process can be seen as something akin to flirting with the sensation of "fragmentation," and reassuring oneself through a sense of recovery at that "edge" (Morrison, 1984).

Similarly, in the depth-psychological discussions of narcissistic disturbances, we again see another parallel element that supports, broadens, and subtlely shifts the tone of Machiavellianism. When narcissistic rage is triggered by what a current situation symbolizes, the individual is compelled to vent strong feelings. At the same time, he or she seeks to rationalize this venting to him or herself and others as justified, as a response appropriate to the situation. The testing-psychology association of risk taking and impulsiveness with Machiavellianism does not hint at its emotional origins. The narcissistic profile associable with Machiavellianism from the depth-psychology level offers clues on this point. The Mach "knack" in question may be rooted in the experience of managing narcissistic rage. Of course the social psychological context in which the ".05 sense" arises warns us that in the range of expression elicited in the laboratory, rage is too extreme to expect from the Mach. We cannot say the Machs of the social psychology laboratory rage. The hypothesis here is that they are showing us the skill formed of experiences in managing feelings that involve an urge to go beyond limits. It seems reasonable that narcissistic rage may represent that urge, and the ability to present well and rationally bind and focus such hostility is the skill in stopping at the limit one is compelled to seek. These limits serve as last warnings before entering dangerous emotional territory and also as the outer bounds of situational plausibility for one's behavior. The depth perspective suggests and warns that Machiavellians do indeed know this domain well, are drawn to it, are practiced in rationalizing their attraction to it, cling to it, and are fundamentally sound enough to apply the brakes.

Of course the depth psychology perspective has no need to see this as a fully conscious activity. Indeed, as we see, the TAT findings reported here distinguish between low and high Machs by suggesting the emotional conditions under which Machs begin to slip beyond playing the limits and into the relatively unencumbered expression of rage.[10] It is important to make clear however that the typical Machiavellian limits-establishing and limits-management would represent not the acting out of a narcissistic rage but the signs that it is held in check.[11]

To summarize, the observed .05 syndrome combined with the MMPI impulsiveness and presenting well items suggest there is something being pushed to limits and being held in check. The rage theme in the narcissistic profile begins to supply a name for what that checked energy is.

The high Mach's advantage over low Machs is not only tied to the face-to-face dimension in ambiguous situations, but is more specifically traceable to a high Mach superiority in having one's claims recognized in interpersonal exchange. This again, could be interpreted on the depth-psychology level as the manifestation of a narcissistic sense of entitlement that one would expect to be displayed in a pressing, persistent, highly insistent manner in many cases. Pursuing this line of reasoning, the social psychology distinction between high and low Mach orientations to others is also paralleled by the differences between narcissistically defective and healthfully empathic response to others. The former is understood as more self-absorbed, "shallow," and opportunistic.

Thus, according to Christie and Geis (1970):

> low Machs lose by opening themselves emotionally to others, by taking others' needs and concerns as their own. Highs win by being polite . . . they do not take his needs personally but rather use them impersonally . . . both high and low Machs are "sensitive" to others—but in quite different ways. High Machs appear sensitive to information *about* the other person. They respond to cognitive, discriminative labels and explicit cues, particularly those that are relevant to planning strategy in the situation. Low Machs appear more

---

[10]In some ways the TAT suggests a sexually-tinged and sadistic rage along the lines of Kohut's (1985) Mr. P.

[11]This is not the same as arguing that the absence of something shows its presence, because we are working here with the given of the ".05 syndrome" of the social psychology observation, not a ".50 syndrome."

sensitive to the other person as a person, from his point of view, and in terms of his feelings, wishes, and expectations (p. 304)

The self-focused orientation leading to a certain shallowness and shall we say, a tendency to hear but not listen to others, seems consistent both with narcissistic deficiencies and Machiavellianism. The association to the latter is reflected not only in the excerpt just given, but also in a very interesting impression Christie and Geis (1970) reported regarding high Mach's perceptions of the relation of others to themselves. Early Mach research suggested that "while low Machs take others personally, highs take others *as objects* viewed in relation to themselves as fixed reference point" (p. 309, italics added). At the same time:

> Highs fail to discriminate between others because they do not go to the other, but stay within their own cognitive frame of reference, maintaining perspective on the situation as a whole.

> For example, high Machs were more accurate in guessing how others had differed from themselves in answering the Mach scale, without discriminating (as lows did) whether their target person was higher or lower in Machiavellianism. One way to have accomplished this would be for the high Mach to have established a definition of where *he* stood vis-á-vis others in the preceding interaction. Not moving emotionally to where others "were" would account for failing to discriminate between high- and low-Mach target persons, while maintaining a self-definition as a fixed reference point would account for accuracy later in inferring how another differed from oneself. Low Machs could infer later where the other must "be" on the Mach scale, because they had moved to where others were in the preceding interaction, but because they had moved, they had no fixed reference point of "self vis-a-vis others" from which to infer how others differed from themselves – and in fact, called him "closer" than his (previously given) responses actually were. (p. 305)

It is a rather counter-intuitive argument to the effect that Machiavellianism implies sensitivity to differences and reduced sensitivity to the direction of these differences. Of course it is possible that the passage just cited may "overexplain" an artifactual element in the corpus of Mach data. Accepting its thrust however, the general point seems clearly to be that Machiavellianism reflects a self-preoccupied world view with others seen as tools for and confirmants of that view. With a diminished emotional significance for others, the emphasis is now on "the situation" Seeing others as tools and information in service of the self-preoccupied view leads to a lesser interest in the individual as a person and a greater interest in his potential as a tool for use at the moment.

Consider the determined self-centeredness of high Machs compared to the apparent accomodatingness of low Machs: It seems fair to say that in this emotional ecology, the very carnivorous have the very herbivorous in trouble. The implication seems to be that the dismissal of others' interests and views occurs with a certain inattentiveness to those others, except for what is required to sort them out as alien. The latter reading shows an accuracy born of emotional investment, but from the egocentric perspective.

Machiavellianism is clearly associated with inherent "leadership behavior," however, the term in the Mach literature appears to have been used in a generic, irreducible sense in some of the research reported. That is, it has been used in the sense of asking who in a group seemed to be "the leader." Individuals respond as their intuitive understanding of the term moves them (and we must assume variously) in classic social psychological research fashion. Indeed, there seems little question of this connection especially in terms of leadership as "taking over" in a loosely structured group situation (Christie & Geis, 1970, p. 309). However, as we see later and as the early Mach work can be read to imply (Christie & Geis, 1970), *formal official* position holding, and consequently official enactment, is not the sense of "leadership" involved here. Of course as we have seen in the other aspects of Mach research, the Machiavellian as "leader" in the sense of taking over a loose group, is also a leader in the sense of "quintessential gamesman." He or she is most likely to scramble to the top of the heap—heaping on others as allegedly needed. These issues in the relationship between Machiavellianism and the *gamut* of senses of leadership, include the question of behavior as a model for vicarious learning by followers. This is linked to leadership in the mass communications age on the one hand, and the depth psychology dynamics of empathic processes on the other. We take it up again in a later chapter.

CONCLUSION

In summary, my first purpose in this chapter has been to describe the major dynamics of Machiavellianism as it has taken shape in social psychology. Second, I have sought to indicate how the depth-psychological understanding of narcissistic development and its vicissitudes variously parallels, supplements, and modifies the Machiavellian picture. The goal is a sturdy, hybridized view of the manipulative personality.

Further toward this goal, the next chapter completes the exploration of manipulativeness on the individual personality level. It adds the "third" psychological dimension by exploring the MMPI and TAT data collected on a group of volunteers who were also tested and scored for their Machiavellianism. This includes a report and brief further discussion of the results of an empirical test which linked narcissistic personality characteristics with Machiavellianism. Thus, the final product of chapters 3 and 4 should be a multifaceted view of the individual psychology of manipulativeness. It should provide both a supporting framework and an implement for probing manipulativeness at organizational and societal levels. There individuals act on one another through webs of institutional forces as well as directly.

4

The Manipulator in Profile:
A Psychological Test Description

As indicated in the preceding chapter, this stage of our inquiry completes the individual-level profile of manipulativeness by conducting a "testing psychology" exploration of Machiavellianism. Also it provides empirical findings to link the narcissistic profile with the Machiavellian profile at the level of quantitative data analysis, supplementing the preceding theoretical discussion of that linkage. The result is a profile in three psychologies on the individual level, with which we may venture forth to further "emergent" levels of analysis, for the purpose of pondering manipulativeness.

If the preceding three chapters have echoed one consistent theme, it is that every discipline has what might be called its paradigmatic emphases. As chapter 3 noted, Machiavellianism is overwhelmingly a creature of social psychology and the small-group laboratory. The questionnaire that identifies Machiavellianism has been used to trace its effect on the actings out of laboratory subjects. Elements in the accumulated body of findings are sometimes drawn from clusters of closely linked experiments and sometimes from eclectically scattered efforts. The latter range over a variety of vocational (Klein, 1969; Siegel, 1973), topical (Drory & Gouskinos, 1980), and disciplinary (Campbell, 1981) interests.

What most of these efforts have in common is a quality inherent in the majority of contemporary social psychology investigations: There is an emphasis on what bearers of a given trait *do*—how they behave in specified generic social situations. Technically, the subjects' behavior differences in the laboratory suggest analogous behaviors in the generic social situations. More frequently, it seems really to be assumed that laboratory behaviors are behaviors in the generic social situation, for which the laboratory game is now the leading case.

As a device for sorting persons to enter these laboratory experiences, the Mach scale has been analyzed rather thoroughly. It has been broken down into subscales measuring various dimensions of Machiavellian orientations (tactics, views, morality; Christie & Geis, 1970). In the Mach V version it is buffered by the social desirability of responses. Various measures of intelligence have been correlated with it. (No significant correlations were found.) An interesting conglomeration of "measures of general cantankerousness" has even been correlated with the Mach test with ambiguous results. Christie and Geis reported these findings in introducing the Mach scale. Occasionally, in the more recent literature, some research on the scale itself reappears, sometimes using the scale to make a point about scale construction per se (Kreitler & Kreitler, 1981). The point is that although the construction of a scale to discriminate behaviors in the social psychological context often entails some analysis of its characteristics as an instrument, the social psychological emphasis is on the scale as a predictor of what people will do in generic social situations. Its value is in the behavioral differences among subjects that it will predict. The natural social psychology focus is on *what Machs do socially*. The composite picture suggested by accumulated research provides only an implicit, understandably impressionistic picture indirectly, of *who Machs are psychologically*.

Perhaps because of Christie and Geis' conviction that Machs could not suffer "gross psychopathology" if they are able to see others keenly, and because results they summarized of an MMPI administration showed none of the more traditional "clinical" scale to correlate with Mach scores—but probably more because social psychologists not clinical psychologists tend to study Machiavellianism—the relatively limited pursuit of who Machs are psychologically has focused on nonclinical concepts. These include concepts like cognitive complexity (Sypher, Nightingale, Vielhaber, & Davenport-Sypher, 1981) and leadership ability (Drory & Gouskinos, 1980). Some exceptions to this trend are discussed shortly.

As the small-group, social psychological research on Machiavellianism continues to accumulate more information on how Machs act in generic social situations, it seems worthwhile even for the research agenda on Machiavellianism per se, to balance the enterprise with further attention to who Machs are psychologically. There would seem to be value in attempting to sketch a personality profile of Machs using clinical diagnostic tests. Such an approach offers a supplement to the accumulated ad hoc, more inferential picture, available as something of a byproduct of the traditional social psychology approach. Of course the still more general concern behind this book creates another strategic motive for probing who Machs are psychologically aside from what they do socially, and for doing so for reasons apart from mainstream interdisciplinary issues.

In an attempt to help fill this gap, two testing psychology studies (as we have been calling them) were undertaken for this volume: a group of volunteers were administered the Minnesota Multi-Phasic Personality Inventory (MMPI) and the Thematic Aperception Test (TAT). The purpose was to collect data out of which a profile of the personality characteristics that would tend to be associated with Machiavellian persons could be fashioned. This chapter is devoted to the report of the data, and presentation and discussion of the profile.

This chapter is organized as follows: When a work spans several styles of scholarship, decisions about presentation are required. As the chapters accumulate, a hypothetical reader may find the treatment of subject matter in his or her own discipline more drawn out than necessary, whereas treatment of material in another discipline is less explained than needed.

Because this chapter involves original research undertaken for this volume, I felt it advisable to "show it" rather than merely to "characterize it." In trying to strike a reasonable balance between belaboring the disciplinarian and losing the nondisciplinarian, I have been willing to assume a modest extra effort from each. I have decided to present the material assuming a social science audience that is psychologically sophisticated but not necessarily containing psychologists of a specialty close to the specific subject matter here. Given that this problem in deliberately multiperspective work is probably not fully soluable—and in any event not fully soluable from the writer's side alone—we may as well proceed.

In gathering the subjects for this research, the conventional resort to the student population prevailed for reasons of administrative feasibility on the assumption that rather generic personality features are being explored.

THE MMPI WORK

Male student volunteers ($N = 112$) were paid $3 an hour to complete the Mach IV and Mach V questionnaires. All subjects were students at a large, urban, public university operating at the time with a relatively "open admissions" policy, and were recruited from classes in a wide variety of subjects.

Mach IV is a series of 20 statements keyed positively or negatively to represent presumed "Machiavellian" precepts. Subjects respond by indicating the extent of their agreement with each statement according to a 7-point scale ranging from "strongly agree" to "strongly disagree." Subject selection of the "strong" position in the appropriately keyed direction scores 7 points on an item; the "strong" position in the inappropriate direction scores 1 point. Intermediate positions receive corresponding intermediate scores on the 7-point scale. The scores for the total of 20 questions are summed to yield a Mach IV score.

Mach V is a series of 20 three-statement groups. In each three-statement group, one statement is a Mach item, two are not. The two that are not are drawn from scales known to be unrelated to Machiavellianism. All three statements in each group are rated for social desirability. One of the two nonMach statements corresponds in social desirability to the Mach statement. The other nonMach statement is opposite in social desirability from the Mach statement. Subjects are required to indicate with an "M," which one of the three statements is most like them, and with an "L," which one of the statements is least like them, thus omitting one statement in each three-statement grouping.

A slightly complicated scoring system is then applied, which is detailed by Christie and Geis (1970) where complete versions of both Mach IV and V also appear. Suffice it to say, for our purposes, that a 7-point range for each of the 20 three-statement groups is again involved. Mach V scores are then produced on a range equivalent to Mach IV. The intention of the Mach V format is to take account of a potential confounding effect of the social desirability of test items' influencing subjects' willingness to acknowledge identification with Machiavellian precepts. The combination of "most like me," "least like me" and omitted responses to each three-statement grouping is scored from 1 to 7 points depending on the overt Machiavellianism or antiMachiavellianism associated with the particular pairings chosen. A full explication of the theory generating the scoring formula would be a considerable digression here. The interested reader is again referred to Christie and Geis.

Typical Mach statements are: "Honesty is the best policy in all cases" (negatively keyed); "It is wise to flatter important people" (positively keyed); "It is hard to get ahead without cutting corners here and there" (positively keyed). The Mach scale is further subdivided into three subscales pertaining to, respectively: tactics, views, and morality.

Following a practice favored in the earlier Machiavellianism research, care was taken to screen subjects for consistent performance across Mach IV and V before comparing Mach scores with scores on other tests. This precaution has not been taken in all published Mach research. Some earlier research outside the Christie–Geis group has been based on only one or the other version. Very recent research has used only the Mach V, and some research has involved only some subsets of the Mach question items. The precaution of screening subjects for consistent scoring across both versions of the Mach test was followed here for two reasons.

The prevailing overview of the nature of Machiavellianism is still largely that offered by the Christie–Geis group, despite useful supplementing implications that the latest research has suggested here and there. Research probing that overview with testing instruments should work with a measure of Machiavellianism that corresponds to the original research on which the bulk of our picture of Machiavellianism is still based.[1]

Also, a not insignificant number of subjects taking both Mach IV and V show score differences across the two tests. The use of a criterion of consistent scoring is necessary to clarify that this personality dimension is assessed as accurately as possible for subjects whose behavior will be the basis of further insight into Machiavellianism as part of an inquiry into manipulativeness.

Thus, in accord with the procedure followed by the Christie–Geis group, a median split was established for the Mach IV and for the Mach V scores of the initial 112 volunteers in this research. Subjects were labeled as "high" or "low" depending on which side of the median they fell. Consistent scorers are defined as those who fall above or below the median on both test versions.

In this research, 76 of the 112 volunteers were consistent scorers. Of these, 46 were successfully recalled to complete the MMPI–TAT examinations, and paid at the same $3 an hour rate. (There were no significant score differences between subjects successfully and unsuccessfully recalled for further testing.) Consistent Mach scoring was based on medians of 78 for Mach IV and 82 for Mach V, with a theoretical range of 20 to 140 for each test and a combined two-test range of 40 to 280. Means and standard deviations for the combined Mach scores of successfully retrieved subjects were 161.8 and 28.1 respectively. Let us first consider the relationship between Machiavellianism and MMPI scores.

The MMPI is a series of statements referring to the individual. Subjects answer true or false to each. The test is classified as an objective as opposed to a projective test. In its fullest form, it consists of 4 validity scales, 10 "clinical" scales, and an ever-increasing number of "research" scales and subscales, with this latter grouping being the most recent additions. Scales are formed from groupings of 566 questions in all. Scores on individual scales consist of total

---

[1]Of course these characterizations apply to a psychological community not including those normally concerned with the psychoanalytic, self-psychology concepts adapted to a discussion involving Machiavellianism in chapter 3. It would be misleading to suggest they have been part of this research tradition – again reflecting an unfortunate fragmentation in the psychological disciplines.

appropriate responses to positively and negatively keyed items comprising the scales. Scale composition is by and large based on empirical findings that groups of diagnosed pathological individuals are distinguished from normals by differences in preferred responses. This is believed to occur for reasons that are theoretically coherent in varying degrees for the various scales. The strength of the MMPI lies partly in the theoretical consistency and justification that some see for some scales, and more in the incredible mass of data on which it was based and continually supported, and in its bedrock anchoring in traditional clinical diagnostic practice since the 1940s. The test has been translated into 115 languages and is currently used in 46 countries. Graham (1977) and Dahlstrom, Welsh, and Dahlstrom (1972) are the universally accepted guides to this intricate instrument. The MMPI scale descriptions here are drawn directly from Graham. His item descriptors and summaries are used throughout.

MMPI results in this research (test administration form R) are reported on 44 subjects. Two subjects in the group of 46 were deleted from the MMPI analysis because their scores on the "Cannot Say" validity scale were above 30. This scale measures the total number of items omitted or answered both true and false. The cut-off score of 30 on this scale follows conservative clinical procedure for eliminating possibly invalid profiles. MMPI scores on each of the scales were correlated (Pearson's R) with the sum of Mach IV and V scores for each subject.

Table 4.1 reports the MMPI scales that showed a correlation with combined Mach scores (henceforth "Mach scores") at the $p < .05$ level rounded to two places, two-tailed. Without excessive distraction with detail, suffice it to say that conventional clinical practice involves the measurement of MMPI scales in various forms involving the use of certain constants derived from some of the MMPI scales and added to others. In this data, validity scales are reported as "raw without K." Other scales are reported in "raw score" and "raw without K" forms, as applicable.

The interpretation of MMPI profiles is at root a clinical exercise. In its native domain of the clinical, therapeutic setting, the MMPI as with all tests, is best interpreted in the holistic context of a multifaceted contact with a patient. Of course its research use on aggregates of subjects is known to clinical fields as well. But this is always an adaptation from the original purpose.

Equally supportable alternative rules of profile interpretation exist in clinical circles. Clinicians variously emphasize absolute values on scales, relative elevations or depressions on scales, subscale conformity with a gross picture, consistency across clusters of scales, behavioral confirmation of

Table 4.1
Correlations of MMPI Scales with Mach Score Significant at $p < .05$[a]

MMPI	Scale	Correlation with Mach
L	(Lie)	−.39
K	(Correction factor plus)	−.29
R	(Repression)	−.31
Ca	(Caudality)	+.33
Re	(Social Responsibility)	−.30
Pr	(Prejudice)	+.36
Cn	([Self-]Control)	+.31
MAS	(Manifest Anxiety)	+.31
D2	(Psychomotor Retardation)	−.44
HY2	(Need for Affection)	−.38
HY4	(Somatic Complaints)	+.32
PA3	(Naivete)	−.47
MA2	(Psychomotor Acceleration)	+.39
Mf1	(Narcissism-hypersensitivity)	+.41

[a]two-tailed

profile implications, confirmation by other tests, and so on. When researchers aggregate data on groups of subjects, the comparison of isolated scales is much more prevalent, although some of the choices of various clinical criteria for labeling are still relevant, and are indeed variously adopted in the research. Thus, a brief clarification is in order regarding the philosophy of interpretation guiding this research.

The goal is to deepen the understanding of the personality dynamics underlying Machiavellianism. It is this feature of personality, not the whole complexion of the test group or individuals in it, that is of interest. In constructing the heuristic device of the "Machiavellian profile" then, we are reconstructing an artist's composite of "the Machiavellian" as seen through those tests, but it is of course an abstraction. It is based on stringing together the personality features that are associated with the scales showing a significant correlation with Mach scores for the test group. The overall pattern displayed in the scales constitutes the Mach personality profile in testing psychology terms. Of course the actual people who served as subjects are many things besides being Machiavellian. The "profile" produced is not the only one such individuals with elevated Machiavellianism scores may show— but it is the profile they should show to the extent their Machiavellianism is an organizing feature of their personalities. Thus, in this sense, it is a profile of Machiavellianism per se. Furthermore, as we shall see in later chapters, to the extent that our society increasingly produces persons disposed to interact via manipulativeness—either because of shifting patterns of individual development or related institutional cues, the abstracted composite profile representing no persons in particular, may represent an increasingly greater part of all persons in general.

Thus, what we here reconstitute in an individual vocabulary certainly can be used to suggest what underlies Machiavellianism. Also, the more that Machiavellianism is central to a given individual's personality it can be used to explain what is likely to underlie the personality of that individual. However, as we see, the profile may also be used to shed light on the psychological dynamics reflected in the tenor of organizational life or even developments within a sociopolitical system, in so far as these are influenced by Machiavellianism in one way or another.

The latter extension becomes appropriate by degree. We are right to do it the more that Machiavellianism—or a partially related concept of manipulativeness appropriate to the viewer's level of analysis—drives the action in such other frameworks. Thus, the profile provided here is relevant to understanding anything from a small dimension of some people's personalities to the major themes of the Western psyche and institutions, depending on one's experiences and intellectual sense of where a large portion of the world is going. The latter dimensions of the problem are taken up in the following chapters.

These considerations make clear that a description of a phenotypic interpersonal orientation formed on the notion of "the manipulator" (here as "the Machiavellian") is not synonymous with the data on a test group. As noted, the latter is a collection of complex persons who may be other things besides being Machiavellians. Group data suggest broad dynamics; they point out directions of association between personality dimensions rooted in clinical conceptualizations, and the more superficial (in the literal sense of being at the surface) Machiavellianism.

From this perspective, the approach to the data in this chapter is to focus on the MMPI-defined personality dimensions that seem not to be associated with Machiavellianism by chance, those that correlate at the conventional .05 level or better. These are taken as signs of the underlying personality dimensions whose collective display we expect to be enhanced as the Machiavellian orientation predominates in a society, and that we associate with more Machiavellian people in such societies.

In the following section I briefly describe each MMPI scale that proved to be significantly correlated with Machiavellianism. This naturally entails the gradual assembly of a cumulative profile of "the Machiavellian" in terms of the MMPI.

THE SCALE FINDINGS

The L Scale. The L scale's most immediate application is in identifying people who are likely to be lying on the MMPI, usually as a tactic for presenting well. Christie and Geis reported that Wrightsman and Cook (1965) administered Mach IV and the four validity scales (which include L and K), finding a correlation of −.27 between Mach IV and K and −.40 between Mach IV and L. These findings are closely confirmed in the results reported here.

These L-scale findings suggest more than the observation that lying on such tests decreases as Machiavellianism increases. The usual conclusion of basic Mach veracity can be supplemented with further information that the L-scale scores are known to provide. Low L scores traditionally suggest self-confidence, social perceptiveness and ease, and effectiveness in leadership roles. For Machs, the latter might be related not only to the preceding characteristics, but also to some persistence or assertiveness in communication. Most interestingly, lowered L scores are also associated with the tendency to be perceived by others as cynical and sarcastic. The data suggest that increasing Machiavellianism is associated with lower L-score characteristics.

The K Scale. The K scale was originally designed as a more subtle test of subject tendencies to control self-presentation in the MMPI. Subsequently it was found to offer much richer information. Graham noted that the inference of personality characteristics from K scores should be conditioned by knowledge of the socioeconomic status (SES) of subjects. Students at the university where the data were collected, fall broadly in the upper working-class to lower middle-class range. Low scores in general for such a group are "normal." This research did not control for SES, but the K-score pattern here is consistent with the correlations reported by others. Descriptors for average and low K scores differ noticeably, and often with regard to items that seem Mach relevant. Under these circumstances it seems best to limit the suggestion of associated personality characteristics to the broader narrative, summary characteristics Graham associated with average K scores and to take seriously only the "low even for SE status" kinds of descriptions that are most consistent with the prevailing picture of Machiavellianism. Thus, Graham (1977) noted that people whose K scores are appropriate to their SES are well adjusted, independent, capable of dealing with daily problems, ingenious, and resourceful. "They are clear thinking, and they approach problems in a reasonable and systematic way. In social situations, they mix well with other people, are enthusiastic and verbally fluent, and tend to take an ascendant role" (p. 24). Further characteristics associated with SES-appropriate K scoring include high intellectual abilities and interests. If high intellectual abilities are understood as problem-solving skills rather than IQ, this element is consistent with what we know of Machs.

The overall picture of low K scores after socioeconomic considerations are taken into account is something of a disturbed profile. Interestingly, however, note the characterization Graham (1977) offered of such excessively low K scores as regards their outlook toward life: "Their outlook toward life is characterized as cynical, skeptical, caustic, and disbelieving, and they tend to be quite suspicious about the motivations of other people" (p. 24).

The remaining scales discussed in this chapter that correlated significantly, two-tailed, with Machiavellianism are the "research scales" of the MMPI and several of the Harris subscales. Relatively less is understood about these scale groups than about the clinical and validity scales, although they are coming into increasing use. Consider first the research scales significantly correlated with Mach scores.

The R (Repression) Scale. Graham noted that factor analyses of the MMPI have repeatedly suggested two major factors. The R scale was assembled to measure one of them. The data reported here suggest a tendency to low R scoring as Machiavellianism increases.

The R scale taps a variety of specific characteristics. Graham (1977) summarized the low R scorer as "rather outgoing, emotional, and spontaneous in his/her life style, and such an individual takes an ascendant role in interpersonal relationships" (p. 84). The item descriptors from which this overview is condensed seem to suggest conceptually, two subgroups of traits: a not too congenial, relatively more Mach-consistent cohort of characteristics, and a remaining group of "bubblier" descriptors. The latter may be interpretable less sanguinely in the context of increasing Machiavellianism, given other pieces of the Machiavellian picture.

Thus, of the 14 specific descriptors associated with low R scoring noted by Graham, consider the following 8 as a thematic subgroup: outgoing (but in the sense of outspoken and talkative); spunky (but in the sense of daring); informal; dominant; aggressive, bossy; self-seeking, self-indulgent; shrewd, wary, guileful, deceitful; and sarcastic, argumentative. The remaining descriptors are as follows: excitable, emotional; enthusiastic; robust, jolly; impulsive; courageous.

Consider the less sanguine interpretation of the "bubblier" second group of low R descriptors just noted. In the context of an emerging larger picture, it begins to suggest an enthusiasm for action, action-pressing, confident overture making, a risk-prepared profile that succeeds in conveying a somewhat engaging element. This seems compatible with the obviously more Mach-suggesting first grouping of low R descriptors. It should be noted here, however, that with the R-scale descriptors as well as those in some of the other scales as described, there is a certain low level but persistent undercurrent, whereby descriptors suggesting emotionality crop up in association with Machiavellianism. This may provide a clue in specifying a somewhat complex dynamic behind the "cool Mach syndrome." This point is elaborated in later sections of this chapter and also is consistent with aspects or the picture of narcissistic disturbance discussed in chapter 3.

The Ca (Caudality) Scale. Relatively little is known about the Ca scale, originally designed to assist in locating brain damage. There is no reason to pursue any implications for normals. As more is learned about the scale some relevance may develop on the general dimension of bio-political analysis. It is reported here for the record.

The Re (Social Responsibility) Scale. Re scores tend to decrease as Machiavellianism increases. Graham (1977) summarized low Re scorers as follows:

> Low Re scorers do not see themselves and are not seen by others as willing to accept responsibility for their own behaviors. They are lacking or deficient in dependability, trustworthiness, integrity, and sense of responsibility to the group. They are less likely than high Re scorers to be in positions of leadership and responsibility. Low Re scorers are also less rigid than high Re scorers in acceptance of values and are more willing to explore other values. Younger persons with low Re scores tend to deny the value system of their parents and to substitute another value system for the parental one. Older persons with low Re scores question or deny their most recently held value system and may have adopted new religious or political outlooks. (p. 101)

Christie and Geis noted DeMiguel's findings suggesting that high Machs are less likely to accept their parents as role models. Touhey suggested that Machiavellianism might be viewed as a failure to establish identification with parents. Touhey (1973) also found a negative correlation between Machiavellian personality traits and attraction to similar attitudes (Touhey, 1977). These findings interpreted in the context of low Re scores may suggest that Machiavellians are likely to raise Machiavellian children because their children may be unlikely to identify with them, indeed often fail to do so, become relatively Machiavellian, and reject their parents' values and reject attitudes similar to those with which they struggle internally at some level.

This again raises issues in the language of self-psychology to which we return at the end of this chapter.

Without forcing a particular causal sequence on these matters, low Re-score predictions for younger persons seem well attuned to the issues in child rearing raised in the Machiavellianism research. The implication that low Re scores for older persons may be associated with recent political disillusionment, and that this may be associated with elevated Mach scores is a suggestive area of further research for political science.

Further pursuing the implications of the low Re-scorer profile for insight into Machiavellianism, the observation of underrepresentation in leadership positions must be interpreted cautiously. These generalizations related to low Re are based on studies that focused on formal hierarchic position. The Mach preference for informality and ambiguity conveys another more behavioral, socially generic sense of "leadership" to which the Graham characterization seems not to speak.

The Pr (Prejudice) Scale. The Pr scale was developed to identify anti-Semitic bigotry and seems to compare consistently with other known constructs tapping such dimensions (Graham, 1977). The specific descriptors and general summary overview offered by Graham seem to focus broadly on themes of suspiciousness, distrust, resentment, and being closed-minded. High Pr scores tend to be overrepresented in lower social classes.

The 12 specific descriptors Graham (1977) associated with high Pr scores seem conceptually to echo three themes: disquieted self-image, assumption of others' interests in tension with one's own, and a resulting combativeness/aggressiveness in search of focus. Such personality aspects might be compatible with increasing Machiavellianism, implying that the cool syndrome high Machs present could conceivably be associated with some difficulties deeper under the surface. This too may bespeak a more complicated emotionality for high Machs than we can observe in strategic laboratory situations.

The Cn (Control) Scale. This scale measures self-control, in the sense of holding oneself together and being able to function well, especially in the face of internal difficulties. In a sense it was designed to measure the ability to keep one's act outwardly together. The higher the Cn score the presumably greater this ability. The research reported here indicates that Cn score increases as Machiavellianism increases. High Cn scores for persons with normal clinical scales suggest an individual who is "reserved and unemotional" (Graham, 1977, p. 106). This broadly conforms with the cool Mach profile. High Cn scores for persons with psychological problems reflected in elevated clinical scales, indicates an ability to control those problems and to strategically present themselves favorably.

Additional item descriptors of high Cn scorers show very Mach relevant characteristics (Graham, 1977). There are seven in all. Three show clear gaming-relevant advantages that would be expected from what we know of high Machs in the laboratory: described by others as sophisticated and realistic; impatient with naive, moralistic, and opinionated people; explores and experiments with the environment even though it may involve risk of social disapproval. Two descriptors are consistent with the possible subsurface unrest, and are highly consistent with aspects of the narcissistic disturbance profile discussed in chapter 3. They are awareness of own weaknesses; inwardly sensitive to social criticism. Two remaining descriptors conform to themes associated with low Re scores that were also associated with increasing Machiavellianism. They are nonacceptance of traditional religious beliefs and rebelliousness toward authority.

The MAS (Manifest Anxiety) Scale. The data here indicate that increases in MAS scores are significantly associated with increasing Machiavellianism. Graham's item descriptors for MAS scoring are quite succinct:

1. reports numerous physical or somatic complaints,
2. feels excited or restless much of the time,
3. has difficulties in concentrating,
4. lacks self-confidence,
5. overly sensitive to the reactions of others, and
6. feels unhappy and useless.

Graham also noted that MAS elevation indicates a view of the environment as threatening, combined with a sense of vulnerability to outside control. For Machs, this would be consistent with a view of the social world as highly competitive and presenting frequently stressful situations that have an organized, intentional cause; *someone* must be in charge when things happen, if not necessarily oneself. Also plausible for the emerging Mach picture, high MAS scorers tend to be oriented more toward the present than the future, and tend to be recency-oriented in developing expectations. They would seem to be both "what have you done for/to me lately?" and "here and now" minded.

The anxiety measured by the MAS is a trait rather than state anxiety. It is not temporary in response to superficial, highly transitory, situational changes. Trait anxiety is sometimes referred to as "drive level." As Spence and

Spence (1966) noted, high drive level, high MAS persons generally show superior performance on simple tasks compared to low drive persons, but as tasks become more complex, high drive persons' performances tend to be inferior to lows', *ceteris paribus*. This seems broadly attributable to an anxiety interference. Broadly speaking, the tendency to high MAS scoring reveals a tendency to an acquired general anxiousness.

Harris Subscales

It has long been observed that any given MMPI scale can tap what may be viewed as several personality dimensions. Many researchers have devised subscales of MMPI scales in an attempt to parse out the several personality dimensions assumed to be intermingled within a given MMPI scale. The Harris subscales are the best known and most widely used subscales of this type. There are 28 Harris subscales.

Scores on each of the Harris subscales were generated for the subjects of this research, and were correlated with subject Mach scores, as was done for all MMPI scale scores proper. Five Harris subscales correlated significantly with Mach scores ($p < .05$, two-tailed) as reported in Table 4.1.

The full implications of Harris subscales are not as well understood clinically, as are the implications of validity, clinical, and research scales. However, the subscales are considered useful adjuncts to clinical interpretation in the context of the fuller MMPI profile, and this is the context in which they are interpreted here.

The D2 (Psychomotor Retardation) Subscale. Graham reported that Calvin (1974) found the D2 subscale to be two-dimensional, encompassing both degree of interest in life activities and hostility manifestation. Graham's descriptors associated with depressed D2 scoring conform to this two-dimensional theme. His first three descriptors clearly pertain to life activities and his fourth to hostility. His descriptors for depressed D2 scoring are as follows:

1. describes himself/herself as active and involved,
2. has no difficulty getting started on things,
3. views everyday life as interesting and rewarding, and
4. admits to having hostile and aggressive impulses at times.

These characteristics are likely to be associated with increasing Machiavellianism.

The HY2 (Need for Affection) Subscale. This scale is significantly, negatively correlated with Mach scores. A tendency to depressed HY2 scores would thus be associated with increasing Machiavellianism. Graham offered three descriptors for depressed HY2 scoring:

1. has very negative, critical, and suspicious attitudes toward other people;
2. sees others as dishonest, selfish, and unreasonable; and
3. admits to negative feelings toward other people who are perceived as treating him/her badly.

This subscale is described as measuring the need for affection, apparently on the strength of the extra-test correlates of elevated subscale scoring. The fear that affection will be withheld in response to frank self-disclosure, and a consequent reluctance to disclose, and to be overly concerned with presenting well, characterize elevated HY2 scoring. Depressed scoring, associated with Machiavellianism, is characterized by a lack of such concerns and the expression of thematically opposite attitudes reflected in the specific descriptors associated with lowered HY2 scores.

It should be noted in the context of the broader Machiavellianism picture, that the tendency to depressed HY2 scores as Machiavellianism increases does not reflect an affective neutrality or indifference. Rather, it reflects a capacity for frank expression of negative feelings toward specific others linked to the perceived experience of having been treated badly. In this sense, the label of this subscale is perhaps too broad, judged by its specific descriptors, at least for the depressed end of the scale. The generalization to a statement of overall need is difficult to establish rationally. Although the answer may lie in the larger observed clinical context of low-scale scoring, the literature on this point is very scant. Thus, for example, psychodynamic interpretations of need and need expression would not necessarily assume a directly observable, and necessarily positive, relationship between overt need expression and the valence of deep-seated need. The association of Machiavellianism with narcissistic disturbance in chapter 3 also suggests the subtlety possibly involved in the simultaneous defense of indifference and aloofness, and feelings of loneliness, with the additional experience also of feelings of superiority at times.

The HY4 (Somatic Complaints) Subscale. The significant positive correlation between HY4 and Mach scores suggests that increased tendencies to somaticize are associated with increasing Machiavellianism. Graham's descriptors for elevated HY4 scores focus on two themes. The major theme, reflected in the scale title, is somatic complaints. Also, there seems to be a second, subsidiary theme related to affectivity. Two descriptors appear to comprise the latter theme: "utilizes repression and conversion of affect"; and "expresses little or no hostility toward other people." This latter theme bears some discussion in the context of the larger Mach profile.

Given the dominant theme of the HY4, somatic complaints subscale, it seems clear that Machiavellianism is associated with somaticizing. This is consistent with the hypocondriasis common to the depth profile of narcissistic disturbance (Muslin & Val, 1987). Regarding the secondary theme of affectivity in HY4 and its interpretation in the Mach context, several other scales already described provide a context for interpretation. L- and K-scale correlations with Machiavellianism suggested apparent cynicism and sarcasm, caustic manner, skepticism, and so on. The Pr (prejudice) scale analysis was interpreted as reflecting a combativeness/aggressiveness ready to focus on socially identified outgroups. D2 (psychomotor retardation) suggested a hostile dimension, but one that had to do with admission of occasional impulses. HY2 (need for affection) indicated negative attitudes toward others that are linked to perceived incidents of prior bad treatment by the others. Again, these elements of focusable, bounded, hostile energy, of impulse combined with energy expended for its control, and of the cynical outlook — are familiar elements from the narcissistic disturbance profile.

I suggest that the HY4 description of little or no hostility toward others be interpreted as an absence of a *generalized* social hostility, or unfocusable anger. This implies that Pr combativeness/aggressiveness focused on socially cued outgroups, D2 hostile impulsiveness of situational specificity, and HY2 negative feelings contingent upon perceived prior offense, are not inconsistent with HY4 "expressions of little or no hostility towards other people." This is because the former descriptors are all group or incident specific. The HY4 seems to be tapping the absence of a more generalized interpersonal hostility or anger. Its co-occurrence with the HY4 characteristic of a tendency to convert affect, a function presumably served by somaticizing in this context, would seem to account for the low expressed hostility associated with general HY4 elevation. This suggests that Machiavellianism may represent a comparatively well-managed experience of narcissistic rage in personalities for whom the emotional experience of such rage has been adapted and somewhat muted with the benefit of a *relatively* well-bounded action posture, so that targets can be safely structured into a "game" (see chapter 3 on avenging versus revenging).

The utilization of repression associated with affective conversion in HY4 is more reliably superceded by the significant negative correlation of the repression scale (R) with Machiavellianism. Repression in the sense the MMPI seems to tap would not play a major role in a profile rooted in the concepts of narcissistic disorder. Repression in this sense would seem to be more likely associable with the traditional picture of *neurotic* patterns. A struggle over the banishment to the unconscious of specific thought constellations would not seem to be characteristic of the character-disorder classifications per se. Indeed the pervasive nature of character-disorder themes when they characterize a personality, would seem to make them inherently unlikely to generate repression in any specific sense. Thus the R-scale element in the MMPI profile of Mach sits well with the narcissistic disturbance profile from the depth perspective.

It would seem that Machs tend to convert affect generally, making ready use of somaticizing for the purpose. High manifest anxiety seems further to corroborate this picture because of its thematic consistency with somaticizing. As chapter 3 indicated, it is furthermore expectable from the depth perspective. It too may serve the additional function of converting affect to physical manifestation. Although there is a potential for explosiveness in terms of outburst under perceived stressors, low K scores that warn of social unconventionality, might be read to imply that the perceived stressors may be unconventional as well, compared to low Machs. The implications of this line of interpretation are developed more fully in a later chapter. The point here is simply to explain the consistency of the low HY4 affectivity related subtheme with the picture provided by other scales significantly correlated with Machiavellianism and to also point out the consistency with the narcissistic themes on the depth level.

The PA3 (Naivete) Subscale. As might be expected from the name of this subscale, the data indicate that this scale is significantly, negatively correlated with increasing Machiavellianism. Graham offered three associated descriptors. Again, as indicated in the HY4 discussion, the low opinion of others (Items 1 and 2) is combined with a hostility that is again situationally specific rather than generalized (Item 3). The descriptors are:

1. has rather negative and suspicious attitudes toward other people;
2. sees others as dishonest, selfish, and untrustworthy; and
3. admits to some hostility and resentment toward other people who make demands on or take advantage of him/her.

The MA2 (Psychomotor Acceleration) Subscale. As expected, the psychomotor acceleration subscale correlates significantly positively with Machiavellianism, whereas the psychomotor retardation (D2) subscale correlated significantly negatively. Elevation on the MA2 dimension suggests restlessness, accelerated thought, speech, and motor activity, tendencies to unjustified excitation or elation, easy boredom offset by thrill seeking, and impulses to do shocking or harmful things. This is a picture of a general tendency to tenseness, relieved (we may presume temporarily and unsatisfactorily) by risky and conventional behavior, with a possibly aggressive element.

The Mf1 (Narcissism-Hypersensitivity) Subscale. Based not on subscale work by Harris, but by Graham and others (Graham, Schroeder, & Lilly, 1971), this scale seems to tap narcissistic themes in the sense of Millon's (1981) "clinical psychological" interpretation as presented in the DSM III and discussed in chapter 3. The significant positive correlation of scores on this subscale with Mach scores offers a more direct empirical link via MMPI, between Machiavellianism and narcissistic disturbance – a link chapter 3 pursued in more a priori terms. Given the extensive discussion there, no further elaboration is needed here. It may be useful, however, to enumerate the descriptors Graham reported for high scoring on this scale, which would again be interpretable as increasing tendencies as Mach score increased for an individual:

1. self-centered, narcissistic;
2. concerned about his/her physical appearance;
3. sees himself/herself as extremely sensitive and easily hurt;
4. lacks self-confidence;
5. preoccupied with sexual matters;
6. expresses resentment and hostility toward his/her family; and
7. characterizes other people as insensitive, unreasonable, and dishonest.

These are characteristics well in accord with themes already established in this chapter.

THE MMPI PICTURE OF MACHIAVELLIANISM: OVERVIEW

The preceding MMPI findings appear to suggest that the cool Mach syndrome is the surface sign of a somewhat more complicated emotionality. The presumed affective detachment associated with increased Machiavellianism would appear to be a surface image based on what is now in more "clinical" terms, a more involved affective orientation. The result is a more subtle, more complicated picture that lacks the more quiescent implications of a purely social psychology profile.

Machiavellians are relatively good at holding a not untroubled act together. They are anxious people with a triggerable hostility if not a generalized constant anger. They are active people but also tense, active people. They are generally critical and suspicious with a low opinion of others, showing little *overt* need for affection. Their body complaints, physical preoccupation (somaticizing), and manifest anxiety appear to be part of a general personality dynamic involving the conversion of not inconsiderable emotional disquiet into *overtly* nonemotive forms. What might be expected to appear as a generalized hostility seems kept in check normally by a capacity to focus hostility on specific incidents and specific others; situational rationales and foci for the hostility are successfully retrieved. They are thrill seeking. This may serve as a kind of venting for the energy partly reflected in their generally high reactivity. The conventional guidelines for interpretation suggest this impulse is often checked short of action. One of the most interesting implications of this picture is that under considerable perceived stressing they can "loose their cool" (pun intended). Their overall in-control, comfortably in-charge, and eye-on-the-ball superficial profile is somewhat self-deluding as well.

Their relative unconventionality or disdain for conventional morality shrewdly noted in earlier Mach research, is psychically functional in the short term,[2] for the picture suggested here. Their characteristic tendency to depressed K scoring may be generalized to a characteristic asocialness, a solipsism. There is a pervasive social indifference that is a kind of psychic distancing on the surface. Of course in depth terms, such distancing can be a paradoxically adaptive reaction to the emotional stresses of earlier personality development.

It is possible to argue, from what might be called a fundamentalist social psychology, disciplinary position, that the significant MMPI-scale associations with Machiavellianism are of no theoretical interest in terms of marking out a personality profile, given L-scale association with Machiavellianism. In effect from this view, Machiavellians are not different from others, they just tell the truth about themselves where others will not.

I have rejected this line of interpretation for several reasons. First, it seems unlikely that the difference between what Machiavellianism leads to honesty about, and what its absence leads to concealment about, should amount to a coherent profile. Moreover, the profile is readily compatible with a profile independently established in psychoanalytic terms regarding narcissistic disturbance, a personality orientation hardly reducible to a mere excess of

---

[2]That is, in light of a profile already with a difficulty. See Waelder on secondary gain (1960).

frankness. In accepting the meaningfulness of the MMPI profile associated with Machiavellianism in the face of a fundamentalist argument to see it as an artifact of superficial L-scale scoring, lies a judgment that a broader multidisciplinary approach to this data should commit one to not miss the forest for the trees.

Even if we were to accord the L-scale differences noted a special prominence, it bears stressing that this "honesty" associated with Machiavellianism, in the collection of themes it raises, is a significant statement about the nature of a personality behind it. It seems a paradigmatic pitfall of what I am calling the fundamentalist social psychological perspective in which Machiavellianism was originally rooted, to see social psychological profiles as simple interpersonal styles somehow divorced from deeper issues of personality. People in the small-group laboratory are always more than the collection of behaviors in the laboratory, even as experimenters abstract out those behaviors for some purpose of analysis. We must remember that at times it is necessary to reconstitute the multidimensional sense of the whole personality in assessing the meaning of behavioral findings. There is a danger in social psychology's reducing people to being only what they do at the expense of a broader picture of who they are. For purposes such as ours, it is wise to take a deeper perspective that asks who they are in a wholistic sense, such that they do particular things we observe in their behavior and in the pattern of the items they are comparatively "honest" about. The "honesty" thus becomes a sign of a personality. We know too much about Machiavellians even in the purely social psychological genre, to see them as simply "frank" people.

At the same time, it is also important to resist a paradigmatic fundamentalism from the psychoanalytic side. One occasionally hears the criticism from that quarter that social psychological formulations of personality are hopelessly superficial because the discipline from which they arise does not accept the prominence of the unconscious (or indeed its existence) in shaping human interaction. Here, too, we must remember that we cannot describe a forest *without* trees. It is a core assumption of this volume that, with care, with the understanding that no one discipline's formulations will simply reduce to the other, it is not only possible but fruitful because of the multiple levels of understanding it promises, to probe social phenonomena from each angle simultaneously.

To probe matters further, the same group of volunteer subjects were also administered the TAT.[3] The TAT is a collection of black- and-white cards

---

[3]Except, in this case we were able to recall two more persons, one of whose participation was partial, swelling the group to 45/46.

(here slides) depicting various ambiguous scenes including a person or persons.[4] Subsets of cards are often chosen for given test administrations depending on what the test administrator is interested in exploring in the psychology of given subjects. Cards are chosen based on prevailing assumptions about the types of psychological material that various cards tend to elicit (i.e., "card pull"). Based on the prevailing view of the cool Mach syndrome with its affective detachment and comparative freedom from conventional morality, the earlier MMPI work, and a male test population, and give Bellak's (1975) descriptions of card pull for each card, the TAT administration reported here involved cards 1, 2, 3BM, 4, 6BM, 7BM, 8BM, 12M, 13MF, and 18BM. Standard TAT instructions were given, with the cards converted to slides shown to the test group at common showings scheduled several times over a 1-month period to accommodate the schedules of volunteers. Subjects wrote their responses.

Quantified data were generated as follows: Focusing on the summary story content for each slide, I constructed variables that seemed to capture themes presented in subject responses to a given slide, while blind to the high or low Mach status of the respondents. (A second coder blindly coded 10% of all slide responses, randomly selected, with a coder reliability averaging 89%.) Frequency counts were taken representing the number of responses for each variable for each slide, by the high and low Mach subject groups separately. This approach led to the construction of a series of two by two cross tabulations of high versus low Mach scores by dichotomous categories of the succession of dependent variables I constructed. Restricted to cross-tab distributions with a .05 probability or less, the resulting significant cross tabulations became the basis for interpreting the TAT test differences between high and low Mach groups, and the resulting TAT profile associable with high Machs.

Table 4.2 shows the variables for which high and low Mach groups show a significantly nonrandom distribution, according to the Fisher's Exact, for each TAT card as indicated. Before discussing the summary TAT profile of high Machs suggested by these data, a brief card-by-card description of the findings is useful.

Bellak observed that Picture 1 tends to elicit material indicative of relations to parents, the conflict between autonomy and compliance, achievement concerns, sexual concerns, aggressiveness, and body and self-image. As the table indicates, in response to this picture highs offer significantly fewer stories in which a hero prevails in conflict with authority figures.

In response to Picture 2, which focuses on family relations, autonomy,

---

[4]Except for one card, the ultimate in projective testing, which is totally blank.

Table 4.2

Significant (Fisher's Exact) Cross Tabulations of Dichotomized TAT Variables
by High and Low Mach Scores (N = 45 Subjects; 22/23 Highs, 22 Lows)

TAT picture	Variable	High Machs	Low Machs	P (Fisher's Exact)
1	# of stories where hero prevails in a conflict with authority figures	9% (n=2)	36% (n=8)	.03
2	# of stories distanced or with a regressive aspect	35% (n=8)	9% (n=2)	.04
2	# of stories distanced; regressed; or involving sex	48% (n=11)	18% (n=4)	.03
3BM	# of stories with + or − (valenced) outcomes (hero gratifying or frustrating) on themes of autonomy, revenge, and/or survival	91% (n=20)	55% (n=12)	.01
3BM	# of stories with positive (hero gratifying) outcomes on themes of autonomy, revenge, and/or survival	73% (n=16)	45% (n=10)	.05
3BM	# of stories with references to confinement	27% (n=6)	5% (n=1)	.04
4	# of stories with themes of violence and/or sex	73% (n=16)	32% (n=7)	.01
4	# of stories with + or − (valenced) outcome for stories with male heroes [17 high and 17 low Mach stories had male heroes].	87% (n=15)	12% (n=2)	.00
4	# of stories where outcome is + or − (valenced), all hero formats	91% (n=20)	23% (n=5)	.00
6BM	# of stories introducing third parties	70% (n=16)	27% (n=6)	.00
6BM	# of stories involving death or bad news	78% (n=18)	32% (n=7)	.00
6BM	# of stories introducing third parties *and* death and/or bad news	61% (n=14)	18% (n=4)	.00
6BM	# of stories involving sex or violence or death	52% (n=12)	23% (n=5)	.03
7BM	# of stories whose action is *intra*-dyad	91% (n=21)	55% (n=12)	.01
7BM	# of stories with articulated (valenced) tone for dyadic relationship (supportive, constructive nurturing; strained, competitive; inefficacious, ambivalent)	100% (n=23)	32% (n=7)	.00
7BM	# of stories with positive (supportive, constructive, nurturing) dyadic tone	39% (n=9)	9% (n=2)	.02

82

Table 4.2 (continued)

TAT picture	Variable	High Machs	Low Machs	P (Fisher's Exact)
7BM	# of stories with negative (strained, competitive; or inefficacious, ambivalent) dyadic tone	61% (n = 14)	23% (n = 5)	.00
8BM	# of stories with aggression by hero	43% (n = 10)	73% (n = 16)	.04
12BM	# of stories where the elder figure affects (contributes to) outcome	65% (n = 15)	36% (n = 8)	.04
13MF	# of stories with references to violence and/or death	30% (n = 7)	59% (n = 13)	.04

compliance, Oedipal and sibling material, and tends to readily elicit distancing and regressive responses, highs show significantly more distancing and regressiveness, and when sexual references are added to form a compound category, the greater high Mach tendency to show such combined references is still more significant.

Picture 3BM tends to pull for latent homosexual responses, aggression and depression. High Machs concoct significantly more stories with valenced (i.e., positive or negative but not neutral) outcomes involving struggles for autonomy, survival, and revenge. That is, their stories involve a winner and/or loser in struggles of such types. They also show significantly more positive (hero victory) stories of this type. It is worth noting with special caution because of a notably low n, that at least as a minor subtheme, 3BM elicits significantly more stories from highs involving themes of hero confinement.

In response to Picture 4, which pulls content about male–female relations and triangular jealousy, highs offer significantly more themes of sex and violence, with more valenced (winner and/or loser) outcomes for male story heroes and story heroes in general.

Picture 6BM pulls mother–son, relations with women, and Oedipal material. Here high Machs offer stories that introduce third parties with significantly greater frequency, and that introduce death and/or bad news, and that introduce sex, violence, and/or death.

In response to picture 7BM, which elicits material on father–son relationships and attitudes toward male authority, high Machs offer significantly more intradyad-focused stories, stories in which dyads take a valenced tone (a positive or negative quality from the hero's perspective) with more positive as well as more negatively valenced dyads being each significantly more frequent in their own right.

Picture 8BM tends to draw out aggression, fear of mutilation especially while passive, and arguably according to Bellak, severe latent hostility if violent references are absent.[5] High Machs' stories in response to this slide differ from lows' in that highs offer significantly more stories casting elders in an efficacious role – stories where elders are determinant of the current action and any outcomes described.

Picture 12BM normally pulls themes revealing attitudes about the relation of younger to older men, passive homosexuality, and fear of domination by superiors. Here highs offer significantly more stories casting elders in an efficacious role – stories where elders are determinant of the current action and any outcomes described.

On slide 13MF, highs offer fewer stories involving violence or death. This picture pulls for significant sex conflicts and guilt regarding sex. If detail is found here as with some other detail-laden pictures, obsessive–compulsive tendencies may be revealed. Highs showed none of the latter detail focus here or on relevant other slides.

Slide 18BM pulls generally for anxiety in males. Highs and lows showed no significant differences on this slide regarding themes of sex, violence, victimization, being caught, being helped, or drinking, sleeping, or any common distancing indicator.

These data seem to plausibly suggest the following overview: Highs introduce sex significantly more than lows do in response to pictures that tend to elicit views of family relations (Picture 2); Oedipal concerns (Picture 2); male–female relations where a triangular element is suggested (Picture 4); and mother–son content with Oedipal suggestiveness (6BM). They also show some uncomfortableness with the family scene (Picture 2) in that they offer significantly more stories that are regressed or distanced. The point is not simply that highs will offer such themes, but that they do so significantly more than lows.

Highs introduce violence and death in male–female pictures with triangular or Oedipal-eliciting content (4 and 6BM). However, they introduce significantly less violence and death in 13MF. This picture involves a male

---

[5]Bellak noted that in 8BM, as in 3BM, a weapon (rifle 8BM; pistol 3BM) appears in the pictures, off to the side. He suggested that subjects avoiding the weapon or a violent element in response to these pictures may thereby indicate *latent* hostility (Bellak, 1975, p. 53). Bellak noted the catch-22 danger in this line of interpretation but cited supporting work. I have rejected this interpretation because (a) the catch-22 argument seems cogent on general principles; (b) violence references per se are freely offered in my subject responses over the 10 pictures; (c) while both highs and lows here generally made little of the weapons in their 3BM and 8BM stories, individuals who did seem to react were in any event randomly distributed between high and low groups.

with head buried in the crook of an arm brought up to the face, with a woman in bed behind the male figure. It is the most overt sex picture suggesting sex between heterosexual peers. Highs also show less violence and death in response to 8BM, a picture that is not Oedipal, male–female, triangular jealousy, or mother–son, as are the pictures for which highs offer death/violence responses.

Highs' reactivity to pictures pulling for reactions to authority includes hero failure to prevail over authorities on Picture 1. This picture involves achievement, authority, parents, and sexual adjustment in the context of body self-image. Highs tend to see relations in valenced terms helping and/or hurting, with an intradyad focus featuring authority figures with power (7BM and 12BM). Highs are also more valenced in their views of situations normally eliciting content about male authority, in the context of father–son relations, in particular (7BM); male–female relations and triangular jealousy (picture 4); and, regarding Picture 3BM which normally pulls any concerns about latent homosexuality, aggression or depression. Highs seem to react to stimuli normally taking the latter form as occasions to express concerns about autonomy, survival, and revenge.

Across the 10 TAT pictures, these are themes that highs are significantly more involved with, and that they project onto ambiguous scenes with a frequency significantly different than low Machs. If there is a pattern across these picture responses that highs are featuring in telling us about themselves in contrast to their low Mach counterparts, it would seem to be as follows: Machiavellianism tends to be associated with individuals who view their relations with authority figures in highly competitive terms, attributing considerable efficacy (but given the conflict they inject, not *legitimacy*) to authority. Outcomes are shaped by authoritative actors but Machs will struggle with them, though not without anxiety. Highs may feel weak while struggling for autonomy (especially with the stimulus nudge of a sole picture figure who is a child confronted with a body/self symbol, Picture 1). Or the high may be a more efficacious actor struggling and succeeding against authority in other cases. But, situations involving authority are determined in their outcomes, by the actors, not nature, not "circumstances," not conventions about role prerogatives that others might have come to accept as givens. These situations are thus viewed as competitive, although alliances can be formed. Pictures with male elders elicit these responses. Family, mother–son, triangular, and Oedipal content pictures elicit sex, violence, death, bad news, and third parties' introduction into stories where they are not on the cards. Peer sex and general anxiety-eliciting scenes (13MF, 18BM) show significantly less violence and death or are unremarkable altogether. In a sense, the imputed contexts that agitate highs are circumscribed, and very much focused on the early family constellation. In that constellation reverie, considerable anxiety and anger/revenge sentiments are experienced. Personal adequacy concerns, somewhat physicalized are associated. In general the reaction involved seems somewhat provocative more than withdrawing, but this is less clear as a general statement.

Violent, destructive, competitive, struggling, breaking out, power-oriented themes projected by high Machs seem confined to situations that are competitive, and reminiscent of family dynamics that involve a triangular theme. High Machs may tend further to have some deeper emotional trouble handling these issues, as suggested by the distancing and regressiveness in the face of situations that conjure these associations (Picture 2). However, whatever anxiety these associations may evoke, they are not generalized without restriction (unremarkable 18BM, nonaggressive 8BM and 13MF). It seems that at root, associations to the family, a conventionally acceptable authority figure not in alliance, and triangular jealousies suggesting the parent–child network of associations may be a precondition for the stressful response pattern.

The TAT may suggest a source and psychological focus of the emotional disquiet that Machs express through the MMPI. In the most general terms, Machiavellianism may be associated with relatively poorer intrapsychic resolution of the triangular early family constellation. This is consistent with the self-psychology emphasis on early parental empathic failure in the development of narcissistic disturbance.

With aggressive attitudes toward authority figures to whom high relationship (but not general social) efficacy is attributed in a striving, frequently competitive framework; with situations generally perceived as win–lose struggles; with violence, death, sex, and third parties significantly more injected into mother–son, family, and triangular jealousy scenes; and with the regressive and distancing responses also associated with family scenes—we may have a not unreasonable basis for a line of speculation that emphasizes emotional failures in the early family constellation. Despite the shifting nuance from the language of psychoanalytic self-psychology and narcissistic disturbance to the more analytically classic language of Bellak's "card pull" in the TAT, the pattern seems clear. The MMPI suggests that Machiavellianism involves hostility, but a hostility focused on readily retrievable specific incidents and others. This may be consistent with the high Mach unremarkability in 18BM and less violent-aggressive responses to 13MF and 8BM that generally tend not to pull parental, family, or triangular jealousy content. The thrill seeking suggested by the MMPI and interpreted as possibly a venting of some relative emotional disquiet may be taken as consistent with the violence themes that high Machs introduce on those TAT pictures that now seem to tap the relative difficulties in question.

The disdain for conventional morality associated with Machiavellianism, the implications of the cool Mach syndrome of the small-group laboratory, the affective detachment posited by Christie and Geis, and the MMPI findings, may allow for an interesting psychological explanation in light of the TAT profile.

Elevated Machiavellianism may be the sign of bringing to contemporary interpersonal situations, still unsettled attitudes toward authority—regarding not its efficacy, but rather its legitimacy, the notion of a "rightfulness" or moral justification for the power at its core. Without legitimacy, power is open to questioning; it remains contestable. Machiavellians may represent an ambivalent attitude toward authority and the manifestation of authority in rules. It is an ambivalence in which efficacy but not legitimacy of authority is acknowledged. Complexes of rules for behavior, or conventionally accepted roles for interpersonal situations, may thus invite resistance or expedient reshaping. Machs may replace them with self-serving postures of their own that allow them to display their own power. Perhaps this is because their earlier relationships to authorities in a formative period focused on the family constellation, were comparatively more troubling.

The Mach posture may be attractive because it facilitates the assertion of autonomy and moreover may enhance the opportunity to display autonomy, by "winning" over others, "winning" apart from socially (authoritatively) preferred rules, and "winning" by one's own rules. Machs may replay these issues by winning rather than withdrawing because the experiences with authority figures were inconsistent, ambiguous and somehow not definitive psychologically. Machs may not win by authoritative, "legitimate" rules because that might not be really a victory for them. This level of speculation would be supported by a self-psychological view of the origins of narcissistic disturbance. Psychoanalytic self-psychology locates the genesis of narcissistic disturbance in early parental empathic failure (Muslin & Val, 1987). Machiavellianism may be construable as a social psychological profile that reflects the relatively successfully managed mild narcissistic disturbance.

A possible implication is that Machs are not so much indifferent to conventional social morality per se, as they are focused on a more primitive phase of social adjustment that most people work through on the way to accepting the full trappings and subtleties of public place, public context morality. They are in a sense still negotiating its terms in the initial rule and role-imposing context of an earlier life phase. They are detached from, and cynical toward what may appear as the requirements for behavior and the social rules that they are not prepared to accept (and not prepared in a double sense). They assume others' behaviors are likely motivated by the issues that drive the Mach. They struggle for an inner sense of certainty in relation to the social environment (and consequently to themselves). The result is striving to transcend uncertainty while re-experiencing it as a host of related anxieties and situational challenges engendering a broad cynicism.

Touhey (1973) suggested that Machs may fail to form proper identifications with their parents. Christie and Geis (1970) noted DeMiguel's findings suggesting that high Machs are less likely to accept their parents as role models. These observations are consistent with the speculative line suggested here. Research cited by Christie and Geis indicates that Machiavellianism increases with urbanization, industrialization, and secularization. We discuss this issue at the social-institutional level, but it is also relevant here. These processes can strain or at least invite flux in the basic family context and diminish the felt emotional effectiveness of authority and nurturing figures, and so contribute to pressures in the formative period which could enhance the Machiavellian pattern. This too seems a plausible unifying interpretation consistent with the several psychologies we have been working through.

5

The Manipulative Profile
and Group Context

To this juncture we have a personality profile developed in some depth. Melding three distinctive styles of personality analysis, we have a picture of a highly manipulative personality. The profile incorporates access to an empirical record of favored manipulative ploys and interpersonal style for effecting them, the Machiavellianism literature. The profile also incorporates access to a dynamic theory of inner mental processes, the self-psychology literature on narcissism. In addition, our testing psychology perspective has helped to join the two other elements in a now rather broad and multifaceted picture. With it we are better able to understand the psychic impetus for manipulativeness.

In a way, it seems that the impetus to seize the manipulative position in interaction is born of a pervasive need to be socially, situationally essential. The TAT suggested the panic and furor that can arise at the prospect of displacement in the most basic group, interpersonal setting. Situational activism and control become the self-tonic for temporarily offsetting a diminished, and potentially even fragmented, sense of self. Grandiosity and insecurity inhabit the same inner emotional space. Under the felt stimulation of idiosyncratically meaningful circumstances, the anticipated experience of each extreme element can fuel the experience of the opposite pole. Intensiveness, deflation, and ambivalence can characterize a single-action frame.

Because action from this position serves the purpose of recouping a sense of being vital, the action is understandably not likely to be in service of ideals.

It seems to have the far more immediate purpose of reassurance by confirming a vivid sense of a primitive self.

With this understanding we now come to the point where we can pursue a new order of question: What is the impact of such a personality on the life and performance of the social group?

EPISTEMOLOGICAL CONSIDERATIONS AND THE CONCEPT OF THE GROUP

Unfortunately, the state of the art both in the social sciences and "applied psychoanalysis" is underdeveloped to a degree that requires a digression at this point. Before we can consider the effect of the Machiavellian/narcissistic actor at the group level, it is necessary to clarify the meaning of the term *group* and work through the subtleties in the idea of a "group level" of interpretation. The meaning of the concept is highly varied and worse yet, confounded, especially when viewed across several disciplinary styles.

Most social science work seems commonly to presume a basic three-part hierarchy of levels of analysis: individual, group, and organization. So-called "emergent" properties seem to appear at each level beyond the individual. The problems with this prevalent social science style stem from ambiguities rooted in conceptual underdevelopment. These ambiguities tend to produce confoundings in research. It is useful to consider some of these ambiguities and fashion working positions on them so as to proceed crisply with the understanding of manipulativeness at various levels of generality.

I think it fair to say that it is the convention in political science to see the group as an independent actor and distinct unit of analysis. Presumably it is interposed between individual and organization although the latter boundary is not often specified. I suspect this is in large part a byproduct of the post-Second World War emphasis on the "pluralist" model of American politics.[1] Even the pluralist versus elitist debate could be understood in these terms as a dispute over the comparative merits of interpreting American national events as the product of *inter*group rivalries or *intra*group rivalries, in both cases within an institutional rule framework. This is not gainsaid by the elite school's tendency to emphasize the congeniality of the rules to the common interests of elite, intragroup factions. Although the pluralist versus elitist debate is less the explicit focus of American political theory in the 1980s, part of its legacy is an easy comfort with the idea of the group as a level

---

[1] It should be noted that in Truman's (1971) classic, however, the complexity of the definitional problem is given an attention often lacking in later pluralist work.

of actor and the attendant casual assumption that we know what this means. To my knowledge it is not a debate that ever dwelled very seriously on the inherent epistemological issue of a group actor or some more subtle understanding of the nature of the group as a medium of action, turning instead to case study evidence and counter evidence on group impact.

The psychoanalytic position on the nature of the group as an actor seems characterized by a greater degree of explicit position taking regarding the uniqueness of the group. However, behind some of the more explicit and noteworthy positions that have been taken, murkiness still lingers. Bion's (1961) work on groups is an interesting illustration, in this case especially considering Kernberg's (1984) observation that Bion's key concepts represent "the most important single contribution psychoanalysis has made to small group psychology" (p. 8). Bion wrote:

the apparent difference between group psychology and individual psychology is an illusion produced by the fact that the group provides an intelligible field of study for certain aspects of individual psychology, and in so doing brings into prominence phenomena that appear alien to an observer unaccustomed to using the group. (p. 134)

And then again:

I attach no intrinsic importance to the coming together of the group. It is important that the group should come together sufficiently closely for me to be able to give an interpretation without having to shout it. This means that the number must be limited. The degree of dispersion of the group must similarly be limited because I wish all individuals to have an opportunity of witnessing the evidence on which I base my interpretation. For the same reason the individuals must all collect at the same time. Now this congregation of the group in a particular place at a particular time is obviously very important for the purely mechanical reasons I have just given, but it has no significance whatsoever in the production of group phenomena. The idea that it has springs from the erroneous impression that a thing must necessarily commence at the moment when its existence becomes demonstrable. The point that I would make is that no individual, however isolated in time and space, can be regarded as outside a group or lacking in active manifestations of group psychology, although conditions do not exist which would make it possible to demonstrate it. Acceptance of the idea that the human being is a group animal would solve the difficulties that are felt to exist in the seeming paradox that a group is more than the sum of its members. The explanation of certain phenomena must be sought in the matrix of the group and not in the individuals that go to make up the group. Time-keeping is no function of any part, in isolation, of the mechanism of a clock, yet time-keeping is a function of the clock and of the various parts of the clock when held in combination with each other.

There is no more need to be confused by the impression that a group is more than the sum of its members than it would be to be confused by the idea that a clock is more than a collection of the parts that are necessary to make a clock.

To sum up, there are characteristics in the individual whose real significance cannot be understood unless it is realized that they are part of his equipment as a herd animal and their operation cannot be seen unless it is looked for in the intelligible field of study—which in this instance is the group. You cannot understand a recluse living in isolation unless you inform yourself about the group of which he is a member. To argue that in such a case one is not dealing with a group is merely to prove oneself naively imperceptive. (pp. 132–133)

Thus, it seems that the group is a unique level of analysis from this modern classic of analytic thinking on group behavior. However, its fundamentalness does not clearly distinguish it from the individual level in the sense that the group dimension is so overwhelming as to absorb the individual as an independent actor. It is as if the first two levels of analysis in the conventional three part formula were now condensed so that the individual and group formed a complex single category. From our perspective the issue is further complicated, as Bion eventually noted what is bedrock for him in probing the dynamics of group processes:

There is ample evidence for Freud's idea that the family group provides the basic pattern for all groups. If I have not stressed the evidence for this, it is because that view does not seem to me to go far enough . . . I think that the central position in group dynamics is occupied by the more primitive mechanisms that Melanie Klein has described as peculiar to the paranoid-schizoid and depressive positions . . . In my view it is necessary to work through both the stresses that appertain to family patterns and the still more primitive anxieties of part-object relationships. In fact I consider the latter to contain the ultimate sources of all group behavior. (p. 189)

These Kleinian concepts that Bion found at the root of the group dynamics that he uncovered pertain primarily to infant development in the first year of life. It is fair to say they are intended as a scheme for understanding individual personality development from its earliest stages. Through subsequent life stages they serve as fixation points to which individuals may return in regression under emotional stress—as stops on a descending slope of immaturity. For Bion, groups constantly struggle to maintain mature, structured, cooperative working postures, in the face of a constant pull to a finite collection of regressed behavior patterns.

Thus, it seems that even in Bion's work, the relationship between individual-level and group-level conceptualizations is somewhat problematic. The group is more than the sum of its parts but not in the strict sense of providing genuinely emergent properties. The group simply reveals facets of individual personality that are inherently group focused. However, the model of individual personality resorted to in this context is interpreted as having its roots in the very struggle to individuate—to distinguish the self from the collective. This is a process that is never complete and never irreversible. In an important sense the individual–group distinction is a question of degree of emphasis, pulled from what is in fact a conceptual cycle on the order of group–individual–group.

In general terms, the psychoanalytic view of groups portrays them as a shared state of mind as well as an acting entity. The group works on a task (i.e., serves some ostensible purpose) but also constantly struggles to resist the regressive forces felt individually and shared collectively, always to some degree. The quality and direction of task work is strongly influenced by this struggle. Whether the signs of the ever-present struggle are interpreted in the psychoanalytic dialects of Kleinian splitting and projective identification or Kohut's fragmentation, the challenge is to sustain consolidation simultaneously on two now highly interactive conceptual and empirical levels of individual and group.[2] The case has also been made that regression in individuals and groups, as a kind of interlocking process, is central to leadership in organizations and therefore organizational performance (Kernberg, 1978, 1979).

The idea of this highly permeable distinction between the fundamental struggle of the group and the individual against the forces of regression that are never put to rest, lends some irony to the classic social science position on the conceptual barrier of emergence that exists between individual and group levels. In Eulau's (1969) chapter on Lasswell mentioned in chapter 2, the following also appears:

> But if the behavior of the individuals is observed from the group or macrolevel perspective, it is possible to identify qualities which are new because they do not exist if any one constituent individual is observed as a single unit. For instance, on the microlevel of the individual, no analytic operation whatsoever enables

---

[2]Lofgren (1984) drew out the Kleinian and Kohutian parallels in the underpinnings of the Bion work.

the analyst to describe a group's "cohesion" or "solidarity." (In other words, an individual's *feeling* of solidarity is a property of the individual, not of the group; "group solidarity" is an analytically distinct property of the whole group.) It is for just this reason that the conception of levels of analysis and the notion of emergence are complementary. Emergence entails the appearance of new levels of organization; the recognition of new levels entails a developmental perspective and the need to distinguish between levels of analysis. (p. 28)

This excerpt is part of a larger discussion offering a position that is in some respects similar to Bion's. The point of interest here, however, is the relationship of the individual to the experience of properties emergent at the group level—here, "solidarity." Indeed, it is clear by definition that individuals cannot display *group* solidarity. (However, what they then feel and how they imagine themselves in doing so is in itself a question part and parcel of this issue.) Nonetheless, a key question for our purposes is whether the individual experiences a parallel appropriate to the individual, of the group solidarity process. This sensation would be best named *individual solidarity* as a manifestation of the concept of solidarity on the individual level, processually duplicating the cohesiveness versus fragmentation dynamic on the group level. Now we accept in psychodynamic terms that the individual does experience precisely such a dynamic process, as essential in fact to the maintenance of what Kohut would call "a cohesive," or fully integrated, self (see Kohut, 1978, on "fragmentation," and for the group context of the same concept of failure to maintain cohesiveness, see Kohut, 1985). We have just noted the Kleinian parallel as well.

Thus, what psychoanalysis has to suggest to social science on the issue of distinguishing individual from group levels of analysis and understanding the dynamics of individual versus group action is as follows: Clearly there is no need to suppress a distinction between the two levels. However, key processes of each have been analyzed in ways that suggest, if we wish to see it, a parallel—a correspondence of internal dynamics—between the two levels. So, in the example just given, individuals do indeed struggle to maintain internal "solidarity" (i.e., internal cohesiveness as ego firmness or in self-psychology terms a *cohesive self*). They strive for a sense of self in terms of a cluster of well-integrated "selves" born of the developmental process and carried through life. Moreover, there is a relationship between cohesiveness on such an individual level and the contribution to the group and therefore to the extent of cohesiveness on the group level, qua group. Yet further, the individual experience of the self and the individual experience of the group, and also the group experience of the group and of the individuals in it (as leader and followers and various additional subtypes we may posit) are intimately tied to one another.

THE MANIPULATIVE ACTOR AND THE GROUP PROCESS: SEVERAL GENERIC PERMUTATIONS

If we examine the Machiavellian actor's impact on the group level from the perspective developed in this chapter so far, we are led to ask not only what the manipulator does to the group or in the group, but also at a deeper level, what the manipulator and group do for one another, through what bi-level process and with what effect on the ostensible group purpose. I believe we can come to a relatively concise view on this in psychological terms. It is a view that can be merged with the social-political science perspective on the behavioral issues in groups deliberating significant problems.

Within a group, the actor profile we are now treating as a broadly construed Machiavellian/narcissistic profile is capable of occupying a somewhat charismatic position (for contrasting psychoanalytic and social science perspectives on charisma see Schiffer, 1973; Willner, 1984). Consider a number of the profile elements: High energy investment in personal performance; a well-developed sense of the mood of the group qua group; prowess in the tactics of social encounter; considerable persuasiveness; the chronic need for mirroring support and the prospect of panic should it be withdrawn; and the attraction to grandiose schemes for the self's triumph before an applauding audience. All these suggest such an advantage and the desire to pursue it. However, the prospect of rage and destructive competitiveness beneath the surface, and difficulty in pursuing genuine ideals suggest that the manipulator as charismatic figure offers a risky brand of leadership. It can be self-destructive and collectively destructive for the group now tied to the leader. The strength projected in such leadership is in this sense no greater than the personality strength of the leader, detached as the mission of such a leadership is from any real values other than personal vindication that is sterilely, solipsistically conceived and hence defectively pursued. This apparent strength is at the price of some brittleness. When idiosyncratically key supports are withdrawn, there may be a tendency to crack rather than bend.

Of course the dangers involved appear as a risk and not as an inevitability. We might expect that at least a few obvious group factors can influence the probability that within-group destructiveness will be an outcropping of such leadership. For example, it seems reasonable to speculate in this vein, that the more the members of a group share such a profile, the greater the capacity to deify an individual while the unannointed turn on one another at the same time. The highly manipulative may aggrandize a leader (distinguishable by some feature or circumstance) while effacing one another. In such cases leaders who appear to hold their position by keeping their minions factionalized, may in fact experience the situation quite differently. Their experience may be that what the followers have in common is a fratricidal preoccupation so intense that it necessitates maintaining the fiction that one of the group is above the fray, as the "leader." Such a leader serves a group purpose. He or she is living proof to each disputant that a mirroring vindicator exists to confirm his or her view of self and self-situation. Such leaders may feel they are riding tigers that offer them a petrifying as much as a thrilling experience.

In such cases, if the group task is vague, perennial, procedurally preoccupying, and if outgroup challenges are actually insignificant, the group situation may be sufficiently insulated from reality to allow for ample intense machinations and surface stability at the same time. The tiger ride can be a long one. Of course these are groups trading on a considerable environmental subsidy, but this is not an uncommon condition, particularly in developed Western societies.[3]

Consider the contrasting case now, of the manipulative leader occupying a charismatic position with a group of followers significantly less manipulative in orientation. Let us hold constant for the moment, the assumption of a benign external environment. The group profile suggested would seem to be one of stifled group development and therefore collective immaturity. The vanities and insecurities of self-preoccupied leadership may go without eliciting an effective challenge, but also without an audience that can be effectively mobilized for mature activity. Although such a group may regress to a deferential state it is at the same time not likely to be marshallable for any material efforts. Rather, the suggested image is one of the large echo that accompanies the beating of an empty drum. Perhaps such echoes are loudest as an accompaniment to trivial, ritual group activities whose procedures and potency would seem meaningless to outsiders.

Whether in charismatic positions or in more modern legal/rational positions of formal authority, the inherently manipulative leader with Machiavellian tactical prowess and narcissistically disturbed compulsions would seem to pose the greatest threat in groups who share something of a similar orientation and who find themselves in a turbulent external environment displaying identifiable, threatening, outgroups. Here the expression of group rage focused by and through the leader is likely to mobilize the drives and skills of the group, and set off the regressive internal processes of the group at the same time. I believe this is the general category of situations that gives full vent to the antisocial potentials of destructive yet seemingly sophisticated manipulativeness in the modern society.

---

[3] I am reminded of the comment—whose specific source I cannot recall—by a writer from a developing nation, to the effect that only Americans could produce a literary community preoccupied with novels about the problems of novelists writing novels, whereas other societies' literatures struggled with themes of war, peace, and the land.

EXTENDING THE METAPHOR AND ATTENDANT EPISTEMOLOGICAL CHOICES

The latter issue represents a level of concern that is quite properly not the focus of small-group laboratory research. Small-group research is simply not designed for probing such issues. Concerns appropriate to the broader realm in question cannot be answered with the sharper tools of small-group research and hence we face another academic trade-off of precision against scope. Choices of the latter over the former seem inherent in movement up the ladder of levels of analysis, and the discussion offered in these pages has involved several such choices, for example in pursuing the suggestion of a hybridized connection between Machiavellianism and narcissism.

Arguments for the heuristic value of conceptualizations reflecting such choices are at best self-evident and at worst self-serving. Thus, having chosen a line of inquiry in which a reliance on the presumed value of such conceptual linkages in inherent, it is appropriate to drop the other shoe: It should be noted that at this level of broadened perspective on the social effects of manipulative activist leadership, several independently developed leader profiles merge with the profile developed here. They all share concern with the long-term effects of a contemporary form of leadership that seems to project inner turbulence outward and also introjects an arguably widespread imbalance in contemporary social values. Lasch, aspects of Kohut and Kernberg, several of the more applied Machiavellianism studies, and the more general discussions offered as part of the pure Machiavellianism research speak to these issues from perspectives explicitly dealt with in these pages. At this level of observation however, the stream widens. Maccoby's (1978) concern with the rise of the "gamesman" is an important case in point.

Gamesman Elements

A brief assortment of Maccoby's descriptors of this leading contemporary type, developed through Rorschach testing and interviews of corporate leaders across the United States and later around the Western world, illustrates the parallels at this level:

> At their worst moments gamesmen are unrealistic, manipulative, and compulsive workaholics. Their hyped-up activity hides doubt about who they are and where they are going . . . When they let down, they are faced with feelings that make them feel powerless. The most compulsive players must be "turned on," energized by competitive pressures . . . (pp. 108–109)

[Attributed to a gamesman:] "We can win at any game society can invent."
(p. 123)

More than any other types, gamesmen told us that the ability to dramatize
ideas and to stimulate or activate others were among the most important
abilities for their work. Charles L. Hughes [1965, cited in Maccoby, 1978] . . .
pointed out that extensive research showed that the kind of people who were
most successful in the high technology corporation were those "compulsively
and habitually seeking to win." (p. 105)

[the gamesman] is energized to compete not because he wants to build an
empire, not for riches, but rather for fame, glory, the exhilaration of running
his team and of gaining victories. His main goal is to be known as a winner and
his deepest fear in to be labelled a loser. (p. 100)

The theme suggested in these descriptive phrases seem to echo themes we
have developed in the preceding chapters. However, this time I forego the
twist by twist interweaving of a third suggestive thread. There are after all,
diminishing returns in an exercise that is potentially endless if we assume a
grand theme of contemporary Western society constitutes the underlying
commonality.

Pursuing the manipulative actor as we know him or her through our
phenotypic personality profile, it would appear that groups led by such
persons—charismatically or in rationalized authority—are potentially distorted in their views and excessive in their responses as are their leaders. The
view developed to this point in this chapter is that action at the group level
is a complex interplay of both behavior emergent in the group and the
constant individual–group, psychic interplay. From this perspective we can
enhance the social psychological picture of group processes with an understanding of what the Machiavellian/narcissistic actor brings on the interwoven dimension of individual personality. The point can be amply illustrated by considering the well known and highly influential picture of group
deliberative, decision making processes developed by Janis (1982).

Groupthink and Our Phenotype

The "groupthink" syndrome, exhibits a number of features by now familiar to
us as reflecting narcissistic and Machiavellian themes. Groups suffering
groupthink tend to hold "illusions of invulnerability" and tend to "taking
extreme risks"; they are "inclined to ignore the ethical or moral consequences
of their decisions" (Janis, 1982, p. 174). They take hostile and condescending
views of outgroups; holding "stereotyped views of enemy leaders as too evil to

warrant genuine attempts to negotiate, or as too weak and stupid to counter whatever risky attempts are made to defeat their purposes" (p. 174). Additionally, rules and group patterns develop that serve to wall off dissent from the grandiose group view of itself and its plans, as reflected in the emergence of "mind-guards" and the general group exertion of pressure on members articulating dissenting arguments or concerns (Janis, 1982). The struggle for a continued cohesiveness of group and view, Janis' "concurrence seeking tendency," becomes a kind of collective "presenting well" to self and external viewers.

Melding our orientation with the groupthink focus suggests several interesting speculations. First, and most obviously, is the possibility of supporting this social psychological construct with the notion that in depth terms we are dealing with the possibility of a narcissistically disturbed "group self" (Kohut, 1985). Second, recall the earlier brief observation in chapter 3 regarding the profile of a Machiavellian/narcissistic hybrid, and groupthink. It was to the effect that postures of independence may represent superficial attempts to break from groups, with such attempts failing in the face of deeper pulls toward in-group loyalism. This would seem especially plausible for groups of significant duration or intensity where the latter ties could be cemented beneath the emotional surface.

Based on other elements of the individual profile, we may also derive the warning in this context, that for "groupthinkers," the denigrating attitude toward the outgroups may not only fortify a group's confidence in its own plans. It may also focus considerable hostilities that need to be projected outward, once the anxiety of high-risk deliberations is underway. Thus there may be a built-in escalating tendency in "groupthink" situations populated by Machiavellian/narcissistic manipulators. Hostility toward outgroups, traceable primarily to narcissistic rage, may develop parallel to any negative characterizations of outgroups which serve confidence-building functions. Additionally, consider the earlier association of our manipulative profile with felt pressures to vent angry impulses, but with the capacity to do so in often sophisticatedly masked fashion. One is led to ask whether the modern "crisis player" has a tendency however unconscious its roots and seemingly uncomfortable its experience, to deliberately *fashion crises* (and a group crisis mentality) out of a deep-seated need to experience emotionally primitive territory. The modern proliferation of crisis centers, crisis teams, situation rooms, command centers, and so on, comes to mind in this regard.[4]

---

[4]I stress the implication of our second point here, that this tendency would not be contradicted by the preference for individual postures of swashbuckling independence. The two tendencies may be thought of as the "phobic/counter-phobic" sides of the same psychic coin.

The solutions to groupthink that we would thus be wise to consider may include not only remedies of its deliberation deficiencies, but checks against the "false–positives" mentality of crisis-seeking. The point here is that they may be expectable with Machiavellian/narcissistic manipulators. "False-negatives"—crises denied—may seem less directly explainable in these terms, but I believe in principle they can be accounted for.

The personality profile we have focused on would seem likely to fashion such denials if the occurrence of a specific empirical scenario represented disconfirmation of beliefs and postures narcissistically invested by the time the disconfirming scenario is offered in group deliberations. Denied crises thus would tend to be those that disconfirm significant articles of political and emotional faith for such actors. Their denial would thus be understandable as regressive fixation of the sort described by Bion. His "flight" and "utopian" group mental states come to mind. The occurrence of such crises-*denied* among power circles of personalities with the profile we have explored, can thus coexist with a crisis-*seeking* emotional undercurrent, and with seeming addiction to marathon, intense, professional experiences.

Hardball Politics Themes

Etheredge (1979), in his model of "hardball politics," offered a picture of apparently Western elite, and in a later work (1985) specifically American elite, decision-making circles that offer strong support for this line of argument. Also built upon a seemingly Kohut-oriented picture of the narcissistically disturbed actor, Etheredge's (1979) rich portrait of the hardball politico (his "NP") is described at one point in a way also suggestive of Maccoby's gamesman theme:

> It is important to be clear that what the NP wants primarily is what he conceives to be a feeling of directorship in the unfolding social and political drama of his times. He seeks a position of power less to use power to accomplish certain specific goals than for the gratifications of being engagé and a top dog. Although he may genuinely dedicate himself to certain ideals of grandiose accomplishment, these typically are symbolic and seldom involve thoughtful and well-elaborated programs. The major story is that, above all, he wants to win, and he imagines a better society to follow (although he is vague on details) once his own will occupies the idealized location on the top . . .

> The narcissistic striving of the NP involves also what is known as "mirror transference." That is, he relates implicitly to people (e.g., the public) with the hope and need that they confirm his grandiose strivings, give him public recognition for his accomplishments and vaunted conception of himself. He

seeks an echo of applause, love, and unbounded admiration and respect coming back. And he is certain such response is out there, albeit latent and mobilizable, that "in their heart" the people, the silent majority, know he is right and will eventually respond. It is difficult to say whether the NP seeks love, or unbounded admiration, or status, or unlimited power or success—these connotations all are correlated in high political office. He is on a public ego-trip—in fact, he wants all of them simultaneously. The "public" is not important to him in a genuine sense; he perceives them not as autonomous fellow human beings of equal status and respect with whom he works collaboratively in a specialized role, but as a supporting cast of subordinates bolstering his own psychic economy. He will be a "public servant" but only if he can look down upon (and imagine himself to be looked up to by) the public. Favorable publicity and recognition are, of course, important to the NP "rationally" to be reelected, but his vanity requires these for more than their strategic value. (pp. 4–5)

Etheredge also suggested a possible thematic continuity among no less than 13 other independent strands of personality research across the psychological research spectrum, if they are viewed in terms of their potential compatibility with themes of narcissism. Interestingly, he included the Christie and Geis Machiavellian construct in this group.[5] Thus we see again, that at this level of generalization, many of the formulations of manipulative/exploitive personality types merge to some degree.

We have woven a portrait primarily with the analytical strands of Machiavellianism and narcissism but in this chapter have also augmented it with nuances suggested by some notably related concepts, particularly those of Maccoby, Janis, and Etheredge.

CONCLUSION: GROUP-LEVEL THEMES—THEIR IMPLICIT ANTICIPATION OF ORGANIZATIONAL-LEVEL ISSUES

In this "group-level" chapter, the aim has been some appreciation of the group dynamics involved in the expression of manipulativeness. We have been primarily concerned to stress that the pattern of group level manifestations results from an interplay of our broad phenotypic profile with the emotional needs of the group. For the sake of economy of exposition, members were treated as a subgroup of potential followers and also as a pool of possible rivals to the focal narcissistic actor also seen as a group member. Consistent with several contemporary strands of leadership research (Chemers, 1984; Hol-

---

[5]However, Maccoby's work is not among the group. Neither is it discussed in the 1985 piece.

lander, 1978; Hunt, 1984), it was noted that the resolution of the ever mercurial leader–group relationship is also contingent on the intervening factors of perceived and actual developments in the group's external environment.

As noted in chapter 2, particularly regarding the discussion of de Board's (1978) interesting *Psychoanalysis of Organizations* group-level discussions at the level of analysis employed in this chapter, are often take as "organizational" analysis. This is apparently on the strength of positing a large bureaucratic context for the specific group or generic group construct under analysis. Apparently, organizational behavior then becomes what people do in groups, ostensibly *within* an organization. By implicit extension, an organization as a context must be a network of groups.

I feel dissatisfied with this understanding of when "organizational analysis" is accomplished. This dissatisfaction is predicated not on the assumption that such an understanding is necessarily "wrong" or untenable. Rather, the difficulty with it is that it seems limiting. Perhaps those who prefer it would say "simplifying," but I think not. The epistemology behind the view in question minimizes, and arguably excludes, the idea of "organization" as a truly distinctive level of analysis. I believe that is precisely what it has become in its most effective manifestations.

The more ambitious understanding of the organizational level is very well captured by the more formal "systems theory" view of organizations. Elsewhere, I have described it as the "macro" approach in organization theory, and have laid out what I believe to be each of its key concepts and their relationships. This is in contrast to the more common "micro" view, and its associated constellation of ideas (Lerner, 1986).

Suffice it to say that a multilevel perspective on the manipulative personality profile would seem well served by considering its impact on the organizational level, now understood in macro, systemic terms. This is the first issue taken up in the next chapter.

6

The Manipulative Personality and the Organizational System

The systems view of organization is perhaps best exemplified by the depiction of organizations as *open systems*. In such treatments, an organization is understood as a dynamic interplay of constellations of functions. The constellations of functions, given their relative coherence, are described as *subsystems*.

For some theorists, generic subsystems are finite in number although their forms may be infinite in variety. For such authors, generic subsystems correspond to the "essential" categories of organizational functioning. Thus, for Katz and Kahn (1978) there are five essential functions: production, maintenance, boundary, adaptive, and managerial. All are performed with corresponding structural entities—subsystems—developed to varying degrees. Thus, maintenance functions are performed primarily by the maintenance subsystem, managerial functions by the managerial subsystem, and so on. These subsystems, in complex interplay, form a whole: *the organization*.

In organizations at an advanced degree of development, we would normally expect an advanced degree of structural elaboration to be exhibited by the organization as system. Its constellation of functions is likely to be manifest in fully articulated structures. Alternatively, in less completely evolved, less fully developed systems, these functions may be implicitly exhibited by skeletal structures that have yet to obtain more elaborate and fully individuated status. In the former cases where such elaboration is well advanced, the subsystems that now embody these functional constellations are expressed through concretely identifiable, formally specified organizational units.

THE REFERENTS OF SYSTEMS ANALYSIS

The metaphorical character of systems theory as an intellectual scheme allows for its ever looser imposition upon ever larger social contexts. Thus, ultimately, society per se may be treated as a *system*. In this motif, whole constellations of social institutions serve as subsystems of society as a whole. In such a view, the constellations of institutions are structurally dedicated to serving clusters of social functions, just as substructures within an organization serve the virtually identical list of generic functions intra-organizationally.

Of course, whole modern societies may lack the structural/functional articulateness, the structurally elaborate specificity, of more self-contained entities such as bureaucracies. The latter are the large-scale formal organizations that are usually the implied referent of such theories in much of the social science literature.

Structural/functional "systems theories" of action often merge literatures and concepts with cybernetic theories, theories of artificial intelligence, and theories of so-called *living systems*. The relevant literature is a vague and exceedingly rich mix of a variety of disciplines from anthropology through political science, to biology and engineering, occasionally achieving the tone of a common denominator: *general systems analysis*. Although this world view thus allows the incorporation of the study of individual organizations as well as societies—if not the cosmos—it has a common frame of reference conceptually. That is the antireductionist imagery of the target entity as a relational complex. The complex is analyzed in terms of the structural/functional interplay of its components in dynamic interaction among themselves, and with an environment. The essential analytical problem is the comprehension of the system's dynamics. They are not reducible to some serial aggregation of its "parts"—which have no meaning in isolation.

In its most elaborate formal versions, this systems or "macro" perspective on organization operates with several key, implicit assumptions. Primarily, systems have a somewhat solipsistic, deterministic, inner logic. They evolve and adapt through time, but somewhat as a moving spiral; their patterned form persists while their "progress" in interaction with an environment is discernible. An exhaustive relational determinism is the essence of their operation. "Systems" and thus organizations as systems, have an inherent *automaticity*. It is reflected in the template-confirming elaboration of the pattern of component relationships.

As noted in an earlier chapter, I have sought elsewhere to present these conceptual underpinnings and their implications in contrast to a "micro" view of organizational action (Lerner, 1986) The latter views the organization not as system, but as context for motive-driven actions in a far less determined context. In the micro view the organization is a fairly "empty" space.

For the purpose here, it is not necessary I hope, and not feasible I am sure, to digress further on the epistemology of systems conceptualizations in contrast to more reductionist analysis. Suffice it to say in this context then, that from the formal systems perspective, motive-based, individual, calculating actor behavior is epiphenomenal. The actions of individual actors that are significant constitute enactment of system-significant patterns. Pattern-breaking behavior is system relevant only if it reveals some limits whose repeated violation may undo the system, or edge it to a new state (always anticipatable by its template). Short of errors crossing a critical level, other behavior irrelevant to this system is treatable as mere system "noise." From this view man plans and God laughs, or more to the point, does not notice.

MACRO ANALYSIS AND PERSONALITY: THE TRADITIONAL PSYCHOANALYTIC VIEW

This antireductionist cast to macro, systems conceptualization of large-scale formal organization appears to be the obstacle to a genuine "organizational" analysis of the effect of personality on the collectivity. It accounts for the "stuckness" at the group level of analysis. The several frequent recourses at this juncture provide only partly satisfactory ways around the problem. None of them are fully satisfactory although some are better than others. Without having an ideal solution either, we may hope to employ the best of some of the better ways around. Consider first, a few of the existing alternatives.

Large-scale formal organizations may simply be treated as "the group." Here the loss of continuous interaction in face-to-face contact, and the loss of explicit short-term task must not be considered critical to the application of the "group" concept. Although this disqualifies any clear relevance of contemporary social psychological group research, or should, it is interesting if no more commendable, that psychoanalytic theory is more comfortable with such a loose, nebulous concept of the group. Indeed, the seeds for this psychoanalytic tolerance of such a broad and vague meaning of "group," allowing its easy application to large scale organization – and even society and civilization – are locatable in Freud's own writings. Thus, in a note to his translation of Freud's (1955) introduction to "Group Psychology and the Analysis of the Ego," Strachey wrote:

> "Group" is used throughout the translation of this work as equivalent to the rather more comprehensive German "Masse." The author uses this latter word to render both McDougall's "group," and also LeBon's "foule," which would

more naturally be translated "crowd" in Engish. For the sake of uniformity, however, "group" has been preferred in this case as well, and has been substituted for "crowd" even in the extracts from the English translation of Le Bon. (p. 64)

Here we see a condensation of the meaning of group, crowd, and mass, subsequently leading to generalizations spanning family, the formal military organization, and civilization. This forewarns of the inherent, excessive psychoanalytic readiness to meld these constructs into one loosely agglomerated referent. The subsequent formalization of macro-structural theories of formal organization has left newer images of organization either outside the reach of psychoanalytic theory or, insufficiently demarcated as a context requiring special handling, if psychoanalytic concepts of personality are to apply.

Of course, Freud was aware of this distinction among levels of abstraction, or as he would probably say, degrees of agglomeration. However, it seems primarily the thrust of "Group Psychology and the Analysis of the Ego" that the ties within "artificial groups," which we would call large-scale formal organizations, were seen as weaker than those within the intimate group. Freud saw the dynamic forces at play in his "artificial groups," such as the church and the military, to be representations of more primitive (in a sense prior) intimate group processes.[1]

This idea that the "artificial organization" can only be explained by emphasizing the intimate group's dynamics and their subtly transmuted expression in now displacing aggregates, seems to have fostered the modern psychoanalytic difficulty with large-scale formal organizations. They are treated as somewhat epiphenomenal in contrast to the intimate group. Either intimate-group concepts are "pulled up" to explain "artificial organizations" or "artificial organizations" are analytically decomposed to find their dynamic explanation. The effect has been to try to explain what we would call *macro phenomena* while treating them as on a level of human behavior comprised solely of extensions of lower level forces.[2] My point is not to say this is

---

[1]Freud saw these processes now focused in the case of "artifical groups" on the identification with the leader or "leading idea" as substitute. Thus, he (1955) noted:

> We have hitherto considered two artificial groups and have found that both are dominated by emotional ties of two kinds. One of these, the tie with the leader, seems (at all events for these cases) to be more of a ruling factor than the other, which holds between the members of the group. (p. 100)

[2]Of course Jung reversed these poles in a sense, creating a problem in the opposite extreme. His style of focus on the societal level would not help with the direction of ours, however, and seems to have more in common with the psychological anthropology school noted in chapter 1. (See Bennet, 1967.)

necessarily nonviable, although I admit I have my suspicions. Rather the point is that as a result, the body of knowledge developed at the macrolevel of organizational analysis resists penetration by psychoanalysis because the latter view of organization is so embedded in this particular epistemological position. In this connection it is interesting to note Freud's preference for positing a primal *horde* over a primal *herd*. Strachey observed, "Freud uses the term 'horde' to signify a relatively small collection of people" (Freud, 1955, p. 122).

MACRO ANALYSIS AND PSYCHOANALYSIS: CONTEMPORARY VARIATIONS

In addition to using a very loose notion of group to obscure the micro–macro disjuncture, other implicit "solutions" to the epistemological problem have been known to be applied. At one extreme, we may deny the significance of our *inner* experience of large-scale structural dimensions of organization. At the other extreme, we may reduce the significance of interaction in organizations to the inner experience of face-to-face interaction with formal role occupants. We may claim to capture the essence of the individual–organizational interaction in the unconscious re-experience of emotions felt toward siblings and authority figures, without allowing for the significance of complications arising from large scale. Alternatively, we may even see the organization not literally as a group, but metaphorically as a "group," thereby pushing the problem to the background shadows of analysis without actually solving it.

Kets de Vries and Miller (1984) offered a psychoanalytic perspective on organizational behavior, one that displays great imaginativeness. It creatively overlays schema of individual, group, and dyadic interaction to reconstruct the depth processes influencing outward patterns of organizational performance. At several points, the work may also be read as implicitly illustrating many of the epistemological choices for how to link psychoanalysis and organizational analysis.

Thus, de Vries and Miller observed:

> Our experience with top executives and their organizations revealed that *parallels* could be drawn between individual pathology—excessive use of one neurotic style—and organizational pathology, the latter resulting in poorly functioning organizations. (p. 17, italics added)

In addition to this notion of micro–macro "parallel," de Vries and Miller also employed the concept of organizational culture as a linking concept.

They combine this with an emphasis on the impact of the personality of the senior individual that they believe can have an overwhelming influence in many organizations: "The personality of the top manager can in very important ways influence strategy and even structure. It can certainly influence organizational culture" (p. 18). Elsewhere they also speak of "the *culture* of the organization and the *key individuals who constitute it*" (p. 147, italics added. This idea that individuals somehow "constitute" a culture is the heart of the issue at this juncture).

Then, too, the authors noted a micro–macro link via group concepts, presumably with the organization as the group, as a network of groups, or as dominated by a leading group:

> We believe that intrapsychic fantasies of key organization members are major factors influencing their prevailing neurotic style and that those, in turn, give rise to shared fantasies that permeate all levels of functioning, color the organizational culture, and make for the dominant organizational adaptive style. This style will greatly influence decisions about strategy and structure. (p. 20)

Indeed, the range of referents appears at the outset to be those organizations dominated by a leading group (neurotic or under the influence of a neurotic leader). The authors noted: "Each of these [dysfunctional] organizational types has many characteristics that stem from its dominant neurotic style—that is the shared inner world of the organization's dominant coalition" (p. 23). Interestingly, the shared-group fantasies eventually analyzed in detail, are Bion's except that Bion's pairing mode is more frequently referred to as the "utopian." I take this as a significant choice of emphasis. It can be read to suggest an understandable desire to emphasize phrasing that generalizes to the large-scale organizational medium from what is originally a more intimate, group-level conceptualization.

The point of this discussion of the Kets de Vries and Miller perspective at this juncture is to underscore the difficulty in retaining an antireductionist posture while employing psychoanalytic concepts to study organizations. This is not a dilemma that should be avoided altogether because the depth level of explanation is essential to understanding the power and exploitation dynamics within organizations. It is also not a dilemma that the more sensitive psychoanalytic treatments can avoid.

Kets de Vries and Miller could not avoid it because the range of applied psychoanalysis clearly includes—but includes with festering ambiguities that render analysis problematic—modern society's large-scale formal organizations. Interestingly, some of the more sophisticated psychoanalytic treatments of the micro–macro problem end in metaphorical allusion. Thus, through an unspecified reasoning, Kets de Vries and Miller (1984, p. 163) produce the following table at one point:

Phases of the Working-Through Process (from Kets de Vries & Miller, 1984)

	Manifestations	
Phase	Individual	Organizational
Phase 1: Shock	Numbing, interrupted by panic and outbursts of anger	State of disarray; organizational processes come to a halt or become ritualistic
Phase 2: Disbelief	Yearning and searching for what is lost; disbelief, denial of reality; irrational anger, self-reproach, sadness	Fight/flight and dependency assumptions; reactive posture; past orientation
Phase 3: Discarding	Discarding of old patterns of thinking, feeling and acting; redefinition of oneself; self-examination, disorganization, despair	Acceptance of organizational situation; occasional flight behavior; redefinition of situation; tentative explorations
Phase 4: Realization	Reshaping of internal representational world; acceptance of new reality	Reorganization: proactive posture; future orientation

The limitations of the state of the art that are exemplified in their table concern in this case the lack of an argument working through the derivation of *organizational* manifestations as the proper parallel to the more micro, clinically grounded *individual* manifestations. Note again that the chosen dimension is organizational not group, although the latter receives ample specific treatment by the authors as a distinguishable composite element in formal organizational dynamics.

By emphasizing that the organization has a culture, others have also implied a mechanism for linking micro events and the dynamics of the macro-system. This includes seeing organizational "ritual" as the link between macro features (now culture) and individual behavior (ritual enactment and its attendant individual-level behaviors; Smirich, 1985). However, because the organizational system is also more than a culture, again this creative solution is necessarily a partial one. Still we search for a way to link structural/functional, macro-systemic conceptualizations of organization—and the incorporation of all we have learned at that level—with the psychoanalytic approach and its tremendous advantages.

MACRO ANALYSIS AND PERSONALITY: A LINKAGE
ATTEMPT VIA SELECTED THEMES IN SYSTEMS THEORY

We can supplement the previous general style of approach and so demonstrate one of the ways to make the micro–macro synapse more bridgeable. This involves establishing a linking line of inquiry, a window in, that will connect the personality level and *those variations of systems theory which are less fixed upon the assumption of automaticity* (i.e., exhaustive relational determinism). Indeed, some of the variations on macro theory may be described in these terms. Some exaggerate the stochastic element in systems processes (Cohen & March, 1986; Cohen, March, & Olsen, 1972). Others link the centrality of functions performed within the system by given subsystems, to the degree of structural elaborateness (and hence relational comprehensiveness) for that system. Thus what is less necessary is less organized (Glassman, 1973; Simon, 1969; Weick, 1974, 1978). As a result, relatively "underdetermined" areas of macro structure can be envisioned. The latter theories emphasize that there are relatively more and relatively less systematized aspects of systems, so to speak.

It is reasonable to probe the organizational-level manifestations of personality factors by asking how a phenotypic profile would impact on the dynamics of a system at those junctures of the system that are the most loosely determined, the most loosely linked. This will not make the logic of personality and the logic of organizational systems analysis interchangeable, but it may now make them mutually relevant. This would approximate a narrowing of the inter-level synapse.

These more "variant" versions of macro analysis place great store in analyzing the structure of a system in terms of its internal linkages among subsystems. They raise the analysis of structural linkages to great prominence in understanding the dynamics of the organization. To the extent that an organization has evolved an adaptive structure, the assumption is that its greatest structural elaboration, its fullest structural articulation, is to be found in those areas performing the relatively few key organizational tasks. An organization will be most elaborately developed when it comes to those activities that are crucial for it. Less rigorous structural elaboration is shown by structures performing functions correspondingly less crucial to the organization's coping with the environment (or its own internal support needs that are generated in the course of having to relate to that environment).

This theme has potentially significant implications for our purposes. It suggests a perspective for viewing the interaction of a phenotypic personality with an organizational "system." Moreover, the nature and consequences of the interaction it would seem to point to, in the case of manipulative personalities, rings true (and parsimoniously) with what we know of Machiavellian and narcissistic personality disturbances.

STRUCTURAL AMBIGUITY AND MANIPULATION

A prominent feature of the exploitive pattern established in the small-group laboratory work on Machiavellianism is the apparent need for situational ambiguity. Let us turn the perspective from that of looking over the individual's shoulder to peeking out from the organizational maze. We may infer that the relatively ambiguous structural aspects of the organization are those that are most susceptible to the Machiavellian actor. From what we have said about structural elaborateness and structural underdevelopment, ambiguous structural features may be understood as those whose internal routines and programs are not fully elaborated, presumably for any of the general reasons we earlier noted.

Manipulative actors may be expected to exert their greatest effect on the evolving pattern of an organization through those of their individual level actions that are most relevant to these underspecified sectors of the organizational system. At the same time these are the areas in which manipulativeness will have its greatest success because behavior in them is the least constrained. It is in these areas that the accumulated pattern of micro events will leave macro traces.

This assumption is consistent with some less variant, some "not particularly loose-linked" theories of organization as well. As March and Simon (1958) have observed, organizations are among other things, relatively decomposeable networks, of bundles of programmatic activity, performed through persisting structural forms for such purposes. March and Simon seem not to raise to a major issue how it is that some actions fall within well circumscribed bundles of routine and others do not. They seem to assume actions longstandingly viewed as major business, and as linked by the logic of the situation, tend to be routinized. Still, the idea can be found here as well that there is a noticeable level of organizational activity that occurs under what we are now calling relatively ambiguous structural constraints. While the "loose-linkage" literature would see these actions as likely to fall in the less crucial functional areas for an organization, it would seem more characteristic of March and Simon (and Katz & Kahn, 1978) to expect such activity at the organizational boundaries as well. Here I have in mind internal boundaries among subsystems and the external boundary with the environment, under normal conditions, and with a reasonably stable environment not posing any defined critical threat. In yet another nuanced version of this

general theme, the antecedent structural condition for efficacious manipulation can be traced to "fuzzy-set" conditions of skeletal and therefore vague
bureaucratic mandates creating a highly discretion-intense environment
(Lerner & Wanat, 1983). Thus, if manipulators are drawn to the ambiguous
domain, structurally their effects are most likely to be absorbed and amplified
in the less fully elaborated structural aspects of large-scale, formal organizations.

THE EXPERIENTIAL EFFECT
OF MANIPULATORS IN ORGANIZATIONS

At the risk of sinking further into the armchair, it seems reasonable to suggest
that at the individual level, the sense of the "important" is often self-fulfilling,
in terms of the individually defined experience. On this shorter term dimension, the Machiavellian/narcissistic impact would appear to be highly visible
and at least moderately disequalibrating. However, within generous, long-
term parameters, it appears more self-limiting.

Short-term, individual-level activity not sucked into the vortex of a now
indifferent organizational routine, occurs in a way that is visible for its
obvious impact on the short-term experience of persons. Such activity
manages to be both highly "noticed" and at the same time not systemically
"memorable," so to speak. Thus, individuals caught up in the events so
instigated may be enthused, upset, partisan, or lamenting exclusion—but
always sucked into much ado about nothing (of substance, long term).

Of course it is also true as in biological systems, that some spontaneous
events of mutation may have dramatic long-term effects. Interestingly,
however, mutation is not a favored notion in organization theory, and so we
do not treat it here as a main effect on large-scale formal organizations as
systems, although it deserves some additional comment at another time.[3] To
be sure the systems view of organization has a history entangled with
biological concepts, a matter recently if still atypically, given some thought
(Bendor, 1977; Kaufman, 1985).

The Machiavellian tendency to seize upon ambiguous structural features
was observed in the laboratory as noted earlier, and may serve depth-
psychological purposes as also discussed earlier. It should be pointed out,
however, that systemically structural ambiguity may be manifest not only in

---

[3]Perhaps such reluctance to deal with the concept of mutation stems from its being too close
at first blush to discredited "great man" theories. Because it needn't be on closer inspection, this
is a potentially interesting issue.

underdetermined form but also in "multiply determined" form. With a kind of curvilinear logic, "empty" and "extremely cluttered" structural arrangements may have the same effect. Both lack a fixed correspondence between structure and function. In functional terms, considerable equifinality of outcomes would seem to be the probabilistic element making system determinism less predictable in the specific outcomes it produces. Overdetermination has the same effect as underdetermination ("underspecifying" as it were) in this sense. For this reason, technical experts may often view a rule-cluttered organizational procedure as "wide open" where laymen see it as tortuously rigid (Lerner, 1976b). It should be remembered in what follows, therefore, that "structurally elaborated" is not the same as "rule-intensive." Thus, structurally ambiguous aspects of organization are not just the "empty" zones of organizational structure. They may also be the *excessively* cluttered aspects.

Thus, *short term*, the visibility of self-appointed tinkering, and of forays into high profile activity by our phenotypically manipulative actors may involve self-inflated assertions of expertise. These would be most likely in technically elaborated if not authoritatively prescribed processes. In either such overdescribed or in underdescribed contexts, they may thus lead peers and hierarchic superiors alike to overinvest in dramaturgically inflated, emotionally charged, contrived issues of the moment. As alluded to earlier, well-established, large, highly institutionalized organizations operating as fixed features of the environment may have few "reality tests" imposed on them. Those they experience may occur belatedly, too late for meaningful correction. Such organizations can certainly operate short term. They do so with the distortions induced by the dramaturgical machinations of manipulative actors. They do so in the absence of environmental feedback that might discourage the organizational distraction entailed thereby.

In *short term*, their prophesies of personal and agenda importance are self-fulfilling. However, although we may presume a discernible priority of issues for any logic of the situation when viewed externally, organizations in such circumstances can generally operate oblivious to it. This behavior can present paradoxes. A recent governmental example comes to mind involving priorities for polygraphing minor functionaries for security reasons, while subcontracting the construction of major embassy installations to adversaries. One issue seizes an emotionally overinvested imagination; the other happens to not.

Consider the possible systemic impact of manipulative behavior over the *intermediate* term. Assume still the entree of our phenotypically manipulative actor in ambiguous sectors of organizational routine, where individual efforts enjoy the greatest resonance. The rhetoric, flurrying energy, and emotional drive of the profile we have elaborated can have pronounced behavioral impact on a human collectivity. Such people shake things up. In mechanical imagery, they do not significantly redesign fundamental structures and processes, but they can cause extreme vibration.

We should consider the possibility that this elevated tension, manifest with persuasiveness and selective persistence—but without genuine empathy—can eventually cause withdrawal, chagrin, and quiet alienation in the community of others. The silent physical and motivational exit of such others can diminish the capacity of the organization to navigate, while its structural capabilities and basic formal structure make it systemically capable of far steadier and effective operation.[4]

If we reserve some concept of *long-term* structural effect for our notion of the most basic system features of large-scale formal organization, the macro perspective warns us that however "oddly wired"[5] and emotionally overinvested they may be, individual-level machinations do not engender direct systemic alteration, only indirect effects in glacially gradual evolutionary perspective over many cycles of behavior. Significantly, however, over the intermediate term that for the sake of discussion we may loosely tie to the individual career cycle, the Machiavellian/narcissistic actor in the throes of heavily invested acting out of deeper tensions, may throw organizations into noticeable oscillations as pertains to significant issues of the day. It should be stressed that even shorter term, large-scale formal organizations undertaking activities in those societal sectors susceptible to "irreversible errors," can do extremely serious damage although their organizational systems remain "sound."

THE ERROR OF ATTACKING PERSONALITY PROBLEMS WITH STRUCTURAL SOLUTIONS

Let us grant for the moment that the seeds of such serious dislocation may lie in the impact of a maladaptive personality type with an increasing organizational presence. In this case, the oft-cited remedy, organizational checks and balances schemes, do not avoid the problem. They simply bifurcate the rhetoric with which the problems are acted out. Dramaturgy may simply be

---

[4]One is reminded of Brent Scocroft's comment on the result of the Tower Commission report on the Reagan administration's Iranian affair. He remarked to the effect that the system works but the people didn't use it, from which one might infer in this context that they were in some sense as Scocroft saw it, "not up to it," as it were.

[5]The phrase is Etheredge's (1985).

modified to melodrama of adversary interaction. Our phenotype seeks the adversarial context; emotionally it is indeed a context conducive to acting out.

Thus, for example, precisely because the problem is not in the mechanics of group-deliberative routines, all the group-opening devices scholars may suggest will not ameliorate the underlying problem.[6] I have in mind the Team As and Team Bs; the devil's advocates; the routinized introduction of extraneous experts into deliberative bodies; the cooling-off interim before required final meetings of decision-making bodies; the assignment of critical evaluators – and so on. These devices will not correct disorientations born of any shared characterological deficiencies of the type we are considering, should they be pervasive in a given organization. Such mechanical remedies miss the point.

These devices can indeed work against problems of group-procedural laxity. However, if the problem is maladaptive organizational behavior owing to the cumulative pervasive effect of a maladaptive phenotypic world view, then small-group procedural ploys and mechanical rearrangement of formal unit interfaces do not touch such a cause. They will yield to neurotic enactment as well.

The only "remedy," if is there is one at all, is in the *combination* of such procedural proposals, such organizational checks and balances – and in less mechanical imagery (Landau, 1972), organizational redundancies – with the need to intellectually and emotionally stand apart from the phenotypic excesses under consideration here. Obviously, this further presumes a psychological capacity of actors to do so. Whether this hope is naive is not the issue. Of course it is naive. But insistence on not yielding the social expectation of the necessity to so stand apart represents an *enlightened simplicity*, a matured post-manipulative sophistication.

This point merits further elaboration, but not at this particular juncture. We have yet to complete the consideration of organizational issues associated with the characterological orientation represented in our phenotype.

PERSONALITY AND ORGANIZATIONAL ETHOS

As indicated earlier, the general value framework and attendant ritual elements of organization – so-called organizational culture – provide another dimension for analyzing some aspects of a relation between personality effects

---

[6]I have in mind the particular examples of Janis' (1982) procedural remedies for groupthink, and George's (1972) foreign policy decision making technique of "multiple advocacy."

and macrolevel features. I believe that in elements of the modern organizational ethos, we may see expression of Machiavellian/narcissistic strivings.

Consider the tendency in modern organizations to display loose linkage as
discussed earlier. There is no need to see the phenomenon as simply a macro
"given." A contributory cause of its manifestation in particular organizations
may be that it serves as a systemic expression of intraorganizational,
intergroup rivalry and competitive excess. We can understand it as reflecting
depth motives behind gamesmanship postures. In the organizational cycle,
such themes can easily be perpetuated over "generations" of key organizational actors. Strong bonds within subsystems, and weak bonds among
subsystems, would resonate well with our phenotypic personality's needs.
Such a condition affords the opportunity to define a pool of mirroring
colleagues, in savored contrast with a sea of indifference—or perhaps even
danger. Within otherwise sophisticated organizations, the Balkanization of
loyalties and perspectives despite a seemingly interwoven complex structure,
may reflect the long-term effects of emotional needs and tension at work.

Subtle long-term changes in the tonality of the bureaucratic ethos could be
read in a similar fashion. The officious, petty clerk, obsessively ruminating
over rule infraction while furiously wielding a rubber stamp (an image so
familiar in the 19th-century literature of Europe, not to mention Danny Kaye
movies), was for a time replaced in post-Second World War America by the
repressed if well-pressed "organization man" in gray flannel suit (not to
mention Jack Lemmon movies; Whyte, 1957). In time he was replaced by the
more ominous functionary just taking orders (Howton 1969; Milgram, 1974).
There seems to be occurring yet another subtle shift in the prevailing myth of
the organizational actor: the grandiose rule violator, the Top Gun, the
can-do guy who breaks the rules to save those lessers who live by them. To
the best of my knowledge we are still awaiting the full academization of this
type in the organizational literature.

It is not hard to see, however, where the overall thrust may lead. Consider
the picture: the excessively loose-linked organization, inclined to stressing
internal rivalry among the loose elements as an organizational motif; staffing
with manipulative types of high energy and aggressiveness, given to both
grandiose schemes and sharp deflations. Without restating the full profile and
its implications developed earlier—the image suggests a tendency to distraction with internal competition and a difficulty in sustaining programmatic
policy making and implementation.

MANIPULATIVENESS AND MANAGEMENT

The latter phrase raises further organizational issues of an administrative
cast. In these terms there is another locus of organizational receptivity to our

phenotypic profile, should it begin to persist and proliferate in an organization. I have in mind changes in the function and structure of organizational management.

As noted earlier, Katz and Kahn (1978) exemplify an "essentialist," structural/functional approach to analyzing organizations as systems. It is time to develop this concept and our relation to it a bit further. They offer a universal, essential list of functions with each manifest in an associated subsystem. As previously indicated, there are five of these. The *production* subsystem is focused on primary-task accomplishment. It "keeps the trains running on time" as it were, for any organization. Also, there is a *maintenance* subsystem, which they see as the collection of functions and associated structures for "mediating between task demands and human needs" (Katz & Kahn, 1978, p. 84). Third, Katz and Kahn posited a boundary system with two facets (or sub-subsystems I suppose): One is concerned primarily with processing material and human resources in connection with production. The other is concerned with the "institutional system," presumably with interorganizational relations, with "social support and legitimation," "societal manipulation," and so on. The authors also marked out a separate "adaptive" subsystem, primarily a research and development function now raised to essentialist status. Interestingly, they also separate boundary functions from adaptive functions, contrary to what seems to be the more common tendency to merge the two notions. (Thompson and Wilensky's thinking seems more representative in this regard. See Thompson, 1969; Wilensky, 1969.) In the context of these other subsystems they also posited the managerial.

I believe that Katz and Kahn's sense of the managerial function and of the organizational dynamics traceable to its expression can be used to locate a further structural access point and associated process by which our personality profile, an individual-level phenomenon, can be understood to enact system, structural transformations.

As Katz and Kahn and others have observed, the categories of activities comprising the "managerial function" involve conflict resolution; facilitating, coding, and conveying interunit communication; and conducting subunit boundary activity (Freedman, 1972, cited in Sayles, 1979; Hollander, 1978; Likert & Likert, 1976; Mintzberg, 1973; Sayles, 1979). The lists offered frequently include also, variously nuanced emphases on an interpolating function. This is to say filling procedural gaps in formal routines. To this list of management functions we may also add agenda aggregation, and intraorganizational advocacy of agenda (Kelley, 1976), and facilitating compromise. Rule enforcement is embedded in this constellation as well. In broadest terms, management is a reintegrating, system-monitoring function (Staut & Landau, 1979) It is the primary coordination of the activities of all the subsystems of an organization.

Now, in complex macro-systems formulations, it is usual to see all essential functions reiterated within each subsystem, even though the subsystem itself is primarily identified with one of the essential functions performed for the parent system. Thus for example, the production subsystem displays managerial, adaptive, boundary, and maintenance functions internal to it, with associated structural differentiation to a modest degree. Presumably, this explains accountants in the production department, accountants in the accounting department, and artists in a mining company, for that matter.

The consequence of interest for our purposes is as follows: Those behavioral and attitudinal excesses regarding managerial functions, which are most pronounced in the managerial subsystem, will also appear if somewhat attenuated, in other organizational subsystems as well. These nonmanagerial subsystems display a modest degree of managerial activity for their own internal workings. This represents the faint contribution to general system management that such intrasubsystem activity offers.

Thus, whatever structural receptivity to our phenotypic profile is inherent in managerial subsystems per se, softer echoes of such receptivity are to be expected in the managerial *aspects* of other subsystems. But of course, it matters for one's art whether one is an artist in a mining company or in an art colony. Thus, the expression of our phenotype in the managerial aspects of overtly nonmanagerial subsystems can alter the organizational impact of our phenotype's expression. We consider this subtlety after discussing the stronger and direct link between the actings out of our phenotype and system modification, effected via transformation in the managerial subsystem. The managerial subsystem is the one of the essentialists' list that is most receptive to alteration by any widespread and persistent expression of our phenotype.

The managerial subsystem as enacted by our phenotype, may be expected to show the following distorted signature, as a result of the interplay between phenotype features and the basic performance dynamics of the managerial subsystem per se, as they were previously noted: When enacted by our phenotypic manipulator in full bloom as it were, organizational management is likely to be characterized by a climate of intense general planning (scheming) and at the same time proportionally little implementation or follow through. Strategy and interpersonal tactics should abound; procedure for tangible execution and completion should languish—perhaps by uninterested assignment away to underlings, who feel operationally disadvantaged for being kept at an emotional and procedural distance.

The generals (and colonels who would be generals) are likely to be distanced, procedurally and empathically, from the problems and needs of the spear carriers. In the language of systems, the management subsystem is *leading*, in excess of any environmentally adaptive requirement, and it is excessively detached from the core of organizational action, the subsystem of production (actually moving the mail in the postal system, or producing a reliable widget in the factory). The subtleties of agenda articulation and intramanagerial coalition dynamics (conflict and consensus management) are savored. However, sensitivity to the environment is replaced by an emotionally overinvested, *hyper*sensitivity to false or superficial signals, whose origins are actually internal to the fantasies of the managerial subsystem. The leaders draw intricately on the cave walls and interpret their own pictures as a sign of things to come.

The inside group as emotional support and audience is extolled. Rage and fear may be expressed in exaggerated hostility towards outgroups or even factions of the in-group. Infantile grandiosity is expressed through conceptual mastery of the imagined rococo intricacy of player alignments. Thus, the "details" of empirical task accomplishment become boring and likely to be seen as potentially ensnaring. Status anxiety is high, hence meetings abound. Persistence is of course uncommon, but is potentially rewarded because the organizational memory and attention span is short.[7] The system, as long as it persists, tends to be excessively self-regulating (solipsistic). Environmental shocks are thus severe because they are slow to be acknowledged and early signs are usually mixed. When they occur they are traumatic. Subcritical challenges once acknowledged are demonized in their origins; enemies thus "appear."

Such an organization can be ruthless because its reactions are unmodulated. At the same time, vague enthusiasm and spurious "dedication" are widespread, favored postures. The triggering of key routines requires the sign of rhetorical investment. An aesthetic of elaborateness is favored over one of simplicity. There is a conspicuous consumption of conceptualization over pragmatic action; high-tech is valued over low-tech on grounds other than performance effectiveness.

PHENOTYPIC IMPACT ON ORGANIZATIONAL MANAGEMENT: SYSTEMIC PERSPECTIVE

To summarize so far in purely systems terms, the effect of our phenotype is to make the managerial subsystem leading apart from any justification of environmental adaptation. Internal subsystem coordination mechanisms absorb resources excessively. Substantive coordination with the core produc-

---

[7]These characteristics are reminiscent of the characteristics of "organized anarchies" derived, on other grounds, by Cohen and March (1986; Cohen, March, & Olson, 1972).

tion system is poor despite elaborate channels being developed. Internal monitoring is excessive and although feedback may be monitored, even excessively, it is homeostatic self-monitoring that is focused on. Environmental signals are delayed in processing, poorly absorbed, and when reacted to, overreacted to. Internal boundaries are managed at the expense of external boundaries; growth occurs in maladaptively complicated patterns as opposed to simple and durable ones of equal or greater adaptiveness.

As the managerial subsystem becomes the leading subsystem apart from any environmental demand for such an organizational pattern, its maladaptive consequences may be masked internally. We may expect a corresponding systemic receptivity to parallel elevation of managerial functions within nonmanagerial subsystems. (In Katz & Kahn's, 1978, terms as indicated, these are production, adaptive, maintenance, and support subsystems.) Thus, the contrast effect by which the overinvested managerial subsystem might be distinguishable is masked by corresponding imitation within other sectors. Over the intermediate range, the "remedy" for excessive investment in managerial dynamics is likely to become more managerial investment. The system can approach a black hole state of infinitely regressed self-absorption. A simple extrapolation predicts an end state of implosion. The viability of the system is threatened by the strain of its own self-absorption. Because the self-absorption is frenzied and not lethargic it can appear that the system has "vitality," when viewed briefly or from a great distance.

We may now consider the systemic implications of a parallel inflation of the managerial dimension throughout all subsystems. They would seem to flow quite clearly from the line of inference developed so far. I would suggest two effects in the main. For one, we may expect that within a given nonmanagerial subsystem, management versus subsystem primary roles will be a source of friction. Thus for example, in a primarily engineering, or litigating, or caseworking unit of a larger and similarly oriented subsystem, general managerial and substantively expert authority will vie for primacy. "Professional" management becomes one more expertise and the division of labor among these contending groups represents the boundary of their competing expansions (Hummel, 1987; Johnson, 1972; Lerner, 1976a; Thompson, 1977).

Second, patterns of individual career advancement, as defined through organizational myth and eventually role messages, may involve the transition to "management" with attendant shifts in behavioral and attitudinal expression, as a necessary evolution for the sake of increased organizational power (over people) and control (over programs). Often viewed as a crisis in career identity, this process may constitute a systemic expression of a bipolarization of organizational power and control (Lerner, 1976b). Additionally, it would seem capable of producing a presumably *second, mid-professional* life career crisis of transition in identity.[8] Systemically, the consequences of these two developments may be expressed as a tendency to decentralization (but pervasive expansion) of the managerial function, and the profusion of an organizationally universal "managerial" vocabulary and value orientation. The latter point may be expressed less anthropomorphically as the profusion of organizational patterns of response to the environment that include patterns of interpretation and communication that maximize values associated with the managerial system, often poorly integrated with the requirements of a purer task logic. The system becomes content free as it becomes process heavy.

It may be prudent to briefly reiterate in summary, the thinking behind the suggestion that our phenotype personality is so naturally and easily absorbed by the managerial subsystem in particular. In what sense is the managerial subsystem, or managerial aspect of the organization, more receptive to the orientation and actings out of our phenotype than are other aspects of organization? The themes of contemporary managerial activity emphasize attending to conflicts, nowadays solicitously, but with the mantle of authority to be sure. High-energy agenda articulation and "vision," competitiveness, and taking the role of the leader as model. The themes of innovator and "change agent," and universally appropriate intervener run deeply through the contemporary managerial role. The contemporary manager/administrator/executive/leader is the grand facilitator who is perenially delving in another organizational sector's expertise, arguably never at home exactly, always indispensable, and invited in a sense to succeed where others needing "management" would otherwise go astray, thus acting at the edge, in multiple senses. In this vein it is interesting to contrast the classic administrator as "highest clerk" with the contemporary administrator as "*intrepreneur*" (cf. Gulick & Urwick, 1937; Peters & Waterman, 1982; see also Peters & Austin, 1985; or more academically, McFarland, 1979). In a way, a number of organizational level issues such as this understandably lead to societal-level concerns. They are the subject of the following chapter. Before turning to them, however, a brief summary of the main ideas of this chapter seems in order.

---

[8]Interestingly, the attendant tensions may be somewhat offset on the conscious level by the secondary gain some may experience from "a fresh start." On the individual life cycle and organizational performance in general, see Kets de Vries Miller (1984).

OVERVIEW

We have seen that in the applications of psychological insights, the transition from group level to organizational level is an especially difficult one, more difficult than the individual–group linkage. The latter is more natural because for better or worse, group and individual conceptualizations are more closely linked in their origins. In contrast, the systems conceptualization of organization, which I take as the most distinctive and distinguished interpretation of phenomena in genuinely organizational terms, begins with a set of inherently antireductionist concepts.

Linkage to the organizational level can be approximated in several ways, the most common being in the "as if" motif that is itself accomplishable with varying degrees of explicitness. Although none of them avoid dependence on one's cooperativeness in seeing the metaphor, some can be articulated with greater specification than others. The approximation to linkage favored here was that of focusing on the synapse across levels in greater magnified detail, to expose a linking, transposition process captured in a question: Under what systemic conditions are aspects of organizational structure susceptible to enactment in a way that would betray the elements of the manipulative style, as we have come to understand its full complexity? This led to the related question: What longer term structural transformations could be anticipated as a result of such predictably stylized enactment?

Our answers to these questions led to a focus on the expansion – or suggesting some danger of excess, the inflation – of managerial functions. This was associated with structural responsiveness to the manipulative enactment. The latter occurs in formally defined managerial sectors of a system, and also in the general exaggeration of managerial elements in sectors or "subsystems" ostensibly dedicated to other system functions.

The "manipulative organization" if we were to pursue images in such terms, is thus likely to be one that is both "over-managed," and "over-managing." In summarizing this chapter I do not want to fall into the error of restating it, and so simply observe at this point, that given what has been said in the preceding pages it can be seen as well, that to be so managed is not at all the same as being well, or even consistently, led. This observation is based on the understanding of the several aspects of the individual profile and the group effects they can create, which lack the elements of sustained empathic attention, and consistency in task interest.

In light of these considerations at the organizational level, the astute reader may reasonably pose the following query: "My God, what kind of society are we living in?!" We consider some answers of a sort, in the next and final chapter.

7

The Manipulative Society

So far we have explored the dynamics of the individual personality as they bear on the disposition to be manipulative. Indeed, we have pursued this dimension with a triangulated approach, employing social psychological, psychoanalytic self-psychological, and diagnostic-testing techniques. With the resulting phenotypic profile, we have explored the manifestations and dynamics of manipulative behavior at the group level as well. We disciplined the use of the term *group* to reserve a levels-of-analysis distinction between group, organizational, and societal levels.

This circumscribed concept of the group is more consistent with a social psychology usage than a psychoanalytic usage, as noted in the preceding two chapters. Such a more specified understanding of the group level positioned the analysis to explore systemic, large-scale organizational processes as a distinct level of action having attendant implications of its own regarding the manifestation and impact of manipulativeness. The effect was to raise new issues having to do with the concepts of manipulable as well as manipulating organization. The crucial advantage of so marking out the organizational level as distinct from the generic "group" of psychoanalysis, was to achieve a transformation of conceptualization whereby inherently systemic processes, such as subsystem development and interplay between leading and secondary subsystems, could be accessed in terms of their manifestations of actions by our phenotypic personality. The latter actions are directly observable only in the frames of reference of lower levels of analysis.

EPISTEMOLOGICAL SENSITIVITY
AT THE SOCIETAL LEVEL OF PROBLEM

Now at the societal level, we face a cluster of analytical alternatives. Here we are concerned with broad value themes and commonalities among far ranging institutional patterns. But at the same time, we are also dealing with a level of phenomena and with processes that are recognized, in a completion of the analytic cycle, to impact upon the development once again, of individual personality.

In an earlier book also focused on the multidimensional analysis of a different, but as we have seen, not unrelated middle-range phenomenon (the politicizing of the expert role in collective decision making) I suggested a distinction that also serves well here. For analytic purposes we can distinguish primarily macro from primarily micro effects of societal-level processes. Macro societal-level processes are those most directly and primarily affecting interinstitutional relationships and the broad sociocultural milieu itself. Micro-societal-level processes are those cues of the general social environment to the individual personality ever in formation; such cues are absorbed via the process of social learning as it impacts on the sense of self, as filtered through the lens of individual experience. This vocabulary will help to keep the levels of analysis less tangled.

Indeed, analyzing the societal level, sociocultural and sociopolitical manifestations of a multifaceted and multilevel concept such as manipulativeness is a task for which we lack disciplinary guidance in key respects. Consider a specific example reflecting this dilemma from the body of material presented so far.

We know now for example, that our phenotypic profile has associated with it, the tendency to somaticizing and hypochondria. That is the tendency to transform anxiety into the experience of excessive body and health concerns. We saw this in the MMPI scale correlations with Machiavellianism and in the clinical literature on narcissistic disturbance. As indicated earlier both literatures suggest an increase in the prevalence among the general population of the syndromes they describe. In fact Christie and Geis (1970) observed in this context:

> We have considered bits of data from a variety of contexts to argue that high Machs are more likely to be attracted to and come from nontraditional societies. In the national sample we found adult respondents who were presumably reared under more traditional standards. De Miguel found a positive correlation between Mach V scores and the degree of industrialization of the province in which Spanish students lived and went to school; there is evidence

that high Mach adults were more likely to come from urban rather than rural backgrounds; Oksenberg found that Chinese students in a transitional situation (attending a Western school) had higher scores than those attending a traditional Chinese school in Hong Kong. (p. 356)[1]

Now suppose we ask the obvious kind of question regarding societal-level transformation in this particular regard: For example, what is the societal-level manifestation of a pervasive tendency to somaticizing? May we expect a nation of fiber-consuming joggers? Or might we alternatively see a manifestation of somaticizing in a national preoccupation with the *health of the body politic?* After all, we have recently seen an intense national interest in the at once fearful and thrilling questions: Does the system work? Is the system viable? Is the system "healthy"? Is there a cancer on the Presidency and is it growing? And so on.

Writers for popular audiences and casual intellectual/political forums may be free to stimulate with such metaphorical allusions and bright connections. I too find them provocative and often highly suggestive, to be sure, which is why I just managed to insert a few. However, the commitment to a social scientific level of understanding requires restraint in this domain. This is not a restraint on creativity. Rather the restraint is in the special need for epistemological sensitivity and properly circumscribed and cautious self-control through appropriate prefacing of the metaphors, parallels, and levels-distant manifestations of phenomena first located elsewhere.

THE PHENOTYPE AND MACRO-SOCIAL MANIFESTATIONS: TWO FORMS

In considering the possible macro-societal manifestations of aspects of our phenotype's behavior there are two possible categories of manifestation that bear noting. The most direct societal level manifestations of our phenotype, the conceptually simplest case involving the least transformation of concepts, is the case of prominent individuals in leading positions of potentially widespread impact who display our profile. The applied psychoanalytic literature focusing on history and politics, and particularly the self-psychology school in this tradition, has produced a number of studies of such persons (Strozier & Offer, 1985).

---

[1]On the profusion of the phenotype from the psychoanalytic and applied psychoanalytic perspectives see Basch, 1984; also see Lasch, 1978.

Also, drawing from the somewhat variant perspective of Kernberg, Stern (1987)—still largely in this tradition—has pursued the notion of a special subtype, "the high-achieving narcissist," suggesting that a close variation on our phenotype, construable as a subtype traceable to a special pattern of father–son relationship, is inclined to behavior of the general kind we have discussed, and is also inclined to seeking positions of great prominence where the ability to directly impact on the course of historical and social events is at its greatest. Such work represents an important, and in terms of levels-of-analysis transformations, least complicated case of individual characteristics shaping the historical stream. We can understand the historical uniqueness of the position of a Woodrow Wilson or a Kaiser Wilhelm. When psychobiographies of such persons reveal their similarity to our phenotypic profile, there is little epistemological intricacy required to grasp the point that the societal level impact of such a personality profile can be significant, indeed monumental, and that it can be understood in significant part as a direct acting-out on the stage of history, of individual-level personality predilections.

The second kind of manifestation of our phenotype on the macro-societal level is conceptually more complicated—not necessarily more important, but requiring additional conceptual groundwork. This second sort of phenotypic manifestation on the societal level involves the transformation of aspects of the individual profile into themes or motifs in the sociopolitical culture. This is the domain most susceptible to the risks in drawing societal-level statements directly from elements of the phenotype as noted earlier. The best remedy is not a foolproof one, but it is all we have: the exercise of great care and the expression of possible manifestations with great tentativeness. In a later section of this chapter we discuss societal-level manifestations of the impact of our phenotype in terms that do not involve the simple metaphoric parallel between individual and societal features. This third category of manifestations involves transformation in structural terms on the order of the exaggeration of managerial functions at the organizational level. However, at this juncture, the individual–societal isomorphism is exactly what we are about to pursue with attendant "ifs and buts" as indicated.

The major notion behind this sort of approach begins with a question: If everyone saw the world as our phenotype does, if the outlook of our phenotype expressed what psychoanalysis likes to call a "shared group fantasy" of the most general type, or what in other terms might be called a common Weltanschaung associable with our phenotype, what tensions or themes in our social–political system could we plausibly take as manifestations and (eventually as reinforcements) of this shared world view?

PHENOTYPE ELEMENTS
AND SOCIETAL-LEVEL PARALLELS

We may address the previous question by working through the possible societal parallelisms of several phenotype characteristics developed in earlier chapters. Consider the phenotypic characteristics of thrill seeking and impulses to the harmful and shocking. The phrasing is taken from the discussion of MMPI results in chapter 4, based on scale correlations of MMPI and Mach scores. In chapter 3, where the Machiavellianism-narcissism overlap was discussed, the notion of narcissistic rage and the dynamics of keeping it in check were discussed as well. The pattern of thrill seeking and impulses to be harmful and shocking may be understood as consistent with the dynamics of managing narcissistic rage as well as being interpretable in the testing and diagnostic language of the MMPI. The combined picture in this regard suggests a tension that is held under functional wraps as it were. This is a tension that occasionally vents and that, given the rage element and certain other potentially antisocial features associated through the MMPI, vents with an element of destructiveness. This should include, again from the narcissistic perspective, a desire to display, to draw attention, and hence the value of shocking others. Perhaps the motive to shocking may also serve a self-shocking purpose, and thereby a means of denying or momentarily breaking from, the sense of depletion and deflation also associated with narcissistic disturbance.

But the intricacies of the individual level dynamics aside, the question now is what the society-level features may be that could be construed as parallels of this phenotypic feature. Let us take the concept of such a societal-level feature as a somewhat sublimated, societal-level acting out. Throughout this discussion I confine myself to images from the contemporary American scene.[2]

We are searching for a manifestation of thrill seeking, rationalized and kept in workable, checked form at the societal level. We should expect it from the former observation, to have a rationalized value, a secondary gain. It seems reasonable to expect it would be manifest as a valued outcropping of impulse. It would be grounded in a larger format of behavior that would be kept serviceably compatible with the demands of adult life in a highly corporatized

---

[2]We are all familiar with the tendency in general social commentary to take the contemporary American scene as also applying in vague and partial ways to things Western European and of course, the finer the distinctions are, the less the general allusion across continents holds up. Individual readers more familiar with the ambiance of the European political culture(s) may assess for themselves the extent to which the observations in this section would seem to apply beyond affairs strictly American.

and interdependent society. I would like to suggest we have a candidate in the continued worship of *entrepreneurism*. I would like to mark this out as one possible societal-level manifestation of an aspect of our phenotypic profile.

The Latterday "Entrepreneur" as Phenotypic Expression

Here I use the term *entrepreneurism* to refer not just to a narrow form of economic action, but in a more general way that absorbs the narrow economics term as well. I refer to the image of the risk-taker who seeks to transform and shape the scene as he finds it. The contemporary entrepreneur in these terms takes risks with outward coolness and aplomb.

It is also interesting that he appears to operate from positions where "dues" have allegedly been paid. Let me stop to comment on this point: The latter element seems a necessary prior process that is part of the mythical image. The suggestion here is that the myth of prior justifying experiences may well serve two purposes. It would satisfy the narcissistic sense of specialness and justified entitlement. It would also fortify self-confidence in contemplation of actions for those more conscious of their self-doubt. These are the functions of the prior justifying process myth for the entrepreneurial posture in individual terms.

Societally, the prior process myth, as prerequisite for acceptable entrepreneurial posing, could serve to put an outer limit on the frequency of sanctioned behavior of this type. Support for leaders carrying such a description also fosters an antisystem theme of alienation behind the doings of those in even the highest formal authoritative positions. The plain-speaking, plain-dealing, of the people, antibureaucratic President of the United States, senior governmental official, or major corporate mogul—secures popular identification with the aid of seeming to be apart from the Establishment order as he or she in fact presides over it.

Entrepreneurism in this broader mythic sense represents a simplistic autonomy that can gratify solipsistic grandiose yearnings. One may infer as a prerequisite of mass consumption, that this persona will have elements attached that would resonate with the yearnings and thoughts of our phenotypic personality. These elements can be expected to draw widespread identification precisely to the extent they echo phenotypic sentiments. These signs would include expressions of past personal and current collective victimization, or more mildly, the experience of being unappreciated. They could include the challenge to be rejected if one's interpretation of the current social (consumer, geopolitical) essence does not hit the mark. They could include a suave *or* homespun dismissal of injuries inflicted by smug "theys" (inviting listeners to feel the injustices as well); and the invitation to the listeners to join in shaking things up—preferably selflessly, for the sake of the children, widows, working people, trees, or other unassailable entities.

In general, the image of the latter-day "entrepreneur" in the wider sense, is appealing because it connotes the flurry of exuberant doing that will presumably follow. Of course the actual "doing" remains problematic, as does the ability of a leader in this mold to sustain programmatic efforts capable of producing significant change in the intended direction.

It seems to me part of this socially climatic theme to find associated in identification with the leader persona, mass follower pleasure in the unmasking of miscellaneously alleged prevailing hypocrisy and falseness. Identification with such a persona could also be attractive to ideologues. However, their determinism and their agendas actually miss the tone of the leader's true appeal, and thus the mass following's basis of identification on this dimension.

The irony, the massive inconsistency with reality that renders the picture suspicious and that thus suggests a compensating fantasy is at work, is the underdeveloped value positions of entrepreneurs allegedly championing values: patriotism that violates law and principles of government; religious bigotry in human rights causes; authoritarian elements in populist movements; strategic policy initiatives bereft of coherent policy guidelines; the persistence of shoddy production and deceptive practices in reformed and allegedly revitalized major consumer product corporations—all would illustrate this flaw. The leaders excessively personify the institutions in such modes. They strike their larger than life poses in a mythical context directly contrary to the relentless corporatization and bureaucratization of societal affairs in reality. The actual, deep, enmeshing in bureaucratization absorbs even those who champion the entrepreneurial attack on the problems identified with bureaucratization in the status quo. Thus, Landau (1987) has shown how even in the undertaking of major socioeconomic reforms through the political/administrative system, as in the civil rights and social welfare reform legislation of the 1960s, the inevitably accompanying and ultimately confounding obstacle to success was the inexplicable compulsion to completely revamp the relevant organization/administrative systems. This occurred at the expense of attention to the already formidable problem of implementation, to the extent of denying even a modicum of constancy to the administrative infrastructure in place. Capturing the overheated and antirational tone of the process, she has aptly dubbed it, "hyperinnovation."

The entrepreneurial posture in the larger sense, which I am suggesting as a societally favored mythical framework for leaders consistent with the elements of our phenotype, is distinguishable from genuine innovativeness by its compulsive fascination with "bureaucratized antibureaucratization." This is in direct contradiction of the essence of the antiformalism at the heart of its appeal. We imitate bureaucratic form in perverted efforts at bureaucratic shake-up. Thus, Landau's definition of the orientation as "hyperinnovation." The overheated, distinguishing element in the orientation is what I focus on in suspecting a pathological core in its mass psychological aspects. There seems to be a nihilistic impulse at its deepest roots – a destructive grandiosity. In this sense the connotations suggest a parallel to elements of Maccoby's gamesman profile, and also imply a basis for the popular appeal of such characteristics.

HIGH DRIVE LEVEL AND ITS SOCIETAL MANIFESTATIONS

Let us turn to another element in the phenotypic profile that would appear to have a parallel manifestation on the societal level: high drive level. Recall the association of Machiavellianism with increased drive level, or increased reactivity. Consider the association of narcissism with the general tendency to overcommitment in career (Kohut, 1971, made this observation at several points). Recall the profile of the high achieving narcissist as a politically prominent type (Stern, 1987). All augur for a stress-emphasizing society and polity. Rhetorically, the preferred collective self-image may well involve a chic preoccupation with "burn-out" and "workaholism" imagery in the corporate and government spheres. It is interesting that economics reasoning has frequently led to predictions of a "leisure society." Such predictions may have failed to take into account a white-collar pseudo-professionalism that links personal and public image with frenetic activity levels. Of course this image can neglect attention to real productivity and quality of work. In fact we know that highly reactive personalities performances deteriorate under high stress. In systemic terms, high reactivity could conceivably be manifest in a spurt-ignore-spurt flitting of attention and overcommitment from one social issue (now "crisis") to another.

Indeed, the prevalence in contemporary times of so called "Type A" personalities seems likely to be associable with the dynamics of our phenotype. In some cardiology circles it has been observed, regarding the "Type A" pattern and its origins, that its two essential elements are low self-esteem and insufficient *unconditional* emotional support by parents – especially but not necessarily during early childhood. Its primary behavioral manifestations may be described as impatience and often seething hostility regarding daily life affairs. As a summary of the ultimate maladaptiveness of the syndrome, it has been said that it involves "investing ten dollars of emotion on ten-cent problems." This view bears a strong relationship to the general self-psychology description of the dynamics of narcissistic disturbance. Politically, whole policy complexes, and total national commitments declared in administrative wars on this or that, may occupy center stage for a short while, and then fade into forgetfulness. Our phenotype's profusion may foretell the coming of the Type A polity, as well as the Type A lifestyle.

OUTGROUPS, SOCIETY, AND THEMES OF THE MANIPULATIVE PROFILE

Consider another possible societal-level manifestation of phenotypic features consistent with this genre of theorizing: the ready focus of hostility on outgroups associable with perceived specific wrongs. This is an aspect of the Mach MMPI profile and was suggested as a manifestation of narcissistic tensions. It is most reminiscent of mass society images (Kornhauser, 1959). It is the tendency to find a focus for hostility by linking some others to a perceived specific provocation.

In terms of the mass political culture, this would suggest increasing difficulty in mobilizing public support for limited, measured responses to adversaries. It would suggest the need to recast adversaries as enemies, and a difficulty in pursuing adversarial policies without *stereotyping* enemies. This augurs for strategies vulnerable to massive, rapid escalation and the expressiveness of dramatic gesture. On the face-to-face level, we know that Machiavellians in the laboratory have no need of this when their own, personally defined interests are involved. The composite profile developed here can be read to warn, however, that when called upon to participate in an abstract, collective, adversarial policy, such stereotypes may be necessary.

Indeed, government policies in such an environment may increasingly need to be portrayed on this dimension both for the leaders who find themselves rapidly losing their sense of proportion and for a public conditioned and actively disposed to be aroused this way. One can envision more and more policies about which the public is uninterested on the one hand, and others in which the public is simplistically, inappropriately, and angrily invested on the other. This is an immoderate world of few contingencies and much overinvested imagination (Etheredge, 1985).

Conventional Morality and the Features of Manipulativeness

Whither the conventional morality? One of the most interesting questions in this speculative context is the future of the "conventional morality" to which increasing numbers of people are increasingly indifferent, by developing social convention. It would seem that a manipulative amorality on the theme of "do onto others—first," may be the prevailing "morality." On the other hand, and I would suspect more likely so, the traditional conventional morality may become an increasingly hollow but valuable rhetorical framework, of primary use as a set of justifications for the rejection and punishment of others when tactical considerations and now emotional imperatives so dictate.

On the individual level, expediency can be the prerequisite for such a tactical invocation of the traditional conventional morality. This is simply old-fashioned hypocrisy. However, in broad institutional level terms, we may see the increased display of a social phenomenon perhaps describable as *synthetic public outrage* concurrent with individual cynicism. Thus, increasing numbers of people may come to agree with themes of public rhetoric to the effect that all politicians are corrupt and the effective ones should be reelected, except when their corruption is specifically focused on, in which case their continued presence is intolerable.[3]

Of course, equally visible in the crystal ball at this stage, are other intriguing and very disquieting possibilities. One is that of periodic swings from the demand for government's political pragmatism to the demand for government's moral virtue. A depressing manifestation is that of sterile media wars between elite factions vying for their preferred definitions of sociopolitical sophistication, either as collective level amoral pragmatism, or as a "return to moral foundations" that in fact represents regressed moral fanaticism.

The end result of collective entrapment in the overly manipulative context is contortion on a rack of extremes. One is the assumptive framework of "realpolitick" cynics. The other is the assumptive framework of true believer idealogues. Neither can generate the working assumptions necessary for functional problem solving. Both represent the extremes of the climate that the manipulative phenotype may induce in followers. They are also translatable as difficulties in a narcissism-reminiscent struggle to internalize mature values. On a societal scale, this amounts to so contorting the context of public discourse that it begins to constrain even the leaders who play a prominent role in instigating such deterioration.

AMBIGUOUS INSTITUTIONAL MOTIFS

Consider yet another possible societal-level manifestation of our phenotype's profile: the preference for ambiguous institutional motifs. The preference for and success with ambiguous rule structures associable with our phenotype and discussed in earlier chapters, suggests on the societal level a continued softening of traditional, hierarchical forms institutionally. This has been associated with an increased, generic "politicizing" of intra-organizational life

---

[3]Discourses on the "post-Watergate morality" theme seem to have this common element.

(Lerner, 1976a; Pfeffer, 1981). Because the organizational level also touches on issues of institutional structure, the point bears restating at this juncture. A major implication of this line of reasoning is that the increased acceptance of antihierarchic forms of organizations (Thayer, 1980) may have an explanation other than humanistic enlightenment. Antihierarchic, persuasion-dependent, more interpersonally focused organizational forms, may well be comfortable and preferred organizational formats for increasingly manipulative climates. One reason we may be seeing more "organized anarchies" is because they accommodate an emerging interpersonal orientation that thrives in the ambiguity of such environments (March & Olsen, 1979).

At the same time we should note as has been expressed in the preceding chapter, that ambiguity can be achieved through excessive rule elaborateness. This occurs when the effect of multiples upon multiples of rules generates inconsistency and allows for multiple, competing, tenable interpretations under various rule complexes. In this way the masters of rule intricacy find themselves free again to maneuver. There are precedents for every action. Yet they definitely point to no single required course. As neither elaborate nor minimal rule structures necessarily provide rule clarity, rule ambiguity may occur in either context. Either extreme can be conducive to and reflective of, our phenotype's actings out. Thus, via either route institutions can become vulnerable to the subversion of valid hierarchic structures and delicately balanced rules for sharing power. The latter often constitute the crucial foundation upon which institutional procedures must rest if institutions are to function well and if societal and governmental stability are to be assured (Day & Day, 1977; see also, the Constitution of the United States of America).

The unfolding story of the so-called Iran-Contra Affair is only the latest reminder of the institutional threat posed by compulsive fascination with the back channel, the off-the-shelf procedure, and the covert mode. It offers the thrill of policy at the edge, of grandiose experience, of relish of ambiguity, frantic endeavor, in-group self-fascination, outgroup denigration, self-appointed indispensibility, and collective in-group absorption in normally impenetrable fantasies. In such fantasies, winks pile upon nods to the point of being never disconfirmable to the participants, except by the crashing in of outsiders (at high social cost even then, to be sure).

EXPERTISE, MANIPULATION, AND THE INSTRUMENTAL IMPERATIVE

Rule ambiguity in either extreme, the urge generally to display specialness, and the urge to seize the play in the "game" of encounters—all reinforce and are in turn reinforced by another trend interpretable as a societal-level reflection of the elements of the phenotypic profile. That is the prevalence of an attraction to the posture of the expert. This is a subject I have elsewhere dealt with at length in its own right, as indicated earlier.

Often tied to the concerns about the "technological society," a variety of work in the social sciences has raised the question of the risks of the tyranny of experts (Ellul, 1964; Galbraith, 1958, 1967, 1969; Halberstam, 1972; Lieberman, 1970; Stanley, 1978). I have generally found it useful to approach the notion of expertise by first separating it from issues of substantive task competence. Of course the latter attribute varies widely among those ceded the "expert" mantle. It is also found among those denied it. This conceptual disentangling of actual task prowess from social form facilitates examination of the social dynamics of role interaction in generic expert–layman and expert–politico forms. These are the dyadic forms for much of modern society's decision making.

Although the postures chosen within the expert role can vary and are distinguishable by at least three subtypes I have detected through some small-group experimentation, they can be conceptually ordered to show a varying degree of assertiveness behind their enactment in each case. Of special interest here, they all share a general tendency to exaggerate the relevance of the alleged expertise to absorb aspects of encounter not clearly marked as yielding to any specialized knowledge. The familiar complaint that "everybody's an expert" may be supplemented with the observation that in any event, it seems that everybody *wants* to be one.

The relationship between this phenomenon and our present concern lies in the common impetus for their expression. This has to do with a common theme in the cues from the societal dimension that bear on both manipulativeness and expertise.

In probing the nature of the role of the expert in modern society, I suggested that the micro-societal value at the heart of the relevant socialization process was the pressure to achieve standing in the production-consumption cycle. In this cycle, however, properly democratized economic and social experiences make it ironically, hard to stand out. At the time, I summarized this acquired internalized value as "the instrumental imperative." It is the need to show one counts, to appear indispensable, and to take this reading of one's self according to the tone in which others respond to one's proffered contributions in the apparently pragmatic doings of the day.

The process seems to be a societally generic one, because of a related tendency in our society to instrumentalize (i.e., technologize) all our societal activities as undertakings and challenges. On a related dimension, we thus formally educate *for* everything we need to get done, attach status to being educated to do it, and find persons increasingly identified and valued according to what they *do,* unfortunately synonymous with who they are (to the extent that the latter distinction carries meaning any more).

We are all familiar with the resulting signs: Clerks are management trainees; kitchen workers attend Hamburger University; the unemployed are coaxed to study for a "career" in motorcycle repair; physicians fill out forms on their "productivity"; the gardener is a "lawn specialist." Many white-collar workers identify with job specialization titles that no one outside their organizations can understand at the parties where everyone nonetheless asks and answers some variation on the mandatory status-clarifying question: What are you?

Commonalities between the themes that appear to underlie gravitation to the expert mantle and themes underlying our phenotype are striking. The instrumental imperative or instrumental orientation in social encounter is also central to the Machiavellian construct. The felt need to appear indispensable is an emotional over-shooting of the understandable desire to have an unquestioned place in one's world. It is interpretable as the central narcissistic concern to have a place in the context of self-selfobject relations and the larger world they reflect. The intensity of the need, as a need perennially unfulfilled by subjective standards, reflects the distortion of the need in narcissistic disturbance, and is paralleled by the excessive emphasis on carving out one's place in the climate of the technological society and its worship of expertise. In this important sense, the aura of technologized, instrumentalized interactions and the social framework it encourages, is perhaps one of the most profound expressions of the workings of our phenotype at the societal level, and acts as both cause and effect of the phenomenon at the individual level. These manifestations constitute darker-side variations on the desire to "be somebody." The attendant impact on educational institutions, particularly higher education; the concern with visibility and notoriety instead of trusting accomplishment to be self-evident, or in any case intrinsically measured; the effect on family life—particularly working-class and middle-class life so infused with upward-mobility preoccupations and designs for achieving it—are dramatic effects indeed.

As indicated earlier in this chapter, regarding macro-societal and micro-societal processes, inquiry at the societal level alerts us to institutional pattern changes as well as isomorphic manifestations of a phenomenon explored at lower levels as well. I would like to focus now on what I consider to be two further macro societal changes associable with our phenotype. They constitute systemic developments parallel to those discussed at lower levels of analysis in earlier chapters. As genuine systemic developments, they express institutional transformations and constitute macro-systemic patterns, rather than being simply the signs of a few phenotypic individuals cutting a wide path through contemporary affairs. They are more than metaphoric expressions in aggregate terms, of the phenomena described at the individual level. We consider two such developments. I have in mind the development of what I call the *rule-intensive polity* and also the evolution of the idea of the politicized society. It is easiest to develop them in reverse order.

THE POLITICIZED SOCIETY

In chapter 6, it was suggested that a major organizational-level consequence of the workings of our phenotype was the enlargement of the domain and functions associated with the managerial subsystem. This entailed a corresponding inflation of the managerial elements of other subsystems as well. The argument was a subtle one, and having been developed at length in the previous chapter it may be wise at this juncture to limit recapitulation of the issue and simply note again here what the managerial subsystem functions are generally taken to be. The list included conflict resolution; intensified interunit communication through heavily invested routines for encoding, decoding, and proliferating information; extensive monitoring of internal boundary relations; intensive rule interpolation – the creative filling in of rule gaps – agenda aggregation and articulation; compromise facilitation; rule enforcement; and most broadly, general functional coordination and overall system monitoring.

Political scientists can recognize this list as a list of generic functions of the governmental/political system. Clearly, management is to the organization what politics is to the society; at the societal level the managerial function becomes the political function. It follows that the societal-level effects of our phenotype's proliferation are akin to the effects produced within organizational systems. From a systems perspective, the abstract referent of the organization is capable of absorbing, of applying to societal systems, now seen as macro-social organization (Katz & Kahn, 1979, on the "supra system").

What this leads us to see at this juncture is that the manipulative society is above all a politicized society. In the same way the ever-managed organization, in our contemporary sense of the term *management,* is a politicized organization. It ebbs and flows via nuance, gamesmanship, continual conflict and solution, strategic ploy, and co-optation of interests. It is tinged with pathological motives for its frenetic, often solipsistic concerns. They manifest the litany of pressures, myths, and depth strivings extensively detailed in earlier chapters.

Such a society is not incapacitated – far from it, just as the high-achieving narcissist for example is not incapacitated; just as the Machiavellian, the gamesman, and the hardball player are not incapacitated. Rather, it is frequently tense, frequently deceptive and self-deceptive, grandiose in its plans, and in a deep sense infused with tragic elements amidst outward engagement. It has its "moments" both of functional success and severe internal depletion.

There are several significant contemporary social and political trends others have pointed to which seem to reflect this view. One is an increase in the apparent uninterest of corporate leadership in the intrinsic quality of products or services that constitute the core, the *raison d'etre*, of enterprise. On the corporate side, advertising and marketing eclipse production quality concerns. Merger mania eclipses intrinsic organizational development as a means to "success." Relatedly, the fever of playing at the edge of the system's rules, suggesting the mentality of a *corporate* hard-ball player, results in fortunes followed by investigations, and scandals that threaten the viability of seemingly perennial, institutionalized citadels of the corporate sector.

There would seem to be analogous developments within the polity, regarding governmental institutions. The penchant for self-destructive scandal and policy fiasco has had tragic effects, almost modularly replayable, through several recent administrations, and precociously enacted by candidates not yet in office (formerly a prerequisite for such actings out). Etheredge (1985) seems entirely correct in this respect; institutions infused with our phenotype are not likely to "learn." They are unlikely to extricate themselves from this pattern, unassisted by painful extended reexamination, any more than disturbed personalities can extricate themselves unassisted, from the emotional holes they dig themselves into.

THE LEGALISTIC POLITY

One of the most fascinating related developments in this vein, noted earlier in this chapter, involves what may be described as a tendency to rule-intensive rhetoric for the polity, a framework of mazes and ambiguities highly evolved for extended intricate gaming. While the political elite has long been drawn heavily from the legal profession, the "legalizing" of discourse in the polity is striking. This is in effect a rule-intensifying process. The extended recent public dramas of the Iran-Contra affair and tanker "reflagging" seem good examples of the point at the time of this writing. Monumental issues hinging on the proper understanding and implementation of profound principles of sophisticated government are transposed to a vague miasma of legal technicalities and the acceptable range of their equivocation. Cleverness replaces wisdom; postures replace policy. This devolves to the point that the rewards to the scrupulously attentive observer are confusion and a loss of the intrinsic sense of issue import, to a degree finally equal to that expressed by the avowedly indifferent from the outset.

Pursuing this point in the language of the experiential mode for a bit, it remains to be noted in this regard that it is not only the litigator that has replaced the statesman. This is the transformation, the regression, that competes with maturity in the *formal* procedings of government.

In the more informal but no less central aspects of government, the statesman is challenged by the dopester—worse yet, *the outside* dopester—as authentic framer of political "reality." The journalistic tendency to characterize at the expense of reporting governmental activities, and to be preoccupied with the "horse race" and organizational aspects of electoral campaigns at the expense of probing issue positions, is commonly observed. The structural problems seem to be reflected in the myopic formal training of both the journalists and lawyers. The problem is not only that government is thereby assured of remaining an inherently dilettante vocation. It is also that the outlook on government fostered by those who enact it creates, again in the metaphoric parallel to the deficiencies of our phenotype, an assumptive framework infused with gaming and sensationalism. This is at the expense of a modulated, sobered fusion that would elevate a middle ground, one of mature creativity and sustained problem solving in a clarified value context.

The result is that as the organization is over-managed and underled, the polity is over-politicized and under-governed. Politics and legalism eclipse statesmanship. The vocabulary and concepts that would be needed tools in restoring a balance are correspondingly underdeveloped as a consequence as well as cause. Indeed, for this reason, pursuing the subject any further as a scholarly issue runs the risk of obscuring the problem with a language of polemic. The proper pursuit of this particular issue waits upon the better development of an appropriate conceptual vocabulary and framework, a task for another time.

MANIPULATIVENESS AND THE MULTIPROFESSIONAL INSTITUTION

There is, however, another contemporary institutional pattern that merits mention at this juncture, because it represents a development that has ramifications for our subject. It is again an institutional, and in that sense an organizational, phenomenon. But just as the individual and group levels show a close overlap because of the commonalities in their core concepts, so do systemic organizational and societal levels overlap. I classify the development in question as societal for our purposes because it is traceable to the general proliferation of the expertise mentality more readily than to intraorganizational forces, and that proliferation has been developed here as a societal phenomenon. I have in mind the rise of the *multiprofessional* institutional format.

Medical sociology has long been concerned with the professional bureaucracy. This refers to formal organizations in which hierarchy co-exists with power legitimized by professional standing as opposed to general administrative authority. This has been the theme behind classic analyses of medical schools and hospitals in particular (Bucher & Stelling, 1969; Zald, 1970). But really the essence of the modern hospital – and university, research, and development organization, increasing numbers of government agencies through the career ranks – and indeed the whole class of what Katz and Kahn call "adaptive organizations" (Katz & Kahn, 1978), is that they are *multi*professional. They operate with negotiated arrangements among a variety of independent professions.

Physicians face not only general administrative officers in the hospital, for example. The two share and shape the organizational space with social workers, clergy, pharmacists, psychologists, chemists, attorneys, accountants, engineers, dieticians, nurses, physical therapists, art therapists, public administrationists, MBAs, police and security experts, public relations experts, labor-management experts, risk analysts, and so on. Each group has its credentials, its peer evaluations, its ethics, its behavioral guidelines, ceremonial protocols, career path priorities, and common corpus of acquired professional judgment nurtured through subtle socialization processes. These operate laterally amidst official vertical procedures. This is a logical consequence of expert power's rise. It is the result of the Weberian bureaucracy's modification through survival into the technological age.

The relevance of this observation to our subject at this juncture is that such an environment is extremely conducive to our phenotype's display in several ways. First, as with organized anarchies and loosely coupled systems described in chapter 6, it offers opportunity. Also, for all practical purposes, the concept of career "accomplishment" is limited only by the imaginations of professional groups to create status-significant events, career stages, and obscure benchmarks of accomplishment for a profession's adherents. Thus, the environment offers external motives for endless striving.

The rigors of peer-scrutinized performance in this context often accommodate anxiety as well as ambition. Thus, the context and tenor of the multiprofessional motif as a social form exacerbates our phenotype's display, reiterating the issues developed throughout the preceding chapters. As institutions of generally high social status, it is out of the multiprofessional motif that the models of career behavior are developed. They reinforce the self-fulfilling prophecy of what esteemable adult roles entail. Also, as ongoing systems, they offer this environment to new members, socializing the acceptance of our phenotype's actings out. In these environments, organizational truth rests with those who can put together the coalition that is convincing in the absence of metacriteria. The structure of the situation in any objective sense, competes with the perceptions of the participants. The situations are ambiguous. The perceptions are sophisticatedly complex and diverse, and therefore subtle and ambiguous themselves. Hence, impression management rivals problem management as the medium of choice for those who strive to have an impact on their environment. As we have seen, our phenotypic personality has such strivings at its core, as an orientation to life.

OVERVIEW AND CONCLUSION

This book has tried to convey that the manipulative orientation is no less than the full range of manifestations of this phenotypic profile throughout the levels we have explored. It is an individual outlook, a group tension, an organizational context, and a societal ambience. The multiple manifestations within levels, and conceptual issues of transformation across levels, underscore that our subject has not a single, simple manifestation; the subject is not a simple "it." Rather, we have been concerned with a dimension of action in the most general sense. The analysis undertaken here has been organized in a way that tries to underscore this point.

In this regard, contemporary political science has tended to focus on a narrow aspect of the problem: the effect of certain abstract categories of objective problem properties or "structure" on tactical behavior, assuming emotional inertness for the most part. While the common language again fails to anticipate the needs for makers of scholarly distinctions, it is fair to observe that the manipulativeness under discussion here is conceived as something apart – and from my own perspective which I note but do not advocate – also as something beyond, the rational choice perspective on goal-attaining behavior in a world of others.

The contrast bears probing for the sake of a constructive purpose. Recall the children of chapter 1 who were at odds over playing pirates or neighbors, and whom we left mulling over the suggestion to play the pirate who lived next door. Rational choice theory has helped us to crisply comprehend such conflicts. It may eventually help further to tap the dimension of conciliation through reshaping which the little girl grasped. But beginning with the probing of her insight, and certainly by the time we ponder whether either child will restore much of his favorite game in the context of the new approach, we have entered a realm where a multifaceted and more psychologized perspective is needed.

The disciplinary enterprise needs to add the study of emotionally suffused perceptions that overlap the structure of the "game" in "economic" terms. In a way that highlights my chosen emphasis or reveals my bias as some might say, I have been calling the structural analysis of the game the tactical properties of the relationship. Strategic insight in the sense of a larger meta-perspective on connections between the existing relationship and desired future empirical states, or goals, requires that the understanding of game structure be matched by an understanding of states of mind brought *to* the "game." And, whether we speak of states of mind in terms of assumptive frameworks, inner life, interpersonal orientation, patterns of personality – or whatever style of psychology we choose to connote with choice of phrase – political science would do well to match the study of "rationalized" machination with the study of patterned idiosyncrasy. It cannot prudently dispense with psychological perspectives in the study of calculated conflict. The purpose of this book has been to aid in an aggressive push once again on the psychological side of the enterprise.

The gap of methods and assumptions is wide but not unbridgeable. (As an example of one attempt in this regard see Lerner & Rundquist, 1984.) Indeed, the gap is no greater than that characterizing the differences in approach of "the three psychologies" interwoven in this work.

It is encouraging in this vein, to see that rational choice theorists and theorists of organization have recently shown renewed interest in this dimension of outlooks and action premises that are not well accounted for within the normal framework of rational choice assumptions. Rational choice conflicts lacking "stable solutions," problems explainable only by resort to "institutional rules," and institutional history, or in "pre-gaming" ploys of agenda control – as if they were peripheral and not part of the problem core – are in any event, drawing increasing attention. They obliquely raise the question of psychologized factors in explanation (March & Olsen, 1984; Riker, 1986).

But the domain of attendant issues is more than an uncharted territory beyond the land of rational choice. Nor is it a domain from which it is sufficient to adduce the occasional "psychological variable" merely as another aggregate statistic. At the same time of course, it is not at the other extreme, the only universe of explanation. The goal in this book has simply been to give it more of its due – to show in a Lasswellian sense, the full extent of its multiple levels of manifestation. For although we have focused on a so-called middle-level conceptualization of manipulation, we have treated that concept as a central motif throughout social action. I believe this concept of manipulativeness, as part of a constellation of concepts including authority (and hence legitimization and institutionalization), power, and conflict are the conceptual core of any political science claim to be a discipline that brings something inherently different to the existing body of traditional social sciences.

From this perspective, the exercise offered in these pages sought a psychological perspective on interpersonal machination, group dynamics, organizational/institutional development, and related social forces, which was designed to be as "political" as psychological. By that I mean a focus on the coercive potential; the elastic element in stated arrangements; the problematic possibility in stated conditions. In a sense, it would seem to me that, at its best it is Political Science that deserve the sobriquet "the dismal science." However, that phrase would mean in this vein, the science of what can go wrong in human affairs, of analyzing when and why this happens, so that the "doers" can be helped by the "thinkers" to make things better.

Of course, it is possible to cast a model of manipulation exclusively within each one of the disciplinary perspectives discussed in this volume. The convential disciplinary work available in the several fields touched upon provides the ingredients. Thus, rational choice theory has lately turned more to the consequences of altering institutional ground rules as well as undertaking strategic play within a game as described. This is a disciplinary orientation to manipulativeness.

Systems theory has aspects that concern the "interpolation" functions of extending routines to cover organizationally underspecified domains, thus pointing to the importance of seizing the day by seizing upon ambiguities. Whether the systems view is manifest as pure sociological theory, as management theory in the organizational context, as political theory focused on governmental institutions, or as cybernetic theory, this conceptualization of manipulativeness as coping with the ambiguities of interstices is a systems-based orientation to manipulativeness observable in several disciplines.

As we have also seen, social psychology and other behavioral approaches to personality theory point to interpersonal behavior patterns like Machiavellianism which are understandable as personality profiles related to manipulativeness, albeit without recourse to explanation involving the unconscious as a dimension of the mind. Psychoanalysis, its internal variety duly noted, offers several models of collective and individual disturbance applicable to the issue of manipulativeness, particularly the notion of narcissistic disturbance, thus providing yet another disciplinary perspective.

The emphasis on multiple perspectives has meant a focus on the nuances of disciplinary overlaps and complementarities among disciplinary orientations more than a focus on disjunctures. It bears stressing again however, that it would be naive to portray these disciplines as epistemologically compatible. As disciplines, they are not. The point is that for middle-level concepts – those concepts of universal value, making recurrent appearances across disciplines, but short of autonomous elaboration and development without recourse to established disciplinary frameworks – for those concepts, it is useful to probe disciplinary overlaps for deeper insight.

Disciplines that are hardly interchangeable or intertranslatable on the whole still show some intersection at such conceptual nodes and can be used to highlight one another's contributions, as I have suggested is the case with their insights into manipulativeness in particular. But again, some disciplines' insights are at the boundaries of the concept in question, and some at the core. Thus, even in their overlaps at such nodes, it is also true as this analysis has implied, that when diverse disciplines are brought to bear at a given conceptual node, they cluster in subgroups of relative epistemological compatibility.

Rational choice theory, currently still dominant in political science, obviously sits least well with psychoanalysis, which is in principle more compatible with aspects of testing psychology and psychological anthropology; less so with small-group social psychology – leave us not tediously iterate all combinations in making this point. In the main, the major cleavage among the disciplinary orientations touched upon in this work would seem to be the location of motivational sources in an unconscious with causal impact on overt actions and judgments. Even here however, it is worth simply noting (because elaboration would entail a prohibitive digression) that there is a further difference between epistemological incompatibility and radical differences on what are still primarily questions of emphasis. Thus, it would seem to be more a result of intellectual history and ingrained customary practice, that contemporary social psychology eschews depth psychological, psychoanalytic formulations in devising its variables and explaining its results. In contrast, for rational choice to open itself to depth formulations would be to make itself unrecognizable.

Indeed, the way that these disciplinary orientations have been mixed in this volume has reflected these relative distances among such disciplinary subgroups. They have not figured equally in developing some modal situational overview or actor profile. But, it has been a conviction behind this effort that those less compatible disciplinary orientations need to be noted and to some degree taken account of, if only to reveal the gaps they leave open to others regarding those mid-range issues, like manipulativeness, to which they have given some recognition. The disciplinary walls are becoming too high and too thick. Action in the world we are trying to investigate will not respect our compartments.

It is probably also true that as we labor in the confines of our disciplines, some of us overrate the possibilities in what goes on behind other's walls and some underrate the possibilities. As I have indicated sometimes explicitly and often implicitly in the previous pages, my suspicion is that what goes on within political science in particular and social science in general would lately benefit primarily from more contact with what goes on in depth pyschology — and I believe the reciprocal holds true. But, in attempting to tunnel in several directions the point has been to resist trading one disciplinary confinement for another, like the prisoner in Dumas' novel who labored for years to tunnel an escape, only to emerge in the cell next door. Even if the result is a maze of tunnels into several neighboring cells, at least there will be a better sense of the maze that confines the collective experience.

References

Axelrod, R. (1984). *The evolution of cooperation*. New York: Basic.

Balbus, I. (1982). *Marxism and domination*. Chicago: University of Chicago Press.

Basch, M.F. (1984). The selfobject theory of motivation and the history of psychoanalysis. In P.E. Stepansky & A. Goldberg (Eds.), *Kohut's legacy* (pp. 3–17). Hillsdale, NJ: Lawrence Erlbaum Associates.

Bellak, L. (1975). *The T.A.T., C.A.T., and S.A.T. in clinical use* (3rd ed.). New York: Grune & Stratton.

Bendor, J. (1977). A theoretical problem in comparative administration. *Administration & Society, 8*(4), 481–514.

Bennet, E. (1967). *What Jung really said*. New York: Schocken Books.

Binion, R. (1978). Doing psychohistory. *Journal of Psychohistory, 5*(3), 320–321.

Bion, W. (1961). *Experiences in groups*. New York: Basic Books.

Bock, P. (1980). *Continuities in psychological anthropology*. San Francisco: Freeman.

Bogart, K. (1971). Machiavellianism and individual differences in response to cognitive inconsistency. *Journal of Social Psychology, 85*, 111–119.

Bucher, R., & Stelling, J. (1969). Characteristics of professional organizations. *Journal of Health and Social Behavior, 10*, 3–15.

Burk, R.J. (1970). Methods of resolving superior-subordinate conflict. *Organizational Behavior and Human Performance, 5*, 393–411.

Calvin, J. (1974). Two dimensions or fifty: Factor analysis studies with the MMPI (mimeo). Kent, OH: Kent State.

Campbell, B. (1981). On the utility of trait theory in political science. *Micropolitics, 1*(2), 117–213.

Chemers, M. (1984). The social, organizational, and cultural context of effective leadership. In B. Kellerman (Ed.), *Leadership: Multidisciplinary perspectives* (pp. 91–112). Englewood Cliffs, NJ: Prentice-Hall.

Chonko, L.B. (1983). Job involvement and obsession-compulsion: Some preliminary empirical findings. *Psychological Reports, 53*, 1191–1197.

Christie, R., & Geis, F. (1970). *Studies in Machiavellianism.* New York: Academic Press.

Cohen, M., & March, J. (1986). *Leadership and ambiguity* (2nd ed.). Boston, MA: Harvard Business School Press.

Cohen, M., March, J., & Olsen, P. (1972). A garbage can model of organizational choice. *Administrative Science Quarterly, 17*(1), 1–25.

Coles, R. (1970). *Erik H. Erickson: The growth of his work.* Boston: Little, Brown.

Day, R., & Day, J. (1977). A Review of the current state of negotiated order theory: An appreciation and a critique. *Sociological Quarterly, 18*(1) 126–142.

Dahlstrom, W., Welsh, G., & Dalhstrom, L. (1972). *An MMPI handbook* (revised ed.). Minneapolis: University of Minnesota Press.

de Board, R. (1978). *The psychoanalysis of organizations: A psychoanalytic approach to behavior in groups and organizations.* London: Tavistock.

Devereux, G. (1978). The works of George Devereux. In G. Spindler (Ed.), *The making of psychological anthropology* (pp. 361–406). Berkeley: University of California Press.

Drory, A., & Gouskinos, U. (1980). Machiavellianism and leadership. *Journal of Applied Psychology, 54*(1), 81–86.

Durvin, D. (1984). Group fantasy models and the imposter. *Journal of Psychohistory, 12*(2), 240–250.

Ellul, J.A. (1964). *The technological society.* New York: Vintage.

Etheredge, L. (1979). Hardball politics: A model. *Political Psychology, 1*(1), 3–26.

Etheredge, L. (1985). *Can governments learn? American foreign policy and Central American revolutions.* New York: Pergamon.

Etzioni, A. (1971). *A comparative analysis of complex organizations.* New York: The Free Press.

Etzioni, A. (1983). Toward a political psychology of economics. *Political Psychology, 4*, 77–86.

Eulau, H. (1964). *The behavioral persuasion in politics.* New York: Random House.

Eulau, H. (1969). The maddening methods of Harold D. Lasswell. In A. A. Rogow (Ed.), *Politics, personality, and social science in the twentieth century: Essays in honor of Harold D. Lasswell* (pp. 15–40). Chicago, IL: University of Chicago Press.

Franklin, C., & Jackson, J. (1983). The dynamics of party identification. *American Political Science Review, 77*(4), 957–973.

Freedman, A. (1972). The medical administrator's life: Administration here today and here tomorrow. *Archives of General Psychiatry, 27*, 418–422.

Freud, S. (1955). Group psychology and the analysis of the ego. In J. Strachey (Ed.), *The complete psychological works of Sigmund Freud* (Vol. 18, pp. 69–143). London: Hogarth Press.

Galbraith, J. (1958). *The affluent society.* New York: Mentor.

Galbraith, J. (1967). *The new industrial state.* Boston: Houghton Mifflin.

Galbraith, J. (1969). *How to control the military.* New York: Doubleday.

Galdston, I. (Ed.). (1971). *The interface between psychiatry and anthropology.* New York: Brunner/Mazel.

Galli, I., & Nigro, G. (1983). Relationship between machiavellianism and external control among Italian undergraduates. *Psychological Reports, 53*, 1081–1082.

Geis, F., & Levy, M. (1970). The eye of the beholder. In R. Christie & F. Geis (Eds.), *Studies in machiavellianism* (pp. 210–235). New York: Academic Press.

George, A. (1972). The case for multiple advocacy in making foreign policy. *American Political Science Review, 66*(3), 751–785.

Gilligan, C. (1983). *In a different voice: Psychological theory and women's development.* Cambridge, MA: Harvard University Press.

Glassman, R. (1973). Persistence and loose coupling in living systems. *Behavioral Science, 18*, 83–98.

Graham, I. (1977). *The MMPI: A practical guide.* New York: Oxford University Press.

Graham, J., Schroeder, H., & Lilly, R. (1971). Factor analysis of items on the social intraversion and masculinity-femininity scales of the MMPI. *Journal of Clinical Psychology, 27*, 367–370.

Gulick, H., & Urwick, L. (Eds.). (1937). *Papers on the science of administration.* New York: Institute of Public Administration.

Hacking, I. (1984). Winner take less. *New York Review of Books, 31* (11), 17.

Halberstam, D. (1972). *The best and the brightest.* New York: Random House.

Helco, H. (1977). *A government of strangers: Executive politics in Washington.* Washington: Brookings.

Hollander, E. (1978). *Leadership dynamics.* New York: The Free Press.

Hollon, C. J. (1983). Machiavellianism and managerial work attitudes and perceptions. *Psychological Reports, 52*, 423–424.

Howton, F. (1969). *Functionaries.* Chicago: Quadrangle.

Hughes, C.L. (1965). *Goal setting.* New York: American Management Association.

Hummel, R. (1987). *The bureaucratic experience.* (3rd ed.). New York: St. Martin's Press.

Hunt, J. (1984). Organizational leadership: The contingency paradigm and its challenges. In B. Kellerman (Ed.), *Leadership: Multidisciplinary perspectives* (pp. 113–138). Englewood Cliffs, NJ: Prentice-Hall.

Janis, I. (1982). *Groupthink* (2nd ed.). Boston: Houghton Mifflin.

Jennings, M., & Markus, G. (1984). Partisan orientations over the long haul: Results from the three-wave political socialization panel study. *American Political Science Review, 78*(4), 1000–1011.

Johnson, T.J. (1972). *Professions and Power,* London: MacMillan Press.

Jones, R.E., & White, C.S. (1983). Relationships between machiavellianism, task orientation and team effectiveness. *Psychological Reports, 53*, 859–866.

Jones, R.E., & White, C.S. (1985). Relationships among personality, conflict resolution styles, and task effectiveness. *Group and Organization Studies, 10*(2), 152–167.

Kahn R., Wolfe D., Quinn R., Snoek J., & Rosenthal R. (1964). *Organizational stress: Studies in role conflict and ambiguity.* New York: Wiley.

Katz, D., & Kahn, R. (1978). *The social psychology of organizations* (2nd ed.). New York: Wiley.

Kaufman, H. (1985). *Time, chance, and organizations.* Chatham, NJ: Chatham House.

Kearns, D. (1976). *Lyndon Johnson and the American dream.* New York: Harper & Row.

Kelley, G. (1976). Seducing the elites: The politics of decision making and innovation in organizational networks. *American Management Review, 1*(3), 66–74.

Kernberg, O.F. (1978). Leadership and organizational functioning: Organizational regression. *International Journal of Group Psychotherapy, 28*, 3–25.

Kernberg, O.F. (1979). Regression in organizational leadership. *Psychiatry, 42*, 24–39.

Kernberg, O.F. (1984). The couch at sea: Psychoanalytic studies of group and organizational leadership. *International Journal of Group Psychotherapy, 34*(1), 5–23.

Kets de Vries, M.F.R., & Miller, D. (1984). *The neurotic organization.* San Francisco: Jossey-Bass.

Klein, E.B. (1969). Machiavellianism and other personality attributes of psychiatry residents. *International Journal of Social Psychiatry, 15* (3), 216–222.

Klein, M. (1983). Notes on some schizoid mechanisms. In M. Klein et al., (Eds.), *Developments in psychoanalysis* (pp. 292–320). New York: Da Capo Press. (Originally published 1952)

Kohut, H. (1971). *The analysis of the self.* New York: International Universities Press.

Kohut, H. (1978). *The search for the self.* New York: International Universities Press.

Kohut, H. (1980). From a letter to one of the participants at the Chicago conference on the psychology of the self. In A. Goldberg (Ed)., *Advances in self psychology* (pp. 449-455). New York: International Universities Press.

Kohut, H. (1984). *How does analysis cure?* Chicago: University of Chicago Press.

Kohut, H. (1985). *Self psychology and the humanities.* New York: Norton.

Kornhauser, W. (1959). *The politics of mass society.* New York: Free Press.

Kreitler S., & Kreitler H. (1981). Test item content: Does it matter. *Educational and Psychological Measurement, 43*(1), 635-642.

Kuhn, T. (1963). *The structure of scientific revolutions.* Chicago: The University of Chicago Press.

LaBier, D. (1983). Bureaucracy and psychopathology. *Political Psychology, 2*(4), 223-243.

Landau, M. (1972). *Political theory and political science.* New York: Macmillan.

Landau, M. (1987). *Race, poverty and the cities: Hyperinnovation in complex policy systems.* Institute of Governmental Studies, University of California, Berkeley, working paper.

Lasch, C. (1978). *The culture of narcissism: American life in an age of diminishing expectations.* New York: Norton.

Lasch, C. (1984). *The minimal self: Psychic survival in troubled times.* New York: W. W. Norton

Lasswell, H. (1960). *Psychopathology and politics.* New York: Viking Press.

Lawton, H. (1978). Psychohistory today and tomorrow. *Journal of Psychohistory, 3*(5), 325-356.

Lerner, A. (1976a). *The politics of decisionmaking.* Beverly Hills, CA: Sage.

Lerner, A. (1976b). *Experts, politicians and decisionmaking in the technological society.* Morristown, NJ: General Learning Press.

Lerner, A. (1982). Decisionmaking by organizations. *Micropolitics, 2*(2), 123-152.

Lerner, A. (1986). Ambiguity and organizational analysis: The consequences of micro versus macro conceptualization. *Administration & Society, 17*(4), 461-480.

Lerner, A., & Rundquist, B. (1984). The effect of misperception on strategic behavior in legislative settings: Social psychology meets rational choice. *Political Behavior, 6*(2) 111-127.

Lerner, A., & Wanat, J. (1983). Fuzziness and bureaucracy. *Public Administration Review, 43*, 500-509.

Levine, R. (1973). *Culture, behavior, and personality.* Chicago: Aldine.

Levinson, H. (1972). *Organizational diagnosis.* Cambridge, MA: Harvard University Press.

Levinson, H., & Rosenthal, S. (1984). *CEO.* New York: Basic Books.

Lieberman, J. (1970). *The tyranny of the experts.* New York: Walker.

Likert, R. (1967). *The human organization.* New York: McGraw-Hill.

Likert, R., & Likert, J. (1976). *New ways of managing conflict.* New York: McGraw Hill.

Lodahl, T.M., & Kejner, M. (1965). The definition and measurement of job involvement. *Journal of Applied Psychology, 49*, 24-33.

Lofgren, L.B. (1984). The self in a small group: A comparison of the theories of Bion and Kohut. In P.E. Stephansky & A. Goldberg (Eds.), *Kohut's legacy: Contributions to self psychology* (pp. 203-213). Hillsdale, NJ: Lawrence Erlbaum Associates.

Maccoby, M. (1978). *The gamesman.* New York: Bantam Books.

March, J., & Olsen, J. (1979). *Ambiguity and choice in organizations.* Bergen, Norway: Universitetsforlaget

March, J., & Olsen, J. (1984). The new institutionalism: Organizational factors in political life. *American Political Science Review, 3*, 734-749.

March, J., & Simon, H. (1958). *Organizations.* New York: Wiley.

McFarland, D. (1979). *Managerial innovation in the metropolitan hospital.* New York: Praeger.

Merton, R. (1968). *Social theory and social structure.* New York: The Free Press.

Miller, A.G., & Minton, H. (1969). Machiavellianism, internal-external control and the violation of experimental instructions. *Psychological Record, 19*, 369-380.

Milgram, S. (1974). *Obedience to authority.* New York: Harper & Row.

Millon, T. (1981). *Disorders of personality.* New York: Wiley.

Mintzberg, H. (1973). *The nature of managerial work*. Englewood Cliffs, NJ: Prentice Hall.

Monaco, P. (1978). Comment. *Journal of Psychohistory, 5*(3), 408.

Morrison, A. (1984). Shame and the psychology of the self. In P. Stepansky & A. Goldberg (Eds.), *Kohut's Legacy* (pp. 71–90). Hillsdale, NJ: The Analytic Press.

Muslin, H., & Val. E. (1987). *The psychotherapy of the self*. New York: Brunner/Mazel.

Ornstein, P.H. (Ed.). (1978). *The search for the self: The selected writings of Heinz Kohut, 1950–1978* (Vol. II). New York: International University Press.

Parsons, T. (1951). *The social system*. New York: The Free Press.

Peters, T., & Austin, N. (1985). *A passion for excellence: The leadership difference*. New York: Random House.

Peters, T., & Waterman, R. (1982). *In search of excellence*. New York: Warner books.

Pfeffer, J. (1981). *Power in organizations*. Marshfield, MA: Pittman.

Presthus, R. (1965). *The organizational society*. New York: Vintage.

Riker, W. (1986). *The art of political manipulation*. New Haven: Yale University Press.

Rogow, A. (Ed.). (1969). *Politics, personality, and social science in the twentieth century: Essays in honor of Harold D. Lasswell*. Chicago, IL: University of Chicago Press.

Rubin, J., & Brown, B. (1975). *The social psychology of bargaining and negotiation*. New York: Academic Press.

Sayles, L. (1979). *Leadership*. New York: McGraw-Hill.

Schiffer, I. (1973). *Charisma: A psychoanalytic look at mass society*. New York: The Free Press.

Siegel, J.P. (1973). Machiavellianism, MBAs and managers: Leadership correlates and socialization effects. *Academy of Management Journal, 16*(3), 404–411.

Siegal, S. (1956). The relationship of hostility to authoritarianism. *Journal of Abnormal and Social Psychology 52*, 368–372.

Simon, H. (1969). The architecture of complexity. In J. Litterer (Ed.), *Organizations: Systems, control, and adaptation* (Vol. 2, 2nd ed., pp. 98–114). New York: Wiley.

Smirchich, L. (1985). Is the concept of a culture a paradigm for understanding organizations and ourselves. In P. Frost, L. Moore, M. Louis, L. Lundberg, & J. Martin (Eds.), *Organizational culture* (pp. 55–98). Beverly Hills, CA: Sage.

Solar, D., & Bruehl, D. (1971). Machiavellianism and locus of control. *Psychological Reports 29*, 1079–1082.

Spence, J., & Spence, K. (1966). The motivational components of manifest anxiety: Drive and drive stimuli. In C. Spielberger (Ed.), *Anxiety and behavior* (pp. 291–326). New York: Academic Press.

Stanley, M. (1978). *The technological conscience*. New York: The Free Press.

Stepansky, P.E., & Goldberg, A. (Eds.). (1984). *Kohut's legacy*. Hillsdale, NJ: The Analytic Press.

Stern, A. (1987, June). The achieving narcissist and his father. Paper delivered at the meetings of the International Society for Political Psychology, San Francisco, CA.

Stout, R., & Landau M. (1979). To manage is not to control. *Public Administration Review 39*(9), 148–156.

Strozier, C.B., & Offer, D. (1985). *The leader: Psychohistorical essays*. New York: Plenum.

Sypher, H., Nightingale, J., Vielhaber, M., & Davenport Sypher B. (1981). The interpersonal constructs of machiavellians: A reconsideration. *British Journal of Social Psychology, 20*(3), 219–220.

Thayer, F. (1980). *An end to hierarchy! An end to competition!* New York: New Viewpoints.

Thompson, V. (1969). *Bureaucracy and innovation*. University, AL: University of Alabama Press.

Thompson, V. (1977). *Modern organization* (2nd ed.). University, AL: University of Alabama Press.

Touhey, J. (1973). Child-rearing antecedents and the emergence of machiavellianism. *Sociometry, 36*(2), 194–206.

Touhey, J. (1977). Personality correlates of attraction in response to attitude similarity. *European Journal of Social Psychology, 7*(1), 117–119.

Truman, D. (1971). *The governmental process* (2nd ed.). New York: Knopf.

Waelder, R. (1960). *Basic theory of psychoanalysis.* New York: Schocken Books.

Weick, K. (1974). Middle range theories of social systems. *Behavioral Science, 19,* 357–367.

Weick, K. (1978). Educational organizations as loosely coupled systems. *Administrative Science Quarterly, 23,* 541–552.

Whyte, W.H. (1957). *The organization man.* New York: Anchor.

Wilensky, H. (1960). *Organizational intelligence.* New York: Basic books.

Willner, A. (1984). *The spellbinders.* New Haven: Yale University Press.

Wrightsman, L., & Cook, S. (1965). Factor analysis and attitude change. *Peabody Papers in Human Development, 3*(2).

Zajonc, R. (1965). Social facilitation. *Science, 149,* 269–274.

Zald, M. (Ed.). (1970). *Power in organizations.* Nashville, TN: Vanderbilt University Press.

Author Index

Subject Index

THE WORD LIVES ON

By Frances Brentano

~~~~~~

THE WORD LIVES ON

BIG CATS

THE QUESTING SPIRIT
(*with Halford E. Luccock*)

The Word Lives On

A TREASURY OF
SPIRITUAL FICTION

EDITED BY FRANCES BRENTANO

INTRODUCTION BY
HALFORD E. LUCCOCK

1951

DOUBLEDAY & COMPANY, INC.

GARDEN CITY, N.Y.

COPYRIGHT ACKNOWLEDGMENTS

INDEXED BY AUTHORS

The editor and Doubleday & Company, Inc., thank the many authors, agents, and publishers whose interest, co-operation, and permission to reprint or use have made possible *The Word Lives On*. All possible care has been taken to trace the ownership of every item included and to make full acknowledgment for its reproduction. If any errors have accidentally occurred, they will be corrected with full apology in subsequent editions, provided notification is sent to Doubleday & Company, Inc., the publisher, at 14 West Forty-ninth Street, New York City.

BESS STREETER ALDRICH   318
The Dreams Are Real.* Reprinted from *A Lantern in Her Hand* by Bess Streeter Aldrich by permission of Appleton-Century-Crofts, Inc. Copyright 1928 by D. Appleton & Company.

LEONID ANDREYEV   284
On the Day of the Crucifixion. Reprinted from *The Crushed Flower* by Leonid Andreyev by permission of Alfred A. Knopf, Inc. Copyright 1944 by Alfred A. Knopf, Inc.

SCHOLEM ASCH   281
Into Thy Hands* from *Mary,* by Sholem Asch. Copyright 1949 by Sholem Asch. Courtesy of G. P. Putnam's Sons and Macdonald & Co. Ltd.

JAMES M. BARRIE (Sir)   111
The Last Night from *A Window in Thrums.* Reprinted from Volume III of *The Novels, Tales, & Sketches of J. M. Barrie.* Copyright 1896 by Charles Scribner's Sons; used by permission of the publishers and by courtesy of Hodder and Stoughton, Ltd. *Auld Licht Idylls* and *A Window in Thrums* by James M. Barrie. Copyright 1929 by Charles Scribner's Sons.

FLORENCE MARVYNE BAUER   162
The Waters of Bethesda* from *Behold Your King* by Florence Marvyne Bauer, copyright 1945, used by special permission of the publishers, The Bobbs-Merrill Company, Inc.

JOHAN BOJER   148
A Letter to Klaus Brock. Reprinted from *The Great Hunger* by Johan Bojer by permission of Curtis Brown, Ltd. Copyright 1919 by Moffatt, Yard and Company.

HEYWOOD BROUN (Heywood Campbell Broun)   41, 43, 44
Frankincense and Myrrh; We, Too, Are Bidden; Even to Judas; from *Collected Edition of Heywood Broun.* Copyright 1941 by Heywood Hale Broun. Reprinted by permission of Harcourt, Brace and Company, Inc.

JOHN BUCHAN (Lord Tweedsmuir)   191
An Extract from the Journal of Father Duplessis. Reprinted from *Mountain Meadow* by permission of the Trustees of the Tweedsmuir Estate. Copyright 1940, 1941 by Susan Caroline Tweedsmuir. Published by Houghton, Mifflin Company.

PEARL BUCK   218
One Named Jesus.* Reprinted from *The Young Revolutionist* by Pearl Buck by permission of The Friendship Press and Methuen & Co. Ltd. Copyright 1932 by G. Q. LeSourd.

JOHN BUNYAN   314
Crossing the River.* Reprinted from *Pilgrim's Progress* by John Bunyan.

*An asterisk denotes titles selected by the editor from the text.

Dorothy Canfield   96
As Ye Sow—. Copyright 1947 by Dorothy Canfield Fisher. Reprinted from her
volume, *Four-Square*, by permission of Harcourt, Brace and Company, Inc.

Mary Ellen Chase   243
Reuben's Courtship.* Reprinted from *Silas Crockett* by Mary Ellen Chase. Copyright 1935 by The Macmillan Company and used with their permission.

Ralph Connor (Rev. Charles W. Gordon)   166
The Canyon Flowers. Reprinted from *The Sky Pilot* by Ralph Connor. Copyright
1899 by Fleming H. Revell Company and used with their permission.

A. J. Cronin (Archibald J. Cronin)   302
A Candle in Vienna. Reprinted from *The Reader's Digest*, June 1936, by permis-
sion of A. J. Cronin through Jacques Chambrun, Inc. Copyright, 1946, by The
Reader's Digest.

Lloyd C. Douglas   306
Pentecost.* Reprinted from *The Big Fisherman* by Lloyd C. Douglas by special
permission of the author, Houghton, Mifflin Company, publishers, Peter Davies,
Ltd., London, and Thomas Allen, Ltd., Toronto. Copyright 1948 by Lloyd C.
Douglas.

George Eliot (Mary Ann Evans)   134
In the Prison. Reprinted from *Adam Bede,* by George Eliot.

Rachel Field   33
A Woman of Virtue.* Reprinted from *All This, and Heaven Too.* Copyright 1938
by Rachel Field Pederson and used with the permission of The Macmillan Company and Wm. Collins Sons & Co., Ltd.

Dorothy Canfield Fisher (*see* Canfield)

Kahlil Gibran   241
Rafca, the Bride of Cana. Reprinted from *Jesus, the Son of Man* by Kahlil Gibran,
by permission of Alfred A. Knopf, Inc. Copyright 1928 by Kahlil Gibran.

Elizabeth Goudge   77
Doing Good from *A Pedlar's Pack*. Copyright 1937 by Elizabeth Goudge. Reprinted
by permission of Coward-McCann, Inc. publishers, and Pearn, Pollinger & Higham,
Ltd. agents.

David Grayson (Ray Stannard Baker)   59
A Day of Pleasant Bread. Reprinted from *Adventures in Friendship* by David
Grayson by permission of Doubleday & Company, Inc., and Mrs. Rachel Baker
Napier. Copyright 1910 by David Grayson.

Elgin E. Groseclose   182
The Healing of the Lepers* from *The Persian Journey of the Reverend Ashley
Wishard and his Servant, Fathi* by E. E. Groseclose, copyright 1937, and used by
special permission of the publishers, The Bobbs-Merrill Company, Inc.

Gunnar Gunnarsson   141
Advent* from *The Good Shepherd* by Gunnar Gunnarsson, copyright 1940, and
used by special permission of the publishers, The Bobbs-Merrill Company, Inc.
and Jarrolds Ltd.

James Hilton   268
The War Years.* Reprinted from *Good-bye, Mr. Chips* by permission of James
Hilton, Little, Brown & Company, The Atlantic Monthly Press, and Hodder &
Stoughton, Ltd. Copyright 1934 by James Hilton.

Alice Tisdale Hobart   171
He Sought to Know God* from *Yang and Yin* by Alice Tisdale Hobart, copyright
1936, used by special permission of the publishers, The Bobbs-Merrill Company, Inc.

Zora Neale Hurston   7
The Tablets of the Law* from *Moses, Man of the Mountain,* copyright 1939 by
Zora Neale Hurston, published by J. B. Lippincott Company.

A. S. M. Hutchinson (Arthur Stuart Monteith Hutchinson)   274
God Is Love* from *He Looked for a City.* Copyright 1941 by A. S. M. Hutchinson.
Reprinted by permission of the publishers Duell, Sloan and Pearce and Michael
Joseph, Ltd.

J. H. Ingraham (Joseph Henry Ingraham) 129
   The Baptizing from *The Prince of the House of David* by J. H. Ingraham.
Toyohiko Kagawa 261
   The Last Supper from *Behold The Man.* Copyright 1941 by Harper & Brothers.
Manuel Komroff 199, 331
   Alone the Stranger Passes and Told in the Stars from *In the Years of Our Lord.*
   Copyright 1941, 1942, by Manuel Komroff. Reprinted by permission of Harper &
   Brothers, publishers.
Selma Lagerlöf 73
   In Nazareth from *Christ Legends* by Selma Lagerlöf. Copyright 1908 by Henry
   Holt and Company, Inc. Copyright 1936 by Velma Swanston Howard. Used by
   permission of the publishers.
Margaret Landon 277
   Reconciliation.* Reprinted from *Never Dies the Dream* by Margaret Landon, by
   permission of Doubleday & Company, Inc., and Reinhardt & Evans, Ltd. publishers,
   through the William Morris Agency. Copyright 1949 by Margaret Mortenson
   Landon.
Richard Llewellyn 155
   Faith To Be Healed* from *How Green Was My Valley.* Copyright 1940 by Richard
   D. V. Llewellyn Lloyd and used with the permission of The Macmillan Company
   and Michael Joseph, Ltd.
William J. Locke 227
   Pity Defined.* Reprinted from *Simon the Jester* by permission of Dodd, Mead &
   Company and John Lane The Bodley Head Ltd. Copyright 1910, 1937 by Aimee
   Locke.
Ian Maclaren (Rev. John Watson) 116
   His Mother's Sermon. Reprinted from *Beside the Bonnie Brier Bush* by permission
   of Dodd, Mead and Company and Hodder & Stoughton Ltd. Copyright 1894, 1922
   by Frederick Watson.
Herman Melville 25
   The Sermon. Reprinted from *Moby Dick* by Herman Melville.
Christopher Morley (Christopher Darlington Morley) 67
   Home Again* from *Where the Blue Begins.* Copyright 1922, 1950, by Christopher
   Morley. Published by J. B. Lippincott Company.
Robert Nathan 295
   Home Is In the Heart.* Reprinted from *They Went On Together* by Robert
   Nathan, by permission of Alfred A. Knopf, Inc. and William Heinemann, Ltd.
   Copyright 1941 by Robert Nathan.
John Oxenham (William Arthur Dunkerley) 1, 108
   The First Meeting from *Crossroads, the Story of Four Meetings.* Copyright 1931
   by Longmans, Green & Company, London.
   Of Our Meeting with Cousin John from *The Hidden Years.* Copyright 1925 by
   Longmans, Green and Company, London and New York.
Alan Paton 123
   The Fathers.* Reprinted from *Cry, the Belovèd Country* by Alan Paton. Copyright
   1948 by Alan Paton. Used by permission of the publishers, Charles Scribner's
   Sons and Jonathan Cape Ltd.
Peter Rosegger 222
   Of Love and Joy.* Reprinted from *I.N.R.I. A Prisoner's Story of the Cross* by per-
   mission of Hodder and Stoughton, Ltd. Translated by Elizabeth Lee. Copyright
   1905 by McClure, Phillips and Company.
William Saroyan 327, 89
   All the World Will Be Jealous of Me and Be Present at Our Table, Lord from
   The Human Comedy, copyright 1943 by William Saroyan. Reprinted by permis-
   sion of Harcourt, Brace and Company, Inc. and Faber & Faber Ltd.
Charles M. Sheldon 207
   A New Discipleship.* Reprinted from *In His Steps* by Charles M. Sheldon.

HENRYK SIENKIEWICZ 312
Keeper of the Faith.* Reprinted from *Quo Vadis?* by Henryk Sienkiewicz. Copyright 1896, 1897 by Jeremiah Curtin.

ELSIE SINGMASTER 46
Little and Unknown. Reprinted from *Bred in the Bone* by Elsie Singmaster. Copyright 1925 by Houghton, Mifflin Company.

HOWARD SPRING 228
Sabre in the Hand from *Fame Is the Spur.* Copyright 1940 by Howard Spring. Reprinted by permission of The Viking Press, Inc. and Wm. Collins Sons & Co., Ltd. publishers, through Pearn, Pollinger & Higham, agents.

LOUISE A. STINETORF 233
First Night in Tani.* Reprinted from *White Witch Doctor* by permission of The Westminster Press and Frederick Muller, Ltd. Copyright MCML by Louise A. Stinetorf.

JAMES STREET 235
The Old, Old Story.* Reprinted from *The Gauntlet* by permission of the author through Harold Matson, agent, and Doubleday & Company, Inc. Copyright 1945 by James Street.

WILLLIAM MAKEPEACE THACKERAY 315
Adsum.* Reprinted from *The Newcomes* by William Makepeace Thackeray.

LEO TOLSTOI 267, 316
God's Peace in the Heart.* Reprinted from *Resurrection* by Leo Tolstoi.
A Future Life.* Reprinted from *War and Peace* by Leo Tolstoi.

MARK TWAIN (Samuel Clemens) 246
Wings* from *An Extract from Captain Stormfield's Visit to Heaven.* Copyright, 1909, by Harper and Brothers. Copyright, 1937, by Clara Clemens Gabrilowitsch.

HENRY VAN DYKE 325
A Handful of Clay. Reprinted from *The Blue Flower* by Henry van Dyke. Copyright 1902 by Charles Scribner's Sons, 1930 by Henry van Dyke; used by permission of the publishers.

PIERRE VAN PAASSEN 297
The Unsaid Prayer. Reprinted from *That Day Alone,* by Pierre van Paassen, by permission of The Dial Press, Inc. Copyright 1941 by Pierre van Paassen.

HUGH WALPOLE (Sir) 209
The Life and Death of a Crisis. Reprinted from *Harmer John* by Hugh Walpole by permission of Doubleday & Company, Inc. Macmillan & Company, Ltd., and the Executors of Sir Hugh Walpole's Estate. Copyright 1925, 1926, by International Magazine Company (Harper's Bazaar); copyright 1926 by George H. Doran Company.

PAUL I. WELLMAN 275
The Dedication.* Reprinted from *The Chain,* by permission of the author through Willis Kingsley Wing, agent, and Doubleday & Company, Inc. publishers. Copyright 1949 by Paul Wellman.

H. G. WELLS (Herbert George Wells) 288
Mr. Britling Writes Until Sunrise. Reprinted from *Mr. Britling Sees It Through* by permission of Marjorie Wells for the Executors of H. G. Wells's Estate. Copyright 1916, 1944, by H. G. Wells. Published by The Macmillan Company.

JESSAMYN WEST 248
The Illumination from *The Friendly Persuasion,* copyright 1940, 1943, 1944, 1945, by Jessamyn West. Reprinted by permission of Harcourt, Brace and Company, Inc. and Hodder and Stoughton Ltd.

DOROTHY CLARKE WILSON 14
Priest and Prophet at Bethel.* Reprinted from *The Herdsman* by permission of the author through Willis Kingsley Wing and The Westminster Press, publishers. Copyright 1946 by Dorothy Clarke Wilson.

ELIZABETH YATES 91
Enshrined in the Heart from *Nearby* by Elizabeth Yates. Copyright 1947 by Elizabeth Yates McGreal. Reprinted by permission of Coward-McCann, Inc. and Cassell & Company, Ltd.

The Word Lives On

for

Lowell Brentano

PREFACE

IN COMPILING a "treasury" such as *The Word Lives On,* an editor is always indebted to helpful collaborators as well as to authors, publishers, and literary representatives. Here I give my thanks to just a few of these co-workers:

To Miss Ruth M. Elmquist, editor of *Christian Herald's* Family Bookshelf, who read and analyzed a prodigious amount of material, made innumerable suggestions, and brought personal enthusiasm to our many conferences.

To Dr. Clarence W. Hall, managing editor of *Christian Herald,* whose literary criticism and untiring co-operation helped shape the anthology from its inception.

To Dr. Halford E. Luccock, not only for his Introduction, but also for his generous counsel, encouragement, and inspiration at every turn.

To Miss Margaret R. Weiss, devoted friend and expert editor, without whose assistance this book would not have seen completion.

To the invaluable staff of the Mercantile Library Association of New York, who gave unstintingly of their time, energies, and vast collection of volumes.

FRANCES BRENTANO

CONTENTS

xiii

FAMILY PORTRAIT

THE GOOD SHEPHERD

THE HEALER

"COME, FOLLOW ME"

THESE, MY BRETHREN

MAN'S GLADNESS

GREAT LESSONS

THE WAY OF THE CROSS

THE SPIRIT RETURNS

THE WORD LIVES ON

INTRODUCTION

BY HALFORD E. LUCCOCK

THE WORD LIVES ON is an alluring invitation to travel. The best travel prospectus ever issued was that of Keats, "Much have I travelled in the realms of gold." The reader who gets aboard this ship is in for good sailing to many realms of gold. The passages from novels in this book offer a fascinating itinerary of a specialized sort, one never before arranged, chapters and selections from novels dealing with religion in the broadest sense of that word, as "man's whole bearing toward what seems to him the best or greatest." Another definition of religion, that of William E. Hocking, that "religion is the passion for righteousness and the spread of righteousness felt as a cosmic demand," indicates the basis of the selection of excerpts from fiction. If anyone is laboring under the delusion that fiction portraying religion in life must necessarily be dull or didactic or soporifically solemn, he is due for a surprise, and an exciting one. For here is a God's plenty of dramatic action, of human nature in all varieties of circumstance, of humor, of tragedy and comedy, as created by the imagination of Tolstoi, Herman Melville, George Eliot, Selma Lagerlöf, H. G. Wells, and a score of living writers such as Sholem Asch and Alan Paton.

Frances Brentano's knowledge of fiction dealing with religion is, like Sam Weller's knowledge of London, "extensive and peculiar." She has roamed the years, and the maps of Europe and America, in the making of this anthology. The resulting collection brings to the reader two of the greatest pleasures that literature can bring—recognition and surprise. Some readers will have the delight of the recognition of things they have known and loved, such as Thackeray's chapter on the death of Colonel Newcome from *The Newcomes,* George Eliot's picturing of Dinah Morris from *Adam Bede,* Selma Lagerlöf's beautiful legend of the boyhood of Jesus, the rugged sermon of Father Mapple in *Moby Dick,* Mark Twain's hilarious and penetrating *Captain Stormfield's Visit to Heaven,* and the tender and moving "His Mother's Sermon" from Ian Maclaren's *Beside the Bonnie Brier Bush.*

Here, for many, will also be the distinct pleasure of surprise, of meeting for the first time such memorable stories as those of the Russian Andreyev, "On the Day of the Crucifixion," John Buchan's noble portrayal of his hero from *Mountain Meadow,* Gunnar Gunnarsson's *The Good Shepherd,* and many others. The whole collection gives expression to the conviction of Van Wyck Brooks that "this mood of health, will, courage, faith in human nature is the dominant mood in the history of literature, and writers will return to it as water always rises to the level of its source."

The reading of this book will be a voyage of discovery. For many it will be nothing less than a discovery to realize how much fiction has been concerned with religion in the lives of people. It will be a fresh discovery for others to see how rich in unfailing interest is the whole spread of such fiction.

The selections in this book can render great services to the mind and imagination and spirit.

For one thing, they offer that priceless boon, the multiplication of life. A great American poet once said that if he had a million lives to live, he would like to change his name and address every time he "started life all over again."

The enlargement of experience in the fiction found here brings opening doors into other lives and gives us a new name and house number. We read from Alan Paton's *Cry, the Belovèd Country,* and our address becomes Johannesburg, South Africa. With the deep spiritual experience of "Faith To Be Healed" from Llewellyn's *How Green Was My Valley,* our house number is in a little mining town in Wales, while Jessamyn West makes us at home, in *The Friendly Persuasion,* among the Quakers of Indiana.

Also there can be witnessed in these pages the perpetual miracle of great fiction—that it makes truth come alive. Ideas become flesh and walk on the stage of our imagination. This varied array of life will also be a first aid in understanding the life of our time. From *Yang and Yin,* by Alice Tisdale Hobart, we can learn more of the heart of China than from a mountain of reports. Howard Spring's moving description of the St. Swithin's labor meeting in *Fame Is the Spur* helps us to understand the aspirations of the exploited of our own time, and every time.

This has never been put more vividly than by De Quincey:

Creative literature does restore to men's minds the ideals of justice, of hope, of truth, of mercy, or retribution, which else (left to the impact of daily life in its realities) would languish for want of sufficient illustration. These ideals, were it not for this amazing power of literature, would often remain among us as mere notional forms, whereas by the creative forces of men put forth in literature, they gain a vernal life and germinate into vital activities.

Also, and this is a great service, the literature here presented is an ally of the spiritual life. John Drinkwater puts this service into notable words in his play *Abraham Lincoln* when he says that "when the high soul we celebrate," then, when we recognize "greatness passing by, ourselves are great." Much of the enduring literature of all countries and times is the vision of greatness passing by. We do live by admiration, hope, and love, whenever we read literature which reminds us, that in spite of all the evil in the world, there is yet a capacity for greatness in men and women. When we uncover our heads before the spark of the divine in human life, that is a genuine religious experience.

Perhaps the strongest impression made by the literature here assembled is its timeliness. By this is meant not only that it fits into and makes articulate a strongly evident present-day mood of interest in spiritual forces. There is also the fact that any genuine expression of truth is timeless in its relation to life. In the words of J. Donald Adams, in his *The Shape of Books to Come,* "I think it is time we put an end to the preposterous humbug which maintains that a writer can speak to his own age only when he speaks in terms of its immediate and temporary difficulties. . . . The basic problems of life are repetitive and eternal; they are the individual's relation to himself, to his fellows, and to God. They were essentially the same when slaves toiled to build the Pyramids, or when the tumbrils clattered through the streets of Paris, as they are today in a Pittsburgh steel mill or a New York night club."[1]

We are in the midst of a great change in mood and thought. The last thirty years have driven multitudes of people into skepticism about the saving power of the ingenuities of scientific and mechanical progress. There is a new readiness to look for hope from other sources. The jaunty dismissal of religion as a major factor in life appears strange as we look back at the 1920s.

There are many reasons for the change in mental and spiritual climate, and evidences of it on every hand. Two world wars and their aftermath have played a large part. Reach back into the 1920s and con-

[1] *The Shape of Books to Come,* copyright 1944 by J. Donald Adams, p. 122. Published by The Viking Press, Inc.

sider the report which Professor W. P. Montague gave on the mood of the decade in his book *Belief Unbound,* stating there was a strong confident feeling that religion was no longer necessary, "for it was based on fear and sorrow, and fear and sorrow are no longer major concerns of our serious culture." Try saying this in 1951! Fear stalks down every city street and country lane, and sorrow has entered a billion homes. The truth is, of course, that fear and sorrow are the major concerns of our culture, and to meet them calls for power which nothing but religious faith can supply.

Another reason for the timeliness of the literature gathered in this volume is that a large multitude of persons feel they have had quite enough books devoted to the life histories of moronic nitwits, psychopathic personalities, or thugs who could be more profitably rounded up in a police patrol than in a seven-hundred-page novel. J. Donald Adams, looking over the contemporary scene in 1944, wrote, "I believe that for some time now there has been growing among readers a quiet but stubborn rebellion against a world peopled exclusively by sadists, nymphomaniacs, double crossers, chiselers, half-wits, ape men and other occasional products of the law of natural selection."[2]

Here, then, in Mrs. Brentano's skillfully assembled collection of passages from novels, with a few short stories, will be found a very different gallery of people from that described above. They are the sort of people who live in the pages of great and enduring literature. Their portrayal meets a widespread hunger for affirmation, for faith and hope. *The Word Lives On* in these pages, and offers rich and enlivening adventures.

HALFORD E. LUCCOCK

[2]*The Shape of Books to Come,* p. 186.

THE WORD LIVES ON

The Promise

~~~~~~

THEIR FIRST MEETING

John Oxenham

~~~~~~

John Oxenham uses *Cross-Roads* to highlight four meetings between Dysmas and Jesus in the years spanning the Master's lifetime. This is the first meeting, in which is spoken the prophecy of the Glory-to-come.

IT WAS a cold night up there in the hills, and the men were all gathered close about the fire they had lighted near the entrance to the sheep-fold.

It was little Dysmas's business to keep the fire properly fed. So every now and again he would creep away and come back with another branch and place it carefully on top of the half-burned ones, and he was well repaid for his trouble by hearing it spit and hiss and burst into yellow flame as the withered leaves caught and the sap ran out. But in doing this he missed some of the talk that was going on round the fire.

He was ten years old, this was his first year out with the shepherds, and he was bent on doing his very best to deserve well of them.

Some of the talk he could understand,—as when Gestas said, "They killed a wolf down Tekoa way last week."

He rather wished a wolf would come along their way. It would be rare fun to see them kill it.

But Matthat crushed his hopes with his dry, "It was nought—an ancient beast, cast out, and gone astray."

Some other bits of the gossip round the fire interested him. Stories of the iniquities of the tax-gatherers, and of the foolish rising over there in Iturea, which Rome had trampled out with a heavy heel, as she always did.

"Great foolishness!" commented Old Jeconiah on that. "Why can't they wait? . . . as we others have done all these years. It will be soon now."

"You've preached that these forty years, old one," said Jona. "The Deliverer is always coming but he never comes. Our fathers hoped for him just as we do, and they are dead."

"He is coming, I tell you. It will not be long now, and when he comes Rome will go, and Israel will be a nation once more and will lead the world."

"We have heard it so often—all our lives. One grows tired of hearing it."

"All the same you may live to see it. . . . You young ones are so impatient."

Some of them were men of forty and fifty, but to him they were still young ones, for he had known their fathers and mothers before they were born.

"If Israel loses heart and hope, maybe he will never come. He will not come to a nation without heart and hope."

They had heard him on that subject so often before that they had come not to pay any great heed to him. In fact he rather wearied them.

He was very old. No one knew quite how old he was—far past the ordinary span of life and long past work. But he had been a shepherd all his days, he knew more about sheep and their ways than any of them, and he was more at home in the company of sheep and shepherds than of ordinary men.

And he was something of a seer. During all his lifelong lonely vigils on the hills he had dreamed dreams—chiefly of the coming of the promised Deliverer; and seen visions—mostly of what would happen when he came. And, in the more ordinary affairs of life among his neighbours, he had a reputation for foreseeing and foretelling things —mostly misfortunes—which at times actually came to pass, as misfortunes have a way of doing.

So, though he wearied them with his unwearying positiveness

about the Coming of the Deliverer—which did not come to pass—
he was still held in some esteem by reason of the smaller things that
did.

With his tall figure and bent shoulders, his long grey hair and
flowing beard, and his eyes still bright—especially when he discoursed
on his favourite theme—he looked very like what they imagined the
prophets of old must have been—Moses or Elijah or Isaiah. There
had indeed been no such prophets in their time, but they had their
ideas of what they must have looked like, and that was like Old
Jeconiah.

It was a cold, still night, the sky illimitably black above them, and
the stars shining very near and large and bright. The sheep in the fold
were snuggled close for warmth. The dogs squeezed in between the
men to get their noses as near to the fire as possible, and little Dysmas
fed it with broken branches whenever it began to get low, and found a
dog in his place each time he came back.

"Ay!" said Old Jeconiah musingly, as though he were just thinking
aloud, "don't give up hoping. For if one loses hope there is nothing
left. . . . And one never knows when . . ."

And then it came—that of which they never ceased to tell for the
rest of their lives.

As though one of the great bright stars had fallen right upon them,
they were suddenly enveloped in dazzling light—light so purely white
and wondrous that no man had ever seen the like, and they fell on
their faces in fear.

All except Old Jeconiah. He sat bowed, but gazing with eyes that
shone responsive and triumphant and without fear.

The sheep in the fold woke up and cried out to one another in
wonder. The dogs sat up all abristle and whimpered, for dogs at times
see more than men.

And in the brightness Old Jeconiah saw a being in white—one the
like of whom he had never seen before, and who shone even in the
wonder and splendour of that most wonderful light; and he was not
afraid.

And the Shining One spoke, in a full sweet voice: "Have no fear!
It is good news I am bringing you, news of a great joy that is meant
for all the people. To-day you have a saviour born in the town of
David—the Lord Messiah. And here is proof—you will find a baby
there wrapped up and lying in a stall for cattle. That is he!"

And then—wonder on wonder!—the Shining One was suddenly surrounded by a host of others, and they broke into wondrous song:

> *"Glory to God in high heaven,*
> *And peace on earth for men whom he favours!"*

Joyously and triumphantly they sang, till the whole sky seemed filled with the sound of it.

Then, as suddenly as they came, they were gone, and the earth was dark as before. But up in the black sky the silvery voices grew fainter and fainter till they died away, and the stars twinkled and sparkled as though they knew all about it and were still singing joyously.

Old Jeconiah rose up, tall and straight as if the years had never bowed his broad shoulders; and his face, if they could have seen it, had in it the eagerness of youth and the overpowering joy of his at-last-fulfilled hope.

"Let us go!" he said simply.

"What of the sheep?" asked Matthat.

"The sheep will take no harm this night."

"I will stop with the sheep," said Gestas. He was a heavy, stolid fellow of two-and-twenty. "I would not walk a mile to see any baby that ever was born. I've got one at home that cries night and day."

Old Jeconiah turned to him, but thought better of it and said nothing. It was never any use arguing with Gestas. It was like arguing with a sheep.

"The boy could stop with him," said one.

"Nay," cried little Dysmas, half crying, "I go too!" for he was young and eager, and wanted to see all that was doing.

"Let him come," said Jeconiah. "No man may forbid him." And they set off down the hill in the darkness, Old Jeconiah keeping pace with the best of them; and when they got to the foot of the hill they found that the dogs had come too.

So they came at last to the little town of Bethlehem and found it crowded with many strangers.

Jeconiah went straight to the Khan to pick up what news he could, and found it overflowing. In time he found the harassed master, and held on to his robe till he answered.

"A baby—just born? . . . Look in the stable there. . . . A man came in a while ago saying his wife was taken with child, and that was the only place. It was hard on her, but we're crowded out, you see, with the folks come up for the Census," and he hurried away after his duties.

They went round to the stable, and there, by the dim light of a lantern which hung among the cobwebs from a beam, they found the child with his mother and father, as the angel had said.

When the strangers came in the mother lifted him from the feeding-trough, where he had been lying in the hay, and held him close to her breast.

"May we see the little one who is to save the people?" said Jeconiah very reverently.

And he told her how an angel had come to them, far away in the hills, and bidden them seek the babe in a manger in Bethlehem.

And he told her all that the angel had said, and what the host of angels had sung. And her sweet girlish face was full of wonder and of joy as she heard it all.

She held the little one in the bend of her arm so that they should see him properly, since they had come so far for that purpose.

And Old Jeconiah went close and knelt by him, and looked upon him long and earnestly—gazed deep into his baby eyes, which could not surely have seen much. But yet he seemed to look back at Jeconiah with understanding. And what Jeconiah saw in the baby's eyes he never told, but he probably saw there more than any other would have done.

Little Dysmas had no little brothers or sisters, nor even a father or mother, and he did not care much for babies, unless they were lambs. But the baby's mother he thought was the most beautiful girl he had ever seen, and he stood gazing at her with wide eyes and open mouth, and a strange new feeling inside him, as though he had suddenly found someone to whom he belonged, say a father and a mother and a little brother.

The dogs went sniffing among the cattle, and the cattle swayed about with wide eyes, and snorted and blew at them till the air was full of the sweet wholesome smell of them.

Old Jeconiah bent lower and kissed the soft downy head of the child very gently and reverently, saying, "One day his head will wear a crown."

And he kissed the hand that clasped the child, and said, "Surely you are the most blessed among women, for you have given a new hope to the world," and then, with one last look at them, he turned to go and the rest with him.

And as Matthat went he said, "When he is big enough we will bring him a clean little white lamb to play with," at which the little mother smiled and thanked him, knowing that in a few days they would be far away in their own home.

Outside were many waiting to hear why they had come and what they had heard. And Old Jeconiah told them; and he looked so exactly like one of the prophets of old, with his long hair and flowing beard, that they believed him, not knowing how often before he had been mistaken in the things he foretold.

On the way back he went heavily, as though he had left something behind him. When they came to the foot-hills he sat down by the side of the path, panting and bowed on his staff, and said, "Go on, you others. . . . Get back to the sheep. . . . For me, I would rest awhile," —and then, as though speaking to himself—"My heart has seen its desire and is satisfied. . . . The Wonder of the World! . . . The Wonder of the World! . . . God be thanked! . . . I have seen the beginning. . . . Who shall see the end?"

So, since they could not get him to go on and their sheep claimed them, for Gestas would certainly have fallen asleep, they left him sitting there, and went on their way.

But little Dysmas lingered behind the others and kept looking back. And suddenly he saw the old man's hands slip down his staff and he fell forward with his face on the ground.

Dysmas gave a loud cry and ran back down the hill, and the others came running after him.

But Old Jeconiah was dead, and his face was full of joy and peace. He had seen of the desire of his soul and was satisfied.

So they wrapped him in his robe and bore him up into the hills to his own place.

A Goodly Heritage

THE TABLETS OF THE LAW

Zora Neale Hurston

Miss Hurston's interest in racial lore has permeated her biography of Moses, portrayed not only as a religious leader but as a powerful voodoo man. "The Tablets of the Law" is the Negro folk version of the great moment when Moses descends from the mountain to find the children of Israel worshiping the golden calf.

MOSES LIFTED the freshly chiseled tablets of stone in his hands and gazed down the mountain to where Israel waited in the valley. He knew a great exultation. Now men could be free because they could govern themselves. They had something of the essence of divinity expressed in order. They had the chart and compass of behavior. They need not stumble into blind ways and injure themselves. This was bigger than Israel itself. It comprehended the world. Israel could be a heaven for all men forever, by these sacred stones.

With flakes of light still clinging to his face, Moses turned down the mountain with the tablets of testimony in his hands. He heard nothing earthly nor sensed anything about him until he descended to where Joshua waited for him. With his eyes turned inward, he sat down on a stone opposite Joshua to rest.

"Joshua, I have laws. Israel is going to know peace and justice."

Moses indicated the sacred stones on his lap.

Then from far off a sound, a noise made up of many sounds, came up to Moses and he listened. And his ears accepted what his soul refused. It was a wild and savage shout of voices and drums that Moses heard, but his spirit rejected it, because it injured his vision of destiny for Israel. It clashed with his exalted forty days. It soiled what had passed between him and God. So for a long time Moses sat silent and listened, hoping that he dreamed. Finally he asked Joshua, "Do I hear shouting and singing, Joshua, or is it just a ringing in my ears?"

"It's shouting and singing, Moses."

Moses sat sodden and sad for a long while and then a new hope crept into his voice.

"Do *you* hear anything that sounds like singing and cymbals, Joshua, or does it just sound like that to me because I'm tired and sort of frazzled out?"

Joshua looked at the face of Moses and pitied him.

"I hear a mighty loud noise down below," Joshua evaded.

Moses looked down at the stones in his lap and passed his hand over the carved figures reverently and then he looked back up the mountain as if he would retreat up there. Then he brought his attention back to the tumult below.

"Does it sound like the voice of the people shouting for victory, Joshua? Maybe the Amalekites have come up against Israel while we've been up here with God."

"No, Moses, it's not the voice of mastery that I hear. It's the voice of Israel, but they are not shouting for conquering anybody."

Moses sat and listened for a while longer, shutting his heart against what he feared.

"Well, Joshua," he said haltingly, "do they sound to you like they are crying out for help? They could be overcome, you know, by some nation that might attack, with both of us away."

Joshua listened carefully for a moment. "No, it's not the voice of them that cry for being overcome."

"What do you reckon could have happened to Israel, Joshua?" Moses tried to persevere in his hopes.

"Oh, that's singing and dancing that I hear. Sounds like the dance songs to Apis, the Bull-god, to me. Listen at those drums!"

Moses snatched his face away from Joshua and the last glimmer of light that had clung to his face from God died to ashes.

"Oh, no, Joshua, they couldn't do a thing like that. Not after all we have been through from Egypt on! Not after they cried to God to deliver them from Egypt and its sorrows! Not after the God of the mountain sent me to save them from all harm and danger, and brought them here to the mountain to give them laws and pledges! No, Joshua, they wouldn't be back in unforgetfulness and ingratitude here at the foot of Sinai. They couldn't be howling in idolatry in the very ears of God."

"It certainly is the sound of drumming and chanting to Apis that I hear."

Moses stood up and closed his eyes with the tablets clasped tightly to his breast. Then he started slowly up the mountainside again. "I better go back and talk to God again about Israel. He'd know better what to do than I would." He left Joshua behind him and struggled on back toward God.

But he didn't get far. At first he thought it was the wind scuffling around in the brush. Then he knew it was the Voice that spoke and halted him.

"Moses," it said like a strong breeze in the pine tops, "don't come up here to me. Hurry down!"

"Lord," Moses sobbed, "have they betrayed you?"

"They have betrayed me. They have betrayed you, and most of all they have dirtied their souls by betraying themselves. Go down, Moses, and halt them in their headlong flight. The people that you have brought out of Egypt have soiled themselves and tempted me to destroy them. They are worshiping a calf of gold and giving it the credit for bringing them out of the land of Egypt, and out of the house of bondage. Go stop them before I get too tired of their ingratitude and kill them."

The Voice was gone and the light was gone and Moses turned cold and heavy and went down the mountain like God descending into Eden. First it was the mountain top and then the high shoulder and then the heavy hips of the mountain and then the crumbling ankles of the mountain and then the plain where Israel waited for a sign from God.

So Moses stood before the altar of the golden calf with the tables of stone in his hands. Drunken shouts filled his ears; bodies drunk on the liquor of feeling rocked and reeled and contorted about him with eyes glazed and covered. Aaron with his bearded chin stuck out in front of him was presiding at the altar. His two oldest sons, Abihu and Nadab, chief acolytes in the dance and revel, were shouting and leaping, and thumping their naked bodies and urging the people on.

"Aaron!" Moses cried at him with a stern voice. "Aaron, do you hear me?" Moses had to call three times before Aaron really saw him standing before the altar with the law from Sinai in his hands. Aaron took one long comprehending look and sunk behind the altar on his knees. The eyes of Moses had gutted him. Aaron hid himself behind the pagan altar while Moses towered tall and grim before it with the tablets of God in his hands. All around the spot the tumult boiled, for few had seen with their eyes or heard.

The calf and all its meaning and all the thoughts it collected glimmered and winked at Moses from its altar and suddenly Moses raised one of the tablets with its fine writings and hurled it at the graven image and saw the golden calf topple over on its side. The force of the impact shattered the sacred stone and crumbled it in pieces. Moses lifted the other stone and hurled it, and the calf broke in pieces and the pieces scattered around the altar. But in breaking the calf, the tablets of testimony had been broken to crumbling stone. Moses stood in his wrath and considered. The law from Sinai had broken the idol of Egypt, but the sacred tablets had themselves been destroyed in the clash. Egypt against Sinai. It was going to be a hard struggle.

The crash of stone on metal had attracted attention. Drums faltered and stopped. Dancers paused and looked and saw Moses destroying Apis and froze to sculpture in poses, which broke into flight. Some ran heedless. Some crept off slowly with dazed faces to hiding places. Before Apis and Aaron they were clothed in joy and license. Before Moses and Sinai they were naked to their souls. They slunk into places of concealment as best they could. Moses strode over the huge vacant square of celebration with Joshua at his heels, looking, looking and seeing. Looking inside of people by their outward appearance and sickening at what he saw. He circled and circled and came back to the naked altar and stopped.

Moses found Aaron squatting down behind the altar trying to hide himself. Moses kicked over the altar and snatched Aaron to his feet and looked him dead in the eye. He looked at the man and saw him as he was, stripped of the imitation of dignity that he affected lately; saw him naked of the imitation of himself that he wore as best he might.

"Aaron," he said, "what on earth did these people do to you to make you bring such a sin on everybody like you did?"

Aaron tried to back off but Moses had him by his whiskers and he wouldn't let him go. So Aaron cringed and fawned and said, "Lord, Moses, you're my bossman, and I know it. I wouldn't think of putting

myself on an equal with you. You're a great big high cockadoo and I
ain't nothing. So you oughtn't to be wasting your time getting mad
with me. You done been round these people long enough to know
'em. You know they ain't nothing and if you and God fool with 'em
you won't be nothing neither."

"Aaron, you haven't said a thing yet to excuse yourself for what you
have done. Tell me and tell me quick why you have betrayed God and
the people in the way you have done."

Aaron lifted his hand as if to break Moses' grip on his beard, but
the eye of Moses forbade him. He winced and said, "You oughtn't to
hold my whiskers like that, Moses, the people are looking at us, and
me being a leader——"

"The people are looking at you naked and capering around like an
old goat, too. Let's forget about that while you answer me."

Moses did not miss the look of hatred born of hurt vanity in Aaron's
eyes as he sought to placate Moses by dissembling.

"Now, Moses, you know these people is always up for something
that ain't no good. They don't mean nobody no good including their-
selves. Know what they did? When you didn't come back right away
they was going round behind your back running you down and
scandalizing your name and making out you was dead or done run
on off and they took and brought me all them ornaments, just because
they knowed I used to work in gold, and they told me, we don't know
what become of that man Moses. Make us some gods to march in
front of us instead of that cloud. And they shoved all them earrings
and things in my hands and naturally I didn't want to be bothered
with the things, so just to get 'em out of my hands I took and threw
'em in the fire and what you reckon, boss? All I did was to fling them
earrings into the fire, and out come that calf."

"Aaron, you haven't said a thing yet and that is because you haven't
thought a thing yet, nor felt anything except your own importance.
Your whole body is nothing but a big bag to tote your littleness in."

Moses thrust Aaron from him so roughly that he all but fell. Then
Moses strode away, noting as he went how many people who had
taken no part in the ceremony to the bull. There was open disgust on
the faces of many and that made Moses think. Some were here because of Sinai and all that it meant and some were just here. A divided
people, and that would never do, not at this point in their history. So
Moses made a decision. He straightened his shoulders and marched
to the gate of the camp and lifted both hands in the air.

People saw Moses standing like a crucifix and came. Moses still stood and they kept coming and questioning each other and coming. When a great multitude stood before him, Moses began to speak and cried out, "Who is on the Lord's side? Who is on the Lord's side?" Moses kept crying until the words became a chant. "Who is on the Lord's side?" Israel's ears were wrung. "Who is on the Lord's side?" It woke up fear in the guilty. Israel was stung. "Who is on the Lord's side?" It freshened hope in the hearts of the just. Israel was called. "Who is on the Lord's side?" And some young Levites were the first to come closer and say, "We are, Moses, we are for the Lord of Sinai." Then others joined until thousands upon thousands stood by Moses. Then he said, "You who are on the Lord's side, take your swords in your hands and come to me." The surging multitudes of young men gathered around Moses with ready swords. So Aaron saw one of his sons, Eleazar, and all the other Levites go to Moses with swords and he was afraid to stay away. He came to Moses also with his sword and his censer in his hand and stood.

Moses said, "You all know what a foul thing has happened in Israel today. You know better than I do who the leaders and the agitators were. If this is to be a great nation, it must be purged of such evil-doers, or all Israel must perish. You have your eager weapons, men. Spare not a soul who is guilty." Their swords leaped out of their scabbards like day out of dawn.

The struggle began. Drunken people in hidden places roused from a stupor with their eyes wide open in judgment. Aaron saw two of his sons dragged forth and cut down before his eyes. He dropped his sword and swung his censer in wide arcs to call to the minds of the avengers that he was a priest. He stood between the living and the dead with his censer in his hand, weeping and quaking and cursing. He was afraid to fight, afraid to run and ashamed to cry out loud.

For hours there was fleeing and screaming and hiding and bloody swords. Then there was quiet again in the camp. It only remained to bury the dead. Aaron came creeping and looked down into the faces of Nadab and Abihu, his two dead sons, and wept. The men buried his sons with the other thousand leaders of the revolt slain by the sons of Levi. Aaron started a little song in his heart that went like this: "It's your time now, be mine after while. Oh, it's your time now, but be mine after while, oh, it's your time now, but it'll be mine after while." And from that minute on till the hour he died Aaron kept his eyes on Moses in secret and waited his chance. All he needed was the strength to seize his hour for vengeance. His hate was strong but his heart was weak. From then on for forty years the underhand struggle went on. Sometimes he made an open attack upon Moses when Aaron thought he could succeed, but always the secret struggle went on to destroy him and have Aaron in the saddle. And always the strength of Moses trampled down the weak cunning of Aaron.

Moses was hard on Israel, after that. He felt that only discipline would save what he had begun and so he chastened the people severely. They suffered epidemics of ailments and many discomforts. It was then that he established the House of God. It was called the Tabernacle of the Congregation and Moses set it apart from all other tents, even his own. He pitched it far outside the camp. And when Moses went out to the tabernacle everybody saw him go and everybody was afraid. Would he lift his rod against them? Would he raise that right hand? As Moses went the people stood in their tent doors and watched him pass. And every eye in Israel followed him in fear.

They watched him go inside the door of the new tabernacle and they saw the shimmering cloudy pillar descend and they saw it stand at the door of the tabernacle and in awe they rose as one man and worshiped the God who had chosen to live among them. They heard the Lord talking to Moses from the cloud like two friends talking face to face. They heard Moses tell the Lord, "If you don't go with us, don't send me by myself, Lord. Other people will make a fool out of us."

So the Lord told him, "I'll always be there, Moses, because I love you and I know you by your name."

"Thank you, Lord. One favor more I want to ask you while I am still on pleading terms with mercy."

"What is it, Moses?"

"Lord, I done seen your pillar of fire and your pillar of cloud and heard your voice in rumbling thunder. I done seen the cloudy cloak that hides your glory, but I ain't never seen your glory itself. Lord, be so pleased in your tender mercy as to show me your glory."

The Lord answered Moses and told him, "Moses, I will make all My goodness pass before you. And I will proclaim the name of the Lord before you and I will be gracious to whom I will be gracious, and show mercy unto whom I will show mercy, but, Moses, you just can't see My face, for no man can see My face and live. But, Moses, since it is you that ask me, look, see there is a place by Me and you go and stand upon that certain rock and when My Glory passes by, I'll take you and put you in a crack in the rock, and I will cover you with My hand while I pass by, then I will move My hand and you shall see the back parts of My Glory, but My face you shall never see."

So Moses thanked the Lord for letting him see that much and God told him, "Moses, get you two more nice smooth pieces of stone and bring it up to the top of the mountain so I can put those same laws that you broke upon that golden calf down again. These people need laws and rules to go by."

Moses got up early next morning and took the stones and went up to the top of the mountain and kept company with God again. And when he came down with the law in his hands, the skin of his face was iridescent and shining, but Moses didn't know it himself, that is, until the people gazed at him in awe and talked about his shining face. So they knew that God had covered Moses with His hand in the cleft of the rock and passed His Glory by Moses.

And Moses took the tables of testimony into the tabernacle and the pillar of cloud went in behind Moses and rested on the altar. So that was the first time that God had come inside the house to live with people.

PRIEST AND PROPHET AT BETHEL

Dorothy Clarke Wilson

Bethel of twenty-eight hundred years ago was the scene of freedom betrayed, of social inequity, of tyranny and slavery. It is the prophet Amos who dominates this historical background in Mrs. Wilson's *The Herdsman*—a more human, gentler Amos in his friendship with Hosea, the priest who preached that "a just God requires justice from men."

IN SPITE of the fact that Jeroboam did not visit Bethel during the spring festival—it being the turn of Dan, the center of the other royal sanctuary in the north, to be accorded the honor of his majesty's presence—the feast was by far the most colorful and successful which the citizens of Bethel could remember. The famine was over. The latter rains were falling gently but abundantly. Yahweh, temporarily out of sorts or possibly so busy helping them win their victories that he had slipped up on his agricultural duties, was again smiling on his people. Never had money been so free and plentiful. Streams of produce were pouring constantly from the languid, surfeited body of Egypt into the greedy mouth of Assyria, and Israel was the feeding spoon. She managed to see that a goodly share of nourishment got spilled on the way. Arrogantly confident over her increasing military prestige, she was demanding higher and higher customs from the caravans which passed through her borders—and, by the grace of Yahweh, who had cleverly set his chosen people astride the narrow saddle with their fingers on the reins of the world's commerce, they all had to pass through.

In the weeks preceding the festival the prophetic party had been unusually active. For some reason, possibly because there had been some whisperings in royal circles that the *nabis* were getting to be a parasitic appendage which wasn't worth its keep, its members had become suddenly imbued with a tremendous frenzy of patriotism. Leaving their comfortable quarters in the sanctuary, they had resumed their former habits of dispersing through the country in groups and had been loudly proclaiming that the day of Yahweh was at hand. By the eve of the festival all southern Israel had been plunged into a fever of excitement and expectation.

For the *nabis* had intimated that Yahweh might well choose this feast as the proper time to instigate his great "Day." Whether the consummation of triumph would come all at once, a stroke of lightning, perhaps, which would annihilate all possible and traditional enemies of Israel at one stroke; or whether it would be a slow process, Yahweh himself appearing in some visible form, such as a great winged bull, marshaling his people into armies, and leading them to military victory over all the nations of the earth, not even the *nabis* seemed to know. But whatever it was, all wanted to be there to see it.

Yet there were other emotions than excitement and expectation in the crowds which swarmed through the streets of Bethel. Hosea, alone perhaps of all the temple priests, was conscious of them. His ears were sensitive to murmurs which he heard as he passed the narrow, noisome streets close to the city walls; and his eyes were keen to discern certain small signs of unrest, sometimes no more than the flicker of an eyelash or the repetition of a curious, apparently meaningless gesture.

On the morning of the first day of the feast, while he was enjoying the coveted privilege of attending the high priest in the donning of his garments, he suddenly became bold enough to voice his fears.

Amaziah, his official dignity unenhanced by the fact that his head protruded from one end of his blue linen robe and his overshort legs, garbed in the prescribed linen breeches, from the other, looked first incredulous, then indignant, then finally amused.

"You mean—ungh!—you think there's danger of an—ouch! My shoulder!—an uprising among the down and outs? Pooh! Such an idea is not only impossible—it's ludicrous."

Hosea dropped to his knees to adjust the folds of the blue robe with its wide border of embroidered purple, blue, and scarlet pomegranates alternating with tiny golden bells which tinkled with the slightest movement.

"If my lord the high priest will permit his humble servant to disagree with him," he continued earnestly, "it is not impossible. Hungry, homeless men are always dangerous, and there are thousands of them, my lord, this moment in Israel."

"And I'll wager there's not a man of them," returned Amaziah, his good nature rapidly disappearing, "who won't bring his sheaf to wave and his lamb to be killed for the sacrifice."

"My lord the high priest is right." As he spoke Hosea adjusted the ephod of heavy white linen which fell from armpits to waist but which, unlike his own, was woven with elaborate threads of pure beaten gold interspersed with others of blue, scarlet, and purple. "They will mortgage their sons, if need be, to bring the prescribed offerings, because they are afraid."

"Well, then!" Amaziah was triumphant. "If they're afraid, certainly we don't need to be. And tonight their stomachs will be full."

"It's tomorrow I'm thinking of," returned Hosea with deep concern, "and the day after, and the day after that. Sometime they're going to awaken, my lord. And when they do, they will no longer be afraid. For hunger is a stronger passion than fear."

Amaziah frowned as his new assistant slipped over his head the gold chains which held his heavy jeweled breastplate. Even the sight of the glittering gems—ruby, topaz, emerald, sapphire, diamond, ligure, agate, amethyst, onyx, and jasper, one for each of the ten tribes which had seceded to form the northern kingdom of Israel—failed to arouse within him the customary complacency. He was beginning to wonder if his selection of this quiet young man as his second priest had been a wise choice, after all. It had certainly seemed so, for two reasons: first, that Hosea could be trusted not to use his new office for personal profit; and, secondly, that he consistently refused to accept more than a subsistence wage for his services. Since the high priest was personally responsible for the stipend of his chief assistant, this last consideration had weighed heavily with Amaziah. Now he was not so sure.

"Just what expedient would you suggest?" he asked, leaning forward to focus his pale, nearsighted eyes on his second priest.

Before replying Hosea placed on the well-oiled and elaborately curled coiffure the mitered headdress with its inscribed gold plate. Then he drew a long breath and looked steadily into the narrowed eyes.

"Has it ever occurred to my lord the high priest that the temple of Yahweh could be made a blessing rather than a burden to the poor? That, instead of us, the priests of Yahweh, being fed by them, we might—help to feed?"

"Thank you for your—advice," returned Amaziah evenly. "I shall dispatch a messenger to Samaria immediately requesting an additional squad of *gibborim*."

Turning, he moved away abruptly, the little bells on his blue robe tinkling as he walked.

Before dawn the rocky eminence on which the temple was built was an island surrounded by a vast sea of humanity. The waves kept lapping above the usual high-water mark beyond the flat stone area in front of the great portals, thrusting their fringes almost to the very altar, so that it took the constant vigilance of the temple police, together with the services of a half dozen *gibborim* hastily impressed for the duty, to hold them back. Hosea, whose new duties as second priest included among other more important offices the supervision of the temple guards, was accosted by a worried deputy the moment he left the high priest's chamber that morning.

"There's never been anything like it, sir, not this early in the morning. All down the slope you can't see the earth for people. They're even climbing up the back side by those queer rocks that everybody calls Jacob's Ladder. And they aren't the people who should be in the front rows, sir, next to the altar."

"Who are they, then?"

"The poor, sir. The dregs of the city, who should be at the bottom, not the top. They have all the best places, sir, and when the respectable citizens come, and find their places filled—— What shall we do, sir? Nothing like this has ever happened before!"

"What can you do?"

"Nothing, sir. Absolutely nothing. We've tried——"

"Very well then. Do nothing."

"But—what's going to happen, sir? The temple maidens—— These men have no gifts——"

"Suppose they haven't?" Hosea's tone was still quiet and equable, but there was a sharp glint in his eye which the distressed young deputy found strangely confusing.

"B-but—it will upset everything! N-nothing like this has—has ever happened before——"

"It's happened now," replied Hosea calmly.

Later, as he stood before the altar of incense, weaving his hands in mystic motions above the glowing coals, he was conscious of the excited tension in the human mass behind him. He knew the reason well enough. It was the direct result of the untoward activity of the prophetic party. Unwittingly the *nabis* had fanned the smoldering fires of unrest into fresh flame by their vague promises of an impending golden era. As if the Day of Yahweh, as pictured in the prevailing concept, held any prospect of improvement for the conditions of the poor! How would the *nabis* handle the situation now? he wondered. Put on some frenzied exhibition so fascinatingly repellent that even this fierce new hunger of emotion would be sated?

"Take fragrant powders, myrrh oil, aromatic onycha, and galbanum, with some clear frankincense, and make them into incense, by the art of the perfumers, a preparation which is salted and pure and sacred. Crush some of it small——"

As Hosea sifted over the glowing coals the fragrant compound prescribed long ago, so tradition said, by Moses, his hands trembled. His people, it seemed, were in need of another Moses, someone to lead them out of a more dense and dangerous wilderness than that of Sinai. And there was no Moses. There were only the *nabis,* the poor, decaying shell of an impulse which had once been virulent and fearless, clinging parasitically to a system even poorer and more decaying than itself.

Already in the flat open space behind him they were strumming on their lyres, uttering the low moans which would rise to shrill crescendos of ecstasy. He could sense the tension of the crowd rising in sympathy, its expectant murmurs swell slowly to wild bursts of frenzy. The *nabis* would be leaping into the air now, cutting themselves with knives until the blood spurted forth in torrents. He could feel their motions, beating the air behind him, even though the dignity of his new high office forbade that he should turn his head.

Then he sensed a sudden quiver, followed by a ripple of expectancy which gave way to silence. So the chief *nabi* was going to make prophetic utterance, fling to the hungry throng another honey-coated foretaste of the promised Day of Yahweh! Hosea's gently moving hands became suddenly arrested in mid-air as a clear, commanding, strangely familiar voice rang out:

> "Yahweh has spoken:
> 'For three sins of Damascus,
> Yes, for four, I will not withhold punishment;
> For they threshed the people of Gilead
> With wagons which had teeth of iron!
> Therefore I will send fire to the house of Hazael,
> Which shall consume Benhadad's palaces.'"

Like Hosea's motionless hands, the tension of the crowd hung suspended until the compelling voice had finished its denunciation; then there burst forth a storm of approbation. Huddled into a tight mass, the assembled worshipers generated a swift contagion of excitement. They had expected a speech from the leader of the *nabis,* but this powerful, passionate denunciation was even better than they had hoped. For many of them, unable to see the tall, commanding figure which had suddenly mounted to the open space in front of the gyrating prophets, it was indeed the voice of Yahweh.

"Down with Israel's enemies!" they shouted.

"Praise be to Yahweh!"

"More! Give us more!"

> "Yahweh has spoken:
> 'For three sins of Ammon,
> Yes, for four, I will not withhold punishment;
> For to enlarge their boundaries in Gilead,
> They ripped open the bellies of women with child.'"

"Hear! Hear!" shouted the crowd.

"Down! Down with Ammon!"

As the voice continued, this time with a bitter recounting of the sins of Moab and their resultant punishment yet to come, the cheering crowd abandoned itself still more completely to its emotion. Swaying rhythmically, beating their breasts, moaning undertones of pious appeals to divinity and bitter vituperation of one after the other of their ancient enemies, the people of Israel lifted their faces to the welcome voice which promised vengeance.

And then suddenly the swaying, the beating, the exultant murmuring ceased. There was only the voice, clear and stern and penetrating, whipping through the stunned silence like a cold, devastating wind.

> *"Yahweh has spoken:*
> *'For three sins of Israel,*
> *Yes, for four, I will not withhold punishment;*
> *For you sell good men for silver,*
> *The needy for a pair of shoes.*
> *You trample on the heads of the weak*
> *And deny justice to the poor!*
>
> *" 'You sprawl on garments seized for debt,*
> *Even beside my altars;*
> *In my house you gulp down wine*
> *Which was given for penance;*
> *A father and his son go in to the same woman,*
> *Making mockery of my worship!'*
>
> *"You who long for the Day of Yahweh,*
> *Do you know what that day will bring to you?*
> *It will be as when a man flees from a lion*
> *And a bear meets him;*
> *Or comes home and leans his hand against his wall*
> *And a serpent bites him!*
> *The day of Yahweh shall be danger, not safety,*
> *Gloom and not light, pitch darkness without a ray of*
> *   brightness in it.*
>
> *'Hear what Yahweh has spoken,*
> *Against you, the sons of Israel,*
> *You who call yourselves his 'chosen people':*
> *'Above all other nations on earth*
> *I have blessed you with knowledge and freedom*
> *Therefore I will punish you*
> *For every last one of your sins!' "*

Warmth leaped upward from the glowing coals to the slender fingers poised above the altar of incense so that the tender flesh began to redden painfully, but still the young second priest did not move his hands. It was coldness, not heat, which swept through his body, wave upon wave of it, subjugating all physical functions to such an intense, startled awareness of the spirit that it seemed as if he would never move again.

But he did move. Slowly, disobeying the stern injunction, he turned his head. The *nabis* were still there, sackcloth garments torn, bodies dripping blood, their frenzied transports abruptly quenched. But the space in front of them was empty. Swiftly Hosea scanned the rows of gaping faces. Then, the coldness receding slowly from his body, he turned back to the altar and began again to weave his hands in mystic motions over the glowing coals. There was a sharp command from the high priest, and the voices of the temple chorus burst into the stricken silence. In its usual orderly fashion, but with an undercurrent of emotional tension which was like a boiling spring beneath a frozen surface, the festival service continued.

Amaziah breathed more freely when Hosea had removed from his body the heavy, mitered headdress and the ephod with its ponderous burden of jewels. But the flush on his hard, thin features was not due entirely to the discomfort occasioned by these priestly appendages.

"You're sure," he demanded sharply of the cringing, sackcloth-coated figure which kept bowing itself abjectly, "that it wasn't one of your band? You swear to it?"

"By the altar of sacrifice, yes! And by the altar of incense and the altar of the meal offering and the great golden bull and the sacred stone of Jacob!" With each averment the man who called himself leader of the *nabis* seemed to grovel farther into the rug's rich pile. "After all, my lord the high priest, what would one of us have had to gain?"

Amaziah, who had looked unimpressed both by the oaths and the groveling, nodded thoughtfully. "That's right," he said. "What would you have had to gain? Get out," he ordered the man abruptly.

As the leader of the *nabis* withdrew, still fawning, Hosea wondered what his one-time predecessor, the dauntless Elisha, would have thought could he have looked ahead and beheld this specimen of prophetic leadership.

"We must find the man," said Amaziah abruptly. "He's a dangerous fool—a maniac. I'm amazed that the people didn't rise up and tear him apart for his blasphemy. The—the consummate audacity of the fellow! Have you any idea who he could be?"

Hosea bowed gravely, his handsome, clean-cut features unimpassioned. "You yourself, my lord the high priest, have already named him, have you not? You called him a dangerous fool."

Amaziah stalked back and forth, the small bells tinkling angrily. "Fool! He must be ten fools, all stuffed into one rawhide body. It looked big enough to hold them, what?"

"I did not see him," replied Hosea truthfully.

"Well, you missed something. It was—uncanny. That great bearded, half-naked giant standing there thundering away, like—like Moses when he came down out of the mountain——"

"Moses was not a fool," threw in the younger priest quietly.

"Moses never said the things this maniac did," retorted Amaziah.

"You are right," replied Hosea. "No man ever said them. It's something no one seems ever to have thought of before—the idea of a just God who requires justice from men."

The high priest bent toward him a sharp, narrowed glance, but he did not pursue the subject. He permitted Hosea to remove his blue robe, his undershirt, and linen breeches, and to prepare him further for the ministrations of his slaves, who would anoint and massage him with rare perfumed oils and provide other antidotes of comfort to his day of strenuous exertion.

"Send the chief of the *gibborim* to me," he ordered abruptly when his second priest had finished.

After obeying his command Hosea passed into the outer court containing the gigantic golden bull and the stone on which Jacob was supposed to have laid his head. It was the popular meeting place of the underpriests and doorkeepers, and already they were beginning to gather. Stretching themselves out, as was their custom, on the *simlahs* which had been left at the altar in token of debts contracted, they had supplied themselves with generous portions of the finest libation wine and were smacking their lips in gustatory appreciation of the mountains of extra-fine victuals which had been consecrated that day to the pleasure of Yahweh.

One of them, already in an advanced state of intoxication, had mounted the pedestal of the golden bull and was giving a clever and undeniably ludicrous imitation of the most widely discussed event of the day:

> *"Listen to me, you dullards!*
> *For three cups of wine,*
> *Yes, for four—ulp!—*

I will not withhold—ulp!—the thirst from you;
For you have spilled half of it—ulp!—
On your ephods."

He was quickly dragged from his pedestal, his outburst hushed. "Shut that loose mouth, can't you? It's nothing to joke about."

"Heavens, no! When I looked up and saw him standing there, I thought it was Yahweh himself!"

"Are you sure you saw him? Some said it was just a voice."

"Whatever it was, it sent ice through one's blood!"

"If it was a man, he vanished mighty quickly! Magic——"

"No magic about it! He just slipped into the scum of those front rows."

"I thought once he was talking straight at us. Did you hear——"

"Oh, forget it! Have another drink!"

When Hosea reached home that evening, he found Amos, as he had expected, already there. No words were necessary to establish understanding between them. In the first glance they exchanged both knew that they were in complete sympathy with each other.

At the moment Amos looked far removed from the startling apparition whose words had wreaked havoc throughout all of Bethel. Seated on a mat, he held in his arms the male child which had recently been born to Gomer and Hosea, its tiny body still salted and wrapped round from head to foot with the swaddling cloth. His touch on the soft, light bundle was as gentle as a woman's.

"I used to hold Debby like this," he said smiling. "I'd almost forgotten what a pleasant thing it is to hold a swaddled babe. What have you named him?" he asked Hosea.

Gomer, carrying a big bowl of steaming lentils from the stove to the mat laid for their supper, stopped and glanced expectantly at her husband. "I want to call him Diblaim," she said firmly. Then, darting at the stooped, crippled figure in the corner a glance of malicious triumph which fortunately its weak eyes were unable to see, she added sweetly, "I think one Beeri is enough in a tiny little hovel like this one, don't you?"

The old man was silent. "There could never be enough Beeris," said Amos, directing a swift glance of scorn at Gomer, "if they could all be like this one."

"His name is Jezreel," said Hosea slowly.

"Jezreel!" In her amazement and dismay Gomer almost dropped the steaming bowl.

"His name will be a symbol," continued Hosea quietly, "to remind people constantly of the sins which the house of Jehu has committed. No nation can hold human life lightly and go unpunished. The blood which was shed at Jezreel will surely be avenged."

Gomer stormed and wept and threatened, but to no purpose. Something had happened to Hosea since he had left for the temple before the festival, and though she sensed that in some way Amos was responsible for the change, it was merely a vague, instinctive conjecture. Unable to attend the festivities on account of her newborn child, she had as yet heard no rumor of the unprecedented event which had occurred that morning in front of the temple, and she would not have connected it with Amos if she had. Resentfully she snatched the small, swaddled bundle from her cousin's arms.

"You must leave here tonight," said Hosea in a low voice as soon as she was out of hearing. "Amaziah has already put the *gibborim* on your trail. But you'll be safe as soon as you get across the border into Judah."

They talked together long and earnestly, walking up and down in the moonlit space beneath the olive trees. And then Amos went away. But he did not go by the southern road which followed the great central plateau across the border of Israel toward Jerusalem and thence to Tekoa. Instead he went northward toward Samaria.

THE SERMON

Herman Melville

~~~~~~

Melville's classic of the sea, *Moby Dick,* is an allegory of good and evil, the life struggle, death and resurrection. It is all this and more, for it is a gripping adventure story of life on a whaler, memorable for its pace, excitement, and thrills. Early in the book Father Mapple's sermon on Jonah establishes the greatest lesson of all—that faith alone can save the universe.

FATHER MAPPLE rose, and in a mild voice of unassuming authority ordered the scattered people to condense. "Starboard gangway, there! side away to larboard—larboard gangway, to starboard! Midships! midships!"

There was a low rumbling of heavy sea-boots among the benches, and a still slighter shuffling of women's shoes, and all was quiet again, and every eye on the preacher.

He paused a little; then kneeling in the pulpit's bows, folded his large brown hands across his chest, uplifted his closed eyes, and offered a prayer so deeply devout that he seemed kneeling and praying at the bottom of the sea.

This ended, in prolonged solemn tones, like the continual tolling of a bell in a ship that is foundering at sea in a fog—in such tones he commenced reading the following hymn; but changing his manner towards the concluding stanzas, burst forth with a pealing exultation and joy—

> "The ribs and terrors in the whale,
>   Arched over me a dismal gloom,
> While all God's sun-lit waves rolled by,
>   And lift me deepening down to doom.

> "I saw the opening maw of hell,
>   With endless pains and sorrows there;

Which none but they that feel can tell—
Oh, I was plunging to despair.

"In black distress, I called my God,
When I could scarce believe him mine,
He bowed his ear to my complaints—
No more the whale did me confine.

"With speed he flew to my relief,
As on a radiant dolphin borne;
Awful, yet bright, as lightning shone
The face of my Deliverer God.

"My song for ever shall record
That terrible, that joyful hour;
I give the glory to my God,
His all the mercy and the power."

Nearly all joined in singing this hymn, which swelled high above the howling of the storm. A brief pause ensued; the preacher slowly turned over the leaves of the Bible, and at last, folding his hand down upon the proper page, said: "Beloved shipmates, clinch the last verse of the first chapter of Jonah—'And God had prepared a great fish to swallow up Jonah.'

"Shipmates, this book, containing only four chapters—four yarns—is one of the smallest strands in the mighty cable of the Scriptures. Yet what depths of the soul does Jonah's deep sea-line sound! what a pregnant lesson to us is this prophet! What a noble thing is that canticle in the fish's belly! How billow-like and boisterously grand! We feel the floods surging over us; we sound with him to the kelpy bottom of the waters; sea-weed and all the slime of the sea is about us! But *what* is this lesson that the book of Jonah teaches? Shipmates, it is a two-stranded lesson; a lesson to us all as sinful men, and a lesson to me as a pilot of the living God. As sinful men, it is a lesson to us all, because it is a story of the sin, hard-heartedness, suddenly awakened fears, the swift punishment, repentance, prayers, and finally the deliverance and joy of Jonah. As with all sinners among men, the sin of this son of Amittai was in his wilful disobedience of the command of God—never mind now what that command was, or how conveyed—which he found a hard command. But all the things that God would have us do are hard for us to do—remember that—and hence, He oftener commands us than endeavors to persuade. And if we obey God, we must disobey ourselves; and it is in this disobeying ourselves, wherein the hardness of obeying God consists.

"With this sin of disobedience in him, Jonah still further flouts at God, by seeking to flee from Him. He thinks that a ship made by men will carry him into countries where God does not reign, but only the Captains of this earth. He skulks about the wharves of Joppa, and seeks a ship that's bound for Tarshish. There lurks, perhaps, a hitherto unheeded meaning here. By all accounts Tarshish could have been no other city than the modern Cadiz. That's the opinion of learned men. And where is Cadiz, shipmates? Cadiz is in Spain; as far by water, from Joppa, as Jonah could possibly have sailed in those ancient days, when the Atlantic was an almost unknown sea. Because Joppa, the modern Jaffa, shipmates, is on the most easterly coast of the Mediterranean, the Syrian; and Tarshish or Cadiz more than two thousand miles to the westward from that, just outside the Straits of Gibraltar. See ye not then, shipmates, that Jonah sought to flee world-wide from God? Miserable man! Oh! most contemptible and worthy of all scorn; with slouched hat and guilty eye, skulking from his God; prowling among the shipping like a vile burglar hastening to cross the seas. So disordered, self-condemning is his look, that had there been policemen in those days, Jonah, on the mere suspicion of something wrong, had been arrested ere he touched a deck. How plainly he's a fugitive! no baggage, not a hat-box, valise, or carpet-bag,—no friends accompany him to the wharf with their adieux. At last, after much dodging search, he finds the Tarshish ship receiving the last items of her cargo; and as he steps on board to see its Captain in the cabin, all the sailors for the moment desist from hoisting in the goods, to mark the stranger's evil eye. Jonah sees this; but in vain he tries to look all ease and confidence; in vain essays his wretched smile. Strong intuitions of the man assure the mariners he can be no innocent. In their gamesome but still serious way, one whispers to the other—"Jack, he's robbed a widow;" or, "Joe, do you mark him; he's a bigamist;" or, "Harry lad, I guess he's the adulterer that broke jail in old Gomorrah, or belike, one of the missing murderers from Sodom." Another runs to read the bill that's stuck against the spile upon the wharf to which the ship is moored, offering five hundred gold coins for the apprehension of a parricide, and containing a description of his person. He reads, and looks from Jonah to the bill; while all his sympathetic shipmates now crowd round Jonah, prepared to lay their hands upon him. Frighted Jonah trembles, and summoning all his boldness to his face, only looks so much the more a coward. He will not confess himself suspected; but that itself is strong suspicion. So he makes the best of it; and when the sailors find him not to be the man that is advertised, they let him pass, and he descends into the cabin.

" 'Who's there?' cries the Captain at his busy desk, hurriedly making out his papers for the Customs—'Who's there?' Oh! how that harmless question mangles Jonah! For the instant he almost turns to flee again. But he rallies. 'I seek a passage in this ship to Tarshish; how soon sail ye, sir?' Thus far the busy Captain had not looked up to Jonah, though the man now stands before him; but no sooner does he hear that hollow voice, than he darts a scrutinizing glance. 'We sail with the next coming tide,' at last he slowly answered, still intently eyeing him. 'No sooner, sir?'—'Soon enough for any honest man that goes a passenger.' Ha! Jonah, that's another stab. But he swiftly calls away the Captain from that scent. 'I'll sail with ye,'—he says,—'the passage money, how much is that?—I'll pay now.' For it is particularly written, shipmates, as if it were a thing not to be overlooked in this history, 'that he paid the fare thereof' ere the craft did sail. And taken with the context, this is full of meaning.

"Now Jonah's Captain, shipmates, was one whose discernment detects crime in any, but whose cupidity exposes it only in the penniless. In this world, shipmates, sin that pays its way can travel freely and without a passport; whereas Virtue, if a pauper, is stopped at all frontiers. So Jonah's Captain prepares to test the length of Jonah's purse, ere he judge him openly. He charges him thrice the usual sum; and it's assented to. Then the Captain knows that Jonah is a fugitive; but at the same time resolves to help a flight that paves its rear with gold. Yet when Jonah fairly takes out his purse, prudent suspicions still molest the Captain. He rings every coin to find a counterfeit. Not a forger, any way, he mutters; and Jonah is put down for his passage. 'Point out my state-room, sir,' says Jonah now, 'I'm travel-weary; I need sleep.' 'Thou look'st like it,' says the Captain, 'there's thy room.' Jonah enters, and would lock the door, but the lock contains no key. Hearing him foolishly fumbling there, the Captain laughs lowly to himself, and mutters something about the doors of convicts' cells being never allowed to be locked within. All dressed and dusty as he is, Jonah throws himself into his berth, and finds the little state-room ceiling almost resting on his forehead. The air is close, and Jonah gasps. Then, in that contracted hole, sunk, too, beneath the ship's water-line, Jonah feels the heralding presentiment of that stifling hour, when the whale shall hold him in the smallest of his bowels' wards.

"Screwed at its axis against the side, a swinging lamp slightly oscillates in Jonah's room; and the ship, heeling over towards the wharf with the weight of the last bales received, the lamp, flame and all, though in slight motion, still maintains a permanent obliquity with reference to the room; though, in truth, infallibly straight itself, it but made obvious the false, lying levels among which it hung. The lamp alarms and frightens Jonah; as lying in his berth his tormented eyes roll round the place, and this thus far successful fugitive finds no refuge for his restless glance. But that contradiction in the lamp more and more appalls him. The floor, the ceiling, and the side, are all awry. 'Oh! so my conscience hangs in me!' he groans, 'straight upward, so it burns; but the chambers of my soul are all in crookedness!'

"Like one who after a night of drunken revelry hies to his bed, still reeling, but with conscience yet pricking him, as the plungings of the Roman race-horse but so much the more strike his steel tags into him; as one who in that miserable plight still turns and turns in giddy anguish, praying God for annihilation until the fit be passed; and at last amid the whirl of woe he feels, a deep stupor steals over him, as over the man who bleeds to death, for conscience is the wound, and there's naught to staunch it; so, after sore wrestlings in his berth, Jonah's prodigy of ponderous misery drags him drowning down to sleep.

"And now the time of tide has come; the ship casts off her cables; and from the deserted wharf the uncheered ship for Tarshish, all careening, glides to sea. That ship, my friends, was the first of recorded smugglers! the contraband was Jonah. But the sea rebels; he will not bear the wicked burden. A dreadful storm comes on, the ship is like to break. But now when the boatswain calls all hands to lighten her; when boxes, bales, and jars are clattering overboard; when the wind is shrieking, and the men are yelling, and every plank thunders with trampling feet right over Jonah's head; in all this raging tumult, Jonah sleeps his hideous sleep. He sees no black sky and raging sea, feels not the reeling timbers, and little hears he or heeds he the far rush of the mighty whale, which even now with open mouth is cleaving the seas after him. Aye, shipmates, Jonah was gone down into the sides of the ship— a berth in the cabin as I have taken it, and was fast asleep. But the frightened master comes to him, and shrieks in his dead ear, 'What meanest thou, O sleeper! arise!' Startled from his lethargy by that direful cry, Jonah staggers to his feet, and stumbling to the deck, grasps a shroud, to look out upon the sea. But at that moment he is sprung upon by a panther billow leaping over the bulwarks. Wave after wave thus leaps into the ship, and finding no speedy vent runs roaring fore and aft, till the mariners come nigh to drowning while yet afloat. And ever, as the white moon shows her affrighted face from the steep gullies in the blackness overhead, aghast Jonah sees the rearing bowsprit pointing high upward, but soon beat downward again towards the tormented deep.

"Terrors upon terrors run shouting through his soul. In all his cringing attitudes, the God-fugitive is now too plainly known. The sailors mark him; more and more certain grow their suspicions of him, and at last, fully to test the truth, by referring the whole matter to high Heaven, they fall to casting lots, to see for whose cause this great tempest was upon them. The lot is Jonah's; that discovered, then how furiously they mob him with their questions. 'What is thine occupation? Whence comest thou? Thy country? What people?' But mark now, my shipmates, the behavior of poor Jonah. The eager mariners but ask him who he is, and where from; whereas, they not only receive an answer to those questions, but likewise another answer to a question not put by them, but the unsolicited answer is forced from Jonah by the hard hand of God that is upon him.

" 'I am a Hebrew,' he cries—and then—'I fear the Lord the God of Heaven who hath made the sea and the dry land!' Fear Him, O Jonah? Aye, well mightest thou fear the Lord God *then!* Straightway, he now goes on to make a full confession; whereupon the mariners became more and more appalled, but still are pitiful. For when Jonah, not yet supplicating God for mercy, since he but too well knew the darkness of his deserts,—when wretched Jonah cries out to them to take him and cast him forth into the sea, for he knew that for *his* sake this great tempest was upon them; they mercifully turn from him, and seek by other means to save the ship. But all in vain; the indignant gale howls louder; then, with one hand raised invokingly to God, with the other they not unreluctantly lay hold of Jonah.

"And now behold Jonah taken up as an anchor and dropped into the sea; when instantly an oily calmness floats out from the east, and the sea is still, as Jonah carries down the gale with him, leaving smooth water behind. He goes down in the whirling heart of such a masterless commotion that he scarce heeds the moment when he drops seething into the yawning jaws awaiting him; and the whale shoots-to all his ivory teeth, like so many white bolts, upon his prison. Then Jonah prayed unto the Lord out of the fish's belly. But observe his prayer, and learn a weighty lesson. For sinful as he is, Jonah does not weep and wail for direct deliverance. He feels that his dreadful punishment is just. He leaves all his deliverance to God, contenting himself with this, that spite all his pains and pangs, he will still look towards His holy temple. And here, shipmates, is true and faithful repentance; not clamorous for pardon, but grateful for punishment. And how pleasing to God was this conduct in Jonah is shown in the eventual deliverance of him from the sea and the whale. Shipmates, I do not place Jonah before you to be copied for his sin but I do place him before you as a model for repentance. Sin not; but if you do, take heed to repent of it like Jonah."

While he was speaking these words, the howling of the shrieking, slanting storm without seemed to add new power to the preacher, who, when describing Jonah's sea-storm, seemed tossed by a storm himself. His deep chest heaved as with a ground-swell; his tossed arms seemed the warring elements at work; and the thunders that rolled away from off his swarthy brow, and the light leaping from his eye, made all his simple hearers look on him with a quick fear that was strange to them.

There now came a lull in his look, as he silently turned over the leaves of the Book once more; and, at last, standing motionless, with closed eyes, for the moment, seemed communing with God and himself.

But again he leaned over towards the people, and bowing his head lowly, with an aspect of the deepest yet manliest humility, he spake these words:

"Shipmates, God has laid but one hand upon you; both his hands press upon me. I have read ye by what murky light may be mine the lesson that Jonah teaches to all sinners; and therefore to ye, and still more to me, for I am a greater sinner than ye. And now how gladly would I come down from this mast-head and sit on the hatches there where you sit, and listen as you listen, while some one of you reads *me* that other and more awful lesson which Jonah teaches to *me,* as a pilot of the living God. How being an anointed pilot-prophet, or speaker of true things, and bidden by the Lord to sound those unwelcome truths in the ears of a wicked Nineveh, Jonah, appalled at the hostility he should raise, fled from his mission, and sought to escape his duty and his God by taking ship at Joppa. But God is everywhere; Tarshish he never reached. As we have seen, God came upon him in the whale, and swallowed him down to living gulfs of doom, and with swift slantings tore him along 'into the midst of the seas,' where the eddying depths sucked him ten thousand fathoms down, and 'the weeds were wrapped about his head,' and all the watery world of woe bowled over him. Yet even then beyond the reach of any plummet—'out of the belly of hell'—when the whale grounded upon the ocean's utmost bones, even then, God heard the engulphed, repenting prophet when he cried. Then God spake unto the fish; and from the shuddering cold and blackness of the sea, the whale came breeching up towards the warm and pleasant sun, and all the delights of air and earth; and 'vomited out Jonah upon the dry land;' when the word of the Lord came a second time; and Jonah, bruised and beaten—his ears, like two sea-shells, still multitudinously murmuring of the ocean—Jonah did the Almighty's bidding. And what was that, shipmates? To preach the Truth to the face of Falsehood! That was it!

"This, shipmates, this is that other lesson; and woe to that pilot of the living God who slights it. Woe to him whom this world charms from Gospel duty! Woe to him who seeks to pour oil upon the waters when God has brewed them into a gale! Woe to him who seeks to please rather than to appall! Woe to him whose good name is more to him than goodness! Woe to him who, in this world, courts not dishonor! Woe to him who would not be true, even though to be false were salvation! Yea, woe to him who, as the great Pilot Paul has it, while preaching to others is himself a castaway!"

He drooped and fell away from himself for a moment; then lifting his face to them again, showed a deep joy in his eyes, as he cried out with a heavenly enthusiasm,—"But oh! shipmates! on the starboard hand of every woe, there is a sure delight; and higher the top of that delight, than the bottom of the woe is deep. Is not the main-truck higher than the kelson is low? Delight is to him—a far, far upward, and inward delight—who against the proud gods and commodores of this earth, ever stands forth his own inexorable self. Delight is to him whose strong arms yet support him, when the ship of this base treacherous world has gone down beneath him. Delight is to him, who gives no quarter in the truth, and kills, burns, and destroys all sin though he pluck it out from under the robes of Senators and Judges. Delight—top-gallant delight is to him, who acknowledges no law or lord, but the Lord his God, and is only a patriot to heaven. Delight is to him, whom all the waves of the billows of the seas of the boisterous mob can never shake from this sure Keel of the Ages. And eternal delight and deliciousness will be his, who coming to lay him down, can say with his final breath—O Father!—chiefly known to me by Thy rod—mortal or immortal, here I die. I have striven to be Thine, more than to be this world's, or mine own. Yet this is nothing: I leave eternity to Thee; for what is man that he should live out the lifetime of his God?"

He said no more, but slowly waving a benediction, covered his face with his hands, and so remained kneeling, till all the people had departed, and he was left alone in the place.

A WOMAN OF VIRTUE

Rachel Field

All This, and Heaven Too is the life story of Rachel Field's own great-aunt, Mlle. Henriette Deluzy des Porte, who became closely involved in the sensational murder trial of the Duc de Praslin. Although acquitted, she found life extremely difficult in France, and through the efforts of Henry Field, a young minister, came to America. "A Woman of Virtue" tells of Henriette's first meeting with her future husband's family in their austere New England parsonage.

THE SUN was setting behind the hills that enclosed the Housatonic valley as they turned into the village street under great arching elm trees on either side. At the far end the slim white tip of another steeple rose above more trees; and nearer by, the substantial houses with their lawns and gardens were all warm with reflected brightness from the western sky. A far clock was striking six, and the delicious smell of freshly baked bread met them even before they came in sight of the square brick parsonage.

Boney quickened her pace from jog to spirited trot. They rattled into the yard almost before Henriette realized that she had reached the end of her journey. In the reunion with Henry, in the beauty and sense of complete well-being that had taken possession of her as they traveled those miles together, she had forgotten her weariness and all her doubts and misgivings. Now they rose to engulf her as she faced the meeting upon which so much depended. For herself, she did not mind if this family disapproved of her. She had met far too much antagonism in the last few years to be easily dismayed. But for Henry's sake she cared to make a good impression upon these people. His eyes were so loving and anxious she must not fail him.

A girl in a blue cotton dress was bending over a flower bed; but at the sound of wheels she set down her watering can and came hurrying with outstretched hands. She was young and fair, with broad brows under smoothly parted hair and clear, thoughtful eyes that lighted in eager responsiveness.

"She is kind and intelligent," Henriette decided after the introductions were over and they walked together up the flagstone path between orange lilies and phlox. "We shall be friends."

Submit Dickinson Field, mother of seven sons and two daughters, stood in the doorway, a small woman nearing seventy in a plain cotton dress and lawn cap and kerchief. She had been beautiful in her youth, and in age she was still lovely to look upon with the fine features and color only a little dimmed by years of activity and fulfillment. Her eyes were soft and kind in their framework of delicate wrinkles, and her lips kept a half-smile even in repose. "I have given my best to life," that radiant old face seemed to be saying unconsciously, "and it has given its best to me in return." Henriette felt the warmth behind the greeting in the hand that closed over her own.

"Come in," she said with cordial scrutiny. "Come in and rest you. My, but you're a little body to have come across all that water!"

"But I did not swim the Atlantic, you know," Henriette responded with a smile.

"My boys and girls are all travelers, too," the pleasant old voice was going on. "Emilia Ann lived ten years in Turkey; Stephen's in California; David and Cyrus and Henry and Mary Elizabeth here are all back from far parts; and Timothy——"

She broke off and turned away. She could never speak of this second son without tears, for Timothy had been lost at sea somewhere off the coast of South America fifteen years before.

"Yes," she went on, "they all want to see far places but me. I've been content to stay at home and let them see the world instead."

"They have brought the world to you, madame," Henriette told her while Henry beamed upon them both.

("So far, so good," Henriette thought as she put on a fresh dress and brushed her hair. "But I have not met his father.")

The room she had been given was simple to the point of bareness, but the curtains and bed linen were snowy white, the homemade rugs and blankets woven in plain, soft colors. The bed, the chest of drawers, the washstand, and two chairs were of cherry and maple. She liked the variation from the mahogany, walnut, and rosewood of city houses. There was no wardrobe, merely a row of wooden pegs for her dresses, and the mirror was very small. Evidently the matter of feminine adornment played little part in this household. Yet both mother and daughter had been appropriately and freshly dressed, and one of them must have taken pains to arrange the glass vase of flowers on the chest. She fastened a tea rose in the ruffles of her green and white muslin before she answered the ringing of the supper bell. Henry waited at the foot of the stairs to conduct her to his father. The pressure of his hand was reassuring, though she also felt that he was bracing himself for the meeting.

The Reverend David Dudley Field had a presence that filled the house with Old Testament dignity, though he was less tall and commanding than she had expected. As he rose from his chair to greet her, Henriette was struck by the spare erectness of his figure and by the angular beauty of his features. The silver-white hair that almost touched his shoulders grew away from the high dome of forehead that dominated the whole face. The eyes were deep-set and searching. Later she was to discover that they were blue and capable of kindness as well as intensity, but on that first meeting they appeared dark and almost fanatical under jutting gray brows. For the rest, his nose was long, large, and straight; the cheekbones, high; the chin, sharply prominent, and the mouth, tight-lipped. A somber austerity wrapped him like a mantle, and behind that stern old face the flame of the spirit was almost visible. So, Henriette thought, the prophets of old must have looked—Isaiah, Ezekiel, and Jeremiah. He would never falter in performing whatever the Lord might call upon him to do. Almost, she believed him capable of sacrificing a son or a daughter to the Will of God, as Abraham had been called upon to offer up Isaac.

Yet he turned fond eyes upon his two children and spoke grave words of welcome to their guest.

"Mrs. Field"—he addressed his wife as formally as if they were not nearing the completion of fifty years of married life—"let us go in to supper now, for Henry and I must uncover the young melon plants before dark."

Henriette stood with bowed head at her place while he delivered the blessing before their meal. He seemed, she thought, to be speaking with an intimate Presence to whom he was used to confiding the simple details of garden and barn as well as more complex matters of the spirit.

Supper, in this New England household, delighted her with its simple perfection. Fresh bread and butter and cottage cheese; a platter of cold meat; a pitcher of milk and a bowl of strawberries were spread on the table with its white cloth and willowware china. A country girl who helped in the kitchen took her place among them as a matter of course and was included in the family conversation.

"Jonathan raised these strawberries," Mrs. Field explained with pride. "He's promised us a mess of early peas soon. I expect you've had them for weeks in New York. The season's later up here in Berkshire. Jonathan's very pleased with his garden. He'll want to show it to you, Miss Desportes."

Mary Elizabeth was almost as eager as Henry to talk of world affairs. She had traveled with Cyrus and his wife and showed unusual gifts of observation and insight in her questions and comments. Besides studying the classics under her father's instruction, she had attended a female institute in Albany. Like Henry she expressed herself well, and Henriette discovered that she had already contributed a number of articles to newspapers upon her foreign experiences. It was pleasant to compare personal reactions to European cities, and to discuss the latest news from France, Italy, and England. Between Mary Elizabeth and her father a peculiar bond existed. Though he seldom joined in the conversation, Henriette noticed that he listened with interest and watched this youngest daughter with tender regard. Once only he addressed their visitor directly, and she was startled by his reference to Paris and by his giving the French pronunciation to her name.

"I found Paris a beautiful city, Mademoiselle Desportes," he remarked. "There were great extremes of poverty and vice as against ostentation and luxury, but no more than in other capitals, and the French people impressed me by their buoyancy and thrift and by their good manners."

His son and daughter exchanged amused glances.

"We never worried about Father wandering the streets of Paris by himself," Henry explained. "Stephen told me that someone always brought him back to their hotel if he lost his way."

Henriette thought that such a remarkable old face would have awed any Frenchman into respectful solicitude. Yet she felt before him something of what she had felt when she had faced the Judge and Chancellor in the courtroom. It was as if his austere goodness made others turn inner scrutiny upon their own shortcomings. One felt this Minister of the Gospel not only had been chosen to exhort the faithful, but also had been endowed with an almost supernatural power to wrestle with the hosts of Satan. Her own worthiness was about to be tested by unflinching standards. Woe to her if she should be found wanting in his eyes.

They rose from the table. Henry and his father went out to the garden; Mary Elizabeth and the helper went into the kitchen to wash and wipe the dishes, while Henriette and her hostess repaired to the parlor. An overflowing workbasket was brought out, and Mrs. Field drew close to the window to make the most of the failing light. Henriette watched her bent over yarn and knitting needles as a woolen sock lengthened under her busy old fingers.

"Yes," she looked up and smiled, "I can knit socks with my eyes shut, all but turning heels. My sons still like to wear the kind I make. I used to be a good hand at spinning wool and flax when I was younger, but with the mills turning out such good cloth it hardly pays to do your own weaving nowadays. I make my husband's shirts still, and I always wash and starch them and his stocks myself. These socks are for Stephen in California," she added, holding out the half-finished piece of knitting, "but dear knows how long it will take to send them so far!"

Henriette offered to help with some mending, but her hostess would not hear of it.

"No, no, you sit and rest yourself. This first evening it's your privilege to be idle. Tomorrow you can lend me a hand with a quilt I'm patching if you've a mind to and Henry makes no objection. He'll want to take you calling, maybe. He's told everyone on both sides of the street all about you."

"Henri is too kind and generous, madame," she ventured. "I am sometimes fearful that he does not see faults in those he——" She broke off, not wishing to commit herself too far.

"Yes, I know, he believes the best of everyone. All Henry's geese were swans when he was little, and now he's a man it's the same way. Not that I mean you by that," she added with her wise, disarming smile.

"Henri has—has told you of me?"

"There, I can never get used to your saying his name in French. Makes him sound so outlandish some way, but I guess he likes to hear you do it. Yes, whatever you do and say suits him. I've known that a long time now. He's told us plenty about you and your troubles, too. You've had more'n your share, but I hope you've seen the last of 'em."

"Thank you." Henriette was touched by the genuineness of the old woman's sympathy. "My troubles seem very far off here in your house where it is so serene and comfortable. I do not wish to bring them into your midst, for I have respect for a family such as yours, and though it would be an honor to become a part of it, perhaps I have no right—after what has happened. There are many who believe the worst of me, madame, things that I could not even speak about to you. To the day I die this tragedy will be with me. I cannot unravel the tangle of my life and knit it over again as you might unravel that yarn in your hands."

"I guess there's not a one of us but would like to pick up a few dropped stitches," the kind voice answered as the needles clicked on in the gathering twilight. "No, you're not the first to wish you could make over the past, and you won't be the last, if that's any comfort. But I say, never put the past between yourself and the future. If Henry loves you and you love him, that's for you both to decide."

"Oh, madame, your life has been sweet and good and beautiful with no dark places to mar it. I can see that, and so perhaps you do not know what evil things the world can say and think. Suppose, for argument's sake, that I had committed grave wrong. Would you wish your son to marry such a woman then?"

"I'd rather see a son of mine married to a woman that loved him——" The needles stayed poised in stillness before the voice went on in soft conviction: "Yes, I'd rather he did, even if she might have fallen from grace, than to have him marry without love. There, don't you ever press me so hard again, and never let Mr. Field hear me say such a thing. It's heresy, maybe, but women know some things that men can never fathom for all their learning."

Mary Elizabeth came in just then, and their conversation ended. After she had set an oil lamp on the table, she brought a large Bible which she laid in readiness.

"Father and Henry are through in the garden," she told her mother. "They're washing up in the kitchen and will be ready for prayers in a few minutes."

Presently the two men and the young household helper appeared and took their places about the table. Mrs. Field laid down her work and joined them. It was absolutely still in the cool parlor, except for the fitful, sleepy calling of birds in near-by trees. The lamplight threw a warm circle about the reverent small group and a heavy sweetness from rose bushes laden with bloom came in through the open windows.

"Let us turn to the Book of Proverbs for our evening lesson." The Reverend David Dudley Field took up the Bible and began to turn its worn leaves. Deep and compelling as the tones of a bell, his voice reached out to the farthest corners of that quiet room.

"Who can find a virtuous woman? for her price is far above rubies. The heart of her husband doth safely trust in her, so that he shall have no need of spoil. She will do him good and not evil all the days of her life. She seeketh wool, and flax, and worketh willingly with her hands. She is like the merchants' ships; she bringeth her food from afar. She riseth also while it is yet night, and giveth meat to her household . . ."

Henriette kept her eyes fixed on the folded hands in her lap. She dared not raise them to the face of the preacher, or to Henry, whose look would have been too hopeful for her to bear. She could only listen with the blood throbbing at her temples, knowing that she had been singled out for this particular challenge.

"With the fruit of her hands she planteth a vineyard . . ." The words continued. *"Her candle goeth not out by night. She layeth her hands to the spindle, and her hands hold the distaff. She stretcheth out her hand to the poor; yea, she reacheth forth her hands to the needy. She is not afraid of the snow for her household . . ."*

A great gray-green moth fluttered close to the lamp. But the voice did not falter. Henriette looked up and saw the hand that brushed it away. In the light that long forefinger made her think of those solemnly pointing New England steeples. She was struck by the resemblance.

"Her husband is known in the gates, when he sitteth among the elders of the land. . . . Strength and honour are her clothing; and she shall rejoice in time to come. She openeth her mouth with wisdom; and in her tongue is the law of kindness. She looketh well to the ways of her household, and eateth not the bread of idleness. Her children shall arise up, and call her blessed; her husband also, and he praiseth her. Many daughters have done virtuously, but thou excellest them all. Favour is deceitful, and beauty is vain: but a woman that feareth the Lord, she shall be praised. Give her of the fruit of her hands; and let her own works praise her in the gates."

Long after prayers were over and they had gone their separate ways for the night, Henriette lay in the darkness, hearing the echo of those verses from Proverbs. They mingled strangely with the faint guttural

of frogs in some far meadow and the chirping of crickets like summer's own throbbing pulse. Yes, she knew why Henry's father had
chosen that passage. She and he understood each other all too well,
though gulfs of age and tradition and different beliefs separated them.

"Search your heart, O strange woman," were the words he had been
asking her, "and see if you can do all this for my son."

The Star of Christmas

FRANKINCENSE AND MYRRH
WE, TOO, ARE BIDDEN
EVEN TO JUDAS

Heywood Broun

In his syndicated newspaper column Heywood Broun created many vignettes of lasting value. The three which follow reveal his deep and joyous feeling for the spirit of Christmas.

FRANKINCENSE AND MYRRH

ONCE there were three kings in the East and they were wise men. They read the heavens and they saw a certain strange star by which they knew that in a distant land the King of the world was to be born. The star beckoned to them and they made preparations for a long journey.

From their palaces they gathered rich gifts, gold and frankincense and myrrh. Great sacks of precious stuffs were loaded upon the backs of the camels which were to bear them on their journey. Everything was in readiness, but one of the wise men seemed perplexed and would not come at once to join his two companions, who were eager and impatient to be on their way in the direction indicated by the star.

They were old, these two kings, and the other wise man was young. When they asked him he could not tell why he waited. He knew that his treasuries had been ransacked for rich gifts for the King of Kings. It seemed that there was nothing more which he could give, and yet he was not content.

He made no answer to the old men who shouted to him that the time had come. The camels were impatient and swayed and snarled. The shadows across the desert grew longer. And still the young king sat and thought deeply.

At length he smiled, and he ordered his servants to open the great treasure sack upon the back of the first of his camels. Then he went into a high chamber to which he had not been since he was a child. He rummaged about and presently came out and approached the caravan. In his hand he carried something which glinted in the sun.

The kings thought that he bore some new gift more rare and precious than any which they had been able to find in all their treasure rooms. They bent down to see, and even the camel drivers peered from the backs of the great beasts to find out what it was which gleamed in the sun. They were curious about this last gift for which all the caravan had waited.

And the young king took a toy from his hand and placed it upon the sand. It was a dog of tin, painted white and speckled with black spots. Great patches of paint had worn away and left the metal clear, and that was why the toy shone in the sun as if it had been silver.

The youngest of the wise men turned a key in the side of the little black and white dog and then he stepped aside so that the kings and the camel drivers could see. The dog leaped high in the air and turned a somersault. He turned another and another and then fell over upon his side and lay there with a set and painted grin upon his face.

A child, the son of a camel driver, laughed and clapped his hands, but the kings were stern. They rebuked the youngest of the wise men and he paid no attention but called to his chief servant to make the first of all the camels kneel. Then he picked up the toy of tin and, opening the treasure sack, placed his last gift with his own hands in the mouth of the sack so that it rested safely upon the soft bags of incense.

"What folly has seized you?" cried the eldest of the wise men. "Is this a gift to bear to the King of Kings in the far country?"

And the young man answered and said: "For the King of Kings there are gifts of great richness, gold and frankincense and myrrh.

"But this," he said, "is for the child in Bethlehem!"

WE, TOO, ARE BIDDEN

THE ANGEL of the Lord said to the shepherds, "And this shall be a sign unto you: Ye shall find the babe wrapped in swaddling clothes, lying in a manger."

They made haste to go to Bethlehem to see the thing which had come to pass. "For unto you," the angel said, "is born this day in the city of David a Saviour, which is Christ the Lord."

But as they journeyed to Bethlehem they fell into a discussion as to just how they should find the place where the infant lay. The shepherds were not folk familiar with the town, even though it lay a short journey from the fields in which they tended their flocks. Besides, they knew that many from the country roundabout had gone to Bethlehem in compliance with the decree of Caesar Augustus that all the world should be taxed. Indeed, one of the group grumbled, "In Bethlehem there be many mangers, and how are we to find the one?"

And the youngest shepherd said, "It will be made known to us."

The night was bright with stars and the way more easy than they had expected. In spite of the late hour many walked in the narrow streets of Bethlehem, and from all the houses there came a clatter. The shepherds stood for a moment in some perplexity as to the appointed place. The noises of the town were confusing to men who had been standing silent under starlight.

And suddenly the volume of voices increased, and down the street there came a caravan of camels. Upon the backs of the beasts sat great bearded men, and with them they brought sacks of precious stuffs and huge treasure chests from distant kingdoms. The air was filled with the pungent tang of spice and perfume.

The startled shepherds stood against the wall to let the cavalcade of the mighty pass by. And these wise men and kings seemed to have no doubt as to their destination. They swept past the inn and dismounted at the door of a stable. Servants took the burdens from the backs of the camels, and the kings and the wise men stooped and went in through the low door of the stable.

"It is there the child lies in the manger," said one of the shepherds and made as if to follow, but his fellows were abashed and said among themselves, "It is not meet that we should crowd in upon the heels of the mighty."

"We, too, are bidden," insisted the youngest shepherd. "For us, as well, there was the voice of the angel of the Lord."

And timidly the men from the fields followed after and found places near the door. They watched as the men from distant countries came and silently placed their gifts at the foot of the manger where the child lay sleeping. And the shepherds stood aside and let the great of the earth go out into the night to take up again their long journey.

Presently they were alone, but as they had no gifts to lay beside the gold and frankincense they turned to go back to their flocks. But Mary, the mother, made a sign to the youngest shepherd to come closer. And he said, "We are shepherds, and we have come suddenly from the fields whence an angel summoned us. There is naught which we could add to the gifts of wise men and of kings."

Mary replied, "Before the throne of God, who is a king and who is a wise man, you have brought with you a gift more precious than all the others. It lies within your heart."

And suddenly it was made known to the shepherd the meaning of the words of Mary. He knelt at the foot of the manger and gave to the child his prayer of joy and of devotion.

EVEN TO JUDAS

"Last night before I went to sleep, I chanced to read in an evening paper a story by a columnist which appealed to me so much as a Christmas sermon that I am going to read to you from it. Here is his parable."

We were sitting in a high room above the chapel and although it was Christmas Eve my good friend the dominie seemed curiously troubled. And that was strange, for he was a man extremely sensitive to the festivities of his faith.

The joys and sorrows of Jesus were not to him events of a remote past but more current and living happenings than the headlines in the newspapers. At Christmas he seems actually to hear the voice of the herald angels.

My friend is an old man, and I have known him for many years, but this was the first time the Nativity failed to rouse him to an ecstasy. He admitted to me something was wrong. "Tomorrow," he said, "I must go down into that chapel and preach a Christmas sermon. And I must speak of peace and good-will toward men. I know you think of me as a man too cloistered to be of any use to my community. And I know that our world is one of war and hate and enmity. And you, my young friend, and others keep insisting that before there can be brotherhood there must be the bashing of heads. You are all for good-will to men, but you want to note very many exceptions. And I am still hoping and praying that in the great love of God the final seal of interdiction must not be put on even one. You may laugh at me, but right now I am wondering about how Christmas came to Judas Iscariot."

It is the habit of my friend, when he is troubled by doubts, to reach for the Book, and he did so now. He smiled and said, "Will you assist me in a little experiment? I will close my eyes and you hold out the Bible to me. I will open it at random and run my fingers down a page. You read me the text which I blindly select."

I did as he told me and he happened on the twenty-sixth chapter of St. Matthew and the twenty-fifth verse. I felt sorry for him, for this was no part of the story of the birth of Christ but instead an account of the great betrayal.

"Read what it says," commanded the dominie. And I read: "Then Judas, which betrayed Him, answered and said, 'Master, is it I?' He said unto him, 'Thou hast said.' "

My friend frowned, but then he looked at me in triumph. "My hand is not as steady as it used to be. You should have taken the lower part of my finger and not the top. Read the twenty-seventh verse. It is not an eighth of an inch away. Read what it says." And I read, "And He took the cup, and gave thanks, and gave it to them, saying, 'Drink ye all of it.' "

"Mark that," cried the old man exultantly. "Not even to Judas, the betrayer, was the wine of life denied. I can preach my Christmas sermon now, and my text will be 'Drink ye all of it.' Good-will toward men means good-will to every last son of God. Peace on earth means peace to Pilate, peace to the thieves on the cross, and peace to poor Iscariot."

I was glad, for he had found Christmas and I saw by his face that once more he heard the voice of the herald angels.

LITTLE AND UNKNOWN

Elsie Singmaster

~~~~~~

A collection of Elsie Singmaster's delightful stories about the Shindledecker sisters has been drawn together for *Bred in the Bone*. A memorable Christmas gift in "Little and Unknown" fulfills the heart's desire of two lonely old women.

. . . PHILIP HERR who stopped each morning for the Shindledeckers' milk arrived exactly with the sunrise. Five objects waited for him at the gate, the two sisters, the dog, the cat and the milk can. He was a good-natured man who did many favors for his friends and Tilly was prepared to meet him when he brought Betsey home and present him with a jar of canned cherries and a plate of doughnuts.

Betsey sighed before and after she stepped into the wagon; before with regret because she must leave Tilly, and after with joy because she was going to drive under the wide sky and ride in the trolley car and see the streets of Lanesville and go up and down the busy market and talk to Mahala and other acquaintances.

"Good-bye once more!" she cried. "Keep the door locked and the dog by you!"

Herr joked about the tight fit that he and Betsey made on the seat of the wagon.

"Now Tilly and I would fit better. Why doesn't Tilly go?"

"She's crowd-shy," explained Betsey. "When she sees people she gets all queer. She always was that way."

Herr was not talkative and he left Betsey to her own pleasant thoughts. She watched the sun climbing up the bright sky, she breathed in the fresh air, she observed the abundance of the crops, the height of the corn, the luxuriance of the tobacco. At the tobacco she shook her head sadly; it was hard to make allowance for this particular weakness of mankind, by which even the plain people grew rich. As they went on, the trees disappeared; there were no beautiful primeval groves like that back of the Shindledecker house and only a few large single trees; every foot of soil was made to work.

As the trolley car bore down upon her Betsey grew nervous, but seeing a number of plain bonnets, she concluded that she could do what others could, and climbed aboard. In the car were representatives of the sects which she and Tilly had discussed, elderly Mennonite women dressed like herself, Mennonite men with bearded chins and flat round hats, rosy-cheeked Dunkers with taller hats and equally plain clothes, Amish people in similar garb and with little children dressed exactly like themselves. All the adults carried baskets and Betsey's horseradish added a new odor to an atmosphere already perfumed with fresh bread and spices and sweet flowers. There were other odors not quite so pleasant; a trained nose would have detected cup-cheese and sauerkraut.

The car ambled slowly across the fertile plain and through several villages and at last reached the outskirts of Lanesville, a city of about seventy thousand. In the morning sunshine even the brick houses set singly and in blocks lost their homeliness. Young trees had been planted to take the place of magnificent growth cut ruthlessly away, and there were well-tended gardens. Passengers were still entering and Betsey took her basket on her lap in order to allow a slender girl in worldly clothes to sit beside her.

"Move a little over," she urged hospitably. "You don't have all your share."

"I have enough," answered the stranger.

Her appearance shocked Betsey. It was not her bobbed and golden hair—that was hidden under her hat—but her excessive slenderness, her excessively red lips, and a distressed expression in her unnaturally large eyes. Her voice was weak and it sounded frightened. Betsey was shy, but she was even more sympathetic than shy.

"Don't you feel so good?" she asked kindly.

"Not so very," confessed the girl.

"Have you a fever?"

"No, I guess not."

There was a blue shade about her mouth and a slight unnaturalness about her body which would have diagnosed her case for a more experienced eye than Betsey's. Suddenly she began to talk rapidly and to twist her hands together.

"It's my husband that's so bad."

"Your husband! Are you married?"

"I've been married three years."

"Such a little thing, married!"

"He's sick and he's had to give up work. He's in a poolroom and they won't keep his place for him."

Betsey did not know what a poolroom was, but she could guess what it might mean to lose one's place.

"*Ach,* that's too bad!"

"I came out here to see this doctor."

"This powwow doctor?" Betsey spoke gravely. The powwow doctor of whom even Betsey knew, an ignorant woman who laid on hands and pronounced sacrilegious sentences, had hundreds of patients. "Could she powwow for your husband when he's not along?"

"She told me what to do for him and she powwowed for me. I must go back to my work again."

"What is your work?"

"I manicure."

"I don't know what that is," confessed Betsey.

"I treat the hands."

"A sort of doctor?"

"You could call it that."

Moved by pity, Betsey did suddenly an inconsidered, uncharacteristic and incredible thing.

"What you need is to eat," she declared. "You come to us once and spend a day. Come in the early trolley and get off at Dan Webber's creamery. There Herr is always with our milk can. We have plenty of milk and plenty of good pie. We are great believers in pie." The girl rose and Betsey seized her by the arm. She saw the poor, thin creature sitting at the table and heard herself saying, "*Ach,* a little more! Just a little more!" She repeated the explicit directions. "Shindledecker is my name, remember, Betsey Shindledecker. We have a dog, but you don't need to be afraid. Herr will holler to us from the gate."

The girl looked at her as at a prodigy, half admiring, half distrusting.

"Remember!" said Betsey.

Betsey was going through the streets of Lanesville and up and down the aisles of the market, not in reality, but in recollection, and Tilly sat opposite her on the settle, enchanted. Betsey was tired but she slipped off her shoes and propped up her feet on the rung of a chair and talked on and on. Her gray shawl and stiff bonnet lay across the settle; beside them stood her basket filled with small cucumbers and heads of cauliflower. Outside there was darkness and the tang of frost, but inside all was bright and warm. Tilly's eyes remained fixed on her sister's face; to be alone for one day was enough for Tilly.

"What people I saw!" said Betsey. "Plain people and fancy people and young and old and fat and thin. I first went to the curb market, to see how it was. My, it was nice! Beans and corn and potatoes and red beets and tomatoes and cakes and pies and chickens and cup-cheese and peaches and plums and pears and sauerkraut and flowers—such flowers I don't believe it gives anywhere else in the world.

"There I saw old friends. Sallie Eshelman was at her stall. You wouldn't believe how fat she is, Tilly. She's yet such a talker, almost all about eating, what her man likes to eat and what her children like to eat. It's not necessary for her to say what she likes to eat; she eats everything she can lay hands on, I bet. She told me about a big funeral and that too was about eating. She said it was a good funeral but they didn't have enough milk in the mashed potatoes."

Tilly uttered a disapproving snort, unwilling to interrupt the recital by a word.

"It stood a Yankee woman by me who asked how we should cook this and how we should cook that. She said to the butcher, 'Do we boil this meat or fry it?' and all the time it was pork roast she bought. You can hardly believe such a thing. She wasn't such a young one, either.

"Then I went to the indoor market, to Ebersole's stall. Mahala wasn't there, but her boy was. He's the beardiest Amishman you ever saw, Tilly, though he's good-looking too. His hair is long like they have it and his beard is thick and curly, but he can't be over nineteen. Mahala don't come often any more; he says she's so fleshy. He's not much for talking; he takes after his Pop, surely not after Mahala. The horseradish went like wildfire."

"It is wildfire," put in Tilly, sniffing reminiscently.

"It was all sold till I made the rounds, and then I got the cauliflower and the little pickles. I think he's more settled than he was; his eyes didn't roam so like last year. I think he was looking at the girls; now perhaps he's picked one out.

"Such stuff, Tilly! Hooked rugs and braided rugs, and a live gander with a bag over him, and paper flowers and old quilts—it's wonderful what the English people will pay for trash—and dried corn and greens —you couldn't say all the things in a day.

"Here I met poor Zinn, and I said to him 'How are you? I guess you

have by this time a house full of little ones,' and he began to cry, Tilly
—what do you think of that? He said, 'She won't have children.' Just
that way he said it, right out. 'She won't have children.' He said she was
of the world's people, she cared only for vanity."

Without warning and to the inexpressible amazement of Betsey,
Tilly burst into tears.

"What ails you?" asked Betsey in deep concern.

"I was all day alone and I had long thoughts. I thought again what
would become of all our nice things. I thought of Mom's washbowl with
the little birds on the edge for holding the soap and I thought of our
blue glass pitchers and other glass things and I said to myself, 'What
will we do?'."

"We're yet here, both of us," said Betsey. "And the Lord will take
care of those things like he always took care of us."

"It's so," said Tilly, trying to check her tears.

Betsey changed to a more cheerful subject.

"You'll be surprised to hear that I've invited company to see us."

"I hope not Eleazar Herr who wanted us to believe that the end of
the world was coming, nor that Cora woman that wanted to buy our
things," said Tilly, trying to smile.

"No, none of those people. This is a stranger that sat along with me
in the trolley and told me her troubles. She looks about sixteen years
old, but she's married already three years. Her man has something to
do with swimming, and he's sick."

"He might well be, swimming in this cool weather!"

"Yes, he's sick and they put him out of his place, and now she must
earn the living. She's herself a sort of hand-doctor, if you know what
that is. She had been to the powwower for him and her, and she had
faith."

"A lot of good it will do her to have faith in the powwower!"

"What she needs is eating. So I told her to come out once and we
would give her milk and also pie. It wondered me if she ever got anything good and solid."

"When will she come?" Tilly's tears were quite dry.

"I don't know; perhaps she can't come right away on account of her
work. I saw yet many other people—there was Thomas Bashore from
the mountain—my, but he's a fine, unworldly man! I saw William
Hershey—he had already this year's *schnitz* to sell, and I saw a fire
engine going out practicing, and autos and autos and autos. It's surely
wonderful what one can see."

"You don't think this young woman might come to-morrow?" asked Tilly.

"I don't believe she could get off, week-days."

"Then Sunday? Perhaps she could come early and go with us to meeting."

"Perhaps." Betsey rose and stretched her arms; then she began to unpack her basket. "Let us call this a day," she said wearily.

It was Thanksgiving evening and the odor of turkey and mince pie lingered in the Shindledecker kitchen. The Improved New Mennonites did not believe in elaborate celebration of holidays, but on Thanksgiving and Christmas they feasted. The sun had not been visible all day and now there was a gentle but ominous tinkle against the window. Winter was apparently beginning at last and that with a hailstorm.

Betsey sat in her armchair sewing and Tilly watched her hungrily. When Betsey finished joining long strips of woolen material, Tilly would braid them. She was not allowed to do any finer work and very little of any sort lest she lose what vision remained. She sat awhile on the settle, then she walked to the window, then she tried a rocking chair, then she came back to the settle. The cat followed her with his sleepy eyes; he had ceased to jump into her lap, because he frequently had to jump out in two seconds, and she resented his desertion though she was responsible for it. The dog lay on his rug by the stove; now and then he opened one beautiful eye and looked at Betsey.

Betsey talked on and on placidly, thinking it best to pay no attention to Tilly's nervous state. Her own inner being was nervous also; she had cheerfully and tenderly suffered many things since Tilly had had to lay down her needle.

"We often wished we had a new vegetable," said Betsey. "I heard of one, called okra. Is not that a queer name? You put it in soup. I thought in spring we would plant some where we had the spinach last year. We're not much for spinach; we're more for boiled dandelion."

Tilly made no answer.

"I was thinking of an old story I once heard." How Betsey racked her brain for old stories! How she wished that it was not sinful to invent stories! "It was that one about when Sarah Fleisher and little Peter Eicholtz were baptized. Do you remember that, Tilly?"

"How should I not?" asked Tilly impatiently. "You told it only a few weeks ago."

Tilly moved from the settle to the window and Betsey cast after her a despairing glance.

"Shall I read?"

"No, thank you. I'm too nervous; it seems as though everything in me were going round and round. I wonder how that young woman's poor man is."

"I guess he's better by this time," said Betsey. The young woman had not come, and her failure to appear preyed on Tilly's mind. Betsey tried to distract her attention. "I dreamed the other night I was married and living far away and I fought my way home through snow. It was a bad dream. I came down William Hershey's road and I met Thomas Bashore, and he said to me, 'Run, run!' but why I don't know. I thought someone was after me with the axe. My! I was glad when I got home and was not married!"

"I would like to have little ones like William Hershey's," said Tilly. "I wouldn't care how I got them."

Betsey found something shocking in this remark. She bent her head closely over her sewing while Tilly seated herself in the rocking chair. It could not be that Tilly was losing her mind!

"You can begin to braid any time," she said brightly.

"Why should I? I can't braid anyhow more than an hour." Tilly's voice grew scornful. "I think that strange young woman fooled you, Betsey. What work could a man have with swimming in winter? And what doctoring could a woman do for the hand? You might be a doctor for the foot, but the hand gets no wear and tear. She never meant to come. Pie!" Intense mockery lengthened the word indefinitely. "She was baffling you. Pie! What did she care for pie? Or milk? I'll bet she drinks something stronger than milk, law or no law. Perhaps she's for liquor like those who take trucks through at night. Perhaps that's the sort of work her husband has. Perhaps——"

Her scornful invention failing, Tilly moved over to the settle and took her place in the corner, while Betsey racked her brain for some subject which was interesting and not irritating.

"Tilly," she said at last. "Would you like to sing?"

Tilly's eyes brightened and Betsey did not observe that their gleam was wicked.

"Yes," she said. "I'll sing."

Betsey reached for the hymnbook which lay near her on the window sill. It contained five hundred hymns—what a deep well to draw from! Strangers found it a curious book, printed as it was with differently shaped notes, a triangle for *g,* a diamond for *b,* and so forth. Betsey's heart danced with happiness; there was nothing like singing to promote contentment.

"What shall we sing?"

Tilly had not waited for the hymnal; Tilly had begun. She did not sing "In the Sweet By and By," or "We're Marching to Zion," or, "Oh, to Be Over Yonder"; she sang a shocking verse.

> *"Zu Lauterbach hab' ich mein' Strumpf verlor'n*
> *Und ohne Strumpf geh' ich nicht heim,*
> *Drum kehr' ich wieder nach Lauterbach hin*
> *Und kauf' mir ein' Strumpf für mein Bein."*

"Tilly!" protested Betsey.

Tilly sang the song a second time. Roughly translated, it meant, "In Lauterbach I lost my stocking and without my stocking I won't go home. So back I'll go to Lauterbach and buy one for my leg."

"Where did you learn such a song?"

"Ach, that I knew from my childhood, and you too." Tilly's tone was insolent. "If it hadn't been that that young Yankee was all the time baffling you, she might 'a' come out once and spent the night and we could 'a' sung for her."

"Let's sing Number Thirty-six," proposed Betsey, turning tremulously from page to page. Number Thirty-six was "My Soul, Be on Thy Guard" to the tune Laban. No one ever needed the stirring admonition more than Tilly at this moment.

"No," said Tilly. "I have another song. I heard men singing it back in the woods, and it goes,

> *"There's a hole in the bottom of the sea,*
> *There's a hole in the bottom of the sea,*
> *There's a hole in the bottom of the sea,*
> *There's a hole in the bottom of the sea."*

"That's the Sweet By and By tune!" cried Betsey, scandalized. "Don't, Tilly!"

"There's the chorus to it yet," said Tilly. She sang so wildly and loudly that the dog gave a yelp and the cat leaped to the mantel. "It says,

> *"Fill the hole,*
> *Fill the hole,*
> *There's a hole in the bottom of the sea.*

Fill the hole,
Fill the hole,
There's a hole in the bottom of the sea."

Betsey closed her hymnal and lifted her sewing, in every motion the dignity of one who has done all and, doing all, has failed.

"I'm going to bed," announced Tilly.

"Yes, well," said Betsey, still composed and unresentful.

Listening to the footsteps above, she sewed on. When she heard the ropes of the bed creak, she put her sewing down and laid her head on her folded arms. The sleet had grown heavier and was driven by a stronger wind. The ropes of the bed ceased to creak, the uneasy cat returned to his throne, there was no sound but the sharp tap, tap on the window, like a thin hand rapping.

After a long time, startled by a touch upon her knee, Betsey lifted her head with a jerk. The Airedale dog had crossed the room and placed himself beside her, his short tail in rapid motion. Betsey smiled at him and, placing a hand on either side of his long jaws, looked deep into his eyes. She believed for an instant that their wistfulness was intelligent, then she shook her head and, rising ponderously, went about her bedtime tasks.

The Shindledeckers sat together in their kitchen. It was a clear, still Christmas Eve, moonless, but bright with stars. Tilly was idle from necessity, Betsey because industry seemed inappropriate to this holy time. They observed the occasion in no other way; the trimming of a tree was a worldly ceremony and they had never believed that Santa Claus came down the chimney. The boys who went from door to door masked and playing Belsnickel did not leave the distant village lights, and this evening was certain to be like any other quiet evening.

Betsey talked slowly and steadily and Tilly answered politely. Tilly had grown quieter; but when Betsey stared into the fire, the better to shape the thought she wished to express, a desperate look came into Tilly's half-darkened eyes.

"We have everything, pretty near." Betsey's voice was placid, yet a keen observer would have caught here also a discordant undertone. "We have our good solid house and our nice field and our woods. Even if we should never get us any more clothes we would still have enough till—till"—Tilly looked up sharply. Was Betsey going to begin again about dying?—"for a couple o' years yet anyhow.

"We have"—Betsey found it necessary to take a long breath—"we have it good compared with many. Think how poor Job Sharretts was murdered on the mountain, and think how Calvin Weikert was took up for it. Think——"

The temptation to be sardonic was too much for Tilly.

"You think we ought to be thankful no one ever wanted to murder us, and we never wanted to murder anybody?"

"We ought to be thankful for everything that's good," answered Betsey. "There's poor Thomas Bashore whose wife went off and is now with her worldly people."

"You have right," agreed Tilly. "I'm glad my husband has not gone from me to live with worldly people."

"And there was that Cora woman who came to buy our old things—how restless! Her eyes went round and round; it was plain she had found no peace."

Tilly regarded her sister with an unmistakable glare, not directed at her personally, but at her sentimental ideas.

"We have God," declared Betsey defiantly. "And our meeting, and each other, and this nice home and our dog and our cat and——"

The dog lifted his head and grinned. Tilly grinned also with exactly the same expression, at once wise and silly, intelligent and blank. She began to talk, now with frantic eagerness, now with a slow drawl, now as if mocking herself. She changed her seat from the settle to the rocking chair and flung herself back and forth, the black ties of her coif dancing in the breeze created by her motions. She expressed no light sudden wish, but a passionate longing, old as her maturity.

"If we had a little girl between us we could bring her up right. She could sit on the low stool and make patchwork and when she was done she could play with the cat and the dog. I'd like to bring up a little girl, not to be worldly, but to be plain, to be 'little and unknown, loved by God alone,' as it says on the towel. I would teach her to quilt. Nobody quilts right any more. No!" Tilly interrupted herself. "You would have to teach her to quilt. She could go to meeting and play in the cemetery with William Hershey's little ones. Perhaps she could someday marry one of those little boys. I would not want her to stay single like us. I could teach her cooking, funnel cakes and pie, and soap-making and everything else. I would make her an accomplished child, not such a *shussle* like some. I would——"

"You would what?" asked Betsey. Tilly had shown no such interest in anything for weeks—this was the old Tilly.

Tilly lay back in her chair, exhausted by her ardor.

"Nothing," she said wearily. She mocked herself again, tapping herself on the forehead. "I have one rafter too few in my little house."

Again Betsey was alarmed. A deep though vague discomfort in her own breast had terrified her for weeks. Could it be that both she and Tilly were growing strange? Surely God would not visit them with so terrible an affliction after their quiet, devout lives! As though the evil she dreaded were taking corporeal shape, she heard a creeping, stealthy step. Was the door locked? Happily she could see from where she sat the bolt secure in the hasp.

She looked at Tilly but Tilly was watching the dog. He had lifted his head and now he got to his feet with motions so careful and slow that he made no sound. He went quietly with a feline swing of his body toward the door and stood with his ears cocked.

"I heard someone walking," whispered Tilly. She looked up at the clock—it was half-past seven. "Who can it be at this late hour?"

"Nobody," answered Betsey nervously. "Come back, Whiskey, and lay down." The cat uttered a low miaow. "And you be quiet."

There was suddenly a loud knock.

"Boys playing a joke on us," guessed Betsey.

"Or perhaps Cora come back with her man and her big wagon to fetch our things."

Betsey half rose from her chair.

"I'll ask them through the door what they want."

There was a louder knock. Tilly seized Betsey by the arm.

"It might be liquor people. They know we don't sympathize with them. Let's turn out the light and go upstairs! Let's——"

Tilly's voice trailed away, her jaw dropped and the skin of her cheeks quivered. From outside came a strange, small smothered cry.

"What is it?" said Betsey hoarsely.

Madness was upon poor Tilly; she leaped from her chair and began tugging at the heavy bolt.

"Are you going to open?" shrieked Betsey.

"To be sure I'm going to open!" Tilly's trembling hands succeeded in their endeavor, the bolt slid back and she opened the door, not gingerly or carefully, keeping her foot against it and putting her eye to the crack, but wide. Without stood a shrewd, sober-looking woman with a bundle in her arms. It was from the bundle that the cry came.

"Are you Betsey Shindledecker?" asked the stranger.

"Yes," said Betsey and Tilly with one voice.

The stranger looked from one to the other.

"Which is Betsey?"

"I am," answered Betsey.

Tilly stepped back, her intent eyes now on the bundle, now on Betsey, in a glance which was not good to see.

"Come in," invited Betsey.

The stranger went directly to the settle. She handled the bundle briskly and expertly, laying it on her knees and beginning to unroll the voluminous wrappings.

"It was here when I started," she said pleasantly. Her keen eyes traveled from one object to another; she saw the beautiful old pieces of furniture and glass and china, the well-fed dog and cat. The dog watched her with profound interest and the cat's eyes gleamed. She saw the broad bosom and the kind arms of Betsey; at Tilly shrinking back into the shadow she did not seem to look.

At last, reaching the core of her bundle, she slid forward so that the light shone full upon it.

"There!" she cried. "What do you think of that?"

The dog took a step nearer, the cat rose and arched his back, Betsey sat down on the settle and leaned forward. The face of Tilly, pale and bright-eyed, peered from the shadows like a mask hung on a wall. She meant to ask a question, but only her lips shaped the words, no breath made them audible. The question was, "Is it a little girl?"

Betsey looked at the woman and reckoned her age.

"Whose is this dear child?"

"Yours," answered the brisk voice.

"Mine!" said Betsey with a start.

The stranger was very clever; she did not answer at once, but occupied herself with straightening the baby's clothes and lifting it to her shoulder. Its tiny head sank into the hollow of her neck, its mouth curved suddenly and its blue eyes opened.

"Yours," she said at last. "A young woman died in the Lanesville hospital last week, a widow, without friends. She said she was acquainted with you and she wanted us to ask you whether you would take her baby. She said she was to visit you, but her husband had died and she had had too much sickness and trouble."

Betsey and Tilly looked at each other.

"See!" cried Betsey. "She would have come if she could! She was no Yankee and no baffler!"

"She was a good, hard-working little thing," went on the stranger.

"There was nothing wrong with her or her husband except misfortune. They were entirely without friends. This is a lovely baby—would you be willing to keep her for a little while and see whether you liked her? This would be a home such as any child might be glad to have, and she would make you happy."

There was a long silence, then the woman addressed the shadows in the corner of the room. She understood the existence of strange subtleties in human character and human relations and she wished to make no mistake.

"Come see her!"

Tilly's step lagged, not with unwillingness but with weakness. She sat down beside the settle in the rocking chair which she had a little while ago swung back and forth in rage. Then the strange woman made a mistake in spite of her shrewdness; she handed the baby toward its legal inheritor.

"Do you want her?"

Betsey did not take the baby; she leaned back and folded her arms, pressing them tight against her throbbing heart.

"Tilly will have to decide," said she coolly. "If she says to take her I'm willing."

"I would have to tend her most of the time," stipulated Tilly hoarsely. "That would have to be understood. You have good eyes, and you could sew for her, but I would have to tend her and prepare her food and hold her."

"Fix it any way you like." Betsey's tone was level and constrained, as though she feared to disturb a quivering needle settling to the pole.

"Well, then," consented Tilly. "I'm willing."

Outside the closed door, the stranger stood still. She said that she would visit the sisters and their charge regularly, but she did not believe they heard a word. She could see nothing inside the house—the Shindledeckers curtained their windows closely—but she could hear. It must be the thin sister who was speaking.

"How ashamed I am of the way I have acted before you and God, Betsey! We can get her baptized when she's old enough and we can train her to be 'little and unknown, loved by God alone,' as it says on the towel. We can teach her everything it is needful to know. She can sit on the little stool that we sat on and she can wash her hands at the brown bowl with the doves on the edge and she can have our things."

There was silence except for the creaking of a rocking chair, then a little whimper.

"Let's sing for her," suggested the same voice.

The hole in the bottom of the sea was apparently filled; Tilly returned to the original words, and Betsey joined with her deep alto.

> *"In the sweet by and by,*
> *We shall meet on the beautiful shore;*
> *In the sweet by and by,*
> *We shall meet on the beautiful shore."*

The stranger went down the path. Seated in her little car, beside a broad basket, empty of all but a blanket, she looked up at the stars, then far away to where the horizon glowed faintly above Lanesville, then back at the dim house, almost lost against the thick grove. She looked at it a long time, her eyes piercing the walls, her ears listening to the song. The tune had changed; the sisters were singing "Holy Night, Silent Night."

"What happiness!" said the stranger, as, smiling soberly, she drove away.

A DAY OF PLEASANT BREAD

David Grayson

~~~~~~

Rediscovering that the rich as well as the poor often need to be included in our hearts at Christmas time, David Grayson here mirrors the joys and pleasures of a simple homespun life.

THEY HAVE all gone now, and the house is very still. For the first time this evening I can hear the familiar sound of the December wind blustering about the house, complaining at closed doorways, asking questions at the shutters; but here in my room, under the green reading lamp, it is warm and still. Although Harriet has closed the doors, covered the coals in the fireplace, and said good-night, the atmosphere still seems to tingle with the electricity of genial humanity.

The parting voice of the Scotch Preacher still booms in my ears:

"This," said he, as he was going out of our door, wrapped like an Arctic highlander in cloaks and tippets, "has been a day of pleasant bread."

One of the very pleasantest I can remember!

I sometimes think we expect too much of Christmas Day. We try to crowd into it the long arrears of kindliness and humanity of the whole year. As for me, I like to take my Christmas a little at a time, all through the year. And thus I drift along into the holidays—let them overtake me unexpectedly—waking up some fine morning and suddenly saying to myself:

"Why, this is Christmas Day!"

How the discovery makes one bound out of his bed! What a new sense of life and adventure it imparts! Almost anything may happen on a day like this—one thinks. I may meet friends I have not seen before in years. Who knows? I may discover that this is a far better and kindlier world than I had ever dreamed it could be.

So I sing out to Harriet as I go down:

"Merry Christmas, Harriet"—and not waiting for her sleepy reply, I go down and build the biggest, warmest, friendliest fire of the year. Then I get into my thick coat and mittens and open the back door. All around the sill, deep on the step, and all about the yard lies the drifted snow: it has transformed my wood pile into a grotesque Indian mound, and it frosts the roof of my barn like a wedding cake. I go at it lustily with my wooden shovel, clearing out a pathway to the gate. . . .

All the morning as I went about my chores I had a peculiar sense of expected pleasure. It seemed certain to me that something unusual and adventurous was about to happen—and if it did not happen offhand, why, I was there to make it happen! When I went in to breakfast (do you know the fragrance of broiling bacon when you have worked for an hour before breakfast on a morning of zero weather? If you do not, consider that heaven still has gifts in store for you!)—when I went in to breakfast, I fancied that Harriet looked preoccupied, but I was too busy just then (hot corn muffins) to make an inquiry, and I knew by experience that the best solvent of secrecy is patience.

"David," said Harriet presently, "the cousins can't come!"

"Can't come!" I exclaimed.

"Why, you act as if you were delighted."

"No—well, yes," I said, "I knew that some extraordinary adventure was about to happen!"

"Adventure! It's a cruel disappointment—I was all ready for them."

"Harriet," I said, "adventure is just what we make it. And aren't we to have the Scotch Preacher and his wife?"

"But I've got such a *good* dinner."

"Well," I said, "there are no two ways about it: it must be eaten! You may depend upon me to do my duty."

"We'll have to send out into the highways and compel them to come in," said Harriet ruefully.

I had several choice observations I should have liked to make upon this problem, but Harriet was plainly not listening; she sat with her eyes fixed reflectively on the coffeepot. I watched her for a moment, then I remarked:

"There aren't any."

"David," she exclaimed, "how did you know what I was thinking about?"

"I merely wanted to show you," I said, "that my genius is not properly appreciated in my own household. You thought of highways, didn't you? Then you thought of the poor; especially the poor on Christmas Day; then of Mrs. Heney, who isn't poor any more, having married John Daniels; and then I said, 'There aren't any.'"

Harriet laughed.

"It has come to a pretty pass," she said, "when there are no poor people to invite to dinner on Christmas Day."

"It's a tragedy, I'll admit," I said, "but let's be logical about it."

"I am willing," said Harriet, "to be as logical as you like."

"Then," I said, "having no poor to invite to dinner, we must necessarily try the rich. That's logical, isn't it?"

"Who?" asked Harriet, which is just like a woman. Whenever you get a good healthy argument started with her, she will suddenly short-circuit it, and want to know if you mean Mr. Smith, or Joe Perkins's boys, which I maintain is *not* logical.

"Well, there are the Starkweathers," I said.

"David!"

"They're rich, aren't they?"

"Yes, but you know how they live—what dinners they have—and besides, they probably have a houseful of company."

"Weren't you telling me the other day how many people who were really suffering were too proud to let anyone know about it? Weren't you advising the necessity of getting acquainted with people and finding out—tactfully, of course—you made a point of tact—what the trouble was?"

"But I was talking of *poor* people."

"Why shouldn't a rule that is good for poor people be equally as good for rich people? Aren't they proud?"

"Oh, you can argue," observed Harriet.

"And I can act, too," I said. "I am now going over to invite the Starkweathers. I heard a rumour that their cook has left them and I expect to find them starving in their parlour. Of course they'll be very haughty and proud, but I'll be tactful, and when I go away I'll casually leave a diamond tiara in the front hall."

"What *is* the matter with you this morning?"

"Christmas," I said.

I can't tell how pleased I was with the enterprise I had in mind: it suggested all sorts of amusing and surprising developments. Moreover, I left Harriet, finally, in the breeziest of spirits, having quite forgotten her disappointment over the non-arrival of the cousins.

"If you *should* get the Starkweathers——"

" 'In the bright lexicon of youth,' " I observed, " 'there is no such word as fail.' "

So I set off up the town road. A team or two had already been that way and had broken a track through the snow. The sun was now fully up, but the air still tingled with the electricity of zero weather. And the fields! I have seen the fields of June and the fields of October, but I think I never saw our countryside, hills and valleys, tree spaces and brook bottoms, more enchantingly beautiful than it was this morning. Snow everywhere—the fences half hidden, the bridges clogged, the trees laden: where the road was hard it squeaked under my feet, and where it was soft I strode through the drifts. And the air went to one's head like wine!

So I tramped past the Pattersons'. The old man, a grumpy old fellow, was going to the barn with a pail on his arm.

"Merry Christmas," I shouted.

He looked around at me wonderingly and did not reply. At the corners I met the Newton boys so wrapped in tippets that I could see only their eyes and the red ends of their small noses. I passed the Williams's house, where there was a cheerful smoke in the chimney and in the window a green wreath with a lively red bow. And I thought how happy everyone must be on a Christmas morning like this! At the hill bridge who should I meet but the Scotch Preacher himself, God bless him!

"Well, well, David," he exclaimed heartily, "Merry Christmas."

I drew my face down and said solemnly:

"Dr. McAlway, I am on a most serious errand."

"Why, now, what's the matter?" He was all sympathy at once.

"I am out in the highways trying to compel the poor of this neighbourhood to come to our feast."

The Scotch Preacher observed me with a twinkle in his eye.

"David," he said, putting his hand to his mouth as if to speak in my ear, "there is a poor man you will na' have to compel."

"Oh, you don't count," I said. "You're coming anyhow."

Then I told him of the errand with our millionaire friends, into the spirit of which he entered with the greatest zest. He was full of advice and much excited lest I fail to do a thoroughly competent job. For a moment I think he wanted to take the whole thing out of my hands.

"Man, man, it's a lovely thing to do," he exclaimed, "but I ha' me doots—I ha' me doots."

At parting he hesitated a moment, and with a serious face inquired:

"Is it by any chance a goose?"

"It is," I said, "a goose—a big one."

He heaved a sigh of complete satisfaction. "You have comforted my mind," he said, "with the joys of anticipation—a goose, a big goose."

So I left him and went onward toward the Starkweathers'. Presently I saw the great house standing among its wintry trees. There was smoke in the chimney but no other evidence of life. At the gate my spirits, which had been of the best all the morning, began to fail me. Though Harriet and I were well enough acquainted with the Starkweathers, yet at this late moment on Christmas morning it did seem rather a hare-brained scheme to think of inviting them to dinner.

"Never mind," I said, "they'll not be displeased to see me anyway."

I waited in the reception room, which was cold and felt damp. In the parlour beyond I could see the innumerable things of beauty—furniture, pictures, books, so very, very much of everything—with which the room was filled. I saw it now, as I had often seen it before, with a peculiar sense of weariness. How all these things, though beautiful enough in themselves, must clutter up a man's life!

Do you know, the more I look into life, the more things it seems to me I can successfully lack—and continue to grow happier. How many kinds of food I do not need, nor cooks to cook them, how much curious clothing nor tailors to make it, how many books that I never read, and pictures that are not worth while! The farther I run, the more I feel like casting aside all such impedimenta—lest I fail to arrive at the far goal of my endeavour.

I like to think of an old Japanese nobleman I once read about, who ornamented his house with a single vase at a time, living with it, absorbing its message of beauty, and when he tired of it, replacing it with another. I wonder if he had the right way, and we, with so many objects to hang on our walls, place on our shelves, drape on our chairs, and spread on our floors, have mistaken our course and placed our hearts upon the multiplicity rather than the quality of our possessions!

Presently Mr. Starkweather appeared in the doorway. He wore a velvet smoking jacket and slippers; and somehow, for a bright morning like this, he seemed old, and worn, and cold.

"Well, well, friend," he said, "I'm glad to see you."

He said it as though he meant it.

"Come into the library; it's the only room in the whole house that is comfortably warm. You've no idea what a task it is to heat a place like this in really cold weather. No sooner do I find a man who can run my furnace than he goes off and leaves me."

"I can sympathize with you," I said, "we often have trouble at our house with the man who builds the fires."

He looked around at me quizzically.

"He lies too long in bed in the morning," I said.

By this time we had arrived at the library, where a bright fire was burning in the grate. It was a fine big room, with dark oak furnishings and books in cases along one wall, but this morning it had a dishevelled and untidy look. On a little table at one side of the fireplace were the remains of a breakfast; at the other a number of wraps were thrown carelessly upon a chair. As I came in Mrs. Starkweather rose from her place, drawing a silk scarf around her shoulders. She is a robust, rather handsome woman, with many rings on her fingers, and a pair of glasses hanging to a little gold hook on her ample bosom; but this morning she, too, looked worried and old.

"Oh, yes," she said with a rueful laugh, "we're beginning a merry Christmas, as you see. Think of Christmas with no cook in the house!"

I felt as if I had discovered a gold mine. Poor starving millionaires! But Mrs. Starkweather had not told the whole of her sorrowful story.

"We had a company of friends invited for dinner to-day," she said, "and our cook was ill—or said she was—and had to go. One of the maids went with her. The man who looks after the furnace disappeared on Friday, and the stableman has been drinking. We can't very well leave the place without someone who is responsible in charge of it —and so here we are. Merry Christmas!"

I couldn't help laughing. Poor people!

"You might," I said, "apply for Mrs. Heney's place."

"Who is Mrs. Heney?" asked Mrs. Starkweather.

"You don't mean to say that you never heard of Mrs. Heney!" I exclaimed. "Mrs. Heney, who is now Mrs. 'Penny' Daniels? You've missed one of our greatest celebrities."

With that, of course, I had to tell them about Mrs. Heney, who has for years performed a most important function in this community. Alone and unaided, she has been the poor whom we are supposed to have always with us. If it had not been for the devoted faithfulness of Mrs. Heney at Thanksgiving, Christmas and other times of the year, I suppose our Woman's Aid Society and the King's Daughters would have perished miserably of undistributed turkeys and tufted comforters. For years Mrs. Heney filled the place most acceptably. Curbing the natural outpourings of a rather jovial soul, she could upon occasion look as deserving of charity as any person that ever I met. But I pitied the little Heneys: it always comes hard on the children. For weeks after every Thanksgiving and Christmas they always wore a painfully stuffed and suffocated look. I only came to appreciate fully what a self-sacrificing public servant Mrs. Heney really was when I learned that she had taken the desperate alternative of marrying "Penny" Daniels.

"So you think we might possibly aspire to the position?" laughed Mrs. Starkweather.

Upon this I told them of the trouble in our household and asked them to come down and help us enjoy Dr. McAlway and the goose.

When I left, after much more pleasant talk, they both came with me to the door seeming greatly improved in spirits.

"You've given us something to live for, Mr. Grayson," said Mrs. Starkweather.

So I walked homeward in the highest spirits, and an hour or more later who should we see in the top of our upper field but Mr. Starkweather and his wife floundering in the snow. They reached the lane literally covered from top to toe with snow and both of them ruddy with the cold.

"We walked over," said Mrs. Starkweather breathlessly, "and I haven't had so much fun in years."

Mr. Starkweather helped her over the fence. The Scotch Preacher stood on the steps to receive them, and we all went in together.

I can't pretend to describe Harriet's dinner: the gorgeous brown goose, and the apple sauce, and all the other things that best go with it, and the pumpkin pie at the end—the finest, thickest, most delicious pumpkin pie I ever ate in all my life. It melted in one's mouth and brought visions of celestial bliss. And I wish I could have a picture of Harriet presiding. I have never seen her happier, or more in her element. Every time she brought in a new dish or took off a cover it was a sort of miracle. And her coffee—but I must not and dare not elaborate.

And what great talk we had afterward!

I've known the Scotch Preacher for a long time, but I never saw him in quite such a mood of hilarity. He and Mr. Starkweather told stories of their boyhood—and we laughed, and laughed—Mrs. Starkweather the most of all. Seeing her so often in her carriage, or in the dignity of her home, I didn't think she had so much jollity in her. Finally she discovered Harriet's cabinet organ, and nothing would do but she must sing for us.

"None of the newfangled ones, Clara," cried her husband: "some of the old ones we used to know."

So she sat herself down at the organ and threw her head back and began to sing:

> *"Believe me, if all those endearing young charms,*
> *Which I gaze on so fondly to-day——"*

Mr. Starkweather jumped up and ran over to the organ and joined in with his deep voice. Harriet and I followed. The Scotch Preacher's wife nodded in time with the music, and presently I saw the tears in her eyes. As for Dr. McAlway, he sat on the edge of his chair with his hands on his knees and wagged his shaggy head, and before we got through he, too, joined in with his big sonorous voice:

> *"Thou wouldst still be adored as this moment thou art——"*

Oh, I can't tell you here—it grows late and there's work to-morrow—all the things we did and said. They stayed until it was dark, and when Mrs. Starkweather was ready to go, she took both of Harriet's hands in hers and said with great earnestness:

"I haven't had such a good time at Christmas since I was a little girl. I shall never forget it."

And the dear old Scotch Preacher, when Harriet and I had wrapped him up, went out, saying:

"This has been a day of pleasant bread."

It has; it has. I shall not soon forget it. What a lot of kindness and common human nature—childlike simplicity, if you will—there is in people once you get them down together and persuade them that the things they think serious are not serious at all.

HOME AGAIN

Christopher Morley

Where the Blue Begins, a whimsical, allegorical satire on life in the United States, has an entirely canine cast of characters. Mr. Gissing, the philosophical bachelor hero, leaves his comfortable house at Canine Estates and his three adopted puppies in the care of Mrs. Spaniel. In his quest for the "immortal blue," he becomes, in turn, a floorwalker in a department store, a lay preacher, and an able seaman. Finally he gives up his search and returns home in time to celebrate Christmas.

HE RAN up the path to the house. The scuffled ragged garden lay naked and hard. At the windows, he saw with surprise, were holly wreaths tied with broad red ribbon. On the porch, some battered toys. He opened the door.

A fluttering rosy light filled the room. By the fireplace the puppies —how big they were!—were sitting with Mrs. Spaniel. Joyous uproar greeted him: they flung themselves upon him. Shouts of "Daddy! Daddy!" filled the house, while the young Spaniels stood by more bashfully.

Good Mrs. Spaniel was gratefully moved. Her moist eyes shone brightly in the firelight.

"I knew you'd be home for Christmas, Mr. Gissing," she said. "I've been telling them so all afternoon. Now, children, be still a moment and let me speak. I've been telling you your Daddy would be home in time for a Christmas Eve story. I've got to go and fix that plum pudding."

In her excitement a clear bubble dripped from the tip of her tongue. She caught it in her apron, and hurried to the kitchen. . . .

The children insisted on leading him all through the house to show how nicely they had taken care of things. And in every room Gissing saw the marks of riot and wreckage. There were tooth-scars on all furniture-legs; the fringes of rugs were chewed off; there were prints of mud, ink, paints, and whatnot, on curtains and wallpapers and coverlets. Poor Mrs. Spaniel kept running anxiously from the kitchen to renew apologies.

"I *did* try to keep 'em in order," she said, "but they seem to bash things when you're not looking."

But Gissing was too happy to stew about such trifles. When the inspection was over, they all sat down by the chimney and he piled on more logs.

"Well, chilluns," he said, "what do you want Santa Claus to bring you for Christmas?"

"An aunbile!"   ⎫   ⎫ Groups
"An elphunt!"   ⎬ exclaimed ⎨ Bunks
"A little train   ⎭   ⎭ Yelpers.
with hammers!"

"A little train with hammers?" asked Gissing. "What does he mean?"

"Oh," said Groups and Bunks, with condescending pity, "he means a typewriter. He calls it a little train because it moves on a track when you hit it."

A painful apprehension seized him, and he went hastily to his study. He had not noticed the typewriter, which Mrs. Spaniel had—too late— put out of reach. Half the keys were sticking upright, jammed together and tangled in a whirl of ribbon; the carriage was strangely dislocated. And yet even this mischance, which would once have horrified him, left him unperturbed. It's my own fault, he thought: I shouldn't have left it where they could play with it. Perhaps God thinks the same when His creatures make a mess of the dangerous laws of life.

"A Christmas story!" the children were clamouring.

Can it really be Christmas Eve? Gissing thought. Christmas seems to have come very suddenly this year, I haven't really adjusted my mind to it yet.

"All right," he said. "Now sit still and keep quiet. Bunks, give Yelpers a little more room. If there's any bickering Santa Claus might hear it."

He sat in the big chair by the fire, and the three looked upward expectantly from the hearthrug.

"Once upon a time there were three little puppies, who lived in a house in the country in the Canine Estates. And their names were Groups, Bunks, and Yelpers."

The three tails thumped in turn as the names were mentioned, but the children were too excitedly absorbed to interrupt.

"And one year, just before Christmas, they heard a dreadful rumour."

"What's a rumour?" cried Yelpers, alarmed.

This was rather difficult to explain, so Gissing did not attempt it. He began again.

"They heard that Santa Claus might not be able to come because he was so behind with his housework. You see, Santa Claus is a great big Newfoundland dog with a white beard, and he lives in a frosty kennel at the North Pole, all shining with icicles round the roof and windows. But it's so far away from everywhere that poor Santa couldn't get a servant. All the maids who went there refused to stay because it was so cold and lonely, and so far from the movies. Santa Claus was busy in his workshop, making toys; he was busy taking care of the reindeer in their snow-stables; and he didn't have time to wash his dishes. So all summer he just let them pile up and pile up in the kitchen. And when Christmas came near, there was his lovely house in a dreadful state of untidiness. He couldn't go away and leave it like that. And so, if he didn't get his dishes washed and the house cleaned up for Christmas, all the puppies all over the world would have to go without toys. When Groups and Bunks and Yelpers heard this, they were very much worried."

"How did they hear it?" asked Bunks, who was the analytical member of the trio.

"A very sensible question," said Gissing approvingly. "They heard it from the chipmunk who lives in the wood behind the house. The chipmunk heard it underground."

"In his chipmonastery?" cried Groups. It was a family joke to call the chipmunk's burrow by that name, and though the puppies did not understand the pun they relished the long word.

"Yes," continued Gissing. "The reindeer in Santa Claus's stable were so unhappy about the dishes not being washed, and the chance of missing their Christmas frolic, that they broadcasted a radio message. Their horns are very fine for sending radio; and the chipmunk, sitting at his little wireless outfit, with the receivers over his ears, heard it. And Chippy told Groups and Bunks and Yelpers.

"So these puppies decided to help Santa Claus. They didn't know exactly where to find him, but the chipmunk told them the direction, and off they went. They travelled and travelled, and when they came to the ocean they begged a ride from the seagulls, and each one sat on a seagull's back just as though he was on a little airplane. They flew and flew, and at last they came to Santa Claus's house. Through the stable-walls, which were made of clear ice, they could see the reindeer stamping in their stalls. In the big workshop, where Santa Claus was busy making toys, they could hear a lively sound of hammering. The big red sleigh was standing outside the stables, all ready to be hitched up to the reindeer.

"They slipped into Santa Claus's house quickly and quietly, so no one would see or hear them. The house was in a terrible state, but they set to work to clean up. Groups found the vacuum cleaner and sucked up all the crumbs from the dining-room rug. Bunks ran upstairs and made Santa Claus's bed for him and swept the floors and put clean towels in the bathroom. And Yelpers hurried into the kitchen and washed the dishes, and scrubbed the pots, and polished the egg-stains off the silver spoons, and emptied the ice-box pan. All working hard, they got through very soon, and made Santa Claus's house as clean as any house could be. They fixed the window-shades so that they would all hang level, not just anyhow, as poor Santa had them. Then, when everything was spick and span, they ran outdoors again and beckoned the seagulls. They climbed on the gulls' backs, and away they flew homeward."

"Was Santa Claus pleased?" asked Bunks.

"Indeed he was, when he came back from his workshop, very tired after making toys all day——"

"What kind of toys did he make?" exclaimed Yelpers anxiously. "Did he make a typewriter?"

"He made every kind of toy. And when he saw how his house had been cleaned up, he thought the fairies must have done it. He lit his pipe, and filled a thermos bottle with hot cocoa to keep him warm on his long journey. Then he put on his red coat, and his long boots, and his fur cap, and went out to harness the reindeer. That very night he drove off with his sleigh packed full of toys for all the puppies in the world. In fact, he was so pleased that he loaded his big bag with more toys than he had ever carried before. And that was how a queer thing happened."

They waited in eager suspense.

"You know, Santa Claus always drives into the Canine Estates by the little back road through the woods, where the chipmunk lives. You know the gateway, at the bend in the lane: well, it's rather narrow, and Santa Claus's sleigh is very wide. And this time, because his bag had so many toys in it, the bag bulged over the edge of the sleigh, and one corner of the bag caught on the gatepost as he drove by. Three toys fell out, and what do you suppose they were?"

"An aunbile!"

"An elphunt!"

"A typewriter!"

"Yes, that's quite right. And it happened that the chipmunk was out that night, digging up some nuts for his Christmas dinner, a little sad because he had no presents to give his children; and he found the three toys. He took them home to the little chipmunks, and they were tremendously pleased. That was only fair, because if it hadn't been for the chipmunk and his radio set, *no one* would have had any toys that Christmas."

"Did Santa Claus have any more typewriters in his bag?" asked Yelpers gravely.

"Oh, yes, he had plenty more of everything. And when he got to the house where Groups and Bunks and Yelpers lived, he slid down the chimney and took a look round. He didn't see any crumbs on the floor, or any toys lying about not put away, so he filled the stockings with all kinds of lovely things, and an aunbile and an elphunt and a typewriter."

"What did the puppies say?" they inquired.

"They were sound asleep upstairs, and didn't know anything about it until Christmas morning. Come on now, it's time for bed."

"We can undress ourselves now," said Groups.

"Will you tuck me in?" said Bunks.

"You're sure he had another typewriter in his bag?" said Yelpers.

They scrambled upstairs.

Later, when the house was quiet, Gissing went out to the kitchen to see Mrs. Spaniel. She was diligently rolling pastry, and her nose was white with flour.

"Oh, sir, I'm glad you got home in time for Christmas," she said.

"The children were counting on it. Did you have a successful trip, sir?"

"Every trip is successful when you get home again," said Gissing. "I suppose the shops will be open late to-night, won't they? I'm going to run down to the village to get some toys."

Before leaving the house, he went down to the cellar to see if the furnace was all right. He was amazed to see how naturally and cheerfully he had slipped back into the old sense of responsibility. Where was the illusory freedom he had dreamed of? Even the epiphany on the hilltop now seemed a distant miracle. That fearful happiness might never come again. And yet here, among the familiar difficult minutiæ of home, what a lightness he felt. A great phrase from the prayer-book came to his mind—"Whose service is perfect freedom."

Ah, he said to himself, it is all very well to wear a crown of thorns, and indeed every sensitive creature carries one in secret. But there are times when it ought to be worn cocked over one ear.

He opened the furnace door. A bright glow filled the fire-box: he could hear a stir and singing in the boiler, and the rustle of warm pipes that chuckled quietly through winter nights of storm. Over the coals hovered a magic evasive flicker, the very soul of fire. It was a pentecostal flame, perfect and heavenly in tint, the essence of pure colour, a clear immortal blue.

Among the Children

IN NAZARETH

Selma Lagerlöf

In later years Selma Lagerlöf rechronicled the beautiful old tales learned at her grandmother's knee for her little volume, *Christ Legends*. Jesus and Judas as childhood playmates provide the theme of "In Nazareth."

ONCE, when Jesus was only five years old, he sat on the doorstep outside his father's workshop, in Nazareth, and made clay cuckoos from a lump of clay which the potter across the way had given him. He was happier than usual. All the children in the quarter had told Jesus that the potter was a disobliging man, who wouldn't let himself be coaxed, either by soft glances or honeyed words, and he had never dared ask aught of him. But, you see, he hardly knew how it had come about. He had only stood on his doorstep and, with yearning eyes, looked upon the neighbor working at his molds, and then that neighbor had come over from his stall and given him so much clay that it would have been enough to finish a whole wine jug.

On the stoop of the next house sat Judas, his face covered with bruises and his clothes full of rents, which he had acquired during his continual fights with street urchins. For the moment he was quiet, he neither quarreled nor fought, but worked with a bit of clay, just as Jesus did. But this clay he had not been able to procure for himself.

He hardly dared venture within sight of the potter, who complained that he was in the habit of throwing stones at his fragile wares, and would have driven him away with a good beating. It was Jesus who had divided his portion with him.

When the two children had finished their clay cuckoos, they stood the birds up in a ring in front of them. These looked just as clay cuckoos have always looked. They had big, round lumps to stand on in place of feet, short tails, no necks, and almost imperceptible wings.

But, at all events, one saw at once a difference in the work of the little playmates. Judas' birds were so crooked that they tumbled over continually; and no matter how hard he worked with his clumsy little fingers, he couldn't get their bodies neat and well formed. Now and then he glanced slyly at Jesus, to see how he managed to make his birds as smooth and even as the oak-leaves in the forests on Mount Tabor.

As bird after bird was finished, Jesus became happier and happier. Each looked more beautiful to him than the last, and he regarded them all with pride and affection. They were to be his playmates, his little brothers; they should sleep in his bed, keep him company, and sing to him when his mother left him. Never before had he thought himself so rich; never again could he feel alone or forsaken.

The big brawny water-carrier came walking along, and right after him came the huckster, who sat joggingly on his donkey between the large empty willow baskets. The water-carrier laid his hand on Jesus' curly head and asked him about his birds; and Jesus told him that they had names and that they could sing. All the little birds were come to him from foreign lands, and told him things which only he and they knew. And Jesus spoke in such a way that both the water-carrier and the huckster forgot about their tasks for a full hour, to listen to him.

But when they wished to go farther, Jesus pointed to Judas. "See what pretty birds Judas makes!" he said.

Then the huckster good-naturedly stopped his donkey and asked Judas if his birds also had names and could sing. But Judas knew nothing of this. He was stubbornly silent and did not raise his eyes from his work, and the huckster angrily kicked one of his birds and rode on.

In this manner the afternoon passed, and the sun sank so far down that its beams could come in through the low city gate, which stood at the end of the street and was decorated with a Roman Eagle. This sunshine, which came at the close of the day, was perfectly rose-red—as if it had become mixed with blood—and it colored everything which came in its path, as it filtered through the narrow street. It painted the potter's vessels as well as the log which creaked under the woodman's saw, and the white veil that covered Mary's face.

But the loveliest of all was the sun's reflection as it shone on the little water-puddles which had gathered in the big, uneven cracks in the stones that covered the street. Suddenly Jesus stuck his hand in the puddle nearest him. He had conceived the idea that he would paint his gray birds with the sparkling sunbeams which had given such pretty color to the water, the house-walls, and everything around him.

The sunshine took pleasure in letting itself be captured by him, like paint in a paint pot; and when Jesus spread it over the little clay birds, it lay still and bedecked them from head to feet with a diamond-like luster.

Judas, who every now and then looked at Jesus to see if he made more and prettier birds than his, gave a shriek of delight when he saw how Jesus painted his clay cuckoos with the sunshine, which he caught from the water pools. Judas also dipped his hand in the shining water and tried to catch the sunshine.

But the sunshine wouldn't be caught by him. It slipped through his fingers; and no matter how fast he tried to move his hands to get hold of it, it got away, and he couldn't procure a pinch of color for his poor birds

"Wait, Judas!" said Jesus. "I'll come and paint your birds."

"No, you shan't touch them!" cried Judas. "They're good enough as they are."

He rose, his eyebrows contracted into an ugly frown, his lips compressed. And he put his broad foot on the birds and transformed them, one after another, into little flat pieces of clay.

When all his birds were destroyed, he walked over to Jesus, who sat and caressed his birds—that glittered like jewels. Judas regarded them for a moment in silence, then he raised his foot and crushed one of them.

When Judas took his foot away and saw the entire little bird changed into a cake of clay, he felt so relieved that he began to laugh, and raised his foot to crush another.

"Judas," said Jesus, "what are you doing? Don't you see that they are alive and can sing?"

But Judas laughed and crushed still another bird.

Jesus looked around for help. Judas was heavily built and Jesus had not the strength to hold him back. He glanced around for his mother. She was not far away, but before she could have gone there, Judas would have had ample time to destroy the birds. The tears sprang to Jesus' eyes. Judas had already crushed four of his birds. There were only three left.

He was annoyed with his birds, who stood so calmly and let themselves be trampled upon without paying the slightest attention to the danger. Jesus clapped his hands to awaken them; then he shouted: "Fly, fly!"

Then the three birds began to move their tiny wings, and, fluttering anxiously, they succeeded in swinging themselves up to the eaves of the house, where they were safe.

But when Judas saw that the birds took to their wings and flew at Jesus' command, he began to weep. He tore his hair, as he had seen his elders do when they were in great trouble, and he threw himself at Jesus' feet.

Judas lay there and rolled in the dust before Jesus like a dog, and kissed his feet and begged that he would raise his foot and crush him, as he had done with the clay cuckoos. For Judas loved Jesus and admired and worshiped him, and at the same time hated him.

Mary, who sat all the while and watched the children's play, came up and lifted Judas in her arms and seated him on her lap, and caressed him.

"You poor child!" she said to him, "you do not know that you have attempted something which no mortal can accomplish. Don't engage in anything of this kind again, if you do not wish to become the unhappiest of mortals! What would happen to any one of us who undertook to compete with one who paints with sunbeams and blows the breath of life into dead clay?"

DOING GOOD

Elizabeth Goudge

Notable among English writers of today for her delineation of children and their elders, Elizabeth Goudge brings a full measure of understanding, tenderness, and humor to *A Pedlar's Pack*. "Doing Good" illustrates what happens when children take a lesson too literally.

IN THE AUTUMN OF 1891, when Colette and Colin du Frocq were aged respectively eight and eleven years old, they had mumps. Eighteen ninety-one was ever afterwards referred to by Rachell, their mother, as "the frightful mumps year." Not that the mumps in itself was frightful; it was not; Colette and Colin suffered the affliction in its mildest form and their exuberant spirits and excellent health seemed quite unimpaired, but in their swollen condition they could not go to church with the rest of the family on Sundays, but remained at home to be taught Scripture by Rachell, and the consequences of her religious teaching were quite dreadful.

She didn't know why. All she did was to tell them Bible stories, explaining the meaning and pointing the moral to the best of her ability, and they promptly went out and did appalling things, doing them moreover as a result of her teaching and in a truly Christian spirit. . . . On the final mumps Sunday Rachell came to the conclusion that if there is anything more dangerous to property than vice it is morality.

And yet it was her own fault. So vivid was her imagination that a story retold by her put on so many frills and embroideries in the retelling that it was scarcely recognizable in its original form. She was one of those, of whom the world is not worthy, who delight to leave a story better than they find it. She did this with the story of the Good Samaritan on the last Sunday of September, 1891, and the consequences were with her for years.

The three of them sat together, that Sunday morning, in the parlor of the old farmhouse of Bon Répos. Pools of sunshine lay on the floor and the room was very still. There seemed no sound in all the world but Rachell's lovely voice, flowing on like a song, and the distant accompaniment of the murmuring sea. . . . For Bon Répos was the loveliest house in the loveliest island of the Channel Islands and the sound of the sea accompanied every thought and word and action from its birth to its death, so constant a friend that it was hardly noticed.

The room where they sat was very old and very lovely, and the china and furniture that lived in it lived there because they were beautiful and because Rachell was a woman who knew how to match a jewel with its setting.

She herself was a jewel and so, in their different ways, were Colette and Colin. Rachell was a tall, stately woman with a glorious crown of dark hair and warm, compassionate eyes. She sat now in a low chair, the folds of her black Sunday silk billowing round her and the cameo brooch in the bosom of her dress rising and falling with every soft movement of her breast. Her beautiful, shapely hands held her open Bible but, carried away by her own eloquence as she was, she entirely neglected to verify the statements that she made, an omission that she afterwards regretted.

In front of her, on two footstools, their eyes fixed on her face, sat her offspring. Colette in her white Sunday starched muslin, with her golden curls and her amber eyes, was a rather substantial symphony in white and gold. For Colette was on the stout side. In the years to come, when her lover put his arms about her and strained her to his bosom —and who could doubt that anything so adorable as Colette would have a lover—he would have a decided armful and there would be something considerable to strain. Colin in his white sailor suit was a complete contrast to his sister. He was slender and dark and vividly alive and had quick, bird-like movements that contrasted amusingly with Colette's stately perambulations, so reminiscent of Queen Victoria at the less slender periods of her illustrious life. They both of them looked extremely devout but in the case of Colin this was an illusion only.

"I am going to tell you the story of the Good Samaritan," said Rachell earnestly.

"What did he have for breakfast?" interrupted Colin.

"Eggs," said Rachell, never at a loss for an answer.

"How many?" asked Colette, whose appetite was enormous and who always secretly hankered after several eggs for her breakfast instead of the regulation one.

"Three," said Rachell, who had always imagined the Good Samaritan as one of those large, benevolent men who need a lot of nourishment.

"Then he was *not* good," said Colin, "he was greedy. When I said to you last Wednesday, 'Mother, may I have another egg?' you said, 'Don't be greedy, Colin.'"

"Ah, but he didn't eat the eggs," said Rachell hastily. "Just as he was going to crack the top off the first one he looked out of the window and saw a poor, hungry little boy, and he picked up his breakfast, the eggs and the toast and everything, and took it out to the poor little boy."

"Didn't he have *any* breakfast, then?" asked Colin.

"No, he was so good that he gave it all away."

"What a giddy goat," said Colin, to whose practical nature the extravagant charity of the elect made no appeal, and his attention wandered to the worms he was harboring in his pocket until his religious duties were over and he could go and fish in the pond.

But Colette, who had a beautiful, saintly disposition, had taken the incident of the eggs very much to heart. She leant forward, her eyes wide and absorbed, her expression that of one of Reynolds' fat-necked cherubs. "Mother," she said, "did he give away *all* the eggs?"

"Yes, darling."

"Didn't he keep even one for himself?"

"No, he gave them all."

"Then, Mother, oughtn't we to give away things that we have to poor people?"

Rachell hastened to improve the shining moment. "Yes, darling, of course we ought. It says so in the Bible again and again."

"And we ought to give all? Like the Good Samaritan and the widow with her mite?"

"Er—yes, darling," said Rachell, with only the slightest hesitation. . . . Really, it was impossible to explain to children that if we all took the Bible quite literally in the nineteenth century the State would be quite unable to support the number of workhouses that would be required.

"What's a mite?" asked Colin. "I thought it was a kind of little worm that lived in cheese."

"I think we had better go on with the story now," said Rachell, who felt that they were running off the rails even before they could be said to have got firmly on them. "Well, when the Good Samaritan had finished his breakfast——"

"But he didn't have any," interrupted Colin.

"No more he did. Well, anyway, he was going on a long journey, so he saddled his ass——"

"Where was he going to?" asked Colette. "Was he going to see his father and mother?"

"Yes, darling, but don't interrupt. . . . And he put on his beautiful, best striped cloak——"

"Did he wear wool next to his skin?" asked Colin.

"Children," said Rachell, "I think you must be quite quiet while I tell you this story."

There was a note in her voice that they knew and respected and they said not one word more, indeed after two minutes they did not want to, for the story enthralled them. Such a clear painter of word pictures was Rachell that they saw it all. They saw the Good Samaritan, clothed in his best blue cloak with the yellow stripes and with a turban thing on his head, jogging along the white, dusty road on his ass, with a hot, blue sky arching over his head and the dust giving him a tickle in the throat. They saw him give a little start as he saw a huddled object lying at the side of the road on ahead of him. At first he thought it was a man but then he knew it couldn't be because another man on ahead of him, when he saw the huddled object, only passed by on the other side. It must be a dead animal, the Good Samaritan probably thought, and it must be very dead indeed or the other man wouldn't have put himself to all the trouble of passing by on the other side. But when he got up to the huddled object it was a man, a poor creature who had been set upon and robbed and hurt most dreadfully. The Good Samaritan was so angry with the man who had passed by on the other side that he went beetroot in the face with rage, and jumping off his ass, he hurried to the poor wounded man and asked him gently if it hurt, and if so, where. The wounded man said it did hurt, and everywhere, and he was thirsty, so the Good Samaritan gave him his water bottle to drink from and let him have the very last drop, even though his own throat was tickling more and more with the dust, and he lifted him on his own ass and took him to an inn and looked after him, binding up his wounds and pouring in oil and wine to make him better. Colette and Colin could see it all, they could smell the blood soaking into the dust and feel how lovely and cool the water was to the poor man's throat, and the oil and wine, even though the remedy seemed odd for wounds, they felt to be doubtless very soothing.

The story affected them both differently. To Colin's adventurous disposition it was a glorious idea for a game; to Colette's pious one it was an example of benevolence that must immediately be followed. But they both wanted to know the end and felt the one provided by Holy Writ to be most unsatisfactory, entirely neglecting, as it did, even to indicate the future history either of the Good Samaritan or of the poor wounded man. Did he get quite well afterwards, Colette wanted to know, and were the Good Samaritan's father and mother pleased to see him, and were they all happy ever afterwards? She got so tearful about the uncertainty of the whole thing that Rachell hastened to comfort her. Yes, she said, the Good Samaritan's father and mother were very pleased to see him, and when the poor wounded man got quite well the Good Samaritan fetched him to live with the father and mother and look after their pigs and everybody, including the pigs, lived happy ever after.

At the midday family dinner Colette was very silent, her jaws champing up and down busily and her mind occupied, not for the first time, with the extraordinary inconsistency of grownups. Her mother had that morning told her, quite definitely, that one should give away all that one had to the poor, and yet here they all were, her father and mother, her three elder sisters, herself and Colin, gobbling up roast mutton and onion sauce, with apple tart to follow, and apparently giving not one thought to the poor. It was all very puzzling and Colette heaved a great sigh, caused partly by repletion and partly by the disturbed condition of her mind.

Colin, too, was wondering a little at the curious habits of his elders. The conversation, to which Colette was paying no attention, had turned upon some poor fisherman's boy who lived down at Breton Bay, a hamlet only a short way from Bon Répos. He had been left an orphan, it appeared, and the uncle and aunt who had taken him in treated him shamefully.

"Sophie says they beat him," said Michelle, the eldest du Frocq, retailing the gossip of an old servant. "And they don't give him enough to eat. The child's becoming quite an idiot through ill-treatment."

"Beasts!" said Peronelle, the second du Frocq, scarlet with indignation. "Why doesn't someone do something about it? Could I have some more tart, please, Mother?"

"Someone should adopt the poor child," said Rachell.

"Cases like that ought to be seen to," pronounced André, her husband.

So like grownups, thought Colin. Always saying that so-and-so should be done but never doing it themselves. It exasperated him. Not that he felt any particular pity for the little boy, for never having seen misery in any form, pity was not as yet a part of his make-up, but statements that were not at once followed by vigorous action seemed to him useless and stupid. He himself, if he said he was going to put his pet rat in a sister's bed, immediately put his pet rat in a sister's bed, and braved the consequences. Inaction and hesitation in any form infuriated him, as they did Peronelle. . . . For a second their eyes met, both pairs ablaze with indignation, and something unseen, but important in its consequences, passed between them.

After dinner, as always on a Sunday afternoon, they made a tour of inspection. The farm did not do too badly, for André du Frocq had been left sufficient money by a brother to pay a competent bailiff to be a better farmer than he was himself. He meanwhile, comfortably removed from the burden and heat of the day, was a poet and a philosopher, one of those who inform a world not removed from the burden and heat of the day that life is good. . . . He was not, perhaps, always believed, but in his chosen vocation he was a happy man.

They looked at the well-stocked garden and the fat pigs and the sleek cows and the fussy hens and, last of all, they looked at their apples. Most of the orchards on the Island that year had failed to bear, and the du Frocq orchard had also not done its duty, but one particular apple tree had borne nobly. Lovely, russet-brown apples tinged with scarlet lay in luscious rows in the apple room.

"Aren't they lovely?" breathed Michelle.

"We must be careful of them," said Rachell, almost reverently. "They must last till Christmas. . . . André, let's go in."

The family separated, Rachell and André for their Sunday siesta in the parlor, the three elder girls to read in the kitchen and Colette and Colin to play in the garden.

"You're not to go out, children," was Rachell's parting remark. "You must promise me to stay in the garden."

"Promise," said Colette.

"Darling Mother," said Colin, not committing himself.

Rachell, satisfied, left them.

They trotted round the house to the kitchen garden behind, so as to be beyond the prying eyes of their sisters.

"Let's play at being the Good Samaritan," said Colin, "and you can be the ass."

But Colette shook her yellow curls. "Not if it's upstairs," she said. She had eaten a very large dinner and she was feeling her weight. What she wanted to do for the present was to sit quietly in a fat heap at the end of the garden and just wonder about things.

"Lazy little cabbage," said Colin scornfully, and left her.

Colette did not mind being scorned, the very good frequently are, and she was used to it. She ran down to the bottom of the garden, where beautiful umbrellas of rhubarb sprouted beside the gate that led on to the road. This was one of her favorite spots for wondering but today she had not time to wonder a single wonder, for peeping through the bars of the gate was a little, dirty boy. His face was thin, and furrowed by tear marks running through grime, and his dark eyes were the eyes of a rabbit caught in a trap. His jersey was torn and his toes were coming through his boots.

Colette's heart seemed to turn right over. She had a compassionate heart and it not infrequently performed these somersaults but, unlike most hearts, when it turned right way up again it immediately goaded her into action. In the twinkling of an eye she had taken off her best strap shoes and thrust them through the bars at the little boy. . . . He remained tepid. . . . "I'd rather have something to eat, mamzelle," he muttered hoarsely.

Not a bit discouraged, Colette restored the shoes to her feet and sped into the house to the larder. . . . But Rachell, remembering the attacks of hunger that sometimes seized Colin in the middle of a Sunday afternoon, had locked the larder. . . . For a moment Colette was near tears and then she suddenly remembered the apples. "They must last till Christmas," Rachell had said, but then she had also said, "We must give away all that we have to the poor," and the only thing to be done with the conflicting commands of grownups was to obey the one that seemed most applicable at the moment. . . . She sped to the apple room.

"How many would you like?" she asked, returning with a pinafore full.

"How many have you got?" he asked.

"There's a sackful there," puffed Colette.

"Then could I have the sackful, mamzelle?" he breathed earnestly.

"Could you eat all that?" asked Colette, overcome with admiration for a feat of appetite that even surpassed anything of her own.

"No, mamzelle, but I could sell them." He leaned nearer to her, trembling all over, his face white beneath its grime. "If I could buy myself tidy clothes I could get work. . . . Like this they would not take me." Colette, looking at his rags, agreed that perhaps they wouldn't.

"Come with me to get the apples," she whispered.

"I daren't," he said.

Something of his animal fear and trembling haste passed into Colette. She made three journeys to the apple room and back, bouncing along at a pace that was not in the least reminiscent of Queen Victoria, and at the end of ten minutes the sack was full and on his back and he was staggering off down the road, panting with eagerness and not even waiting to say thank you. . . . Not that she minded. She always gave for the sake of the person to whom she gave and with no thought of herself.

Turning back from the gate, flushed with benevolence, she found herself face to face with Colin, who was coming down the path attired in Peronelle's new striped silk dressing gown, with a towel twisted turbanwise round his head and his dog Maximilian attached to his person by a rope. In one hand he held a bottle of cod-liver oil and in the other a bottle of turpentine.

"I'm the Good Samaritan," he announced, "and Maximilian is the ass since you wouldn't be."

"What's the cod-liver oil and the turpentine for?" asked Colette.

"The oil and the wine to pour into the wounds," he said, and hitching up his dressing gown, he opened the gate.

"You mustn't go out," remonstrated Colette. "Mother said not to."

"I didn't promise not to, I wasn't such a giddy goat, I just said, 'Darling Mother,' and left it at that." And Colin stalked out of the gate and down the road. . . . Colette watched him, green with envy. She would have liked to go too, but already, young as she was, she was terribly handicapped by an active conscience, and duty kept her tethered.

Colin trudged down the white, dusty road beneath the hot, blue sky of Palestine, his noble ass lolloping behind. The sun scorched him and the dust tickled his throat and the dressing gown was distinctly hot, but he did not mind these things because he was good, and nothing, in stories, that is, ever upsets the good.

Presently, the heat of the sun being what it was, he turned to the right and plunged down a leafy lane. There was nothing in the story about the Good Samaritan turning sideways but one might as well be comfortable as not. At the bottom of the first lane he turned to the left into a second, a lovely lane with a stream running down it. This was a short cut to the town and was very well known to Colin, whose private business frequently took him townwards unknown to his parents, yet today, his own character being changed, the character of the lane was changed, too. It was not an Island lane any longer, it was a dusty track crossing the treeless fields of the Holy Land, and at any moment now he might come upon that prostrate figure by the roadside. . . . Already he could smell the blood soaking into the dust. . . . He jerked the rope to accelerate the movements of the ass and took a firmer grip on the bottle of cod-liver oil.

Therefore it was a distinct surprise, when he turned a corner, to come face to face with not one prostrate figure but four. Four boys were kicking and sprawling and cursing together in the middle of the path, a confused mass of arms and legs and shouts, and all round them rolled russet-brown apples tinged with scarlet. For a moment Colin stood still, nonplussed, for the thing was not working out according to plan. Then he realized what had happened. The Good Samaritan had arrived upon the scene a shade too soon and the thieves were caught in the act. All the better. With a yell of triumph he flung the dressing gown from him into the stream and rushed to the rescue. The noble ass, showing all his teeth and brandishing his tail like a banner of war, leaped into the fight, too, and instantly there began such a bloody battle as the water lane has not seen before or since. Colin was a magnificent fighter, second to none, and Colette's little, dirty boy fought with the courage of desperation and the others with the courage of greed. They all five— six, counting Maximilian—bit and scratched and punched and kicked with incomparable vigor, while the sun and moon and stars stood still to watch, and victory, as always in Holy Writ, went to the righteous. The robbers were vanquished at last and fled home to their mothers in a pitiable state. . . . But not before they had somehow succeeded in gathering up most of the apples.

The Good Samaritan and the poor wounded man sat up and looked at each other. The story was now progressing along the proper lines except that the Good Samaritan was rather the worse wounded of the two. One of his eyes was closed up and his nose was bleeding, and he had a horrid cut on his cheek given him by the bottle of turpentine, which had had the bad taste to get itself smashed in the middle of the *mêlée*. The bottle of cod-liver oil had not smashed, but the cork had come out, and it had emptied itself in a slimy mess all over Maximilian.

"They *were* thieves all right, weren't they?" demanded Colin, his one eye sparkling with interest.

"Trying to steal my apples they were," growled the wounded man, and swore. "I'll kill 'em, so I will, when next I catch 'em."

Colin cast his eye upon the few bruised apples that were left. . . . Russet and scarlet. . . . Nowhere but at Bon Répos did one see such apples. . . . He leaped to his feet.

"Thief!" he yelled. "You stole those from Bon Répos. Thief! Thief! *Sal petit cochon!*"

At this dreadful island insult the wounded man also leaped to his feet. "Liar!" he shouted. "Liar! I didn't steal 'em!"

Out shot their fists and the whole thing began all over again. Backwards and forwards they swayed, pommeling and thumping, Maximilian prancing round and barking ecstatically. Then with a thud they came down on the path, the Good Samaritan gloriously on top. . . . With the courtesy of the victor, he instantly removed himself and assisted the vanquished to sit up.

"What's your name?" he demanded.

"Pierre," growled the wounded one.

Colin wiped blood out of his eye and had a good look. In the final scuffle Pierre's jersey had been completely torn off him, and Colin saw a bony back with long weals across it. . . . He had never seen such a thing before and he felt suddenly sick. . . . Then he remembered the conversation at dinner and gripped Pierre's arm.

"Are you the boy who lives at Breton Bay and whose uncle beats him?" he demanded.

Pierre nodded indifferently. "I didn't steal those apples, m'sieur," he pleaded. "The mamzelle at Bon Répos gave them to me."

"Which mamzelle?" asked Colin.

"The nice fat little one."

The description was adequate and Colin believed him and nodded. Then he sat back on his heels wondering what to do next. What with his eye and his nose and his bruises, he felt a little heavy and confused, and the sight of the weals on Pierre's back had done something to him. For the first time in his life he was overwhelmed by pity, a sensation apparently situated in the pit of the stomach, and it made him feel quite queer. In its confusion his mind went groping back to the story he was acting and instantly light dawned. The wounded man had been taken by the Good Samaritan to live with his father and mother and look after the pigs. . . . A good deal had taken place first, but the story was now being re-enacted in a compressed form and there wasn't time for everything. . . . "Come on," he said to Pierre, and dragged him to his feet.

When the family assembled in the kitchen for tea Colin was not there, but as all the attention was focused upon Colette his absence was hardly noticed.

Colette's disposition was the very reverse of secretive, and at each meal it was usually her habit to tell everyone exactly what she had done since she last took nourishment. She recounted the afternoon's adventure with placidity and a certainty of approval, touching lightly upon her mother's remarks of the morning and dwelling at length upon the hunger of the little boy. If the silence that followed her narration was ominous she was too much occupied in not biting over the jam in the middle of her doughnut to notice it.

Rachell, with the ease of long practice, recovered quickly from the shock and silenced the outcry of the rest of the family with a swift look. "*All* the apples, darling?" she asked faintly.

"All," said Colette. "You said this morning one must give all," and she gave a little crow of pleasure as she found the jam and bit deep into it.

"Is it better for the community at large that the young should be instructed in the rudiments of religion by their mothers or by Holy Church?" asked André mildly, but no one answered him, for Colin and Pierre had appeared in the doorway.

At the sight of her son's torn and bloodstained garments Rachell nearly fainted, but then she perceived the bloom of health on his cheek, recovered, and arose in her wrath.

"Colin, what on earth have you been doing?" she demanded. "And who is this little boy?"

"He's Pierre," said Colin, "and he's come to live with us. I've told him he's to live with us and he says he'd like to. . . . He's the wounded man and I'm the Good Samaritan."

Rachell swayed where she stood. "Peronelle," she said, "take them away and wash them."

Peronelle the practical was already on her feet, and had haled them upstairs in the twinkling of an eye, but in twenty minutes she was back again, her lovely face glowing with eagerness.

"Mother!" she cried, "it *is* the little boy!"

"What little boy?" asked Rachell weakly.

"The one Sophie told us about. The one you said someone should adopt. And Father said cases like that ought to be seen to."

"By the parish," said André hastily.

"The parish!" cried Peronelle scornfully. "The parish indeed! Think of Oliver Twist. A child like that wants love and he is going to get it. I've told him he shall stay with us. He's a darling. He shall be our boot boy and help in the garden and with the pigs."

"Peronelle, is this my house or yours?" demanded Rachell, enraged. "I tell you I will not have it turned into a workhouse without my permission. You children have already made me take on the most incompetent maidservant ever endured, simply as an act of charity, and I cannot and will not have a second of the species about the place. . . . It's too much. . . . It's simply too much." Her lovely eyes, full of angry tears, sought her husband's. "André, for pity's sake go and deal with it."

André looked up and cleared his throat deprecatingly. This, his children knew, was a sure sign that he was about to do as he was told, and Peronelle flew round the table and wound her arms round his neck.

"Keep him, Father," she whispered into his left ear, "keep him!" Her arms round him were trembling and her cheek against his was hot. . . . A tear fell and trickled down his neck. . . . Caught as he was between the devil and the deep sea of two lovely, determined women, and both of them his, he capitulated to the one whose arms were round his neck.

"I think, dear," he said to his wife, "that since all this is the result of your own religious teaching——"

"Very well," said Rachell, her eyes blazing. "You are of course master in your own house."

This was a statement that she frequently made in moments of wrath, and André, who wasn't, often wondered if she really believed it.

"Yes, dear," he said gently, "and I should like the little boy to stay."

It was the first time he had ever won a victory over her, and from then on there was almost a martial note in his poems.

But by night Rachell's sense of humor had come to the rescue and she was ashamed of herself. . . . Also Peronelle had shown her the scars on Pierre's back and she had cried for pity.

"Poor little soul!" said she to André, as she stood in front of her looking glass brushing out her long hair for the night. "I'm so glad, darling, that you gave in to me and decided to keep him after all."

André, who was sitting up in the four-poster reading a book, started slightly and then smiled.

"Yes, dear," he said sweetly, "I am glad, too. I am always glad when your romantic heart triumphs over my more practical one."

His wife looked at him affectionately. He looked so funny sitting up in bed in his white nightshirt, rather like a gnome with his gray beard and ruffled hair and his spectacles on the end of his nose. She wondered if the people who read his beautiful poems pictured him as an exquisite young man in a black velvet coat with a lily in his buttonhole. They would, perhaps, get a shock if they saw him, but she herself preferred him as he was. She was much blessed in her husband, she considered, and sometimes, but not always, in her children.

"Those young wretches!" she sighed. "All my apples gone and my house turned into an orphanage without my leave. . . . If I have any more children, André, I shall bring them up heathens."

André glanced up over his spectacles. "I think, dear," he said, "that in teaching religion to children emphasis should be laid on those stories that encourage reverence for parental property."

Rachell, her hairbrush raised, paused. "Are there any?" she asked.

BE PRESENT AT OUR TABLE, LORD

William Saroyan

William Saroyan's *The Human Comedy* is the story of an American family in wartime, and especially of Homer Macauley, who—like Saroyan himself—went to work as a messenger in a telegraph office of the San Joaquin Valley. Homer's breakfast-table prayer expresses an important truth: "Everybody is somebody . . . and everybody believes."

WHEN HOMER sat down at the breakfast table his sister Bess and his mother were waiting for him. The family bowed their heads a moment, lifted them and began to eat.

"What prayer did you say?" Bess said to her brother.

"The prayer I *always* say," Homer said, and then quoted it, saying the words exactly as he had learned to say them when he had scarcely known how to speak.

> *Be present at our table, Lord.*
> *Be here and everywhere adored.*
> *These creatures bless, and grant that we*
> *May feast in Paradise with Thee.*
> *Amen."*

"Oh, that's old," Bess said, "and besides, you don't even know what you're saying."

"I know all right," Homer said. "I may say it a little too swiftly because I'm hungry, but I know what it means. It's the spirit of the thing that counts anyway. What prayer did *you* say?"

"You've got to tell me first what the words mean," Bess said.

"What do *you* mean what do they mean?" Homer said. "They mean exactly what they say."

"Well," Bess said, "what *do* they say?"

"Be present at our table, Lord," Homer said. "Well, that means—Be present at our table, Lord. Lord means a lot of things, I guess, but I guess all the things it means are good. Be here and everywhere adored —well, that means let good things be loved here and everywhere else. These creatures—that means us, I guess—everybody. Bless—that means —well, bless. Bless means to forgive, maybe, I guess. Or to love, maybe, or to watch over, or something like that. I don't know for sure but I guess it's something like that. And grant that we may feast in Paradise with Thee. Well, that means exactly what it says. Just grant that we may feast in Paradise with Thee."

"Who is *Thee?*" Bess said.

Homer turned to his mother. "Doesn't the prayer mean," he said, "that if people are right, they feast in Paradise every time they sit down at a table? Thee is good things, isn't it?"

"Of course," Mrs. Macauley said.

"But isn't Thee *somebody?*" Bess said.

"Sure," Homer said. "But I'm somebody too. Ma and you and everybody is somebody. Grant that this world is Paradise and that everybody we ever have food with is somebody. Bess," Homer said impatiently, "it's a table prayer, and you know as well as I do what it means. You just want to mix me up. Well, don't worry. You can. I guess *anybody* can mix me up, but it doesn't make any difference because I *believe*. Everybody believes. Don't they, Ma?"

"Of course they do," Mrs. Macauley said. "If you don't believe, you're not alive. And you can't feast at all, let alone in Paradise—no matter how laden with wonderful food your table is. It's faith that makes anything wonderful—not the thing itself."

ENSHRINED IN THE HEART

Elizabeth Yates

Nearby is a timely novel about a timeless problem: the relationships between peoples of different backgrounds and beliefs. It is the story of Mary Rowen, a young teacher who imbues the small New England village of Nearby with a living democracy that works. Her understanding of others' needs—especially her love for children—raises teaching to a fine art and builds a strong sense of lasting values.

THE FOLLOWING Friday afternoon Mary told the children, when they assembled after the noon recess, that there would be no separate classes but that all would work together during the remaining periods on one subject—English. A slight murmur of approval ran through the older children; the younger ones looked excited as always at the thought of anything new. Mary had contemplated asking their choice of a book for discussion, but knowing their tastes would be diverse, she made her own choice.

Matt would have said, "Airplanes."

Patsy, "A book about a baby."

Gwen, "Don't care so long as it has a horse in it."

And the little ones would clamor for *Mother Goose,* though some of them might be too tongue-tied with delight to make their wish audible.

She decided to give them something she liked; so a slim little volume, long loved and gently handled, came with her that Friday in her luncheon box. Anyone opening it might have seen the inscription made when she was a child of six by an aunt who had long since died. "To little Mary, hoping she will love this book as I have. Mary, always treat good books as your best friends." From the first she had cherished the tales by Hans Andersen. All through her childhood she had loved them, and even now the simple stories with their delicate joys and exquisite sadness could cast a spell over her. Some quality of veracity made them constantly appealing to her. Fairy tales they might be, sometimes cloaking parables, sometimes indulging in purest fancy, but they were told by one who had been to those far fay lands and who had learned their secret language.

Opening the book, she read the children two or three of the shorter stories. Some of them entered into the spirit slowly, but soon they were all spellbound—from the rangy eighth-graders who already were looking ahead into life, to the little ones for whom the dialogue between toys was most understandable, to the outdoor ones who sympathized with the plight of the fir tree, and to the natural-born farmers who took the story of "The Buckwheat" to heart. Mary finished her reading with that story, looking up and at the enchanted faces as she read the last words: " 'I, who now repeat the story, heard it from the talkative Sparrows, who told it me one evening when I asked them for a tale.' "

The room was very quiet when she closed the book, a quietness broken only by subdued requests for more.

"I wish you'd tell us something about the writer of those stories," Emily Bruce said.

"I hoped someone would ask for that," Mary smiled, "for it always seems to me that enjoyment of a book is measured in some degree by an interest in the author."

"Please, please, Miss Rowen, tell us about Hans Christian Andersen," a chorus of voices echoed through the room until Mary's nod of agreement silenced them in anticipation.

Easily and persuasively, more through her own deep love than too much knowledge, she took them with her to the little town in Denmark where Hans Christian Andersen was born in 1805.

"His father was a cobbler, his mother was a washerwoman, and they were very poor, so much so that their home consisted of a single room with a great bed and a shoemaker's bench and a cupboard that held books from which Hans's father would read. There was, as well, a little kitchen of shining pots and pans. A ladder went out onto the roof to the gutters between the houses and there Hans's mother kept a chest filled with soil. That was their garden and, small as it was, it gave herbs and vegetables for their use.

"The little home was clean and Hans's mother kept it fresh with green branches from the forest. Everything the boy needed seemed to be there with a full measure of kindness. There was no poverty of love in that home. Hans was imaginative. He used to go about with his eyes half-shut, dreaming of wonderful things. He was very ambitious, and though he was not sure of what he was going to do in the world he knew that it would be something important. Perhaps he would be a great actor, he told himself; then he wondered if that was vanity, deciding it was not since something within him told him it so clearly. But, vanity or not, the desire to be great lifted him out of want and ignorance into education and freedom.

"In his home he was treated with tenderness and respect to his individuality; later he would write for children with respect to their individuality. From his mother came queer tales of ghosts and goblins that filled him with a terror of the dark; from his father came wisdom and a great love for the Bible. The two, meeting in Hans, made of him the first modern writer for children; he held one hand on the past but his eyes looked ahead."

"When did he start to write his stories, Miss Rowen?" Fingal asked.

"Not for some time, because he was sure he was going to be an actor —the way Diane is." Mary looked at the little girl so captured by the story. No one laughed as they once had at Diane and her absurdities. If Hans Andersen had dreamed of being an actor and then had become a writer, what might not Diane Carson do? Suddenly it was no joking matter, this of what each one of them would do in life; it was deeply serious and no one of them could begin thinking of it too soon.

"His thoughts were all on the theater," Mary went on. "He had a toy theater of his own and he used to spend much time with it, producing plays and thinking of the part he would play on the stage one day. His mother, watching him bent over bits of silk, his fingers curiously deft with a needle as he made costumes for his actors, often declared that she would make a tailor of him. There was little in the boy with his yellow shock of hair, loose gangling limbs, and high voice to hint of the hopes he held. But when Hans was fourteen and his father died, it was to the opera house at Copenhagen that he went to find work.

"He had small means to aid him but he had something that was sufficient for any need—an absolute conviction that God was guiding him. Later in his life he wrote with feeling, "There is a loving God who directs all things for the best.' At Copenhagen he called on a famous actress and, while waiting for the doorbell to be answered, dropped on his knees on the door mat and prayed to be led aright.

"Neither ballet nor theater proved to be the place for the country boy and, though his high voice seemed to show possibilities, it broke under training and ruled out singing as a career. Hans was ridiculed. He nearly starved. But he had always felt that suffering must come before accomplishment, so he held on. He distrusted himself but at the same time knew he was destined for greatness. He longed to make friends, for it was his nature to attach himself to people, to love everyone and everything, but life for him lay in lonely and difficult ways. His enthusiasm and devotion were not to be ignored, however, and soon a rich citizen of Copenhagen, Jonas Collin, took him under his patronage and saw that he was educated properly.

"Hans's natural ability was freed and he began to write. He wrote plays and novels which made quite a stir in the Denmark of the 1830s but which are little read now. Then, one by one, he began to write simple stories, fairy tales, that took hold of people's imaginations. The real Hans was speaking. In the quietness of his study he prayed, 'Let me never write a word of which I shall not be able to give an account to Thee,' for, as in his childhood, he felt that God was watching him and that all the good that came to him came from God.

"The world of daisies and fir trees, of great oaks and tiny mice, of mermaids and elfin creatures had always been his world. These were things that he understood and they, in their way, had been kind to him while the world of men had mocked him. So it was of this world that he wrote. Never far removed from childhood himself, he brought through his tales what he knew as a child to other children. With simplicity of telling, he mingled legend, superstition, memories of the Bible with his own intuitions.

"Dew, wind, rain, an old street lamp, storks nesting on a chimney, all were friends of his, having ways of their own that he understood. The language of the birds was not strange to him, nor were the thoughts of a tree. Every fence, every flower, a battered toy or a sailing ship could tell him a story which he retold to the world. As he found his true genius his fame rose, in a way he never could have dreamed in the long-ago days in Odense. He traveled much, had many friends, and loved once deeply, but he never married. When he died in 1875 Denmark honored him as one of her best-loved sons, but he was repaid in other ways. He had always longed for affection; now it was his in rich measure as he came to be enshrined in the hearts of children all over the world." Mary held up the little volume from which she had first read. "Would you like to hold this book in your hands?"

"Yes," they cried excitedly, and the crimson volume that had companioned Mary for so many years started on its journey around the schoolroom.

It was given reverent treatment, gazed at with longing eyes, touched caressingly. Nezar stroked it as he might a kitten. Diane clasped it to her heart dramatically and said, "I love books." Matt looked at his hands to be sure they could not soil it, then because he was the last to receive the book he returned it to Mary.

"I wish I could write a book," Nezar said.

Mary smiled dubiously, thinking of Nezar's strangely unholy compilations of words; but before she could make any reply most of the children were expressing the same desire.

"Why don't you, then?" Mary flung out the challenge to them all. "Write a story, bind it in some way, make it as like an actual book as you can, and have them all ready for this same period next week."

A collective smile ran over the room, then a backwash of doubt erased it.

"What should it be about?" Constance Lovering asked.

"Something near your heart. Something real to you," Mary said. "When Hans Christian reached too far he failed; when he took what was close at hand he gave it immortality—and himself too. Nothing is too trivial to call forth a story. The way you think about it will give it significance. Be very honest with yourselves and write of something near you that you really know about."

The afternoon had gone and it was soon time for dismissal. Nezar looked up at Mary as he passed her desk on his way out.

"I know what I'm going to write about," he said, his pale face gleaming as if a light had been turned on behind it.

Patsy stopped at Mary's desk. "I never knew how wonderful books were." She picked up the crimson volume and held it to her cheek. "Why, they have thoughts—somebody's thoughts—and we can know them just by reading. It's lovely to think that we can buy them when they're so precious."

"And borrow them for nothing except the respect we pay them," Mary reminded her.

"Gosh, Miss Rowen," Andy said, "I never knew a book meant so much. It's just like a person coming to see you."

And so, in varying degrees of dawning appreciation of books and the part they played in the scheme of things, they went home on their self-appointed tasks of writing and making books.

AS YE SOW—

Dorothy Canfield

~~~~~~

Dorothy Canfield's outstanding contribution to literature is her portrayal of plain living and high thinking in family life. With a delightful blend of the practical and the spiritual, her Vermont mother, in "As Ye Sow—," brings courage to a challenging problem and proves that "a loving heart is the beginning of all knowledge."

CASUALLY, not that she was especially interested, just to say something, she asked as she handed out the four o'clock pieces of bread and peanut butter, "Well, what Christmas songs are you learning in your room this year?"

There was a moment's pause. Then the three little boys, her own and the usual two of his playmates, told her soberly, first one speaking, then another, "We're not going to be let to sing." "Teacher don't want us in the Christmas entertainment." Their round, eight-year-old faces were grave.

"Well—!" said the mother. "For goodness' sakes, why not?"

Looking down at his feet, her own small David answered sadly, "Teacher says we can't sing good enough."

"Well enough," corrected his mother mechanically.

"Well enough," he repeated as mechanically.

One of the others said in a low tone, "She says we can't carry a tune. She's only going to let kids sing in the entertainment that can carry a tune."

David, still hanging his head humbly, murmured, "She says we'd spoil the piece our class is going to sing."

Inwardly the mother broke into a mother's rage at a teacher. "So that's what she says, does she? What's she *for,* anyhow, if not to teach children what they don't know. The idea! As if she'd say she would teach arithmetic only to those who are good at it already."

The downcast children stood silent. She yearned over their shame at failing to come up to the standards of their group. "Teachers are callous, that's what they are, insensitively callous. She is deliberately planting an inferiority feeling in them. It's a shame to keep them from going up on the platform and standing in the footlights. Not to let them have their share of being applauded! It's cruel."

She drew in a deep breath, and put the loaf of bread away. Then she said quietly, "Well, lots of kids your age can't carry a tune. Not till they've learned. How'd you like to practice your song with me? I could play the air on the piano afternoons, after school. You'd get the hang of it that way."

They brightened, they bit off great chunks of their snacks, and said, thickly, that that would be swell. They did not say they would be grateful to her, or regretted being a bother to her, busy as she always was. She did not expect them to. In fact it would have startled her if they had. She was the mother of four.

So while the after-school bread-and-butter was being eaten, washed down with gulps of milk, while the November-muddy rubbers were taken off, the mother pushed to the back of the stove the interrupted rice pudding, washed her hands at the sink, looked into the dining room where her youngest, Janey, was waking her dolls up from naps taken in the dining-room chairs, and took off her apron. Together the four went into the living room to the piano.

"What song is it your room is to sing?"

"It came upon the midnight—" said the three little boys, speaking at once.

"That's a nice one," she commented, reaching for the battered songbook on top of the piano. "This is the way it goes." She played the air, and sang the first two lines. "That'll be enough to start on," she told them. *"Now—"* she gave them the signal to start.

They started. She had given them food for body and heart. Refreshed, heartened, with unquestioning confidence in a grownup's ability to achieve whatever she planned, they opened their mouths happily and sang out.

> *"It came upon the midnight clear*
> *That glorious song of old."*

They had evidently learned the words by heart from hearing them.

At the end of that phrase she stopped abruptly, and for an instant bowed her head over the keys. Her feeling about Teacher made a right-about turn. There was a pause.

But she was a mother, not a teacher. She lifted her head, turned a smiling face on the three bellowing children. "I tell you what," she said. "The way, really, to learn a tune is just one note after another. The reason why a teacher can't get *every*body in her room up to singing in tune is because she'd have to teach each person separately—unless they happen to be naturally good at singing. That would take too much time, you see. A teacher has such a lot of children to see to."

They did not listen closely to this. They were not particularly interested in having justice done to Teacher, since they had not shared the mother's brief excursion into indignation. But they tolerated her with silent courtesy. They were used to parents, teachers, and other adults, and had learned how to take with patience and self-control their constantly recurring prosy explanations of things that did not matter.

"Listen," said the mother, "I'll strike just the two first notes on the piano—'It came——'" She struck the notes, she sang them clearly. Full of good will, the little boys sang with her. She stopped. Breathed hard.

"Not quite," she said, with a false smile, "pret-t-ty good. Close to it. But not quite, yet. I think we'd better take it *one* note at a time. Bill, *you* try it."

They had been in and out of her house all their lives, they were all used to her, none of them had reached the age of self-consciousness. Without hesitation, Bill sang, "I-i-it—" loudly.

After he had, the mother, as if fascinated, kept her eyes fixed on his still open mouth. Finally, "Try again," she said. "But first, *listen.*" Oracularly she told them, "Half of carrying a tune is listening first."

She played the note again. And again. And again. Then, rather faintly, she said, "Peter, you sing it now."

At the note emitted by Peter, she let out her breath, as if she had been under water and just come up. "Fine!" she said. "Now we're getting somewhere! David, your turn." David was her own. "Just that one note. No, not *quite*. A little higher. Not quite so high." She was in a panic. What could she do? "Wait," she told David. "Try just breathing it out, not loud at all. Maybe you can get it better."

The boys had come in a little after four. It was five when the telephone rang—Bill's mother asking her to send Bill home because his

Aunt Emma was there. The mother turned from the telephone to say, "Don't you boys want to go along with Bill a ways, and play around for a while outdoors? I've got to get supper ready." Cheerful, sure that she, like all adults, knew just what to do, relieved to see a door opening before them that had been slammed shut in their faces, and very tired of that one note, they put on their muddy rubbers and thudded out.

That evening when she told her husband about it, after the children had gone to bed, she ended her story with a vehement "You never heard anything like it in your life, Harry. Never. It was appalling! You can't *imagine* what it was!"

"Oh, yes I can too," he said over his temporarily lowered newspaper. "I've heard plenty of tone-deaf kids hollering. I know what they sound like. There *are* people, you know, who really *can't* carry a tune. You probably never could teach them. Why don't you give it up?"

Seeing, perhaps, in her face, the mulish mother-stubbornness, he said, with a little exasperation, "What's the use of trying to do what you *can't* do?"

That was reasonable, after all, thought the mother. Yes, that was the sensible thing to do. She would be sensible, for once, and give it up. With everything she had to do, she would just be reasonable and sensible about this.

So the next morning, when she was downtown doing her marketing, she turned in at the public library and asked for books about teaching music to children. Rather young children, about eight years old, she explained.

The librarian, enchanted with someone who did not ask for a light, easy-reading novel, brought her two books, which she took away with her.

At lunch she told her husband (there were just the two of them with little Janey; the older children had their lunch at school), "Musical experts say there really is no such thing as a tone-deaf person. If anybody seems so, it is only because he has not had a chance to be carefully enough trained."

Her husband looked at her quickly. "Oh, all right," he said, "all *right!* Have it your own way." But he leaned to pat her hand. "You're swell," he told her. "I don't see how you ever keep it up as you do. Gosh, it's one o'clock already."

During the weeks between then and the Christmas entertainment, she saw no more than he how she could ever keep it up. The little boys had no difficulty in keeping it up. They had nothing else to do at four o'clock. They were in the indestructible age, between the frailness of infancy and the taut nervous tensions of adolescence. Wherever she led they followed her cheerfully. In that period of incessant pushing against barriers which did not give way, she was the one whose flag hung limp.

Assiduous reading of those two reference books on teaching music taught her that there were other approaches than a frontal attack on the tune they wanted to sing. She tried out ear-experiments with them, of which she would never have dreamed, without her library books. She discovered to her dismay that sure enough, just as the authors of the books said, the little boys were musically so far below scratch that, without seeing which piano keys she struck, they had no idea whether a note was higher or lower than the one before it. She adapted and invented musical "games" to train their ear for this. The boys standing in a row, their backs to the piano, listening to hear whether the second note was "up hill or down hill" from the first note, thought it as good a game as any other, rather funnier than most because so new to them. They laughed raucously over each other's mistakes, kidded and joshed each other, ran a contest to see who came out best, while the mother, aproned for cooking, her eye on the clock, got up and down for hurried forays into the kitchen where she was trying to get supper.

David's older brother and sister had naturally good ears for music. That was one reason why the mother had not dreamed that David had none. When the two older children came in from school, they listened incredulously, laughed scoffingly, and went off to skate, or to rehearse a play. Little Janey, absorbed in her family of dolls, paid no attention to these male creatures of an age so far from hers that they were as negligible as grown-ups. The mother toiled alone, in a vacuum, with nobody's sympathy to help her, her great stone rolling down hill as fast as she toilsomely pushed it up.

Not quite in a vacuum. Not even in a vacuum. Occasionally the others made a comment, "Gee, Mom, those kids are fierce. *You* can't do anything with them." "Say, Helen, an insurance man is coming to the house this afternoon. For heaven's sake keep those boys from screeching while he is here. A person can't hear himself think."

So, she thought, with silent resentment, her task was not only to give up her own work, to invent and adapt methods of instruction in an hour she could not spare, but also to avoid bothering the rest. After all, the home was for the whole family. They had the right to have it the background of what *they* wanted to do, needed to do. Only not she. Not the mother. Of course.

She faltered. Many times. She saw the ironing heaped high, or Janey was in bed with a cold, and as four o'clock drew near, she said to herself, "Now today I'll just tell the boys that I can *not* go on with this. We're not getting anywhere, anyhow."

So when they came storming in, hungry and cheerful and full of unquestioning certainty that she would not close that door she had half-opened for them, she laid everything aside and went to the piano.

As a matter of fact, they were getting somewhere. She had been so beaten down that she was genuinely surprised at the success of the exercises ingeniously devised by the authors of those books. Even with their backs to the piano, the boys could now tell, infallibly, whether a second note was above or below the first one. Sure. They even thought it distinctly queer that they had not been able to, at first. "Never paid any attention to it, before," was their own accurate surmise as to the reason.

They paid attention now, their interest aroused by their first success, by the incessant practicing of the others in their classroom, by the Christmas-entertainment thrill which filled the schoolhouse with suspense. Although they were allowed no part in it, they also paid close attention to the drill given the others, and sitting in their seats, exiled from the happy throng of singers, they watched how to march along the aisle of the Assembly Hall, decorously, not too fast, not too slow, and when the great moment came for climbing to the platform how not to knock their toes against the steps. They fully expected—wasn't a grown-up teaching them?—to climb those steps to the platform with the others, come the evening of the entertainment.

It was now not on the clock that the mother kept her eye during those daily sessions at the piano, it was on the calendar. She nervously intensified her drill, but she remembered carefully not to yell at them when they went wrong, not to screw her face into the grimace which she felt, not to clap her hands over her ears and scream, "Oh, horrible! *Why* can't you get it right!" She reminded herself that if they knew how to get it right, they would of course sing it that way. She knew (she had been a mother for sixteen years) that she must keep them cheerful and hopeful, or the tenuous thread of their interest and attention would snap. She smiled. She did not allow herself even once to assume the blighting look of patience.

Just in time, along about the second week of December, they did begin to get somewhere. They could all sound—if they remembered to sing softly and to "listen to themselves"—a note, any note, within their range, she struck on the piano. Little Peter turned out, to his surprise and hers, to have a sweet clear soprano. The others were—well, all right, good enough.

They started again, very cautiously, to sing that tune, to begin with "It ca-ame—" having drawn a deep breath, and letting it out carefully. It was right. They were singing true.

She clapped her hands like a girl. They did not share her overjoyed surprise. That was where they had been going all the time. They had got there, that was all. What was there to be surprised about?

After that it went fast; the practicing of the air, their repeating it for the first skeptical and then thoroughly astonished Teacher, their triumphant report at home, "She says we can sing it good enough. She says we can sing with the others. We practiced going up on the platform this afternoon."

Then the Christmas entertainment. The tramping of class after class up the aisle to the moment of footlighted glory; the big eighth-graders' Christmas pantomime, the first-graders' wavering performance of a Christmas dance as fairies—or were they snowflakes? Or perhaps angels? It was not clear. They were tremendously applauded, whatever they were. The swelling hearts of their parents burst into wild hand-clapping as the first grade began to file down the steps from the platform. Little Janey, sitting on her mother's lap, beat her hands together too, excited by the thought that next year she would be draped in white cheesecloth, would wear a tinsel crown and wave a star-tipped wand.

Then it was the turn of the third grade, the eight- and nine-year-olds, the boys clumping up the aisle, the girls switching their short skirts proudly. The careful tiptoeing up the steps to the platform, remembering not to knock their toes on the stair treads, the two lines of round faces facing the audience, bland and blank in their ignorance of —oh, of everything! thought David's mother, her hand clutching her handbag tensely.

The crash from the piano giving them the tone, all the mouths opened,

"It came upo-on the midnight clear
That glorious song of old."

The thin pregnant woman sitting in front of the mother leaned to the shabbily dressed man next to her, with a long breath of relief. "They do real *good,* don't they?" she whispered proudly.

They did do real good. Teacher's long drill and hers had been successful. It was not howling, it was singing. It had cost the heart's blood, thought the mother, of two women, but it was singing. It would never again be howling, not from those children.

It was even singing with expression—some. There were swelling crescendos, and at the lines

> *"The world in solemn stillness lay*
> *To hear the angels sing."*

the child-voices were hushed in a diminuendo. Part of the mother's very life had been spent in securing her part of that diminuendo. She ached at the thought of the effort that had gone into teaching that hushed tone, of the patience and self-control and endlessly repeated persistence in molding into something shapely the boys' puppy-like inability to think of anything but aimless play. It had taken hours out of her life, crammed as it was far beyond what was possible with work that must be done. Done for other people. Not for her. Not for the mother.

This had been one of the things that must be done. And she had done it. There he stood, her little David, a fully accredited part of his corner of society, as good as anybody, the threat of the inferiority-feeling averted for this time, ready to face the future with enough self-confidence to cope with what would come next. The door had been slammed in his face. She had pushed it open, and he had gone through.

The hymn ended. The burst of parental applause began clamorously. Little Janey, carried away by the festival excitement, clapped with all her might—"learning the customs of her corner of society," thought her mother, smiling tenderly at the petal-soft noiselessness of the tiny hands.

The third grade filed down the steps from the platform and began to march back along the aisle. For a moment, the mother forgot that she was no longer a girl, who expected recognition when she had done something creditable. David's class clumped down the aisle. Surely, she thought, David would turn his head to where she sat and thank her with a look. Just this once.

He did turn his head as he filed by. He looked full at his family, at his father, his mother, his kid sister, his big brother and sister from the high school. He gave them a formal, small nod to show that he knew they were there, to acknowledge publicly that they were his family. He even smiled, a very little, stiffly, fleetingly. But his look was not for her. It was just as much for those of his family who had been bored and impatient spectators of her struggle to help him, as for her who had given part of her life to roll that stone up hill, a part of her life she never could get back.

She shifted Janey's weight a little on her knees. Of course. Did mothers ever expect to be thanked? They were to accept what they received, without bitterness, without resentment. After all, that was what mothers worked for—not for thanks, but to do their job. The sharp chisel of life, driven home by experience, flaked off expertly another flint-hard chip from her blithe, selfish girlhood. It fell away from the woman she was growing to be, and dropped soundlessly into the abyss of time.

After all, she thought, hearing vaguely the seventh-graders now on the platform (none of her four was in the seventh grade), David was only eight. At that age they were, in personality, completely cocoons, as in their babyhood they had been physical cocoons. The time had not come yet for the inner spirit to stir, to waken, to give a sign that it lived.

It certainly did not stir in young David that winter. There was no sign that it lived. The snowy weeks came and went. He rose, ravenously hungry, ate an enormous breakfast with the family, and clumped off to school with his own third-graders. The usual three stormed back after school, flinging around a cloud of overshoes, caps, mittens, windbreakers. For their own good, for the sake of their wives-to-be, for the sake of the homes which would be dependent on them, they must be called back with the hard-won, equable reasonableness of the mother, and reminded to pick up and put away. David's special two friends came to his house at four to eat her cookies, or went to each other's houses to eat other cookies. They giggled, laughed raucously, kidded and joshed each other, pushed each other around. They made snow forts in their front yards, they skated with awkward energy on the place where the brook overflowed the meadow, took their sleds out to Hingham Hill for coasting, made plans for a shack in the woods next summer.

In the evening, if the homework had been finished in time, they were allowed to visit each other for an hour, to make things with Meccano, things which were a source of enormous pride to the eight-year-olds, things which the next morning fell over, at the lightest touch of the mother's broom.

At that age, thought the mother, their souls, if any, were certainly no more than seeds, deep inside their hard, muscular, little-boy flesh. How do souls develop? she wondered occasionally, as she washed dishes, made beds, selected carrots at the market, answered the telephone. How do souls develop out of those rough-and-ready little males? If they do develop.

David and Peter, living close to each other, shared the evening play-hour more often than the third boy who lived across the tracks. They were allowed to go by themselves to each other's house, even though it was winter-black at seven o'clock. Peter lived on the street above theirs, up the hill. There was a short cut down across a vacant lot, which was in sight of one or the other house, all the way. It was safe enough, even for youngsters, even at night. The little boys loved that down-hill short cut. Its steep slope invited their feet to fury. Never using the path, they raced down in a spray of snow kicked up by their flying overshoes, arriving at the house, their cheeks flaming, flinging themselves like cannon balls against the kitchen door, tasting a little the heady physical fascination of speed, on which, later, as ski-runners, they would become wildly drunken.

"Sh! *David!* Not so *loud!*" his mother often said, springing up from her mending at the crash of the banged-open door. "Father's trying to do some accounts," or "Sister has company in the living room."

Incessant acrobatic feat—to keep five people of different ages and personalities, all living under the same roof, from stepping on each other's feet. Talk about keeping five balls in the air at the same time! That was nothing compared to keeping five people satisfied to live with each other, to provide each one with approximately what he needed and wanted without taking away something needed by one of the others. (Arithmetically considered, there were of course six people living under that roof. But she did not count. She was the mother. She took what she got, what was left. . . .)

That winter, as the orbits of the older children lay more outside the house, she found herself acquiring a new psychological skill that was almost eerie. She could be in places where she was not, at all. She had an astral body which could go anywhere. Anywhere, that is, where one of her five was. She was with her honey-sweet big daughter in the living room, playing games with high-school friends (was there butter enough, she suddenly asked herself, for the popcorn the young people would inevitably want, later?). She was upstairs where her husband sat, leaning over the desk, frowning in attentiveness at a page of figures—that desk light was not strong enough. Better put the floodlight up there tomorrow. She was in the sun porch of the neighbor's house, where her little son was bolting Meccano-strips together with his square, strong, not-very-clean hands—his soul, if any, dormant far within his sturdy body. She floated above the scrimmage in the high-school gym, where her first-born played basketball with ferocity, pouring out through that channel the rage of maleness constantly gathering in his big frame which grew that year with such fantastic rapidity that he seemed taller at breakfast than he had been when he went to bed. She sent her astral body upstairs to where her little daughter, her baby, her darling, slept with one doll in her arms, and three others on the pillow beside her. That blanket was not warm enough for Janey. When she went to bed, she would put on another one.

She was all of them. First one, then another. When was she herself? When did *her* soul have time to stretch its wings?

One evening this question tried to push itself into her mind, but was swept aside by her suddenly knowing, as definitely as if she had heard a clock strike, or the doorbell ring, that the time had passed for David's return from his evening play-hour with Peter. She looked at her watch. But she did not need to. A sixth sense told her heart, as with a blow, that he should before this have come pelting down the hill, plowing the deep snow aside in clouds, hurling himself against the kitchen door. He was late. Her astral self, annihilating time and space, fled out to look for him. He must have left the other house some time ago. Peter's mother always sent him home promptly.

She laid down the stocking she was darning, stepped into the dark kitchen, and put her face close to the window to look out. It was a cloudless cold night. Every detail of the back-yard world was visible, almost transparent, in the pale radiance that fell from the stars. Not a breath of wind. She could see everything: the garbage pail at the wood-shed door, the trampled snow of the driveway, the clothes she had washed that morning and left on the line, the deep unbroken snow beyond the yard, the path leading up the hill.

Then she saw David. He was standing halfway down, as still as the frozen night around him.

But David never stood still.

Knee-deep in the snow he stood, looking all around him. She saw him slowly turn his head to one side, to the other. He lifted his face towards the sky. It was almost frightening to see *David* stand so still. What could he be looking at? What was there he could be seeing? Or hearing? For as she watched him, the notion crossed her mind that he seemed to be listening. But there was nothing to hear. Nothing.

She did not know what was happening to her little son. Nor what to do. So she did nothing. She stood as still as he, her face at the window, lost in wonder.

She saw him, finally, stir and start slowly, slowly down the path. But David never moved slowly. Had he perhaps had a quarrel with Peter? Had Peter's mother been unkind to him?

It could do no harm now to go to meet him, she thought, and by that time, she could not, anxious as she was, not go to meet him. She opened the kitchen door and stepped out into the dark, under the stars.

He saw her, he came quickly to her, he put his arms around her waist. With every fiber of her body which had borne his, she felt a difference in him.

She did not know what to say, so she said nothing.

It was her son who spoke. "It's so still," he said quietly in a hushed voice, a voice she had never heard before. "It's so still!"

He pressed his cheek against her breast as he tipped his head back to look up. "All those stars," he murmured dreamily, "they shine so. But they don't make a sound. They—they're *nice,* aren't they?"

He stood a little away from her to look up into her face. "Do you remember—in the song—'the world in solemn stillness lay'?" he asked her, but he knew she remembered.

The starlight showed him clear, his honest, little-boy eyes wide, fixed trustingly on his mother's. He was deeply moved. But calm. This had come to him while he was still so young that he could be calmed by his mother's being with him. He had not known that he had an inner sanctuary. Now he stood in it, awe-struck at his first sight of beauty. And opened the door to his mother.

As naturally as he breathed, he put into his mother's hands the pure rounded pearl of a shared joy. "I thought I heard them singing—sort of," he told her.

Family Portrait

OF OUR MEETING WITH COUSIN JOHN

John Oxenham

The Hidden Years creates for Jesus the childhood that is not in the Bible. All the incidents are seen through the eyes of his loving young friend and neighbor. The story told here with unique spiritual quality illuminates the striking contrast between Jesus and his cousin John.

AT TIMES when we could get a whole day off, we would go along the valley towards the Plain of Esdraelon and strike up through the olive groves and over the hills to Nain, to see Arni and his mother.

It was a glorious tramp, for the Great Plain, with the Kishon wandering through it in wide curves on its way to the sea, was a wonder in itself, and Jesus made it still more wonderful by the stories he told of the great things that had happened there. While we lay in the grass on a hilltop and ate our meal, he told of King Joram and Ahaziah and Jehu the furious driver, and of Elijah and Elisha and of Judith and the Assyrian King.

And there, just in front of us, was Mount Gilboa, where Saul and Jonathan were killed. And on the other side was Tabor. It was a wonderful place.

We were lying there one such day when Jesus, who had been gazing very intently across the valley towards Gilboa, said, "Who is this, I wonder?" And I saw a very long way off a small black figure coming from the direction of Mount Gilboa.

When the stranger drew near to the olive groves that lay about the foot of our hill, Jesus suddenly sprang up and gave a great "Hallo! Hallo!" and Tobias barked loudly.

The stranger stopped and stared at us under his hand and then came striding on through the grove and straight up towards us. Jesus ran down to meet him with Tobias racing and bounding beside him. There was no mistaking who this strange-looking figure was, and I stared my hardest at him. We had queer people passing through the village at times, but I had never seen anyone quite as queer as this.

In the first place, his skin was burned red-brown with the sun, almost black—what you could see of it, and that was only part of his face and his arms and legs. And all the rest of him was shaggy hair. The hair of his head was, as the ox-man had said, like a horse's mane that had never been trimmed and it tumbled wildly about him. And his coat was hair of the same kind and very shaggy, and round his middle he had a wide leather band. His hand was hard and bony but looked very strong, and in it he grasped a long thick stick which was taller than himself.

"You are my Cousin John," I heard Jesus say.

"And you are Jesus ben Joseph!"

"I've been hoping you would come," said Jesus. "It's a long time since we've seen one another," and they came up the hill together.

And as they came John was gazing at Jesus all the time in the most curious, searching way. He had very bushy brows and his eyes were set deep under them, and they burned in their hollows like live coals in the dark.

His voice was vibrant and sonorous but rather harsh. I thought he probably talked much aloud to himself in the deserts where he lived and perhaps shouted and sang. There was none of the roundness and sweetness, as of a flute, or at times as of a silver trumpet, that was in Jesus's voice.

"And you spend all your time in the open, Cousin John?" asked Jesus.

"Where should one live better than under God's sky?" and he threw his arms up with a strange wild gesture.

"I love the open, too," said Jesus, "especially the hilltops——"

"Ay—the hilltops! One feels nearer to God on the hilltops . . . And at night . . . ah—the nights! The firmament showeth His handiwork!

And at dawn . . . The morning stars sing together! I would live not in a house—no, not in Herod's palace."

"But how do you live? What do you eat, if you're forever wandering on the hilltops and never go home?"

"Eat? I eat what God gives me to eat. He feeds the ravens and He feeds me. The earth is full of things to eat—wild carobs, and honey, and now and again a fig, some dates, some grapes."

"But how do you serve Jah by roaming about the hills?" persisted Jesus.

"I am learning. Sometime I shall know. And you?"

All the while he spoke his burning eyes were fixed hungrily on his cousin's face.

"I?" said Jesus. "I live with my father and mother, and help in my father's business."

"You make ox yokes," with a touch of scorn again.

"And good ones, too. I serve Jah by making the best yokes that can be made."

"And life is corrupt and the world is going down into darkness."

"Deliverance will come."

"Ay—how and when?" with a hungry look at him.

"With the promised Messiah . . . But when . . . we know not. They say very soon now."

"I grow sick with waiting. Every day but makes His task the harder."

"With God no task is hard. He made the world. He will save it. Else why did He make it?"

"Ay—why? why? I often wonder. For He can find no joy in it."

"It's a very beautiful world," said Jesus softly, and his eyes roved lovingly from Gilboa to the great plain with its silver river and on to Carmel.

"But for the men in it . . . All spoiled by His own creatures. Why does He suffer them? Break it all up! Drown it as in the time of Noah and begin afresh!"

"That would be to confess failure," said Jesus thoughtfully. "And He cannot fail."

"A terrible world . . . a terrible world," said John, and fell silent with the thought of it.

"You will come home with me, Cousin John?" said Jesus presently, for the sun was sinking towards the sea beyond Carmel. "My father and mother would wish to see you, and you don't come too often."

"I would see them, too. Joseph and Mary are dear to my father and mother. But I will sleep without."

"You shall sleep where you will if you won't take my bed."

"I have not slept on a bed since I have had any say in the matter."

Jesus was about sixteen years old at the time when he and John met and John was a little older. He was taller than Jesus and very lean and hard. But they seemed to me as different in nearly all things as the day is from the night and I could never have felt towards John as I did towards Jesus.

THE LAST NIGHT

James M. Barrie

As *Margaret Ogilvy* is Barrie's literary tribute to his mother, *A Window in Thrums* immortalizes his native village. "The Last Night" is a boy's farewell to his parents on the eve of his departure for the city. In its mood of haunting tenderness, it reveals the power of religious faith in the sacred circle of Scottish family life.

"Juist another sax nichts, Jamie," Jess would say, sadly. "Juist fower nichts noo, an' you'll be awa." Even as she spoke seemed to come the last night.

The last night! Reserve slipped unheeded to the floor. Hendry wandered ben and but the house, and Jamie sat at the window holding his mother's hand. You must walk softly now if you would cross that humble threshold. I stop at the door. Then, as now, I was a lonely man, and when the last night came the attic was the place for me.

This family affection, how good and beautiful it is. Men and maids love, and after many years they may rise to this. It is the grand proof of the goodness in human nature, for it means that the more we see of each other the more we find that is lovable. If you would cease to dislike a man, try to get nearer his heart.

Leeby had no longer any excuse for bustling about. Everything was ready—too soon. Hendry had been to the fish-cadger in the square to get a bervie for Jamie's supper, and Jamie had eaten it, trying to look as if it made him happier. His little box was packed and strapped, and stood terribly conspicuous against the dresser. Jess had packed it herself.

"Ye mauna trachle (trouble) yersel, mother," Jamie said, when she had the empty box pulled toward her.

Leeby was wiser.

"Let her do't," she whispered, "it'll keep her frae broodin'."

Jess tied ends of yarn round the stockings to keep them in a little bundle by themselves. So she did with all the other articles.

"No' at it's ony great affair," she said, for on the last night they were all thirsting to do something for Jamie that would be a great affair to him.

"Ah, ye would wonder, mother," Jamie said, "when I open my box an' find a'thing tied up wi' strings sae careful, it a' comes back to me wi' a rush wha did it, an' am as fond o' thae strings as though they were a grand present. There's the pocky (bag) ye gae mi to keep sewin' things in. I get the wifie I lodge wi' to sew to me, but often when I come upon the pocky I sit an' look at it."

Two chairs were backed to the fire, with underclothing hanging upside down on them. From the string over the fireplace dangled two pairs of much-darned stockings.

"Ye'll put on baith thae pair o' stockin's, Jamie," said Jess, "juist to please me?"

When he arrived he had rebelled against the extra clothing.

"Ay, will I, mother?" he said now.

Jess put her hand fondly through his ugly hair. How handsome she thought him.

"Ye have a fine brow, Jamie," she said. "I mind the day ye was born sayin' to mysel 'at ye had a fine brow."

"But ye thocht he was to be a lassie, mother," said Leeby.

"Na, Leeby, I didna. I kept sayin' I thocht he would be a lassie because I was fleid he would be; but a' the time I had a presentiment he would be a laddie. It was wi' Joey deein' sae sudden, an' I took on sae terrible aboot 'im 'at I thocht all alang the Lord would gie me another laddie."

"Ay, I wanted 'im to be a laddie mysel," said Hendry, "so as he could tak Joey's place."

Jess's head jerked back involuntarily, and Jamie may have felt her hand shake, for he said in a voice out of Hendry's hearing—

"I never took Joey's place wi' ye, mother."

Jess pressed his hand tightly in her two worn palms, but she did not speak.

"Jamie was richt like Joey when he was a bairn," Hendry said.

Again Jess's head moved, but still she was silent.

"They were sae like," continued Hendry, " 'at often I called Jamie by Joey's name."

Jess looked at her husband, and her mouth opened and shut.

"I canna mind 'at you ever did that?" Hendry said.

She shook her head.

"Na," said Hendry, "you never mixed them up. I dinna think ye ever missed Joey sae sair as I did."

Leeby went ben, and stood in the room in the dark; Jamie knew why.

"I'll just gang ben an' speak to Leeby for a meenute," he said to his mother; "I'll no be lang."

"Ay, do that, Jamie," said Jess. "What Leeby's been to me nae tongue can tell. Ye canna bear to hear me speak, I ken, o' the time when Hendry an' me'll be awa, but, Jamie, when that time comes ye'll no forget Leeby?"

"I winna, mother, I winna," said Jamie. "There'll never be a roof ower me 'at's no hers too."

He went ben and shut the door. I do not know what he and Leeby said. Many a time since their earliest youth had these two been closeted together, often to make up their little quarrels in each other's arms. They remained a long time in the room, the shabby room of which Jess and Leeby were so proud, and whatever might be their fears about their mother, they were not anxious for themselves. Leeby was feeling lusty and well, and she could not know that Jamie required to be reminded of his duty to the folk at home. Jamie would have laughed at the notion. Yet that woman in London must have been waiting for him even then. Leeby, who was about to die, and Jamie, who was to forget his mother, came back to the kitchen with a happy light on their faces. I have with me still the look of love they gave each other before Jamie crossed over to Jess.

"Ye'll gang anower, noo, mother," Leeby said, meaning that it was Jess's bed-time.

"No yet, Leeby," Jess answered, "I'll sit up till the readin's ower."

"I think ye should gang, mother," Jamie said, "an' I'll come an' sit aside ye after ye're i' yer bed."

"Ay, Jamie, I'll no hae ye to sit aside me the morn's nicht, an' hap (cover) me wi' the claes."

"But ye'll gang suner to yer bed, mother."

"I may gang, but I winna sleep. I'll aye be thinkin' o' ye tossin' on the sea. I pray for ye a lang time ilka nicht, Jamie."

"Ay, I ken."

"An' I pictur ye ilka hour o' the day. Ye never gang hame through thae terrible streets at nicht but I'm thinkin' o' ye."

"I would try no to be sae sad, mother," said Leeby. "We've ha'en a richt fine time, have we no?"

"It's been an awfu' happy time," said Jess. "We've ha'en a pleasant-ness in oor lives 'at comes to few. I ken naebody 'at's ha'en sae muckle happiness one wy or another."

"It's because ye're sae guid, mother," said Jamie.

"Na, Jamie, am no guid ava. It's because my fowk's been sae guid, you an' Hendry an' Leeby an' Joey when he was livin'. I've got a lot mair than my deserts."

"We'll juist look to meetin' next year again, mother. To think o' that keeps me up a' the winter."

"Ay, if it's the Lord's will, Jamie, but am gey dune noo, an' Hendry's fell worn too."

Jamie, the boy that he was, said, "Dinna speak like that, mother," and Jess again put her hand on his head.

"Fine I ken, Jamie," she said, " 'at all my days on this earth, be they short or lang, I've you for a staff to lean on."

Ah, many years have gone since then, but if Jamie be living now he has still those words to swallow.

By and by Leeby went ben for the Bible, and put it into Hendry's hands. He slowly turned over the leaves to his favourite chapter, the fourteenth of John's Gospel. Always, on eventful occasions, did Hendry turn to the fourteenth of John.

"Let not your heart be troubled; ye believe in God, believe also in Me.

"In My Father's house are many mansions; if it were not so, I would have told you. I go to prepare a place for you."

As Hendry raised his voice to read there was a great stillness in the kitchen. I do not know that I have been able to show in the most im-perfect way what kind of man Hendry was. He was dense in many things, and the cleverness that was Jess's had been denied to him. He had less book-learning than most of those with whom he passed his days, and he had little skill in talk. I have not known a man more easily taken in by persons whose speech had two faces. But a more simple, modest, upright man, there never was in Thrums, and I shall always revere his memory.

"And if I go and prepare a place for you, I will come again, and receive you unto Myself; that where I am, there ye may be also."

The voice may have been monotonous. I have always thought that Hendry's reading of the Bible was the most solemn and impressive I have ever heard. He exulted in the fourteenth of John, pouring it forth like one whom it intoxicated while he read. He emphasized every other word; it was so real and grand to him.

We went upon our knees while Hendry prayed, all but Jess, who could not. Jamie buried his face in her lap. The words Hendry said were those he used every night. Some, perhaps, would have smiled at his prayer to God that we be not puffed up with riches nor with the things of this world. His head shook with emotion while he prayed, and he brought us very near to the throne of grace. "Do thou, O our God," he said, in conclusion, "spread Thy guiding hand over him whom in Thy great mercy Thou hast brought to us again, and do Thou guard him through the perils which come unto those that go down to the sea in ships. Let not our hearts be troubled, neither let them be afraid, for this is not our abiding home, and may we all meet in Thy house, where there are many mansions, and where there will be no last night. Amen."

It was a silent kitchen after that, though the lamp burned long in Jess's window. By its meagre light you may take a final glance at the little family; you will never see them together again.

HIS MOTHER'S SERMON

Ian Maclaren

In his writings Ian Maclaren tried to brighten lives that had become embittered by harsh experience and deprivation. "His Mother's Sermon" reveals the deep religious sentiment and feeling that he knows will best touch the hearts of the outwardly dour Scottish peasantry. In essence, it is a tribute to the strong ties of family love and the undying influence of a mother on her son.

HE WAS an ingenuous lad, with the callow simplicity of a theological college still untouched, and had arrived on the preceding Monday at the Free Kirk manse with four cartloads of furniture and a maiden aunt. For three days he roamed from room to room in the excitement of householding, and made suggestions which were received with hilarious contempt; then he shut himself up in his study to prepare the great sermon, and his aunt went about on tiptoe. During meals on Friday he explained casually that his own wish was to preach a simple sermon, and that he would have done so had he been a private individual, but as he had held the MacWhammel scholarship a deliverance was expected by the country. He would be careful and say nothing rash, but it was due to himself to state the present position of theological thought, and he might have to quote once or twice from Ewald.

His aunt was a saint, with that firm grasp of truth and tender mysticism whose combination is the charm of Scottish piety, and her face was troubled. While the minister was speaking in his boyish complacency, her thoughts were in a room where they had both stood, five years before, by the death-bed of his mother.

He was broken that day, and his sobs shook the bed, for he was his mother's only son and fatherless, and his mother, brave and faithful to the last, was bidding him farewell.

"Dinna greet like that, John, nor break yir hert, for it's the will o' God, and that's aye best.

"Here's my watch and chain," placing them beside her son, who could not touch them, nor would lift his head, "and when ye feel the chain about yir neck it will mind ye o' yir mother's arms.'

"Ye 'ill no forget me, John, I ken that weel, and I'll never forget you. I've loved ye here and I'll love ye yonder. Th'ill no be an 'oor when I'll no pray for ye, and I'll ken better what to ask than I did here, sae dinna be comfortless."

Then she felt for his head and stroked it once more, but he could not look nor speak.

"Ye 'ill follow Christ, and gin He offers ye His cross ye'll no refuse it, for He aye carries the heavy end Himsel. He's guided yir mother a' thae years, and been as gude as a husband since yir father's death, and He 'ill hold me fast tae the end. He 'ill keep ye too, and, John, I'll be watchin' for ye. Ye 'ill no fail me," and her poor cold hand that had tended him all his days tightened on his head.

But he could not speak, and her voice was failing fast.

"I canna see ye noo, John, but I know yir there, an' I've just one other wish. If God calls ye to the ministry, ye 'ill no refuse, an' the first day ye preach in yir ain kirk, speak a gude word for Jesus Christ, an', John, I'll hear ye that day, though ye 'ill no see me, and I'll be satisfied."

A minute after she whispered, "Pray for me," and he cried, "My mother, my mother."

It was a full prayer, and left nothing unasked of Mary's Son.

"John," said his aunt, "your mother is with the Lord," and he saw death for the first time, but it was beautiful with the peace that passeth all understanding.

Five years had passed, crowded with thought and work, and his aunt wondered whether he remembered that last request, or indeed had heard it in his sorrow.

"What are you thinking about, aunt? Are you afraid of my theology?"

"No, John, it's no that, laddie, for I ken ye 'ill say what ye believe to be true withoot fear o' man," and she hesitated.

"Come, out with it, auntie: you're my only mother now, you know," and the minister put his arm round her, "as well as the kindest, bonniest, goodest auntie ever man had."

Below his student self-conceit he was a good lad, and sound of heart.

"Shame on you, John, to make a fool o' an auld dune body, but ye'll no come round me with yir flattery. I ken ye ower weel," and as she caught the likeness in his face, her eyes filled suddenly.

"What's the matter, auntie? Will ye no tell me?"

"Dinna be angry wi' me, John, but a'm concerned aboot Sabbath, for a've been praying ever syne ye were called to Drumtochty that it micht be a great day, and that I micht see ye comin' tae yir people, laddie, wi' the beauty o' the Lord upon ye, according tae the auld prophecy: 'How beautiful upon the mountains are the feet of him that bringeth good tidings, that publisheth peace,'" and again she stopped.

"Go on, auntie, go on," he whispered; "say all that's in yir mind."

"It's no for me tae advise ye, who am only a simple auld woman, who kens naethin' but her Bible and the Catechism, and it's no that a'm feared for the new views, or aboot yir faith, for I aye mind that there's mony things the Speerit hes still tae teach us, and I ken weel the man that follows Christ will never lose his way in ony thicket. But it's the fouk, John, a'm anxious aboot, the flock o' sheep the Lord hes given ye tae feed for Him."

She could not see his face, but she felt him gently press her hand, and took courage.

"Ye maun mind, laddie, that they're no clever and learned like what ye are, but juist plain country fouk, ilka ane wi' his ain temptation, an' a' sair trachled wi' mony cares o' this world. They 'ill need a clear word tae comfort their herts and show them the way everlasting. Ye 'ill say what's richt, nae doot o' that, and a'body 'ill be pleased wi' ye, but, oh, laddie, be sure ye say a gude word for Jesus Christ."

The minister's face whitened, and his arm relaxed. He rose hastily and went to the door, but in going out he gave his aunt an understanding look, such as passes between people who have stood together in a sorrow. The son had not forgotten his mother's request.

The manse garden lies toward the west, and as the minister paced its little square of turf, sheltered by fir hedges, the sun was going down behind the Grampians. Black massy clouds had begun to gather in the evening, and threatened to obscure the sunset, which was the finest sight a Drumtochty man was ever likely to see, and a means of grace to every sensible heart in the glen. But the sun had beat back the clouds on either side, and shot them through with glory, and now between piled billows of light he went along a shining pathway into the Gates of the West. The minister stood still before that spectacle, his face bathed in the golden glory, and then before his eyes the gold deepened into an awful red, and the red passed into shades of violet and green, beyond painter's hand or the imagination of man. It seemed to him as if a victorious saint had entered through the gates into the city, washed in the blood of the Lamb, and the after-glow of his mother's life fell solemnly on his soul. The last trace of sunset had faded from the hill when the minister came in, and his face was of one who had seen a vision. He asked his aunt to have worship with the servant, for he must be alone in his study.

It was a cheerful room in the daytime, with its southern window, through which the minister saw the roses touching the very glass and dwarf apple trees lining the garden walks; there was also a western window that he might watch each day close. It was a pleasant room now, when the curtains were drawn, and the light of the lamp fell on the books he loved, and which bade him welcome. One by one he had arranged the hard-bought treasures of student days in the little bookcase, and had planned for himself that sweetest of pleasures, an evening of desultory reading. But his books went out of mind as he looked at the sermon shining beneath the glare of the lamp, and demanding judgment. He had finished its last page with honest pride that afternoon, and had declaimed it, facing the southern window, with a success that amazed himself. His hope was that he might be kept humble, and not called to Edinburgh for at least two years; and now he lifted the sheets with fear. The brilliant opening, with its historical parallel, this review of modern thought reinforced by telling quotations, that trenchant criticism of old-fashioned views, would not deliver. For the audience had vanished, and left one careworn but ever beautiful face, whose gentle eyes were waiting with a yearning look. Twice he crushed the sermon in his hands, and turned to the fire his aunt's care had kindled, and twice he repented and smoothed it out. What else could he say now to the people? and then in the stillness of the room he heard a voice, "Speak a gude word for Jesus Christ."

Next minute he was kneeling on the hearth, and pressing the *magnum opus,* that was to shake Drumtochty, into the heart of the red fire, and he saw, half-smiling and half-weeping, the impressive words, "Semitic environment," shrivel up and disappear. As the last black flake fluttered out of sight, the face looked at him again, but this time the sweet brown eyes were full of peace.

It was no masterpiece, but only the crude production of a lad who knew little of letters and nothing of the world. Very likely it would have done neither harm nor good, but it was his best, and he gave it for love's sake, and I suppose that there is nothing in a human life so precious to God, neither clever words nor famous deeds, as the sacrifices of love.

The moon flooded his bedroom with silver light, and he felt the presence of his mother. His bed stood ghostly with its white curtains, and he remembered how every night his mother knelt by its side in prayer for him. He is a boy once more, and repeats the Lord's Prayer, then he cries again, "My mother! my mother!" and an indescribable contentment fills his heart.

His prayer next morning was very short, but afterwards he stood at the window for a space, and when he turned, his aunt said:

"Ye will get yir sermon, and it will be worth hearing."

"How did ye know?"

But she only smiled, "I heard you pray."

When he shut himself into the study that Saturday morning, his aunt went into her room above, and he knew she had gone to intercede for him.

An hour afterwards he was pacing the garden in such anxious thought that he crushed with his foot a rose lying on the path, and then she saw his face suddenly lighten, and he hurried to the house, but first he plucked a bunch of forget-me-nots. In the evening she found them on his sermon.

Two hours later—for still she prayed and watched in faithfulness to mother and son—she observed him come out and wander round the garden in great joy. He lifted up the soiled rose and put it in his coat; he released a butterfly caught in some mesh; he buried his face in fragrant honeysuckle. Then she understood that his heart was full of love, and was sure that it would be well on the morrow.

When the bell began to ring, the minister rose from his knees and went to his aunt's room to be robed, for this was a covenant between them.

His gown was spread out in its black silken glory, but he sat down in despair.

"Auntie, whatever shall we do, for I've forgotten the bands?"

"But I've not forgotten them, John, and here are six pair wrought with my own hands, and now sit still and I'll tie them round my laddie's neck."

When she had given the last touch, and he was ready to go, a sudden seriousness fell upon them.

"Kiss me, auntie."

"For your mother, and her God be with you," and then he went through the garden and underneath the honeysuckle and into the kirk, where every Free Churchman in Drumtochty that could get out of bed, and half the Established Kirk, were waiting in expectation.

I sat with his aunt in the minister's pew, and shall always be glad that I was at that service. When winter lies heavy upon the glen I go upon my travels, and in my time have seen many religious functions. I have been in Mr. Spurgeon's Tabernacle, where the people wept one minute and laughed the next; have heard Canon Liddon in St. Paul's, and the sound of that high, clear voice is still with me, "Awake, awake, put on thy strength, O Zion"; have seen High Mass in St. Peter's, and stood in the dusk of the Duomo at Florence when Padre Agostino thundered against the evils of the day. But I never realized the unseen world as I did that day in the Free Kirk of Drumtochty.

It is impossible to analyze a spiritual effect, because it is largely an atmosphere, but certain circumstances assisted. One was instantly pre-possessed in favor of a young minister who gave out the second para-phrase at his first service, for it declared his filial reverence and won for him the blessing of a cloud of witnesses. No Scottish man can ever sing,

> "God of our fathers, be the God
>   Of their succeeding race,"

with a dry heart. It satisfied me at once that the minister was of a fine temper when, after a brave attempt to join, he hid his face and was silent. We thought none the worse of him that he was nervous, and two or three old people who had suspected self-sufficiency took him to their hearts when the minister concluded the Lord's prayer hurriedly, having omitted two petitions. But we knew it was not nervousness which made him pause for ten seconds after praying for widows and orphans, and in the silence which fell upon us the Divine Spirit had free access. His youth commended him, since he was also modest, for every mother had come with an inarticulate prayer that the "puir laddie wud dae weel on his first day, and him only twenty-four." Texts I can never re-member, nor, for that matter, the words of sermons; but the subject was Jesus Christ, and before he had spoken five minutes I was con-vinced, who am outside dogmas and churches, that Christ was present. The preacher faded from before one's eyes, and there rose the figure of the Nazarene, best lover of every human soul, with a face of tender patience such as Sarto gave the Master in the Church of the Annun-ziata, and stretching out His hands to old folk and little children as He did, before His death, in Galilee. His voice might be heard any moment, as I have imagined it in my lonely hours by the winter fire or on the solitary hills—soft, low, and sweet, penetrating like music to the secret of the heart, "Come unto Me . . . and I will give you rest."

During a pause in the sermon I glanced up the church, and saw the same spell held the people. Donald Menzies had long ago been caught into the third heaven, and was now hearing words which it is not lawful to utter. Campbell in his watch-tower at the back had closed his eyes, and was praying. The women were weeping quietly, and the rugged faces of our men were subdued and softened, as when the evening sun plays on the granite stone.

But what will stand out forever before my mind was the sight of Marget Howe. Her face was as white as death, and her wonderful gray eyes were shining through a mist of tears, so that I caught the light in the manse pew. She was thinking of George, and had taken the minister to her heart.

The elders, one by one, gripped the minister's hand in the vestry, and, though plain, homely men, they were the godliest in the glen; but no man spoke save Burnbrae.

"I a' but lost ae fairm for the Free Kirk, and I wud hae lost ten tae be in the Kirk this day."

Donald walked with me homewards, but would only say:

"There was a man sent from God whose name was John." At the cottage he added, "The friend of the bridegroom rejoiced greatly because of the bridegroom's voice."

Beneath the honeysuckle at his garden gate a woman was waiting.

"My name is Marget Howe, and I'm the wife of William Howe of Whinnie Knowe. My only son wes preparin' for the ministry, but God wanted him nearly a year syne. When ye preached the Evangel o' Jesus the day I heard his voice, and I loved you. Ye hev nae mither on earth, I hear, and I hae nae son, and I wantit tae say that if ye ever wish tae speak to ony woman as ye wud tae yir mither, come tae Whinnie Knowe, an' I'll coont it ane of the Lord's consolations."

His aunt could only meet him in the study, and when he looked on her his lip quivered, for his heart was wrung with one wistful regret.

"Oh, auntie, if she had only been spared to see this day, and her prayers answered."

But his aunt flung her arms around his neck.

"Dinna be cast doon, laddie, nor be unbelievin'. Yir mither has heard

every word, and is satisfied, for ye did it in remembrance o' her, and
yon was yir mither's sermon."

THE FATHERS

Alan Paton

The murder of a liberal white industrialist in South Africa by the
son of a Zulu parson engenders new understanding of the race problem. Paton catches the power of spiritual comfort in desolation, the
beauty and strength of forgiveness, in this dramatic meeting between
the two fathers who are "brothers under the skin."

ONE of the favourite nieces of Margaret Jarvis, Barbara Smith by name,
had married a man from Springs, and both Jarvis and his wife, on a
day when the Court was not holding the case, went to spend a day
with them. He had thought it would be a good thing for his wife, who
had taken the death of their son even more hardly than he had feared.
The two women talked of the people of Ixopo and Lufafa and High-
flats and Umzimkulu, and he left them and walked in the garden, for
he was a man of the soil. After a while they called to him to say they
were going into the town, and asked if he wished to go with them. But
he said that he would stay at the house, and read the newspaper while
they were away, and this he did.

The newspaper was full of the new gold that was being found at
Odendaalsrust, and of the great excitement that still prevailed on the
share-market. Someone with authority was warning people against
buying at higher and still higher prices, and saying that there was no
proof that these shares were worth what they were fetching, and that
they might come down after a while and cause much loss of money
and much suffering. There was some crime too; most of the assaults reported were by natives against Europeans, but there was nothing of the
terrible nature that made some people afraid to open their newspapers.

While he was reading there was a knock at the kitchen door, and he went out to find a native parson standing on the paved stone at the foot of the three stone steps that led up to the kitchen. The parson was old, and his black clothes were green with age, and his collar was brown with age or dirt. He took off his hat, showing the whiteness of his head, and he looked startled and afraid and he was trembling.

— Good morning, umfundisi, said Jarvis in Zulu, of which he was a master.

The parson answered in a trembling voice, Umnumzana, which means Sir, and to Jarvis' surprise, he sat down on the lowest step, as though he were ill or starving. Jarvis knew this was not rudeness, for the old man was humble and well-mannered, so he came down the steps, saying, Are you ill, umfundisi? But the old man did not answer. He continued to tremble, and he looked down on the ground, so that Jarvis could not see his face, and could not have seen it unless he had lifted the chin with his hand, which he did not do, for such a thing is not lightly done.

— Are you ill, umfundisi?

— I shall recover, umnumzana.

— Do you wish water? Or is it food? Are you hungry?

— No, umnumzana, I shall recover.

Jarvis stood on the paved stone below the lowest step, but the old man was not quick to recover. He continued to tremble, and to look at the ground. It is not easy for a white man to be kept waiting, but Jarvis waited, for the old man was obviously ill and weak. The old man made an effort to rise, using his stick, but the stick slipped on the paved stone, and fell clattering on the stone. Jarvis picked it up and restored it to him, but the old man put it down as a hindrance, and he put down his hat also, and tried to lift himself up by pressing his hands on the steps. But his first effort failed, and he sat down again, and continued to tremble. Jarvis would have helped him, but such a thing is not so lightly done as picking up a stick; then the old man pressed his hands again on the steps, and lifted himself up. Then he lifted his face also and looked at Jarvis, and Jarvis saw that his face was full of a suffering that was of neither illness nor hunger. And Jarvis stooped, and picked up the hat and stick, and he held the hat carefully for it was old and dirty, and he restored them to the parson.

— I thank you, umnumzana.

— Are you sure you are not ill, umfundisi?

— I am recovered, umnumzana.

— And what are you seeking, umfundisi?

The old parson put his hat and his stick down again on the step, and with trembling hands pulled out a wallet from the inside pocket of the old green coat, and the papers fell out on the ground, because his hands would not be still.

— I am sorry, umnumzana.

He stooped to pick up the papers, and because he was old he had to kneel, and the papers were old and dirty, and some that he had picked up fell out of his hands while he was picking up others, and the wallet fell too, and the hands were trembling and shaking. Jarvis was torn between compassion and irritation, and he stood and watched uncomfortably.

— I am sorry to detain you, umnumzana.

— It is no matter, umfundisi.

At last the papers were collected, and all were restored to the wallet except one, and this one he held out to Jarvis, and on it were the name and address of this place where they were.

— This is the place, umfundisi.

— I was asked to come here, umnumzana. There is a man named Sibeko of Ndotsheni——

— Ndotsheni, I know it. I come from Ndotsheni.

— And this man had a daughter, umnumzana, who worked for a white man uSmith in Ixopo——

— Yes, yes.

— And when the daughter of uSmith married, she married the white man whose name is on the paper.

— That is so.

— And they came to live here in Springs, and the daughter of Sibeko came here also to work for them. Now Sibeko has not heard of her for these twelve months, and he asked—I am asked—to enquire about this girl.

Jarvis turned and went into the house, and returned with the boy who was working there. You may enquire from him, he said, and he turned again and went into the house. But when he was there it came suddenly to him that this was the old parson of Ndotsheni himself. So he came out again.

— Did you find what you wanted, umfundisi?

— This boy does not know her, umnumzana. When he came she had gone already.

— The mistress of the house is out, the daughter of uSmith. But she will soon be returning, and you may wait for her if you wish.

Jarvis dismissed the boy, and waited till he was gone.

— I know you, umfundisi, he said.

The suffering in the old man's face smote him, so that he said, Sit down, umfundisi. Then the old man would be able to look at the ground, and he would not need to look at Jarvis, and Jarvis would not need to look at him, for it was uncomfortable to look at him. So the old man sat down and Jarvis said to him, not looking at him, There is something between you and me, but I do not know what it is.

— Umnumzana.

— You are in fear of me, but I do not know what it is. You need not be in fear of me.

— It is true, umnumzana. You do not know what it is.

— I do not know but I desire to know.

— I doubt if I could tell it, umnumzana.

— You must tell it, umfundisi. Is it heavy?

— It is very heavy, umnumzana. It is the heaviest thing of all my years.

He lifted his face, and there was in it suffering that Jarvis had not seen before. Tell me, he said, it will lighten you.

— I am afraid, umnumzana.

— I see you are afraid, umfundisi. It is that which I do not understand. But I tell you, you need not be afraid. I shall not be angry. There will be no anger in me against you.

— Then, said the old man, this thing that is the heaviest thing of all my years is the heaviest thing of all your years also.

Jarvis looked at him, at first bewildered, but then something came to him. You can only mean one thing, he said, you can only mean one thing. But I still do not understand.

— It was my son that killed your son, said the old man.

So they were silent. Jarvis left him and walked out into the trees of the garden. He stood at the wall and looked out over the veld, out to the great white dumps of the mines, like hills under the sun. When he turned to come back, he saw that the old man had risen, his hat in one hand, his stick in the other, his head bowed, his eyes on the ground. He went back to him.

— I have heard you, he said. I understand what I did not understand. There is no anger in me.

— Umnumzana.

— The mistress of the house is back, the daughter of uSmith. Do you wish to see her? Are you recovered?

— It was that that I came to do, umnumzana.

— I understand. And you were shocked when you saw me. You had no thought that I would be here. How did you know me?

— I have seen you riding past Ndotsheni, past the church where I work.

Jarvis listened to the sounds in the house. Then he spoke very quietly. Perhaps you saw the boy also, he said. He too used to ride past Ndotsheni. On a red horse with a white face. And he carried wooden guns, here in his belt, as small boys do.

The old man's face was working. He continued to look on the ground, and Jarvis could see that tears fell on it. He himself was moved and unmanned, and he would have brought the thing to an end, but he could find no quick voice for it.

— I remember, umnumzana. There was a brightness in him.

— Yes, yes, said Jarvis, there was a brightness in him.

— Umnumzana, it is a hard word to say. But my heart holds a deep sorrow for you, and for the inkosikazi, and for the young inkosikazi, and for the children.

— Yes, yes, said Jarvis. Yes, yes, he said fiercely. I shall call the mistress of the house.

He went in and brought her out with him. This old man, he said in English, has come to inquire about the daughter of a native named Sibeko, who used to work for you in Ixopo. They have heard nothing of her for months.

— I had to send her away, said Smith's daughter. She was good when she started, and I promised her father to look after her. But she went to the bad and started to brew liquor in her room. She was arrested and sent to gaol for a month, and after that of course I could not take her back again.

— You do not know where she is? asked Jarvis.

— I'm sure I do not know, said Smith's daughter in English. And I do not care.

— She does not know, said Jarvis in Zulu. But he did not add that Smith's daughter did not care.

— I thank you, said the old man in Zulu. Stay well, umnumzana. And he bowed to Smith's daughter and she nodded her acknowledgement.

He put on his hat and started to walk down the path to the back gate, according to the custom. Smith's daughter went into the house, and Jarvis followed the old man slowly, as though he were not following him. The old man opened the gate and went out through it and closed it behind him. As he turned to close it he saw that Jarvis had followed him, and he bowed to him.

— Go well, umfundisi, said Jarvis.

— Stay well, umnumzana. The old man raised his hat and put it back again on his head. Then he started to walk slowly down the road to the station, Jarvis watching him until he was out of sight. As he turned to come back, he saw that his wife was coming to join him, and he saw with a pang that she too walked as if she were old.

He walked to join her, and she put her arm in his.

— Why are you so disturbed, James? she asked. Why were you so disturbed when you came into the house?

— Something that came out of the past, he said. You know how it comes suddenly?

She was satisfied, and said, I know.

She held his arm more closely. Barbara wants us for lunch, she said.

The Good Shepherd

THE BAPTIZING

J. H. Ingraham

The Prince of the House of David is the life of Jesus from his baptism in Jordan to his crucifixion on Calvary. The incidents are told in a series of letters from Adina, a Jewess sojourning in Jerusalem, to her wealthy father in Egypt. "The Baptizing" is one of the most poignant of the scenes depicted in Ingraham's classic—a continued best seller from 1851 to 1901.

MY DEAR FATHER:

I will commence this letter by entreating you not to let any prejudice lead you to reject, without examination, belief of the events which have formed the subject of my recent letters to you. Please, my honored and beloved father, please to consider impartially the things of which I have written, the preaching of John, and his baptism of Jesus, whom, before ten thousand people, he declared to be MESSIAS, to whom he bore witness, and how the voice of God proclaimed from Heaven that He was "His beloved Son!" Think of all this, and ask yourself seriously, "Is not this the Christ?"

This question need not pass far on its way ere it finds a response from *my* lips and heart: "Yes, He is the Christ, and I will believe in Him!"

I can see you look both displeased and grieved. But you have no reason to fear that I shall do or believe aught that will bring shame on your gray hairs, or your name. If thou art a Jew, and proud of being descended from the lineage of the Patriarchs who walked with the Lord, I am also equally proud of my nation and of my faith. In believing Jesus of Nazareth to be the Messias of God, I do not make myself less a Jewess; but, without believing it, my dear father, I could not be completely a Jewess. Has not the Messias of our nation been the burden of Judah's prayer and of Israel's hope, for ages? Does not the belief that Messias cometh constitute one of the great characteristics of the Jewish race?

I shall wait for your next parcel of letters with the deepest solicitude, in order that I may know what your decision is in reference to these extraordinary things which are coming to pass. You will not hear them only from my letters, dear father, for the report of these wonders is broad-cast over the land, and men who witnessed the baptism of Jesus will, no doubt, report in Egypt what then took place. Merchants of Damascus and of Cairo were present, leaving their trains of camels a little way off; and Arab horsemen sat in their saddles on the outside of the crowd; while Roman soldiers, strangers from Persia and Edom, and even the merchants from Media, with numerous people, Gentiles as well as Jews, were seen mingled with the multitude. This thing, therefore, was not done in a corner. The voice I plainly heard, and understood every word! It seemed to me to come from the far blue depths of Heaven, with the clearness of a trumpet, and the sonorous majesty of thunder. But the light which descended was the most dazzling that human eyes ever encountered; and though when descending with the velocity of lightning, it seemed like a lance of fire; yet, upon reaching the sacred head of Jesus, it assumed, as I before stated, the shape of a dove; and, resting upon Him, cast over His whole person a glittering splendor, like the sun. This lasted for full a minute, so that all eyes beheld it, and then followed the voice from the skies! While thousands either stood stupefied, or fell upon their faces in adoration and fear, He withdrew himself from the multitude, no one knew how, save two persons, whose eyes never wander from him. These were the cousin of Mary, John, and Lazarus, the brother of Mary and Martha.

The people, after recovering a little from their amazement and awe, were looking for Him, and inquiring whither he had gone, some gazing into the water, some towards the wilderness, some even gazing upwards into Heaven, of which last I was one, as if they expected to behold Him ascending upon a chariot of dazzling clouds towards the throne of His God and Father. The general impression was that he had been translated to Heaven; and some wept that a prophet was sent to be taken so soon; some doubted, and called it magic and sorcery; and others, who were doubtless filled with their own wickedness, mocked, and said the voice was thunder, and the light lightning. But the majority believed, and greatly rejoiced at what they had seen and heard. The prophet John, of Jordan, looked constantly around for Jesus, and then, with his hands clasped together and uplifted, gazed heavenward.

The excitement which the sudden disappearance of Jesus produced led to a universal separation of the multitude, who dispersed in all directions, forgetting John the Baptizer, whom they had hitherto followed.

Rabbi Amos and our party remained standing near the water, for he did not wish us to be lost in the retiring throngs, and he also desired to speak with John, who stood alone in the midst of the water, precisely where he had baptized Jesus. Not one of his disciples remained with him. Rabbi Amos drew near, and said to him:

"Holy prophet, knowest thou what man, if man he may be called, was just baptized by thee?"

The prophet bent his looks with tearful tenderness upon Rabbi Amos, and said, plaintively and touchingly:

"This is He of whom I spake—— After me cometh a man which is preferred before me, for He was before me. And I knew Him not; but He that sent me, to baptize with water, the same said unto me, Upon whom thou shalt see the Spirit descending and remaining on Him, the same is He that baptizes with the Holy Ghost. And I saw the Spirit descending like a dove, and I saw and bear record this is the Son of God!"

"And whither, oh, holy prophet of Jordan," asked Rabbi Amos, with deep and sacred interest, "whither has He departed?"

"That I know not! He must increase and I must decrease, whether He remaineth on earth or has been taken up into Heaven! My mission is now drawing to its close: for He to whom I have borne witness is come."

"And is He come to depart so soon forever?" I asked, with deep interest; "shall we behold Him no more?"

"The hidden things belong to God. I know not whence He came nor whither He has gone! for I knew Him not in all His glory, but only as a prophet and son of man, until the Spirit descended and abode upon Him. Ye have heard my testimony that this is the very Messias, the Christ, the Son of God!"

Thus speaking, he turned and walked out of the water on the side towards Bethabara, and disappeared among the trees that fringed the bank. The face of Rabbi Amos was grave and thoughtful. I said, "Uncle, dost thou believe all that thou hast seen and heard?"

"I know not what to say," he answered, "only that the things which I have beheld this day are evidences that God has not forgotten his people Israel!" We left the banks of the Jordan in silence and awe, and remounting our mules, we returned towards my uncle's house at Gilgal. On the way we constantly passed crowds of people who were riding and walking; and all were in high talk about the wonderful events which had taken place at the river. The impression seemed universally to be that Jesus had gone up into Heaven after he was baptized.

But, my dear father, it is with deep joy that I am able to tell you that this wonderful person is still on the earth. I stated that my cousin John, and Lazarus, the Secretary of the Scribes, had kept their eyes upon Him from the first, and that they had seen Him pass down the river, where some projecting and overhanging trees hid Him at once from view. Though they often lost sight of Him, they yet followed, and at length came in view of Him, as he was leaving the river bank, and going towards the desert. But one of the young men said to the other:

"Let us not fail to overtake Him, and follow Him whithersoever He may go; for with Him must be the well of life, as He is so highly favored of God."

So they ran very swiftly, and at length coming near Him, called, "Master, good master, stay for us, for we would follow and learn of thee!"

He stopped, and turned upon them a visage so pale, and marred with sadness and anguish, that they both stood still and gazed upon Him with amazement at beholding such a change. Lazarus, who had been so long his bosom friend, wept aloud. "Weep not! thou shalt see me another day, my friends," He said. "I go now to the wilderness, in obedience to the Spirit which guideth me thither. Thou shalt, after a time, behold me again. It is expedient for you that I go whither I go."

"Nay, but we will go with thee," said Lazarus, earnestly. "If thou art to endure evil, we will be with thee."

"There must be none to help. There must be none to uphold," He said firmly, but sadly. "I must tread the wine press of temptation alone!"

He then left them, waving His hand for them to go back. They obeyed sorrowfully, wondering what His words meant, and wherefore it was needful for Him to go into the desert, where certain mysterious trials seemed to wait for Him. From time to time the two young men looked backward to watch the receding figure of the Christ, till they no longer distinguished Him in the distance.

The two friends came on to the house of Rabbi Amos, at Gilgal, the same night, and there Lazarus made known to us what I have just related. It affected us all deeply, and we sat together late at night upon the porch under the fig trees, talking of Jesus, and we wept to think that He was driven by some destiny, unknown and unfathomable by us, to dwell alone in the wilderness.

Now, my dear father, how wonderful is all this! That a great prophet is among us cannot be denied. Rabbi Amos advises all persons to wait patiently the issue, for if God has sent a Prophet, He must have a mission, which, in due time, He will come forth from the wilderness to deliver. In my next I may be able to write you something further touching the development of that which remains so much enveloped in mystery. May the God of our father's house come forth indeed from the Heavens, for the salvation of His People.

Your devoted and loving

ADINA.

IN THE PRISON

George Eliot

Modeling the characters of Mrs. Poyser and Dinah Morris, the Methodist preacher, on members of her own family, George Eliot framed a remarkable picture of English village life of a hundred years ago in *Adam Bede*. Throughout the novel Dinah Morris lives by the Word in faith and works. Here she comes to bring comfort to one whose indiscretion is her own undoing.

As DINAH crossed the prison court with the turnkey, the solemn evening light seemed to make the walls higher than they were by day, and the sweet pale face in the cap was more than ever like a white flower on this background of gloom. The turnkey looked askance at her all the while, but never spoke: he somehow felt that the sound of his own rude voice would be grating just then. He struck a light as they entered the dark corridor leading to the condemned cell, and then said in his most civil tone, "It'll be pretty nigh dark in the cell a'ready; but I can stop with my light a bit, if you like."

"Nay, friend, thank you," said Dinah. "I wish to go in alone."

"As you like," said the jailer, turning the harsh key in the lock, and opening the door wide enough to admit Dinah. A jet of light from his lantern fell on the opposite corner of the cell, where Hetty was sitting on her straw pallet with her face buried in her knees. It seemed as if she were asleep, and yet the grating of the lock would have been likely to waken her.

The door closed again, and the only light in the cell was that of the evening sky, through the small high grating—enough to discern human faces by. Dinah stood still for a minute, hesitating to speak, because Hetty might be asleep; and looking at the motionless heap with a yearning heart. Then she said, softly—

"Hetty!"

There was a slight movement perceptible in Hetty's frame—a start such as might have been produced by a feeble electrical shock; but she did not look up. Dinah spoke again, in a tone made stronger by irrepressible emotion—

"Hetty . . . it's Dinah."

Again there was a slight, startled movement through Hetty's frame, and without uncovering her face, she raised her head a little, as if listening. . . .

"Hetty," she said, gently, "do you know who it is that sits by your side?"

"Yes," Hetty answered, slowly, "it's Dinah."

"And do you remember the time when we were at the Hall Farm together, and that night when I told you to be sure and think of me as a friend in trouble?"

"Yes," said Hetty. Then, after a pause, she added, "But you can do nothing for me. You can't make 'em do anything. They'll hang me o' Monday—it's Friday now."

As Hetty said the last words, she clung closer to Dinah, shuddering.

"No, Hetty, I can't save you from that death. But isn't the suffering less hard when you have somebody with you, that feels for you—that you can speak to, and say what's in your heart? . . . Yes, Hetty: you lean on me: you are glad to have me with you."

"You won't leave me, Dinah? You'll keep close to me?"

"No, Hetty, I won't leave you. I'll stay with you to the last. . . . But, Hetty, there is some one else in this cell besides me, some one close to you?"

Hetty said, in a frightened whisper, "Who?"

"Some one who has been with you through all your hours of sin and trouble—who has known every thought you have had—has seen where you went, where you lay down and rose up again, and all the deeds you have tried to hide in darkness. And on Monday, when I can't follow you,—when my arms can't reach you,—when death has parted us,—He who is with us now, and knows all, will be with you then. It makes no difference—whether we live or die, we are in the presence of God."

"Oh, Dinah, won't nobody do anything for me? *Will* they hang me for certain? . . . I wouldn't mind if they'd let me live."

"My poor Hetty, death is very dreadful to you. I know it's dreadful. But if you had a friend to take care of you after death—in that other world—some one whose love is greater than mine—who can do everything? . . . If God our Father was your friend, and was willing to save you from sin and suffering, so as you should neither know wicked feelings nor pain again? If you could believe He loved you and would help you, as you believe I love you and will help you, it wouldn't be so hard to die on Monday, would it?"

"But I can't know anything about it," Hetty said, with sullen sadness.

"Because, Hetty, you are shutting up your soul against him, by trying to hide the truth. God's love and mercy can overcome all things —our ignorance, and weakness, and all the burthen of our past wickedness—all things but our wilful sin; sin that we cling to, and will not give up. You believe in my love and pity for you, Hetty; but if you had not let me come near you, if you wouldn't have looked at me or spoken to me, you'd have shut me out from helping you: I couldn't have made you feel my love; I couldn't have told you what I felt for you. Don't shut God's love out in that way, by clinging to sin. . . . He can't bless you while you have one falsehood in your soul; his pardoning mercy can't reach you until you open your heart to him, and say, 'I have done this great wickedness; O God, save me, make me pure from sin.' While you cling to one sin and will not part with it, it must drag you down to misery after death, as it has dragged you to misery here in this world, my poor, poor Hetty. It is sin that brings dread, and darkness, and despair: there is light and blessedness for us as soon as we cast it off: God enters our souls then, and teaches us, and brings us strength and peace. Cast it off now, Hetty—now: confess the wickedness you have done—the sin you have been guilty of against your heavenly Father. Let us kneel down together, for we are in the presence of God."

Hetty obeyed Dinah's movement, and sank on her knees. They still held each other's hands, and there was long silence. Then Dinah said—

"Hetty, we are before God: he is waiting for you to tell the truth."

Still there was silence. At last Hetty spoke, in a tone of beseeching—

"Dinah . . . help me . . . I can't feel anything like you . . . my heart is hard."

Dinah held the clinging hand, and all her soul went forth in her voice:

"Jesus, thou present Saviour! Thou hast known the depths of all sorrow: thou hast entered that black darkness where God is not, and hast uttered the cry of the forsaken. Come, Lord, and gather of the fruits of thy travail and thy pleading: stretch forth thy hand, thou who art mighty to save to the uttermost, and rescue this lost one. She is clothed round with thick darkness: the fetters of her sin are upon her, and she cannot stir to come to thee: she can only feel her heart is hard, and she is helpless. She cries to me, thy weak creature. . . . Saviour! it is a blind cry to thee. Hear it! Pierce the darkness! Look upon her with thy face of love and sorrow, that thou didst turn on him who denied thee; and melt her hard heart.

"See, Lord,—I bring her, as they of old brought the sick and helpless, and thou didst heal them: I bear her on my arms and carry her before thee. Fear and trembling have taken hold on her; but she trembles only at the pain and death of the body: breathe upon her thy life-giving Spirit, and put a new fear within her—the fear of her sin. Make her dread to keep the accursed thing within her soul: make her feel the presence of the living God, who beholds all the past, to whom the darkness is as noonday; who is waiting now, at the eleventh hour, for her to turn to him, and confess her sin, and cry for mercy—now, before the night of death comes, and the moment of pardon is for ever fled, like yesterday that returneth not.

"Saviour! it is yet time—time to snatch this poor soul from ever-lasting darkness. I believe—I believe in thy infinite love. What is *my* love or *my* pleading? It is quenched in thine. I can only clasp her in my weak arms, and urge her with my weak pity. Thou—thou wilt breathe on the dead soul, and it shall arise from the unanswering sleep of death.

"Yea, Lord, I see thee, coming through the darkness, coming, like the morning, with healing on thy wings. The marks of thy agony are upon thee—I see, I see thou art able and willing to save—thou wilt not let her perish for ever.

"Come, mighty Saviour! let the dead hear thy voice; let the eyes of the blind be opened: let her see that God encompasses her; let her tremble at nothing but at the sin that cuts her off from him. Melt the hard heart; unseal the closed lips: make her cry with her whole soul, 'Father, I have sinned.' . . ."

"Dinah," Hetty sobbed out, throwing her arms round Dinah's neck, "I will speak . . . I will tell . . . I won't hide it any more."

But the tears and sobs were too violent. Dinah raised her gently from her knees, and seated her on the pallet again, sitting down by her side.

It was a long time before the convulsed throat was quiet, and even then they sat some time in stillness and darkness, holding each other's hands. At last Hetty whispered—

"I did do it, Dinah . . . I buried it in the wood . . . the little baby . . . and it cried . . . I heard it cry . . . ever such a way off . . . all night . . . and I went back because it cried."

She paused, and then spoke hurriedly in a louder, pleading tone.

"But I thought perhaps it wouldn't die—there might somebody find it. I didn't kill it—I didn't kill it myself. I put it down there and covered it up, and when I came back it was gone. . . . It was because I was so very miserable, Dinah . . . I didn't know where to go . . . and I tried to kill myself before, and I couldn't. Oh, I tried so to drown myself in the pool, and I couldn't. I went to Windsor—I ran away—did you know? I went to find him, as he might take care of me; and he was gone; and then I didn't know what to do. I daredn't go back home again—I couldn't bear it. I couldn't have bore to look at anybody, for they'd have scorned me. I thought o' you sometimes, and thought I'd come to you, for I didn't think you'd be cross with me, and cry shame on me: I thought I could tell you. But then the other folks 'ud come to know it at last, and I couldn't bear that. It was partly thinking o' you made me come toward Stoniton; and, besides, I was so frightened at going wandering about till I was a beggarwoman, and had nothing; and sometimes it seemed as if I must go back to the Farm sooner than that. Oh, it was so dreadful, Dinah . . . I was so miserable . . . I wished I'd never been born into this world. I should never like to go into the green fields again—I hated 'em so in my misery."

Hetty paused again, as if the sense of the past were too strong upon her for words.

"And then I got to Stoniton, and I began to feel frightened that night, because I was so near home. And then the little baby was born, when I didn't expect it; and the thought came into my mind that I might get rid of it, and go home again. The thought came all of a sudden, as I was lying in the bed, and it got stronger and stronger . . . I longed so to go back again . . . I couldn't bear being so lonely, and coming to beg for want. And it gave me strength and resolution to get up and dress myself. I felt I must do it . . . I didn't know how . . . I thought I'd find a pool, if I could, like that other, in the corner of the field, in the dark. And when the woman went out, I felt as if I was strong enough to do anything . . . I thought I should get rid of all my misery, and go back home, and never let 'em know why I ran

away. I put on my bonnet and shawl, and went out into the dark
street, with the baby under my cloak; and I walked fast till I got into
a street a good way off, and there was a public, and I got some warm
stuff to drink and some bread. And I walked on and on, and I hardly
felt the ground I trod on; and it got lighter, for there came the
moon—— Oh, Dinah, it frightened me when it first looked at me out
o' the clouds—it never looked so before; and I turned out of the road
into the fields, for I was afraid o' meeting anybody with the moon shining on me. And I came to a haystack, where I thought I could lie
down and keep myself warm all night. There was a place cut into it,
where I could make me a bed; and I lay comfortable, and the baby
was warm against me; and I must have gone to sleep for a good while,
for when I woke it was morning, but not very light, and the baby was
crying. And I saw a wood a little way off . . . I thought there'd perhaps be a ditch or a pond there . . . and it was so early I thought I
could hide the child there, and get a long way off before folks was up.
And then I thought I'd go home—I'd get rides in carts and go home,
and tell 'em I'd been to try and see for a place, and couldn't get one.
I longed so for it, Dinah, I longed so to be safe at home. I don't know
how I felt about the baby. I seemed to hate it—it was like a heavy
weight hanging round my neck; and yet its crying went through me,
and I daredn't look at its little hands and face. But I went on to the
wood, and I walked about, but there was no water . . ."

Hetty shuddered. She was silent for some moments, and when she
began again, it was in a whisper.

"I came to a place where there was lots of chips and turf, and I
sat down on the trunk of a tree to think what I should do. And all
of a sudden I saw a hole under the nut-tree, like a little grave. And it
darted into me like lightning—I'd lay the baby there, and cover it
with the grass and the chips. I couldn't kill it any other way. And
I'd done it in a minute; and, oh, it cried so, Dinah—I *couldn't* cover
it quite up—I thought perhaps somebody 'ud come and take care of it,
and then it wouldn't die. And I made haste out of the wood, but I
could hear it crying all the while; and when I got out into the fields, it
was as if I was held fast—I couldn't go away, for all I wanted so to go.
And I sat against the haystack to watch if anybody 'ud come: I was
very hungry, and I'd only a bit of bread left; but I couldn't go away.
And after ever such a while—hours and hours—the man came—him in
a smock-frock, and he looked at me so, I was frightened, and I made
haste and went on. I thought he was going to the wood, and would

perhaps find the baby. And I went right on, till I came to a village, a long way off from the wood; and I was very sick, and faint, and hungry. I got something to eat there, and bought a loaf. But I was frightened to stay. I heard the baby crying, and thought the other folks heard it too,—and I went on. But I was so tired, and it was getting towards dark. And at last, by the roadside there was a barn—ever such a way off any house—like the barn in Abbot's Close; and I thought I could go in there and hide myself among the hay and straw, and nobody 'ud be likely to come. I went in, and it was half full o' trusses of straw, and there was some hay, too. And I made myself a bed, ever so far behind, where nobody could find me; and I was so tired and weak, I went to sleep. . . . But oh, the baby's crying kept waking me; and I thought that man as looked at me so was come and laying hold of me. But I must have slept a long while at last, though I didn't know; for when I got up and went out of the barn, I didn't know whether it was night or morning. But it was morning, for it kept getting lighter; and I turned back the way I'd come. I couldn't help it, Dinah; it was the baby's crying made me go: and yet I was frightened to death. I thought that man in the smock-frock 'ud see me, and know I put the baby there. But I went on, for all that: I'd left off thinking about going home—it had gone out o' my mind. I saw nothing but that place in the wood where I'd buried the baby . . . I see it now. O Dinah! shall I allays see it?"

Hetty clung round Dinah, and shuddered again. The silence seemed long before she went on.

"I met nobody, for it was very early, and I got into the wood. . . . I knew the way to the place . . . the place against the nut-tree; and I could hear it crying at every step. . . . I thought it was alive. . . . I don't know whether I was frightened or glad . . . I don't know what I felt. I only know I was in the wood, and heard the cry. I don't know what I felt till I saw the baby was gone. And when I'd put it there, I thought I should like somebody to find it, and save it from dying; but when I saw it was gone, I was struck like a stone, with fear. I never thought o' stirring, I felt so weak. I knew I couldn't run away, and everybody as saw me 'ud know about the baby. My heart went like a stone: I couldn't wish or try for anything; it seemed like as if I should stay there for ever, and nothing 'ud ever change. But they came and took me away."

Hetty was silent, but she shuddered again, as if there was still something behind; and Dinah waited, for her heart was so full, that tears must come before words. At last Hetty burst out, with a sob—

"Dinah, do you think God will take away that crying and the place in the wood, now I've told everything?"

"Let us pray, poor sinner: let us fall on our knees again, and pray to the God of all mercy."

ADVENT

Gunnar Gunnarsson

The Icelandic shepherd, Benedikt, journeys into the grim mountain wastelands on his twenty-seventh rescue of the sheep missed in the annual roundup. As he sets out on his feats of endurance and patience, he reflects on the deeds of the Good Shepherd of us all.

WHEN a holy season approaches men make ready for it, each after his own manner and kind. There are many ways. Benedikt too had a way all his own; and this was his way: At the beginning of the Christmas season, that is, when the weather permitted, if possible on the first Sunday of Advent, he would pack food, changes of socks and several pairs of new leather shoes in a knapsack, and with these a small oil stove with a can of kerosene and a small flask of spirits. Then he would take the way to the mountains, the desolate mountains of Iceland, where at this season of the year nothing was to be found but birds of prey, hard and cruel as winter itself, foxes, and a few scattered sheep, lost and wandering about.

And it was for the sake of these very sheep that he went forth, animals which had not been found at the regular autumn in-gathering. They must not be allowed to perish up there from hunger and cold merely because none would take the trouble or the risk to seek them out and bring them home. They too were living creatures of God and he felt a kind of responsibility for them. His aim then was simple enough—to find them and bring them safe and sound under shelter before the great festival should spread its benediction over the earth, and bring peace and satisfaction in the hearts of men who have done their best.

Benedikt was always alone on this Advent Journey of his—that is, no man went with him. To be sure he had his dog along and his bell-wether. The dog he had at this time was called Leo, and as Benedikt put it, he earned his name, for truly he was a Pope among dogs. The wether was named Gnarly; that was because he was so tough.

These three had been inseparable on these expeditions for a number of years now, and they had gradually come to know one another with that deep-seated knowledge perhaps to be found only among animals of such divergent kinds that no shade of their own ego or own blood or own wishes or desires could come between them to confuse or darken it. There really was a fourth member of the band, the sleek-maned horse, Faxe, but unfortunately he was too heavy and his feet were too small to wade through the deep light snow of early winter; and besides he was not capable of enduring many days of hard work on the slender rations with which the other three made out. Benedikt and Leo were sorrowful and troubled when they had said farewell to him, even though only for a week. Gnarly took this dispensation of Providence as he took everything else, with the greatest of calm.

So the three of them journeyed through the winter day, Leo in front; in spite of the cold his tongue was hanging comfortably out of the right side of his mouth; Gnarly next in an imperturbable trot; last of all Benedikt, trailing his skis behind him. Down here in this in-habited country the snow was still too light and soft to hold up a man on skis; he had to stamp his way through the snow and sometimes his feet struck against frozen clods and stones—phew! It was a hard matter to make much speed, but aside from this there was no great difficulty. Leo, after the manner of dogs, was interested in everything and in the best of humor. At times he could no longer hold himself in and had to break away; then he would come charging back to Benedikt in wide leaps with the snow spraying about him, leaping up at him, barking, stretching against him, asking to be praised and petted.

"Yes, you are really a Pope," Benedikt would say then.

That was his pet name for his comrade, and from his mouth could come no higher praise.

At present the three were making their way through settled country toward Botn, the last farm before you come to the mountains. They had the whole day before them and were making easy going of it, following the paths from one farm to another, pausing to greet the people and their dogs.

"But at least have a cup of coffee."

"No, thank you, not today."

They wanted to reach their goal early, so instead of coffee they would take a drink of milk—all three of them. Again and again Benedikt was called on to give his opinion as to the weather prospects. Of course, they only meant . . . they would not for anything be importunate or prophesy evil . . . but surely there was no harm in asking the question. And someone might add, for instance, "Well, the only thing that I wanted to say was . . . I suppose Leo is a dog who can find his way even in the dark and in the whirl of a snowstorm?" They would bring it up as a sort of joke and would take care not to look up, would take care not to call attention even with a glance to the dour and threatening clouds in the heavens. And then they would add quickly, "Of course he can find his way, the big cur."

"All three of us can find our way," Benedikt would answer calmly, and empty the cup of milk. "Many thanks."

"As to that," the peasant would joke, "I would trust Leo the most, except for Gnarly," and then he would disappear for a moment in the house and bring out some tidbit, something for the dog to gnaw on. Benedikt at such times did not say anything about Leo's being a regular Pope, but he merely nodded to the dog to take his time about eating, that they would wait until he was through. Meantime Gnarly would be getting a handful of good, sweet meadow hay. Then they would start on again, the three of them.

Benedikt had not been to church today. He had put it off, had not found time for it. If he expected to arrive at a reasonably sensible hour and rest sufficiently to prepare him for the early morning awakening and the long march of the morrow, then he would have to make full use of this day from the first light on. It was principally on Gnarly's account that he was taking the first day's journey so easily. Let it be understood that Gnarly was thoroughly capable and well deserved the name he bore, but one must be careful and not overdo him at the very first. So that Benedikt really could not take the longer road around by the church. On the first Sunday of Advent this wandering through the tilled land to the edge of the heath was his church-going. Besides, before setting out, he had sat down on the edge of his bed in the farmhands' room and read a passage from the Scripture, the twenty-first chapter of Matthew—Jesus' entry into Jerusalem. But to accompany it he had to imagine the ringing of bells, the singing of hymns in the little sod-roofed church, and the wise, calm exposition of the gospel by the old pastor. And he *could* imagine it too, so well that it was all real to him.

So now he was pushing through the snow—white as far as the eye could reach, gray white under winter skies in the evening, the ice on the lake covered with rime or a light drift of snow. Only the low flat craters rising here and there out of the snow outlined the greater or lesser rings of their funnels in a kind of a warning pattern in all this waste of snow. But what sort of a warning was it they wanted to give? Could anyone ever find out? Perhaps those crater mouths were saying, "Let everything freeze, let stone and water grow stiff, let the air freeze and come down in white flakes like a bridal veil, like a shroud upon the earth, let the breath in your mouth freeze, and the hope in your heart and the blood in your veins grow cold in death. Deep down below the fire still lives." Perhaps that is what they said. And what did they mean by it? Or perhaps they were saying something else. But in any case if you looked away from these black rings everything was white, even the lake in the valley—a glittering white surface, smooth and slick as a parlor floor. For whom? Whom did it invite to the dance?

As though born of all this whiteness, against which only the black crater rings showed, and scattering gray lava pillars towered, ghost-like here and there, there lay a benediction over this Sunday in the mountains that laid hold on the heart; an immeasurable solemnity, white as innocence itself, surrounded the peaceful Sabbath smoke from the low-lying farmhouses scattered far and wide, one from another, almost vanishing in the waste of snow—an inconceivable peace filled with unbelievable promise—Advent—Advent. Yes, Benedikt took the word in his mouth guardedly, that great, quiet, strange, and yet at the same time intimate, word—for Benedikt perhaps the most personal of all words. It is true he did not know precisely what it meant, but there was an expectation in it, a getting ready, that he felt. In the course of years this word had come to contain for him almost the entire meaning of his life. And what was his life? What was the life of men on earth anyhow, except a service, imperfect, never to be finished, upheld, nevertheless, and justified by expectation and preparation?

And then they came to another farmhouse and everyday life met them again with its peasant hospitality.

"At least have a cup of coffee."

"We are, to tell the truth, somewhat pressed for time, the days are so short, so thank you very much."

The farmer took a long careful look at the sky and confessed frankly that he had no great opinion of the weather.

"Well, we just have to take the weather as God sends it," said Benedikt.

The farmer, for his part, only hoped that the storm would not break before night set in. Talk like this was especially displeasing to Benedikt. So then they must be on their way.

"Are they really good for anything, these companions of yours?" asked the farmer. He did not want to let the man go on; perhaps he was seeing him for the last time, who knows? Anyway he had had such a peculiar dream—as real as life: A storm gathering around these three—it would test their very souls, if not worse.

"Isn't Gnarly really a bother to you? Can you depend on him and the dog?"

"Can I depend on him?" answered Benedikt. "All three of us are up to anything."

One should not say things like that in the hour of danger. One should not defy the powers so arrogantly. The farmer stood and watched them go. There they went, the three of them—Benedikt, Leo, and Gnarly; and a man, doubt-filled, deeply moved, dissatisfied with himself, with them, with the world, remained behind them, looked after them, and chewed tobacco. Who in the world could understand people like that—to risk everything, even life? And for what? For a few sheep that belonged to others. For Benedikt had only a very few, and none of his were missing.

It is likely that Benedikt did not understand the cautious peasant either. In any case the three went on their way, rejoicing that today was a good day which no one might spoil—Advent. And as Benedikt's head was so filled with thoughts of the holy significance of this day, and of the Scripture lesson he had read, he got to thinking that this must have been the very day, hundreds of years ago, that Jesus had made his entry into Jerusalem. For he was only a simple man, un-learned in the finer matters of history and theology; good will and devotion often crowded out facts in his mind. And it seemed to him that he could feel in the very air plain traces of that great event, that the day had taken on something of its peculiar sacred character, and had kept it on down through the centuries. Benedikt could see

Him plainly before his eyes, going into the great city, splendid in the rays of the sun. He had seen it—its white temple and houses in a picture Bible—and Jesus riding on the ass in the midst of it. The branches that the people cut down from trees and spread out before the feet of the ass looked like frost flowers on a window-pane. But they were not white, he knew that—they were green, full of sap, and something of the sunshine was clinging to their leaves. And suddenly the words of the old Book rang out almost audibly through the air, as though the ether-waves had preserved them, and one need only lend an ear: "Behold thy King cometh unto thee, meek, and sitting upon an ass, and a colt the foal of an ass."

Meek! That was a word Benedikt could understand. He could understand how the Son of God could be meek and riding upon the foal of an ass, for of all things living and dead nothing is too small for service, and there is nothing that is not consecrated through service. Even the Son of God. And only through service. Benedikt felt that he knew that little ass and knew exactly how he felt, and how God's Son felt in that holy hour. He could see plainly before his eyes the people spreading their best clothes on the road. And then he heard some say, "Who is this man?" Really! "Who is this Man?" For they did not recognize the Son of God. And yet they should have known Him, for on that perfect and simple countenance shone a smile, only a little overshadowed for sorrow that they knew Him not. That their eyes were so blind, that the mirrors of their hearts were so tarnished. And at the sight of that troubled smile something, a flash of fire, went through Benedikt's heart. How blind they must have been! To stand face to face with their Redeemer and not recognize Him. As for him, he was convinced that he would have recognized Him from the first glance. And he would have joined himself unto Him at once and helped Him drive the insolent ones out of the Holy of Holies and overthrow the chairs of the money-changers and the tables of those that sold doves.

At this thought Benedikt pushed back his leather cap and dried his forehead. Walking was no exertion for him now, but these war-like thoughts were driving the sweat from his every pore, for he was a man of peace. Never even in his dreams had he thought of violence against his fellow-men—at least not since he was grown. But the words of the Saviour, "My house shall be called the house of prayer: but ye have made it a den of thieves," awakened burning anger in him.

Just to think—how it would be for the merchant to set up shop and begin his usual cheating in the old sod-covered church. Then there would be an end of all peace. And with these words of Jesus ringing in his ears he felt himself ready for anything that might be required of him—under the leadership of the Master. Money-changers—oh-ho! Sellers of doves—ha! ha! Sellers of anything—he knew what they were like. Only he would think of them as little as possible. And again he wiped his forehead, for he knew some who bought and sold, the merchant, and a few peddlers—of course it was all right to say anything at all about them, but the idea of having to attack them with his fists— well, he was not that kind of man.

So Benedikt had his thoughts, joys, and worries, while all about him the gray day gradually grew dark, the full moon lighted up, a pale torch behind the clouds, and from time to time peeped out fleetingly against the silver sky of evening. Benedikt did not think very much about himself and his journey. Why should he? As the day gradually died, he became, to the eye, only one more vague shadow against the landscape. And yet it was a question whether his conception of himself was not still more formless and confused. He was only a farmhand, a laborer, and had been all his life. Or more precisely half hired man, half tenant. Indeed, there was something halfway, indeterminate about him all the way through. Half good, half bad; half man, half beast of burden. Yes, that was really the way it was. In the summer he worked for wages on the farm where he lived the whole year. In the winter he would take care of the sheep there in return for food and a few clothes. Only a short time in the spring and autumn and then during his wanderings in the mountains before Christmas was he his own master. To be sure he had his own stable and barn for his horse, and he had his sheep and the hay which he mowed on Sundays after church in a rented meadow. So he had a good time of it and he was only a simple man and a servant; and he neither hoped nor strove to become anything greater—not even in heaven. At least no longer. Those days were past—the days and nights when he dreamed dreams and felt yearnings now and then after fortune and freedom. Past—and it was better so, for only in those times had he felt the lack of freedom. Since then he had become more of a man—at least he had become a man. And he hoped that that, too, was not vanity and sinful arrogance.

Well, in any case he was now an aging man—fifty-four, and now there were no longer very many or very long false paths on which he could lose his way. Fifty-four years—and this was the twenty-seventh time that he had come this way. He knew precisely, for he had kept

account from year to year—twenty-seven. When he was twenty-seven
he had come the first time, and twenty-seven times he had wandered
thus, through the land, to the mountains, usually on Advent Sunday,
as today. Ah, yes! time slips away. Twenty-seven years—so deeply
buried lay his dreams, those dreams that only God and he himself
knew about. And the mountains where he had cried them aloud in
his anguish. But at the very first of all his journeys he had left them
behind and there they lay safely buried. Or perhaps they were not so
safely buried? Could it be that they wandered about in the loneliness
of the mountains, like restless spirits that live out their fleeting, perverse lives in the waste of snow and weathered stone? Could it be in
reality those same dreams which drove him up there every winter—
to see if they had not yet lost the edge of their keenness and had sunk
into the earth? But he shook off the thought. No, he was surely not
such a pitiful thing as that.

A LETTER TO KLAUS BROCK

Johan Bojer

Through disaster, suffering, and sacrifice, Peer Holm—the hero of
Bojer's *The Great Hunger*—exemplifies the soul's longing for the
Divine. In his final letter to Klaus Brock he summarizes the tragedies
that have tried his spirit but left it undaunted in its aspiration.

DEAR KLAUS BROCK,

I write to tell you of what has lately happened to us here, chiefly
in the hope that it may be some comfort to yourself. For I have discovered, dear friend, that this world-sorrow of ours is something a
man can get over, if only he will learn to see with his own eyes and
not with those of others.

Most men would say things have steadily gone from bad to worse
with me, and certainly I shall not pretend to feel any love for suffering in itself. On the contrary, it hurts. It does not ennoble. It rather

brutalises, unless it becomes so great that it embraces all things. I was once Engineer in charge at the First Cataract—now I am a blacksmith in a country parish. And that hurts. I am cut off from reading because of my eyes, and from intercourse with people whose society would be a pleasure because there are no such people here. All this hurts, even when you've grown used to it—a good thing in itself it is not. Many times I have thought that we must have reached the very bottom of the inclined plane of adversity, but always it proved to be only a break. The deepest deep was still to come. You work on even when your head feels like to split; you save up every pin, every match; and yet the bread you eat often tastes of charity. That hurts. You give up hoping that things may be better some day; you give up all hope, all dreams, all faith, all illusions—surely you have come to the end of all things. But no; the very roots of one's being are still left; the most precious thing of all is still left. What can that be, you ask?

That is what I was going to tell you.

The thing that happened came just when things were beginning to look a little brighter for us. For some time past my head had been less troublesome, and I had got to work on a new harrow—steel again; it never lets one rest—and you know what endless possibilities a man sees in a thing like that. Merle was working with fresh courage. What do you think of a wife like that? taking up the cross of her own free will, to go on sharing the life of a ruined man? I hope you may meet a woman of her sort one day. True, her hair is growing grey, and her face lined. Her figure is not so straight as once it was; her hands are red and broken. And yet all this has a soul of its own, a beauty of its own, in my eyes, because I know that each wrinkle is a mark left by the time when some new trouble came upon us, and found us together. Then one day she smiles, and her smile has grown strained and full of sadness, but again it brings back to me times when both heaven and earth breathed cold upon us and we drew closer to each other for warmth. Our happiness and our sufferings have moulded her into what she now is. The world may think perhaps that she is growing old; to me she is only more beautiful than before.

And now I am coming to what I was going to tell you. You will understand that it was not easy to send away the two children, and it doesn't make things better to get letters from them constantly begging us to let them come home again. But we had still one little girl left, little Asta, who was just five. I wish you could have seen her. If you were a father and your tortured nerves had often made you harsh and unreasonable with the two elder ones, you would try—would you not?—to make it up in loving-kindness to the one that was left. Asta—isn't it pretty? Imagine a sunburnt little being with black hair, and her mother's beautiful eyebrows, always busy with her dolls, or fetching in wood, or baking little cakes of her own for father when mother's baking bread for us all, chattering to the birds on the roof, or singing now and then, just because some stray note of music has come into her head. When mother is busy scrubbing the floor, little Asta must needs get hold of a wet rag behind her back and slop away at a chair, until she has got herself in a terrible mess, and then she gets smacked, and screams for a moment, but soon runs out and sings herself happy again. When you're at work in the smithy, there comes a sound of little feet, and "Father, come to dinner"; and a little hand takes hold of you and leads you to the door. "Are you going to bath me to-night, father?" Or "Here's your napkin, father." And though there might be only potatoes and milk for dinner, she would eat as if she were seated at the grandest banquet. "Aren't potatoes and milk your favourite dish, father?" And she makes faces at you in the eagerness of her questionings. At night she slept in a box at the foot of our bed, and when I was lying sleepless, it would often happen that her light, peaceful breathing filled me too with peace; and it was as if her little hand took mine and led me on to sleep itself, to beautiful, divine sleep.

And now, as I come to the thing that happened, I find it a little hard to write—my hand begins to tremble. But my hope is that there may be some comfort in it for you too, as there has proved to be for Merle and me in the end.

Our next neighbours here were a brazier and his wife—poor folks, like ourselves. Soon after we first came I went over to have a talk with him. I found him a poor wizened little creature, pottering about with his acids, and making a living as best as he could, soldering and tinning kettles and pans. "What do you want?" he asked, looking askance at me; and as I went out, I heard him bolt the door behind me. Alas! he was afraid—afraid that I was come to snatch his daily bread from him. His wife was a big-boned fleshy lump of a woman, insolent enough in her ways, though she had just been in prison for criminal abetment in the case of a girl that had got into trouble.

One Sunday morning I was standing looking at some apple trees in bloom in his garden. One of them grew so close to the fence that the branches hung over on my side, and I bent one down to smell the blossom. Then suddenly I heard a cry: "Hi, Tiger! catch him!" and the brazier's great wolf-dog came bounding down, ready to fly at my throat. I was lucky enough to get hold of its collar before it could do me any harm, and I dragged it up to its owner, and told him that if anything of the sort happened again I'd have the sheriff's officer after him. Then the music began. He fairly let himself go and told me what he thought of me. "You hold your jaw, you cursed pauper, coming here taking the bread out of honest working people's mouths," and so on. He hissed it out, flourishing his arms about, and at last it seemed to me he was fumbling about for a knife or something to throw at my head. I couldn't help laughing. It was a scene in the grand style between two Great Powers in the world-competition.

A couple of days later I was standing at the forge, when I heard a shriek from my wife. I rushed out—what could be the matter? Merle was down by the fence already, and all at once I saw what it was—there was Asta, lying on the ground under the body of a great beast.

And then—— Well, Merle tells me it was I that tore the thing away from the little bundle of clothes beneath it, and carried our little girl home.

A doctor is often a good refuge in trouble, but though he may sew up a ragged tear in a child's throat ever so neatly, it doesn't necessarily follow that it will help much.

There was a mother, though, that would not let him go—that cried and prayed and clung about him, begging him to try once more if nothing could be done. And when at last he was gone, she was always for going after him again, and grovelled on the floor and tore her hair— could not, would not, believe what she knew was true.

And that night a father and mother sat up together, staring strangely in front of them. The mother was quiet now. The child was laid out, decked and ready. The father sat by the window, looking out. It was in May, and the night was grey.

Now it was that I began to realise how every great sorrow leads us farther and farther out on the promontory of existence. I had come to the outermost point now—there was no more.

And I discovered too, dear friend, that these many years of adversity had shaped me not in one but in various moulds, for I had in me the stuff for several quite distinct persons, and now the work was done, and they could break free from my being and go their several ways.

I saw a man rush out into the night, shaking his fist at heaven and earth; a madman who refused to play his part in the farce any more, and so rushed down towards the river.

But I myself sat there still.

And I saw another, a puny creature, let loose; a humble, ashen-grey ascetic, that bent his head and bowed under the lash, and said: "Thy will be done. The Lord gave, the Lord hath taken away——" A pitiful being this, that stole out into the night and disappeared.

But I myself sat there still.

I sat alone on the promontory of existence, with the sun and the stars gone out, and ice-cold emptiness above me, about me, and in me, on every side.

But then, my friend, by degrees it dawned on me that there was still something left. There was one little indomitable spark in me, that began to glow all by itself—it was as if I were lifted back to the first day of existence, and an eternal will rose up in me, and said: Let there be light!

This will it was that by and by grew and grew in me, and made me strong.

I began to feel an unspeakable compassion for all men upon earth, and yet in the last resort I was proud that I was one of them.

I understood how blind fate can strip and plunder us of all, and yet something will remain in us at the last, that nothing in heaven or earth can vanquish. Our bodies are doomed to die, and our spirit to be extinguished, yet still we bear within us the spark, the germ of an eternity of harmony and light both for the world and for God.

And I knew now that what I had hungered after in my best years was neither knowledge, nor honour, nor riches; nor to be a priest or a great creator in steel; no, friend, but to build temples; not chapels for prayers or churches for wailing penitent sinners, but a temple for the human spirit in its grandeur, where we could lift up our souls in an anthem as a gift to heaven.

I could never do this now. Perhaps there was nothing that I could do any more. And yet it seemed to me as I sat there that I had conquered.

What happened then? Well, there had been a terrible drought all that spring—it is often so in this valley. The eternal north wind sent the dry mould sweeping in clouds over the whole countryside, and we were threatened with one of our worst years of scarcity if the rain didn't come.

At last people ventured to sow their corn, but then the frosts set in, and snow and sleet, and the seed froze in the earth. My neighbour the brazier had his patch of ground sown with barley—but now he would have to sow it again, and where was he to get the seed? He went from farm to farm begging for some, but people hated the sight of him after what had happened about Asta—no one would lend him any, and he had no money to buy. The boys on the roads hooted after him, and some of the neighbours talked of driving him out of the parish.

I wasn't able to sleep much the next night either, and when the clock struck two I got up. "Where are you going?" asked Merle. "I want to see if we haven't a half-bushel of barley left," I said. "Barley—what do you want with barley in the middle of the night?" "I want to sow the brazier's plot with it," I said, "and it's best to do it now, so that nobody will know it was me."

She sat up and stared at me. "What? His—the—the brazier's?"

"Yes," said I. "It won't do us any good, you know, to see his bit of field lying bare all summer."

"Peer—where are you going?"

"I've told you," said I, and went out. But I knew that she was dressing and meant to come too.

It had rained during the night, and as I came out the air was soft and easy to breathe. The morning still lay in a grey half-light with yellow gleams from the wind-clouds to the north. The scent of the budding birches was in the air, the magpies and starlings were up and about, but not a human soul was to be seen; the farms were asleep, the whole countryside was asleep.

I took the grain in a basket, climbed over the neighbour's fence and began to sow. No sign of life in the house; the sheriff's officer had come over and shot the dog the day before; no doubt the brazier and his wife were lying sleeping, dreaming maybe of enemies all around, trying their best to do them harm.

Dear friend, is there any need to tell the rest? Just think, though, how one man may give away a kingdom, and it costs him nothing, and another may give up a few handfuls of corn, and it means to him not only all that he has, but a world of struggle and passion before he can bring his soul to make that gift. Do you think that is nothing? As for me—I did not do this for Christ's sake, or because I loved my enemy; but because, standing upon the ruins of my life, I felt a vast responsibility. Mankind must arise, and be better than the blind powers that order its ways; in the midst of its sorrows it must take heed that the god-like does not die. The spark of eternity was once more aglow in me, and said: Let there be light.

And more and more it came home to me that it is man himself that must create the divine in heaven and on earth—that that is his triumph over the dead omnipotence of the universe. Therefore I went out and sowed the corn in my enemy's field, that God might exist.

Ah, if you had known that moment! It was as if the air about me grew alive with voices. It was as though all the unfortunates I had seen and known were bearing me company; more and more they came; the dead too were joined to us, an army from times past and long ago. Sister Louise was there, she played her hymn, and drew the voices all together into a choir, the choir of the living and the dead, the choir of all mankind. See, here are we all, your sisters and brothers. Your fate is ours. We are flung by the indifferent law of the universe into a life that we cannot order as we would; we are ravaged by injustice, by sickness and sorrow, by fire and blood. Even the happiest must die. In his own home he is but on a visit. He never knows but that he may be gone tomorrow. And yet man smiles and laughs in the face of his tragic fate. In the midst of his thraldom he has created the beautiful on earth; in the midst of his torments he has had so much surplus energy of soul that he has sent it radiating forth into the cold deeps of space and warmed them with God.

So marvellous art thou, O spirit of man! So god-like in thy very nature! Thou dost reap death, and in return thou sowest the dream of everlasting life. In revenge for thine evil fate thou dost fill the universe with an all-loving God.

We bore our part in his creation, all we who now are dust; we who sank down into the dark like flames gone out;—we wept, we exulted, we felt the ecstasy and the agony, but each of us brought our ray to the mighty sea of light, each of us, from the negro setting up the first mark above the grave of his dead to the genius raising the pillars of a temple towards heaven. We bore our part, from the poor mother praying beside a cradle, to the hosts that lifted their songs of praise high up into boundless space.

Honour to thee, O spirit of man. Thou givest a soul to the world, thou settest it a goal, thou art the hymn that lifts it into harmony; therefore turn back into thyself, lift high thy head and meet proudly the evil that comes to thee. Adversity can crush thee, death can blot thee out, yet art thou still unconquerable and eternal.

Dear friend, it was thus I felt. And when the corn was sown, and I went back, the sun was glancing over the shoulder of the hill. There by the fence stood Merle, looking at me. She had drawn a kerchief forward over her brow, after the fashion of the peasant woman, so that her face was in shadow; but she smiled to me—as if she, too, the stricken mother, had risen up from the ocean of her suffering that here, in the daybreak, she might take her share in the creating of God. . . .

FAITH TO BE HEALED

Richard Llewellyn

The blackening of the valley by the encroachment of mining interests forms the background for Llewellyn's story of the Morgans, a South Wales family. The following passage is Huw Morgan's recollection of an episode in his childhood, in which tragedy is averted by the Reverend Mr. Gruffydd's faithful ministrations.

MY FATHER brought the new preacher in to see me before my mother came from Bronwen's, and Mr. Nicholas, the colliery manager, and Dr. Richards stood in the doorway because the kitchen was full up with girls and women, all cooking or cutting bread and butter.

"This is Huw, Mr. Gruffydd," said my father. "Huw, this is the Reverend Mr. Merddyn Gruffydd, the new preacher. Bow your head, my son."

"Leave your head on the pillow," said the Reverend Mr. Gruffydd, and he was looking at me, and frowning. "Huw Morgan, never let that light go from your eyes. Never mind how long you are here. Do you want to go out with the other boys?"

"Yes indeed, Mr. Gruffydd," I said.

"Are you sure you will go from here one day?" asked Mr. Gruffydd, smiling now.

"Yes," I said. "I am, sir."

"Good," said Mr. Gruffydd. "And not a doubt about it, never mind what all the doctors have got to say."

Of course, that was a cut for Dr. Richards, in fun, mind, so everybody laughed except the doctor.

"The boy will be no better for those ideas, Mr. Gruffydd," Dr. Richards said. "Nature must take her course."

"Nature," said the Reverend Mr. Gruffydd, "is the handmaiden of
the Lord. I do remember that she was given orders on one or two occasions to hurry herself more than usual. What has been done before
can also be done again, though perhaps not so quickly, indeed. Have
you faith, Huw, my little one?"

"Yes, sir," I said, and I was on fire.

"Good," said the Reverend Mr. Gruffydd, "you shall see the first
daffodil out upon the mountain. Will you?"

"Indeed I will, sir," I said, and his hand was cool on my forehead.

"God bless you, little Huw," said the Reverend Mr. Gruffydd. "I will
come to see you every day. Yes?"

"Yes, sir," I said. . . .

. . . It was a long time after that . . . but I was making progress,
with the help of the Reverend Mr. Gruffydd. Every day he called in to
see me, sometimes for a minute in the early morning, or at night, and
sometimes, but few and far, in the afternoons for an hour at a time. He
was a hard-working man, with a conscience that would not allow him
to rest idle. Day in and day out, he was over the mountain to see people
and ask them why they were not at Chapel, or to sit with the sick, or
to talk to old people who could not walk the miles across the gorse on
a Sunday to come and pray.

From him I learnt our history. Caradog, Cadwaladr, Lud, Coel,
Boadicea, all the princely, shining host passed into my keeping and
from me to little Gareth, who was old enough now to understand all
that was said to him. I saw in his eyes the light that Mr. Gruffydd must
often have seen in mine.

"Men who are born to dig coal," Mr. Gruffydd said to me, "need
strength and courage. But they have no need of spirit, any more than
the mole or the blind worm. Keep up your spirit, Huw, for that is the
heritage of a thousand generations of the great ones of the Earth. As
your father cleans his lamp to have good light, so keep clean your
spirit."

"And how shall it be kept clean, Mr. Gruffydd?" I asked him.

"By prayer, my son," he said, "not mumbling, or shouting, or wallow-
ing like a hog in religious sentiments. Prayer is only another name for
good, clean, direct thinking. When you pray, think well what you are

saying, and make your thoughts into things that are solid. In that manner, your prayer will have strength, and that strength shall become part of you, mind, body and spirit. Do you still want to see the first daffodil out upon the mountain, my son?"

"Indeed I do, Mr. Gruffydd," I said.

"Pray, my son," he said, and left. . . .

That morning Mr. Gruffydd came to the house early and opened the door of the kitchen so that the sun shone in all round him. Big he looked, and full of happy purpose.

"Good morning, Mrs. Morgan," he said.

"Good morning, dear Mr. Gruffydd," said my mother, in surprise. "There is good to see you."

"I have come for Huw," he said, as though he was asking to take a loaf for old Mrs. Llywarch.

"Huw?" my mother asked, and looked over the table at me with her eyebrows almost touching this little blue cloth.

"Yes," said Mr. Gruffydd, "this is the morning he has been waiting for."

I looked at Mr. Gruffydd and knew. But my mother was still in fog with her.

"The daffodils are out, Mama," I said.

"Oh, Huw," my mother said, and put down the bread knife, and turned her head away.

"Where are your clothes, Huw?" he asked me, but quiet, and looking at my mother's back.

"Under my pillow, sir," I said.

"Your pillow?" he said.

"For these months," I said, "ready for to-day."

"Come you, then," he said, and smiling he was. "You shall bring back a posy fit for a queen for your brave mother, is it?"

"Indeed I will," I said, and back I pulled the pillow, and out came my clothes that I had made ready ever since I had put my mind to the matter.

Pain there was, and a helpless feeling in all my bones, but I was determined to have those clothes on. On they went, and no nonsense, though the stockings were big and the trews too short, but I had grown and got thin, so it was no use to grumble.

There is a sight I must have looked when I put my legs out and stood up. But neither Mr. Gruffydd nor my mother looked at me, so I was spared to blush and very thankful.

"Up on my back, Huw," Mr. Gruffydd said, and bent his knees so that I could put my arms about his neck. I shall never forget how shocked I was to find myself up on the shoulders of a minister. It seemed wrong to be so familiar. But there I was, and carried to the door.

"He will be back in two hours, Mrs. Morgan, my little one," said Mr. Gruffydd.

"God bless you," my mother said, and still not looking.

"Good-bye, our Mam," I said, with my legs falling about at the back. "Get ready the big pot for the daffodils. I will have an armful for you, and some for Bron."

Outside, then, and through the blessed curtains of air, spun with morning mist and sunshine, blown upon us by wind from the southeast and the draughts that played in the Valley.

"Are you right, Huw?" Mr. Gruffydd asked me. "Am I too quick?"

"No indeed, Mr. Gruffydd," I said. "Go, you."

"Right," he said. "Here is the road, and up by there are the daffodils. Tight, now."

For the first few minutes I was shutting my eyes to get used to the sunshine, so raw and pure and shining white. Then I got used to it and less tears came and I was able to see without screwing up my eyes and having to blink.

The first thing I saw was the slag heap.

Big it had grown, and long, and black, without life or sign, lying along the bottom of the Valley on both sides of the river. The green grass, and the reeds and the flowers, all had gone, crushed beneath it. And every minute the burden grew, as cage after cage screeched along the cables from the pit, bumped to a stop at the tipping pier, and emptied dusty loads on to the ridged, black, dirty back.

On our side of the Valley the heap reached to the front garden walls of the bottom row of houses, and children from them were playing up and down the black slopes, screaming and shouting, laughing in fun. On the other side of the river the chimney-pots of the first row of houses could only just be seen above the sharp curving back of the far heap, and all the time I was watching, the cable screeched and the cages tipped. From the Britannia pit came a call on the hooter as the cages came up, as though to remind the Valley to be ready for more filth as the work went on and on, year in and year out.

"Is the pit allowed to do this to us, Mr. Gruffydd?" I asked him.

"Do what, my son?" Mr. Gruffydd asked.

"Put slag by here," I said.

"Nowhere else to put it, my son," he said. "Look up by there at the top of the mountain, by the Glas Fryn. There are the daffodils, see."

And indeed, there they were, with their green leaves a darker sharpness in the grass about them, and the yellow blooms belling in the wind, up by the Glas Fryn and all along the Valley, as far as I could turn my head to see.

Gold may be found again, and men may know its madness again, but no one shall know how I felt to see the goldness of daffodils growing up there that morning. The Glas Fryn was the nearest place to our house where they grew. It was later that I pulled bulbs to grow in our garden, but the garden was so small and the earth so blind with dust from the slag that they gave up trying and died.

But that morning Mr. Gruffydd put me down among them all, close to them, where I could take them in my hands to breathe the cool breath of them and give thanks to God.

Below us, the river ran sweet as ever, happy in the sun, but as soon as it met the darkness between the sloping walls of slag it seemed to take fright and go spiritless, smooth, black, without movement. And on the other side it came forth grey, and began to hurry again, as though anxious to get away. But its banks were stained, and the reeds and grasses that dressed it were hanging, and black, and sickly, ashamed of their dirtiness, ready to die of shame, they seemed, and of sorrow for their dear friend, the river.

"Will the salmon come up this year, Mr. Gruffydd?" I asked him.

He was quiet a moment, feeling for his pipe.

"I am told," he said, "that no salmon have been seen these two years."

"And no trout either, then?" I said.

"I am afraid not, Huw," he said. "They cannot face that black stretch, there."

"Good," I said. "No one shall tell me again that fish have got no sense with them. Pity, I do think, that more of us are not thinkers like the fish."

"Collect your flowers, Huw," he said. "Two hours I said to your Mama. She will be waiting."

There is pity that we cannot dig all round the growing flowers and take earth and all with us. It is hurting to have to break the stems of blossoms and see them lose their rich white blood only for the pleasure of putting them in a pot of water. Still, I had promised, and there it was. So break them I did, an armful of them, and up on Mr. Gruffydd's back, and off home, down the mountain.

There is pleased were the people to see me, indeed. Every door was open, and as we passed, the women ran out to wave to me and wish we well.

Up at our house, my mother was waiting with Bronwen and Angharad in the doorway.

"Well," said my mother.

"Let me have him from you, Mr. Gruffydd," Angharad said, and put her arms about my waist, but I pushed her away.

"Go on with you, girl," I said, "I am walking now."

And walk I did, though a bit like an old spider with a drop too much in him. The wall was my friend till I came to my father's chair, and into that I fell.

"Good," said Mr. Gruffydd, and my mother was making noises under her breath.

"There is hungry I am," I said.

"Wait you," said my mother. "You shall have a breakfast like your father now this minute. Cup of tea for Mr. Gruffydd, Angharad. You are standing there fast to the floor, girl."

Bronwen came in with the daffodils in the pots and beautiful she looked with the gold shining into her face.

"Soon you shall take little Gareth for walks, is it, Huw?" she said, and pulling a blossom out here, and pushing another in by there.

"No," I said. "Soon I will be going to school and finishing and then down the pit with Dada."

"Why down the pit, Huw?" Mr. Gruffydd asked me. "Why not to school and college, then university and then a doctor or a lawyer?"

"Yes," said my mother. "Indeed that is beautiful. Dr. Huw Morgan, and your own house and a lovely horse and trap. With a good black suit and a shirt with starch. Oh, there is good, Huw, my little one. There is proud would I be."

"I will not be a doctor, Mama," I said. "Not six months ago and Dr. Richards said I would never put my feet on the floor. This morning I went up on the mountain. To-morrow I will go and the next morning and all the mornings to come. I will not be a doctor."

My mother gave Mr. Gruffydd his cup of tea, and started to hit sparks out of the fire, so I knew she had plenty to say but holding it because of Mr. Gruffydd.

"Say what is in your mind, Mrs. Morgan," he said, and smiling he was.

"Here is a pack of obstinate donkeys I have got for boys," my mother said, and angry, too, turning to me and throwing the poker wherever it went. "Like old mules, they are. If you say something that is good, no. If you say something that is bad, no. Whatever you say, no. They are the ones who know. If Dr. Richards is an old fool, does it mean that you cannot go to school and do better? Have sense, boy. You are not old enough to talk."

"Yes, Mama," I said, and the bacon smelt so good it was sending spit bubbling in my mouth.

"We shall see," said Mr. Gruffydd, and he stood to go. "On Sunday, he shall come to Chapel and sit in the choir. And he shall sing a solo. That will keep his mind awake till then."

"Oh, Mr. Gruffydd," my mother said, "there is pleased Gwilym will be. Thank you, indeed."

"And no more talk of doctors or lawyers," Mr. Gruffydd said. "There is more than enough talking done by them without us wasting our time with them. To-morrow morning, Huw."

"Yes, Mr. Gruffydd," I said, "and thank you."

"God bless you, my son," he said, and smiled at my mother and went.

The Healer

~~~~~~

THE WATERS OF BETHESDA

Florence Marvyne Bauer

~~~~~~

Mrs. Bauer bases her novel *Behold Your King* on the last two years of the life of Jesus. "The Waters of Bethesda" takes the reader directly into the atmosphere of that momentous period when the lessons taught by the Nazarene at once awakened and empowered men into action. Such a one was Jonathan, a young Cyrenian Jew, who was later to become a devoted follower of Jesus.

IDDO followed Jonathan with obvious reluctance, scuffing his sandals as he walked backward, pausing to throw pebbles across the ditch and upward toward the Tower of Antonia sitting in cold majesty on its height, showing to his master in every way a young servant could that he obeyed under protest.

Then, with sudden shout, he ran to overtake Jonathan, pointing back to something the young man did not turn to see.

"What ails you, lad?" asked the master.

"The Nazarene!"

Jonathan's eyes lighted with interest and he paused, turning to search the street for the rabbi's tall form. "I do not see him," he said and turned back toward the pool.

"He is coming down the hill. See, even now he is turning this way!"

Jonathan glanced over his shoulder, but politely continued walking.

"Do you think he will go to the pool also?" asked Iddo.

Jonathan shrugged and turned into a street which climbed by steps up the hill toward Bethesda's highest level. "Watch," he commanded Iddo. "We will follow him when he has passed by."

They were only a few steps behind the rabbi from Nazareth as he walked into the first of the porches which surrounded the pool. Jonathan, who had drawn his cloak closely around him, saw that the rabbi did not remember to catch his garments close but wound slowly among the dirty and diseased forms which covered the floors of the five porches, picking his way carefully that he might not further injure the poor wretches.

Suddenly he stopped. He bent to lift an emaciated child and hold her close on his left arm while he parted her eyelids with the fingers of his right hand. Jonathan, shuddering within himself at thought of contact with the grimy creature, saw the besmirched little face grow lax in wonder, as dark eyes opened wider and wider and moved from one object to another. The little head with its matted crinkly hair turned slowly and the dark eyes sought the face of the rabbi, staring for a moment into his smiling ones, and then moved on to gaze around in amazement and growing delight.

With a sudden scramble, she wriggled down from the rabbi's arms and started to run, at first staggeringly and then more strongly as she gained strength. As she ran she uttered joyous little noises which made Jonathan's heart swell within him in quick sympathy. The rabbi turned with a broad smile to watch her progress. Jonathan was only dimly conscious of her as she passed, for his eyes now met those of the Nazarene. For a moment the two tall young Jews stared at each other in quickly tensed perception. The smile faded from the rabbi's tender mouth and he turned to go. Jonathan felt strangely weak, frightened, as though he had been before a bar of justice and stood condemned.

A sudden clamor arose from the multitude. Shrieks of entreaty, screams of petition, piteous cries and challenging shouts filled the air. The floors of the galleries seemed suddenly alive as maimed creatures wriggled toward the young Nazarene and other cripples writhed and twitched their way across the undulating mass of bodies.

An overpowering stench, the acrid odor of sweaty unwashed humanity, made breathing difficult. Jonathan gagged and roused himself. He was like one impotent. Movement required his going among those wriggling bodies and he cringed at thought of it. He saw no opening on any side. He and Iddo stood as on an island in a swirling stream.

He felt the lad pressing against his side, felt Iddo's head buried in his flowing sleeve, felt his own body quiver as the floundering wretches surged against his legs. He raised despairing eyes to find the young rabbi. The man from Nazareth was standing quite still among a thicket of upraised talons, a look of unspeakable yearning upon his face.

A sudden shriek of unintelligible words froze the undulating motion of the gallery floors, as everywhere wretches waited breathless to hear the words. "The angel! The waters! The angel has come!"

Again there was motion, again the gallery floors seemed like a turbulent stream, but now the flow was toward the pool, and its waters became fouled with wriggling, scrambling forms. The rabbi from Nazareth watched the twisting and turning of the crippled creatures, his face both sad and wistful. Then he looked up.

His eyes again met those of Jonathan. Once more the young Cyrenian had the feeling that he stood before a bar of judgment, that the evidence against him far outweighed that in his favor. His eyes dropped away from those calm ones which seemed to search his heart and mind and soul. The depression settling over his spirit was like a weight upon his chest, making breathing difficult and temptingly undesirable. He had never known complete despair before. He had thought he knew, when he found Elizabeth was lost to him, but this despair was something deeper, more profound than that, with a quality strangely clinging as if he could never completely rid himself of it; no, not after years of trying, or even after centuries.

After a time he found himself walking along the Street of the Cheesemongers, with Iddo guiding him as he would have guided a blind man. He heard but dimly the cries of the shopkeepers and the shrill haggling of the buyers. He shook his head. What ailed him? Why should he have such a weight within him? And then he was entirely roused by Iddo shaking his arm.

"Of a truth, you'll need a ceremonial cleansing now!" said the boy accusingly. "I will too!" When Jonathan made no answer, Iddo went on, half crying, "You walked us through the midst of that crowd of beggars, and they pushed us and clawed at us and spat upon us when we threw them no alms!"

Jonathan still made no answer. He had such a sense of unworthiness within himself that this contact with the unwashed humanity of Jerusalem streets seemed of little importance to his dazed mind.

Never afterward could he tell how he and Iddo got to the house of Joseph, or to the Temple for cleansing and sacrifice. Iddo had been master, for he himself was too fatigued, too heavy of spirit, to make plans and carry them out. It was as though his mind had been absent from his body.

Indeed, it was not until the following morning that his mind began to clear and to function in a normal manner. Thinking back over his experience at the Bethesda Pool, he decided that his physical discomfort and violent disgust, coupled with his excited amazement at the healer's opening of blind eyes, had somehow affected his mind. Not that this explanation satisfied him, for deep within himself he knew that his state had been directly due to the influence of the healer. Yet the man had said no word to him.

What had there been about the Nazarene's gaze that could have given him such a sense of guilt? Why should he, Jonathan, a righteous Israelite according to the Law, have that deep feeling of judgment and condemnation? That horrible hopelessness? As he thought of the calm and lustrous eyes of the Galilean, a kind of resentment began to take possession of Jonathan. Who was this Nazarene anyway?

The young Cyrenian sat up and swung his legs over the side of his bed. He was not going to think about that man any longer. He was, after all, only a carpenter from a small town in Galilee of the Gentiles. In the act of rising from the couch, Jonathan sat down again. A carpenter? What then made him different from other men? And he was different. His personality, his manner of teaching, his trends of thought, all were different.

Nathanael of Cana had said this carpenter was Messiah, had insisted on it with quiet conviction. Yet this man of Nazareth was plainly a man. Was he also angel? He showed powers over disease greater than was common to man. The prophets of old had shown similar powers. Did these powers come from an angelic source?

Nicodemus had said he believed the rabbi a teacher sent from God. Did he also believe he was Messiah, as Nathanael did? He acknowledged the teachings of the Nazarene more profound than any he had heard before, confessed that he did not understand them fully. Nicodemus was a master in Israel. Could this humble carpenter be wiser in truth than Nicodemus? Could this carpenter be Messiah?

With a sigh Jonathan gave it up. It was a mystery he could not solve this morning. His head ached and his body felt old and tired. He threw himself back on his divan and called for Iddo to read aloud to him.

THE CANYON FLOWERS

Ralph Connor

~~~~~~

The Sky Pilot dramatizes the adventures of a tubercular pastor sent out to minister to miners and lumbermen in the remote wilds of Canada. When tragedy strikes a young untamed girl and dooms her to a life of suffering, the Sky Pilot comes to her aid in building a new perspective. He tells her this little story to help her solve the eternal problem of the existence of pain and evil under a God who is all-good.

THE Pilot's first visit to Gwen had been a triumph. But none knew better than he that the fight was still to come, for deep in Gwen's heart were thoughts whose pain made her forget all other.

"Was it God let me fall?" she asked abruptly one day, and The Pilot knew the fight was on; but he only answered, looking fearlessly into her eyes:

"Yes, Gwen dear."

"Why did He let me fall?" and her voice was very deliberate.

"I don't know, Gwen dear," said The Pilot steadily. "He knows."

"And does He know I shall never ride again? Does He know how long the days are, and the nights when I can't sleep? Does He know?"

"Yes, Gwen dear," said The Pilot, and the tears were standing in his eyes, though his voice was still steady enough.

"Are you sure He knows?" The voice was painfully intense.

"Listen to me, Gwen," began The Pilot, in great distress, but she cut him short.

"Are you quite sure He knows? Answer me!" she cried, with her old imperiousness.

"Yes, Gwen, He knows all about you."

"Then what do you think of Him, just because He's big and strong, treating a little girl that way?" Then she added, viciously: "I hate Him! I don't care! I hate Him!"

But The Pilot did not wince. I wondered how he would solve that problem that was puzzling, not only Gwen, but her father and The Duke, and all of us—the *why* of human pain.

"Gwen," said The Pilot, as if changing the subject, "did it hurt to put on the plaster jacket?"

"You just bet!" said Gwen, lapsing in her English, as The Duke was not present; "it was worse than anything—awful! They had to straighten me out, you know," and she shuddered at the memory of that pain.

"What a pity your father or The Duke was not here!" said The Pilot, earnestly.

"Why, they were both here!"

"What a cruel shame!" burst out The Pilot. "Don't they care for you any more?"

"Of course they do," said Gwen, indignantly.

"Why didn't they stop the doctors from hurting you so cruelly?"

"Why, they let the doctors. It is going to help me to sit up and perhaps to walk about a little," answered Gwen, with blue-gray eyes open wide.

"Oh," said The Pilot, "it was very mean to stand by and see you hurt like that."

"Why, you silly," replied Gwen, impatiently, "they want my back to get straight and strong."

"Oh, then they didn't do it just for fun or for nothing?" said The Pilot, innocently.

Gwen gazed at him in amazed and speechless wrath, and he went on:

"I mean they love you though they let you be hurt; or rather they let the doctors hurt you *because* they loved you and wanted to make you better."

Gwen kept her eyes fixed with curious earnestness upon his face till the light began to dawn.

"Do you mean," she began slowly, "that though God let me fall, He loves me?"

The Pilot nodded; he could not trust his voice.

"I wonder if that can be true," she said, as if to herself; and soon we said good-by and came away—The Pilot, limp and voiceless, but I triumphant, for I began to see a little light for Gwen.

But the fight was by no means over; indeed, it was hardly well begun. For when the autumn came, with its misty, purple days, most glorious of all days in the cattle country, the old restlessness came back and the fierce refusal of her lot. Then came the day of the round-up. Why should she have to stay while all went after the cattle? The Duke would have remained, but she impatiently sent him away. She was weary and heart-sick, and, worst of all, she began to feel that most terrible of burdens, the burden of her life to others. I was much relieved when The Pilot came in fresh and bright, waving a bunch of wild-flowers in his hand.

"I thought they were all gone," he cried. "Where do you think I found them? Right down by the big elm root," and, though he saw by the settled gloom of her face that the storm was coming, he went bravely on picturing the canyon in all the splendor of its autumn dress. But the spell would not work. Her heart was out on the sloping hills, where the cattle were bunching and crowding with tossing heads and rattling horns, and it was in a voice very bitter and impatient that she cried:

"Oh, I am sick of all this! I want to ride! I want to see the cattle and the men and—and—and all the things outside." The Pilot was cowboy enough to know the longing that tugged at her heart for one wild race after the calves or steers, but he could only say:

"Wait, Gwen. Try to be patient."

"I am patient; at least I have been patient for two whole months, and it's no use, and I don't believe God cares one bit!"

"Yes, He does, Gwen, more than any of us," replied The Pilot, earnestly.

"No, He does not care," she answered, with angry emphasis, and The Pilot made no reply.

"Perhaps," she went on, hesitatingly, "He's angry because I said I didn't care for Him, you remember? That was very wicked. But don't you think I'm punished nearly enough now? You made me very angry, and I didn't really mean it."

Poor Gwen! God had grown to be very real to her during these weeks of pain, and very terrible. The Pilot looked down a moment into the blue-gray eyes, grown so big and so pitiful, and hurriedly dropping on his knees beside the bed, he said, in a very unsteady voice:

"Oh, Gwen, Gwen, He's not like that. Don't you remember how Jesus was with the poor sick people? That's what He's like."

"Could Jesus make me well?"

"Yes, Gwen."

"Then why doesn't He?" she asked; and there was no impatience now, but only trembling anxiety as she went on in a timid voice: "I asked Him to, over and over, and said I would wait two months, and now it's more than three. Are you quite sure He hears now?" She raised herself on her elbow and gazed searchingly into The Pilot's face. I was glad it was not into mine. As she uttered the words, "Are you quite sure?" one felt that things were in the balance. I could not help looking at The Pilot with intense anxiety. What would he answer? The Pilot gazed out of the window upon the hills for a few moments. How long the silence seemed! Then, turning, looked into the eyes that searched his so steadily and answered simply:

"Yes, Gwen, I am quite sure!" Then, with quick inspiration, he got her mother's Bible and said: "Now, Gwen, try to see it as I read." But, before he read, with the true artist's instinct he created the proper atmosphere. By a few vivid words he made us feel the pathetic loneliness of the Man of Sorrows in His last sad days. Then he read that masterpiece of all tragic picturing, the story of Gethsemane. And as he read we saw it all. The garden and the trees and the sorrow-stricken Man alone with His mysterious agony. We heard the prayer so pathetically submissive and then, for answer, the rabble and the traitor.

Gwen was far too quick to need explanation, and The Pilot only said, "You see, Gwen, God gave nothing but the best—to His own Son only the best."

"The best? They took Him away, didn't they?" She knew the story well.

"Yes, but listen." He turned the leaves rapidly and read: " 'We see Jesus for the suffering of death crowned with glory and honor.' That is how He got His Kingdom."

Gwen listened, silent but unconvinced, and then said slowly:

"But how can this be best for me? I am no use to anyone. It can't be best to just lie here and make them all wait on me, and—and—I did want to help daddy—and—oh—I know they will get tired of me! They are getting tired already—I—I—can't help being hateful."

She was by this time sobbing as I had never heard her before—deep, passionate sobs. Then again The Pilot had an inspiration.

"Now, Gwen," he said severely, "you know we're not as mean as that, and that you are just talking nonsense, every word. Now I'm going to smooth out your red hair and tell you a story."

"It's *not* red," she cried, between her sobs. This was her sore point.

"It is red, as red can be; a beautiful, shining purple *red,*" said The Pilot emphatically, beginning to brush.

"Purple!" cried Gwen, scornfully.

"Yes, I've seen it in the sun, purple. Haven't you?" said The Pilot, appealing to me. "And my story is about the canyon, our canyon, your canyon, down there."

"Is it true?" asked Gwen, already soothed by the cool, quick-moving hands.

"True? It's as true as—as—" he glanced round the room, "as the *Pilgrim's Progress.*" This was satisfactory, and the story went on.

"At first there were no canyons, but only the broad, open prairie. One day the Master of the Prairie, walking out over his great lawns, where were only grasses, asked the Prairie, 'Where are your flowers?' and the Prairie said, 'Master, I have no seeds.' Then he spoke to the birds, and they carried seeds of every kind of flower and strewed them far and wide, and soon the Prairie bloomed with crocuses and roses and buffalo beans and the yellow crowfoot and the wild sunflowers and the red lilies all the summer long. Then the Master came and was well pleased; but he missed the flowers he loved best of all, and he said to the Prairie: 'Where are the clematis and the columbine, the sweet violets and wind-flowers, and all the ferns and flowering shrubs?' And again he spoke to the birds, and again they carried all the seeds and strewed them far and wide. But, again, when the Master came, he could not find the flowers he loved best of all, and he said: 'Where are those, my sweetest flowers?' and the Prairie cried sorrowfully: 'Oh, Master, I cannot keep the flowers, for the winds sweep fiercely, and the sun beats upon my breast, and they wither up and fly away.' Then the Master spoke to the Lightning, and with one swift blow the Lightning cleft the Prairie to the heart. And the Prairie rocked and groaned in agony, and for many a day moaned bitterly over its black, jagged, gaping wound. But the Little Swan poured its waters through the cleft, and carried down deep black mould, and once more the birds carried seeds and strewed them in the canyon. And after a long time the rough rocks were decked out with soft mosses and trailing vines, and all the nooks were hung with clematis and columbine, and great elms lifted their huge tops high up into the sunlight, and down about their feet clustered the low cedars and balsams, and everywhere the violets and wind-flowers and maiden-hair grew and bloomed, till the canyon became the Master's place for rest and peace and joy."

The quaint tale was ended, and Gwen lay quiet for some moments, then said gently:

"Yes! The canyon flowers are much the best. Tell me what it means."

Then The Pilot read to her: "The fruits—I'll read 'flowers'—of the Spirit are love, joy, peace, long-suffering, gentleness, goodness, faith, meekness, self-control, and some of these grow only in the canyon."

"Which are the canyon flowers?" asked Gwen softly, and The Pilot answered:

"Gentleness, meekness, self-control; but though the others, love, joy, peace, bloom in the open, yet never with so rich a bloom and so sweet a perfume as in the canyon."

For a long time Gwen lay quite still, and then said wistfully, while her lip trembled:

"There are no flowers in my canyon, but only ragged rocks."

"Some day they will bloom, Gwen dear; He will find them, and we, too, shall see them."

Then he said good-by and took me away.

He had done his work that day.

HE SOUGHT TO KNOW GOD

Alice Tisdale Hobart

Yang and Yin epitomizes the conflict between Eastern and Western thought in the life story of Peter Fraser, an American medical missionary to China. The incident, "He Sought to Know God," based on historical fact, relates one of the grim experiments he made in the interest of medical science.

A HUMBLE PATIENT who had the sickness that caused spitting of blood, so well-known among Chinese of all classes—Dr. Fraser called it "tuberculosis"—had been sent to the new Mission sanitarium out in the hills beyond the city. Quite suddenly the man developed appendicitis.

"We'll have to operate," Peter said, as he talked the case over with Lo Shih. "But it'll be difficult because of the condition of his lungs. I'll have to work very fast. We can't keep him under ether long."

Sen Lo Shih was assisting at all operations now. He had even given the anesthetic in certain easy cases, when Miss Powell, the white nurse, was unusually busy. But he liked better to do as he was doing today—hand Dr. Fraser the instruments. Then he could give his full attention to the technique of the operation. The swiftness and certainty with which the doctor cut reminded him of his father's vigorous brush strokes. He coveted such mastery of hand. He thought of surgery as an art. Today he especially admired Peter's lightning swiftness.

The operation was nearly completed. There was a little gasp from Miss Powell. Dr. Fraser gave one quick glance, leaned down, placed his lips against the patient's, forcing his own breath into his lungs. Soon the man was breathing again. Peter went on with his work.

Lo Shih was aghast. Over and over Dr. Fraser had impressed upon him that to "eat" the breath of a person who had this sickness was to eat the sickness. Had this careful scientist committed that carelessness which he so sternly preached against?

After the operation, following his usual habit, Peter took Lo Shih into his office, discussing the case with him. "In a properly equipped hospital there would have been a pulmotor. In this case, it was necessary for me to act in that capacity."

A new vista opened before Sen Lo Shih. Dr. Fraser had risked his own life for this humble man, to whom he had no responsibility except as doctor to patient. The Confucian doctrine taught the relationship of son to father, pupil to teacher, friend to friend, but here was a relationship that transcended those personal ones—the doctor to his case, the workman to his task.

Heretofore, Lo Shih had accepted the popular belief of the city that Dr. Fraser was here to make money. Even according to Lo Shih's standard of wealth as he had known it in his father's dwelling, Peter showed signs of riches. This great brick house in which he lived, for instance. Now he glimpsed Peter's life as one of service. The Superior Man serving! His father had taught him that *the path of the Superior Man leads in the end to that which even the sage does not discern.* Here was something which the sages of his country had not seen. Did this teaching of the sage called Christ take one a little farther along the hidden way? That alien symbol of the cross seemed suddenly to take on meaning.

A few evenings later, just before Lo Shih left the house for the laboratory, he came into Peter's study, sitting silently by the desk.

"Is there something you wish to ask me?" asked Peter.

"I would like to accept the teachings of Christ," answered Lo Shih.

"It is not often that a Confucianist, trained as you have been to the Confucian doctrines, turns away from them to Christianity," said Peter, a little astonished.

Lo Shih had been sitting with his legs crossed, the skirt of his gown caught over one knee. His hands were behind his head, a pose he had acquired from Peter. At Peter's words, he sat up straight. "I am still a Confucianist. I simply go a little farther along the hidden way." That Peter had shown him that way, he did not mention.

"You would like me to tell Mr. Baker that you wish to join the church?" asked Peter, puzzled.

"Join the church?" said Lo Shih. "What has that to do with me? This is a personal matter."

"Yes, it is a personal matter," answered Peter.

"We have a custom," Lo Shih went on. "As you know, our fathers or our teachers give us a literary name. I should like it if you would select for me a Christian name."

After a little, Peter said very gently, "I will give you the name of John."

"It shall be used only by the honored teacher," said Lo Shih. He rose. "If *Fei I Sheng* will excuse me, I will attend the flukes."

As the year drew to its close, both of them came to think of little else but Sen Lo Shih's future. Both realized that what he needed now was to go to a well-equipped medical school.

Peter had always thought it would be easy to get assistance for his promising pupil. Had Lo Shih been a member of the church, it would have been—there were scholarships for such. He longed to help him out of his own salary, but every cent he could spare went to Diana and Mei Mei. Even though they were living with Diana's mother, the expense of keeping them in America was a severe drain upon his salary.

One day in the very late spring, Lo Shih said quite simply, "It seems to me wise, if I am to become a good surgeon, that I study in America. Would my teacher and friend lend me the money?"

It was a hard thing for Peter to refuse. He had to tell Lo Shih that he had no money.

For a Chinese gentleman, Lo Shih was almost hasty in his reply. Eagerly he urged Peter to think no more of the matter. "There is a relative of my father who wishes to give me the money. Please, it is not important." He wanted to relieve Peter of the embarrassment of his failure to understand the Confucian relationship of teacher to pupil.

The Superior Man would have considered it a high honor to be given the opportunity to help a scholar, even if it were necessary to borrow the money.

Lo Shih did not tell Peter what obligation the loan of the money from his uncle carried—that his uncle had no children, wanted to arrange a marriage for him in order to perpetuate the family. This Lo Shih accepted. The tradition of his race to preserve the harmony of the *yin* and *yang* was strong within him. Man bowed to the mysterious forces of life and death, flowing and ebbing, making the universe.

What he did not wish to do was to take a concubine, and this his uncle had made a part of the bargain. Lo Shih was to remain six months in his uncle's house after his marriage. If there were no promise of a child, then he was to take a concubine. Only when he had a son was he to start for America.

Peter felt relieved to know Lo Shih had relatives. He had thought them all dead except for Sen S Mo, but the ramifications of a Chinese family, he knew, were great. Evidently, they had not been exterminated. In fact, Peter remembered now that an aged man had been coming, of late, to see Sen Lo Shih. Lo Shih had not said who he was, only that he had recently come from a far-distant province. The old man's hair was snow white—very unusual for a Chinese—and his goatee was streaked with white. It had not occurred to Peter that he was a relative. He had not the fine, thin features of Scholar Sen Lo Shih, nor their nobility.

Sen Lo Shih came to say polite good-by to his teacher, holding out his long slender hand, after the custom of the West.

"Please sit down for a little, Lo Shih," said Peter. "There is a custom in my country," he went on, "that a teacher sometimes gives a pupil a gift. I should like to give you a copy of our Classic, the Bible, to put beside your Confucian Classics. It portrays a finer era than any other— the Christian era."

Lo Shih had stood to take the proffered gift, when suddenly the decorum under which Peter had seen him for all these years was rent asunder. "A finer era—your Christian era! You can say that, knowing what your opium has done to us! The Christian nations have despoiled us and weakened us. They have used their strength to force opium on us, force our land away from us. They have raped us!" Lo Shih was trembling from head to foot.

Peter had listened spellbound to this outburst. Then, suddenly, he, too, was angry. "Sit down," he said. "Calm yourself. Do not think you can shirk your responsibility like this. The blame is not all to those who exploit the weak. Why are you weak? What right have you to be weak? What right have you to harp on equality if you are weak? You praise yourself for your submission. In your submission, you have been the accomplices to what you so dramatically call the raping of your country. At Geneva in the conferences over opium your countrymen have made impotent many a plan for control by trying to hide the fact that native opium is again being grown. Take your share of responsibility like a man!" Peter sank down in his chair. He, too, was trembling.

Across the ashes of their anger, they sat silently facing each other.

"What have I done?" thought Peter. "After all these years of careful building to gain the confidence of this lad, almost son to me, I have destroyed everything in one burst of anger."

As the minutes passed, and Lo Shih did not speak, Peter tried to think of something to say to right things. There was nothing. The evil had been done, he grieved.

And then, gradually, he perceived that this silence between them was comfortable and natural. There was no necessity for speech. The strains and stresses of two sensitive men of different races, trying to adjust themselves to each other, were over. All the stubborn nationalism of each had burned up in their separate angers. All pretense, all hidden grievances, now that they had been spoken, seemed to have lost their potency. For a long time they sat thus in the darkening room, barely able to make out the outlines each of the other, their spirits meeting in understanding. At last Lo Shih rose to go.

"You will let me know, Lo Shih, what university you choose?" asked Peter. "When I go home in a year, I shall hope to see you. Here are letters of introduction to friends of mine in America. If you are near them, go to see them." And he handed Lo Shih a packet of letters held together with a rubber band.

That Peter heard nothing further from Sen Lo Shih did not worry him. In their bursting anger and the ensuing silence, understanding had gone very deep. They both, Peter felt, needed to withdraw, each into his own people. Each should let go the other for a little. To Peter, that one spirit ever pierced its way through the accumulated layers of everyday living to the hidden centers of another human being always partook of the nature of a miracle. That it pierced through when those layers would seem naturally to be too thick to penetrate was indeed mysterious. But despite all the contrary forces existing between himself and Sen Lo Shih, they had reached understanding.

Through all these months that Peter had worked with Sen Lo Shih in the laboratory, in spite of almost negligible progress with the experiment, he had never doubted his final success. But now, without the stimulus of Lo Shih's mind and the actual help he gave, Peter began to wonder if he were not attempting the impossible. He hadn't sufficient time. But even more, he was realizing he lacked the proper equipment for scientific research. He could not afford a micrographic camera to record the steps of his experiment. He needed a thermostat for accurate temperature control.

He was lonely, too. He seemed to have no vital touch with any human being.

The day was very hot. The Great Heat had begun. Peter was half across the city on his way to the tuberculosis sanitarium, when he remembered he had not brought money to pay the attendants. He was near the office of the Great American Oil Company. The oil company often cashed checks for the missionaries of the city, but the traditional antagonism between business and Missions had kept Peter from asking this favor. Today, he decided, he'd take advantage of their courtesy. It was too hot to go back.

As he turned into the Great Street where the office building stood, he was thinking what a strange relationship Missions had to American business—at once despised by it and made its expression. The business men openly said that they had little use for Missions, and yet men who had made their fortunes in these very businesses were putting large sums into Mission undertakings such as the centralized hospitals Diana had been anxious for him to enter. Was it an effort to transcend the material world they lived in, or to regiment the spirit to business enterprise? Peter, with his continual struggle to free himself from the sterility of form, was apprehensive.

He was ushered into the manager's office. Behind a flat-topped desk, swept clean of papers except for one sheet on which he seemed to be doing some figuring, sat a neat, very businesslike American.

"Well, what can I do for you?" the man asked. His brown eyes seemed to be taking Peter in from head to foot. The doctor felt awkward, standing there under such keen scrutiny. He stated his errand, feeling the man wished him to waste no time.

"Gladly, Dr. Fraser. But won't you sit down, if you're not in too much of a hurry? My name's Chase—Stephen Chase. I've heard of you often in the city. I owe a lot to your profession." He liked this lean, tall doctor, with his sensitive face.

Peter sat down. A warm sense of companionship came over him at this disarming friendliness.

"I lived in Manchuria a long time, but I've recently come from the Upper Yangtse. Do you know that part of the country?"

"No," said Peter. "I've always lived here."

"I've heard about your work," said Stephen. "I've heard you did a good deal in cleaning up opium in this province."

"Yes, we've got it under control here."

"The sad thing about it is," said the other, "it's creeping in again. On the upper river, it's bad. The war lords find it's the best crop for their use—easily transported, brings the highest returns. Why, I've seen a hundred men at a time trekking it across country under military escort. My adviser up there, a man named Ho, says the back country is full of it."

"Just what do you think that will mean? A return to the old conditions?" asked Peter.

"It's a bad combination—the war lords are greedy, the people submissive."

Peter went away disturbed over the prospect, but stimulated, too, by the contact with this man of other experience. He had liked his social outlook.

So had begun a friendship between the two. Although never going beyond the office, it steadily deepened. Peter often stopped for a half-hour's chat with this countryman of his, who accepted him so naturally. They talked a good deal about the Chinese. Each appreciated the other's deep knowledge of this alien race. Each profited by checking his knowledge against that of another good observer. Chase spoke often of the man named Ho he knew up-river. Peter spoke often of Sen Lo Shih.

One day Chase sent a note to Peter, asking if he would come to see his wife. She was not well, he said.

At the door of his apartment above the office, Chase, looking a little anxious, met him. "I think my wife is only tired," he said, "but I've persuaded her to see you."

Peter wondered what the wife of his friend would be like.

"Hester, this is Dr. Fraser," Chase said to a woman lying on a wicker chaise-longue in the hall.

"We find this the coolest spot in the house." Mrs. Chase spoke languidly.

Peter marked that she looked frail. He noticed at once the sensitive curve to her mouth, and the expressive, well-kept hands. "These women of the business community don't have enough to do," he thought.

"You have no children, your husband tells me." Very gently, he added, "Have you ever had any?"

"Yes . . . one," was her quiet reply.

As she spoke, he saw the eyes of wife and husband meet, saw the deep understanding between them. He saw something else that he felt Chase did not know—that for his sake this woman held her own powers in abeyance because for some reason they would conflict with his.

"Are you by any chance a musician?" he asked.

"How did you know?" she asked in surprise. "I play the violin. I mean, I did. There's no opportunity for music out here."

He went away pondering. It had been a shot in the dark, asking if she were a musician. There was about her some frustration. Was there always more cost to one than to the other in marriage? he wondered. There hadn't been, at first, for Diana and him. It seemed, as he thought of it, that they had held in their hands that perfect thing, growth of each within the circle of their union.

Except for his odd hours with Chase, Peter liked best to be with the Chinese. He was beginning to feel more at home with them than with his own people. They had that art of never obtruding their personalities, and Peter was seeking solitude. He did not miss Diana so poignantly as he had at first, although the wound of absence was always there. Not only in his moments on the city wall did he seek solitude, but even when he was in the midst of his crowded hospital or the intimacy of the compound, he shut himself off into some deep inner aloneness where he sought answer to a question asserting itself more and more in his mind of late.

Slowly he was coming to the conclusion that if he were to learn how the fluke infested human beings, he must make his research in America, where he could have a properly equipped laboratory. In such a laboratory, he felt certain he could complete the scientific data, give his knowledge of this disease not only to China, but to the world. The problem was to get the ova to such a laboratory. He could not take a sick Chinese to America—but he himself could enter sick.

Summer passed into fall and then winter. During his vacation, Peter had gone to the canal area and again collected snails. He'd make one more effort. For the careful incubation of the ova, he had no time, but he could study the snails. He might find the organism there, and he might yet learn how the disease was transmitted. Doggedly, he set to work.

One morning he rose early. Not wishing to arouse Wang Ma, he made himself a cup of coffee over a native charcoal stove he had in his laboratory. He would put in a quiet hour of work before the hospital awoke for the day. Skillfully he took one of the tiny snails brought from a caltrop field, mounted it on a slide, slipped it into place under the microscope and started to focus the lens. The lens was broken.

No one knew how it had happened. The coolie who cleaned the room declared he had not touched it. Well, it didn't matter how it had happened. It was broken. He couldn't afford a new one.

He kept seeing in his mind the laboratory at his old school—its efficient equipment. And again that thought, that he might carry the disease in his own body. Strange, that no one knew how to keep man from being infected, and yet easy to infect himself with the live flukes.

Not so dangerous a thing that he need hesitate. There was practically no chance of death. But how great would be the ravages on his system he could not say. Recovery varied greatly with the individual. Some were never really well, once infected, even though the parasite were eliminated. All, afterward, seemed more vulnerable to other diseases. A fit body had always been a passion with Peter, and through all the years of working with disease, he had kept his original feeling that disease was unclean. He had already run the chance of tuberculosis in that unpremeditated act in the hospital. Deliberately to bring disease into his body—it was from this he drew back. He should not draw back. Other physicians had done far more heroic acts to trace disease, even accepting death.

What was his responsibility to Diana? That he should consult her about this step, he did not consider necessary, as once he would have. Love for her had come to mean care for her—no longer a sharing of his thoughts and problems. If he were to weaken his body, it seemed to him, he should take extra precaution for Diana, because there was that one chance in a million that the disease might take his life. According to his contract, the Mission would support her, but he'd like her to have a little more. He ought to arrange an insurance. How should he do it?

He thought of his friend, Chase. He would know the business end. He sought him out in his office, taking a check as a pretext for his visit. But he realized, when he got there, that it was going to be difficult telling Chase what he had come to tell. Somehow the whole matter took on a different aspect here, among the things of business, where everything was checked up in dollars and cents.

When he came in, Chase was giving orders to the head of a boat *hong*. The fellow had been up to some sharp practice, and Chase was "putting the fear of God into him," he told Peter after the man had gone. For the moment there seemed to Peter to be nothing to draw them together. Why should he have come to this man for help in a matter he shrank from telling anyone? And then he realized there was no reason to tell why he wanted the insurance. All he needed to know from Chase was how to go about it.

"There's a business matter I'd like to discuss with you," he began.

"Yes?" said Chase.

"It's a question of insurance, something more than the Mission gives in the way of protection. What would you advise?"

"Insurance is high for any man in this country," answered Chase. "At best a man out here is considered a good deal of risk. For a man past thirty, it's almost prohibitive."

"How much?" asked Peter. He gasped at the figure Chase named.

"Of course," added Chase, "you're very fit. Anyone can see that. That would lower the rate. I'll see what I can do for you . . . I've a friend in the business. I'll let you know when I've talked to him. He'll come and see you . . . examination, and so on, you know."

Two weeks later, the policy was signed.

The time of Peter's going to America was only a few days away. He had gone early to his laboratory. Through all the years of his life he had sought to know God. He never had, except as he had seen Him revealed through other human beings. At times, when he had been with Stella, he had felt close to some revelation. He bowed his head on the laboratory table. The familiar cries of the city came up to him.

More vividly than he had ever seen them in life, he saw the men, women and children of China, depleted by this parasite. The youth of China, with flat chests, thin narrow shoulders. He saw the struggle that lay ahead of these boys and girls. Only an abortive democracy had been born in this land. The agony of real creation lay darkly hidden, as all creation was. It was these boys and girls who must bear that agony.

He reached out his hand, took the cup standing on the table, and drank what he had prepared for himself. He could not fail to be infected.

Man turns away from a secret act. Even when it is wholly good, some sense of guilt goes with it. Peter was drawn as if by a magnet back to Chase. This time he found himself confiding in him. Was it because Chase seemed so entirely apart from his own life?

"But you shouldn't have taken out insurance without explaining," Chase exclaimed impetuously, when Peter had finished.

"You mean . . . you think . . . but I couldn't tell them this. No one in the world knows it. It's . . . it's my own private business."

"You've told me."

"You're the only one."

Stephen Chase felt an odd tightening in his throat. Here again was friendship, and into his mind came the memory of his friend Ho. He remembered that first drawing together in friendship, and Ho's remark, "You think of business; we think of relationship." Two standards pulling at him. It was essential that he save for this idealist his self-respect.

"I'm sorry I spoke so hastily," he said. "I was looking at it as a business man would. You've looked at it—well, as an idealist would. And perhaps you're right. It's not a thing to tell just anyone. It's quite your own business, as you say."

Chase felt oddly humble before this man, and yet he continued to be a little shocked at his business ethics. The next week, he took out a policy for himself, to average the risk.

"Strange act on my part," Stephen said to himself. "However, very Chinese . . . the way they would settle an insult, I'm settling an obligation. But neither the friend nor the insurance company knows about it." He smiled to himself.

THE HEALING OF THE LEPERS

Elgin E. Groseclose

The Persian Journey tells how Reverend Ashley Wishard was sent out to bring religion and science to the Mohammedans. In "The Healing of the Lepers" he discovers that science fights a losing battle against Moslem fatalism unless fortified by the simple faith of the Gospel.

ASHLEY WISHARD rode on in silence, puzzled and distressed at his failure to make any impression upon the Persian boy. It was not his first failure—his servant Fathi, quiet, suave, never outspoken, presented a blank wall to him when he began to get beyond the obvious and attempt to lead the understanding into an appreciation of the springs of the Promethean spirit of the West. With Kazim, with Fathi, with others with whom he talked, it was invariably the same—polite interest, an expression of wonder, usually the set phrase "God is great," and beyond that, nothing.

It was, he appreciated, the *kismet of* the East, the profound sense of the majesty and might of God, the insignificance of man, and the impossibility of communion between the two. Petitions might go up to Him; He might be propitiated by the fivefold devotion—prayer, fasting, alms giving, pilgrimage and the recitation of the creed—but God Himself was a treasure house to which there was no key. He might unlock His mysteries, but man, never. How could man, who was finite, understand or approach God, who was infinite? In the face of such a concept it was inconceivable that man should ever be master of his destiny. If a wall fall, it was an act of God, for which man was not responsible. If a plague decimated the population, it was the same— futility to attempt to stay the hand of God by medical science. If slavery, social injustice, tyranny, or natural calamity prevailed, nothing remained but to accept these things passively, as the acts of a Will to which the will of man might not, could not, be opposed. God is great.

In that phrase was summed up the Moslem's attitude toward life, and before such a fanatic faith in the authority and the wisdom of God, how was one to oppose against it the Christian belief that God was a father, and that man might commune with God as a child speaks to its parent, and that unto as many as received Christ, "to them gave he power to become the sons of God."

Ashley could appreciate this attitude of the Moslem; he had caught the same spirit in many Christians whose eyes were focused on the Old Testament rather than the New, those who considered for instance the cry of Job regarding Him

Which commandeth the sun, and it riseth not; and sealeth up the stars.

Which alone spreadeth out the heavens, and treadeth upon the waves of the sea. . . .

For he is not a man, as I am, that I should answer him, and we should come together in judgment.

Neither is there any daysman betwixt us, that might lay his hand upon us both.

To one who looked upon God in this light, and with the blind faith and fanatic devotion to his belief which the Moslem exhibited, it was inconceivable that an Intercessor should exist, and that man, through that Intercessor, might approach the eternal Throne, yes, that it might be possible, through the grace of that Intercessor, and by His power, to "enter into the treasures of the snow," to know "by what way the light is parted," perhaps, in time, even to "bind the sweet influences of the Pleiades, or loose the bands of Orion." . . .

"Can leprosy be cured?" asked Fathi Ashraf, as they rode along.

"We cannot say so positively," replied Ashley, "but enough that in many cases patients are discharged from the leprosaria and returned to their homes. Thanks to Hansen, the Norwegian, the bacillus was finally isolated in 1873, and with the bacillus known we can be confident eventually of making cures as surely as in the case of tuberculosis or syphilis. A number of remedies are being used, the most efficacious being injections of an ester of chaulmoogra oil, although mercury solutions have been used and are being experimented with. The treatment is somewhat painful in its early stages, and it must be continued for several years to get results, and the patient must be kept under constant observation and care to guard against a relapse.

"The chief scourge of the leper has not been his leprosy but man's inhumanity," he continued. "For two thousand years Christian nations

supinely followed the law of Moses, rather than the injunction of
Christ, and treated the leper as unclean, to be driven from city gates
and condemned to live alone. But the method of dealing with leprosy
is not isolation but treatment. Isolation kills hope and breaks down the
spiritual vitality upon which all treatment must be based. The first step
is to restore the mental attitude of the patient, and then build up his
recuperative powers by proper nourishment and care."

Fathi appeared satisfied, for he did not ask further questions. They
rode on in silence.

As they mounted the ridge of red hills, the path grew rocky and
steep, and the rising sun beat down upon their company, upon the
rocks which in turn reflected the hard light and heat into their faces.
The horses slackened their gait, and Ashley, Fathi, Kazim, the
katkhoda's servants, all became uncommunicative, passive, like the
patient donkeys that had been trotting along at their unvarying gait
the whole morning. The plain below was now a great bowl of light;
the hills ahead, hard as flint.

Presently they had crossed the ridge and were descending into a
desolate, barren valley. Not a village, not an oasis of green in this
seared, pock-marked depression. No sign of life save for a cluster of
huts in the distance, set against the brassy slopes of the mountain, and
near which a yellow stream of water flowed. The water of the stream
was not of the life-giving variety; it was sulphurous, brackish, impossible to drink. Here and there in the valley were glittering areas of salt.

Here it was that a colony of fifty to a hundred lepers lived, living in a
desolation of desolation, exiled from the villages which were their
homes, exiled from friends and relatives, exiled from God it seemed,
separated from everything that one associates with the earth and its
goodness.

The huts in which they lived proved, on nearer approach, even more
miserable than they seemed at a distance. What had once been a mud
wall surrounded the village, but it was broken and crumbling and in no
place higher than a man's waist.

A few human beings were creeping about the decaying hovels. The
huts were not much higher than a man's head, and the doorways were
nothing more than apertures at the bottom of the wall—small on purpose so that the inhabitants might more easily defend themselves
against the prowling desert jackals. Some of these apertures had shreds
of gates hanging precariously on rusty hinges; others had none.

As Ashley and his company drew up beside the wall, a cluster of ragged beings formed on the opposite side, salaaming. One, an old man with knotted fingers, whispered a greeting. His tongue had been eaten out by the disease of which he suffered.

As Ashley saw the actual condition of the lepers, an uncontrollable resentment arose within him at the attitude to which Kazim had given words. It seemed impossible to him that men should exist in such condition. What ignorance, what perversity, he exclaimed to himself, what unwillingness to accept truth! In India, he had visited the leper colonies under the care of the various medical missions, and he had seen what restoration of health and sound body had been effected by intelligent medical care. That was the work of intelligence, of the Promethean spirit which dares do what seems impossible.

But before this terrible misery what could he here alone accomplish? It would take months, even years, of patient administration to cleanse this lazaret. Give him a staff of doctors, and money enough, and it could be done. But what could he do now? A single injection of mercury salts, from his meager stock of medicine, would cause more pain than cure.

What could he offer them at this moment?

Fortunately, there was something within Ashley Wishard besides thought, something beyond logic. He did not recognize it, though in time he would, but of its own accord it sprang into being. Even as his thought was depressed by what he saw, his spirit was astir, rising by some unwilled urge, to meet the challenge. While Ashley was thinking, he leaped from his horse, and saluted the lepers:

"*Salaam aleikum* [Peace be with you]. The *katkhoda* of the village of Ismet has of his bounty sent you wheat. Have you a headman to make the division?"

"Yes, *sahib*," croaked the old man who had first greeted him.

Fathi Ashraf set to work getting the grain unloaded and distributed, putting it up in sacks and in quantities proportioned to need as the village elder indicated, all the time keeping his work at a safe distance from the lepers, and cautioning them with gentle but firm remonstrances to stay at a distance. Ashley Wishard, meantime, laid out gauze and antiseptics, and donning his surgeon's robe and rubber gloves, prepared to examine the condition of the lepers. As he directed them to approach one by one, Fathi Ashraf turned from his work.

"Master," he exclaimed in consternation, "you will not be touching them? The disease will enter into you."

"Some risk, but slight," replied Ashley with as much professional unconcern as he could muster. "A minimum if one uses care."

But it was a courageous task, for Ashley, for all his brave talk, was not sure of his ground. To a wholesome dread of infection, which even his medical training could not wholly eradicate, was added the realization that his professional experience with the disease was very limited. And not only his professional skill, but all professional skill. For despite the achievements of medical science, the mystery of how life is sustained is as distant as ever. Science, which could make an automobile, could not make a frog; science, which could breathe life into a water-like liquid, could not breathe it into a human being. And what is an atom of hydrogen, for instance, compared to a drop of blood?

This discovery of the limits of scientific achievement, brought to him under such circumstances, struck him with tremendous impact. His eyes were suddenly opened to the paltry area dominated by the mind in contrast to the tremendous field of the unknown, and filled him with an awe and dread at the infinity of the universe. He saw life, for a moment, with the eyes of the Moslem, the finitude of man, the infinitude of God, and he quaked inwardly with the thought of human futility.

Ashley went about his task with outward calm.

Leprosy, he saw, was not ordinarily a painful disease, since it attacks the nerves and deadens them; nor was it always a loathsome disease, since the sores it forms are what is known as "dry." It becomes loathsome in its advanced stages, when the affected parts begin to drop off, or develop malformations. Many of the lepers here were in that stage of the disease. Some had their fingers drawn into knots until their hands were useless, others had bulbous legs that ended in mere stumps of feet; all, of course, were incapacitated for labor, and it was this inability to look after themselves, with no one else to help them, that rendered their condition especially pitiful. And it moreover added to their own distress, for, being unable to supply their wants, they fell ill to other ailments, some of which were more to be feared than the leprosy itself, such as malaria, dysentery, and syphilis.

The expressions on the faces of these lepers were horrible under the influence of the disease. Some were leonine, the effect of the thickening of flesh and its folding in heavy, vertical lines that lent an appearance of ferocity. With others, the skin had atrophied and hung in despondent wrinkles on the face, giving a lugubrious aspect to the expression. Others wore the look of a living corpse—eyes paralyzed and always open, with a fixed and stony gaze, lips paralyzed, leaving the mouth inert with drooping corners and the face mournful.

Some of the lepers, those suffering from malaria, for instance, Ashley Wishard was able to minister to. For them, quinine, of which he had ample supply in his kit, and which he parceled out in capsules, with explicit instructions as to its use. Two of the lepers were suffering so, quaking and shivering as they came forward, that Ashley decided that an immediate injection by hypodermic was necessary. He ordered them to bare their elbows while he got out his syringe and needle and set an alcohol lamp to burning.

Fathi and the *katkhoda's* servants ceased the distribution of grain to watch with awe, as the missionary got ready his instruments, sterilized them, drew a tourniquet around the arm in preparation for an injection of quinine dihydrochloride, and then carefully administered it. When he had finished, he again carefully sterilized the instruments, washed his hands with germicidal solution, and put the case back into its container.

The two malaria sufferers lay on a piece of sacking, shivering.

"There is nothing more that medical science can do here in an afternoon," said Ashley solemnly, as he strapped his kit back on the saddle. He decided that he must write to the Church of the Age about these lepers. Perhaps he could get money to take care of them properly. At least he hoped so.

The men were gathering in the pack animals and preparing to depart when Fathi Ashraf asked hesitantly:

"Perhaps, master, if you read them something from the *Injil,* it might comfort them."

Ashley looked at his servant in wonder. Fathi had asked him to read to these lepers something from the New Testament, something from the story of Jesus! Ashley had thought of doing this but he had been afraid that it might seem as though he were forcing his message, compelling unwilling attention in payment for medical services. Doctor Winthrop had cautioned him, in their conferences before he had left America, to avoid forcing his gospel down the throats of people. "You must be patient, and give only to those who ask. In time, they will ask, for seeing your good works, they will want to know the secret of Christian benefactions."

"Do you think they would like for me to read to them?" Ashley asked.

"Yes, *sahib,* please tell us about Jesus," spoke up one of the crowd of lepers who were gathered about respectfully.

"Have you heard of Jesus, then?" Ashley asked.

He knew of course that every Moslem who read his Koran had heard of Jesus, whom the prophet Mohammed had characterized as a lesser prophet. Besides, the Nestorians and Armenians had their churches in all the larger towns. Nevertheless, he did not expect these Moslem lepers to be familiar with His story.

"Yes, *sahib,* we have heard of the Saviour," the old man said. "One was here—a *firenghi*—many years ago—who told us about the Saviour, and read to us His story, and we have kept our memory of Him as one who blesses children and lepers, and makes sweet the path of darkness. We have long hoped that some would come again who would tell us more of the Saviour."

Ashley had not used the word "Saviour" in speaking of Jesus. Indeed, he seldom did, not only because it was a term offensive to the Moslem, but partly, perhaps, because of his own cast of mind, which was of that modern mold of thought which apparently has little consciousness of the need of a saviour, being sufficient unto itself, confident of its own power, and desiring only an Intelligence which will illuminate the path of forward progress.

The use of the word "Saviour" was like an electric shock, touching him in recesses of his spirit which he himself had seldom entered, and filling him again with the sense of profound personal inadequacy.

Ashley opened his Testament and, addressing the lepers, began to read the story of the raising of Lazarus:

"Now a certain man was sick, named Lazarus, of Bethany, the town of Mary and her sister Martha . . .

"Therefore his sisters sent to him, saying, Lord, behold, he whom thou lovest is sick.

"When Jesus heard that, he said, This sickness is not unto death, but for the glory of God, that the Son of God might be glorified thereby."

When Ashley came to the word *Esau* (Jesus) in his reading there was a responsive murmur among the lepers, and a nodding as at the entrance of a friend.

Ashley continued reading, and in doing so his imagination was awakened to the reality of the historical event in a way that it had never been awakened before. Like most modern religionists he ignored the actualities of these stories and at most accepted them in a symbolic, mystical sense. They were out of the natural order, did not fit into scientific concepts of natural law, hence they could not be, or if they were, were true only in a preternatural sense. And natural law, of course, though it was at best nothing more than a conceptual generalization of a human mentality, was, in the modern world at least, more absolute than deity itself, and conceptions of deity had to fit into natural law, rather than natural law adjusting itself to deity.

Of course, the keener scientists were beginning to recognize the limits of their "law" and their concepts, and, particularly since the discoveries of the erratic nature of electrons, were beginning to suspect the possibility of individuality, free choice and even divinity; but these were but a minority, and the ordinary scientist, and the ordinary student who followed in the tradition, still clung to this arrogant belief in the absoluteness of their system. And Ashley Wishard, born and bred in that environment, had not escaped infection by that attitude.

But now, it seemed, the doors were opening to him, and he began to catch a glimpse of the profound naturalness of religion, the intimacy and the reality of the spirit, and the perfect historicity of Biblical miracle.

Ashley came to the words:

"Then when Jesus came, he found that he had lain in the grave four days already."

The lepers had been listening eagerly, but at this point, the entrance of the Saviour upon the scene of death ready to grapple with that eternal mystery, the sighing of the lepers was audible. Ashley could scarcely continue his reading. They are thinking, he said to himself, how long will it be until the Death that now has his hands laid upon them will be challenged by his Master? He surveyed the wretched group about him. In their faces he saw, beyond dispute or doubt, a light of hope and faith, a faith of a quality which he himself, he painfully realized, had never possessed.

He continued with his reading:

"Jesus . . . cometh to the grave. It was a cave, and a stone lay upon it.

"Jesus said, Take ye away the stone. Martha . . . saith unto him, Lord, by this time he stinketh: for he hath been dead four days. . . .

"Then they took away the stone from the place where the dead was laid.

And Jesus lifted up his eyes and said, Father, I thank thee that thou hast heard me. . . .

"And when he had thus spoken, he cried with a loud voice, Lazarus, come forth.

"And he that was dead came forth, bound hand and foot with grave-clothes: and his face was bound about with a napkin."

As Ashley finished his reading, exclamations of *"Alhamdulillah"* (Praise God) and *"Allahu Akbar"* (God is Great) were gasped.

Ashley wanted to flee; he wanted to go somewhere away and think and pray, for the distress of his soul. For these lepers, for whatever cause, perhaps from their very misery—were more prepared to accept the truth of the gospel than he, who was its professed minister and evangel. But he could not flee; he must speak to them. Here was mystery which he had not entered, had not sought to enter, but which he was called to illuminate. He could only speak to them with such light as he possessed and hope and trust that his speech might not be such as darkens counsel with words without knowledge. He began:

"I do not come to you as Jesus, healing your wounds, casting forth the leprosy from you, or raising you from the dead. But I come with a message of hope that some day, perhaps unto you, these things shall be accomplished, for we have been commanded by Jesus to go into the world and cast forth devils, restore the blind to sight, heal the lepers, and raise the dead.

"And if God's Son has so commanded us, shall God withhold from us the power to do these things? Shall we make brick without straw?

"But we know these things shall be done, for our Master has taught us that we are the children of God, partaking of the power and nature of Godhead. And that knowledge inspires us to seek for the secrets by which man may arise to the power of God, that we may be no longer children, but attain to the manhood and the inheritance, and, so attaining, do the will of God.

"In that knowledge and in that confidence men have learned the secrets of light and darkness, and how to restore sight, and to heal many sicknesses. We have confidence that the disease of which you suffer will yet be subdued by the grace of God. Already there is an oil, a medicine, which has power to stay the progress of the disease. Men, inspired by the faith given us in the teachings of Jesus Christ, are now seeking to wrest the furthest secrets of the disease. God willing, this knowledge, and the fruits of this knowledge, shall be brought to you, and in that hope accept my service not as fruit, but as harbinger of fruit, not as cure, but the hope of cure, and wait in patience, in the knowledge that men regard you in kindness, as children of God and as their brothers, and wish you well."

Ashley Wishard closed abruptly, lifted his hand in benediction, mounted and rode off, followed by Fathi and the rest of the company.

When at a distance from the village, he turned in his saddle to look back. The lepers were struggling over the sacks of grain, but two or three stood by the wall watching his party as they rode away. Were they wondering, he thought, whether they too would ride away one day?

AN EXTRACT FROM THE
JOURNAL OF FATHER DUPLESSIS

John Buchan

A remote North Canadian valley is the setting for *Mountain Meadow,* the last of John Buchan's adventure stories. Mystery, travel, and speculation upon life and death play a part in the fate of a man who knows he will die within a year.

IN THIS JOURNAL, which I have now kept for more than twenty years, I shall attempt to set down what I remember of my friend. I call him my friend, for though our intercourse was measured in time by a few weeks, it had the intimacy of comradeship in a difficult undertaking. Let me say by way of prologue that during our friendship I saw what is not often vouchsafed to mortal eyes, the rebirth of a soul.

In the fall I had talked with L. at Fort Bannerman. He was clearly a man in bad health, to whom the details of living were a struggle. I was impressed by his gentleness and his power of self-control, but it was a painful impression, for I realised that it meant a continuous effort. I felt that no circumstances could break the iron armour of his fortitude. But my feeling for him had warmth in it as well as respect. We had been soldiers in the same campaign, and he knew my home in France.

When things became bad early in the New Year, I was in doubt whom to turn to. Father Wentzel at Fort Bannerman was old and feeble; and I could not expect the Police to spare me a man. Besides, I wanted something more than physical assistance. I wanted a man of education who could understand and cope with the Hares' *malaise*. So when one of L.'s guides reached the camp in early February, I thought at once of him, and ventured to send him a message.

It was a shot at a venture, and I was not prepared for his ready response. When he arrived with Galliard I was surprised by the look of both. I had learned from Father Wentzel that Galliard was a man sick in the spirit, and I knew that L. was sick in body. Now both seemed to have suffered a transformation. Galliard had a look of robust health, though there was that in his manner which still disquieted me—a lack of confidence, an air of unhappy anticipation, a sense of leaning heavily upon L. As for L., he was very lean and somewhat short of breath, but from my medical experience I judged him to be a convalescent.

The first day the party spent with me I had light on the situation. L. was all but cured—he might live for years with proper care. But proper care meant life in the open, no heavy duties, and not too much exertion. On this, one of the hunters, Louis Frizelle, insisted passionately. Otherwise, he said, and Galliard bore him out, that in a little time he would be dead. This L. did not deny, but was firm in his resolution to take up his quarters in the camp and to devote all his powers to saving what was left of the Hare tribe. On this decision plans were made, with the successful result explained in the Police corporal's report, which I here incorporate. . . .

At first I thought that L.'s conduct was that of a man of high humanitarian principles, who could not witness suffering without an attempt at relief. But presently I found that the motives were subtler, and if possible nobler, and that they involved his friend, Galliard. L., not being of the Church, made no confessions, and he did not really speak of himself, but in the course of our work together I was able to gather something of his history.

We talked first, I remember, about the war in Europe. I was deeply apprehensive about the fate of my beloved France, which once again in my lifetime would be bled white by war. L. seemed curiously apathetic about Europe. He had no doubts about the ultimate issue, and he repeated more than once that the world was witnessing again a contest between Death and Life, and that Life would triumph. He saw our trouble with the Hares as part of the same inscrutable purpose of the Almighty, and insisted that we were on one battle-front with the allies beyond the Atlantic. This he said often to Frizelle, whom it seemed to comfort.

I observed that as the days passed he showed an increasing tenderness towards the Hares. At first I think he regarded their succour as a cold, abstract duty. But gradually he began to feel for them a protective and brotherly kindness. I suppose it was the gift of the trained lawyer, but he mastered every detail of their tribal customs and their confused habits of thought with a speed that seemed not less than miraculous. He might have lived most of his life among them. At first, when we sat at the conferences and went in and out of the huts, his lean, pallid face revealed no more than the intellectual interest which might belong to a scientific enquirer. But by degrees a kind of affection showed in his eyes. He smiled oftener, and his smile had an infinite kindliness. From the beginning he dominated them, and the domination became in the end, on their part, almost worship.

What is the secret, I often ask myself, that gives one human being an almost mystical power over others? In the War I have known a corporal have it, when it was denied to a general of division. I have seen the gift manifest in a parish priest and lacking in an archbishop. It does not require a position of authority, for it makes its own authority. It demands a strong pre-eminence in brain and character, for it is based on understanding, but also, I think, on an effluence of sincere affection.

I was puzzled at first by the attitude of Galliard. He was a Catholic and had resumed—what he had for a time pretermitted—the observances of the Church. He came regularly to Mass and confession. He was ultimately of my own race, though *Les Canadiens* differ widely from *Les Français de France*. He should have been easy for me to comprehend, but I confess that at first I was at a loss. He was like a man under the spell of a constant fear—not panic or terror, but a vague uneasiness. To L. he was like a faithful dog. He seemed to draw strength from his presence, as the mistletoe draws strength from the oak.

What was notable was his steady advance in confidence till presently his mind was as healthy as his body. His eye cleared, his mouth no longer twitched when he spoke, and he carried his head like a soldier. The change was due partly to his absorption in his work, for to L. he was a right hand. I have rarely seen a man toil so devotedly. But it was largely due to his growing affection for L. When the party arrived from the mountains, he was obviously under L.'s influence, but only in the way in which a strong nature masters a less strong. But as the days passed, I could see that his feeling was becoming a warmer thing than admiration. The sight of L.'s increasing weakness made his face often a tragic mask. He fussed as much as the elder Frizelle over L.'s health. He would come to me and implore my interference. "He is winning," he would repeat, "but it will be at the cost of his life, and the price is too high."

Bit by bit I began to learn about Galliard, partly from L. and partly from the man himself. He had been brought up in the stiff tradition of *Les Canadiens,* had revolted against it, and had locked the door on his early life. But it was the old story. His ancestry had its revenge, a revenge bound to be especially harsh, I fancy, in the case of one of his breeding. He had fled from the glittering world in which he had won success, and from a devoted wife, to the home of his childhood. And here came a tangle of motives. He had in his blood the pioneer craving to move ever farther into the wilds; his family, indeed, had given more than one figure to the story of Arctic exploration. He conceived that he owed a duty to the family tradition which he had forsaken, and that he had to go into the North as an atonement. He also seems to have conceived it as part of the penance which he owed for the neglect of his family religion. He is a man, I think, of sentiment and imagination rather than of a high spirituality.

But his penance turned out severer than he dreamed. He fell into a *malaise* which, it is my belief, was at the bottom the same as the Hares' affliction, and which seems to be endemic in the North. It may be defined as fear of the North, or perhaps more accurately as fear of life. In the North, man, to live, has to fight every hour against hostile forces; if his spirit fails and his effort slackens, he perishes. But this dread was something more than a rational fear of a potent enemy. There was superstition in it, a horror of a supernatural and desperate malevolence. This set the Hares mooning in their shacks awaiting death, and it held Galliard, a man of education and high ability, in the same blind, unreasoning bondage. His recovered religion gave him no defence, for he read this fear as part of the price to be paid for his treason.

Then L. came on the scene. He saved Galliard's life. He appeared when Frizelle, in a crazy fit, had deserted him, and he had come from

England in the last stage of a dire sickness to restore Galliard to his old world. In L.'s grim fortitude Galliard found something that steadied his nerves. More, he learned from L. the only remedy for his *malaise*. He must fight the North and not submit to it; once fought and beaten, he could win from it, not a curse, but a blessing.

Therefore he eagerly accepted the task of grappling with the Hares' problem. Here was a test case. They were defying the North; they were resisting a madness akin to his own. If they won, the North had no more terrors for him—or life either. He would have conquered his ancestral fear.

Then something was added to his armour. He had revered L., and soon he came to love him. He thought more of L.'s bodily well-being than of his own nerves. And in forgetting his own troubles he found they had disappeared. After a fortnight in the camp he was like the man in the Scriptures out of whom the evil spirit was cast—wholly sane and at peace, but walking delicately.

But L. was my chief concern. I have said that in him I witnessed the rebirth of a soul, but that is not quite the truth. The soul, a fine soul, was always there. More, though not of the Church, I do not hesitate to say that he was of the Faith. *Alias oves habeo quae non sunt ex hoc ovili.* But he had been frozen by a hard stoicism which sprang partly from his upbringing and partly from temperament. He was a strong man with an austere command of himself, and when he had to face death, he divested himself of all that could palliate the suffering, and stood up to it with a stark resolution which was more Roman than Christian. What I witnessed was the thawing of the ice.

He had always bowed himself before the awful majesty of God. Now his experience was that of the Church in the thirteenth century, when they found in the Blessed Virgin a gentle mediatrix between mortal and divine. Or perhaps I should put it thus: that he discovered that tenderness and compassion which Our Lord came into the world to preach, and, in sympathy with others, he lost all care for himself. His noble, frosty egoism was merged in something nobler. He had meant to die in the cold cathedral of the North, ceasing to live in a world which had no care for life. Now he welcomed the humblest human environment, for he had come to love his kind; indeed, to love everything that God had made. He once said (he told me he was quoting an English poet) that he "carried about his heart an awful warmth like a load of immortality."

When I first met him at Fort Bannerman, he seemed to me the typical Englishman, courteous, aloof, the type I knew well in the War. But now there seemed to be a loosening of bonds. He talked very little, but he smiled often, and he seemed to radiate a gentle, compelling courtesy. But there was steel under the soft glove. He had always the air of command, and the Hares obeyed his lightest word as I am certain they never obeyed any orders before in their tribal history. As his strength declined, he could speak only in a whisper, but his whispers had the authority of trumpets. For he succeeded in diffusing the impression of a man who had put all fear behind him and was already in communion with something beyond our mortality.

He shared his confidences with no one. Galliard, who had come to regard him with devotion, would never have dared to pierce his reserve. I tried and failed. With him I had not the authority of the Church, and, though I recognised that he was nearing death, I could not offer the consolations of religion unless he had asked for them. I should have felt it an impiety, for I recognised that in his own way he was making his soul. As the power of the sun waxed, he liked to bask in it with his eyes shut, as if in prayer or a daydream. He borrowed my Latin Bible and read much in it, but the book would often lie on his knees while he watched with abstracted eyes the dazzle of light on the snow of the far mountains.

It is a strange fact to chronicle, but I think his last days were his happiest. His strength was very low, but he had done his work and the Hares were out of the pit. Galliard tended him like a mother or a sister, helped him to dress and undress, keeping the hut warm, cooking for him and feeding him. The hunters, the Frizelles and the Hares, came to see him on every return journey. Old Zacharias would remain for hours near his door in case he might be summoned. But all respected his privacy, for they felt that he had gone into retreat before death. I saw him oftenest, and the miracle was that, as the spring crept back to the valley, there seemed to be a springtime in his spirit.

He came often to Mass—the last occasion being the High Mass at Easter, which for the Hares was also a thanksgiving for recovery. The attendance was now exemplary. The little church with its gaudy colouring—the work of old Brother Onésime, and much admired by Father Wentzel—was crowded to the door. The Hares have an instinct for ritual, and my acolytes serve the altar well, but they have none for music, and I had found it impossible to train much of a choir.

L. would sit in a corner following my Latin with his lips, and he seemed to draw comfort from it. I think the reason was that he was now sharing something with the Hares, and was not a director, but one of the directed. For he had come to love those poor childish folk. Hitherto a lonely man, he had found a clan and a family.

After that Easter Sunday his body went fast downhill. I do not think he suffered much, except from weakness. His manner became gentler than ever, and his eyes used often to have the pleased look of a good child. He smiled, too, often, as if he saw the humour of life. The huskies—never a very good-tempered pack, though now they were well fed—became his friends, and one or two of the older beasts would accompany him out-of-doors with a ridiculous air of being a bodyguard. One cold night, I remember, one of them suddenly ensconced itself in an empty box outside the presbytery door. I can still hear L. talking to it. "I know what you're saying, old fellow: 'I'm a poor dog and my master's a poor man. I've never had a box like this to sleep in. Please don't turn me out.'" So there it remained—the first time I have seen a husky with ambitions to become a house-dog.

He watched eagerly for the signs of spring. The first was the return of the snow buntings, shimmering grey flocks which had wintered in the South. These he would follow with his eyes as they fluttered over the pine woods or spread themselves like a pied shadow on the snow. Then the mountain we call Baldface suddenly shed most of its winter covering, the noise of avalanches punctuated the night, and the upper ribs were disclosed, black as ink in the daytime, but at evening flaming into the most amazing hues of rose and purple. I knew that he had been an alpinist of note, and in these moments I fancy he was recapturing some of the activities of his youth. But there was no regret in his eyes. He was giving thanks for another vision of the glory of God.

The last time he was able to go abroad, Galliard and I assisted him down to the edge of the lake. There was still a broad selvedge of ice —what the Canadian French call *batture*—but in the middle the ice was cracking, and there were lanes of water to reflect the pale blue sky. Also the streams were being loosed from their winter stricture. One could hear them talking under their bonds, and in one or two places the force of water had cleared the boulders and made pools and cascades. . . . A wonderful thing happened. A bull moose, very shaggy and lean, came out of the forest and stood in an open shallow at a stream's mouth. It drank its fill, and then raised its ugly head, shook it, and stared into the sunset. Crystal drops fell from its mouth, and the setting sun transfigured the beast into something magical, a beneficent dragon out of a fairy-tale. I shall never forget L.'s delight. It was as if he had his last sight of the beauty of the earth, and found in it a pledge of the beauty of Paradise, though I doubt if there will be anything like a bull moose in the Heavenly City. . . .

Three days later he died in his sleep. There was no burial, for Galliard wished the interment to be at his old home in Quebec. The arrival of two of the R.C.M.P. made it possible to convey the body to Fort Bannerman, whence it would be easy to complete the journey by air.

Such is my story of the end of a true-man-at-arms whose memory will always abide with me. He was not of the Church, but beyond doubt he died in grace. In his last hours he found not peace only but beatitude. *Dona aeternam quietem, Domine, et lux perpetua luceat ei.*

"Come, Follow Me"

ALONE THE STRANGER PASSES
Manuel Komroff

In the Years of Our Lord, Komroff's novel of the life and times of
Jesus, is wholly in keeping with the spirit and mood of the gospel version, but re-created with new clarity, new vision, and immediacy to the
soul of man. The chapter which follows reveals Jesus himself moving
quietly among his followers with gentleness and healing.

. . . A BLIND BEGGAR who spent his days seated on the ground beside
the gate, with his clay saucer beside him, suddenly stood up, breathed
deeply and followed the stranger into the city streets.

"There, see," said one of the soldiers. "Blind Saul seems to know
whom to follow. Perhaps he has heard of this Prophet who comes
from the desert to preach to multitudes."

"Do you believe," asked one of the soldiers, "that this Prophet can
perform miracles?"

"No. Certainly not."

"He seems just like you or me and I can believe none of the stories
about him."

"Well, if I saw it with my eyes, then I might believe," added one.

With such meaningless chatter and with the recounting of some
of the tales of this Prophet, the soldiers at the city gate spent the last
quarter-of-an-hour before the night-watch took over their duties.

In the meantime the blind beggar Saul followed the stranger. That strange and unexplained power given to those who live in darkness led him on and on. At times he was but a pace or two behind the stranger. But at other moments he fell eight or ten paces behind because he paused to listen.

He heard all but he saw nothing. And all twelve events which followed occurred in rapid succession. All twelve occurred in almost twelve short minutes.

Blind Saul heard the voice of a young woman singing. The voice came from an open window. But he did not see that she was seated before her mirror and was combing her hair and admiring the beauty of the reflection in the glass. The shadow of the stranger walking in the street was reflected by the low evening light across the wall of her room. Suddenly her singing stopped and the comb fell from her hand.

She spoke to someone close by and her words were heard by the blind beggar Saul.

"How long will my beauty last!" she exclaimed.

"A few years more," replied a woman's voice.

"And then?"

"Look about you and see."

"And I too will be old."

"And live for many years, I hope."

"Just now," said the girl, "I saw a shadow cross the mirror and suddenly it all came to me."

For a brief moment she was silent.

"Come, speak, child. Say what it is that came to you," said the voice.

"I don't know how to say it. But the pleasure has suddenly left me. I loved to see myself in the mirror and admire my hair and eyes and lips and now . . . It was as though a shudder passed through me and made me drop the comb. Something inside has changed and I cannot say what it is."

"Perhaps, my child, you have lost your vanity."

"Would that be good?"

"Yes, my child; very good."

"Then I have lost it; it is gone forever."

Across the street another girl was standing in the window and suddenly she turned to speak with her sister. The blind beggar Saul heard her say: "I just saw her drop the comb from her hand. All day long she looks at herself in the glass. And do you want me to tell you something? For a long time I have watched her with eyes of envy. I was envious of her beauty, her jewels, her silk garments, the wealth and comfort of her home; of everything about her I was envious. But now I feel sorry for her and I no longer envy anything she possesses."

"What has made this sudden change in you, dear sister?"

"I don't know."

The Stranger passed on in silence and the blind beggar followed.

As they passed the open shop of a coppersmith, the apron-boy stopped hammering and spoke to the old man.

"Master," he said, "why don't you take the money home? It is not safe here in the shop."

"No one knows it is here."

"I know it is here and I must confess to you that it is a temptation."

"How is that?"

"Well, I have a key to the shop and at night . . . Take it home. It is not safe here."

"And if you took the money, where would you go?"

"Ah! That's the point that makes it hard. I would have to leave Jerusalem and flee into Galilee."

"You planned it?"

"I was thinking about it and . . ."

"And what?"

"Well, just now it came to me that it is all foolish. The money would do me no good for I could never see my mother again and . . . Forgive me, master. I tell you the truth. It is a temptation to anyone. Take the money home."

"I will; for it says in the great scroll that a tempter is as evil as the one who is tempted."

The boy went on with his hammering and blind Saul hurried away, for the Stranger was now some distance ahead.

Now the shadow of the Stranger crossed the open archway of a tavern. The inn-keeper was sitting at a table with two of his customers and all three men stirred slightly and watched the shadow pass across the wall.

Then for some unknown reason the inn-keeper rose up and called aloud: "All my life flows away in nothingness. As though the bung were knocked out of my barrel and the wine pours down a gutter. Why, I ask you!" And he shook the one who was a heavy drinker and shouted in his ear. "And you, too, what good are you! Take your drunkenness elsewhere. Your company only breeds indolence. For years I have been lazy and the filth in this place . . . Look at it! Filthy squalor! No more, no more!" He reached for the broom and began sweeping his floor with great vigor.

The drunkard arose, a little unsteadily, and said: "Fill up the big beaker; I will pay and drink it down and go. If you do not like my company I will go. Fill it up to the brim. It is a league to the bottom."

The inn-keeper filled the cup to the very top. The eyes of the drunkard gazed deep into the red wine as though it were a pool into which he was about to dive. Then suddenly with a quick brush of his arm he swept it off the table.

"The wine! The wine!" cried the third man, rising from his seat. "You have spilled it over the floor!"

"Good wine," laughed the drunkard. "Let it spill. I am not its slave any more. I have been drunk long enough and now . . . Now there is a new world for me to see."

When he had spoken these words he threw two shekels upon the table and left the tavern.

The third man, who was horrified at the waste of the wine, stood speechless. The inn-keeper took up the broom again and spoke to him.

"Never mind the wine. He paid for it, not you. But it hurts you just the same. Yes, I know. And when you are dead, what will you do with it?"

"With what?"

"The money. The pennies, the shekels, the talents. You have gathered them together and like the wine on the floor, someone will some day spill them about. Your greed will do you no good."

"Greed!" His mouth opened in amazement.

"Yes, you. Greed and you are one. Must I tell you what you already know?"

"I work and save and struggle. Yet you call it greed."

"With you, it is greed. Ask any child in the street. You are a miser and your children only wait for you to die."

"And then it all will be squandered?"

"Yes. Poured away like the wine on the floor."

"I believe it," spoke the miser after a slight pause. "And I leave now with more reason and understanding than I ever had before. You will see me again, but in the meantime, do not despise me."

Blind Saul heard the miser's steps leaving the tavern and he hurried ahead to catch up with the Stranger. So much seemed to happen in so short a while. So much, so much!

A few steps further down the narrow street toward the bazaar the blind beggar heard loud and angry shouts. Ungovernable seemed the temper of this man, shouting at his wife. And the wife shouted back with vile curses and at the same time pinched and smacked her child. The husband shouted, the woman cursed, and the child screamed.

And then suddenly, as though cut with a knife, all was silent.

The man laughed and then he spoke softly. "The supper is late and the soup is cold. Those two things do not go together, for even late supper is hot. Ha, ha! My temper mounts high and what is the result?"

"True, true," said the wife in a sobbing voice. "Your temper rises and I curse you for you cannot listen to reason. The pot was cracked and I lost half the soup before I could pour it over into another. That is why it is both cold and late. And the injustice of your wrath brings out the terror and cruelty in my nature."

Then she hugged the child, whom she had pinched and smacked a minute before, and she wept large tears and kissed it; a hundred affectionate kisses she poured over the child's face.

"We are fools, both of us," said the husband. "Forgive me."

The blind beggar ran on and now found himself in the heart of the bazaar. Some were buying, others selling, and some haggling. A score of voices came to his ears from many directions.

But out of all this din and commotion he suddenly heard clearly the voice of a merchant close by.

"Wait," said the merchant, "before I wrap it up. I lied to you. I exaggerated the value a little. Now I am cool and reason has control. The value is there and it is worth what I ask. Take it or leave it. I have often lied but today it has just occurred to me that it serves no purpose. Shall I wrap it up?"

"Yes. Wrap it up. I knew you lied."

And from another part of the bazaar he heard an old woman call to her customer: "Wait a moment. The eggs in the basket were not counted strictly. Two are missing. Here, add these two and the count will be right. There can be no profit in cheating."

The blind man walked on a pace or two and he heard another voice say: "A man is happy when he loses something and he finds it again. And I come to make you happy."

"How can you make me happy?" said the other voice.

"Very easily." He rang a gold coin on the counter. "Here, take it. The coin is yours."

"Yes, it is mine, but how . . ."

"Ask no questions. Be happy. What you lost you have found."

"But how did it come to you?"

"Well, I could tell you I found it and someone informed me it was yours. Or I could tell you it rolled off your counter and I picked it up last week but did not have a chance to bring it to you before. Or I could tell you a long story about a man and a boy and a camel. All these tales would explain it perfectly. Only the truth is simpler."

"Then what is the truth?"

"I stole it last week and suddenly this evening I felt quite miserable and . . . It burned a hole in my pocket. I am glad to give you what is yours and I would even pay a second coin to ease bad conscience."

The sound of a trumpet interrupted the voices. This was the signal for the closing of the city gates.

The blind beggar heard the tramp of the soldiers of the night-watch as they left their garrison. The bells in the wall towers were rung as an additional warning. The day was over and those who had stalls in the bazaar began taking down the awnings and packing away for the night.

The Stranger hurried now toward the city gate. And the blind beggar followed him as closely as he could through the crowded streets. One more voice he was to hear before the Stranger passed through the gates and into the vast country beyond. It was the voice of a young man which seemed to come through an open window facing upon the street.

"If I have been a cruel master, then forgive me. Your days and hours belonged to me, and your lives and souls I counted also as mine. But now I know that your lives and souls belong elsewhere. And if the days and hours have been long and the tyranny sometimes unbearable, now I want to repair some of the wrong between us. Call the ironsmiths and let the chains be removed. Those who would remain will remain as free-men. And those who would go, they also shall go as free-men. Each will have a paper sealed with my ring. You who were slaves are now men. With these words I set you free."

The tower bells rang out as the Stranger hurried toward the gate, which was about to close.

The soldiers held ready the heavy bars which bolted the great doors.

They waited for him to pass and then slowly they moved the massive doors and bolted them. The blind beggar Saul stood in the archway. Between him and the Stranger he heard the great doors lock.

"There now, Saul," said one of the soldiers, addressing the blind man. "You followed him through the streets and you are still blind."

"Only my eyes are blind. My understanding sees more than most."

"You should have begged him to perform the miracle they say he has done in Galilee and make your blind eyes see. If we saw your sight returned to you, then we would believe some of the stories we hear about him."

"I followed him," said Saul, "and with my ears I heard everything, and although blind, I have seen in so short a time more than all of you who have eyes."

"And what have you seen with your hollow eyes?"

"I followed him and wherever his shadow passed the evil was cast down. Twelve times, in as many minutes, his shadow changed the course of human events. Twelve times were twelve evils hurled to the ground."

"What evils?" asked one.

"Twelve evils, each different," said the blind man. "I know they were twelve for I counted them."

"Name the twelve evils," challenged one of the soldiers.

"Yes, I could name them for you. Each one of them. There was a boy who worked for a coppersmith and he was fighting with the evil of *temptation* and he told his master the truth and threw it off. And then in a tavern there were three evils hurled to the ground. *Indolence, drunkenness* and *greed*. But first, the very first, I had almost forgotten. A girl in the grip of *vanity* suddenly dropped her comb and also the *envy* of her neighbor was cast out of the window. These were the first two and added to the four I have already mentioned, it makes six in all."

"How six?" asked one.

"I will repeat the evils in the order I heard them this evening. *Vanity, envy, temptation, indolence, drunkenness* and *greed*. The man who drank too much dashed the cup to the floor and the cup was not empty either."

"Yes, that is six," admitted one of the soldiers.

"Then I will go on. There was *anger* in a husband and *cruelty* in the wife who pinched her child. And then we went into the bazaar and I heard a liar confess the *lie* and the woman who *cheated* in counting the eggs into the basket made good her mistake. And so these four evils are *wrath, cruelty, lying* and *cheating*. These four added to the other six makes ten."

"Two more."

"The last two you may not believe, but I heard the ring of a golden coin upon the counter myself. The thief returned it. *Stealing* is an evil. And finally I heard a man set free his slaves and end the *tyranny* which held them in an iron grip. And tyranny is an evil as great as any. Altogether there were twelve."

"And the Prophet from the desert, did he speak?" asked one.

"No. Not one word. He passed in silence and he was unnoticed by the crowds in the streets. But wherever his shadow crossed, there the events were changed."

"I do not believe a word you say!" cried one in a loud voice.

"I do not ask you to believe." With these words the blind man bent down to the ground and his groping hand found the clay saucer which he had left when he rose to follow the Stranger. "There!" he cried, and he flung out the few coppers from the dish. "I am richer than all of you! And what is more, blind as I am, I see more than all."

He pounded his staff upon the pavement and started off for that hovel which he called his home.

At the same time, a short distance from the walls of Jerusalem, the Stranger passed beneath an old cedar tree. Looking back, he could see in the falling light the shadowy figure of a sentinel pacing along the top of the city wall.

Beside him was the heavy trunk of the old cedar tree but the sun had already set in the heavens and no finger traced out the red muscles and limbs of those two eternal wrestlers, man and the evil monster. Twelve times they have clashed. Twelve falls and twelve victories have taken place and now they seemed merged together and in peace.

The bells in the wall towers ceased their clanging, but the metal tongues still swayed and touched lightly the quivering rims to sound a far-away and muffled note. It was as though weary bells were clanging softly in their sleep and sending out their deep low echoing notes to be part of the vast dark night.

Alone the Stranger walked.

A NEW DISCIPLESHIP

Charles M. Sheldon

~~~~~~

In His Steps is a story of the way that standards of society would be improved by a return to the simple teachings of Jesus. The sermon of Henry Maxwell on the Raymond movement shows how true Christianity could provide the only weapon with which to fight the advancing selfishness of our age.

"What would Jesus do? Is not that what the disciple ought to do? Is he not commanded to follow in His steps? How much is the Christianity of the age suffering for Him? Is it denying itself at the cost of ease, comfort, luxury, elegance of living? What does the age need, more than personal sacrifice? Does the church do its duty in following Jesus, when it gives a little money to establish missions or relieve extreme cases of want? Is it any sacrifice for a man who is worth ten million dollars simply to give ten thousand dollars for some benevolent work? Is he not giving something that costs him practically nothing, so far as any personal pain or suffering goes? Is it true that the Christian disciples to-day in most of our churches are living soft, easy, selfish lives, very far from any sacrifice that can be called sacrifice? What would Jesus do?

"It is the personal element that Christian discipleship needs to emphasize. 'The gift, without the giver, is bare.' The Christianity that attempts to suffer by proxy is not the Christianity of Christ. Each individual Christian, business man, citizen, needs to follow in His steps along the path of personal sacrifice for Him. There is not a different path to-day from that of Jesus' own times. It is the same path. The call of this dying century, and of the new one soon to be, is a call for a new discipleship, a new following of Jesus, more like the early, simple, apostolic, Christianity when the disciples left all and literally followed the Master. Nothing but a discipleship of this kind

can face the destructive selfishness of the age, with any hope of overcoming it. There is a great quantity of nominal Christianity to-day.
There is need of more of the real kind. We need a revival of the
Christianity of Christ. We have, unconsciously, lazily, selfishly, formally, grown into a discipleship that Jesus Himself would not acknowledge. He would say to many of us, when we cry, 'Lord, Lord,' 'I
never knew you.' Are we ready to take up the cross? Is it possible for
this church to sing with exact truth,

> 'Jesus, I my cross have taken,
> All to leave and follow thee?'

If we can sing that truly, then we may claim discipleship. But if our
definition of being a Christian is simply to enjoy the privileges of
worship, be generous at no expense to ourselves, have a good, easy
time surrounded by pleasant friends and by comfortable things, live
respectably, and at the same time avoid the world's great stress of sin
and trouble because it is too much pain to bear it—if this is our definition of Christianity, surely we are a long way from following the
steps of Him who trod the way with groans and tears and sobs of
anguish for a lost humanity, who sweat, as it were, great drops of
blood, who cried out on the upreared cross, 'My God! My God! why
hast thou forsaken me!'

"Are we ready to make and live a new discipleship? Are we ready to
reconsider our definition of a Christian? What is it to be a Christian?
It is to imitate Jesus. It is to do as He would do. It is to walk in His
steps."

THE LIFE AND DEATH OF A CRISIS

Hugh Walpole

One of Walpole's Polchester novels, *Harmer John,* recounts the story of a triumphant fight for beauty and truth. Bewildered by opposition from every side, Harmer visits the Rectory of Glebeshire and there with his friend Wistons examines the possible paths his life and career may take.

It was with a heavy heart that Harmer John set off for Pybus St. Anthony. He was experiencing that loneliness belonging to lovers who are too confident. We are so close together that not God Himself can separate us—one body, soul and spirit. Then, in a moment of time, a word, a phrase pokes up its ugly face and there is no relationship at all—strangers in a strange place.

As he walked down the long Polchester platform to find the little local train, lonely by itself like a poor relation, his love for Maude constricted his heart, hurting him physically. She seemed to accompany him down the platform, treading lightly at his side, and saying to him again and again: "Am I not worth everything? Is there anything of more value than me? Surrender yourself. Will you give me up for a shadow?"

As he climbed into the stuffy, tight little compartment he knew that the crisis of all his life had climbed in with him. He had, in fact, never known any crisis before. Life had been direct. First there had been his mother to protect, and he had protected her; then there had been his father to fight, and he had fought him; then there had been his living to earn, and he had earned it; then there had been his work to love, and he had loved it. It was when the other loves had come to him that the struggle had begun, love of beauty, love for his friend and love for a woman.

As he sat there and saw the little fields, brilliantly lit by the evening sun, the hedges like wet lines of paint, the cottages so characteristic of Glebeshire in their isolated defiant pastures, his heart ached as though he were saying farewell to it all. And yet he could formulate nothing. His problem was a wood in front of him, into whose heart he had not yet penetrated. He knew that Wistons would help him.

He was the only traveller to alight at Pybus St. Anthony. The little village was dead and bright like a picked bone as he walked up the sunny hill. Maude was still with him, walking beside him and saying, "Am I not of more value . . . ?"

He turned to the left at the top of the hill, walked down a little by-road; he opened a white gate sorely in need of paint, pushed up a weed-stained drive and saw the Rectory, bare, four-square, unadorned, impersonal. When the old Glebeshire servant answered his ring and he stood in the hall he felt as though nothing had been done to this house for ever and ever. And it did not care that anything should be done. If help were offered it would refuse it. The pictures would fall from the walls, the fresh wall-paper wither, the stair-rods trip the unwary. Everywhere was the proud spirit of resistance. The old servant ushered Johanson into Wistons' study. It was exactly as he had anticipated it—absolutely spare, distempered white, a table, a crucifix, a photograph of Leonardo's "Last Supper," a wall of grimy and dishevelled books.

Wistons looked pleased to see his visitor. For the first time in their acquaintance there was something warm in his greeting. They talked a little, trivially, and very soon went into the other room for supper.

Wistons did not apologise for the food which was bad—poorly cooked turbot, cold beef and hard potatoes that clung sullenly to their jackets, apple tart with pastry of lead. Wistons did not apologise, and Johanson did not consider it. He ate heartily and happily. His mind had cleared. His depression had retreated like a defeated enemy. They achieved during the meal that relationship that was to last to the end. It was not so personal as friendship; it was rather the frank intimacy of two human beings who recognise in one another those two great qualities, reality and honesty. Whatever the future might bring, they would always meet with interest and, cataloguing in their minds the true human beings they had known, they would remember one another.

After supper they went out into the little garden. The moon was a sickle of apricot, the scent of the flowers lay thickly on the evening air, peace flowed like a river down the hill. They sat on two old shabby garden chairs and Johanson faced his problem.

"I must settle it now," he said, leaning forward, and staring at the sky that flowed above the sharp wall of the garden like a stream of pale lemon-coloured water. Tiny clouds of gold moved on a faint wind. Wistons, a true observer of men, studied his face as he talked. Although it had in the curve of the mouth and the determination of the chin a man's character, its roundness, the simplicity of the blue directness of the eyes, the buoyancy of the brow, had still the happy unclouded kindliness of the boy who has not yet learnt to distrust.

The brows drew together in perplexity as a boy's might. Wistons knew that the man was face to face with the first real trouble of his life. "I must settle it now, but what is it I must settle? Sometimes I fancy that I am inventing all my trouble, making it up like a story. Perhaps you shall tell me that, sir, when I have finished, but I don't think you shall. When I first came it was all simple. I was lucky and got my work quickly and made friends. No man ever was helped so fast in a foreign town. Shouldn't I then be satisfied? Here I had my work that I could do, and I was not lonely, and then I fell in love and was loved too. Should I not have been happy, sir? But I was. I have always been happy. But from the first there were something more. There was two things. First, I don't hope you shall think me foolish. There has always been a place I dream of in my sleep. I saw it first as a little boy when my father had beaten me and I slept because I was tired. It were always the same place, a house, empty but for a few things, very clean and shining with sun. Long stairs with the sun gleaming on them, open doors and mirrors with green trees reflected, running water. I myself placed some things there, a statue of Donatello, the Leonardo "Virgin of the Rocks." There was always birds singing, water running, trees and a line of hills. It is so real to me I could tell you of the marks on the walls, the hollow in the hill and the thin white road out of my window. I were very happy there. Secondly, there were the Cathedral. You know the Brytte Monument and the young man who made it? I seem to have known him and spoken to him. And when I were with him I had ideas that I couldn't control—my own work, the gymnastics and the rest, was unimportant and didn't matter. I wanted what he too had wanted, to make a beautiful place with beautiful people. Just one place, or one street even, or one house. But that were not my business. My business were clear—to do my work and mind my own affairs.

"Then when I fell in love everything was lost in that. I had never been in love before. I loved her the moment I saw her, but for some time I did not know that she loved me, and then when she said that

she did, oh, sir, wasn't I happy? For a time I seemed to have everything. I sang all day, and every one else was singing too. My work grew
and grew; every one was more kind and more kind. All was made
clear and straight for me. Perhaps I were too happy. I had suspicions of
being too comfortable. I don't know what it were, but I began to dream
again and then to watch the people around me. I saw that some of them
were for using me, not badly, you know, sir, but for their own purpose,
not caring for me and my work for what was good in it, but only for
what helped what *they* wanted me to do. Do I make it clear?"

"Perfectly," said Wistons.

"Then there came two things. I have a friend. His daughter came
home. She had once been unhappy and unfortunate here. You know,
of course, sir, who I mean. People were cruel to her. I had not thought
they would be so narrow or so self-righteous. Perhaps I am not to blame
them, but they are hurting her because they like to hurt, not because
they are shocked by what she did. It makes them feel better to make her
feel worse.

"And then there were Seatown. I went down one afternoon. Oh, sir,
it is terrible, the dirt, the walls tumbling, the windows broken, the
smell, the rags. In such a town as this, so beautiful, so old, so happy, to
have such!

"It's only a little place, one street, fifty houses. One day would pull
it down. I was made unhappy by that. You told me once I couldn't
build before I pulled down. Perhaps that is true. But what right had I
to say anything? It were not my business. I am a stranger. And deep
in my heart I don't wish to change people. I am not confident enough
of my own goodness to teach others. But if we were all at it together,
not because we were better than others, but because we all saw the
same thing to do and set about to do it!

"Then the lecture came. It were a success, you know. I was happy
for most of it, seeing my friends there pleased in front of me, but at
the last, when I came to make a speech, I were in a moment ashamed.
What was I doing standing there glorifying myself? This wasn't the
work I intended. I wanted to make a speech speaking of Seatown, and
all working together for one beautiful place that the world might see
and so make more beautiful places. But I was frightened. I knew I
should make some angry, should lose some friends and most of all dis-
appoint my girl. I was afraid. It was the most shameful moment of my
life and I went from the lecture and hid myself.

"After that everything was clear. Certain in the town made me see that it were not my business to say anything were wrong with the town or the people in the town. One important gentleman told it me quite plainly, and that I must give up the daughter of my friend if I would go on to be a success here. Then my girl—she is Miss Maude Penethen, sir, and I lodge with her mother—she is young, and she wants me to be the greatest success the town has ever seen. That she must have—success for me, you understand, not for herself. She wants everybody to like me, you see.

"With every hour from the lecture I see more clearly I must make a choice. I must be quiet about Seatown, I must not see my friend's daughter, I must do what certain gentlemen and ladies of the town tell me, and then I shall be a true success here. I shall marry and have money and build a big business, later perhaps in Drymouth and then in London. I know I can because I have that practical gift. But if I try to change anything, be myself, and keep my integrity and freedom, I am ruined here, and so it will be everywhere. Always the same in every place. And perhaps I shall do nothing in the end. Just be a failure, you see. But if I work here at my gymnastics I *must* do good. And Miss Penethen she won't love me if I'm not as she thinks moral, if I am friends with people who she thinks are wicked. She must be happy and see me happy too. I understand her so well. She is young and beautiful, and she is proud of me. If she's no longer proud she don't love me. So I must do what every one tells me or I lose my work, my girl and my friends. And for what do I lose them? For a dream, an idea. And why should I meddle with other people? But how can I live and not be honest? How can I live and not be honest?"

He ended with that despairing cry.

He had poured out his words tempestuously, but Wistons had understood him.

"This question of honesty," Wistons said at last, "aren't you making too much of it? It is not, I think, of such overwhelming importance these days. Your trouble comes down to very little if you look it in the face. To get on, to make a good job out of the material world, to put money by, to live on twenty-four hours a day according to a sharp materialistic pattern, to study success as an art—all of that is the point in these days when God has been proved a liar and all religions a sham. Where's your trouble? Stay here quietly, do what you're told for a year or two, give up ridiculous dreaming, get power and position and then, when you're really strong in the place, pull down Seatown if you like."

"You!" said Johanson. "You to advise that!"

"Well, why not? What do we think of honesty when, to take only a small example, at this very moment one of the principal dignitaries of my church is neglecting his ecclesiastical duties (for which by the way he is quite decently paid) in order to earn easy money by writing sensational articles in the daily press? The thing is as old as the world. You wish to give up your home, your job, your love, because one or two old houses are falling into ruin, and a lady of your acquaintance has not been sufficiently called on. Folly!"

Johanson answered.

"Why are you so bitter about life? Has every one always disappointed you? Have no one been true or honest?"

"I am not bitter," Wistons answered. "I was putting a point of view to you that many very good people hold, and with much justice, I daresay. When I was a young man I had a friend who came up from the provinces to London. He was a painter. For some while he made very little progress. He was a hard-headed, clever fellow with no nonsense about him, but he had, rather to his own surprise, a very warm heart. He thought that this got in the way of his success, so he did what he could to cool it. Great fame came to him in a night. That was the critical moment of his life. He might have been contented with that— it was enough to content any man. He might have sat down, thought less of himself and his career, learnt to love his wife, who was charming. But he chose the other. He wanted more success and more money and more and more and more. He got rid of his wife, who was, I daresay, tiresome from the successful point of view. He got fatter and fatter and ever more deeply concentrated upon himself. He is, I admit, a very happy man."

"You think he's done wisely?" Johanson asked.

"Yes. He's concentrated upon certainties. He has possessions that he can finger, a stomach that needs an ever-widening waistcoat, motor cars and a fine sum at the Bank. He is laughed at and sneered at, but he comforts himself with the thought that those who laugh at him are the jealous, unsuccessful ones. He has touched on certainties. And what are the other things? The spiritual life? What man or woman alive to-day but has doubts of its existence? God, Christ, the Saints? Does not book after book seek to prove them fairy-tales? This death— has it not a tangible stink of corruption about it that is never out of our nostrils? Art, friendship, love, are they not for ever fading and failing? What are we but a little gas and water, formed for an instant, blown back into æther a moment later? Why think of others who think only of themselves? Why pray vainly to a God who is not there? Why study the life and words of a Christ whose every movement is riddled with modern suspicion? Why cheat ourselves with all this illusion? No, let us clutch our certainties. You are a fool, Johanson; you are giving up something for nothing—for nothing at all save certain defeat. What can you do in this place with your reforms? You are a foreigner. I told you before and I tell you again that they will not let you take one single step against their will. And why should they? This is their town, they have built it on certain moralities, certain social laws. Those moralities and those laws make them safe. They have to protect their wives, their children, their earthly property, their heavenly souls. You come from outside and attack them. Why should they not defend themselves?"

"I will not attack them," Johanson answered fiercely. "I told you I would not wish that. I have no right, as you say, and no desire. But I must be honest. I must not be something that I am not. I would say to them, 'I think in this way and in this, but that are only myself.' I must not lie about myself."

"Yes," answered Wistons, "but you are against them, and the things you want may seem to a few others desirable, and so a little group will grow, and that group will not be contented, as you are, with simply stating their ideas. They will want to put them into practice. Then hostilities begin whether you wish it or no."

"It is more simple than you suppose," Johanson said in a little while. "I have no doubt that it is right to do. I must not agree to what I know to be wrong, I am not to interfere with others, but my own integrity is to be protected at every cost. At almost every cost. Here is the struggle, you see. I love that girl, Mr. Wistons, with heart and soul and body. If I for a moment look over the wall and see myself without her it is terrible, standing alone in the world. Once that were possible. I did not mind to be alone, but now that I have been close to her, to be alone will be a terror. I love her body, but much more I want her for my companion, some one who knows my troubles and I knows hers, some one I can always talk with, some one who is true whatever else may happen, some one who knows me and loves me although they knows me. Some one half me and I half them. She is not very wise, perhaps, she is young. She can't think of two things at once, and she must have some things or she is angry; and she values some things falsely. We shall quarrel—perhaps often—but my heart shall be hers and hers mine. I love her so that if I can't have her I can never be intimate with any one again."

They sat in silence. After a long time Johanson said, almost timidly, "What am I to do, Mr. Wistons? What am I to do? I can't lose her."

"And must you lose her," Wistons asked gently, "if things go badly with you in the town? Doesn't she care for you more than that?"

"She is very young," Johanson answered, "and she is jealous. She loves me, I am sure, but she has been spoilt. She wants her way. I know that if we were married a year or more I could control her, but now, if I don't promise not to see my friend's daughter, I'm afraid her jealousy shall, at some moment, separate us."

"Then go on for a year with your work," said Wistons, "be married, keep quiet for a while about Seatown. That will come right if you wait. There are others besides yourself who are moving in that."

"And give up my friend?" Johanson asked.

"Oh, you can be diplomatic about that. Go there a little less, not see the daughter privately . . ."

"But they are my friends," Johanson broke in. "Do you think at once they would not see that I was as the rest of the town? 'Yes,' I say to them, 'I love my girl, and she doesn't like that I come here. So we meet in secret, you understand?' Oh yes, *they* understand! Only a little flush in the face, a little dropping of the eyes, but Tom Longstaffe's heart is hurt for ever and I have been false to my word. No, no—— No, no, no!"

"Then," said Wistons quietly, "you must persuade the lady you love, explain to her. If she loves you——"

"If she did not love me," Johanson broke in, "I could, perhaps. But she are jealous because she love me. Jealousy is so strong that the one who has it cannot reason. They can only cry out like they have been wounded. It is not themselves, but a disease in their stomach like a cancer. And when it is cured they wonder they have had it. . . ." He sat there, his hands clasped tightly together. In a voice full of pain he said at last: "Oh, Mr. Wistons, show me how to keep her, and yet be honest, show me how."

"There is no way to show you. This is something you must fight out with your own soul as I have had to fight it out and many another man. Your real life is at stake now."

"You believe, then, in a real life?" Johanson said urgently. "My dreams aren't all mist, my desires not all untrue, there is something——?"

"I believe," said Wistons, "that if God Himself came flaming before us here in this poor garden and commanded us to put away our superstitions, to bury our beliefs, to abandon our little shreds of ideals, to think only of the material life because there was none other, to know that Christ Jesus was a sham and a fake, to practise selfishness and gain and worldly success, to put heaven away from our eyes and to pray no more, I believe that behind this thunder there would be a still small voice comforting us and bidding us still believe——

"If the spirit of man is a delusion and a joke, then it is a joke of so much greater power, glory, hope and comfort than any serious word that I will go to my grave feeding it, caring for it, giving it all I have."

"I know how loose words are," Wistons went on quietly after a little while. "What have I said that means anything or that can't mean anything you like to make it? But what I know is that there is more in life than anything that men can do or say, that there is an immortal spirit whose history, whose struggles, whose victories and defeats give the whole meaning to this life which is only one short paragraph in the book of that greater life. These are our fleshly conditions and we must obey them, but through them, always, we must be waiting, listening, for ever at attention to catch the movement of that other life. Your honour, your courage, your self-sacrifice, your gentleness, kindliness, if you lose these things you had as well be a sheep's carcass hanging in any butcher's. That I *know* to be true." Then he added, "There's a storm coming. I've felt the thunder over the hill a long time back. The breeze has gone."

He came over to Johanson and put his hand on his shoulder. "Come into the house and drink some bad coffee."

Johanson stood up.

"No, thank you. I think I'll be off. I'm going to walk back and I'll not be caught by the storm."

Wistons answered, "Very well. I won't keep you." He added slowly, "I've not been much help to you. It's my fate never to help the people I want to, but I doubt in this whether any one could help you much. It's your own fight."

"Yes, it's my own fight." Johanson shook himself like a dog coming out of water. "But you have helped me. Immense. I don't know which way it will be, but whatever way it is, I shall never forget what you have said."

Wistons nodded his head.

"All right, then. Come up again some time. I shall always like to see you. I wish you luck."

They shook hands and Johanson strode away.

ONE NAMED JESUS

Pearl Buck

~~~~~~

In *The Young Revolutionist,* Pearl Buck traces a Chinese youth's
disillusionment with his temple gods, with his service to Sun Yat-
sen's army, with the whole ideology of modern revolutionary China.
"One Named Jesus" shows how Ko-sen's hope and salvation lie in the
Christian medical missionary work to which he finally dedicates himself.

THEN ONCE he had opened the gates of speech it seemed to Ko-sen that
he could tell his father and his mother and Siu-may everything and
indeed that he must tell them, to ease his own heart. And evening after
evening when they had eaten their rice they sat and Ko-sen told them
and they could not hear enough of all he had seen and learned. And
they marveled much, his father most that Ko-sen had learned to read,
and he found a bit of paper that he had picked up on the street and he
brought it to Ko-sen and Ko-sen read it easily enough, for it was one
of the leaflets that revolutionists scatter as they go. His father laughed
with delight to hear it, not that he had understood what it said but because of his pride in his son.

And Ko-sen's mother marveled most because he had passed through
such peril and that he came out alive and she must hold his hand and
smooth it and weep a little. As for Siu-may she must weep when she
heard of Fah-li and of his sad end, and indeed when Ko-sen told of the
hospital they all listened in silence and Ko-sen's father's mouth was
ajar to hear of what they did and his mother cried out, "Now I would
never dare to enter such a place!" But Siu-may, when she heard that
there were women there who learned and worked and were free,
yearned to be like them and when she heard of the white-robed one
she murmured,

"Oh, I wish I were in such a place!"

Then when all had been told Ko-sen sat musing and thinking and at last he said,

"Well do I know I cannot be as I was before when my life was bound up in this little village. I have heard the call of the revolution and go I must to do something for my country but I do not know what."

And when he had said this Ko-sen knew that the thing in his heart which was waiting for him he had now faced and brought out into the light. But his mother asked fearfully,

"You do not mean you would go back into wars again, my son?"

"No, not that," replied Ko-sen slowly, his eyes fixed on the light of the flaming candle, "no, not when they cut down my ten lads like that —and the one I saw lying on the ground was a farmer such as I might have been had I lived my life as I was born. No, my country is bigger than they told me and we are all in it." And he thought a while and he said, "There must be another way to serve my country if I could see that way."

But they could not help him, these three simple people who had never traveled ten miles away from their own village and who when Ko-sen spoke of ships upon the river and of battlefields could not see what he meant them to see and it was as though he spoke of dreams to them. Therefore they went to bed each thinking as each was able of what they had heard.

But Ko-sen could not sleep of nights, and day after day he worked in the fields with his father and now having told all he was very silent again, thinking of what the future must be and of what he must do with this life of his. And thinking he came to be very glad for all his young captain had told him and taught him.

"Whether he was right or wrong," Ko-sen thought, "he waked my heart and he made me see what my country is and that it is not only a little village and an old temple. But I cannot serve my country in the way he taught me. I cannot serve her by war and death, that I know, for so Fah-li died, and who knows how many like him I might kill if I set my arm to it? No, there must be another way."

But he could not find it.

Then one evening in the early summer when the young rice was be-ing planted in the flooded fields and the peaches were turning red upon their branches, and all the world was full of life and growing, it came to Ko-sen what he must do. It came as effortlessly and as suddenly as though a bird flying past had lighted unexpectedly on his shoulder. He

straightened his back from the field in which he stood and he said to
his father,

"My father, I see the way—I see what I am to do!" And when his
father paused and looked at him without understanding, Ko-sen explained,

"Father, when I look back over my days I see that there was one
place where life was made and saved and it was in that place where
Fah-li died. True, he died, but he died how happily and they did what
they could. I never saw death so clean and like a child's sleep, and it
was so strange the love they had for him that I cannot understand it
even now, seeing Fah-li was not of their clan or blood. But I must go
back and ask them to take me as apprentice and learn of them and so
shall I serve my country best."

And his father looked at him patiently and humbly, his hands still
fumbling about the watery roots of the rice plant he held, and he said,

"Well, my son, you must do as you will, for these are new times and
I cannot judge. It is not as it was in my young days when we had not
heard of revolutions and we did not see the gods crumbling on their
faces. But there is your sister and well I wish you would stay until she
is wed and my duty done."

Then Ko-sen seemed to see light fall upon an unending road and he
spoke as fast as he could think and he said,

"But, my father, my father, there are women there, many of them,
who learn also, and why may not Siu-may go there with me and work
together with me? I can help her and so may we be free indeed. My
father, it is a new day—I saw women in the ranks of soldiers, even!
How much better in this other service!"

His father rose then also and he looked at Ko-sen for a time. And
he saw Ko-sen's face and Ko-sen's eyes were staring into the sky and
he was smiling, satisfied with what he had thought of, dreaming of the
days to come. And this was because Ko-sen saw himself in that life,
busy, learned in the way of saving others like Fah-li, free from the old
fears of temple and priest and battle; and he saw Siu-may looking as
that white-robed one had looked who tended Fah-li, moving swiftly
and silently as she had moved upon her free and competent feet. Yes,
he would go back and he would say,

"I and my sister, we will take service under you for our country's
sake. We are revolutionists, we two. Teach us how to save our people."

"My son," said Ko-sen's father gently, "tell me what service this is of
which you speak. Under whose name is it?"

Ko-sen looked at his father out of his dream and collected himself. What service? He remembered suddenly that he did not even know the name of the hospital or of the doctors or anyone. He only knew that there was some spirit there common to them all. What had that white-robed one told him? He knit his brows, remembering, and looking earnestly at his father he said,

"The master there—I think they told me the master there is one named Jesus. It is under him we would take service for our country."

These, My Brethren

OF LOVE AND JOY

Peter Rosegger

Albert Schweitzer describes Rosegger's *I.N.R.I.* as one of the most beautiful fictional versions of the life of Jesus. Konrad Ferleitner, condemned as a political offender, spends his last prison days in writing down what he recalls about the great story of the Gospel. In this chapter he blends the lessons of love, humility, and true Christian simplicity.

ELSEWHERE Jesus's fame had become so great that all men came to Him. The poor crowded to Him in order to eat at His table where the word had become flesh. The rich invited Him to their houses, but He mostly declined those invitations, accepting, however, one here and there.

He Himself went to those who humbly remained in the background and yet desired to go to Him. A man lived in the district whose greatest desire was to see the Prophet. When he heard that Jesus was coming his way, he began to tremble and to think what he should do. "I should like to meet Him face to face, and yet dare not venture to go to Him. For I have a bad reputation as a publican, and am not worth much any way. Then He is always accompanied by so many people, and I am short and cannot see over their heads." When Jesus approached, the man climbed a bare sycamore-tree and peeped between the branches.

Jesus saw him, and called out: "Zacchæus, come down from the tree! I will come and visit you to-day."

The publican jumped down from the tree and went over to Him, and said humbly: "Lord I am not worthy that you should go to my house. Only say one word to me, and I shall be content."

The people wondered that the Prophet should so honour this person of somewhat doubtful character. Zacchæus was almost beside himself to think that the Master should have recognized and spoken to him. He set before his guest everything that his house afforded. Jesus said: "These things are good. But I want the most precious thing you possess."

"What is that, sir?" asked Zacchæus in terror, for he thought he had given of his best. "Everything I possess is yours."

Then Jesus grasped his hand, looked at him lovingly, and said: "Zacchæus, give me your heart!"

The man became His follower.

One day He was dining with a man who was very learned and a strict censor of morals. Several of His disciples were among the guests, and the talk, partly intellectual and partly guided by feeling, turned on the Scriptures. At first Jesus took no part; He was thinking how much pleasanter it would be to hear simple talk at His mother's fireside at home than to dispute with these arrogant scholars about the empty letter. But He was soon drawn into the conversation. Some one mentioned the commandment which enjoins a man to love his neighbour, and, as often happens, the simplest things became confused and incomprehensible in the varied opinions of the worldly-wise. One of the guests said: "It is remarkable how we do not reflect on the most important things because they are so clear; and yet if we do reflect on them by any chance, we don't understand them. So that I really do not know who it is I should love as myself."

"Your neighbour!" the disciple Matthew, who was sitting by him at table, informed him.

"That is all right, my friend, if only I knew who was my neighbour! I run up against all sorts of people in the day, and if one of them trips me up, he is my neighbour for the time being. At this moment I have two neighbours, you and Zachariah. Which of the two am I to love as myself? It is only stated that you shall love one. And if it's you or Zachariah, why should I love either of you more than the Master who sits at the other end of the table and is not my neighbour!"

"Man! that is an impertinent speech," said the disciple Bartholomew reprovingly.

"Well then, put me right!" retorted the other.

The disciple began, and tried to explain who the neighbour was, but he did not get very far, his thoughts were confused. Meanwhile the question had reached the Master. Who is, in the correct sense of the term, one's neighbour?

Jesus answered, by telling a story: "There was once a man who went from Jerusalem to Jericho. It was a lonely road, and he was attacked by highwaymen, who plundered him, beat him, and left him for dead. After a while a high priest came by that way, saw him lying there, and noticing that he was a stranger, passed quickly on. A little later an assistant priest came by, saw him lying there, and thought: He's either severely wounded or dead, but I'm not going to put myself out for a stranger; and he passed on. At last there came one of the despised Samaritans. He saw the helpless creature, stopped, and had pity on him. He revived him with wine, put healing salve on his wounds, lifted him up, and carried him to the nearest inn. He gave the host money to take care of the sufferer until he recovered. Now, what do you say? The priests regarded him as a stranger, but the Samaritan saw in him his neighbour."

Then they explained it to themselves: Your neighbour is one whom you can help and who is waiting for your help.

The disciple Thomas now joined in the conversation, and doubted if you could expect a great prince to dismount from his horse and lift a poor beggar out of the gutter.

Jesus asked: "If you rode by as a great prince and found Me lying wretchedly in the gutter, would you leave me lying there?"

"Master!" shouted Thomas in horror.

"Do you see, Thomas? What you would do to the poorest, you would do to Me."

One of the others asked: "Are we only to be kind to the poor, and not to the rich and noble?"

And Jesus said: "If you are a beggar in the street, and a prince comes riding past, there's nothing you can do for him. But if his horse stumbles and he falls, then catch him so that his head may not strike against a stone. At that moment he becomes your neighbour."

Then some whispered: "It often seems as if He desired us to love all men. But that is too difficult."

"It's very easy, brother," said Bartholomew. "To love the millions of men whom you never see, who do not do you any harm, that costs nothing. Hypocrites love in that way. Yet while they claim to love the whole human race, they are hard on their neighbour."

"It is easy to love from afar," said Jesus, "and it is easy to love good-tempered and amiable men. But how is it when your brother has wronged you, and is always trying to do you harm? You must forgive him, not seven times, but seventy times seven. Go to him in kindness, show him his error. If he listens to you, then you have won him. If he does not heed you, repeat your warning. If still he heeds you not, seek a friendly intermediary. If he will not heed him, then let the community decide. And only when you see your brother saved and contented will you be glad again."

While they were talking thus, a young woman pushed her way into the room. She was one of those who followed Him everywhere, and waited impatiently at the door while the Master visited a house. Bending low, almost unnoticed, she hurried through the crowd, stooped down before Jesus, and began to rub His feet with ointment from a casket. He calmly permitted it; but His host thought to himself: No, He is no prophet, or He would know who it is that is anointing His feet. Isn't she the sinner of Magdala?

Jesus guessed his thoughts, and said: "My friend, I will tell you something. Here is a man who has two debtors. One owes him fifty pence, and the other five hundred. But as they cannot pay he cancels both the debts. Now say, which of them owes him most gratitude?"

"Naturally him to whom the most was remitted," answered the host.

And Jesus: "You are right. Much has been remitted to this woman. See, you invited Me to your house, your servants have filled the room with the scent of roses, although fresh air comes in through the windows. My ear has been charmed with the strains of sweet bells, and stringed instruments, although the clear song of birds can be heard from without. You have given Me wine in costly crystal goblets, although I am accustomed to drink out of earthen vessels. But that My feet might feel sore after the long wandering across the desert only this woman remembered. She has much love, therefore much will be forgiven her."

One day when the Master had gone down to Capernaum He noticed that the disciples who were walking in front of Him were engaged in quiet but animated talk. They were discussing which of them was most pleasing to God. Each subtly brought forward his meritorious services to the Master, his sacrifices, his renunciations and sufferings, his obedience to the teaching. Jesus quickly stepped nearer to them, and said: "Why do you indulge in such foolish talk? While you are boasting of your virtues, you prove that you lack the greatest. Are you the righteous that you dare to talk so loudly?"

Whereupon one of them answered timidly: "No, sir, we are not the righteous. But you yourself said that there was more rejoicing in heaven over penitents than over righteous men."

"There is rejoicing over penitents when they are humble. But do you know over whom there is greater rejoicing in heaven?"

By this time a crowd had formed round Him. Women had come up leading little children by the hand and carrying smaller ones in their arms in order to show them the marvellous man. Some of the boys got through between the people's legs to the front in order to see Him and kiss the hem of his garment. The people tried to keep them back so that they should not trouble the Master, but He stood under the fig-tree and exclaimed in a loud voice: "Suffer the little ones to come unto Me!" Then round-faced, curly-headed, bright-eyed children ran forward, their skirts flying, and crowded about Him, some merry, others shy, and embarrassed. He sat down on the grass, drew the children to His side, and took the smallest in His lap. They looked up in His kind face with wide-opened eyes. He played with them, and they smiled tenderly or laughed merrily. And they played with His curls, and flung their arms round His neck. They were so trustful and happy, these little creatures hovering so brightly round the Prophet, that the crowd stood in silent joy. But Jesus was so filled with blessed gladness that He exclaimed loudly: "This is the Kingdom of Heaven!"

The words swept over the crowd like the scent of the hawthorn. But some were afraid when the Master added: "See how innocent and glad they are. I tell you that he who is not like a little child, he shall not enter the Kingdom of Heaven! And woe to him who deceives one of these children! it were better he tied a millstone round his neck and were drowned in the sea! But whosoever accepts a child for My sake accepts Me!"

Then the disciples thought they understood over whom there was joy in heaven, and they disputed no longer over their own merits.

PITY DEFINED

William J. Locke

~~~~~~

With a bit of deft narrative, William J. Locke represents the hero of his novel *Simon the Jester* taking a walk in the East End of London. Along the way, his friend Campion, who has found his vocation in service to mankind, makes some enlightening remarks.

AN ANAEMIC, flirtatious group passed us, the girls in front, the boys behind.

"Good Heavens, Campion," says Simon, "what *can* you do?"

"Pity them, old chap," he returned quickly.

"What's the good of that?"

"Good? Oh, I see." He laughed with a touch of scorn. "It's a question of definition. When you see a fellow-creature suffering and it shocks your refined susceptibilities, you say, 'poor devil,' and pass on, you think you have pitied him. But you haven't. You think pity's a passive virtue. But it isn't. If you really pity anybody, you go mad to help him—you don't stand by with tears of sensibility running down your cheeks. You stretch out your hand, because you've got to. If he won't take it, or wipes you over the head, that's his look-out. You can't work miracles. But once in a way he does take it, and then—well, you work with all your might to pull him through. And if you do, what bigger thing is there in the world than the salvation of a human soul?"

"It's worth living for," said I.

"It's worth doing any confounded old thing for," he declared.

I envied Campion as I had envied no man before. He was alive in heart and soul and brain; I was not quite alive even yet. But I felt better for meeting him. I told him so. He tugged his beard again and laughed.

"I am a happy old crank. Perhaps that's the reason."

SABRE IN THE HAND

Howard Spring

Against a superb panorama of politics, economic revolution, and social progress, Howard Spring's *Fame Is the Spur* projects the figure of a poor boy whose ambitions drove him to become a peer. The labor meeting at St. Swithin's catches him at the very peak of his first success, blending elements of sincere romanticism and political finesse.

THERE ARE people alive today who remember that meeting in St. Swithin's, and, indeed, any one who attended it could hardly forget it. It started off as a commonplace Labour propaganda meeting. The chairman bellowed his hearty platitudes, and caused Ellen to colour with confusion as he expressed his pleasure in seeing, on the same platform with Hamer Shawcross, the mother who had been all in all to him. The man from Leeds followed with a witty, racy speech; and Arnold, whom Pen had implored to do his best, not to be left in the lurch, certainly did do his best: as good a speech as he had ever delivered. Pen flushed with pleasure as he sat down, and looked along the table toward Hamer Shawcross, as if to say: "Beat that!" Hamer did not catch her eye, and she was startled by the abstracted look upon his face, as though his mind were miles away.

Then the chairman called upon him, with a flowery reference: "Mr. Hamer Shawcross, the thews and sinews of the campaign we are waging in this constituency." Nearly every one there knew him by this time, and when he rose a great wave of cheering broke towards him. In the midst of it, he turned, and to everybody's amazement, mounted the pulpit steps. This little action was so unexpected that the cheering died down, and by the time he faced them, leaning slightly forward with the weight of his body resting on the hands that grasped the pulpit rail, there was a profound silence into which his first quietly-spoken words fell with effect. "My friends. I have come up here because I am going to preach to you from the word of God."

He stood up straight, pushed back the wave of hair that fell across his forehead, and looked round the chapel: at the crowded floor, with people standing at the back, jamming the doors, at the galleries that could not take another man, and then down at the long table below him: Ellen's red glass cherries, Ann's hair coloured like white honey, the gleaming bald patch of the man from Leeds. Never before had he had such an audience. Only a fool would waste it by standing down there. Here he was commanding, isolated, Hamer Shawcross, Shawcross of Peterloo.

He took a Bible from his pocket, placed it on the lectern, and opened it at the twenty-first chapter of the Revelation of St. John. "I saw a new heaven and a new earth."

Before he was done, there was not a man or woman in the audience who had not seen it, too. There was no "St. Swithin's" about that address. It was only when he had finished that people noticed he had spoken for an hour. It was the longest speech he had made. He did not use a note. All the immortal promises of the chapter threaded themselves through a masterpiece of romantic oratory. He shall wipe away every tear. There shall be no mourning, nor crying, nor pain, any more. The old things are passed away. The old things. He went through them all—the old things that every one there knew too well: the sorrows of the poor. Passed away! They held their breath, those people. They saw the widow's tears assuaged, they saw a world of plenty and themselves living in it with freedom and joy. They saw Jerusalem come down from Heaven and dwelling among men, in England's green and pleasant land.

He didn't mention, as Pen Muff noted, a single thing that you could call a fact. He didn't mention the candidate or the party; but only a fool could have missed the implications of his splendid imagery. This was a possible world he was painting for them: let them go out and get it. They would get it when the old things were passed away.

They were spell-bound, and knew not whether they were listening to speech or sermon; but they felt they could listen for ever to this shepherd leading them to delectable mountains. The healing of the nations . . . no curse any more.

There are those who say that this was the greatest speech Hamer Shawcross ever delivered—and there were close on fifty years of speech-making still before him. There are those who say that it was pure fustian, a shameless harping on the emotions of lives starved of the beauty he promised them, desolate for the hope he conjured up, hungry for the food he spread as plentifully and deceptively as banquets laid before Tantalus.

He himself has left in the diary a comment on this occasion which, whatever else it was or did, gave him the reputation, which he never afterwards lost, of being the greatest romantic orator of his party.

"After Tom Hannaway had left me, I wrote what I had to do for the *Courier* and then I lay on the bed in Arnold's hut, thinking of the meeting that night in Selby Street chapel. I wanted to finish up the campaign on a high note, an appeal to the hearts of the people, because I believe that through their hearts, not their heads, one can get their votes. The fact of the meeting being in a chapel made me think of that twenty-first chapter. Rightly handled, the promises could seem heavenly or earthly. Years before, when I was a local preacher, I had dealt with this theme. I had liked it so much that I took it round: I preached on it in every chapel in the circuit. So it was firmly in my mind. I don't forget those things. I made no notes, but lay on the bed, half-asleep, half-awake, letting the thing saturate my mind and trying over some good phrases. Tom went at two. I lay on the bed till six, and then went down to Lizzie Lightowler's.

"As soon as I started I knew it was going to be good. There is sometimes a resistance about an audience. You have to beat them down. This audience 'went under' at once. It was as though they were hypnotized. And I myself felt, after I had been speaking for a little while, as though I were being used for the promulgation of truths that came from outside me. Often as I had spoken on this theme, never had I felt such conviction of the beauty and truth of what I was saying: so much so that I could almost literally see a world of peace and justice descending before my eyes and displacing the stony streets of St. Swithin's. It was an experience of a peculiar sharpness and sweetness.

"Some time before this, I had come upon John Addington Symonds's great hymn and had made up my mind that the meeting should end, unexpectedly, with the singing of it. I believe in the value of such dramatic moments. So I had arranged with Lizzie Lightowler to have the verses of the hymn prepared on slides and to have a man with a lantern in the gallery. A screen was hung behind the pulpit, where the choir usually sits, and, though no one but me and Mrs. Lightowler knew it, there was a man in the organist's seat.

"I had not realized, when these arrangements were made, how well they were going to fit into the occasion. I ended by speaking of Labour's crusade for universal peace, because that's what I had to do—make these people feel that they were crusaders, not mere voters bought with a pint of Lostwithiel's beer or a Labour promise of another sixpence a week.

"When I had finished I stood where I was. Most of the lights were lowered, and the lantern shone the first verse on to the screen, as the organist played a well-known hymn tune to which it could be sung. When he began it a second time, they had tumbled to it, and started to sing:

> '*These things shall be! A loftier race*
> *Than e'er the world hath known shall rise,*
> *With flame of freedom in their souls*
> *And light of knowledge in their eyes.*'

"It was amazing. The hymn was, of course, the perfect conclusion to what I had been saying, and as I listened to its harmonies swelling through the hot crowded chapel, I knew that I had succeeded: that these people were seeing not a provincial by-election but a purpose to which lives might be dedicated.

"I stood there till the last verse began:

> '*New arts shall bloom of loftier mould,*
> *And mightier music thrill the skies*
> *And every life shall be a song*
> *When all the earth is paradise.*'

"I did not wait for the end of it. Half-way through the verse I walked down the pulpit steps. Jimmy Newboult saw me coming, picked up the sabre, and came to meet me. He walked before me to the vestry. When the others came in, I was too weak to stand. Pen Muff gave me a drink of cold tea out of a bottle. My mother was on the verge of tears. She said: 'It was beautiful. I wish Gordon could have heard it.' Ann Artingstall was crying without restraint. Arnold Ryerson took my hand and said: 'It was enough to make the very stones stand up and testify.'"

The Bradford boiler-maker and the man from Leeds went away together. Pen Muff took Ellen to the house in Thursley Street. Ann and Lizzie suggested supper at Ackroyd Park. Hamer merely shook his head, and they understood his mood and left him. Arnold said: "Are you walking up to Baildon, Hamer?" and Hamer said: "Yes—alone, if you don't mind, old man." Then Arnold went, too, and no one was left in the vestry but Hamer and Jimmy Newboult.

Hamer sagged in the chair, his long legs outstretched. Jimmy loitered about uncertainly, his lean face, that had those almost white eyebrows and lashes that often go with red hair, lit with livelier fanatical fires than usual. The sabre lay on the table.

Presently, Hamer got up. "Well, Jimmy," he said in a voice utterly weary, "that's the end of it. That's all we can do. Thank you, and good-bye."

Then Jimmy did a surprising thing. He picked up the sabre by the point, knelt suddenly on one knee, and tendered the hilt toward Hamer's hand. Hamer divined the boy's intention, hesitated, wondering, perplexed. What would people say? . . . He looked down at the burning bush of Jimmy's bowed head, and laid the sabre lightly upon his shoulder. Jimmy got up. "Now I am your man," he said. "Call me when you want me." He seized his hat and rushed out of the room.

Hamer thoughtfully buckled on the scabbard, thrust the steel home. The little incident shook him, and uplifted him, more than anything that had happened that night. It might have been ridiculous, farcical. But it wasn't. He thought of Jimmy's white, dedicated face. No, it wasn't. It was beautiful.

A couple of hours later he climbed the wall into the intake. He leaned upon the cold stones and looked out over the moor stretching away in shadowy undulations beneath the stars. His exhaustion was gone. He felt the lightness, the joyful relief, of the creator when his task is done. He leaned there for a long time, the events of the evening defiling in a satisfying procession before his inner eye. Far off a star tore from its moorings and streamed across the dark ocean of the night.

FIRST NIGHT IN TANI

Louise A. Stinetorf

In *White Witch Doctor* Ellen Burton faces life as a medical missionary in the Belgian Congo, armed only with a sense of humor, a knack of praying with a scalpel in her hand, and a love of people that transcends race or color. Her introduction to the African tribe, to whom she was to devote twenty-five very full years, takes place in "First Night in Tani."

Dr. Early opened a tin box in which he kept his Bible safe from mold and the ravages of white ants. "Time for prayer meeting," he announced simply.

For a moment I wondered desperately if I might not plead extreme fatigue and so be excused, but while I was searching for words, my host went on.

"For days our people have talked of little else than your coming. They will all be at church tonight to see you and to talk with you afterward. I have told them that you will have a message for them."

"A—a message?" I stammered.

"I shall read a chapter from the Bible and there will be a hymn or two, and then we will turn the meeting over to you," Dr. Early was saying.

It had never occurred to me that I, of all people, would be expected to preach. I gasped out as much, ending with a lame: "Why, I—I have never even gotten up and testified in meeting. Goodness knows, I'm not a preacher or any other kind of public speaker. . . ."

We stared at each other for perhaps ten seconds, then he put his hand on my shoulder and pushed me through the open door of the church.

The next half hour was a confusion of shining black faces and of hymns sung in nonsense syllables. I opened my mouth and tried to carry the familiar tunes in a string of la-la-la's but my tones were an embarrassing falsetto against that background of guttural sound, and finally I stopped and merely listened. Everywhere I turned my eyes, gleaming faces broke into smiles.

Then I was standing behind the pulpit with a hundred faces before me, each one upturned in bright expectation. And there wasn't a thing in my mind except the memory of the flowers just outside the walls and the torchlighted path and, beyond the dancing shadows, perhaps a hungry leopard. I looked down at my congregation helplessly; it was banked in tiers, according to age and sex. First the very old men, then the middle-aged ones, then the boys. Then the elderly women, the middle-aged ones, and the young girls. And behind the banks of black polls, most of them shaven clean, a thin row of white faces. Through the open door I could see many torches flaring, their handles driven into the soft soil beside the path. And beyond the dancing shadows, God only knew how many hungry leopards were lurking.

"There is a tribe of people who live far away across many miles of jungle and sea," I began, and before my voice had died away, Dr. Early, who was standing beside me, translated my words into Hausa.

"These people are fond of an old saying which runs: It is better to light a candle—a torch, I mean—than to curse the darkness!"

I am a nurse and not a preacher. But surely God was with me that evening and put words into my mouth—or else my people at Tani, black and white, for all their human frailties, are the most gracious in the world. On countless occasions since, when I have had to stand before a group of men and women in a strange village, one of my safari *boys* has whispered in my ear: "Tell them what you told us that first night in Tani, *mama*. That a woman over her cooking fire in the evening, although she is nothing but a pair of hands and stupid as a hen, is safer than the strongest man who rails against the night but does not gather sticks for a blaze. Then tell them that love of others lights up the soul——"

That first night I couldn't have said all the things for which they later gave me credit because I was too ignorant of Africa. But before I left the Tani Station, the women no longer sat behind the men in church. The benches were divided with an aisle running down between them, and the women sat on one side, the men on the other. We made that much social progress in a little over a year, which is phenomenal speed for any primitive community. People have told me that my first sermon was the starting point, and the statement always warms my heart.

THE OLD, OLD STORY

James Street

London Wingo is James Street's protagonist in *The Gauntlet,* which presents the struggles of this young Protestant minister and his wife Kathie to keep both their parish and their spiritual integrity. "The Old, Old Story" brings out the contrast between the new minister and the old—between two figures strongly reminiscent of Paul and Timothy.

THE NOVICE was presented to the congregation by the veteran preacher announcing, in a sonorous voice, that "today's Bible reading will be done by Brother London Wingo." He pronounced the name slowly, carefully, then nodded slightly to the young minister and took a seat in one of the upholstered oak chairs that stood beside the high-backed big chair.

London, striving for dignity and reserve, got deliberately to his feet and stood by his chair for a second. His knees were weak and he was waiting for strength to flow into them before he began the long walk from his chair to the pulpit, a distance of about eight feet. There was a tight knot in his stomach and a lump in his throat, and he was on the verge of panic, although there was no visible evidence of his nervous state. At that minute London Wingo wasn't a preacher with a message of comfort, but an actor facing a critical audience. He felt the sweat pop out on his forehead, and his palms suddenly were moist. He took the few steps to the pulpit, and his heart beat a peal of triumph because he made the journey without mishap.

The Scofield Bible was in his left hand, and he put the Book on the pulpit and his hand on the Book and surveyed the congregation. He was still trembling inside, and the color had mounted to his brown cheeks. Outwardly, however, he gave the impression of calmness and confidence. He tried to make it appear that this was just another sermon to him. He had preached before. Of course never on such an occasion, but, after all, he was an experienced man on his feet. That's the way he tried to appear. His front, as false as it was, deceived most of the people, but not Burl Ducksworth and Charlie Moffett.

Satisfied that his appearance was impressive, London flipped through his Bible. He had his place well marked, but the gesture suggested that he knew the Book. He rested his hands on the edge of the pulpit and said, "Our reading today . . ."

At the sound of the first words Honeycutt, who had been leaning forward, tense and prayerful, relaxed in his chair and smiled. The young preacher's tone was well pitched. The sound of his voice came back to London and encouraged him. He had a sickening dread that a frog might be in his throat, or that he would hiccup.

"Our reading today is from Paul's letter to the Hebrews, written from Italy, and is among the last letters written by the great apostle."

He squared his shoulders and changed his voice to a conversational tone, as though he were talking to a group of friends. "There are many scholars who doubt if Paul even wrote this letter and there is reason for doubt. It is written in a style utterly different from Paul's other letters. It is not so much a letter as a sermon to the Jews in which he tries to convince them that Judaism has been superseded by the religion that Paul preached."

The explanation was not necessary at all, but London couldn't miss the opportunity of showing his knowledge and seminary training. Most of the congregation simply gawked at him and had no idea what he was talking about and didn't care. They wanted to hear God's Word.

London sensed that and cut short his own words, as much as he hated to, and turned to the words of Paul, reading:

"'Now faith is the substance of things hoped for, the evidence of things not seen. . . . By faith Abel offered unto God a more excellent sacrifice than Cain. . . . By faith Enoch was translated that he should not see death. . . . By faith Noah, being warned of God of things not seen as yet, moved with fear, prepared an ark to the saving of his house. . . .'"

On and on he read, as though hypnotized by the sound of his own voice.

He read the entire chapter and let his words trail off as an actor recites his last lines, reluctant to make his exit. Then he looked down at the people and his heart sank. Many of them were restless. They didn't like long Bible readings. To most of them, church was a duty, even a habit, and seldom a pleasure. They didn't understand the dramas and poems of the Scriptures and were easily bored. Each knew a few popular quotations from the Bible and was satisfied and didn't want to change.

The older members were looking critically at London when he turned from the pulpit and sat down. Then some of the people exchanged glances. Charlie Moffett looked over at Burl Ducksworth and shook his head. Tama Ducksworth leaned heavily against the back of the hard pew, then wiggled, scratching between her shoulders. The custodian, old man Alvin Thigpen, who always sat in the rear of the church, already was dozing, and down front little Cush Carter, son of the undertaker, snatched at a fly that had come to life and was buzzing in the warm air.

Brother Honeycutt was solemn as he stepped to the pulpit, and his mind was not on the procedure of service, for he was worrying about London, who had muffed his first appearance by trying to be profound. Josie Moffett sang a solo during the offertory, and Honeycutt made the announcements—"Regular meeting of the B.Y.P.U. and the Missionary Society. Prayer meeting Wednesday night."

Then the old man frowned, and the furrows of his face formed a web of lines. He wanted so much to tell London what to do and how to do it. The inspiration came just when he was so troubled. He fumbled through his songbook, seeking a number, and, not finding it immediately, began turning the pages rapidly. Still it escaped him, so he turned to the index, found what he was seeking, and smiled, and the lines left his face. He fixed his eyes on the people and they were still. "Let us stand and sing Number 19—'Tell Me the Old, Old Story.'"

The pianist was surprised, as that song was not on the order of hymns for the service. She, too, flipped through her book until she found it. The congregation arose, and Josie Moffett sang the first word, pitching the tune. Honeycutt waved his arms, keeping time. "Come on, everybody sing. The old, old story of Jesus and His love. Come on, Brother Wingo. Join us."

London stood by the old preacher and sang. He was not a good singer, but his voice was passing fair. And he enjoyed singing. At first he was thinking of how his voice sounded, and the words and the message of the words were lost to him. And then that for which Honeycutt had prayed came to pass. The words became a message to the young man. "Tell me the old, old story." The orthodox might have said it was the Holy Spirit talking to the Lord's servant, the bewildered young preacher. Others might have said it was London's subconscious mind working through an association of thoughts. His mother used to sing that song when she worked about her house. And many times he had heard Kathie humming it without being aware that she was humming it. That memory brought Page Musselwhite to his mind, and he remembered what Page had said. "Preach Christ and Him crucified. That's the old story."

He forgot that the people were watching him and sang out the words, and when the song was ended he stepped back to his chair and bowed his head and prayed, whispering, "Lord, help me to do my best." He forgot about himself, even the quest.

His head was still bowed when the choir began singing softly:

> *"I come to the garden alone,*
> *While the dew is still on the roses,*
> *And the voice I hear,*
> *Falling on my ear,*
> *The Son of God discloses.*
> *And He walks with me, and He talks with me,*
> *And He tells me I am His own.*
> *And the joys we share as we tarry there,*
> *None other has ever known."* *

There was no false pride in London's bearing when he stepped back to the pulpit to preach. He felt humble, yet he felt clean and good, and strong. His eyes were moist, and he was not ashamed of his emotions. He looked at the people and they looked at him and the church was hushed. Even old man Thigpen was awake, and the fly had buzzed away and little Cush Carter was quiet.

The young preacher pushed aside his notes and began talking. His voice was as clear as a bell on the desert. The sermon he had worked on so laboriously was forgotten and he talked of Jesus, of the young man who came out of the wild hills of Galilee, a melting pot of Jews and Phoenicians, Syrians, Arabs, and Greeks.

"Jesus was of the people," he said. "He came from the people, poor people who were crying for a revelation from God or a revolution among men. Jesus, this Joshua of Nazareth, was a mystic and, yes, He

*From "In the Garden," by C. Austin Miles. Copyright, 1940, renewal, by the Rode-heaver Company.

worked in mysterious ways because He worked for God, and God's ways are mysterious.

"He came not in purple robes or with a diadem, but He came with the most powerful weapon of all time—Truth. Jesus is Truth, and Honor, and Justice, and Mercy. It was He who first preached that all men are equal in the sight of God and He gave His life for that truth. It was He who ridiculed and scorned the vicious doctrine of a chosen people, of a spiritual aristocracy, of a race of the elect. He defied His people's leaders and preached a brotherhood of man, Jew and Gentile, black and white and yellow. That's why they killed Him—His own people."

London forgot that a congregation was listening to him. He was talking to Page, and Kathie was nodding her proud little head in approval. He spoke of Galilee and the pool of Siloam and of Jordan. And as he talked one could almost hear the breeze rustling in the olive trees and feel the heat of the Holy City and see the flocks grazing beyond the David Wall.

"He, this carpenter, this worker of wood, brought a new law—Love thy neighbor as thyself. He was the revelation from God and He preached a revolution, a revolution of the spirit—the brotherhood of humanity. You are your brother's keeper, for we all are a part of humanity, and humanity is a storm-beaten island in a sea of misery, and when one grain of dust, just one man, is lost from this island and falls into the sea, then we all are the losers. . . ."

At that moment London Wingo was very near to the truth he was seeking, almost to the mountaintop of his quest. And so early in his ministry.

The people were looking up at him, a strange light on their faces. They had drunk the wine of those old words a hundred times, and still they were thirsty. They had feasted on the substance of the story a thousand times, and still they hungered. He didn't choose his words but let them pour out, and they fell on the people as rain falls on a thirsty field, and bore fruit in the people's resolve to live closer to God henceforth. Only wise old Honeycutt knew that in a few minutes the rain would pass and that the field would thirst again, for the spirit must be watered every day.

London concluded his sermon with the parable of the good Samaritan and stood there a few seconds, looking at the people and then out at the linden tree. There was nothing else to be said, so he picked up his Bible and turned and walked down from the rostrum and into the study, closing the door behind him. He had done his best and he knew it was good. He heard the people shuffling to their feet, and then came their voices singing, "How Firm a Foundation, Ye Saints of the Lord."

He didn't hear Brother Honeycutt enter the room, and when he turned the old preacher was beside him, smiling, although his good eye was swimming in tears, and the tears were on the lashes under his other eye. He put his hand on the young preacher's arm and said, "And Paul wrote to Timothy, saying, 'This charge I commit unto thee, son Timothy.' The Lord was with you, boy."

"Thank you, sir. I did my best. I changed my sermon at the last minute."

"Uh-huh. I figured you did. Now come on with me and shake hands with the folks." He stepped to the door. "Just one thing, I've been circulating around among the deacons. I dropped hints that another church is after you. I don't know that that's not true."

Man's Gladness

~~~~~~

RAFCA, THE BRIDE OF CANA

Kahlil Gibran

~~~~~~

In *Jesus, The Son of Man,* Gibran allows the Young Man of Nazareth's contemporaries to speak for themselves, revealing his power and charm over their thoughts, actions, and lives. Rafca's recollection of her wedding brings a tender, womanly warmth to the miracle of Cana.

THIS HAPPENED before He was known to the people.

I was in my mother's garden tending the rose-bushes, when He stopped at our gate.

And He said, "I am thirsty. Will you give me water from your well?"

And I ran and brought the silver cup, and filled it with water; and I poured into it a few drops from the jasmine vial.

And He drank deep and was pleased.

Then He looked into my eyes and said, "My blessing shall be upon you."

When he said that I felt as it were a gust of wind rushing through my body. And I was no longer shy; and I said, "Sir, I am betrothed to a man of Cana in Galilee. And I shall be married on the fourth day of the coming week. Will you not come to my wedding and grace my marriage with your presence?"

And He answered, "I will come, my child."

Mind you, He said, "My child," yet He was but a youth, and I was nearly twenty.

Then he walked on down the road.

And I stood at the gate of our garden until my mother called me into the house.

On the fourth day of the following week I was taken to the house of my bridegroom and given in marriage.

And Jesus came, and with Him His mother and His brother James.

And they sat around the wedding-board with our guests whilst my maiden comrades sang the wedding-songs of Solomon the King. And Jesus ate our food and drank our wine and smiled upon me and upon the others.

And He heeded all the songs of the lover bringing his beloved into his tent; and of the young vineyard-keeper who loved the daughter of the lord of the vineyard and led her to his mother's house; and of the prince who met the beggar maiden and bore her to his realm and crowned her with the crown of his fathers.

And it seemed as if He were listening to yet other songs also, which I could not hear.

At sundown the father of my bridegroom came to the mother of Jesus and whispered saying, "We have no more wine for our guests. And the day is not yet over."

And Jesus heard the whispering, and He said, "The cup bearer knows that there is still more wine."

And so it was indeed—and as long as the guests remained there was fine wine for all who would drink.

Presently Jesus began to speak with us. He spoke of the wonders of earth and heaven; of sky flowers that bloom when night is upon the earth, and of earth flowers that blossom when the day hides the stars.

And He told us stories and parables, and His voice enchanted us so that we gazed upon Him as if seeing visions, and we forgot the cup and plate.

And as I listened to Him it seemed as if I were in a land distant and unknown.

After a while one of the guests said to the father of my bridegroom, "You have kept the best wine till the end of the feast. Other hosts do not so."

And all believed that Jesus had wrought a miracle, that they should have more wine and better at the end of the wedding-feast than at the beginning.

I too thought that Jesus had poured the wine, but I was not astonished; for in His voice I had already listened to miracles.

And afterwards indeed, His voice remained close to my heart, even until I had been delivered of my first-born child.

And now even to this day in our village and in the villages near by, the word of our guest is still remembered. And they say, "The spirit of Jesus of Nazareth is the best and oldest wine."

REUBEN'S COURTSHIP

Mary Ellen Chase

The saga of three generations of Maine seafaring men is recorded in *Silas Crockett*. Mary Ellen Chase treats the love idyll of Reuben Crockett and Huldah Barrett with warm nostalgic beauty and deep feeling for the New England character.

REUBEN'S COURTSHIP of Huldah Barrett was for a long time only in his mind. Except for the stout certainty of Susan and the active memory of his grandmother, women had heretofore played no part at all in his life. But now that Huldah had come into his thoughts, his mind suddenly opened in an odd way as though after walking through a shadowy and quite satisfying wood, he had come suddenly and without warning into the full sunlight of a summer field.

It was months before he saw anything at all of Huldah beyond her presence at church, and she would have been startled enough had she known the part she was already playing in his life. It was not, in fact, until June after their meeting in October that he became so bold as to call upon her. Searching about for some reason or excuse which might explain his coming to the old Stevens' house, he discovered in a shop in Rockland a set of excellent photographs of some of the Maine lighthouses—Portland Head Light ringed with winter surf, the great shaft of Petit-Manan shadowy in thick weather, the lonely outpost of Saddle-back Ledge, Matinicus Rock deep in January snow, the windblown spruces of Heron Neck, black behind its white tower. He selected eight of these and had them mounted on sheets of white cardboard. They would look well on the walls of her schoolroom. Reuben sat on in the Barrett sitting-room for an hour with Huldah after he had presented his pictures with explanations of how he thought they might interest her children at school.

"I think it's a wonderful thing to know the world," he said, as he stood again before the pictures now on Huldah's mantel, "and I've often wished I could. But if you can't go to foreign countries, then I think it's a good thing to know the state you live in and a coast like this."

Huldah was direct and frank with Reuben in her delight over his gift. She should choose her favourite she said—she thought it was Petit-Manan, but she would have to sleep on it—and keep it on her desk in her own room there at home. It would help no end when she was correcting examples in cube root, which she thought the worst and most senseless exercise in all Greenleaf's arithmetic.

Now that he had opened the way and had not been repulsed, Reuben spent every Saturday evening with Huldah and saw her home from prayer-meeting on Sunday nights as well. The village began early to accept their keeping company and to talk about it with generous approbation, overlooking even the discrepancy in age. Reuben Crockett had never looked at any one else in all his life, and now that he had, it was a good thing, might loosen him up a bit and make him more like other folks. As for Huldah, such a woman had not come to Saturday Cove for years, with ideas and standards that were fast slipping in a changing age. She was one in a thousand, and any man who could get *her* might count himself fortunate.

Reuben's entrance into her life was not without difficulties although the difficulties were a hundredfold outweighed by the compensations. Huldah's mother was not by nature a buoyant woman. She harboured, indeed nourished many ills both of the flesh and of the spirit, and she found occasion to speak of them during the hours that Reuben and Huldah spent playing with her the new game of *flinch*. Moreover, she looked warily upon Reuben's invasion of her life with her daughter, a life which she had until now assumed was to be entirely her own. She had a way of making them both uncomfortable in her presence, which resulted, once she was absent, in an extreme sense of comfort one in the other. Long before Reuben had told Huldah that he loved and wanted her, he had told her everything else he had ever thought, known or experienced in twenty-six years.

Huldah was one of the relatively few persons in this world who find life by giving it away, wholly and unequivocally. Upon her and others like her is the gospel paradox built and fulfilled. Whatever she received came flowing back, begotten, born, and nourished by what she had given. She did not have to wait many days for her bread cast upon the waters. She was an example, people said, to the young and un-decided at the seasons of revival still held at the turn of the century, of the power of God and His grace in a human heart. When Reuben came in Huldah's thirty-first year, the necessity for God was well-established within her. She could not do without Him. With Reuben's entrance into her days and hours and minutes, she found much of her love for him in her love for God, and her love of God in him. But she did not recognize the new and mutual dependence of these loves, one upon the other, and would have been genuinely puzzled at any such suggestion, which in her time and place and by the people whom she knew was never even surmised.

Reuben felt sure that Huldah could not have been surprised when, after he had told her everything else in his world, he got around to telling her of his love. Nor was she. Nor was either of them unduly distressed over the apparent necessity of waiting for each other. They could wait more easily upon the certainty of a few untrammelled hours each week together than they could face the certainty of more trammelled hours with Susan and Huldah's mother to reckon with.

When all the trying realities of the whole matter had been once faced for good and all, as was Reuben's way, he and Huldah entered upon one of those long courtships of which most rural villages in New England and elsewhere bear record. By the time four years had gone by, Saturday Cove ceased talking about it—the pity that two persons, one of whom was already in advanced years for marriage, could not spend their lives together, the once-persistent query as to whether Reuben Crockett might not do better with the odds so against him to seek elsewhere, the almost certain conjectures that unless time intervened and that hastily, the Crockett name was doomed to cessation with the death of Reuben.

Perhaps, indeed, Saturday Cove had been more anxious over their long-deferred marriage than were either Reuben or Huldah. As for Reuben, the very creation of love in his life was so overwhelming a thing that he could wait more patiently than most for its consummation. He could never become entirely accustomed to the way it heightened perceptions and experiences, forever bringing to shining points what before had been flat surfaces—the birds in spring when he left the house early to rejoin his boat, sure that Huldah would be at her door to say good-bye, the rugged outlines of the coast, his new understanding of the lives of the men with whom he worked, even the blessing of rainy days which seemed to him to halt time and give him a chance to live over his new life in his mind. Now the most concrete and repeated happenings put an edge upon themselves, cutting deeply into the succession of his days, things such as selecting with Huldah the evening hymns for church and, after church was over, staying behind with her to close the wheezy organ, pile the hymn books neatly, turn out the hanging lamps, and see that the old stove was safe.

At Huldah's suggestion Reuben became the new superintendent of the Sunday-school in 1904. He still retained enough of his old life to be surprised at the way he stood before the school, gave out the hymns for Huldah to play, and even made a few remarks of his own about the lesson to be taught in the various classes. These things now in his new freedom seemed natural and easy; and when in church he heard the minister read the morning lesson from the Psalms,

Bring my soul out of prison that I may praise Thy name,

he knew precisely what the words meant and understood that he now had no need to make the prayer.

WINGS

Mark Twain

~~~~~~

Mark Twain's irrepressible sense of humor is nowhere more provocative than in his *Extract from Captain Stormfield's Visit to Heaven.* The following discussion between the Captain and Sandy McWilliams illuminates one aspect of fashions in Heaven.

I HAD BEEN HAVING considerable trouble with my wings. The day after I helped the choir I made a dash or two with them, but was not lucky. First off, I flew thirty yards, and then fouled an Irishman and brought him down—brought us both down, in fact. Next, I had a collision with a Bishop—and bowled him down, of course. We had some sharp words, and I felt pretty cheap, to come banging into a grave old person like that, with a million strangers looking on and smiling to themselves.

I saw I hadn't got the hang of steering, and so couldn't rightly tell where I was going to bring up when I started. I went afoot the rest of the day, and let my wings hang. Early next morning I went to a private place to have some practice. I got up on a pretty high rock, and got a good start, and went swooping down, aiming for a bush a little over three hundred yards off; but I couldn't seem to calculate for the wind, which was about two points abaft my beam. I could see I was going considerable to looard of the bush, so I worked my starboard wing slow and went ahead strong on the port one, but it wouldn't answer; I could see I was going to broach to, so I slowed down on both, and lit. I went back to the rock and took another chance at it. I aimed two or three points to starboard of the bush—yes, more than that— enough so as to make it nearly a head-wind. I done well enough, but made pretty poor time. I could see, plain enough, that on a head-wind, wings was a mistake. I could see that a body could sail pretty close to the wind, but he couldn't go in the wind's eye. I could see that if I wanted to go a-visiting any distance from home, and the wind was ahead, I might have to wait days, maybe, for a change; and I could see, too, that these things could not be any use at all in a gale; if you tried to run before the wind, you would make a mess of it, for there isn't any way to shorten sail—like reefing, you know—you have to take it *all* in —shut your feathers down flat to your sides. That would *land* you, of course. You could lay to, with your head to the wind—that is the best you could do, and right hard work you'd find it, too. If you tried any other game, you would founder, sure.

I judge it was about a couple of weeks or so after this that I dropped old Sandy McWilliams a note one day—it was a Tuesday—and asked him to come over and take his manna and quails with me next day; and the first thing he did when he stepped in was to twinkle his eye in a sly way, and say,—

"Well, Cap, what you done with your wings?"

I saw in a minute that there was some sarcasm done up in that rag somewheres, but I never let on. I only says,—

"Gone to the wash."

"Yes," he says, in a dry sort of way, "they mostly go to the wash—

about this time—I've often noticed it. Fresh angels are powerful neat. When do you look for 'em back?"

"Day after tomorrow," says I.

He winked at me, and smiled.

Says I,—

"Sandy, out with it. Come—no secrets among friends. I notice you don't ever wear wings—and plenty others don't. I've been making an ass of myself—is that it?"

"That is about the size of it. But it is no harm. We all do it at first. It's perfectly natural. You see, on earth we jump to such foolish conclusions as to things up here. In the pictures we always saw the angels with wings on—and that was all right; but we jumped to the conclusion that that was their way of getting round—and that was all wrong. The wings ain't anything but a uniform, that's all. When they are in the field—so to speak—they always wear them; you never see an angel going with a message anywhere without his wings, any more than you would see a military officer presiding at a court-martial without his uniform, or a postman delivering letters, or a policeman walking his beat, in plain clothes. But they ain't to *fly* with. The wings are for show, not for use . . . that's all, only just for show."

THE ILLUMINATION

Jessamyn West

Quaker life in Indiana during the Civil War fills *The Friendly Persuasion* with a homespun humor and charm. In this episode Jess Birdwell and his preacher wife Eliza gain insight into the importance of illumination both in the home and in the heart.

IT WAS a May morning, early. The morning of a piece-meal flicker-light day. It was the time of the return of shadows. The time once again when there was sun enough and leaf enough to give some variety to the monotony of a wall or strip of land.

Jess sat on his side of the bed putting his foot into a white wool sock. He gazed at the sunlight coming through the east windows, like water tinged with a little squeezed juice from a red geranium, he decided. He had a head full of quizzical ideas about himself and the world—at the minute his foot was busy feeling its way into the sock, and his eye with watching the sun set the water pitcher on the floor. There it was on the gray rag carpet.

"Appears to be a big-eared animal," he said, figuring it out finally.

Eliza, who had the May morning in her veins but was giving no thought to it, gartered her stockings neatly with the soft pieces of rolled red silk she used. Since she was a Quaker, Eliza didn't hold with distracting the eye of man with violent colors. But under three skirts, knee-high and visible only to God, she didn't reckon it mattered. And she knew it was there.

"Thee's choosing a poor time to be fanciful, Jess," she said. "I can feel all the steps I got to take before night jolting my spine right now. Kitchen to dining room. Dining room to kitchen." She got up from her side of the bed and walked to the middle of the room, where she gave a little bounce.

"Tickled?" Jess asked.

"Gratified," she said without studying about it. "Praising God in his glory. It'll be a convenience. Beautiful at night. Shining through the trees, too. To say nothing of the novelty."

"It was my idea," Jess reminded her.

"Thee was the vessel. The Lord filled thee."

Jess was used to that. Eliza had given God the credit for all he'd ever done.

She had on all but her dress now. It was hard to say what was plumpness and what was starch. There was plenty of both. "Stir thy stumps, Jess," she said, "twenty people for supper—thirty, maybe, and thee shilly-shallying in thy shirttail at six in the morning."

Jess smiled on her fondly. The best training for a woman, he figured, was to put her early in the pulpit. It didn't cut down any on her flow of talk, but it bettered it, and relieved the pressure. A pity neither of his daughters had pulpit leanings. He pulled his nightshirt over his head. There was more warmth under it than outside.

"I got more heat than the sun," he said.

Eliza didn't encourage him to talk. He watched her, her plump fingers flying in and out of her still black hair. Like birds at dusk. That was his own thought of them. The pleasing thoughts God let him have!

So long as he had a head and shoulders to lodge it, he would never be bereft. He was jolted from daylight to dark with pleasing ideas. Whether God was the fount of all he could not say, but for their having he was grateful.

Eliza looking in her mirror saw him naked behind her. She took an eye off her plaiting.

"At thy age," she said through her hairpins.

Jess came to life. "I ain't never been this age before," he complained. "Thee seems never hard put for what's becoming to thy years." He meant it. Whatever she did was becoming, waking or sleeping. A child in her arms or tanning its behind, she had a face of love and beauty. What could a man ask further—with that face opposite him for forty years and ideas popping in his mind like firecrackers? He buttoned his shirt meditatively.

Eliza's face got pink. She'd never learned to take a compliment—and she'd had two a day for forty years. They made her feel uneasy—as if she weren't taken for granted like sun and moon. "Don't put on thy good shirt, now," she said sharply. "Save it till evening—there's a mort of work to be done—unless thee plans to sit in the parlor saving thy strength for the Illumination."

Jess slowly pulled off the fresh shirt. "The Illumination," he said. "So that's what thee calls it? Sounds Biblical. The Annunciation, The Transfiguration. The Illumination. Sounds as if the Lord Himself had a hand in it."

Eliza bridled. "Thee'd be a sorry piece—saying He hadn't. But what," she asked reasonably, "would thee call it, Jess Birdwell? Thee's rigged up a gas plant in the cellar—we light the jets tonight and ask in the neighbors. That's the Illumination. Does thee feel marble cake, coconut drops, floating island, and French custard ice cream will be a sufficiency as dessert, Jess?"

"Scanty pickings," he said. "Scanty pickings. No pie."

Eliza's black eyes searched her husband's face anxiously until she saw his Adam's apple fluttering.

"Pie's kind of commonplace," she said.

The bedroom door opened without a knock. In the doorway stood a figure half-way between all known stopping places. A face too sharp-cut for a Negro—too dark for anything else—too much mustache for a woman, too much bosom for a man.

"Preacher," she intoned, "gravy's gobbling up the skillet, morning's gobbling up the day, pretty soon the daylight's going far away." Then she waited.

"That's pretty, Emanuela," said Eliza. "One of thy best. We'll be right down."

Emanuela walked away limber-legged, satisfaction oiling her knee-hinges.

"There's nothing about that woman I like," said Jess. "Calls thee 'preacher.' Always rhyming. No answer unless she can rhyme it."

Eliza was leaving the room, her Bible for breakfast Scripture reading in her hand. "After twenty years, Jess, thee might be reconciled."

"I'm still sane," the old man said. "Though after twenty years it's a wonder."

Eliza was going light-foot down the stairs. "Thee get thy sanity down to the breakfast table," she called back. "Feed it some ham and gravy. Don't get stuck up there preening thyself on it."

Jess stood fully dressed but not descending. It was his morning's pleasure to stand thus at the day's rim as over a pool of water before plunging in. There was no telling what the day might hold—what vexations seize him belowstairs. Or what joys. He stood now, uncommitted to either, his own man, as silent and at peace as the clapper in a ropeless bell. Silent—silent. Here now at six o'clock in the morning with the pink light on the gray carpet, and the bed not yet made up, shutting out the night, he, Jess Birdwell, sixty-two years old, stood committed as yet to nothing but the unraveling of his own soul.

"Taste eternity," he said aloud, "on a May morning in a white clapboard house on the banks of the Muscatatuck. How to taste it—there's so much of it and none you want to waste."

Gratingly his strong finger stroked his long Irish upper lip—his eyes sharply focused on something beyond the chamber's edge. Then he walked slowly to the secretary which stood between the two south windows and took down Janney's *Life of William Penn*. With the stub pencil he always carried in his shirt pocket he wrote quickly, "Eternity," the soft blunt pencil set firmly down, "is experienced in life by sampling as many of the elements as is possible."

Around the sentences went quotation marks and under them the words, "From the writings of Dr. Samuel Johnson." Jess's books were filled with sentences of his own with other men's names under them. He was not a wasteful man, he was pious and he was Irish. The good thoughts God gave him he would save. He kept his stub pencil handy to write them down. But say he wrote them himself—he was too bashful for that—it would plague him to death to have it thought he set himself up to be a John Greenleaf or Henry Wadsworth. So his books were filled with wisdom from Charles Lamb and John Milton and John Woolman. When once in a while he had a thought he was convinced was true, but maybe not one a writer'd like to own, he labeled it "Anon."

"Sample as much as possible," he said to himself, put back the book, shut the secretary, and descended to the day that lay belowstairs, waiting.

Jane bent over the hearth in the sitting room, turkey brush in hand, brushing up the night-before's ashes. She was bent, but not brushing.

"Well, daughter," said Jess.

"Good morning, pa," the girl said soberly, not lifting her eyes to peer beyond the blinkers of her black frizzed bangs.

"Thee's like a witch, with thy broom—bent double and ready to fly."

"A witch," Jane said, standing bolt upright and staring her father sadly in the eye. Then tears rolled out of her own gray eyes and down to the corners of her crooked mouth.

"Hoity-toity!" her father sighed. There was scarcely a word safe to say to fifteen-year-olds. They took exception to Holy Writ itself. Thinking to take her mind off the witch business, if that was what upset her, he said, "Thee have a fever blister on thy lip, Jane?"

Then Jane sobbed, threw down the wing brush, cried, "Oh, pa," and ran to the kitchen.

Now I'm in the day and fairly launched, Jess thought, and walked into the kitchen.

There Jane sat at the breakfast table, her head in her arms, and Eliza faced him, her black eyes crackling. "A pretty way to start a day of celebration with twitting thy daughter about her looks."

"Twitting!" Jess said aghast. He wouldn't twit a shooting enemy about his looks. There was nothing so personal as looks.

"Call her first a witch—then take notice of a blemish that's plaguing her."

A witch—old, bent, ugly. A fever blister—a blemish big as a mountain and visible miles off and akin to leprosy in repulsiveness. I got to re-travel so many miles to get back to fifteen, he thought, and even that don't turn the trick for I ain't female.

He sat down to the table. "Ever hear the word bewitching, Jane?" he asked. Jane raised her sorrowing head. "Bewitching. Like a witch. I don't know about now—but when I was a young blade, there was nothing a man could say in way of praise beyond that. Bewitching. Thy mother was bewitching. Don't thee ever read poetry, Jane? Bee-stung lips? A fev—a fullness such as thine is highly regarded."

Jane's sniffs were drying up. Eliza's eyes had given over blazing. The four of them, Jess and Eliza, Jane and Emanuela, sat at the breakfast table. The hired man had eaten earlier.

"Let us return thanks," said Jess, and the four heads bowed in silent prayer.

Jess meditated on God but asked for nothing. Eliza talked with her Father of gifts and wants alike. Emanuela floated wordless before a blazing throne. Jane prayed, "Take away my fever blister, take away my fever blister." Then being of a reasonable and conciliatory nature, "Or if Thee'd rather just make it invisible. Thee has the power, O Lord," she reminded Him. "Make it invisible for the Illumination."

The other three heads lifted while Jane's was still bowed. Eliza said, "Help thyself to the gravy, Jane."

Prayer was a solace, but there were twenty—thirty people coming for supper, and solace didn't chew like bread.

Jane raised her head and looked about the table. No one was paying any attention to her fever blister. Perhaps it was already invisible. She helped herself to ham and gravy and soda biscuits, eating with lifted lip.

Eliza planned her day like a general: terrain to be covered, redans thrown up, posts held. She gave out the commissions: "Emanuela, thee's not to set foot outside the kitchen today. Thee's to take care of the cooking. The chickens and ham should go on now. Those hens are all muscle. I'll make the floating island myself, and the corn pudding."

Emanuela drew a long breath to show speech was welling up. "Preacher, while your back is turned none of the vittles will be burned."

Jess swallowed heavily.

> "Emanuela, it's time thee's learned
> Prose is nothing to be spurned."

"Jess, Jess," Eliza chided. This was no day to get a rhyming hoe-down started between those two. It could go on till candlelighting time with Jess the winner, Emanuela sulking in her room, and Eliza with the work to do.

"Jane," she said, "thee's to redd up the bedrooms, get fresh flowers, dust, set tables, and be at all times near at hand. No dallying down by the branch."

"Yes, ma," said Jane.

"Jess, thee set this down on paper."

"Otherwise," Jess said, "it might slip my mind slick as a whistle."

"Bring up from the spring-house dill pickles, the sour cream jar, the apple butter, and all yesterday's milk. Bring up from the ice-house enough ice for the freezing. Go out to the south wood lot and see if there's dogwood blooming there we could use as table flowers. Take a bucket of hot water and see that all signs of thy ducks is off the back steps. Go out——"

"Whoa there!" said Jess. "Whoa there! When that's done I'll come back for further orders."

They darted like needles through the morning—they wove the bright May morning into a fabric strong enough to support a party. Eliza and Emanuela filled in the groundwork sturdy and firm while Jane and Jess feather-stitched around the edges. Jane sang while she dusted, not clearly, because of her sore lip.

> *"I am a stranger here*
> *Within a foreign land.*
> *My home is far away,*
> *Upon a coral strand."*

She believes it, Jess thought, listening to her loud and sorrowing voice. She ain't used to Indiana yet. Life's a shock to the young. Shock to have an old man for a father instead of an angel. Shock to eat ham gravy instead of honey dewdrops. And to like ham gravy. That's the worst shock of all. Find yourself fitting into this sorry world.

Jane came down the back steps, walking carefully so's not to disturb the flowers she was carrying. "Look, pa," she cried. "Isn't it beautiful?"

Jess didn't care for it much. The old gravy bowl, mounded high as a lump of raising bread with white bridal wreath in the center, had red geraniums running in a scarlet circle round the outer edge.

"I just got to find something blue," Jane said. "One big blue flower or four little ones would do it. To go right in the center of the white. Then look what I've got, pa. Red, white, and blue."

Jess saw it otherwise. Blue eye with red rim. Bad case of pink-eye's what it'll look like, he thought, but said nothing.

Red, white, and blue. If he'd been of a suitable age how'd his Quaker principles've stood up during the war? Had he been in his prime could he have held out against fighting for what he believed in? Union and the slaves free? The Lord didn't ask me to make that decision. But it goes against the grain now to have to take these things, things I most believe in, from men I never laid eyes on. He watched a cloud shadow pass over the pail of cooling water at his feet.

Eliza came down the steps bouncing. "Cold water'll never do the trick," she said.

"Time was," Jess answered, "when thee'd of been too fine-haired to direct me in dousing duck manure off the back steps."

She nodded her head, remembering that girl.

"Was we better then, Jess?" she asked. "When we's young? When we couldn't bear nought but flowers and sweet words? Couldn't bear to have a mouse die—let alone a bird? Thought hens unladylike for laying eggs? Now I say clean off the duck dung like 'draw up a chair.' And none of this world's beauties break my heart any more—no, nor words, any more, Jess, like once I cried for 'As for man, his days are as grass: as a flower of the field so he flourisheth.' Is it gaining or losing, Jess?"

She hoisted her gray chambray skirts so Jess's final swishing would not spatter them.

"Both, both," he said, leaning on his broom. This was a way he seldom saw Eliza. Ordinarily she fit snug and without questioning into one of her two worlds, this world of work, the next of love.

"Both," he repeated. "The thing being to taste each in its turn."

Eliza shook her head. "I don't know."

The shadows of morning had shortened. Fingers of light came through the leafing maple onto her kitchen-warmed face. Enoch's voice came up from the west forty in the kind of guttural horse talk he used in plowing. Jane walked by not seeing them, intent on her red, white, and blue. Emanuela clanged like a forge in the kitchen. Far off, on a farm out of sight, a dog barked as if to someone returning after long absence.

"The mind," said Eliza, puzzled, to her husband, "the live mind can hardly take in the idea of death."

"No need," Jess said. "No need. It ain't in nature."

"We ought to prepare."

"This is preparing," he answered, lifting his face to the sky.

Jane was finished with her work. She went from room to room, leaning in their doorways, seeing their perfection and seeing Jane, stepping under the gaslights tonight, fair as the Illumination itself. She stepped across a threshold to tauten a coverlet or pick up a fallen petal, and stepped back, to watch the room silent in its waiting.

She had not looked in a glass at her fever blister since morning. She trusted the Lord and felt it to be invisible.

Eliza said, "I've got to have a body bath." She hadn't planned on it. Not on getting that hot. She washed in a corner of the kitchen while Emanuela kept her eyes modestly on the cast-iron kettles.

The day's light flowed over the edge of the western hills. Mud daubers left the road puddles with their last loads for home. The Muscatatuck moved like steel under the light-drained sky. The curtains in the parlor lifted a little in the wind off the river.

Eliza was getting panicky—the way she always did before a doings —fearful maybe the knives had been left off the table, or the salt out of the gravy.

Jess went upstairs to get into his First Day shirt.

"Don't thee leave thy dirty shirt on the floor," Eliza called after him.

He put it in the closet, and as he stood in his undershirt and work pants the thought came to him: Better see if the gas plant's working. Sixty years of living had convinced him that something wry and sardonic had a hand in the world's management, something that arranged for invitations to be sent out to Illuminations and then put a stop to the gas supply. It didn't make the old man bitter—it made him alert. When he was bested he listened for that far-off laugh—when things went without a hitch, he laughed himself.

He went downstairs silent as shadow in the shadowy house. In the parlor he turned the jet, heard the gas whisper like a snake, set his match to it, saw its tongue of flame.

Eliza crackled in, sweet with soap and sunlight. "If Stephen were home from school, could join us here and see the lighting . . ."

Eliza's muted voice said what perfection that would have been. Steve was the youngest, the child from whose eyes her lost Sarah looked; without him no occasion, however festive, was complete.

"The boy has his studies to think of," Jess said.

Eliza nodded. Then she looked about concerned. This was the hour when she always feared no one would come to the party.

"Jess," she whispered, "what if no one comes? What'll we do with all the food? I've been casting up in my mind what to do with the food."

"Thee never remembers from one time to the next, does thee?" Jess asked patiently. "Surreys'll be turning off the pike in ten minutes."

"Then why's thee standing here in thy underwear? Ten minutes and the house'll be full of people and thee in thy underwear." She pushed him toward the stairs. "It's enough to rile a saint. Hustle into thy clothes."

The old man hustled.

By the time the threads of his silk tie were catching on his rough fingers, he heard, as he had said they would, the wheels of the first surrey become silent as they turned off the pike's gravel on to the soft dust of the Maple Grove drive.

He lingered at the stairhead before descending. The balloon of party preparations which had swollen to vast proportions now burst belowstairs.

People can't be that glad to see each other, he thought. They's taken aback to feel so little joyful and talk loud to hide it. Half the evening passes before it's natural to them.

"Jess, Jess," came Eliza's voice. "It's time for the lighting. We're waiting for thee to set the match to them."

He walked downstairs slowly. A party for him was like a thunderstorm—a fine sight to see, and music to the ears, but nothing to be caught plumb in the heart of.

"Howdy, Jess, howdy."

"Think it's safe, does thee?"

"Cost a mint of money, I reckon."

"The Illumination, eh? Well, light up."

Jess set matches to the jets, and parlor and sitting room, dining room and parlor-bedroom were light-struck as flowers at midday, clear and shining and orderly as petals beneath the yellow lights. The faces turned upward as if to a marvel—and it was a marvel, here in the backwoods a house lit with something flowing up through pipes from the cellar. No lamps to be washed and filled, no coal-oil splashing over the cornmeal and sugar on trips home from town.

"The Illumination," Jane whispered, marveling, yellow lights in her gray eyes as she looked upward.

They were all there: the Griffiths, the Hoopers, the Peases, the Armstrongs: Quakers who dressed plain and Quakers who didn't. The Reverend Godley and his wife from the Rush Branch neighborhood.

Lidy Cinnamond, beautiful but somewhat sad; grieving, Jane hoped, for Stephen, her absent brother. The Venters from down the pike. Talking naturally now beneath the artificial lights, and drifting more often past the dining room, where the cold foods were already set out on the table.

In the kitchen was the crisis of dishing up, but it was over in a minute: chicken with dumplings like yellow clouds floating on top, coleslaw in green and white glacier drifts, and mashed potatoes like cloud and snow together were carried in by Emanuela.

Eliza stood in the doorway, untying her apron. "Friends," she said, "supper is ready."

They were twenty-eight at table. Young and old. Oldsters for whom food had a meaning, and young'uns—and in-between, those whose hearts had not yet fed, and who could eat on bread or stone, so little were they centered in swallowing, so much in seeing, searching.

Eliza was the minister at table, but it was a man's place to return grace. Grace was silent, except on occasions like this—with Methodists present who liked to hear what people were saying to God.

Jess shut his eyes. "Father, for food and friends we thank Thee. Amen." It was over before the youngest had started to peek.

After supper there was a little lull. The men talked crops while the women cleared dishes and had some final bites under the excuse of not letting anything waste.

This was a Quaker home and play-party prancing would never shake its floors—but the songs could be sung even if the feet couldn't be lifted.

As Jess walked outside, "Skip to My Lou" was being sung in the parlor and he thought he could hear Jane's eager, asking voice above the others. He walked up to the little rise they called the pasture knoll where he could see the house, have a look at the fireworks from a sheltered spot.

From the pasture knoll the house was a shell of light. The night was mild and from the raised windows light fell out in golden bars across the dark earth. Jess nodded his head, approving—for man whose time on earth is so short it was a brave job, this installing gaslights and eating chicken dumplings like children of eternity. Considering man's lot nobody could berate him, if he chose to molder in some dark corner, thinking on the sorry upshot of it all. Taste all, he thought, taste all.

As he leaned on the fence that separated pasture from orchard, he heard someone come up the orchard side of the knoll, heard the fence creak as it was leaned against.

"Well, Mr. Birdwell," said a thin grasshopper voice, "I see you're pouring it out tonight."

"Pouring it out?" Jess asked. Thinking he meant the lights, but, knowing old Eli Whitcomb, not sure.

"The money," Eli said, "the money," and he moved nearer so that his smell, like leaves wet with the first fall rains, was stronger in the May night than anything spring could muster.

"A lot of money going down the drainpipe, there. Food and lights nobody needs. Don't it irk you?"

The old coot ain't ashamed of being a miser, Jess thought. No need my being ashamed for him. For the first time in his life he spoke to the man he knew his forty-year neighbor to be: said farewell to make-shifts and politeness and plunged right into that hard core where Eli lived.

"Money," he said. "Thee prizes it above all else?"

"No," said old Eli Whitcomb, "not money. Anything you can get your hands on. Anything you can count or weigh or measure. There's nothing else to rely on. Looky," he said, and beat out his words on Jess's arm with a finger as light as a withered flower stalk. "What's the main idea behind this world? A wasting away—a wasting away. Trees rotting. Ground carried off by the rivers. The sun getting less hot. Iron rusting. I run counter to that. I put a stop to it. God don't care. Wreckage is His nature. It ain't mine. I save. Piles of everything. Boxes, papers, I get old papers from as far as Kokomo. Nails, money too. I save all. Me alone. Against the drift. The rest of you letting it run down the spout."

Jess turned to the old fellow he couldn't see. "I never figured it in that light."

"Of course you didn't. If you had there'd be none of that."

He pointed to the house. "Devouring, gnawing away. I got to get home," he said abruptly. "A little of a sight like that is as much as I can stomach. Clean against reason. Farewell, Jess Birdwell. You got it in you to've been a credit to the world if things'd taken another drift."

He went away in the May night with the sound of leaf brushing against leaf.

"Eli," Jess called after him, "Eli, is thee happy?"

"Not in sight of that," he said, and Jess knew he was looking at the house, "but against I get home, see what one man's done by way of putting a check to the wasting away of the world, I reckon I will be."

Jess leaned back against the fence, arms stretched along the top rails. "Well, well," he said.

Here where the woods had been so thick a star could be seen only if a leaf was lifted by the wind, here where the Indians had trod silent-foot, here he, Jess Birdwell, the Quaker, stood under the open sky regarding his farm land, his house, his family.

He turned and looked in the direction old Eli had gone. "That's another way if I don't misdoubt."

He walked into the house and up the back stairs to his and Eliza's chamber. He lit a lamp and took down the book he'd written in that morning, and under his morning's writing he set down, "One or many —it don't matter. Eternity's how deep you go."

Not a finished way of saying it, he thought, but for the first time he signed his own name. "Eternity's the depth you go. Jess Birdwell."

He closed the book and replaced it, turned the light low and walked down the front stairs. Oldsters were sitting at ease, talking and listening while the young people were singing,

> *"Oh, when I'm gone, don't you, don't you grieve,*
> *Oh, when I'm gone, don't you, don't you grieve after me."*

Jane came to the bottom stair and looked up at him.

"Where's thee been, pa?"

"Outside to see the lights—from outside."

"How's it look from outside, pa?"

"Like an oversize lightning bug."

"I just love Illuminations. Don't thee, pa?"

"Well," said Jess, "they's much to be said for them." Then he joined the young folks in their singing,

> *"Oh, when I'm gone, don't you, don't you grieve after me."*

Great Lessons

~~~~~~

THE LAST SUPPER

Toyohiko Kagawa

~~~~~~

Behold The Man is another famous novelized biography of Jesus, beginning at the death of John the Baptist and concluding with the scene between Christ and Thomas on the Sunday evening following Easter. "The Last Supper" is a colorful three-dimensional canvas of this momentous event in the life of Jesus.

JESUS was looking around the table, which boasted no lamb, although it was the feast before the Passover.

"Tonight," he said, "I am become the lamb."

The disciples, Mary saw, were more than ever mystified. She stood unobtrusively in the shadow by the stairway entrance, her heart beating fast again, and anguished she knew not why. Perhaps there were things she could do to help in the service of the meal, but she could make no move toward the table. She was aware that something of solemn poignant import was transpiring.

Although the disciples had eaten, Jesus now broke more bread and lifting up his eyes in thanks, said: "Take, eat: this is my body."

Strange words, and stranger still the gloom which pressed into the room now, thick as fog. Again Mary felt that tearing at her throat of withheld sobs. Never—never before had she felt thus in the presence of Jesus of Nazareth. Could it be that he had had some terrible forewarning of disaster? It was true that for many months now the priests and Pharisees had been plotting against him. She remembered the proclamations posted after the resurrection of Lazarus, when the chief priests feared his swelling popularity. Anyone telling the whereabouts of Jesus of Nazareth to Annas and Caiaphas was to have thirty pieces of silver. Jesus had retired then into a city called Ephraim on the edge of the wilderness. Disguised so that none might follow her and discover where he dwelt, Mary had gone to him at intervals to bring what news there was. Once she had come upon him tending sheep on a hillside and his face had been calm as the countryside bordering the Jordan, and in his eyes the vision of skies. Picking up one of the little shaky-legged lambs, he had held it in his arms lovingly, and said what he had just now spoken to the disciples: "I am become the lamb." He had talked to her about scriptural prophecies, but she had understood little of what he said, for her heart was heavy, fearing for his safety. On the way to Ephraim she had torn down all the proclamations she could find concerning the reward for Jesus' capture. She told him this, but he only smiled, saying: "My time is not yet come."

Relief had flooded her heart, hearing that. "My time is not yet come." But now—now was his time come? Nay, she would not believe it. Was not the power of one who could raise the dead, four days entombed, sufficient to conquer any mortal malice? Had not Jesus said: "I and my Father are one"? Yea, despite the hatred and plotting of the chief priests, the Pharisees and jealous scribes, the Master would, must, be victorious.

Jesus had taken the wine jug now and was filling the cups of the eleven. "This is my blood of the new testament shed for the remission of the sins of many." Silently the cups were passed to each in turn. Many hands trembled, Mary saw, spilling the wine. In the face of every man was the dark print of bewildered fear and sorrow. Seeing this, her own inexplicable despair increased.

Jesus said, his eyes going tenderly from face to face as if he, younger than many of his disciples, were a father and they confused children to whom only maturity could bring proper knowledge: "Drink you all of it."

Putting down his cup, Jesus lifted his eyes to heaven, "The time has come when the Son of man must be glorified. I tell you, I will not drink of the fruit of the wine until I drink it anew with you in my Father's kingdom."

Slow tears were falling from the eyes of John, glittering briefly in the moonlight pouring through the east window of the room. Watching, Mary stood motionless. Young Mark had long since gone down the stairs, but she had hardly been conscious of his going.

Again, Jesus' voice: "Little children, yet a little while I am with you. You shall seek me and shall not find me: and as I told the Jews, Whither I go, you cannot come; so I say to you now likewise."

Peter leaned across the table and said with loud, rebellious insistence: "Master, where are you going? Wherever you go, there will I go, also."

Jesus smiled affectionately. "Whither I go, you cannot follow me now; but you shall follow me afterwards."

"But, Master, why cannot I follow you now? I will lay down my life for your sake." His tone was strained, but full of courage.

Jesus took up his cup, empty now, and looked for a long moment into the bottom. Then he raised his eyes, and in them was stark, clear discernment.

"Will you indeed lay down your life for my sake, Peter? Verily, verily, I say unto you the cock shall not crow, until you have thrice denied me."

Peter's eyes went wide with hurt. "Never, Master!" With one hand, he brushed away tears which glistened suddenly upon his brown hard cheeks.

The next words Jesus spoke took some of the ache from Mary's throat.

"Let not your heart be troubled: you believe in God, believe also in me. In my Father's house are many mansions: if it were not so, I would have told you. I go to prepare a place for you. And if I go and prepare a place for you, I will come again, and receive you unto myself; that where I am, there you may be also."

Now he spoke, thought Mary, as of old. With courage and with confidence.

"And whither I go you know, and the way you know."

Thomas frowned. "Lord, we don't know whither you go; and how can we know the way?"

Jesus' voice was clear and firm. "I am the way, the truth, and the life: no man comes to the Father, except by me."

Philip said eagerly: "Master, show us the Father."

Surprise and grief mingled on the Master's countenance. "Have I been so long time with you, Philip, and yet have you not known me? He that has seen me has seen the Father; and why then do you say, Show us the Father?"

Philip dropped his eyes, although the rebuke was gentle. His hands gripped the table tensely.

"Don't you understand that I am in the Father and the Father in me? Indeed, the very words I speak unto you, I speak not of myself, and the Father dwelling in me does the works."

Silence for a time. And the white April moon, a little past the full, illumined the dimly lighted chamber. Jesus' eyes were on it as he spoke again. "The prince of this world comes, but has nothing in me."

Mary pondered the words. Whether he meant Herod or the authority of Rome, she did not know. Perhaps it was neither, but Satan. If so, it was true that in the mind of Jesus of Nazareth, Satan could find nothing with which to work. He had no foothold there.

Jesus said gravely: "Greater love has no man than this, that he lay down his life for his friends."

James, son of Zebedee, cried chokingly: "Master!"

Peter hid his face, and Mary saw tears trickle through his calloused fingers. Andrew and Thomas were weeping, too.

The songs of the pilgrims, gathered in Jerusalem for the Passover, echoed from all parts of town. Jesus was silent as if listening to the chanting voices.

But Simon the Zealot, who all this while had remained speechless save for his burning eyes which vividly expressed his thoughts, cried out now: "Lord, do not desert us!"

Jesus said plainly: "I tell you the truth. It is necessary that I go away."

"Nay, Master!" protested James the Less.

"If I go not away," said the Nazarene gently, "the Comforter will not come unto you; but if I depart, I will send Him unto you." The moonlight streaming through the window made a nimbus about his head.

Mary found herself upon her knees in the attitude of prayer—found, too, that her tears were falling slowly, one by one upon the floor.

"I have yet many things to say unto you," went on the Master, "but you cannot bear them now."

He had but to look at each face, torn by grief, fear, bewilderment, to know that there was not strength enough yet in these men to bear any further load of agonized knowledge, Mary thought. In herself, too, she was aware of frightened weakness.

Jesus' voice roused her again from the gloom which threatened to stop her ears and blind her eyes. She was possessed with the feeling of necessity. She must remember to treasure up these words for the future. . . .

"Howbeit when he, the Spirit of truth is come, he will guide you into all truth: for he shall not speak of himself; but whatsoever he shall hear, that shall he speak: and he will show you things to come."

No sound in the room but the sobbing of Thomas, and the torn breathing of the other disciples. The olive oil lamps were burning low. It was time, Mary told herself, to go below for the cruse to refill them. Her mind, blown like a bird in a windstorm, fastened with relief on something solid. A duty to be performed. A service for the Master.

She got to her feet, her limbs still trembling, and felt her way to the stairs. She was both loath to leave and eager to be gone. Halfway descended, she heard Jesus begin again to speak, but what he was saying she was too far away by then to hear.

Only the mother of Mark was in the kitchen, and her back was toward Mary. Mary was grateful. She wanted no one to be alarmed by the pattern of anguish upon her face. In haste, she found the cruse, stepping lightly to the shelf where it stood. When Mark's mother became aware of her presence, Mary had turned back, one foot upon the stair.

"Is there anything the Master needs?" asked the older woman.

Mary's throat hurt. Is there anything the Master needs? Dear Father in heaven! Food, drink, apparel, these things could be supplied. But what he needed now, no man could give him. From his own inner store he must provide himself. But that secret place held all the treasure of earth and heaven.

She swallowed. "He has everything, I believe."

Mary climbed again. Up, up the steps. Led by a voice speaking with sorrowful assurance.

"Verily, verily, I say unto you, That you shall weep and lament, but the world shall rejoice: and you shall be sorrowful, but your sorrow shall be turned into joy."

Joy! Spoke he in this hour of joy? When, but a little while ago, he had foretold his own doom? When his disciples wept? When he had said plainly he must leave them? Surely it was a contradiction. Then Mary remembered. "The flesh profits nothing. It is the Spirit that quickens." Did he then weep for the suffering of the flesh, while at the same moment rejoicing in the everlasting strength of the truth which he so oft declared made free?

His voice faded, though she could tell that he still spoke. When she reached the room, she found that Jesus had left his place at the table, and was standing before the window.

When Mary entered with the cruse of oil, he turned and faced his disciples, huddled like sheep where he had left them.

"These things I have spoken unto you, that in me you might have peace. In the world you shall have tribulation: but be of good cheer; I have overcome the world."

One by one the grief-stricken men lifted their heads. Jesus, his hands clasped behind him, lifted his eyes again to the starry spring sky.

"Father, the hour is come: glorify Your son, that Your son also may glorify You: as You have given him power over all flesh, that he should give eternal life to as many as You have given him."

Eternal life! Mary stood still. He was still speaking, but now she heard not his words for joyful relief. Eternal life! He would not leave them, then. Surely the giver of everlasting life died not. What she had feared, what they all who loved him had feared, would not, after all, come to pass.

She was still standing and the lamps were still unfilled.

Jesus said: "Let us sing an hymn."

It was their custom to conclude a meal with singing. One by one, the eleven straightened. John's voice was lifted first after the Master's, trembling a little, but growing stronger. Then Peter's. Then James'. Soon they were all joined in the harmony of praise, a chorus of untrained, yet well-blended voices. As they sang, Mary saw, strain lessened.

When they had finished, there was silence. Moments stretched long and taut.

Then the Master lifted his hand.

"Arise, let us go hence."

GOD'S PEACE IN THE HEART

Leo Tolstoi

This is one of the many passages of *Resurrection* concerned with our reliance, not on our own understanding, but upon the divine wisdom. At the peak of a storm the hero Nekhlyudov suddenly realizes the true way to inner peace.

... Nekhlyudov sat down on the doorstep, and inhaling the warm air, balmy with the strong fragrance of fresh birch leaves, he gazed for a long time into the gradually darkening garden. He listened to the thumping of the mill-wheel, to the nightingales, and some other bird that whistled monotonously in a bush close by ... in the east, behind the barn, gleamed the light of the rising moon; and heat lightning, with more and more frequency, began to illumine the tumble-down house and the blooming, over-grown garden. There was thunder in the distance, and a black cloud spread over a good part of the sky ...

The bright moon, now almost full, rose above the barn. Dark shadows deepened across the yard, but the iron roof of the neglected house shone bright.

Nekhlyudov recalled how in the garden at Kuzminskoye he had meditated on his life and tried to decide what he was going to do; and he recalled how perplexed he had become, how incapable of making any decision, so manifold were the difficulties each problem had presented. He now asked himself the same questions, and was astonished how simple it all was. It was simple because he no longer thought of what would happen to himself; he thought only of what he ought to do. And strangely enough, while he could not decide what he had to do for himself, he knew beyond any doubt what he had to do for others. ...

The black cloud now blotted out the whole sky; lightning flickered vividly across the yard and the old house with its dilapidated porches;

the thunder crashed overhead. The birds had all stopped singing, but the leaves began to rustle and the storm-wind reached the step where he was sitting. One drop splashed down, and another; then they came down in a torrent. . . . Nekhlyudov went into the house.

"Yes, yes," he thought, "the work which our life accomplishes, the whole of this work and its true meaning is not, and can never be, intelligible to me. . . . Why should my friend die, and I remain alive? . . . For what purpose was Katyusha born? To what end was my madness? Why did this war come about? And why later did I lead such a dissolute life? To answer these questions, to understand the whole of the Master's work is not within my power; but to do his will, which is written down in my conscience, that is entirely within my power; that much I know with certainty. And when I do his will, then assuredly I have God's peace in my heart."

THE WAR YEARS

James Hilton

In *Good-bye, Mr. Chips,* James Hilton brings to life a lovable English schoolmaster whose eccentric ways earn him the affection and loyalty of all the boys at Brookfield. The war years of 1914–18 found Mr. Chips teaching Latin, serving as Acting Head of the school for the duration, and making his own special contribution to his pupils' character and spirit.

THE War years.

The first shock, and then the first optimism. The Battle of the Marne, the Russian steam-roller, Kitchener.

"Do you think it will last long, sir?"

Chips, questioned as he watched the first trial game of the season, gave quite a cheery answer. He was, like thousands of others, hopelessly wrong; but, unlike thousands of others, he did not afterward conceal the fact. "We ought to have—um—finished it—um—by Christ-

mas. The Germans are already beaten. But why? Are you thinking of
—um—joining up, Forrester?"

Joke—because Forrester was the smallest new boy Brookfield had
ever had—about four feet high above his muddy football boots. (But
not so much a joke, when you came to think of it afterward; for he was
killed in 1918—shot down in flames over Cambrai.) But one didn't
guess what lay ahead. It seemed tragically sensational when the first
Old Brookfieldian was killed in action—in September. Chips thought,
when that news came: A hundred years ago boys from this school
were fighting *against* the French. Strange, in a way, that the sacrifices
of one generation should so cancel out those of another. He tried to
express this to Blades, the Head of School House; but Blades, eighteen
years old and already in training for a cadetship, only laughed. What
had all that history stuff to do with it, anyhow? Just old Chips with one
of his queer ideas, that's all.

1915. Armies clenched in deadlock from the sea to Switzerland. The
Dardanelles. Gallipoli. Military camps springing up quite near Brookfield; soldiers using the playing fields for sports and training; swift
developments of Brookfield O.T.C. Most of the younger masters gone
or in uniform. Every Sunday night, in the Chapel after evening service,
Chatteris read out the names of old boys killed, together with short
biographies. Very moving; but Chips, in the black pew under the
gallery, thought: They are only names to him; he doesn't see their
faces as I do. . . .

1916. . . . The Somme Battle. Twenty-three names read out one
Sunday evening.

Toward the close of that catastrophic July, Chatteris talked to Chips
one afternoon at Mrs. Wickett's. He was overworked and overworried
and looked very ill. "To tell you the truth, Chipping, I'm not having too
easy a time here. I'm thirty-nine, you know, and unmarried, and lots of
people seem to think they know what I ought to do. Also, I happen to
be diabetic, and couldn't pass the blindest M.O., but I don't see why I
should pin a medical certificate on my front door."

Chips hadn't known anything about this; it was a shock to him, for
he liked Chatteris.

The latter continued: "You see how it is. Ralston filled the place up
with young men—all very good, of course—but now most of them
have joined up and the substitutes are pretty dreadful, on the whole.
They poured ink down a man's neck in prep one night last week—silly
fool—got hysterical. I have to take classes myself, take prep for fools

like that, work till midnight every night, and get cold-shouldered as a slacker on top of everything. I can't stand it much longer. If things don't improve next term I shall have a breakdown."

"I do sympathize with you," Chips said.

"I hoped you would. And that brings me to what I came here to ask you. Briefly, my suggestion is that—if you felt equal to it and would care to—how about coming back here for a while? You look pretty fit, and, of course, you know all the ropes. I don't mean a lot of hard work for you—you needn't take anything strenuously—just a few odd jobs here and there, as you choose. What I'd like you for more than anything else is not for the actual work you'd do—though that, naturally, would be very valuable—but for your help in other ways— in just *belonging* here. There's nobody ever been more popular than you were, and are still—you'd help to hold things together if there were any danger of them flying to bits. And perhaps there *is* that danger. . . ."

Chips answered, breathlessly and with a holy joy in his heart: "I'll come. . . ."

He still kept on his rooms with Mrs. Wickett; indeed, he still lived there; but every morning, about half-past ten, he put on his coat and muffler and crossed the road to the School. He felt very fit, and the actual work was not taxing. Just a few forms in Latin and Roman History—the old lessons—even the old pronunciation. The same joke about the Lex Canuleia—there was a new generation that had not heard it, and he was absurdly gratified by the success it achieved. He felt a little like a music-hall favorite returning to the boards after a positively last appearance.

They all said how marvelous it was that he knew every boy's name and face so quickly. They did not guess how closely he had kept in touch from across the road.

He was a grand success altogether. In some strange way he did, and they all knew and felt it, help things. For the first time in his life he felt *necessary*—and necessary to something that was nearest his heart. There is no sublimer feeling in the world, and it was his at last.

He made new jokes, too—about the O.T.C. and the food-rationing system and the anti-air-raid blinds that had to be fitted on all the windows. There was a mysterious kind of rissole that began to appear on the School menu on Mondays, and Chips called it *abhorrendum*— "meat to be abhorred." The story went round—heard Chips's latest?

Chatteris fell ill during the winter of '17, and again, for the second time in his life, Chips became Acting Head of Brookfield. Then in April Chatteris died, and the Governors asked Chips if he would carry on "for the duration." He said he would, if they would refrain from appointing him officially. From that last honor, within his reach at last, he shrank instinctively, feeling himself in so many ways unequal to it. He said to Rivers: "You see, I'm not a young man and I don't want people to—um—expect a lot from me. I'm like all these new colonels and majors you see everywhere—just a war-time fluke. A ranker—that's all I am really."

1917. 1918. Chips lived through it all. He sat in the headmaster's study every morning, handling problems, dealing with plaints and requests. Out of vast experience had emerged a kindly, gentle confidence in himself. To keep a sense of proportion, that was the main thing. So much of the world was losing it; as well keep it where it had, or ought to have, a congenial home.

On Sundays in Chapel it was he who now read out the tragic list, and sometimes it was seen and heard that he was in tears over it. Well, why not, the School said; he was an old man; they might have despised anyone else for the weakness.

One day he got a letter from Switzerland, from friends there; it was heavily censored, but conveyed some news. On the following Sunday, after the names and biographies of old boys, he paused a moment and then added:—

"Those few of you who were here before the War will remember Max Staefel, the German master. He was in Germany, visiting his home, when war broke out. He was popular while he was here, and made many friends. Those who knew him will be sorry to hear that he was killed last week, on the Western Front."

He was a little pale when he sat down afterward, aware that he had done something unusual. He had consulted nobody about it, anyhow; no one else could be blamed. Later, outside the Chapel, he heard an argument:—

"On the Western Front, Chips said. Does that mean he was fighting for the Germans?"

"I suppose it does."

"Seems funny, then, to read his name out with all the others. After all, he was an *enemy*."

"Oh, just one of Chips's ideas, I expect. The old boy still has 'em."

Chips, in his room again, was not displeased by the comment. Yes, he still had 'em—those ideas of dignity and generosity that were be-coming increasingly rare in a frantic world. And he thought: Brookfield will take them, too, from me; but it wouldn't from anyone else.

Once, asked for his opinion of bayonet practice being carried on near the cricket pavilion, he answered, with that lazy, slightly asthmatic intonation that had been so often and so extravagantly imitated: "It seems—to me—umph—a very vulgar way of killing people."

The yarn was passed on and joyously appreciated—how Chips had told some big brass hat from the War Office that bayonet fighting was vulgar. Just like Chips. And they found an adjective for him—an ad-jective just beginning to be used: he was pre-War.

And once, on a night of full moonlight, the air-raid warning was given while Chips was taking his lower fourth in Latin. The guns began almost instantly, and, as there was plenty of shrapnel falling about outside, it seemed to Chips that they might just as well stay where they were, on the ground floor of School House. It was pretty solidly built and made as good a dugout as Brookfield could offer; and as for a direct hit, well, they could not expect to survive that, wherever they were.

So he went on with his Latin, speaking a little louder amid the reverberating crashes of the guns and the shrill whine of anti-aircraft shells. Some of the boys were nervous; few were able to be attentive. He said, gently: "It may possibly seem to you, Robertson—at this par-ticular moment in the world's history—umph—that the affairs of Cæsar in Gaul some two thousand years ago—are—umph—of some-what secondary importance—and that—umph—the irregular conjuga-tion of the verb *tollo* is—umph—even less important still. But believe me—umph—my dear Robertson—that is not really the case." Just then there came a particularly loud explosion—quite near. "You cannot—umph—judge the importance of things—umph—by the noise they make. Oh dear me, no." A little chuckle. "And these things—umph—that have mattered—for thousands of years—are not going to be—snuffed out—because some stink merchant—in his laboratory—invents a new kind of mischief." Titters of nervous laughter; for Buffles, the pale, lean, and medically unfit science master, was nicknamed the Stink Merchant. Another explosion—nearer still. "Let us—um—resume our work. If it is fate that we are soon to be—umph—interrupted, let us be found employing ourselves in something—umph—really appro-priate. Is there anyone who will volunteer to construe?"

Maynard, chubby, dauntless, clever, and impudent, said: "I will, sir."

"Very good. Turn to page forty and begin at the bottom line."

The explosions still continued deafeningly; the whole building shook as if it were being lifted off its foundations. Maynard found the page, which was some way ahead, and began, shrilly:—

"*Genus hoc erat pugnae*—this was the kind of fight—*quo se Germani exercuerant*—in which the Germans busied themselves. Oh, sir, that's good—that's really very funny indeed, sir—one of your very best——"

Laughing began, and Chips added: "Well—umph—you can see—now—that these dead languages—umph—can come to life again—sometimes—eh? Eh?"

Afterward they learned that five bombs had fallen in and around Brookfield, the nearest of them just outside the School grounds. Nine persons had been killed.

The story was told, retold, embellished. "The dear old boy never turned a hair. Even found some old tag to illustrate what was going on. Something in Cæsar about the way the Germans fought. You wouldn't think there were things like that in Cæsar, would you? And the way Chips laughed . . . you know the way he *does* laugh . . . the tears all running down his face . . . never seen him laugh so much. . . ."

He was a legend.

With his old and tattered gown, his walk that was just beginning to break into a stumble, his mild eyes peering over the steel-rimmed spectacles, and his quaintly humorous sayings, Brookfield would not have had an atom of him different.

November 11, 1918.

News came through in the morning; a whole holiday was decreed for the School, and the kitchen staff were implored to provide as cheerful a spread as war-time rationing permitted. There was much cheering and singing, and a bread fight across the Dining Hall. When Chips entered in the midst of the uproar there was an instant hush, and then wave upon wave of cheering; everyone gazed on him with eager, shining eyes, as on a symbol of victory. He walked to the dais, seeming as if he wished to speak; they made silence for him, but he shook his head after a moment, smiled, and walked away again.

It had been a damp, foggy day, and the walk across the quadrangle to the Dining Hall had given him a chill. The next day he was in bed with bronchitis, and stayed there till after Christmas. But already, on that night of November 11, after his visit to the Dining Hall, he had sent in his resignation to the Board of Governors.

When school reassembled after the holidays he was back at Mrs. Wickett's. At his own request there were no more farewells or presentations, nothing but a handshake with his successor and the word "acting" crossed out on official stationery. The "duration" was over.

GOD IS LOVE

A. S. M. Hutchinson

In this brief selection from *He Looked for a City,* John Brecque summarizes his working philosophy of life. Despite disappointments and vicissitudes in his thirty years of service in a country parish, his faith that "God is love" remains an unfailing refuge.

IT WAS his simplicity that caused him (John Brecque) to earn the love of what were perhaps the "right" people. Jokes are subtleties of thought. He could not see them because he had no subtlety. He was not ingenious. He was ingenuous. When he delivered his text in his pulpit he would invariably, before he began to expound it, pause a moment, smiling down upon his people. He had only one dogma, that God was love; that love, when all-embracing, was God.

At least in their simplicity of thought and diction all his sermons created among those to whom he ministered as it were a little heart of response within a husk of indifference. At St. Luke's he was seeking to serve God among a social class unrepresented in his previous experience in Orders. In the Fields at Brodham his people had been shabby, at Knipstone rough. Here he found himself among a people (above the Banks) of means; some of greater, some of less, but none without. They were leisured. Their chief preoccupation was to fill their time.

The emptiness of these people of Upton Springs was, in fact, a spiritual emptiness. Hope Hubbard, with those gleaming eyes of his observing it among his own following from his own pulpit of St. Monica's, with that pungent tongue of his scourged it. The vicar of St. Luke's, seeing good, and only good, in all, felt towards his sufferers from it as feels a fond parent towards the child whom illness keeps in bed. There was the sunshine outside. Here was the sufferer unable to enjoy it. Draw back the curtains, open wide the casements, wheel the cot to the window. Have love for all in your heart. Give entry thus to Christ. Realize then the surging within you of His strength.

THE DEDICATION

Paul I. Wellman

John Carlisle, an ascetic young minister whose story is told in *The Chain,* successfully ran the gamut of materialistic obstacles and petty parish politics in the town of Jericho, Kansas. In "The Dedication" the whole community unites in honoring a man who never wavered from his faith—who lost his life to live again in eternity.

IN THE CHANCEL the Bishop began the prayer of dedication, raising his hand toward the rood beam.

"*. . . Vouchsafe, we beseech thee, that this memorial which we now dedicate may be enduring witness before all thy people of the faithful service of thy servant John Carlisle, whom thou hast seen fit, in thine infinite wisdom, to take into the glory of thy nearer Presence . . .*"

Gilda sat, with her hand in the curve of her husband's arm, in an attitude which bespoke a mood surrendered to memory.

She remembered how Carlisle looked the last time she saw him, when his spirit had departed his frail body. He had been conscious only a little time the evening after the operation, long enough to smile at Gilda and Murray, and to whisper a few words.

"It makes me happy . . . to see you two together . . ."

He thanked Murray, and said: "You have become a dedicated doctor and as such you will know and follow the precepts and example of the Great Physician . . ."

And to Gilda: "My dear . . . the world will be richer for your having lived in it . . ."

His last concern in this life was for his humble friends, Pawnee and Big Hoob. He learned with sorrow of Pawnee's death that afternoon.

"There was so much in him that was good," he said.

And of Big Hoob: "Tell him to comfort himself. Death does not matter when the peace of Eternity is before you. He will learn to live on his own strength."

Then forgetfulness came, his eyes closed, and his soul passed on to the home it had so ardently desired.

Had he failed? He had accomplished in his life but little, it seemed, of what he had set out to do. People will still be people, as the Bishop once had said, and one of the difficulties with humanity is that it has human nature.

Gilda looked down upon him. He seemed asleep, and his face, with the white bandages about his head, had the appearance of a very spiritual, very fervent, very selfless monk of some strange white hooded order. Upon it was the fullness of peace which often is attained before the Great Change, as if his spirit already were bravely seeking the comradeship of heaven.

Once she had felt dry and weary, as if she were an old woman who had passed through a life of suffering until acute feeling could no longer exist in her. Then this strange man had given her the inspiration to live again, to know joy, to feel love, to praise God for her happiness.

Because even in the subduing thought that he was gone she was not unhappy, at least with the unhappiness of despair. An inherent fearlessness of character always had been part of her; now she trusted, and in the trust wherein John Carlisle had died happily she felt the completeness of a nature clothed in impregnable armor, armor which would uphold and protect her spirit for all time to come.

She thought of the chain which would be with him in death as it had been in life. Murray's words returned to her, when he told her of what a chain represented to him: *Life, I suppose. Events and people, separate, yet linked together . . .*

Sometimes Murray's perception was wonderfully delicate and profound, even poetic.

Carlisle's chain was like life, his expression of it, and of his soul. The perfected circle, which Murray had refused to permit the doctors to cut, was a symbol of Eternity itself, which has no beginning and no end. Once she had been unwilling to consider the fundamental meanings of things, because within her nature was that which shrank from a full acceptance of the spiritual. Now she accepted and saw clearly.

In the chain was beauty as well as cruelty, the triumph of the soul over the body. All at once it seemed to her that it held the key to the great Overscheme. She had Murray, and the splendor of love; and she had just seen the emptiness of death's victory, which has no power over the soul. All things fell into order, rounded to a flawless circle. She felt the completeness and beauty of a realization of supreme perfection.

Gilda beheld the calmness of Carlisle's face at rest, and it seemed to her there need be no tears in this presence. She thought of his prayer:

"Life is eternal; and love is immortal, and death is only a horizon; and a horizon is nothing save the limit of our sight . . ."

A horizon . . . where earth meets the wondrous downcurve of heaven; beautiful, because it is not an ending but a promise.

Upon his face was a smile, like that of one who dreams and knows his dream will one day be fulfilled.

She felt Murray take her hand. Together they went out of the room, and left him with his constant lovely dream.

RECONCILIATION

Margaret Landon

Present-day Bangkok is the setting for *Never Dies the Dream,* the story of a teaching missionary, India Severn. Among her many problems is the adaptation of her pupils and associates to new concepts of Christianity, education, and Western culture. This selection exemplifies the most basic reconciliation of all those that she tried to establish at Jasmine Hall School.

RATHER DIFFIDENTLY as the days went on, Angela began to ask questions that concerned India herself, where she had grown up, where she had gone to school, what her childish interests had been. Like her other questions, it seemed more than a device to fill empty hours. She was piecing together the pattern of Jasmine Hall to satisfy some need within herself.

India, who rarely thought about her childhood, obligingly brought out of her memory incidents she had not called to mind in years. What had she worn to dancing school? Well, high-buttoned shoes, of course, and a red velvet dress with a lace collar, and an ermine coat her father had given her. How foolish for a child of ten to have an ermine coat, but her father had been like that.

Had she been an only child? Yes. Her one brother died in infancy. Was her mother pretty? Very beautiful and very gay, the despair of her plainer daughter. Everyone had loved her mother. She always remembered her as surrounded by people. When her father made money they gave dinner parties for twenty or more. She could see her mother now, dressed in satins and velvets and jewels. Then, when things went badly, the jewels disappeared, and there were small suppers, but people seemed to come just the same.

What had her father been like? A big man who tumbled and teased her and bought her expensive gifts. Once she had had a doll from Paris with a trunkful of clothes, and another time he had given her a dollhouse like a mansion, furnished throughout, with a family of dolls to live in it. He had made and lost several fortunes on the grain exchange. The family was always up or down. Perhaps that was why she never worried about money.

Had she been a good child? Not too difficult, except for her habit of bringing home all the cats and dogs in the neighborhood. The only time she remembered causing a scandal was when the boy sitting behind her in school dipped the ends of her curls into his inkwell. The ink had dripped onto her favorite dress of gray nun's veiling with a white embroidered collar that her mother had brought her from New York. She had stood up and hit him over the head with her geography until the teacher pulled her away. Then she had wept for the dress until the school sent her home. Ralph, that was his name. A horrid boy! He'd grown up to be president of a large bank in Chicago.

Had her family objected when she decided to become a missionary? Not really objected. They were a religious family. Her mother was an Episcopalian and her father a Presbyterian. She thought they were more troubled when she told them that she had broken her engagement to the boy who had been her constant companion since she was fifteen. But they had always let her have her own way. They hadn't been happy about her determination to go to college either, but they had yielded, and in the end she thought they understood.

"And so you never married?"

"And so I never married." India repeated the words noncommittally.

Angela felt the closing of a door and changed the subject. "How did you happen to choose Siam?"

"When I was a junior in college I heard Dr. Eugene Dunlap speak at chapel. He'd been a missionary in Siam since shortly after the Civil War. He was a very great and simple man, and what he said impressed me."

"There must have been more to it than that."

"Yes, of course there was. I'd always had a longing to be of use, but that isn't the whole story either. My religious experience had deepened in college until sharing it seemed the most important thing in life."

Angela pondered this for a moment. "Isn't it almost impertinent to try to win other races to our religion?"

"Not unless you believe that truth and beauty have national boundaries."

"But what is truth?"

India looked at her strangely, hearing Pilate's question on her lips, then answered by quotation: *"Jesus saith unto him, I am the way, the truth, and the life: no man cometh unto the Father, but by me."*

"You believe Christianity true, then, and all other religions false?"

"Perhaps not so much false as shadows, and God the substance."

Then feeling the explanation inadequate, India went on, after a search for words: "I suppose the basic problem in all life is the problem of good and evil. The knowledge of what constitutes good and what constitutes evil is a universal possession, at least in some degree. It isn't the knowing that's difficult, it's the doing. *For the good that I would I do not: but the evil which I would not, that I do.* We of the Christian communion believe that the conflict can be resolved only when man is reconciled to God through Christ. It's the possibility of reconciliation and the resulting power for good that we try to share with all mankind, not just the knowledge of what is good and what is evil. Put that way, does it still seem an impertinence?"

"No," Angela said slowly, but India could not be sure whether she spoke from conviction or courtesy. "But how can you prove anything like that to people who don't believe in God?"

"How many things can be proved, outside of mathematical equations and some physical facts? I can testify to my own experience of the power of God in the human heart. I wouldn't try to do more. Most people believe in a Supreme Being anyway."

Angela hesitated. "What about modern science and the Bible?"

"Well, what about it?"

"Doesn't it disprove the Old Testament stories like the creation?"

"That can be argued, but it's not a particularly profitable argument. So I'll beg the question and answer with the words of—wasn't it Mark Twain?—who said: It isn't the parts of the Bible I can't understand that trouble me, but the parts I understand too well. *Love thy neighbor as thyself. Pray for them which despitefully use you, and persecute you. Forgive us our trespasses, As we forgive those who trespass against us.*"

"Yes, but look at the way some Christians behave."

"Granted. Those commands are often honored in the breach, and yet outside of the Christian church where do you find the stubborn conviction that the poor, the sick, the filthy, and the leper are worthy of reverence in the form of care because man was made in the image of God? Hospitals, schools, all the attempts of our imperfect civilization to solve the problems of the individual come out of the concept of man's importance as something more than an animal. For if God so loved the world that He sent His only begotten Son into the world for us, then we must be worth something in His sight. And by that measure we're worth something to men who follow His teachings. Strip us of this valuation and what is left? Besides, not all men fail to live up to the standards of their faith. I know many whom I honor for their service to mankind, and their lives are a testimony to me of the truth of what they believe."

It was Angela who spoke next, and the simplicity of her words silenced India.

"As yours is to me," she said.

The Way of the Cross

~~~~~~

INTO THY HANDS

Sholem Asch

~~~~~~

Following *The Apostle* and *The Nazarene,* Asch's *Mary* brings fresh color to the story of the birth and growth of Christianity. Here the universal theme of a mother's love for her son reaches new glory in the drama of Mary's love for Jesus.

GOLGOTHA was quiet again. The crowd that had followed the condemned man to his execution to see if he was indeed the Messiah had wearied of waiting for a miracle and had dispersed at last. The sixth hour was approaching; the sun stood at its zenith and it was almost time to bring the paschal offering into the Temple.

The cross against which Yeshua was nailed was somewhat taller than the other two. Of the three bodies, Yeshua's alone still showed symptoms of life. Robbed of its garment, it looked pale, almost white under the sun. It writhed briefly with a snake-like movement as Yeshua tried to straighten himself on his impaled feet. Blood ran in trickles from his scalp where plaited thorns wreathed his black hair and dried against his sharp, protruding ribs. His thin arms, transfixed to the crossbar, sagged from the weight of his body as it strained from the cross. The soldiers, when they stripped him, had left only the four-cornered ritual shirt whose fringes could be seen to flutter lightly, pointing the breeze.

It was all silent now. The Roman quaternion that had been detailed to this crucifixion were squatting away at some distance. They were casting lots for Yeshua's cloak that lay before them, flecked with incrusted gore. Their captain every now and then glanced at the crucified one to see if he would not produce a miracle at this late hour. The sight of the white body stirred points of anxiety in his eyes and, averting his head, he returned to his brooding.

On another part of the hill, a good distance from the site of the crosses, a woman in black lay on her face, whimpering to herself. Under Yeshua's cross stood Rabbi Nicodemon, Yeshua's childhood friend. Aged and gray before his time, he swayed back and forth in prayer, a *tallith* pulled over his head. Again and again his hands reached out toward Yeshua's body; his inflamed eyes, which had cried much, scanned Yeshua's face, and his lips murmured endlessly:

"Yeshua, holy man of God, give us a sign, forsake us not in our darkness. Tell us who you are."

The other Jew with Nicodemon was the rich Joseph of Arimathea. His handsome head with its dark fringe of beard was raised toward Yeshua. Sorrow and veneration lay heavy on his features, and he said:

"By the living God, they have killed him for whom we waited all our days!"

And Yeshua, as if he had heard the words, murmured in a dying voice:

"Father, forgive them, for they know not what they do."

And when Yeshua had spoken these words, behold, a somber cloud shaped like a giant fist over Jerusalem, and suddenly a midnight darkness over all the earth, and this although the day had not begun to wane.

And then it was that a small group of three was seen ascending the slope. In the middle went an old, bowed woman, draped in black, and she was upheld on one side by a woman and on the other by a tall massive man clothed in a shroud-like sheet.

It was Miriam, coming to see the dying of her son. In obedience to his word, she had avoided seeing him while he fulfilled his ministry on earth. Now she was led by her sister, the faithful Mariama, who had come with Yeshua to the very foot of the cross, and by Jochanan, Yeshua's best-loved disciple, to see the visage of her son in the hour of his glory, even as he had foretold.

They approached with halting, shuffling steps till Miriam was face to face with her son. Then they retreated from her—but a little space only, lest she fall, being unsupported.

Miriam's eyes remained open. She saw the body of her son convulsing with pain, and she looked unblinking with large wounded eyes. This was the body she had held in her arms, that she had bathed and aneled, often and often since the day of his birth. Now she gazed at its bruises and lacerations, and the red welts where the soldiers' whips had struck.

She looked at his head. His hair which she had often smoothed with oil was dressed with his life's blood. It trickled steadily from his brow, and Miriam's eyes traced every stream to its gash. She looked up at his hands that had often lain in her own, and her glance followed the nails through his palms where the stigmata were beginning to fester.

She did not weep at the sight. The lines of her face were hard and set, as though the muscles had been arrested forever. Only her eyes were strangely dilated and the whites were shot with a red tracery of veins so that they seemed like open wounds.

At last her gaze met Yeshua's; imperceptibly, her lips began to move; lightly at first, then with a flying flutter; and, almost inaudibly, the words came with the tremor of her breath:

"Tinoki, tinoki, tinoki . . ."

The son's body winced on the cross. His ribs shifted under their skin; for one fleeting moment the muscles of his body tensed and Miriam caught his word:

"Emi!"

She swayed as if to fall. Strong arms held her from behind, and as her son's voice said, "Behold thy mother!" she fell back in Jochanan's embrace. And even then she did not close her eyes, but continued to meet the gaze of her child. She felt her life falling away, falling away like an old garment. A new life was entering her. She was no longer her own person only; she was one with her child. In his glance she was nailed with him to the rood. Her body burned with his pain, the sting of gall and vinegar was on her tongue, and as her consciousness fled into darkness, she heard these words,—

"Into Thy hands I commend my spirit"—and knew not whether he or she had spoken them.

ON THE DAY OF THE CRUCIFIXION

Leonid Andreyev

In times of stress, petty annoyances often serve to distract the individual from awareness of the cosmic events taking place before his eyes. For Leonid Andreyev's hero the immediate physical pain of his own toothache transcends the soul-searing drama of the crucifixion.

ON THAT terrible day, when the universal injustice was committed and Jesus Christ was crucified in Golgotha among robbers—on that day, from early morning, Ben-Tovit, a tradesman of Jerusalem, suffered from an unendurable toothache. His toothache had commenced on the day before, toward evening; at first his right jaw started to pain him and one tooth, the one right next the wisdom tooth, seemed to have risen somewhat, and when his tongue touched the tooth, he felt a slightly painful sensation. After supper, however, his toothache had passed, and Ben-Tovit had forgotten all about it—he had made a profitable deal on that day, had bartered an old donkey for a young, strong one, so he was very cheerful and paid no heed to any ominous signs.

And he slept very soundly. But just before daybreak something began to disturb him, as if some one were calling him on a very important matter, and when Ben-Tovit awoke angrily, his teeth were aching, aching openly and maliciously, causing him an acute, drilling pain. And he could no longer understand whether it was only the same tooth that had ached on the previous day, or whether others had joined that tooth; Ben-Tovit's entire mouth and his head were filled with terrible sensations of pain, as though he had been forced to chew thousands of sharp, red-hot nails. He took some water into his mouth from an earthen jug—for a minute the acuteness of the pain subsided, his teeth twitched and swayed like a wave, and this sensation was even pleasant as compared with the other.

Ben-Tovit lay down again, recalled his new donkey, and thought how happy he would have been if not for his toothache, and he wanted to fall asleep. But the water was warm, and five minutes later his tooth-ache began to rage more severely than ever; Ben-Tovit sat up in his bed and swayed back and forth like a pendulum. His face became wrinkled and seemed to have shrunk, and a drop of cold perspiration was hanging on his nose, which had turned pale from his sufferings. Thus, swaying back and forth and groaning for pain, he met the first rays of the sun, which was destined to see Golgotha and the three crosses, and grow dim from horror and sorrow.

Ben-Tovit was a good and kind man, who hated any injustice, but when his wife awoke he said many unpleasant things to her, opening his mouth with difficulty, and he complained that he was left alone, like a jackal, to groan and writhe for pain. His wife met the undeserved reproaches patiently, for she knew that they came not from an angry heart—and she brought him numerous good remedies; rats' litter to be applied to his cheek, some strong liquid in which a scorpion was preserved, and a real chip of the tablets that Moses had broken. He began to feel a little better from the rats' litter, but not for long, also from the liquid and the stone, but the pain returned each time with renewed intensity.

During the moments of rest Ben-Tovit consoled himself with the thought of the little donkey, and he dreamed of him, and when he felt worse he moaned, scolded his wife, and threatened to dash his head against a rock if the pain should not subside. He kept pacing back and forth on the flat roof of his house from one corner to the other, feeling ashamed to come close to the side facing the street, for his head was tied around with a kerchief, like that of a woman. Several times children came running to him and told him hastily about Jesus of Nazareth. Ben-Tovit paused, listened to them for a while, his face wrinkled, but then he stamped his foot angrily and chased them away. He was a kind man and he loved children, but now he was angry at them for bothering him with trifles.

It was disagreeable to him that a large crowd had gathered in the street and on the neighboring roofs, doing nothing and looking curiously at Ben-Tovit, who had his head tied around with a kerchief like a woman. He was about to go down, when his wife said to him:

"Look, they are leading robbers there. Perhaps that will divert you."

"Let me alone. Don't you see how I am suffering?" Ben-Tovit answered angrily.

But there was a vague promise in his wife's words that there might be a relief for his toothache, so he walked over to the parapet unwillingly. Bending his head on one side, closing one eye, and supporting his cheek with his hand, his face assumed a squeamish, weeping expression, and he looked down to the street.

On the narrow street, going uphill, an enormous crowd was moving forward in disorder, covered with dust and shouting uninterruptedly. In the middle of the crowd walked the criminals, bending down under the weight of their crosses, and over them the scourges of the Roman soldiers were wriggling about like black snakes. One of the men, he of the long light hair, in a torn blood-stained cloak, stumbled over a stone which was thrown under his feet, and he fell. The shouting grew louder, and the crowd, like colored sea water, closed in about the man on the ground. Ben-Tovit suddenly shuddered for pain; he felt as though some one had pierced a red-hot needle into his tooth and turned it there; he groaned and walked away from the parapet, angry and squeamishly indifferent.

"How they are shouting!" he said enviously, picturing to himself their wide-open mouths with strong, healthy teeth, and how he himself would have shouted if he had been well. This intensified his toothache, and he shook his muffled head frequently, and roared: "Moo-Moo. . . ."

"They say that He restored sight to the blind," said his wife, who remained standing at the parapet, and she threw down a little cobblestone near the place where Jesus, lifted by the whips, was moving slowly.

"Of course, of course! He should have cured my toothache," replied Ben-Tovit ironically, and he added bitterly with irritation: "What dust they have kicked up! Like a herd of cattle! They should all be driven away with a stick! Take me down, Sarah!"

The wife proved to be right. The spectacle had diverted Ben-Tovit slightly—perhaps it was the rats' litter that had helped after all—he succeeded in falling asleep. When he awoke, his toothache had passed almost entirely, and only a little inflammation had formed over his right jaw. His wife told him that it was not noticeable at all, but Ben-Tovit smiled cunningly—he knew how kind-hearted his wife was and how fond she was of telling him pleasant things.

Samuel, the tanner, a neighbor of Ben-Tovit's, came in, and Ben-

Tovit led him to see the new little donkey and listened proudly to the warm praises for himself and his animal.

Then, at the request of the curious Sarah, the three went to Golgotha to see the people who had been crucified. On the way Ben-Tovit told Samuel in detail how he had felt a pain in his right jaw on the day before, and how he awoke at night with a terrible toothache. To illustrate it he made a martyr's face, closing his eyes, shook his head, and groaned while the gray-bearded Samuel nodded his head compassionately and said:

"Oh, how painful it must have been!"

Ben-Tovit was pleased with Samuel's attitude, and he repeated the story to him, then went back to the past, when his first tooth was spoiled on the left side. Thus, absorbed in a lively conversation, they reached Golgotha. The sun, which was destined to shine upon the world on that terrible day, had already set beyond the distant hills, and in the west a narrow, purple-red strip was burning, like a stain of blood. The crosses stood out darkly but vaguely against this background, and at the foot of the middle cross white kneeling figures were seen indistinctly.

The crowd had long dispersed; it was growing chilly, and after a glance at the crucified men, Ben-Tovit took Samuel by the arm and carefully turned him in the direction toward his house. He felt that he was particularly eloquent just then, and he was eager to finish the story of his toothache. Thus they walked, and Ben-Tovit made a martyr's face, shook his head and groaned skillfully, while Samuel nodded compassionately and uttered exclamations from time to time, and from the deep, narrow defiles, out of the distant, burning plains, rose the black night. It seemed as though it wished to hide from the view of heaven the great crime of the earth.

MR. BRITLING WRITES UNTIL SUNRISE

H. G. Wells

~~~~~~

Mr. Britling Sees It Through, H. G. Wells's chronicle of the years
1914–18, describes the effects of war on an English family, their American guest and German tutor. The story concludes with a letter to the
young German's parents, in which Mr. Britling sets forth his emergent
philosophy of war and faith—as appropriate to the modern world as
it was for his own day.

ON THE TOP of Mr. Britling's desk, beside the clock, lay a letter, written
in clumsy English and with its envelope resealed by a label which
testified that it had been "OPENED BY CENSOR."

The friendly go-between in Norway had written to tell Mr. Britling
that Herr Heinrich also was dead; he had died a wounded prisoner in
Russia some months ago. He had been wounded and captured, after
undergoing great hardships, during the great Russian attack upon the
passes of the Carpathians in the early spring, and his wound had mortified. He had recovered partially for a time, and then he had been
beaten and injured again in some struggle between German and Croatian prisoners, and he had sickened and died. Before he died he had
written to his parents, and once again he had asked that the fiddle he
had left in Mr. Britling's care should if possible be returned to them.
It was manifest that both for him and them now it had become a symbol with many associations.

The substance of this letter invaded the orange circle of the lamp;
it would have to be answered, and the potentialities of the answer were
running through Mr. Britling's brain to the exclusion of any impersonal
composition. He thought of the old parents away there in Pomerania—
he believed, but he was not quite sure, that Heinrich had been an only
son—and of the pleasant spectacled figure that had now become a
broken and decaying thing in a prisoner's shallow grave. . . .

Another son had gone—all the world was losing its sons. . . .

He found himself thinking of young Heinrich in the very manner, if with a lesser intensity, in which he thought about his own son, as of hopes senselessly destroyed. His mind took no note of the fact that Heinrich was an enemy, that by the reckoning of a "war of attrition" his death was balance and compensation for the death of Hugh. He went straight to the root fact that they had been gallant and kindly beings, and that the same thing had killed them both. . . .

"I must write a letter to the old father and mother," Mr. Britling thought. "I can't just send the poor little fiddle—without a word. In all this pitiful storm of witless hate—surely there may be one greeting—not hateful.

"From my blackness to yours," said Mr. Britling aloud.

He would have to write it in English. But even if they knew no English some one would be found to translate it to them. He would have to write very plainly.

DEAR SIR,

I am writing this letter to you to tell you I am sending back the few little things I had kept for your son at his request when the war broke out.

Especially I am sending his violin, which he had asked me thrice to convey to you. Either it is a gift from you or it symbolised many things for him that he connected with home and you. I will have it packed with particular care, and I will do all in my power to ensure its safe arrival.

I want to tell you that all the stress and passion of this war has not made us here in Matching's Easy forget our friend your son. He was one of us, he had our affection, he had friends here who are still his friends. We found him honourable and companionable, and we share something of your loss. I have got together for you a few snapshots I chance to possess in which you will see him in the sunshine, and which will enable you perhaps to picture a little more definitely than you would otherwise do the life he led here. There is one particularly that I have marked. Our family is lunching out-of-doors, and you will see that next to your son is a youngster, a year or so his junior, who is touching glasses with him. I have put a cross over his head. He is my eldest son, he was very dear to me, and he too has been killed in this war. They are, you see, smiling very pleasantly at each other.

If you think that these two boys have both perished, not in some noble common cause but one against the other in a struggle of dynasties and boundaries and trade routes and tyrannous ascendancies, then it seems to me that you must feel as I feel that this war is the most tragic and dreadful thing that has ever happened to mankind.

If you count dead and wounds this is the most dreadful war in history;

for you as for me, it has been almost the extremity of personal tragedy. . . .
Black sorrow. . . .

But is it the most dreadful war?

I do not think it is. I can write to you and tell you that I do indeed believe
that our two sons have died not altogether in vain. Our pain and anguish
may not be wasted—may be necessary. Indeed they may be necessary. Here
am I bereaved and wretched—and I hope. . . .

War is a curtain of dense black fabric across all the hopes and kindliness
of mankind. Yet always it has let through some gleams of light, and now—I
am not dreaming—it grows threadbare, and here and there and at a thousand points the light is breaking through. We owe it to all these dear
youths——

His pen stopped. . . .

Three hours later Mr. Britling was working by daylight, though his
study lamp was still burning, and his letter to old Heinrich was still no
better than a collection of material for a letter. But the material was
falling roughly into shape, and Mr. Britling's intentions were finding
themselves. It was clear to him now that he was no longer writing as
his limited personal self to those two personal selves grieving, in the
old, large, high-walled, steep-roofed household amidst pine woods, of
which Heinrich had once shown him a picture. He knew them too
little for any such personal address. He was writing, he perceived, not
as Mr. Britling but as an Englishman—that was all he could be to them
—and he was writing to them as Germans; he could apprehend them
as nothing more. He was just England bereaved to Germany bereaved. . . .

And to that he wrote, to that dimly apprehended figure outside a
circle of the light like his own circle of light—which was the father of
Heinrich, which was great Germany, Germany which lived before and
which will yet outlive the flapping of the eagles. . . .

Our boys, *he wrote,* have died, fighting one against the other. They have
been fighting upon an issue so obscure that your German press is still busy
discussing what it was. . . .

What have we been fighting for? What are we fighting for? Do you
know? Does any one know? Why am I spending what is left of my substance and you what is left of yours to keep on this war against each other?
What have we to gain from hurting one another still further? Why should
we be puppets any longer in the hands of crowned fools and witless diplo-
matists? Even if we were dumb and acquiescent before, does not the blood

of our sons now cry out to us that this foolery should cease? We have let these people send our sons to death.

It is you and I who must stop these wars, these massacres of boys. . . .

I do not think you Germans realise how steadily you were conquering the world before this war began. Had you given half the energy and intelligence you have spent upon this war to the peaceful conquest of men's minds and spirits, I believe that you would have taken the leadership of the world tranquilly—no man disputing. Your science was five years, your social and economic organisation was a quarter of a century in front of ours. . . . Never has it so lain in the power of a great people to lead and direct mankind towards the world republic and universal peace. It needed but a certain generosity of the imagination. . . .

But your Junkers, your Imperial court, your foolish vicious Princes; what were such dreams to them? . . . With an envious satisfaction they hurled all the accomplishment of Germany into the fires of war. . . .

Your boy, as no doubt you know, dreamt constantly of such a world peace as this that I foreshadow; he was more generous than his country. He could envisage war and hostility only as misunderstanding. He thought that a world that could explain itself clearly would surely be at peace. He was scheming always therefore for the perfection and propagation of Esperanto or Ido, or some such universal link. My youngster too was full of a kindred and yet larger dream, the dream of human science, which knows neither king nor country nor race. . . .

These boys, these hopes, this war has killed. . . .

That fragment ended so. Mr. Britling ceased to read for a time. "But has it killed them?" he whispered. . . .

"If you had lived, my dear, you and your England would have talked with a younger Germany—better than I can ever do. . . ."

He turned the pages back, and read here and there with an accumulating discontent.

"Dissertations," said Mr. Britling.

Never had it been so plain to Mr. Britling that he was a weak, silly, ill-informed and hasty-minded writer, and never had he felt so invincible a conviction that the Spirit of God was in him, and that it fell to him to take some part in the establishment of a new order of living upon the earth; it might be the most trivial part by the scale of the task, but for him it was to be now his supreme concern. And it was an almost intolerable grief to him that his services should be, for all his desire, so poor in quality, so weak in conception. Always he seemed to

be on the verge of some illuminating and beautiful statement of his
cause; always he was finding his writing inadequate, a thin treachery
to the impulse of his heart, always he was finding his effort weak and
ineffective. In this instance, at the outset he seemed to see with a
golden clearness the message of brotherhood, or forgiveness, of a common call. To whom could such a message be better addressed than to
those sorrowing parents; from whom could it come with a better effect
than from himself? And now he read what he had made of this message. It seemed to his jaded mind a pitifully jaded effort. It had no
light, it had no depth. It was like the disquisition of a debating society.

He was distressed by a fancy of an old German couple, spectacled
and peering, puzzled by his letter. Perhaps they would be obscurely
hurt by his perplexing generalisations. Why, they would ask, should
this Englishman preach to them?

He sat back in his chair wearily, with his chin sunk upon his chest.
For a time he did not think, and then, he read again the sentence in
front of his eyes.

These boys, these hopes, this war has killed.

The words hung for a time in his mind.

"No!" said Mr. Britling stoutly. "They live!"

And suddenly it was borne in upon his mind that he was not alone.
There were thousands and tens of thousands of men and women like
himself, desiring with all their hearts to say, as he desired to say, the
reconciling word. It was not only his hand that thrust against the obstacles. . . . Frenchmen and Russians sat in the same stillness, facing
the same perplexities; there were Germans seeking a way through to
him. Even as he sat and wrote. And for the first time clearly he felt a
Presence of which he had thought very many times in the last few
weeks, a Presence so close to him that it was behind his eyes and in his
brain and hands. It was no trick of his vision; it was a feeling of immediate reality. And it was Hugh, Hugh that he had thought was
dead, it was young Heinrich living also, it was himself, it was those
others that sought, it was all these and it was more, it was the Master,
the Captain of Mankind, it was God, there present with him, and he
knew that it was God. It was as if he had been groping all this time in
the darkness, thinking himself alone amidst rocks and pitfalls and piti-
less things, and suddenly a hand, a firm strong hand, had touched his
own. And a voice within him bade him be of good courage. There was
no magic trickery in that moment; he was still weak and weary, a dis-

couraged rhetorician, a good intention ill-equipped; but he was no longer lonely and wretched, no longer in the same world with despair. God was beside him and within him and about him. . . . It was the crucial moment of Mr. Britling's life. It was a thing as light as the passing of a cloud on an April morning; it was a thing as great as the first day of creation. For some moments he still sat back with his chin upon his chest and his hands dropping from the arms of his chair. Then he sat up and drew a deep breath. . . .

This had come almost as a matter of course.

For weeks his mind had been playing about this idea. He had talked to Letty of this Finite God, who is the king of man's adventure in space and time. But hitherto God had been for him a thing of the intelligence, a theory, a report, something told about but not realised. . . . Mr. Britling's thinking about God hitherto had been like some one who has found an empty house, very beautiful and pleasant, full of the promise of a fine personality. And then as the discoverer makes his lonely, curious explorations, he hears downstairs, dear and friendly, the voice of the Master coming in. . . .

There was no need to despair because he himself was one of the feeble folk. God was with him indeed, and he was with God. The King was coming to his own. Amidst the darknesses and confusions, the nightmare cruelties and the hideous stupidities of the great war, God, the Captain of the World Republic, fought his way to empire. So long as one did one's best and utmost in a cause so mighty, did it matter though the thing one did was little and poor?

"I have thought too much of myself," said Mr. Britling, "and of what I would do by myself. I have forgotten *that which was with me*. . . ."

He sighed.

He looked at the scattered papers, and thought of the letter they were to have made.

His fatigue spoke first.

"Perhaps after all I'd better just send the fiddle. . . ."

He rested his cheeks between his hands, and remained so for a long time. His eyes stared unseeingly. His thoughts wandered and spread and faded. At length he recalled his mind to that last idea. "Just send the fiddle—without a word."

"No. I must write to them plainly.

"About God as I have found Him.

"As He has found me. . . ."

He forgot the Pomeranians for a time. He murmured to himself. He turned over the conviction that had suddenly become clear and absolute in his mind.

"Religion is the first thing and the last thing, and until a man has found God and been found by God, he begins at no beginning, he works to no end. He may have his friendships, his partial loyalties, his scraps of honour. But all these things fall into place and life falls into place only with God. Only with God. God, who fights through men against Blind Force and Night and Non-Existence; who is the end, who is the meaning. He is the only King. . . . Of course I must write about Him. I must tell all my world of Him. And before the coming of the true King, the inevitable King, the King who is present whenever just men foregather, this blood-stained rubbish of the ancient world, these puny kings and tawdry emperors, these wily politicians and artful lawyers, these men who claim and grab and trick and compel, these war makers and oppressors, will presently shrivel and pass—like paper thrust into a flame. . . ."

Then after a time he said:

"Our sons who have shown us God. . . ."

He rubbed his open hands over his eyes and forehead.

The night of effort had tired his brain, and he was no longer thinking actively. He had a little interval of blankness, sitting at his desk with his hands pressed over his eyes. . . .

He got up presently, and stood quite motionless at the window, looking out.

His lamp was still burning, but for some time he had not been writing by the light of his lamp. Insensibly the day had come and abolished his need for that individual circle of yellow light. Colour had returned to the world, clean pearly colour, clear and definite like the glance of a child or the voice of a girl, and a golden wisp of cloud hung in the sky over the tower of the church. There was a mist upon the pond, a soft grey mist not a yard high. A covey of partridges ran and halted and ran again in the dewy grass outside his garden railings. The partridges were very numerous this year because there had been so little shooting. Beyond in the meadow a hare sat up as still as a stone. A horse neighed. . . . Wave after wave of warmth and light came sweeping before the sunrise across the world of Matching's Easy. It was as if there was nothing but morning and sunrise in the world. . . .

HOME IS IN THE HEART

Robert Nathan

The cruelties and hardships of war lose their stark horror for one mother who draws inspiration from the comforting counsel of a preacher. Warmed by the same spirit that made France great, she gains new insight into the sanctity of home and peace.

THERE WERE rumors of defeat; but there was no talk of peace. If the war was lost, it was lost; they hadn't wanted it, those people stumbling along the road in the retreat; they had given up their homes, and their possessions, but they'd rather never see them again, than have the country surrender.

The night before she got to Willow Bend, Mom lay on the bare floor of an empty mill, next to a preacher and his family. There were others there, too; the preacher spoke, his voice filled the dusty, echoing structure as though it were a church. Mom lay and listened to what he had to say. It wasn't a sermon, exactly, but it did her good.

"It's the cynics who have lost this war," the preacher said: "the men who wouldn't fight for what they believed. Pious men, too, mostly; but they wouldn't fight for God, or for their neighbors. Only for themselves, in self-defense, and after they'd been struck. That isn't what God likes to see in a man; nor Jesus, either. One thing or the other, is what it ought to be. Turn the other cheek, said Christ; and Jehovah said unto Joshua, Fear not, neither be thou dismayed: take all the people of war with thee, and arise, go up to Ai."

He continued, in a sterner voice: "I've watched this war come upon us. Nobody wanted it; and so nobody thinks he's to blame. But I say that those are to blame who wouldn't step out and fight when the first injustice was done. I say those are to blame who went into their houses and hid when the alarm bells rang far away, in another country. I say those are to blame who left mercy to lie bleeding on the street, and passed by on the other side. I heard them say it was no war of theirs, and my heart was sick for them, and for the world."

"Well," said Mom, "they've got it now; and where they wanted it, right in their own front yard."

"You tell them, lady," said a man's voice from the darkness.

"Spain was the first," said the preacher, "that was no war of ours. And we had none of Finland, either. We have not fought for the right, but for our own skins, and the hand of God is heavy on us for that account."

A woman's voice cut in, trembling and sharp. "We've fought for our homes," she said. "What more do you want?"

"Where is man's home?" asked the preacher gently. "Is it a yard of earth, where he raises a wall, and burns a fire against the cold? I tell you that man's home is not in walls of stone or wood. It is in his heart, or nowhere."

He was silent. Someone said Amen softly; and others whispered Amen. It seemed to Mom as if the darkness itself breathed, as if the dusty air of the mill were vibrant with spirit.

She slept well that night. When she awoke, the preacher and his family were already gone. But Mom remembered his words; she didn't hold much with religion, but while she walked that day, she thought about them. It's a fact, she thought, we haven't fought for our homes— not in the truest way of speaking. For when we speak of home, we mean something more than four walls and a door. Home is a feeling; it's where our spirit is, is home. It's where we have our peace, it's where we try to gather together the things that are right, and good. Well . . . if we've lost our home, it's because we got mixed up. There were too many telling us what was right and what was wrong; they cut things up too fine, they got us confused.

You have to look at things whole, like the preacher said. The trouble with us was, we were too busy, each in his own back yard, doing for himself. We had forgot that home was all the little back yards, everywhere.

Win or lose, we'll have to build all over again. We'll have to build from the ground up, solid and good, for all men to admire, for all people to see. A place to live in, a place to keep the things in that are good, and right. A place to have our peace.

THE UNSAID PRAYER

Pierre van Paassen

Pierre van Paassen's *That Day Alone* is a series of sketches, anecdotes, and short stories based on the Nazi occupation of western Europe. Though called upon many times during the holocaust to bring hope to the bereaved, Reverend Baxter here learns with newfound humility that he cannot intone the "unsaid prayer."

His HANDS trembled a little as he poured himself a cup of tea. There had been so much work that day. First there had been the evacuation of a hundred children from the village. That was in the morning. Then there had been a tedious delay at the railway station, when a last minute checkup revealed that two of the children were missing. Could it be that they were among the victims of last night's air raid? Perhaps the morrow would tell, when the wardens should have removed the debris above the shelter near the church. Then there had been a burial. That had taxed his strength to the utmost. He had been with the parents of William Gillespie, a pilot in the R.A.F., who had been shot down over Middlesex a few days before. What could one say to a father and mother of an only son? That he had died so that England might live? That sounded quite inspiring and touching in official orations, but Mr. and Mrs. Gillespie were amongst his dearest parishioners. He had to give them a ray of hope, something to cling to in their cruel bereavement. . . .

The Reverend Thomas Baxter heaved a deep sigh. He was no longer a young man. He was verging on sixty-three years, though he bore few of the signs of age; his hair was rather grizzled, but not grey; his eye was mild, but clear and bright. Mr. Baxter had come to Hampton Road forty years ago. It was his first parish; it would probably be his last. He had dreamed of retiring in a few years and devoting the remaining years of his life to some scholarly work from which the arduous duties of a rural dean of the Church of England had kept him thus far. But his wife had fallen ill, and then the war had come. Now there could be no thought of retiring, of course.

He drank his tea in silence and looked around the room. This was not his own home. His own home lay in ruins, next to the battered church. This was one of Sir Henry Matthews' cottages, which had been placed at his disposal after those first aerial onslaughts on East Anglia. His wife lay in the next room, a helpless invalid. His daughter was busy in the kitchen.

It was evening, and he was tired, but he dreaded the coming night. Would the Germans return as they had done on the previous ten nights? Would they again make Hampton Road one of their targets? The bombings had riddled Mr. Baxter with fear. But he had had to put a brave face on it and go out after the all-clear signal and speak to people and pretend that he was, if not unconcerned, at least not upset but calm and collected. In short, he had to set an example to others.

At William Gillespie's grave that afternoon he had spoken from the text: "Who for the joy that was set before Him endured the cross." He thought of it now. Was that the right word to have said? And then he thought of the government's announcement that it was framing its policy on the assumption that the war would last three years or more. That was the thing that had disturbed him most that day: three more years of war. He thought that there must have been few hearts in England that did not quail for a moment when that announcement came. It was all well and good to pretend to grin and say: "We are Englishmen: we can take it and hold our thumbs up in the air," but Englishmen were only human beings, too, after all.

Mr. Baxter wondered how much more his parishioners could stand of the sleepless nights and constant bombing. And yet, more was to come apparently, for what else could the government's announcement mean? In his imagination, the prospects of the future tended to grow more and more terrifying. The calamities in store assumed almost monstrous proportions. . . .

His wife was calling from the other room, and he and his daughter reached her bedside simultaneously. "Have you heard from Gilbert?" the woman asked. She referred to their son, a lieutenant in the tank corps, now on duty in Europe. He had a letter from Gilbert, he reassured her, and the boy was doing well. He was going to read the letter more carefully as soon as he had washed up. He had only glanced at it in the afternoon when the mailman had pushed it in his hands. He asked his wife if she would like some tea, but she did not answer him.

As he spoke, the sirens began to wail. The woman on the bed stirred restlessly. "Who is that crying?" she said. "Someone is crying!"

Father and daughter exchanged a significant look. Mrs. Baxter's mind was wandering again; the weeks and weeks of fever had affected her brain. Mr. Baxter felt his wife's forehead and stooped down to kiss her. Then he walked back into the sitting room and took his son's letter from his pocket. He turned at once to the last page, the page that had disturbed him most when he had glanced at it in the afternoon. The boy's letters had been so optimistic in the past, so full of good cheer, that this latest message with its note of somber despair had upset him the more.

"It is your conviction, I know," his son had written him, "that what we are facing is the consequence of sin and that it is not for us to apportion the guilt. . . . But the consequences of sin fall upon the innocent and the guilty alike. Here in the first line, between two raids, two bombardments, two attempts to dig a hole in the night, with dead men all around me, what remains of life? Is not this punishment too great?"

Mr. Baxter looked up. The droning of airplanes filled the dark sky above. "Here they are again," he muttered. There was a muffled crash in the distance. He went back to the sickroom. "Isn't it early in the year for thunder, Thomas?" his wife asked him. There was another crash, nearer this time. "They are bombing the church again," said his daughter, as she stepped into the room. "But they are swinging to the north. Hear, that is the sound of our fighters. They are attacking them. . . ."

Mr. Baxter was holding his wife's hand in his. In the other hand he held his son's letter. He glanced at it involuntarily by the light of the bed lamp and read: "What else can I tell you? Life? What is it? What remains of it? It is something more than a phantom, a phantom which is itself so inconsistent that it fails to move us. I quit you on these words of Lawrence: 'When things get very bad, they pass beyond tragedy— and then the only thing we can do is to keep quite still—and guard the lost treasure of the soul, our sanity. . . . If we lose our sanity, nothing and nobody in the whole vast realm of space wants us, or can have anything to do with us. We can but howl the lugubrious howl of idiots, the howl of the utterly lost howling their nowhereness. . . .'" Mr. Baxter shuddered. He keenly felt the suffering his boy must have undergone when he wrote those words. And then he thought of the government's announcement again, three more years of war. . . .

It seemed an endless span of time if those years were to be charged with suffering and horror the like of which had never been experienced on earth before. Was it shameful to be afraid of the future? he wondered. He was not afraid of death for himself. What he feared was sudden death or, as he had often said, to be cut off in a flash and to pass to his judgment unshriven. He had always prayed to be spared from sudden death, to be granted at least a moment of recollection, that he could turn his heart again to God in penitence and faith before leaving this life. No, on the whole he was not afraid of death.

He was afraid for his people, his parishioners of Hampton Road, for England. What we are facing? he thought again, as he had written to his son: "What we are facing is the consequence of sin: sin of pride, sin of fatness, sin of self-righteousness. If there were only an acknowledgment of this, if there only would be contrition and penitence, then we could again pray for fortitude. . . ."

The rattle of machine-gun firing in the sky above shook him from his meditation. "They'll soon be coming back this way," said his daughter. "Our fighters are trying to intercept them. I hope they've dropped their bombs elsewhere, so that they will not be forced to unload again in our neighborhood."

He nodded his head. The firing grew heavier. In the distance were some heavy detonations. He thought of the sermon he was to preach the next Sunday. The fortitude for which we ought to pray, he thought, is not that the natural virtue of man which enables him to square his shoulders and determine his course, come what may? The fortitude for which we ought to pray is a gift from the Holy Spirit, a gift which enables us to face the evils we most dread, a gift which enables us to resist mere recklessness—that appearance of courage, which is not true courage. This Christian grace of fortitude would not, to be sure, banish fear. It was not a sort of Dutch courage; but it would enable men to control fear. With Christian fortitude we could, he thought, enter upon arduous tasks with the quiet and steady will that men would naturally bring to bear on relatively easy matters. Christian fortitude would enable men to keep their heads, whether in adversity or prosperity. . . .

There was a knock at the cottage door. Mr. Baxter rose to open. A farmer was standing before him. Could Mr. Baxter come with him quickly, the man was asking. They had just dug a woman out of the ruins, and she was seriously hurt, so seriously that she might die in the night. She had asked for the parson. But would he hurry, please, for there was not much time to lose.

Mr. Baxter went into the bedroom to see that his wife was comfortable. He kissed her on the forehead and tucked the blankets in at the sides. He said to his daughter, as he put on his hat, that he hoped he would not be gone for long. Then he went out with the farmer. The man carried an electric torch to guide their way. To the left, but far away, a house was burning fiercely. "That must be Mr. Mortlock's place," said Mr. Baxter. The farmer said it was. It had been burning for an hour. But in the village it was worse. A whole row of cottages had gone down. "They just toppled over like houses of cards," the man said. "We can't tell how many dead there are. We had only begun to dig when I was sent to fetch you. . . ."

Suddenly the rumble of a bombing squadron was heard approaching from the northwest. "They are coming back from London," said the man. "Our fellows are on their tails." A Very light illuminated the landscape. They could see the skeleton of the burnt-out church, starkly outlined on the knoll. "They are lighting their way home," said the farmer. The bombers were nearly overheard. They were looking for a target on which to unload before flying over the Channel. Fighting planes threw out Very lights to show the oncoming bombers their targets. All at once the air was filled with the crash and thunder of exploding projectiles. The two men crouched behind the trees at the roadside. The bomb fragments whistled about their heads. Mr. Baxter covered his ears with his hands, but his eyes turned in the direction of his own cottage, above which another parachute light was slowly floating to earth. He could hear the whistle of the bombs as they rained down in the vicinity of his home. "Merciful heavens," he said, "if we are going to escape this, it will be a wonder."

There was a deafening series of explosions. By the flash of the striking bombs, he could see his cottage wrapped in flames and smoke. Then, just as suddenly, the flock of raiders passed, and all that could be heard was the rattle of machine guns from the British fighter planes chasing the invaders.

Mr. Baxter ran back to his cottage. He was breathing hard. The farmer was racing along behind him. The first glow of light had appeared in the east when they reached the place. The cottage was a heap of rubble. Mr. Baxter threw off his coat and started to pull at some of the cracked timbers. The two men worked in silence. But they were soon forced to give up. Then Mr. Baxter sat down on the stone bench in front of what had been his house and stared at what had become the tomb of his wife and daughter. It was daylight when the village people came up. The parson was just pulling a sheet of paper from his jacket. On the paper he had written out the prayer he had intended to intone the next Sunday.

He glanced at it and read: "O God, who art the Author of peace and Lover of concord, pour down now upon the German people the blessing of Thy love and understanding, that their hearts may be touched by the grace of Thy Holy Spirit and their minds awakened to the recognition of the universal brotherhood of man. Grant that their eyes may be opened to the truth, and that they may rise from the plane on which men are separated from each other by their prejudices to that plane where they are united by good will and unselfish co-operation. Amen. . . ."

He read the words a second time and shook his head with a deep sigh. Then he tore up the paper.

A CANDLE IN VIENNA

A. J. Cronin

Though best known for his novels, Dr. Cronin has also written a number of inspiring short stories and vignettes. This miniature proclaims the power of abiding faith to withstand even the destruction and carnage of war.

For weeks I had looked forward to my visit to Vienna which in the past I had known so well and loved so much. Yet, since morning, when the transport plane had landed me at the airfield, my mood had grown progressively more bitter. There was no accommodation at the Bristol, and the room they had finally found for me in a drab house in the Kartnerstrasse was sparsely furnished and unheated. For lunch there was only vegetable soup and the inevitable bully beef.

In the afternoon, as I set out in the cutting wind on my tour of inspection, past the shattered Cathedral and the ruins of the Opera House, my heart sank further. Was this the lovely, festive city where I had known such joyful days and exhilarating nights, where I had heard Lehmann sing in *La Bohème* and driven afterward in an open carriage through the gaily crowded thoroughfares to celebrate the *Heurige,* the festival of the new wine? I had come prepared for material destruction, for shattered houses, heaps of rubble, bombed buildings, yes, even for the melancholy spectacle of the blown-up Danube bridges. But I had not foreseen the empty, silent hopelessness which, like a chill miasma, pervaded these gray and dingy shuttered streets.

As it crept into my bones a blind anger grew within me, a sullen resentment against Providence that such things should come to pass. To make matters worse, as the frigid February twilight fell, it began to rain, a heavy, freezing sleet that threatened to penetrate the army mackintosh which I wore over my woolen coat.

I was now somewhere in the eastern suburbs and to escape I took shelter in a neighboring building—a small church which had escaped destruction. The place was empty and almost dark, the shadows relieved only by the faint red flicker of the sanctuary light. Impatiently, I sat down to wait until the worst of the downpour should pass.

Suddenly, I heard footsteps and, turning, I saw an old man enter the church. He wore no coat and his tall figure, gaunt and stiffly erect, clad in a thin, much mended suit, was painfully shabby. As he advanced toward the side altar I observed with surprise that he was carrying in his arms a child, a little girl of about six, dressed also in the garments of poverty. When he reached the railing of the altar he put her down gently. I perceived then, from the helpless movements of her limbs, that she was paralyzed. Still supporting her with great patience, he encouraged her to kneel, arranging her hands so that she could cling to the altar rail. When he had succeeded, he smiled at her, as though congratulating her on her achievement, then he knelt, spare and erect, beside her.

For a few minutes they remained thus, then the old man rose. I heard the thin echo of a small coin falling into the box, then saw him take a candle, light it and give it to the child. She held it in one transparent hand for a long moment while the glow cast a little halo about her, making visible the pleased expression on her pale, pinched features. Then she placed the candle upright on the small iron stand before the shadowed altar, admiring her little gift, dedicating it with the rapt up-turned tilt of her head.

Presently the old man got up again and, lifting the child, began to carry her in his arms out of the church. All the time that I had watched them I had felt myself intruding on their privacy, guilty of a sort of sacrilege. Yet now, though that feeling remained, an irresistible impulse made me rise and follow them to the church porch.

Here, drawn to one side, was a small homemade conveyance—a rickety wooden box with lopsided sticks for shafts, mounted on two old perambulator wheels which had long ago lost their tires. Into this equipage the old man was bestowing the child, spreading an old potato sack across her limbs. Now that I stood close to them I could plainly confirm what I had already suspected. Every line of the old man's drawn face, the cropped gray mustache, the fine nose, the proud eyes under deep brows showed him a true aristocrat, one of those patrician Viennese to whom, through no fault of their own, the war had brought utter ruin. The child, whose peaked features resembled his own, was almost certainly his granddaughter. As with his veined, fine hands he finished tucking the sack around her, he glanced at me. A rush of questions was on my tongue, but something, the spiritual quality of that face, restrained my curiosity. I could only say, with awkwardness:

"It is very cold."

He answered me politely. "Less cold than it has been this winter."

There was a pause. My gaze returned to the child whose blue eyes were fixed upon us. "The war," I said, still looking at her.

"Yes, the war," he answered. "The same bomb killed her mother and father."

Another, and a longer, pause.

"You come here often?" I regretted this crudity immediately it escaped me. But he took no offense.

"Yes, every day, to pray." He smiled faintly. "And also to show the good God we are not too angry with Him."

I could find no reply. And as I stood in silence he straightened himself, buttoned his jacket, picked up the shafts of the little buggy and with that same faint smile, that polite inclination of his head, moved off with the child into the gathering darkness.

No sooner were they gone than I had again an insufferable desire to pursue them. I wanted to help, to offer them money, to strip off my warm coat, to do something impetuous and spectacular. But I remained rooted to the spot. I knew that this was no case for common charity, that anything which I could give would be refused. Instead, it was they who had given something to me. They, who had lost everything, refused to despair; they could still believe. A feeling of confusion rose in me. Now there was no anger in my heart, no concern for my own petty deprivations, but only pity and a pervading sense of shame.

The rain had gone off. But I did not go out. I hesitated. Then I turned and went back toward the little faithful beacon which still burned at the side altar in the no longer empty church. One candle in a ruined city. But while it shone there seemed hope for the world.

The Spirit Returns

PENTECOST

Lloyd C. Douglas

Lloyd C. Douglas's novel, *The Big Fisherman*, weaves legend and history into a humanized portrait of Simon called Peter. The dramatic scene of "Pentecost" lays bare the vision that made Peter the greatest of the disciples and teachers of Christianity.

NEVER had there been a fairer morning in Jerusalem than on this Day of Pentecost.

Since dawn, every road leading into the city had been filling with merry-makers on foot from the provinces, and within an hour the highways were crowded.

Frequently the country people scampered to the hedges, good-naturedly conceding the right of way to impressive caravans from distant lands, unannoyed by the haughty stares of the urbane strangers.

Once within the gaily decorated gates, the festive throng jostled toward the bazaars and food-markets while the sober-faced men of consequence, indifferent to the city's gaiety, proceeded on through to the Sheep Gate and up the steepening Bethany boulevard to Levi's Inn where, after a comforting bath and a change of linen, they would rest until it was time to attend the famous camel-auction in the early afternoon.

Half a block down the hill from Levi's stood a massive old stone structure which had long served as headquarters for the Coppersmiths' Guild. It was an undeniably ugly building but no discredit to the street, for the organization that it housed was one of the most honorable institutions in Jerusalem. The Coppersmiths' Guild had been the first society to volunteer substantial aid to Nehemiah when he rebuilt the city's walls more than four centuries ago.

The high-ceilinged, rectangular second story of the Guildhall, accessible by an outside staircase, was used as an auditorium. It had seating for approximately two hundred and served not only the general conclaves of the Guild but was frequently rented to business conventions with a large non-resident membership.

The hall was open this morning and gradually filling with men of all sorts whose only observable relation to one another was their apparent uncertainty as to the nature of their errand. For the most part they came singly. The majority of them were of middle age, plainly dressed in country garb, and obviously from the provinces. They slowly mounted the stone staircase, diffidently entered the dingy old auditorium, and stood awkwardly for a long moment wondering what was expected of them, for there were no ushers, nor was there anyone in sight who had the appearance of being responsible for the mysterious meeting. After tarrying awhile at the door, the bewildered men from the country found seats and sat down to wait. A sprinkling of well-dressed men of affairs stalked in, one by one; but, for all their urbanity, they seemed quite as confused as the unsophisticated provincials.

Jairus turned to young Joel, as they lingered in the doorway to survey the half-filled room, and asked, "Do you see anyone you ever saw before?" And Joel, craning about, shook his head; but immediately amended his reply to whisper, "Over there is a man I recognize. His name is Micah. He was a laborer in the Tetrarch's vineyard."

"I wonder what brings him here," mumbled Jairus.

"His little girl was blind," said Joel. "Jesus opened her eyes. I saw him do it, sir. Last summer. But I heard, a few days ago, that the child had just died. Of a fever. . . . Maybe that's what brings him here, sir."

"You mean—perhaps Micah thinks that Jesus—now that he is alive again—may give his little girl back to him?"

"I wouldn't know, sir," murmured Joel.

"Do you suppose that all these people knew Jesus?" wondered Jairus.

"It could be, sir."

They found seats near the rear of the hall. Presently a distinguished-looking, smooth-shaven Roman with close-cropped, grizzled hair came in, glanced about, and strode directly to the rear, seating himself at the end of the row but one vacant chair apart from Jairus. They gave each other a brief appraisal without speaking.

For a full quarter-hour there had been no new arrivals. Apparently the company was complete. Now the heavy oaken door began to complain of its rusted hinges. All heads were turned in that direction and mystified eyes watched the massive door slowly close, though no one had touched it. Jairus darted an inquiring glance at the Roman at the same instant that Mencius arched an eyebrow toward Jairus; but neither spoke. The baffled audience again faced forward. The room grew strangely quiet.

Then a giant of a man, seated in the front row, rose and walked confidently to the rostrum. Only a few in the transfixed audience failed to recognize him; but even those who had seen him, again and again, as he stood at the Master's side, protecting him in the crush of great throngs, observed instantly that something had happened to the Big Fisherman.

They hadn't always liked his attitude on those eventful summer days. He had kept the great crowds in order, yes; and he had made the bearers of the sick ones take their turn. But sometimes his manner had annoyed them. It was almost as if he owned the show—and Jesus was his exhibit. Not infrequently some offended man, who had been unceremoniously pushed back into line, would grumble, "Who does that big fellow think he is, anyhow?"

Now it appeared that some sort of miracle had been wrought upon Peter.

For one thing, he had a different face. The former face had been more than a bit bumptious, the darting eyes audacious, the lips inclined to purse protrudingly. The Big Fisherman's new face was refined. All the old deep-chiseled lines carved by habitual brashness and bluster were gone; ironed out as by fire. There were still plenty of lines but they had not been engraved by self-pride: Peter had evidently suffered to earn his new countenance.

Maybe the changed color of his hair had had something to do with the softening and refinement of his face. His heavy thatch, previously black as a raven's wing, had turned gray—in patches. It was sprinkled with gray throughout, but at his temples and where the hair grew low on the middle of his forehead, there were broad strips of white; snow-white! His formerly unkempt black beard had been shortened: it too glistened with white. Peter's face had lost its austerity and had taken on dignity. . . . Mencius, who once had had a fleeting glimpse of the gigantic man running down the street, recognized nothing about him but his extraordinary height, and told Captain Fulvius, when he rejoined *The Vestris,* that the massive Galilean, who directed the meeting on the Day of Pentecost, was the most august and majestic figure he had ever seen.

But perhaps the chief distinction of the transformed disciple was his arresting voice; deep, resonant, commanding. It had the tone of authority. When he began by saying that he was speaking on behalf of the Living Christ to a selected company of men reverently awaiting tidings of him, it was evident in the faces and postures of the audience that Peter's commission was, in their opinion, authentic.

It had been the hope of God from the beginning, he said, that His children would inherit the Kingdom. He had not compelled them to accept its benefits. He had endowed them with free will to claim or refuse their heritage.

But God had not left them in darkness concerning the results of their decisions. Every generation had had its inspired prophets who had entreated men to receive and enjoy their heavenly legacy. Only a few had heeded these messages. The lonely prophets had been imprisoned, flogged, and stoned by the forces of greed and the lust for power.

God had been patient with the evil-doers. Again and again, through the ages, humanity had reaped such appalling harvests of its own misdeeds that even the kings and warriors had stood aghast at the tragedies they had contrived. And always, in the midst of ruin and the fear that had chastened both the just and the unjust, the prophets had shouted, "Now we shall begin anew! We shall rebuild the wastes! We shall repair the world's desolations!"

But when a brief day of peace had brought prosperity, new tyrants rose up and another era of rapine, slavery and slaughter would bring distrust and terror to the children of men. The scepter had passed from one bloody hand to another as the nations clamored for power, and yet more power, over the lives of the helpless.

Here the Big Fisherman, after pausing for a moment, continued in an ominous tone that deepened the silence. He had done with his calm review of mankind's unfortunate history. It was time now for the world to be shaken wide awake. God had sent forth His Son with power to heal the sick, bind up broken hearts, open blind eyes, and proclaim a new era of good will among men.

But the world would not receive him. He had been scorned, whipped, and put to a shameful death! But he had come alive again—and had been seen of many. Now he had returned to his Father's House.

"Think you then," demanded Peter, "that the will of God has been set at naught? Think you that His Spirit will no longer strive with men? I declare to you that our Christ is King! He has begun to reign! And he shall reign until all the kingdoms of this world shall have become his Kingdom!"

For a moment the one hundred and twenty men thought the Big Fisherman's speech had ended, for he stood silent with his head bowed as in prayer. Then he faced them to say impressively:

"We, who confidently believe in him, have been summoned here to receive unmistakable proofs that his Holy Spirit abides with us. And from this day forward we are commissioned to spread the good news of his conquering Kingdom!"

Suddenly Peter drew himself up to his full height and glanced upward as if he had been struck. His auditors straightened and stared. Immediately above the Big Fisherman's head, and touching it, was a shimmering crimson flame—in shape like the flame of a torch! All breathing in the spacious room was suspended.

Then the massive oaken door flew open and banged hard against the wall. There was the deafening roar of a mighty tempest that swept through the hall. The startled men held to their seats and clung to one another as the rushing wind lashed to and fro. It was as if the world had come to an end! Now tongues of flame stabbed through the storm, coming to rest—torch-like—upon the heads of all present! The glow of the fire possessed exhilarating properties. Some of the men shouted ecstatically. Some wept for joy. Strangers grasped the hands of strangers and gazed at one another in wonderment. Jairus put his arm around Joel who was weeping. Mencius put both hands over his eyes and shook his head. Joseph of Arimathaea clutched Hassan's arm.

Now the torch-like flames departed and the tempest roared out as suddenly as it had come. Every man was on his feet, all talking at once, loudly, as if the tempest still raged. Mencius, not one to be easily discomposed, was so utterly stampeded that he turned to Jairus and shouted—in Greek, "This is a most amazing thing, sir!" And Jairus, who didn't know a word of Greek, instantly replied, in that language, "Surely the Lord has visited us!" Young Joel, listening intently, nodded his head; and when Jairus asked him if he had understood what they were saying he said he had, and added, in his own Aramaic, "It is true, sir! God Himself has been in this place!"

But the pandemonium in the Coppersmiths' Guildhall was no secret. The roar of the storm had been heard throughout the city. The urbane guests at Levi's Inn had rushed out into the street to see what was happening. It was evident that the fury of the tempest was confined to the Guildhall. They ran up the stairway, arriving when the tornado had spent itself and all the men in the auditorium were shouting joyfully. Crowding into the room, they stared at the strange scene.

A tall, haughty man from Crete remarked sourly to his bodyguard, in the outlandish dialect of that country—a curious composite of Greek and Egyptian, "Bah! They're all drunk!"

Peter, striding toward the door, answered him in Crete's guttural patois, "These men are not drunk! They are rejoicing because the Kingdom of God is at hand! The world shall have peace! The slaves shall be freed! The Lord has proclaimed a new day!"

"How do you happen to be speaking our language?" demanded the stranger. "You are not a citizen of Crete!"

"I am a citizen of the Kingdom of God!" declared Peter. "And from henceforth that Kingdom includes Crete!"

"You say—all the slaves are to be set free?"

"Yes—and their masters, too. No men can be free while other men are slaves!"

"You should be locked up!" growled the Cretan. "You are speaking treason!"

The controversy was attracting attention. A dozen of the illumined men gathered close and joined in supporting Peter, all of them speaking the barbarous jargon of far-away Crete. The man from that country, with baffled eyes, raised his elbow as if to ward off a blow, and slowly backed toward the door, muttering, "No! No!"

The Guildhall rapidly emptied. The street was packed with a huge crowd of bewildered people. The newly commissioned men, radiant, confident, infiltrated the throng, shouting, "The Kingdom of God has come for all who believe in Him!" They scattered through the city, spreading the news. They were unafraid. They stopped Roman legionaries on the street to announce the new Kingdom; and the legionaries, stunned by their audacity, did not detain them.

That day, three thousand men in Jerusalem said they believed it and would join the disciples in preparing for the reign of peace.

Late in the evening, as the little company of Jesus' Galileans sat together in Benyosef's house, exhausted to the point of speechlessness by the amazing events of the day, Philip, who had spread the tidings to incredulous groups at the camel-auction, remarked, "It is said that the Prince of Arabia has been smitten with paralysis."

Peter made no comment but seemed deeply impressed by this tragedy that had befallen the royal house of Israel's long-time enemy. Presently he arose and seated himself in a far corner of the dimly lighted room, with his elbows on his knees and his head in his hands, apparently wrestling with a difficult problem.

After a half-hour of silent meditation he took leave of them and trudged slowly up the long hill to the Garden of Gethsemane where he knelt beside a great rock and prayed earnestly for guidance. Could it be possible that God might use him as a messenger of good will to hostile Arabia?

KEEPER OF THE FAITH

Henryk Sienkiewicz

~~~~~~

The colorful pageantry of the reign of Nero sets the scene for *Quo Vadis?*, Sienkiewicz's epic of Christian martyrdom. In this pagan world, teeming with intrigue and bloodshed, the Apostle Paul earns his crown of righteousness and remains "keeper of the faith."

IN THAT SAME wonderful evening another detachment of soldiers conducted along the Ostian Way Paul of Tarsus toward a place called Aquæ Salviæ. And behind him also advanced a crowd of the faithful whom he had converted; but when he recognized near acquaintances, he halted and conversed with them, for, being a Roman citizen, the guard showed more respect to him. Beyond the gate called Tergemina he met Plautilla, the daughter of the prefect Flavius Sabinus, and, seeing her youthful face covered with tears, he said: "Plautilla, daughter of Eternal Salvation, depart in peace. Only give me a veil with which to bind my eyes when I am going to the Lord." And taking it, he advanced with a face as full of delight as that of a laborer who when he has toiled the whole day successfully is returning home. His thoughts, like those of Peter, were as calm and quiet as that evening sky. His eyes gazed with thoughtfulness upon the plain which stretched out before him, and to the Alban Hills, immersed in light. He remembered his journeys, his toils, his labor, the struggles in which he had conquered, the churches which he had founded in all lands and beyond all seas; and he thought that he had earned his rest honestly, that he had finished his work. He felt now that the seed which he had planted would not be blown away by the wind of malice. He was leaving this life with the certainty that in the battle which his truth had declared against the world it would conquer; and a mighty peace settled down on his soul.

The road to the place of execution was long, and evening was coming. The mountains became purple, and the bases of them went gradually into the shade. Flocks were returning home. Here and there groups of slaves were walking with the tools of labor on their shoulders. Children, playing on the road before houses, looked with curiosity at the passing soldiers. But in that evening, in that transparent golden air, there were not only peace and lovingness, but a certain harmony, which seemed to lift from earth to heaven. Paul felt this; and his heart was filled with delight at the thought that to that harmony of the world he had added one note which had not been in it hitherto, but without which the whole earth was like sounding brass or a tinkling cymbal.

He remembered how he had taught people love,—how he had told them that though they were to give their property to the poor, though they knew all languages, all secrets, and all sciences, they would be nothing without love, which is kind, enduring, which does not return evil, which does not desire honor, suffers all things, believes all things, hopes all things, is patient of all things.

And so his life had passed in teaching people this truth. And now he said in spirit: What power can equal it, what can conquer it? Could Cæsar stop it, though he had twice as many legions and twice as many cities, seas, lands, and nations?

And he went to his reward like a conqueror.

The detachment left the main road at last, and turned toward the east on a narrow path leading to the Aquæ Salviæ. The red sun was lying now on the heather. The centurion stopped the soldiers at the fountain, for the moment had come.

Paul placed Plautilla's veil on his arm, intending to bind his eyes with it; for the last time he raised those eyes, full of unspeakable peace, toward the eternal light of the evening, and prayed. Yes, the moment had come; but he saw before him a great road in the light, leading to heaven; and in his soul he repeated the same words which formerly he had written in the feeling of his own finished service and his near end,—

"I have fought a good fight, I have finished my course, I have kept the faith. Henceforth there is laid up for me a crown of righteousness."

CROSSING THE RIVER

John Bunyan

~~~~~~

The allegory of *Pilgrim's Progress* traces the path of a soul toward salvation. This excerpt takes Valiant-for-Truth to his journey's end.

_____

AFTER THIS it was noised abroad that Mr. Valiant-for-Truth was taken with a summons by the same post as the other, and had this for a token that the summons was true, That his pitcher was broken at the fountain. When he understood it he called for his friends, and told them of it. Then said he, I am going to my Father's; and though with great difficulty I am got hither, yet now I do not repent me of all the trouble I have been at to arrive where I am. My sword I give to him that shall succeed me in my pilgrimage, and my courage and skill to him that can get it. My marks and scars I carry with me, to be a witness for me that I have fought His battles who now will be my rewarder. When the day that he must go hence was come, many accompanied him to the river side, into which as he went he said, Death, where is thy sting? And as he went down deeper, he said, Grave, where is thy victory? So he passed over, and all the trumpets sounded for him on the other side.

ADSUM

William M. Thackeray

As a picture of English society in the first half of the nineteenth century, *The Newcomes* is a novel without peer. "Adsum" marks the passing of Colonel Newcome, who epitomized the most perfect type of gentleman to be found in the world of fiction.

THE DAYS went on, and our hopes, raised sometimes, began to flicker and fail. One evening the Colonel left his chair for his bed in pretty good spirits, but passed a disturbed night, and the next morning was too weak to rise. Then he remained in his bed, and his friends visited him there. One afternoon he asked for his little gown-boy, and the child was brought to him, and sat by the bed with a very awe-stricken face; and then gathered courage, and tried to amuse him by telling him how it was a half-holiday, and they were having a cricket-match with the St. Peter's boys in the green, and Grey Friars was in and winning. The Colonel quite understood about it; he would like to see the game; he had played many a game on that green when he was a boy. He grew excited; Clive dismissed his father's little friend, and put a sovereign into his hand; and away he ran to say that Codd Colonel had come into a fortune, and to buy tarts, and to see the match out. I *curre,* little white-haired gown-boy! Heaven speed you, little friend!

After the child had gone, Thomas Newcome began to wander more and more. He talked louder; he gave the word of command, spoke Hindustanee as if to his men. Then he spoke words in French rapidly, seizing a hand that was near him, and crying, "Toujours, toujours!" But it was Ethel's hand which he took. Ethel and Clive and the nurse were in the room with him; the nurse came to us, who were sitting in the adjoining apartment; Madame de Florac was there, with my wife and Bayham.

At the look in the woman's countenance Madame de Florac started up. "He is very bad, he wanders a great deal," the nurse whispered. The French lady fell instantly on her knees, and remained rigid in prayer.

Some time afterwards Ethel came in with a scared face to our pale group. "He is calling for you again, dear lady," she said, going up to Madame de Florac, who was still kneeling; "and just now he said he wanted Pendennis to take care of his boy. He will not know you." She hid her tears as she spoke.

She went into the room where Clive was at the bed's foot; the old man within it talked on rapidly for a while: then again he would sigh and be still: once more I heard him say hurriedly, "Take care of him when I'm in India"; and then with a heartrending voice he called out, "Leonore, Leonore." She was kneeling by his side now. The patient's voice sank into faint murmurs; only a moan now and then announced that he was not asleep.

At the usual evening hour the chapel bell began to toll, and Thomas Newcome's hands outside the bed feebly beat time. And just as the last bell struck, a peculiar sweet smile shone over his face, and he lifted up his head a little, and quickly said "Adsum!" and fell back. It was the word we used at school, when names were called; and lo, he, whose heart was as that of a little child, had answered to his name, and stood in the presence of The Master.

A FUTURE LIFE

Leo Tolstoi

With unerring insight into his characters, Tolstoi builds the drama of *War and Peace* against a panorama of Russia during the Napoleonic Wars. The following interlude catches the hero Pierre in the act of convincing his disillusioned friend André that truth lives on.

IN THE EVENING Prince André and Pierre seated themselves in the carriage . . . they approached a river which had overflowed its banks, and they had to cross it in a ferry. While the carriage and the horses were being put on the boat, they walked down to the landing. Prince André, leaning on the balustrade, gazed in silence down the broad stream, which was sparkling in the setting sun. . . .

Pierre broke in upon him. "Do you believe in a future life?" he asked.

"A future life?" repeated Prince André. But Pierre gave him no time to answer, taking this echoing of his own words as a denial, the more so since he knew Prince André's former atheistic convictions.

"You say that you cannot see the kingdom of goodness and truth on earth. Neither have I seen it, nor can anyone see it who looks upon life here as the end of everything. Upon earth, particularly upon this earth," (Pierre pointed to the fields), "there is no truth: all is falsehood and evil; but in the universe, in the whole universe, there is the kingdom of truth; and we who are now the children of earth, in eternity are the children of the universe. Do I not feel that in this countless assemblage of beings, in which Divinity—call it a higher Power, if you wish—is manifested,—I form one link, one step between the lower beings and the higher? Since I clearly see the ladder leading from the plant to man, why should I suppose that it breaks off with me, and does not lead on beyond? I feel that I cannot completely disappear, since nothing in the universe completely disappears, and that I shall always be, just as I have always been. I feel that besides me there are spirits above me, and that truth abides in the universe."

"Yes, that is Herder's doctrine," said Prince André, "but that, my friend, will not convince me; life and death—they alone are what convince a man. What convinces a man is when he sees someone dear to him, in whose life he has been closely bound, but to whom he has done a wrong and wished to make atonement," (Prince André's voice quivered and he turned his face away), "and suddenly this being suffers, is in torment, and ceases to exist—but why? It cannot be that there is no answer! I believe that there is one. That is what convinces a man. That is what has convinced me," said Prince André.

"Why, of course," said Pierre. "Isn't that just what I was saying?"

"No. I only say that no argument will convince a man of the necessity of a future life, except this one: when you go through life hand in hand with another, and suddenly your dear one vanishes *there, into the nowhere;* and you yourself are left on the brink of that abyss looking down into it. And I have looked!"

"Very well. What then? You have known that there is a *There* and a *Someone.* The *There* is the future life, the Someone is *God.*"

Prince André made no reply. The carriage and horse had long since been led out on the further bank and harnessed; the sun was half-hidden beneath the horizon, and the evening frost was beginning to form crystal stars on the puddles ashore, but Pierre and André, to the surprise of the attendants, coachmen and ferrymen, were still standing on the boat talking.

"If God and the future life exist, then truth and virtue exist; and man's highest happiness consists in striving to attain them. We must live, we must love, we must believe," said Pierre, "that we live not only now, on this patch of earth, but that we have lived and will live always in eternity there, in the universe." He pointed to the sky.

Prince André stood leaning on the rail of the ferryboat and listening to Pierre. He never moved his eyes, but gazed steadily at the ruddy reflection of the sun in the deep blue stream. Pierre ceased speaking. There was complete silence. The ferryboat lay moored along the bank, and only the ripples of the current could be heard lapping gently against its sides. It seemed to Prince André that this splashing of the water murmured a refrain to Pierre's words: "That is truth, accept it: that is truth, accept it."

THE DREAMS ARE REAL

Bess Streeter Aldrich

At the age of eighty, Abbie Deal could look back with deep satisfaction on her life as a pioneer wife and mother. One by one, she saw her children attain success through talents she herself had had no opportunity to express. And in her last hours, with a vision of her dead husband before her, she faced eternal life with "courage her lodestar and love her guide, a song on her lips, a lantern in her hand."

GRACE DEAL, in her roadster, went back to summer school early in the morning. John Deal and his family left about the same time for Cedartown. Isabelle and Harrison Rhodes were remaining in Omaha for a few days' visit at Mack's, before making the rounds of the other homes. Abbie rode back with Margaret and Dr. Baker.

On the way, Margaret asked: "Don't you want to go on up to Lincoln with us for a few days, Mother?"

"No. Oh, no," Abbie said hastily. "I'm tired and I'll be real glad to get home again."

When the big car stopped under the Lombardy poplars near the sitting-room porch of the old farmhouse, Margaret got out with her mother and helped her up the short walk to the house.

"I just can't bear to leave you here alone, Mother. Don't you want me to stay all night with you? Fred could run out and get me tomorrow or I could go in on the morning train."

"No. Oh, no. I'm all right. I'm just tired from the excitement. When you're used to being alone you don't mind it a bit."

"Promise me you would call some one on the phone the first minute you didn't feel well."

"I promise. I would call Christine. She's got a phone in now, but she certainly begrudges the money. Anyway, I won't be alone much more this summer. Isabelle will be here next week, and Grace will be home again soon, and Laura is going to come and stay a few days."

When they had gone, Abbie Deal opened some of the windows to air out the house. She had a whimsical notion that the things seemed glad to have her back,—the table where old Doc Matthews had rolled his pills, the walnut cupboard, Will's corner what-not. There was something human about them as though they shared her thoughts,—as though, having come up through the years with her, they held the same memories.

She fed her chickens, watered the sweet-peas, picked the dried leaves off her geraniums, and went over the whole yard as though to greet every bush and shrub after her absence.

For the next few days she went slowly about her household duties with the same little sense of pleasure she always experienced after she had been to one of the children's homes. How could old women bear to sit around with folded hands? What mattered it that the children all had such nice houses, there would never be any real home for her but the old wing-and-upright set in the cedars and poplars.

By Friday night she had accomplished a lot of extra small tasks, setting an old hen that was foolishly wanting to raise a family out of season, gathering some early poppy-seeds and putting fresh papers on her pantry shelves. At five-thirty she started her supper. As she

worked she tried to hum an old tune she had known when she was
young, an old song she had not thought of for years and years, until
Isabelle had sung it over the radio in the winter:

> *"Oh . . . the La . . . dy of . . . the Lea,*
> *Fair and . . . young and . . . gay was . . . she"*

She had to make long pauses between the syllables to get her breath.

> *"Beau . . . tiful . . . exceed . . . ingly*
> *The La . . . dy of . . . the Lea."*

Her voice cracked and went up or down without her volition, so that
even though her mind heard the song, her ear scarcely recognized the
melody.

> *"Many . . . a woo . . . er sought her . . . hand*
> *For she . . . had gold . . . and she . . . had land,*
> *Every . . . thing . . . la la . . . la la"*

She had forgotten what the words were right there.

> *"The La . . . dy of . . . the Lea."*

She was completely out of breath, so that she had to sit down a few
minutes before starting to put her dishes on the kitchen table. As she
sat looking at the old table, she suddenly wished that she could pull it
out, put in all the leaves, set the places for the children and then call
them in from play,—not the prosperous grown people she had been
with so recently in Omaha, but just as they were when they were little.
Queer how plainly she could see them in her mind: Mack's merry
round face with its sprinkling of freckles, Margaret's long dark pig-
tail, her gray eyes and her laughter, Isabelle's reddish-brown curls and
her big brown eyes, Grace's square little body with her apron-strings
always untied, John's serious face,—a sort of little old man who did not
want to be hugged. How real they seemed to her. One could almost
imagine that it was they who were playing "Run, Sheep, Run" out
there now instead of the neighbor children.

Abbie Deal had never forbidden the north-end children access to her
yard, and their high-pitched voices calling "Going east . . . going
west . . ." came to her now from the region of the cottonwood wind-
break. Yes, it sounded for all the world like her own children out
there.

As she got up and went about her supper, putting a little piece of meat on to cook, her mind slipped to the fact that she had promised to make a short talk on the following week at the sixtieth anniversary of the founding of the city of Lincoln. She must begin to think of what she could say. There was plenty to talk about but she dreaded the speaking. She hoped her voice wouldn't quaver and break. That was the trouble of being old. Your body no longer obeyed you. It did unruly and unreasonable things. An eye suddenly might not see for a moment. Your knees gave out at the wrong time, so that when you thought you were walking north, you might find yourself going a little northwest. Your brain, too, had that same flighty trick. You might be speaking of something and forget it temporarily,—your mind going off at a little to the northwest, too, so to speak.

She glanced up to see what time it was, and discovered that the clock had stopped. Whatever had happened to the faithful old thing? It must be wearing out, for she was sure she had wound it.

She opened the door with the little brown church painted on the glass, and reached for the key. Suddenly,—so suddenly that it was like a flash,—a queer feeling came over Abbie Deal. It was unlike any she had ever experienced,—a tightening of the throat and chest as of cold icy hands upon her. She tried to take her arms down from their stretched position, but it was almost impossible to move them for the pain. In a moment the icy hands released their hold upon her as quickly as they had clutched at her, but they left her so weak and shaken that she started into her bedroom holding onto the backs of the chairs.

She lay down on her bed to get herself in hand. There was a sharp pain now in the back of her head and it seemed a little hard to breathe. For a moment she wondered if it could be that her time to die had come. No, that could not be. She was a little sick, but she had been so many times. "I never *do* die," she said to herself and smiled a little at the humor of it.

The sun's rays slanted along the floor from the west sitting-room windows. The meat was cooking, for the air was filled with the odor of it. Robins were singing outside in the poplars. The neighbors' children ran across the yard with cries of "All's out's in free." They would trample the grass a little, but children were worth more than grass anyway. She must not get sick, for she was planning to go to something in a few days. For a few moments she could not think what it was, and then she remembered. It was the old settlers' meeting in Lincoln. There would be a lot of old folks there and they would tell their reminiscences all day. No doubt she would be bored to distraction. Old people usually bored her. No, that was not right. Something was wrong with that thought. She was not young. She was *old*. She, herself, was one of the old settlers. How strange! Well, she would go. Her mind seemed not quite under control. She tried hard to think whether she was to go in the big shining sedan on the straight graveled roads or in the creaking wagon through the long swaying grass. *Blow . . . wave . . . ripple . . . dip. Blow . . . wave . . . ripple . . . dip.* She felt ill. It was the swaying of the prairie grass that made her ill.

If she were taken sick she had promised to do something,—something with the little brown box at the side of the bed. Suddenly, she remembered . . . call Christine. That was it. Good old Christine! . . . Old friends . . . were best. Maybe she ought to call Christine in the little brown box. Her arm slipped around the rolled silk quilt at the foot of the bed. Such a soft silk quilt . . . and an old patched quilt in front of a sheep-shed for a door. There it was again,—her mind going northwest.

The sun slanted farther across the carpet. Whoever was frying that meat was letting it burn. The children shouted very close to the house: "Run, sheep, run." It was nice to know the children were all well and out there playing,—Mack and Margaret, John and Isabelle, Grace and the baby. She hoped they were taking good care of the baby,—the baby with a face like a little white rose. She would let them play on until she got to feeling better, and then she would get up and finish supper.

That queer thought of death intruded itself again, but she reasoned, slowly and simply, with it. If death were near she would be frightened. Death was her enemy. All her life she had hated death and feared it. It had taken her mother, and Will and the baby and countless old friends. But Death was not near. The children playing outdoors, the sun slanting over the familiar carpet, the meat frying for supper,—all the old simple things to which she was accustomed reassured her. A warm feeling of contentment slipped over her to hear the children's happy voices. "All's out's in free," they called. It was almost time for Will to come in to his supper. It was the nicest part of the day—the robins singing in the poplars—the meat cooking—the supper table set —every one coming home—the whole family around the table—all— Will—the children. She must wind the clock before they came in. You—couldn't—stop—Time——

It was hard again to breathe,—the icy pain—in her chest——

Oh . . .

Immediately the children were quiet. The robin had stopped singing. Whoever had been frying meat had removed it from the stove, and some one must have pulled down all the shades. It was strange to have all those things happen at once,—the robin cease singing, the children stop playing, the meat taken from the stove, and the shades pulled down. For a moment it was as though one could neither see nor hear nor smell. At any rate she felt much better. The pressure in her chest and in the back of her head was gone. That was nice. It seemed good to be relieved of that. She breathed easily,—so very easily that she seemed not to be breathing at all. She sat up on the edge of the bed. She felt light, buoyant. "I'll wind the clock and finish supper now and call them in."

Through the semi-darkness of the house there was no sight or sound. But as she looked up, she saw Will standing in the doorway. For a moment she thought he was standing under honey-locust branches in a lane, but saw at once that it was only shadows.

"Well, Will!" She stood up. "I'm so glad you're home. You've been away all day, haven't you? Where were you, Will? Isn't that stupid of me not to remember?" She moved lightly toward him, but suddenly stopped, sensing that for some reason there was a strangeness about his presence. She stood looking at him questioningly, a little confused.

Will was looking intently at her, half-smiling. She would have thought he was joking her—teasing her a little—if his expression had not been too tender for that.

"I don't quite understand, Will. Did you want something of me? . . ." That was a way of Will's,—always so quiet that you almost had to read his mind. There was no answer, but at once she seemed to know that Will was waiting for her.

"Oh, I must tell the children first. They *never* want me to go." She turned to the window. "Listen, children," she called, "I'm going away with Father. If some one would pull up the shades I could see you, but it doesn't really matter. Listen closely . . . I'm only going to be gone a little while. Be good children . . . You'll get along just fine."

She turned to the doorway. "It seems a little dark. You know, Will, I think we will need the lantern. I've always kept the lantern . . ." Her voice trailed off into nothing. For Will was still smiling at her, questioningly, quizzically,—but with something infinitely more tender, —something protecting, enveloping. Slowly it came to her. Hesitatingly she put her hand up to her throat. "Will . . . you don't mean it! . . .

Not *that* . . . not *Death* . . . so *easy?* That it's nothing more than *this* . . . ? Why . . . *Will!"*

Abbie Deal moved lightly, quickly, over to her husband, slipped her hand into his and went with him out of the old house, past the Lombardy poplars, through the deepening prairie twilight,—into the shadows.

It was old Christine Reinmueller who came in and found her.

"Ach . . . Gott!" She wrung her hard old hands. "Mine friend . . . de best voman dat efer on de eart' valked."

The children all came hastily in response to the messages. In the old parlor with the what-not and the marble-topped stand and the blue plush album, they said the same things over and over to each other.

"Didn't she seem as well to you last week as ever?"

"Do you suppose she suffered much?"

"Or called for us?"

"Isn't it *dreadful.* Poor mother . . . all alone . . . not one of us here . . . as though we had all forsaken her just when she needed us most . . . and after all she's done for us . . ."

It was then that little twelve-year-old Laura Deal turned away from the window where she had been looking down the long double row of cedars and said in a voice so certain that it was almost exalted:

"I don't think it's so dreadful. I think it was kind of nice. Maybe she didn't miss you. Maybe she didn't miss you *at all.* One time grandma told me she was the very happiest when she was living over all her memories. Maybe . . ." She looked around the circle of her relatives,— and there was a little about her of another twelve-year-old Child who stood in the midst of his elders in a Temple,—"Maybe she was doing that . . . then."

A HANDFUL OF CLAY

Henry van Dyke

This famous parable carries the Easter message of hope, faith, and rebirth in the eternal spring of the spirit.

THERE WAS a handful of clay in the bank of a river. It was only common clay, coarse and heavy; but it had high thoughts of its own value, and wonderful dreams of the great place which it was to fill in the world when the time came for its virtues to be discovered.

Overhead, in the spring sunshine, the trees whispered together of the glory which descended upon them when the delicate blossoms and leaves began to expand, and the forest glowed with fair, clear colours, as if the dust of thousands of rubies and emeralds were hanging, in soft clouds, above the earth.

The flowers, surprised with the joy of beauty, bent their heads to one another, as the wind caressed them, and said: "Sisters, how lovely you have become. You make the day bright."

The river, glad of new strength and rejoicing in the unison of all its waters, murmured to the shores in music, telling of its release from icy fetters, its swift flight from the snow-clad mountains, and the mighty work to which it was hurrying—the wheels of many mills to be turned, and great ships to be floated to the sea.

Waiting blindly in its bed, the clay comforted itself with lofty hopes. "My time will come," it said. "I was not made to be hidden forever. Glory and beauty and honour are coming to me in due season."

One day the clay felt itself taken from the place where it had waited so long. A flat blade of iron passed beneath it, and lifted it, and tossed it into a cart with other lumps of clay, and it was carried far away, as it seemed, over a rough and stony road. But it was not afraid, nor discouraged, for it said to itself: "This is necessary. The path to glory is always rugged. Now I am on my way to play a great part in the world."

But the hard journey was nothing compared with the tribulation and distress that came after it. The clay was put into a trough and mixed and beaten and stirred and trampled. It seemed almost unbearable. But there was consolation in the thought that something very fine and noble was certainly coming out of all this trouble. The clay felt sure that, if it could only wait long enough, a wonderful reward was in store for it.

Then it was put upon a swiftly turning wheel, and whirled around until it seemed as if it must fly into a thousand pieces. A strange power pressed it and moulded it, as it revolved, and through all the dizziness and pain it felt that it was taking a new form.

Then an unknown hand put it into an oven, and fires were kindled about it—fierce and penetrating—hotter than all the heats of summer that had ever brooded upon the bank of the river. But through all, the clay held itself together and endured its trials, in the confidence of a great future. "Surely," it thought, "I am intended for something very splendid, since such pains are taken with me. Perhaps I am fashioned for the ornament of a temple, or a precious vase for the table of a king."

At last the baking was finished. The clay was taken from the furnace and set down upon a board, in the cool air, under the blue sky. The tribulation was passed. The reward was at hand.

Close beside the board there was a pool of water, not very deep, nor very clear, but calm enough to reflect, with impartial truth, every image that fell upon it. There, for the first time, as it was lifted from the board, the clay saw its new shape, the reward of all its patience and pain, the consummation of its hopes—a common flower-pot, straight and stiff, red and ugly. And then it felt that it was not destined for a king's house, nor for a palace of art, because it was made without glory or beauty or honour; and it murmured against the unknown maker, saying, "Why hast thou made me thus?"

Many days it passed in sullen discontent. Then it was filled with earth, and something—it knew not what—but something rough and brown and dead-looking, was thrust into the middle of the earth and covered over. The clay rebelled at this new disgrace. "This is the worst of all that has happened to me, to be filled with dirt and rubbish. Surely I am a failure."

But presently it was set in a greenhouse, where the sunlight fell warm upon it, and water was sprinkled over it, and day by day, as it waited, a change began to come to it. Something was stirring within it—a new hope. Still it was ignorant, and knew not what the new hope meant.

One day the clay was lifted again from its place, and carried into a great church. Its dream was coming true after all. It had a fine part to play in the world. Glorious music flowed over it. It was surrounded with flowers. Still it could not understand. So it whispered to another vessel of clay, like itself, close beside it, "Why have they set me here? Why do all the people look toward us?" And the other vessel answered, "Do you not know? You are carrying a royal sceptre of lilies. Their petals are white as snow, and the heart of them is like pure gold. The people look this way because the flower is the most wonderful in the world. And the root of it is in your heart."

Then the clay was content, and silently thanked its maker, because, though an earthen vessel, it held so great a treasure.

ALL THE WORLD WILL BE JEALOUS
OF ME

William Saroyan

In this selection from *The Human Comedy* a small child's proverbial question "Why?" leads to an explanation of man's place in the universe.

Music came from the Macauley house on Santa Clara Avenue. Bess and Mrs. Macauley played *All the World Will Be Jealous of Me.* They played the song for the soldier Marcus, wherever he happened to be, because it was the song he loved most. Mary Arena came into the parlor from the house next door, stood beside Bess at the piano and soon began to sing. She sang for Marcus, who was all the world to *her.* The small boy Ulysses listened and watched. Something was mysterious somewhere and he wanted to find out what it was, even though he was half asleep. At last he summoned enough energy to say:

"Where's Marcus?"

Mrs. Macauley looked at the boy.

"You must try to understand," she began to say, then stopped.

Ulysses tried to understand but didn't know just what was to be understood.

"Understand what?" he said.

"Marcus," Mrs. Macauley said, "has gone away from Ithaca."

"Why?" Ulysses said.

"Marcus is in the Army," Mrs. Macauley said.

"When is he coming home?" the little boy said.

"When the War is over," Mrs. Macauley said.

"Tomorrow?"

"No, not tomorrow."

"When?"

"We don't know. We're waiting."

"Then where is my father?" Ulysses said. "If we wait, will *he* come home like Marcus too?"

"No," Mrs. Macauley said, "not that way. He will not come walking down the street, up the steps, across the porch, and on into the house, as he used to do."

This too was too much for the boy, and as there was only one word with which to hope for something like truth and comfort, he said this word:

"Why?"

Mrs. Macauley turned to Bess and Mary. "Death," she said, "is not an easy thing for anyone to understand, least of all a child, but every life shall one day end." She looked now at Ulysses. "That day came for your father two years ago." She looked back at Bess and Mary. "But as long as we are alive," she said, "as long as we are together, as long as *two* of us are left, and remember him, nothing in the world can take him from us. His body can be taken, but not *him*. You shall know your father better as you grow and know yourself better," she said. "He is not dead, because *you* are alive. Time and accident, illness and weariness took his body, but already you have given it back to him, younger and more eager than ever. I don't expect you to understand anything I'm telling you. But I know you will remember *this*—that nothing good ever ends. If it did, there would be no people in the world—no life at all, anywhere. And the world is full of people and full of wonderful life."

The boy thought about this a moment and then remembered what he had witnessed earlier that day.

"What are the gophers?" he said.

His mother was not at all unprepared for such a question. She knew that he had eyes, and beyond eyes vision, and beyond vision heart and passion and love—not for one thing alone, or for one *kind* of thing, but for any and all.

"The gophers of the earth," she said, "the birds overhead, the fish in the sea are all part of the life of things—and part of *our* life. Everything alive is part of each of us, and many things which do not move as we move are part of us. The sun is part of us, the earth, the sky, the stars, the rivers, and the oceans. All things are part of us, and we have come here to enjoy them and to thank God for them."

The little boy accepted this news.

"Then where is Homer?" he said.

"Your brother Homer," Mrs. Macauley said, "is working. Yesterday he found himself a job after school. He will be home after midnight, when you are in bed asleep."

The small boy could not understand. What was work? Why was his brother working? What delight came to a man from working?

"Why is Homer working?" he said.

The two girls sat by patiently, waiting for Mrs. Macauley's answers to the child's questions.

"Your brother Homer is working," she said, "because your brother Marcus is in the Army. Because we must have money with which to buy food and clothing and pay rent—and to give to others whose need is greater than ours."

"*Who?*" Ulysses said.

"Anybody," Mrs. Macauley said. "The poor, for instance."

"Who're the poor?" the boy said.

"Everybody," Mrs. Macauley said, smiling to herself.

Ulysses tried hard to stay awake, but it was no longer possible.

"You must remember," she said, "always to give, of everything you have. You must give foolishly even. You must be extravagant. You must give to all who come into your life. Then nothing and no one shall have the power to cheat you of anything, for if you give to a thief, he cannot steal from you, and he himself is then no longer a thief. And the more you give, the more you will have to give."

Mrs. Macauley looked from the boy to his sister Bess. "Put him to bed," she said.

Bess and Mary took the boy to his room. When they were gone and she sat alone, the woman heard a footstep and turned. There at the door she saw Matthew Macauley as if he were not dead.

"I fell asleep," he said. "I was very sleepy. Please forgive me, Katey."

He laughed as if it were Ulysses laughing, and when Bess came back to the parlor she said, "He laughed just before we tucked him in."

The Word Lives On

TOLD IN THE STARS

Manuel Komroff

In the Years of Our Lord opens with the story of the three kings and the old oracle Xado's prediction: ". . . Your faith will be firm . . . truth will walk through the world unharmed." Here, many years later, it is Pilate who seeks Xado and learns how this prophecy will be fulfilled through the influence of the Word on ages to come.

OUT OF the deep far East came the old oracle Xado. His skin was brown, scorched by the hot sun of the Indies and dried by the winds of desert Persia. He carried a staff cut from the holy acacia wood and with this rod he journeyed the hundreds of leagues from the great mysterious lands of the East. From India, dotted with its fierce stone gods, through the vast snow-covered mountains and into Persia the land of mystery he journeyed. He had climbed the mountain of Elam and spent the night on the very top studying the stars in the heavens. He journeyed through the rocky wilderness of Paran and the hot sands of the wilderness of Zin. And now with staff in hand he walked through the open gate and into the busy paved streets of Jerusalem.

The cloth of his tattered garment, his burnt skin and even the staff in his hand gave him the stamp of one who had come from the far far East. And it was not long before the people of Jerusalem discovered that the great oracle Xado was in their midst.

As he was washing himself at the public fountain rich merchants sent their servants to bow before him and invite him to their homes for rest and refreshment. But he thanked them and sent them away saying he had need of nothing. There was a proud toss of his head.

The servants of the high-priests also came to him but these too he sent away. "I must journey now to the land of Egypt," he said.

The hunch-backed female slave of Pilate came before the oracle and said: "My master sends me. Though he is Governor of all Judea he offers the holy and wise man from the East nothing."

"You come to tell me this?"

"In haste I have been sent."

"Then return," spoke the oracle Xado, "and thank your governor for the nothing he offers. I ask for nothing and I am truly grateful if what I ask for is given me."

"Ah!" said Buncha with a twinkle in her eye. "I see I am no match for you, for the years of my life are only forty and yours are twice forty, and I can barely read the alphabet while you can read the stars in the heavens; and so if my master can give you nothing, then perhaps you could give my master something."

"What have I so precious?"

"Words and prophecy."

"Your master does not believe in the stars."

"He would listen to your words for he has heard of the fame of Xado even in Rome."

"And he sent you to bring me before him?"

"That is it."

"And if I refuse to appear in his presence he will probably send his soldiers to bring me. And what I would not do willingly I will have to do by compulsion."

"No. You are wrong. That is what I said he should do but he has another plan. If you do not come to him, then he will come to you."

"This he said?"

"Yes."

"Then lead the way and take me to him. When governors are humble, then they deserve to hear words of faith and prophecy."

The hunch-backed slave led the way through the streets of Jerusalem and brought the venerable oracle Xado into the presence of Pontius Pilate.

"Long have I heard of the wonders of your prophecies," said Pilate. "Your fame has even traveled to Rome."

The old man bowed in acknowledgment of this compliment.

"Tell me, wise Xado, what brings you into Jerusalem?"

"For the past forty nights have I watched the stars in the sky. I am on my way to the land of Egypt. In Egypt my fathers were born and died and there I will remain the rest of my days and be buried beside my own people. Here in Jerusalem I hoped to see some of those whose names I read clearly in the stars."

"You have but to command, my good Xado, and I will order that they be brought before you. This would be little service indeed for a guest so renowned."

"Ah, Pilate! It is not so easy. Only eleven of the true followers remain and they have already left Jerusalem."

"Then someone else surely you desire to see?"

"No one else."

"You know," said Pilate, "many years ago, it must have been about thirty years ago, when I was still a young man in Rome, little did I imagine I would ever be sitting face to face with the oracle Xado. . . . At that time we heard stories in Rome how once three Eastern kings came to you. And you pointed out a star to them and told them to follow this star for under it a certain child was born. And this child was destined to be king over all. Tell me, Xado, was this a tale of a story-teller or was it true?"

"It was true, Pilate."

"Then what happened to this king?"

"Alas, he is dead."

"Dead? Born only thirty years ago and already dead?"

"Yes. By your command."

"No, no! It could not be. No king came before me. Five years have I been in this wretched hole and . . ."

"By your command," repeated the oracle.

"When? Tell me when I condemned a king."

"Forty days ago. Before the Passover holidays."

"Ah! That was no king. Your stars could not have told the truth."

"The stars have no reason to speak falsely."

"He was one from the desert and the priests arrested him. They called him the King of the Jews only in mockery. I remember clearly now. I could find no guilt in the man. But they cried aloud for him. And I washed my hands of the whole business."

"He was the one. Forty days ago I read the news in the heavens. And because of this innocent man whom you condemned . . ."

"I wanted only peace."

"Because of him, your name will be immortal."

"Because of him?"

"Yes. Only that and nothing else."

"Immortal! . . . Tell me this, wise Xado. Here I have been Procurator of Judea these five long years. How many more years will I remain here as procurator?"

"Five more."

"And after me?"

"You are the last of all. No other governors will Rome send to Jerusalem."

"And those who served as procurators here before me . . . Will their names be forgotten?"

"Perhaps on some dusty page of history their names may be preserved. But only your name will be truly known in all the ages to come."

"The first procurator to come to Jerusalem from Rome was Coponius and soon after there was Marcus Ambivius and he was followed by Annius Rufus. These three were all very distinguished. And they did very well for themselves and went back to Rome laden with wealth."

"They will be forgotten."

"And before me there was Valerius Gratus. He spent six years here in this wretched hole and is now a senator in Rome."

"Only one name of all these will be immortal and that name is Pontius Pilate."

"How strange! And you say five years more I will remain in this place?"

"Yes."

"And then?"

"Wars will drive you out."

"And I will return to Rome?"

"Yes, in poverty and disgrace."

"But you say I will be renowned and my name will be immortal."

"Not in your days, but in the years to come."

"And when you say immortal you mean my name will really be known everywhere?"

"Everywhere and in every land. It will be known as well as Caesar's."

"And all because . . ."

"Because of him."

"How strange are the stars. One could really never imagine such a thing. It is like a dream. Tell me more. What else do you read in the stars?"

"Herod Antipas, the son of the old tyrant Herod who killed the innocents, will fall from his high place. And with him will fall Herodias who plotted for the head of the Baptist John. The Arabian king Aretas, father of the first wife of Herod Antipas, will invade the lands and defeat him. He will flee to Rome to plead before the Emperor but he will not win favor. And he and his dark wife will end their evil days in banishment."

"What else do you read in the stars? The Temple of the Jews . . . Will it remain standing?"

"For forty years more it will stand. And then it will be laid in ruin, as will all the great buildings of Jerusalem."

"And the victors?"

"Rome. The great altar candlesticks and other golden relics sacred to the Jews will be paraded in a march of triumph through the streets of Rome."

"Then out of all this Rome will be the victor?"

"No, not really. The true conquest is of a different order. It will stem from those who have survived. From the eleven faithful followers. Theirs will be the victory and a new faith will be born."

"But they are without arms and can conquer no one."

"Without arms, true. But little by little a great part of the world will come over to their faith. And the teachings of their Master they will make known over the entire world."

"You seem to make this incident into a very big affair."

"Not I. The stars so proclaim. And your name is caught in this net of destiny and will endure the ages."

"And that is why you seek the eleven followers of this one who was condemned?"

"Yes. I hoped to find them here and learn from their own lips how they saw their Master after he rose out of the tomb. He spoke with them as man to man and he commanded them to believe and go out into the world and teach the word that is the true word."

"And what word could be a true word?" asked Pilate.

"Love is a true word. Faith is another word that might well be true."

"I must admit, Xado, that the stars are filled with a great confusion of strange things."

"Out of the confusion comes order and the destiny of all things."

With these words the venerable oracle rose to depart.

"Stay, Xado. I will make a feast for you."

"My eyes have feasted with forty nights of heaven. And such a feast has never been before. In peace I leave you. Egypt calls."

"Come, I will give you beasts of burden that your journey may be less wearisome."

"My heart is light and my staff dots a long track. As I came so I will depart."

He held his acacia staff aloft as a signal of a long farewell and with this gesture left the presence of the Procurator of Judea. When he reached the street, Buncha the slave woman came running after him with a bag of dried dates and other fruit. She pressed it quickly into his hands and without a single word she ran away.

On that very afternoon while the old oracle Xado was leaving the city of Jerusalem to take the road westward toward Bethlehem and Egypt, another wanderer was journeying northward. He had walked the long weary way along the banks of the River Jordan and had now reached the shore of the Sea of Galilee.

Here he paused before the hut of the local tax collector.

"Master, master!" called the clerk, looking up from the counter. "It is you?"

"Yes, Jacob," said Matthew. "I have come to ask a service of you."

"Anything."

"You have heard?"

"Yes, the news has come even here to Galilee. The Teacher, the good One, the One you followed. He is no more."

"Do not say that, Jacob. He is and always will be. We have seen Him again on the Mount where once He preached the sermon to the multitude. And that is why I now come to ask your help."

"Ask anything."

"You have parchment?"

"Yes. Plenty of freshly scraped and squared skins."

"And reeds and ink?"

"Yes."

"Then close up this miserable hovel and take those things with you and lead me to your home. I will dictate to you and as I dictate, so will you write."

Jacob lost no time gathering together the skins and reeds and ink. He closed down the shutters of the hut and conducted his former master, Matthew, to his home. Here they spread the parchment sheets on the table before them and made themselves comfortable.

"While the words are still fresh in my mind," said Matthew, "let us write them down. For never has there been such a tale of wonder since the beginning of time."

"I am ready," said Jacob, dipping a fresh reed in the jar of ink.

"Leave space for the names of the generations which I will record later. Leave a good space. Two palms. And let us begin with His life."

"Begin," said Jacob.

Matthew spoke the words slowly and with great deliberation and as he spoke Jacob, his former clerk, wrote: "Now when Jesus was born in Bethlehem of Judea in the days of Herod the king, behold, there came wise men from the East . . ."

Biographical Notes

BESS STREETER ALDRICH (1881–) Born in Cedar Falls, Iowa, Mrs. Aldrich is a graduate of Iowa State Teachers College, where she prepared for her career in pedagogy. From 1911 until 1918 she wrote under the pen name of Margaret Dean Stevens. Thereafter, having given up teaching, she used her own name as a professional writer and contributed to many of the leading women's magazines. Her popular romantic novels include: *Mother Mason, The Rim of the Prairie, The Cutters, A Lantern in Her Hand, A White Bird Flying, Miss Bishop, Spring Came On Forever, The Man Who Caught the Weather, Song of Years, The Drum Goes Dead,* and *The Lieutenant's Lady*. During this fertile period of authorship she also found time to bring up a family of four children and to have a long, close association with the *Christian Herald*.

LEONID ANDREYEV (1871–1919) Born in Russia, Andreyev studied law at the Universities of Moscow and St. Petersburg. Tired of struggling with an unremunerative practice, he became a police-court reporter for a Moscow newspaper. In 1898 his first short story, "Bargamot and Garaska," attracted the attention of Gorki, whose unstinting praise started him on the road to fame. Becoming more and more conservative, he ardently supported World War I, upheld Kerensky, and revolted violently against the Soviet regime. Finally he retired to Finland, whence he sent out impassioned protests against the Bolshevists. Translations of Andreyev's prolific writings have appeared in all the European languages. Among the principle works available in English are *The Red Laugh* (1904), *The Seven Who Were Hanged* (1909), *Judas Iscariot and Others* (1910), *He Who Gets Slapped* (1916), *The Crushed Flower and Other Stories* (1916), *The Waltz of the Dogs* (1922), and *The Abyss* (1929).

SHOLEM ASCH (1880–) Of Polish birth, Sholem Asch came to the United States to be naturalized at the outbreak of World War I. He was already known throughout the world for novels, short stories, and plays—especially the drama, *The God of Vengeance,* produced by Max Reinhardt in 1910. He still writes in Yiddish, and all his literary creations bear the indefinable stamp of his early training in Hebrew and rabbinical schools. With *Three Cities,* a trilogy written in France in 1925, he entered into a more universal sphere of reference than that of his earlier period of writing. His interest in the destiny of his own people was continued in frequent trips to Europe and a long visit to the Jewish colonies now part of Israel. *The Apostle, The Nazarene,* and *Mary* comprise his second great trilogy and mark him as a writer of epic scope and spiritual power.

(SIR) JAMES M. BARRIE (1860–1937) Educated at Edinburgh University, James M. Barrie studied journalism and became a contributor to various London papers. The publication of *The Little Minister* (1891) established him as a successful novelist, and its subsequent dramatization began his career as a prolific playwright. From 1902 on, his production was almost entirely dramatic, running the gamut from the purely comic to the predominantly tragic—from *Peter Pan* to *Dear Brutus* and *Mary Rose. Margaret Ogilvy* is his great tribute to his mother, and *A Window in Thrums* reveals keen insight into beauties of Scottish family life.

FLORENCE MARVYNE BAUER* Wife of Dr. W. W. Bauer of the American Medical Association and mother of three grown children, Mrs. Bauer was born in Illinois and still lives there. She has written and produced dozens of radio dramas, plays, and pageants, as well as keeping up with her special interests of painting and Bible study. The research she did preparatory to teaching Sunday-school classes provided her with background material for *Behold Your King* and *Abraham, Son of Terah.*

JOHAN BOJER (1872–   ) The dramatization of his novel, *The Power of a Lie,* brought Bojer continental recognition, but it was not until after 1919 that *The Great Hunger* and *The New Temple* won him universal praise. *God and the Woman, The Last of the Vikings, The Emigrants,* and *The Everlasting Struggle* are all aimed to broaden understanding of his beloved "folk by the sea." His French biographer has said of him: "Bojer is of the family of great writer-philosophers."

HEYWOOD BROUN (1888–1939) American newspaper columnist and critic, first affiliated with the New York *Tribune* and later the New York *World,* Heywood Broun gained fame as a syndicated columnist for the Scripps-Howard newspaper chain. He was always concerned with championing the underprivileged and crusading against social injustice. For a time Broun was a radio commentator and once ran unsuccessfully as a congressman from New York City.

*Denotes that date of birth is unavailable but author is still living.

JOHN BUCHAN (1875–1940) This Scottish novelist-historian, Lord Tweedsmuir by rank and title, spent three decades of his life as diplomat, director of information, and Governor General in South Africa, England, and Canada, respectively. A member of Thomas Nelson & Sons, publishers, he edited the Nations of Today series and wrote a massive four-volume *History of the Great War*. His biographies of Scott and Cromwell are outstanding in their field; his romantic fiction includes such popular works as *Prester John, Greenmantle, Hunting Tower, The Three Hostages, John Macnab, The Thirty-Nine Steps,* and *Mountain Meadow*.

PEARL S. BUCK (1892–   ) Coming from Hillsboro, West Virginia, Pearl Buck matriculated at Randolph-Macon Woman's College, Lynchburg. A few years later she went to China and taught in several universities there. Since her return in 1931 she has received degrees from five American universities. With two children of her own, she has adopted, since her marriage to Richard J. Walsh, three boys and a girl. The Nobel prize for literature, 1938, followed several other notable awards. In addition to the biographies of her father and mother, fiction covering aspects of life in America, miscellaneous short stories, essays, and a translation of the classic *Shui Hu Chuan,* her novels about the Chinese hold a unique place in the literature of today. Among those most widely loved are *East Wind, West Wind, The Good Earth, The Young Revolutionist, Pavilion of Women,* and *Peony*.

JOHN BUNYAN (1628–88) Though able to boast of very little literary culture, Bunyan was saturated with the imagery of the Bible, passionate religious convictions, and an overwhelming perception of people and places. His own conversion is described in the extraordinary spiritual autobiography, *Grace Abounding*—which, together with his preaching, led to his arrest at the Restoration under the Conventicle Act. He was imprisoned for twelve years, during which he wrote nine books, including his masterwork, *Pilgrim's Progress*. The latter—combining Puritan theology with a story of great imaginative vitality—is the most famed allegory in the English language, having reached its tenth edition by 1685 (one year after publication).

DOROTHY CANFIELD (1879–   ) A native of Kansas, Dorothy Canfield is a graduate of Ohio University and Columbia University. After her marriage to John R. Fisher in 1907 she moved to one of the Canfield farms in Vermont, which became the locale of many of her stories, including *Hillsboro People, The Brimming Cup,* and *Raw Material. The Montessori Mother* was a pioneer work in English on the Montessori system of child education, and *Understood Betsy* is a study in the development of rural education. Another classic of the democratic ideal at work is her *Seasoned Timber,* the masterly portrayal of a schoolmaster's plea for social justice. Her *Home Fires in France* has been cited as one of the most inspiring books about World War I, and her translation of Papini's *Christ* as one of the finest works of its kind. As a member of the board of judges of the Book-of-the-Month Club, Mrs. Fisher has done much to raise the level and broaden the scope of American literary tastes.

MARY ELLEN CHASE (1887–   ) Born in Blue Hill, Maine, Mary Ellen Chase was educated at the Universities of Maine and Minnesota. For more than twenty years she has been a professor of English at Smith College, devoting much of her time to the writing of essays, belles-lettres, and reference works, as well as articles and stories in leading national magazines. Distinguished in the field of religious literature for such authoritative volumes as *The Bible and the Common Reader* and *Jonathan Fisher, Maine Parson,* her informal autobiography, *A Goodly Heritage,* has become a classic. Her sensitive, almost poetic prose appears at its best in the well-drawn characters of *Mary Christmas, Uplands, Mary Peters, Silas Crockett, Dawn in Lyonesse, Windswept,* and *The Plum Tree.*

RALPH CONNOR (1860–1937) (pseudonym of Charles William Gordon) This Canadian author was born in Glengarry, Ontario, of Scottish descent. In 1870 his family moved to Borra, Ontario, but the wild scenery of Glengarry lingered in his memory and pervaded all his work. After graduating from Toronto University, he studied theology at Knox College and was ordained to the Presbyterian ministry in 1890. In the same year he went to the Canadian Northwest Territories, where he served as a missionary among the miners and lumbermen for three years. In 1894 he became pastor of St. Stephen's Presbyterian Church at Winnipeg. His first novel, *Black Rock,* grew out of a story written for the *Westminster Magazine* at a friend's request. This book was so popular that though he never gave up the ministry he wrote novel after novel (all under the name of Ralph Connor), including *The Sky Pilot, The Man from Glengarry, The Rock and the River, Torches Through the Bush,* and *The Rebel Loyalist.*

A. J. CRONIN (1896–   ) A native of Cardross, Scotland, A. J. Cronin has combined a medical career with a literary career, receiving his M.D. from Glasgow University and a doctorate in literature from Bowdoin University. Practicing in South Wales and London, he became medical inspector of mines and life governor of Sussex General Hospital. He now lives in Connecticut. Since 1930 he has been a prolific writer of best-selling novels, including *Hatter's Castle, Grand Canary, The Stars Look Down, The Citadel, The Keys of the Kingdom, The Green Years,* and *The Spanish Gardener.*

LLOYD C. DOUGLAS (1877–   ) Dr. Douglas is a Lutheran clergy-man whose writings have been a source of lasting inspiration to millions. Up to 1940 his novels dealt with the search for spiritual happiness and inner peace: *Magnificent Obsession* (1929), *Forgive Us Our Trespasses* (1932), *Precious Jeopardy* (1933), *Green Light* (1935), *White Banners* (1936), *Disputed Passage* (1939), *Doctor Hudson's Secret Journal* (1939), and *Invitation to Live* (1940). His writing in the last decade, notably *The Robe* and *The Big Fisherman,* has been more deeply concerned with an interpretation of Jesus' teachings as carried on by his disciples and followers. All his fiction preaches the importance of universal brotherhood and the self-enrichment made possible through serving humanity.

GEORGE ELIOT (1819–80) (pseudonym of Mary Ann Evans) Brought up in a strongly evangelical atmosphere, George Eliot's early schooling was bolstered by extensive reading and study of languages. Later, as a member of the *Westminster Review* editorial staff, she traveled in literary circles and became a friend of J. S. Mill, Harriet Martineau, Herbert Spencer, and G. H. Lewes. Upon publication of her novels—*Adam Bede, The Mill on the Floss,* and *Silas Marner,* recollections of her own early life in Warwickshire—her fame became universal and won her a place among the great English novelists of all time.

RACHEL FIELD (1894–1942) A native of New York, where she attended the public schools, Rachel Field was a special student at Radcliffe College from 1914 to 1918. It was there she first displayed her unusual ability in writing. In 1929 she was awarded the John Newbery medal for the most distinguished contribution to literature for children. Her many juveniles and one-act plays preceded her popular novels: *Time Out of Mind, Fear Is the Thorn, To See Ourselves* (with her husband, Arthur Pederson), *All This, and Heaven Too, And Now Tomorrow.*

KAHLIL GIBRAN (1883–1931) Gibran, the son of an affluent Lebanon family, devoted his early years to the study of music, art, and literature. His reputation and influence traveled far beyond the Near East, with the translation of his work into more than twenty languages. During the last two decades of his life he made his home in New York's Greenwich Village and began writing in English exclusively. *The Prophet, Jesus the Son of Man, The Wanderer,* and *The Garden of the Prophet* are among his most popular volumes. His drawings and paintings, reminiscent of the work of William Blake, have been exhibited in the major capitals of the world.

ELIZABETH GOUDGE (1900–   ) Born in Somersetshire and a graduate of the Art School of Reading University in England, Miss Goudge was a handicraft teacher for ten years before turning to writing as a profession. Since 1932 she has produced many best-selling novels and juvenile stories, for which she has received well-merited awards. Her widely known works include *Island Magic, A City of Bells, A Pedlar's Pack, Towers in the Mist, The Bird in the Tree, Golden Skylark, The Castle on the Hill, The Blue Hills, Green Dolphin Street* (a Literary Guild selection and winner of the Metro-Goldwyn-Mayer Prize), and *Pilgrim's Inn* (another Literary Guild choice and recipient of the Carnegie Medal).

DAVID GRAYSON (1870–1946) (pseudonym of Ray Stannard Baker) This author-statesman, a native of Lansing, Michigan, received a B.S. from Michigan State College, 1889, and an LL.D., 1917, continuing his graduate work in literature and law at the University of Michigan, Amherst College, and Duke University. After newspaper experience, he gravitated to magazine editing and writing, later gaining an intimate knowledge of political history as special commissioner of the Department of State in Great Britain, France, and Italy and as director of the Press Bureau of the American Commission to Negotiate Peace at Paris, 1919. Under his own name he wrote many books dealing with world affairs and with Woodrow Wilson, also acting as technical adviser of the motion picture *Wilson,* 1943–44. As "David Grayson" he vitalized the intrinsic pleasures of everyday living in his series of *Adventures—in Contentment, in Friendship, in Understanding,* and *in Solitude.*

ELGIN E. GROSECLOSE (1899–   ) A native son of Oklahoma, Groseclose holds a bachelor's degree from the University of Oklahoma and a doctorate from the American University in Washington, D.C. His varied career includes working for the Presbyterian Mission School in Iran, the Department of Commerce, United States Trade Commission, Guaranty Trust Company, *Fortune,* Federal Communications Commission, and United States Treasury Department; teaching banking and finance at City College and the University of Oklahoma; and currently heading his own economic-counsel firm. He has won a number of literary awards and the Near East Relief Medal. Author of a series of economic monographs and contributor to financial journals, he has also written several deeply religious novels: *The Persian Journey of the Reverend Ashley Wishard and his Servant Fathi, Ararat,* and *The Firedrake.*

GUNNAR GUNNARSSON (1889–   ) Born of an old Icelandic family, Gunnarsson continued their tradition by spending his boyhood on a farm and attending country school. His first literary efforts were two collections of poetry—forerunners of the epic and elemental beauty of his later fiction. After many years' residence in Denmark and wide travel in Scandinavia, Europe, and North Africa, he bought an old farm near his birthplace in Iceland, where he now lives. His four-volume "Borg" series portrays three generations of an Icelandic farm family.

Among his books available in English are *Guest the One-Eyed* (1930), *Seven Days' Darkness* (1930), *Night and the Dream* (1938), and *The Good Shepherd* (1940), published in England under the title of *Advent*.

JAMES HILTON (1900–   ) This English novelist is best known for his extremely popular novelette, *Goodbye, Mr. Chips* (1935). All his writing is marked by a strong sentimental and adventurous overtone. Among his chief works are *And Now Goodbye, Rage in Heaven, Lost Horizon* (from which comes Shangri-La, the late President Roosevelt's mythical base of an American air-bombing raid on Japan, 1942), *Knights Without Armour,* and *We Are Not Alone. Goodbye, Mr. Chips, Lost Horizon,* and *We Are Not Alone* were brought to life on the screen and featured some of Hollywood's top talent.

ALICE TISDALE HOBART (1882–   ) Born in Lockport, New York, Mrs. Hobart studied at the University of Chicago. After her marriage she made her home in China, which provided the locale for many of her stories and articles. In 1933 the publication of her first novel, *Oil for the Lamps of China,* brought her wide recognition. Since then she has written *Yang and Yin, Their Own Country, The Peacock Sheds His Tail,* and *The Cleft Rock,* as well as contributing extensively to such national magazines as *Atlantic Monthly, Harper's, Century, Asia, Saturday Review of Literature, National Geographic,* and *The American Girl.*

ZORA NEALE HURSTON (1903–   ) Born in Eatonville, Florida, Miss Hurston attended Morgan College and Howard University and received her degree from Barnard College in 1928. She did graduate work in anthropology and later, as a Guggenheim fellow, spent 1936 to 1938 writing on folklore in Haiti and the British West Indies. Currently she heads the drama department of North Carolina College for Negroes in Durham, North Carolina. Her professional honors include the Annisfield Award of one thousand dollars for her autobiography, *Dust Tracks on a Road,* and the Howard University Alumni Award for distinguished postgraduate work in literature. Among her other best-known books are *Jonuh's Gourd Vine* (1934), *Their Eyes Were Watching God* (1937), *Moses: Man of the Mountain* (1939), and *The Voice of the Land* (1945).

A. S. M. HUTCHINSON (1879–   ) Barred from the Army because of poor eyesight, Hutchinson was induced by his family to study medicine and prepare for the medical services of the Indian Army. He began writing for his own amusement, enjoyed it thoroughly, and determined then and there to become a novelist. Later, while serving as editor of the *Daily Graphic,* he wrote his first book, *The Happy Warrior.* This began a long succession of extremely popular works, including *If Winter*

Comes, This Freedom, The Uncertain Trumpet, He Looked for a City, and *The Book of Simon,* which gave a humorously detached account of the development of his small son.

J. H. INGRAHAM (1809–60) A sailor and participant in a South American revolution, Ingraham based his first novels on these early experiences (*The Southwest, by a Yankee,* and tales dealing with such picturesque figures as Captain Kidd and pirate Lafitte). After 1849 he became an Episcopal minister in the South and wrote several biblical romances—among them his best-known work, *The Prince of the House of David.*

TOYOHIKO KAGAWA (1888–   ) This great Japanese minister, Christian socialist, reformer, and author received his training at the Presbyterian College of Tokyo, Kobe Theological Seminary, and Princeton University. His autobiographical novel, *Before the Dawn,* sold 250,000 copies, and his later works have netted an income of more than fifty thousand dollars a year. The royalties from his one hundred and fifty books and pamphlets have been used to maintain a dispensary, a visiting nurse, night schools, and inexpensive dormitories and eating places. In all of his welfare and union work, he has never forgotten the years he spent living in the slums of Kobe, where ten thousand people were huddled into lots six feet square and where he contracted trachoma and tuberculosis from the outcasts he befriended. As literature, his *Meditations on the Cross* and *Meditations on the Holy Spirit* rank even higher than such novels as *A Grain of Wheat* and *Behold The Man.*

MANUEL KOMROFF (1890–   ) Engineering, music, and art first attracted Manuel Komroff as possible careers. His literary activities did not begin until he had gone to Petrograd to become correspondent and later editor of the *Russian Daily News.* When the Bolshevists came into power the newspaper died, and Komroff wandered about the Japanese archipelago and China before returning to his native America. Hard years followed until he landed a staff position with Boni & Liveright— a post he left after the publication of his first novel, *Juggler's Kiss.* It was his second book, *Coronet,* which established him as a popular writer. Two years later *Two Thieves* was published. Before Komroff began writing this story of the pair who were crucified beside Jesus at Calvary, he read fifty-eight volumes and filled 723 pages with notes about Palestine. *In the Years of Our Lord* carries on this same profound research and imaginative re-creation of Jesus and his times.

SELMA LAGERLÖF (1858–1940) Selma Lagerlöf is a Swedish novelist, Nobel prize winner (1909), and the first woman to be elected to the Swedish Academy (1914). Most of her novels and short stories have been translated and command a wide international audience. Among her most famous works are *The Ring of the Löwenskölds,* a series of seven novels; *Invisible Links,* a collection of short stories; and *The Wonderful Adventures of Nils,* a children's tale. In the field of religion, *Christ Legends* has become a classic favorite among young readers.

MARGARET LANDON (1903–   ) Born in Wisconsin, Margaret Landon received her A.B. from Wheaton College and taught at Bear Lake, Michigan, for a year. After her marriage to Kenneth Perry Landon, in 1926, she went with him, under the auspices of the Board of Foreign Missions Presbyterian Church, to Siam, living in Bangkok, Nakon, Sritamarat, and Trang, where she was principal of the Trang Girls' School for five years. There she came to know intimately the endless complications of life in the Orient. Upon returning to the United States in 1937, the Landons and their four children took up residence in Washington, D.C. Her book, *Anna and the King of Siam,* which made motion-picture history, was followed in 1949 by *Never Dies the Dream,* a vivid picture of life and social conditions in the Siam of today.

RICHARD LLEWELLYN (1907–   ) (pseudonym of Richard David Vivian Llewellyn Lloyd) Of Welsh descent, British novelist-playwright Llewellyn was educated at St. David's, Cardiff, and London. Sent to Italy at an early age to learn the fundamentals of hotel management, he studied painting and sculpture in his spare hours away from the hotel kitchen. Working later with an Italian film unit, he learned the rudiments of the cinema and played "extra" parts. He joined the ranks of His Majesty's Regular Army, serving at home and abroad, and subsequently became reporter on a penny film paper. At one time he was assistant director, scenarist, production manager, and director. His mystery play, *Poison Pen,* was produced in England, and his novels, *How Green Was My Valley* (1940) and *None But the Lonely Heart* (1943), were successfully dramatized in motion pictures.

WILLIAM J. LOCKE (1863–1930) Born in Barbados, Locke was educated at Queen's Royal College, Trinidad, and St. John's College, Cambridge. From 1897 to 1907 he served as secretary to the Royal Institute of British Architects, establishing himself as a successful writer of fiction and plays. His *The Morals of Marcus Ordeyne, Simon the Jester,* and, still more, *The Beloved Vagabond* enjoyed wide popularity in England and the United States.

IAN MACLAREN (1850–1907) (pseudonym of John Watson) Born at Manningtree in Essex, Maclaren became minister of Free St. Matthew's, Glasgow, and of Sefton Park, Liverpool. His best-loved works—all dealing with simple rural Scottish life—are *Beside the Bonnie Brier Bush, The Days of Old Lang Syne,* and *Kate Carnegie.*

HERMAN MELVILLE (1819–91) In 1841–42 this native of New York spent eighteen months on a Yankee whaler rounding Cape Horn. Extreme hardships caused him to escape from the ship and take refuge on the Marquesas Islands, where he was captured by the Typees—a tribe of cannibals. His first book, *Typee,* is an account of this adventure. *Moby Dick,* a story of whaling written five years later in 1851, is considered his greatest masterpiece.

CHRISTOPHER MORLEY (1890–   ) Born in Haverford, Pennsylvania, Christopher Morley was educated at Haverford College, becoming a Rhodes Scholar at New College, Oxford, England, 1910–13. Between 1913–40 he served on the editorial staffs of Doubleday and Company, the *Ladies' Home Journal,* Philadelphia *Evening Ledger,* New York *Evening Post,* and the *Saturday Review of Literature.* Morley's volumes of poetry, plays, essays, and belles-lettres have been widely acclaimed; his novels and short stories are equally well regarded for their light, deft touch. In 1928, with Cleon Throckmorton, he founded the Hoboken Theatre, which produced revivals of such plays as *After Dark* and *The Black Crook.* Among the most popular of his novels are *Parnassus on Wheels, The Haunted Bookshop, Where the Blue Begins, Kitty Foyle,* and *The Man Who Made Friends with Himself.*

ROBERT NATHAN (1894–   ) Born in New York, Nathan was educated in Geneva, Switzerland, at Phillips Exeter Academy, and at Harvard, where he was on the staff of the *Harvard Monthly.* Except for two years as a solicitor for a New York advertising firm and another two-year period teaching at the New York University School of Journalism, his time has been devoted exclusively to writing. His first novel, *Peter Kindred,* published in 1919, was semi-autobiographical and quite unlike his later work. He did not, however, become widely known until 1933, with the appearance of *One More Spring,* his delightfully wistful fantasy about the depression. *Journey of Tapiola* and *Portrait of Jennie* were also received enthusiastically by many readers. A painter and an accomplished musician, Nathan composes, plays the piano and cello, and actively participates in athletics as well. He is a charter member of the P.E.N. Club and a member of the National Institute of Arts and Letters.

JOHN OXENHAM (185?–1941) (pseudonym of William Arthur Dunkerley) Manchester-born, Oxenham studied at Victoria University and traveled widely before entering the publishing business. With Robert Barr and Jerome K. Jerome he launched *The Idler* and the weekly *Today.* Subsequently he derived greater satisfaction—and profit—from the purely literary end of publishing. In the course of his newly found career he produced forty-two novels and many volumes of verse, which rolled up enormous sales. After World War I he drew inspiration from the life of Christ, bringing out *The Cedar Box, The Hidden Years, Cross-Roads,* and a whole series of interpretations of the Master and his followers.

ALAN PATON (1903–   ) Born in Pietermaritzburg, South Africa, Paton has dedicated twenty-five years of his life to improving conditions among the underprivileged in his own country. Leaving his teaching post at Maritzburg College, he took over the direction of Diepkloof Reformatory, an institution for six hundred and fifty African delinquents, seven miles from the center of Johannesburg. He soon saw before his own eyes the impact of industrialization on a simple tribal people and began his unceasing fight for social welfare and penal reform. After World War II his avid interest in prison work took him to Scandinavia, England, and the United States. Freed from the heavy responsibilities of his job during this period of travel, he began writing *Cry, The Beloved Country* and completed it in three months.

PETER ROSEGGER (1843–1918) In a lonely mountain region of Austria, Rosegger led the life of a forest peasant until he was eighteen. After a four-year apprenticeship to a traveling tailor, he studied under a scholarship in the commercial school of Graz. Never having had money for books, he learned to make them for himself and devoted ten years to compiling twenty-four magnificent handcrafted volumes. His discovery of print inspired him to write, and within thirty years he produced forty books. Author of tales and novels of Austrian peasant life, Rosegger was awarded the Bauernfeld Prize in 1897. Among his better-known writings are *The Forest Schoolmaster* (an autobiographical novel), *The Godseeker, The Earth and the Fullness Thereof,* and *I.N.R.I.*—all of which show his deep concern with spiritual themes and the serenity that comes from true faith.

WILLIAM SAROYAN (1908–   ) Novelist, playwright, and short-story writer of Armenian parentage, Saroyan is best known for his picturesque characters and impressionistic style. Individual freedom even in stark poverty, essential goodness and romantic aspiration, the American ideal in action—these are the elements out of which he has woven his fine tapestries of whimsey and sentiment. From his pen flows a steady stream of short fiction, including such volumes as *The Daring Young Man on the Flying Trapeze, Inhale and Exhale, The Trouble with Tigers, Love, Here Is My Hat, Peace, It's Wonderful, My Name is Aram, My Heart Is in the Highland,* and *The Beautiful People.* His chronicle of a simple American family, *The Human Comedy,* was warmly received both as a book and as a motion picture. In 1940 *The Time of Your Life* was awarded the Pulitzer prize, which Saroyan modestly refused.

CHARLES M. SHELDON (1857–1946) Born in Wellsville, New York, Dr. Sheldon was graduated from Brown University and Andover Theological Seminary. For three years he served as pastor in Waterbury, Vermont, and from 1889 to 1919 as active pastor and minister-at-large for the Central Congregational Church in Topeka, Kansas. During the period between 1920–25 he was editor-in-chief of the *Christian Herald*. Author of about a dozen novels, this American clergyman is best known for *In His Steps*. His description of a congregation which consistently followed the teachings of Jesus sold millions of copies all over the world but brought little profit to the author because of defective copyright.

HENRYK SIENKIEWICZ (1846–1916) Awarded the Nobel prize for literature in 1905, this widely read Polish author is famous for his series of historical novels, *Fire and Sword, The Deluge, Pan Michael,* and *Quo Vadis?* The last-mentioned work is a novel of Christian martyrs in the days of Nero, which established Sienkiewicz as an internationally renowned literary figure.

ELSIE SINGMASTER (1879–   ) Of Pennsylvania Dutch (German) and English Quaker stock, Elsie Singmaster has spent most of her life in the small towns of Pennsylvania. A Radcliffe graduate and holder of several Litt.D. degrees, her writing career crystallized with her husband's death after only three years of marriage. *Katy Gaumer,* her first novel, appeared in 1915, and was followed by *Basil Everman, Ellen Levis,* and *The Hidden Road. Bred in the Bone,* a volume of short stories, was published in 1925, and within the next two years she wrote *The Book of the United States, The Book of the Constitution,* and *The Book of the Colonies.* Among her more recent popular novels are *The Magic Mirror, The Loving Heart,* and *A High Wind Rising.* Faithful portrayals of human nature in the little Pennsylvania Dutch world she knows so well, her characters and stories have a piquant charm, an artistic integrity, and a warmhearted sincerity that have endeared them to a wide audience.

HOWARD SPRING (1889–   ) Born in Cardiff, Wales, of a large and very poor family, Howard Spring had little in the way of formalized education. Before serving in the Intelligence Section of British General Headquarters during World War I, he was a reporter on the South Wales *Daily News* and the Yorkshire *Observer.* Later he returned to reporting and became literary critic on the London *Evening Standard. My Son, My Son!* was his fifth novel and his first literary success. Among his subsequent best sellers are: *Heaven Lies About Us, Fame Is The Spur, Hard Facts, And Another Thing, Dunkerley's,* and *There Is No Armour.*

LOUISE STINETORF* One of nine children, Louise Stinetorf grew up on an Indiana farm. Upon graduation from Earlham College, she served on a Quaker Mission Board and later went to Palestine as an educational missionary. She interrupted her work with the American Friends Service Committee to take additional study in English literature at Temple University and Bryn Mawr. Frequent vacations spent in Africa have given her authentic and colorful source material for juveniles, short stories, and her first book-length novel, *White Witch Doctor*.

JAMES STREET (1903–   ) Born in Mississippi and currently a resident of North Carolina, James Street was educated at Southwestern Theological Seminary and Howard College. After three years in the ministry, he returned to the newspaper field, living and working in many cities throughout the country. The publication of *Look Away, A Dixie Notebook* in 1936 heralded his entrance into full-time freelance writing. Since then he has written *Oh, Promised Land, In My Father's House, The Biscuit Eater, Tap Roots, By Valour and Arms,* and *The Gauntlet*.

WILLIAM M. THACKERAY (1811–63) Born in Calcutta, Thackeray was educated at Cambridge. Having dissipated his inheritance, he was compelled to support himself by literary hack work and illustrating. His first real popularity came through satirical sketches contributed to *Punch* (published as *The Book of Snobs*), and with serialization of *Vanity Fair* he rose to major rank among English novelists, rivaling Dickens and Fielding in popularity. *Henry Esmond, The Newcomes,* and *The Virginians* are among his best-known novels.

LEO TOLSTOI (1828–1910) Born of an old Russian noble family, Tolstoi at an early age found their gay, shallow social life repellent. After resigning from the Army and journeying abroad, he opened a school for peasant children and spent his spare hours in literary studies. Among his finest works are *War and Peace* and *Anna Karenina,* which reflect the philosophy and aspirations of the Russian people toward self-release. By 1881 he had crystallized a religious doctrine for himself and began to put it into practice. Produced after his conversion, *The Kreutzer Sonata, The Death of Ivan Ilyitch,* and *Resurrection* exhibit strong moral and social elements within their highly imaginative framework.

MARK TWAIN (1835–1910) (pseudonym of Samuel L. Clemens) The work of this great Missouri-born humorist is credited with providing a "lasting monument to a vanished era of American history." From his early Mississippi river-boat experiences to his get-rich-quick schemes in Carson City, Nevada, Mark Twain's literary accounts constitute some of the richest examples of American wit and humor. His pen gave us the classics *Tom Sawyer* and *Huckleberry Finn,* followed by *Innocents Abroad, Roughing It, Life on the Mississippi, The Prince and the Pauper, A Connecticut Yankee,* and *Joan of Arc*.

HENRY VAN DYKE (1852–1933) Nationally prominent as pastor of New York's Brick Presbyterian Church, Henry van Dyke became professor of English literature at Princeton and later Minister to the Netherlands in Wilson's administration. His writings comprise poems, essays, and stories, many of which are based on religious themes. *The Other Wise Man,* a Christmas story of wide appeal, has been translated into many languages, and *The Blue Flower* has become almost a classic because of its wide and lasting popularity.

PIERRE VAN PAASSEN (1895–   ) Born in the Netherlands, Van Paassen received his higher education in Canada and France. In this country, the University of Dubuque, Albright College, and the Jewish Institute of Religion have awarded him doctorate degrees. Before his ordination to the Unitarian ministry in 1946, he spent more than ten years as columnist and roving foreign correspondent for the New York *Evening World* and the Toronto *Star.* Among his most notable books are *The Days of Our Years, The Time Is Now, That Day Alone, The Forgotten Ally,* and *Earth Could Be Fair;* his latest work is *Why Jesus Died,* published in 1949.

HUGH WALPOLE (1884–1941) Born in New Zealand, Walpole was educated at Cambridge, where he wrote two novels before he was twenty. He did not achieve any literary success, however, until several years later, when *Maradick at Forty, Fortitude, The Dark Forest,* and *The Secret City* followed in rapid succession. In addition to his novels about the cathedral town of Polchester, he has written biographies of Joseph Conrad and Anthony Trollope and the Jeremy series for children. *Harmer John* is the precursor of many modern novels dealing with social service, slum clearance, and the ideals of brotherly love.

PAUL I. WELLMAN (1898–   ) Though born in Enid, Oklahoma, Wellman spent most of his first ten years in West Africa, where his father was a medical missionary. After graduation from Fairmount College in Wichita and service in World War I, he joined the staff of the Kansas City *Star* as editorial and feature writer. Author of such distinguished historical works as *Death on the Prairie, Death in the Desert,* and *The Trampling Herd,* he has also written many novels, including *Jubal Troop, Angel with Spurs, The Bowl of Brass,* and the recent best sellers, *The Walls of Jericho* and *The Chain.* Mr. Wellman lives in Westwood, near the campus of the University of California, Los Angeles, and now devotes all his time to the writing of fiction.

H. G. WELLS (1866–1946) Upon commencement from the Royal College of Science and the University of London, Wells taught for a few years. During this period he published *The Time Machine*—the first of a long and entertaining series of scientific fiction. A prolific writer, his published work includes novels of social prophecy, novels of contemporary life, psychological satires on war, Fabian essays, and a monumental work, *The Outline of History,* in collaboration with some of the greatest scientists of our day. Much of the philosophy set forth in such works as *Mr. Britling Sees It Through* applies with surprising accuracy to world problems today.

JESSAMYN WEST* An Indiana Quaker, Jessamyn West was educated abroad, at Whittier College, and at the University of California. A prolific short-story writer, her work has appeared in *Collier's, Atlantic Monthly, Harper's, Ladies' Home Journal,* and *Harper's Bazaar.* In the fall of 1945 a collection of these stories was published under the title *The Friendly Persuasion.*

DOROTHY CLARKE WILSON (1904–) Dorothy Clarke Wilson was born in Gardiner, Maine, and was graduated from Bates College with highest honors and a Phi Beta Kappa key. At Bates she also met her future husband, Elwin L. Wilson, whom she married during his student years at Princeton Theological Seminary. While her husband was serving a small church in Perrineville, New Jersey, there was need for a suitable religious play. Dorothy Clarke Wilson wrote one and has been writing them ever since. She is the author of *Twelve Months of Drama for the Average Church.* At the same time she has produced fiction as well, notably the best-selling novel *The Brother,* about James, the brother of Christ, and *The Herdsman,* about the prophet Amos. Her latest book is *Prince of Egypt,* which won the Westminster $7,500 Fiction Award for 1948.

ELIZABETH YATES (1905–) Born in Buffalo, Elizabeth Yates went on to study in New York City, London, and Paris. While still a student she started her writing career with book reviews and articles. Business took her and her husband, William McGreal, to London from 1929–39. There she published her first book, *High Holiday,* and found material for several volumes of Cornish tales. Since then, living on a farm outside of Peterborough, New Hampshire, where she finds many outlets for community usefulness, she has authored about a dozen gentle, imaginative books for children. A rare feeling for nature and a deep spiritual understanding of her characters mark her novels *Wind of Spring, Nearby, Beloved Bondage,* and *Guardian Heart.*

Index of Titles